D0225661

Dr. Sondra Kathryn Wilson, literary executor and editor of the James Weldon Johnson Papers, is an Associate of the W.E.B. Du Bois Institute, Harvard University. Her past publications include *The Selected Writings of James Weldon Johnson* (Oxford, 1995), *The Crisis Reader* (1999), and *The Opportunity Reader* (1999).

IN SEARCH OF DEMOCRACY

IN SEARCH OF DEMOCRACY

The NAACP Writings of
James Weldon Johnson,
Walter White, and Roy Wilkins
(1920–1977)

Edited by

Sondra Kathryn Wilson

New York   Oxford

Oxford University Press

1999

Oxford University Press

Oxford   New York

Athens   Auckland   Bangkok   Bogotá   Buenos Aires   Calcutta
Cape Town   Chennai   Dar es Salaam   Delhi   Florence   Hong Kong   Istanbul
Karachi   Kuala Lumpur   Madrid   Melbourne   Mexico City   Mumbai
Nairobi   Paris   São Paulo   Singapore   Taipei   Tokyo   Toronto   Warsaw

and associated companies in
Berlin   Ibadan

Copyright © 1999 by Oxford University Press, Inc.

Published by Oxford University Press, Inc.
198 Madison Avenue, New York, New York 10016

Oxford is a registered trademark of Oxford University Press

Library of Congress Cataloging-in-Publication Data
In search of democracy : the NAACP writings of
James Weldon Johnson, Walter White, and Roy Wilkins (1920–1977) /
edited by Sondra Kathryn Wilson.
p.   cm.
Includes bibliographical references and index.
ISBN 0-19-511633-X
1. Afro-Americans—Civil rights—History—20th century—Sources.
2. National Association for the Advancement of Colored People—Archives.
3. United States—Race relations—Sources.   4. Johnson,
James Weldon, 1871–1938.   5. White, Walter Francis, 1893–1955.
6. Wilkins, Roy, 1901– .
I. Wilson, Sondra K.
E185.61.I513   1999
323.1'196073—DC21   98-19625
CIP

1 3 5 7 9 8 6 4 2
Printed in the United States of America
on acid-free paper

To
Myrlie Evers-Williams
who continues the struggle for freedom
and for "... our new day begun."

Jane White Viazzi remembers her father,
Walter White, in the following

Walter White was the father whom I lived with under the same roof for over twenty years of my life but whom I am still coming to know. Through my memories, through his writings, through the research and writings of others such as Sondra Kathryn Wilson, 43 years after his death he is still being revealed to me as extraordinary—for the exceptional breadth of his interests, for his energy and single-mindedness, for his vision of this country. I often wonder what he would make of today's world of black and white, whether the progress made would have given him some satisfaction. Yesterday's world certainly did not. Every injustice against black people made him angry and combative and, of course, still would where injustice still exists.

My father was more often away from home than in it. Countless were the valises my mother packed for him to travel thousands of miles on NAACP business (sometimes to his life's peril). He spent hours with his associates in meetings or on the telephone—a device he would have invented if it didn't already exist. He read and clipped from stacks of daily newspapers in order to keep abreast; we never read a paper that wasn't full of empty spots! He was frequently exhausted in the evenings, often short-tempered, sometimes discouraged, sometimes euphoric, always preoccupied and even obsessed with his assault on every form of American bigotry. Little did it all mean to my little brother and me; those years of overheard talk of cloture, filibuster, Senators Rankin and Bilbo, anti-lynching, disenfranchisement, the Scottsboro boys—all of this was the drumbeat against which our family life pulsated.

But even a selfish child must arrive at the lucid realization that her father is not an ordinary man, that he belongs to the world and she must hand him over. In truth, Walter White was only half alive in any other context than the NAACP and the civil rights struggle. He believed in both passionately, and he believed deeply in his own capacity to further them, which he did for 37 years. And yet today he is little celebrated. Perhaps Dr. Wilson's excellent work will remind us of his importance to the fight which paved the road to the Sixties and the present.

New York City   Jane White Viazzi
July 1, 1998

Foreword

This volume gives readers an intimate look into the workings of the nation's oldest civil rights organization, the NAACP. More importantly, it gives readers a look into the minds of three of the NAACP's most important leaders—James Weldon Johnson, Walter White, and Roy Wilkins. Their collective tenure paralleled the most trying days of the struggle for equal rights. Johnson began just after the nadir; White carried the NAACP through war; Wilkins saw young militants rise to challenge the NAACP's supremacy.

In her Introduction, Sondra Kathryn Wilson outlines the different challenges these very different men faced as white supremacy diminished and then was legally defeated. The generation Johnson and White represent sprang from a population born in the nineteenth century in slavery, freed from servitude by the Civil War, determined to make their way as free women and men, sharing confidence with the slave-born generation that preceded and produced them. Wilkins was born in the twentieth century; his generation was equally determined to make its way in expanded freedom. Opening with Johnson's 1920's reports to the NAACP's Board of Directors and closing with Wilkins's 1976 commentary on the FBI harassment of Dr. Martin Luther King, Jr., these papers cover more than half a century of struggle, failure, and success.

As I write this foreword, black Americans face conditions very different from, but no less daunting than those faced by this remarkable trio in their distinct times. The scientific racism and social Darwinism that characterized these authors' times are too much with us today. We are now three decades past the second Reconstruction, the modern movement for civil rights that Johnson and White helped usher in and Wilkins helped direct and lead. Despite the distance traveled and the victories won, many remain unsure about what the goals of yesterday's movement were, and by and for whom that movement was made.

These pages are instructive. Here in sometimes dry and bureaucratic prose is the language of movement makers, reporting the sometimes gruesome effects of opposing the racial status quo and describing the plans the NAACP is making to ensure that the status quo is opposed. This work is part of a long-needed reappraisal of civil rights history. Now, rather than the towering figures of Kings and Kennedys standing alone, we see an army of anonymous women and men. Instead of famous orations made to multitudes, we now see the planning and work that preceded the triumphant speech. Instead of well-publicized marches and protest, we now see long organizing campaigns and brave and lonely soldiers working in near solitude. And instead of a movement which begins in Montgomery in 1955, we now see a long history of aggressive challenges to white supremacy, and we see how many contributed to the successful whole.

These giants played a role too little known today. During their terms at the NAACP, they sat at the center of black thought and action. They saw the movement shift from a bitter struggle to win elementary civil rights to a post-segregation era with largely politically and economically oriented goals. Johnson might not have dreamed of possibilities that White saw come to pass, and White may not have imagined the world Wilkins eventually saw, but each could convincingly say that he built the steps on which the next man stood.

This excellent collection shows what builders they were, constructing a people's liberation. For some it will be an introduction to unknown figures; for others, an in-depth look at the inner workings of a familiar organization; for all, a reminder of what used to be and a summons to what might lie ahead.

Washington, D.C.   Julian Bond
January 14, 1998

Contents

PART II
The Selected Writings of Walter White, 1929–1955

PART III
The Selected Writings of Roy Wilkins, 1955–1977

IN SEARCH OF DEMOCRACY

Introduction

The National Association for the Advancement of Colored People has been in existence for nearly ninety years. James Weldon Johnson wrote, "I think it is fair to say that there is no phase of race relations in America which the [NAACP] has not profoundly affected."[1] Roy Wilkins called the NAACP the most radical idea of this century—the idea was to abolish legal segregation, a goal the organization achieved in the 1954 *Brown* decision. The trenchant and sweeping apparatus of the NAACP since its inception in 1909 has, without question, been the most effective force for the freedom of black Americans. In short, for most of this century the organization can claim almost monopolistic credit for civil rights achievements. It is likely that without the NAACP, this nation would have lapsed into a kind of moral vacuity.

This collection of writings by James Weldon Johnson, Walter White, and Roy Wilkins, the NAACP's first three African-American secretaries, constructs a narrative that illuminates their courageous role in challenging virtually every form of race discrimination during their successive fifty-seven years of leadership. Their consummate and innovative leadership capacities inspired an oppressed people to see them and their organization as a viable hope for achieving the promise of the U.S. Constitution.

This collection, which comprises more than a half century of racial conflicts in American civil rights history, builds a story that brings the reader face to face with momentous events: rampant lynchings and mob violence, the white primaries, the American occupation of Haiti, the Scottsboro case, two world wars, *Brown vs. Board of Education*, the sit-ins, the March on Washington, the urban riots, and the Kennedy, King, and Evers assassinations. The reader will witness the words and actions of these three leaders who emerge in towering dimensions as they tactically battle the enemies of freedom who used race discrimination in virtually every phase of African-American life to implant roadblocks to justice.

This volume likewise documents the reality and verity that all hearts imbued with morality, regardless of color, seek justice. The pivotal role of white founders and white sustaining members—the Spingarn brothers, Clarence Darrow, Arthur

Garfield Hays, Oswald Garrison Villard, Mary White Ovington, Kivie Kaplan, and countless others—was critical to the development and growth of the NAACP. The coalescing of these white freedom fighters with powerful black civil rights warriors like W. E. B. Du Bois, Charles Hamilton Houston, William Hastie, Ralph Bunche, Robert Weaver, Addie Hunton, Medgar Evers, and Thurgood Marshall propelled the NAACP into the forefront of political and social thought and action.

The most crucial challenge facing James Weldon Johnson during his tenure as leader of the NAACP was the eradication of lynching—what he called the saving of black America's bodies and white America's souls. During his leadership, most of the NAACP's resources were used to fight for passage of a federal anti-lynching bill. Although a federal anti-lynching bill was never passed, through widespread publicity and his intense congressional lobbying efforts, he brought home the facts of the crime to the American people as they had never been brought before. Therefore, Johnson as much as anyone must be credited for the vast reduction in lynchings that occurred by the time he resigned as secretary of the NAACP in 1930.

Racial brutalities and murders were no longer a principal focus of the Association when White became secretary in 1931; therefore, he began to channel the organization's resources in other areas, including the white primaries, restrictive housing covenants, segregation in transportation and places of recreation, and desegregation of public education from primary school to graduate institutions.

Walter White has certainly not received his historical due regarding the quest for freedom in America. He often seems fixed and mired in the 1950s era of the black struggle for freedom. I hope his writings presented here will serve to demonstrate the inaccuracy of such an assumption by underscoring his unique contributions to the African-American journey. Whereas Johnson gave the NAACP 14 years of service but devoted much of his career to creative writing. White spent 37 years with the Association and, as its secretary, used a blending of intelligence, perseverance, audacity, public relations, and a myriad of diverse contacts to become one of the nation's major champions of civil rights.

Walter White died nearly one year after the victorious *Brown* decision, and the task of leadership was handed to Roy Wilkins, who would guide the NAACP through some of the most perilous and momentous times of its existence. His leadership is allied with the 1963 March on Washington, the issues of rising black militancy, and the civil rights acts of 1957, 1964, and 1965. From the mid-1960s until his retirement in 1977, he spent an exorbitant amount of time trying to implement these federal enactments on state and local levels. His leadership is critically important to understanding the black struggle during the modern civil rights movement.

The NAACP began as a board-dominated organization controlled by a few white progressives and the lone African American, the distinguished intellectual William Edward Burghardt Du Bois. A discussion of the rise of black empowerment in the NAACP bureaucracy is presented in the editor's notes. As board member and director of publicity and research, Du Bois also spoke for the NAACP as editor of its official organ, the *Crisis*. The initial by-laws underscored the organization's center of power, stating "that the chairman of the Board shall be the executive officer of the Association with full authority."[2] In the NAACP's early stages, the white board members were indispensable to the objectives of the Association because of their affluence and expertise. Moreover, these spirited reformers believed they could give greater legitimacy and prestige to such a developing black movement.

In short, I hope to show the transformation of the NAACP from an organization founded and run mainly by a few wealthy white progressives to an unparalleled civil rights force empowered by some of the most talented black thinkers of the twentieth century. To illustrate this, I will discuss in the editor's notes how these three leaders consecutively took over the organization's field work, administration, board of directors, and legal department.[3] Further, the reader will witness how their stratagems ultimately set the NAACP on a course of expansion that generated a series of legal victories spawning an unrivaled civil rights revolution that changed the course of American history.

Parts I, II, and III of this volume contain the selected writings of Johnson, White, and Wilkins, respectively. With the exception of two essays, this selection of writings represents speeches, essays, and articles by these three men during their tenures as leader of the NAACP. These works consist of a selection of their monthly reports to the board of directors. The writings presented here document a civil rights organization's bureacratic history and illustrate the passionate declarations of social responsibility by three towering figures of the civil rights movement who were at the center of black thought and action for more than half of the twentieth century.

Johnson, White, and Wilkins accepted the challenge to change the future of this nation. This collection creates a revelant and dynamic present by providing a unique opportunity for reexamination of many unresolved questions. Their collective legacy symbolizes venerable lessons that transcend time. They laid solid stones in the foundation of freedom that all Americans stand upon today. Therefore, it is incumbent upon contemporary men and women who claim the mantle of leadership to build on the work of these statesmen. The challenge of the twenty-first century demands no less.

PART I

THE SELECTED WRITINGS
OF JAMES WELDON JOHNSON,
1920–1937

James Weldon Johnson,
circa late 1920s. From
the collection of
Jewel Sims Okala and
Sondra Kathryn Wilson

Mr. and Mrs. James Weldon Johnson, 1932. From the collection of Jewel Sims Okala
and Sondra Kathryn Wilson

James Weldon Johnson
(June 17, 1871–June 26, 1938)

A *Chronology*

1871   Born to James and Helen Louise Dillet Johnson on June 17, in Jacksonville, Florida.

1884   Makes trip to New York City.

1886   Meets Frederick Douglass in Jacksonville.

1887   Graduates from Stanton School, Jacksonville. Enters Atlanta University Preparatory Division.

1890   Graduates from Atlanta University Preparatory Division. Enters Atlanta University's freshman class.

1891   Teaches school in Henry County, Georgia, during the summer following his freshman year.

1892   Wins Atlanta University Oratory Prize for "The Best Methods of Removing the Disabilities of Caste from the Negro."

1893   Meets Paul Laurence Dunbar at the Chicago World's Fair.

1894   Receives B.A. degree with honors from Atlanta University. Delivers valedictory speech, "The Destiny of the Human Race." Tours New England with the Atlanta University Quartet for three months. Is appointed principal of Stanton School in Jacksonville, Florida, the largest African-American public school in the state.

1895   Founds the *Daily American*, an afternoon daily serving Jacksonville's black population.

1896   Expands Stanton School to high school status, making it the first public high school for blacks in the state of Florida.

1898   Becomes the first African American to be admitted to the Florida bar.

1900   Writes the lyrics to "Lift Every Voice and Sing," with music by his brother J. Rosamond Johnson. Meets his future wife, Grace Nail, in New York.

1901   Is elected president of the Florida Teachers Association. Is nearly lynched in a Jacksonville park; this near lynching makes him realize that he cannot advance in the South.

1902   Resigns as principal of Stanton School to move to New York and form a musical trio—Cole and the Johnson Brothers. As part of this trio he writes over 200 songs, many of which are used in Broadway productions.

1903   Attends graduate school at Columbia University, where he studies with Brander Matthews, professor of dramatic literature.

1904   Writes two songs for Theodore Roosevelt's presidential campaign. Becomes a member of the National Business League, an organization founded by Booker T. Washington. Receives honorary degree from Atlanta University. During this time he meets W. E. B. Du Bois, then a professor at Atlanta University.

1905   With Cole and the Johnson Brothers, goes on European tour. Becomes president of the Colored Republican Club in New York City.

1906   Accepts membership in the American Society of International Law. Is appointed U.S. consul to Venezuela by President Theodore Roosevelt.

1909   Is promoted to U.S. consul to Nicaragua.

1910   Marries Grace Elizabeth Nail, daughter of successful Harlem businessman John B. and Mary Frances Nail, on February 3, in New York City.

1912   Publishes anonymously *The Autobiography of an Ex-Colored Man*, probably the earliest first-person narrative in fiction written by an African American.

1913   Resigns from the consular service because of race prejudice and party politics.

1914   Accepts position at the *New York Age* as contributing editor. Becomes a founding member of the American Society of Composers, Authors, and Publishers (ASCAP). Joins Sigma Pi Phi fraternity and Phi Beta Sigma fraternity.

1915   Becomes member of the NAACP. Puts into English the libretto of *Goyescas*, the Spanish grand opera, which is produced at the Metropolitan Opera House.

1916   Attends the NAACP Conference in Amenia, New York, at the estate of J. E. Spingarn. Delivers speech "A Working Programme for the Future." Joins the staff of the NAACP in the position of Field Secretary.

1917   Publishes volume *Fifty Years and Other Poems*. Publishes poem
        "Saint Peter Relates an Incident of the Resurrection Day." With
        W. E. B. Du Bois, leads over 12,000 marchers down New York's
        Fifth Avenue to protest lynchings and riots. Becomes acting
        secretary of the NAACP. Supports U.S. entry into World War I and
        fights against the atrocities perpetrated against black soldiers.
        Meets Walter White in Atlanta and persuades him to join the staff
        of the NAACP. Attends a conference of the Intercollegiate Socialist
        Society in Bellport, New York, and gives a talk on the contribution
        of the Negro to American culture. With W. E. B. Du Bois, becomes
        a charter member of the Civic Club, a liberal club that grew to be
        a strong influence in the life of black New Yorkers.

1918   Is responsible for an unprecedented increase in NAACP
        membership in one year, particularly in the South, making the
        NAACP a national power.

1919   Participates in converting the National Civil Liberties Bureau,
        a permanent organization, to the American Civil Liberties Union.

1920   NAACP board of directors name him secretary, making him the
        first African American to serve in that position. Based on his
        earlier investigation of the American Occupation of Haiti,
        he publishes four articles on "Self-Determining Haiti" in the *Nation*.

1922   Publishes *The Book of American Negro Poetry*.

1924   Assists several writers of the Harlem Renaissance.

1925   Co-authors with J. Rosamond Johnson *The Book of American Negro
        Spirituals*. Receives NAACP's Spingarn Medal.

1926   Co-authors with J. Rosamond Johnson *The Second Book of American
        Negro Spirituals*. Purchases an old farm in the Massachusetts
        Berkshires and builds a summer cottage called Five Acres.

1927   During the height of the Harlem Renaissance, *The Autobiography of
        an Ex-Colored Man* is reprinted. (The spelling "coloured" was used
        to attract British sales of the book.) *God's Trombones* is published.

1928   Receives Harmon Award for *God's Trombones*. Receives D. Litt. from
        Howard University and Talledega College.

1929   Takes a leave of absence from the NAACP to attend the Third
        Japanese Biennial Conference on Pacific Relations. Receives Julius
        Rosenwald Fellowship to write *Black Manhattan*.

1930   Publishes *Black Manhattan*. Publishes *Saint Peter Relates an Incident*
        in a small private edition. Resigns as secretary of the NAACP on
        December 17.

1931   Publishes the revised and enlarged edition of *The Book of American
        Negro Poetry*. Is honored by the NAACP at a testimonial dinner in
        New York City attended by over 300 guests. Is appointed vice
        president and board member of the NAACP. Accepts Fisk University

appointment as the Adam K. Spence Professor of Creative Literature.

1933   Publishes autobiography *Along This Way*. Attends the Second NAACP Amenia Conference.

1934   Is appointed visiting professor, fall semester, at New York University, becoming the first of his race to hold such a position at the institution. Receives the Du Bois Prize for *Black Manhattan* for the best book of prose written by an African American during a three-year period. Publishes *Negro Americans, What Now?* Is hospitalized at Hubbard Hospital in Nashville, Tennessee, for tonsillitis.

1935   Publishes *Saint Peter Relates an Incident: Selected Poems*.

1938   Dies as the result of an automobile accident in Wiscasset, Maine, nine days after his sixty-seventh birthday on June 26. Funeral held at the Salem Methodist Church in Harlem on Thursday, June 30. Is cremated and interred at the Nail family plot in Green-Wood Cemetery, Brooklyn, New York.

Selected Reports of the NAACP Secretary to the Board of Directors, 1920–1929

Editor's Note

James Weldon Johnson would have been considered a successful man had he remained the principal of Stanton School in his hometown of Jacksonville, Florida. Destiny led him, however, to become the first African American to pass the Florida bar exam and to win international acclaim as a lyricist, poet, novelist, diplomat, and champion of human rights.

When Johnson joined the staff of the NAACP in 1916, the organization lacked the power that comes from substantial and active memberships. Nevertheless, the Association had made great strides in its nine-year existence by effectively using agitation through mass meetings, as well as through newspapers, journals, and other print media. It was increasingly apparent that the NAACP faced an irrefutable increase in relentless race prejudice and discrimination. The board of directors understood that the organization would wither on the vine unless it made more inroads into the black community, and this meant more branches. By now, only 70 branches had been formed and most of them were quiescent and in the North, with a total membership of 9,000. The NAACP's meager yearly income was $14,000, a portion of which came from shriveling black membership dues.[1]

Chairman of the Board J. E. Spingarn set out to find the person who could turn the membership problem around. Reading James Weldon Johnson's *New York Age* column, Spingarn was so impressed by Johnson's well-crafted editorials and intellectual acumen that he convinced the board to hire him as field secretary and organizer.

In the fall of 1916 when Johnson joined the staff, he and W. E. B. Du Bois were the only two African Americans in administrative positions in the NAACP's Fifth Avenue offices. Roy Freeman Nash, a white progressive who had headed a North Carolina NAACP branch, was now secretary. Dedicated board members such as brothers Joel and Arthur Spingarn, Oswald Garrison Villard, and Mary White Ovington volunteered their time to the daily administrative tasks of the organization.

In his new role as field secretary and organizer, Johnson compiled a list of black ministers, heads of schools, and secret fraternal organizations throughout the nation. He used every available opportunity to talk to groups and individuals about the work of the NAACP as an initial bridge between the Association and black communities so that he could increase memberships.

During his early years with the NAACP, he committed the organization to the widest form of publicity against the crime of lynching. Joining the Harlem NAACP branch for a Silent Parade, he and Du Bois led 12,000 men, women, and children down Fifth Avenue to protest the lynchings and mob violence that had occurred during July 1917.

That same year, Roy Nash resigned as secretary. The board of directors was unwilling to replace Nash with a black secretary. However, Johnson was named acting secretary. In 1918 John R. Shillady, a white social worker from Westchester County, New York, was hired as the new secretary. And twenty-four-year-old Walter White of Atlanta, Georgia, was added to the administrative staff as assistant secretary.

After an undistinguished two-year tenure as secretary, Shillady resigned and Johnson, once again, filled in as acting secretary. The Association was now being attacked for its white-controlled board of directors. The initial by-laws of the NAACP underscored the organization's center of power by stating "that the chairman of the Board shall be the executive officer of the Association with full authority."[2]

From the NAACP's inception in 1909 to 1920, four secretaries had been white and generally incompetent. The sensitivity around the race issue that each white secretary faced may have caused some debilitation of leadership. There were charges of white paternalism from within and outside the NAACP. Nevertheless, the board remained adamant in its decision to keep the secretaryship white. Board member and NAACP founder Charles Edward Russell wrote that "a white-controlled board and secretary were necessary in order that the NAACP not isolate itself from the sources of power in American society; otherwise it could cease to exist."[3]

Marcus Garvey was clearly the most outspoken and most vitriolic in his opposition to the NAACP's policy on white leadership. Garvey, who had come to America from Jamaica, West Indies, in 1916 and founded the Universal Negro Improvement Association (UNIA) in 1918, had not sought white patronage for his own organization. Arguing that "[t]he Negro must have a country and nation of his own," he was fast becoming the leader of the largest organization of its type in the world in the history of Africans and their descendants.[4] Not only was he the most widely known black leader in Harlem, but he generated a bond among his international followers that produced a spirited discontent over the loss of independence due to colonialism and oppressive tactics.[5] Newspaper editor T. Thomas Fortune argued that "Garvey had constrained the Negro to think Negro, and that is a great achievement."[6] Johnson and other NAACP officials charged that Garvey, who was not an American citizen and had not conceived a thoughtful and practical plan for black Americans, had taken it upon himself to advocate that blacks forsake their constitutional rights, leave this nation, and go to Africa.

Even the radical *Boston Guardian* editor Monroe Trotter slammed the white-controlled NAACP. Describing his own organization, The Negro American Political League, which was practically threadbare of funds and talent, "as an organization of the colored people and for the colored people and led by the colored people,"[7] Trotter further denounced the NAACP's white leadership policy by asserting that "whites in any racial group would have a moderating function."[8]

Inside the NAACP headquarters Du Bois and Johnson knew that Trotter and Garvey had some merit to their claims against the white-controlled organization. Du Bois wrote during this time that the NAACP could never succeed in America unless it became an organization similar to that of the white philanthropists who were in the Anti-Slavery Society. Du Bois argued that almost everything in the NAACP tended to break "along the color line." He further charged that his well-meaning white colleagues had their limits and that racial distinctions were the basis for his disagreements with them. Moreover, he strongly urged that the new secretary be black because no competent white person could be successful in that role.[9] Du Bois vociferously complained about this inside the offices of the NAACP; however, James Weldon Johnson sought another strategy.

Even though Johnson believed that Garvey and Trotter had some successes, especially Garvey's unique ability to mobilize African Americans, he still maintained that the NAACP was doing the heavy work.

By 1920 Johnson had spent four years building branches across the North and in the difficult South. He had strategically used his position as field secretary and organizer during these years to quietly gather the forces in the field—building armies of members across the nation. Now, for the first time, 95 percent of the NAACP's funding came from black members. Not only had Johnson been adroit at building a strong base in the black community, but the important administrative work was being planned and executed by him and Assistant Secretary Walter White.[10] Johnson and White represented the NAACP in Washington, lobbying congressmen, senators, and cabinet members—in other words, bearing the chief public responsibility for the Association and, in their visible roles, proving themselves effective in the eyes of their race.

Still determined to keep the secretaryship white, the board now had to contend with a burgeoning black NAACP constituency that was growing increasingly impatient with the white-controlled civil rights organization. NAACP Branch Director Robert Bagnall wrote during this time, "Found every branch I visited clamoring for the ratification of Johnson as secretary."[11] Political scientist E. E. Schattschneider observed, "The outcome of all conflict is determined by the scope of its contagion. The number of people involved in any conflict determines what happens. . . . [C]onflicts are won or lost by the success that the contestants have in getting participants involved."[12] Johnson understood the power of the stalwart board. Nevertheless, the expanding and aggressive black constituency he had reared as field secretary began to shift the organization's balance of power. With such an ardent and incensed base of support and no one else contending, the board finally named Johnson secretary in the fall of 1920. About Johnson's tactic, noted political scientist Warren Bennis writes, "nothing serves an organization better than leadership that knows what it wants, communicates those intentions, positions itself correctly, and empowers its [members]."[13]

Johnson must be credited with the advent of black empowerment in the NAACP bureaucracy. After becoming the chief executive officer of the Association, he now had a mollified black constituency that provided him with authority that was at least tantamount to that of the board of directors. His tasks as chief administrative officer included coordinating board, staff, and branches so that the NAACP could handle its growing caseload effectively. Walter White served as Johnson's assistant. And for ten years the two worked amicably and successfully as a team.

Although a federal anti-lynching law was never passed, Johnson's most significant contribution to the civil rights movement was the pivotal role he played in the drastic reduction of lynchings. In 1921 Congressman L. C. Dyer of St. Louis wrote to Johnson about reintroducing an anti-lynching bill in Congress. Johnson made a number of trips to Washington during the greater part of 1922 to lobby for passage of the Dyer Anti-Lynching Bill. The bill passed in the House but failed in the Senate. Afterward, Johnson reflected, "The Dyer Anti-Lynching Bill did not become a law, but it made the floors of Congress a forum in which facts were brought home to the American people as they had never been before."[14]

During the 1920s, as leader of the nation's oldest and largest civil rights organization, Johnson became the foremost champion of civil rights for blacks in America. In the role of chief executive officer, with his subordinates, he consciously placed himself in a position of "first among equals," but always emerging as the consummate leader. He was praised by the board for his velvet glove and smooth approach in getting people to do what he desired for the good of the NAACP. He lost not one of his administrative staff during his ten-year tenure as leader of the Association.

While championing civil rights, Johnson helped to generate and lead the black literary movement of the 1920s known as Harlem Renaissance. His role as a leader of the Harlem Renaissance while simultaneously running the NAACP is legend. The work of extolling his race through the NAACP had given him a high degree of gratification but he experienced some disillusionment as well. After numerous political, economic, educational, and religious strategies had been implemented with only varying degrees of success, he believed there had to be another means to bring about political and social parity in America. He regarded the artistic approach as a means for advancing the cultural dignity of black Americans in national and international life. Johnson's own creative output during his tenure as secretary of the NAACP was exceptional. During the 1920s, he edited pioneering anthologies of black American poetry and spirituals. His most famous work, *God's Trombones: Seven Negro Sermons in Verse*, was published in 1927 at the height of the Harlem Renaissance.

Some historians have written that Johnson's most important contribution to his race was more effectively expressed through his literary works. On the other hand, some assert that his greatest contribution was made through the arena of civil rights. In working to uplift his race through one means or the other, he often used both concomitantly. The fact that he could simultaneously lead the black literary movement and the NAACP illustrates how closely the two objectives were tied. This unique duality distinguishes him as one of the exceptional figures of the twentieth century.

The following selections of Johnson's monthly reports to the board reveal the nature and enormity of his work. It is apparent from these reports that his most laborious and troubling challenge was the NAACP's anti-lynching crusade, what he called "the saving of black America's bodies and white America's souls." In this section, the reader will be made aware of James Weldon Johnson's dedication to the advancement and celebration of his people. Hopefully, this selection of reports will encapsulate the spirit and substance of the race problem in another era and reveal Johnson's consummate leadership style.

Report of the Secretary for the
Board Meeting of December 1920

Anti-Lynching

Since the convening of Congress the National Office has had assurances from both Senator Curtis, who introduced the Anti-Lynching Bill in the Senate, and Congressman Dyer, who introduced the Anti-Lynching Bill in the House, that they will immediately become active in pushing these measures. The branches of the Association have been asked to urge upon their members and others to write their senators and representatives requesting that they vote for these measures.

Congressman Dyer is to be one of the speakers at an Anti-Lynching Meeting which is to be held by the Brooklyn Branch on December 9, at the Academy of Music. The other speakers will be Senator Joseph I. France of Maryland, Mrs. Mary B. Talbert, and the Assistant Secretary [Walter White].

Ocoee, Fla.

The Assistant Secretary, who was sent to investigate the lynching at Ocoee, Fla., on election day, reports the following as his findings:

1. That between thirty and sixty Negroes were killed in election rioting in and near the town of Ocoee, Florida, on November 2;
2. That by flagrant violation of the terms of the United States Constitution and of local election laws, Negroes in Ocoee, Jacksonville, and other Florida towns and cities were prevented from voting;
3. That intimidation by the Ku Klux Klan and other agencies apparently beyond the control of the State of Florida was systematically and persistently practiced against colored people for weeks preceding the election, and especially on the Saturday night immediately preceding;
4. That the election rioting about Ocoee resulted not only in the burning of eighteen Negro houses, but also in the destruction of a school, a church, and a lodge hall;
5. That less than a week after [the] election, citizens of Ocoee publicly boasted of a number of colored people killed in the riots, one white man claiming seventeen colored victims.

The above information was sent to Attorney General Palmer with the statement that sufficient evidence of violence, fraud, and illegality is at hand to make it possible to disqualify the entire vote of the State of Florida. At the same time the Association offered to the Department of Justice its cooperation in an immediate investigation of the atrocities at Ocoee and the terrorization of colored voters by the Ku Klux Klan in Florida and other states.

A reply was received from the Department of Justice to the effect that it would be glad to receive any further information the Association had to give but suggested that the facts be first submitted to our legal adviser in order to determine whether or not the cases presented constitute a violation of rights secured to Negroes under the Federal Constitution or laws as distinguished from the constitutions and laws of the several states involved.

As soon as the Legal Committee has gone over the evidence secured by Mr. White it will be submitted to the Department of Justice.

Since the last report to the Board the following lynchings have occurred:

- Kant Junction, Tenn.: On November 14, Dave Hunt, held for alleged assault on an aged woman, was taken from jail by a mob of about seventy-five men and hanged to a bridge.
- Tylertown, Miss.: On November 10, Ben Jacobs, accused of an attack on a white woman, was lynched.
- Douglas, Ga:. On November 18, two men, Alex Byrd and Willis Ivory, and one woman, Minnie Ivory, charged with the murder of a white man, were taken from a sheriff and two deputies and lynched.
- Tylertown, Miss.: On November 23, Harry Jacobs, brother of Ben Jacobs, on trial for assault on a white woman, was taken from the courtroom and lynched by a mob which broke down the doors to reach him.
- Princeton, Fla.: On November 24, Curley McKelvey was shot by a posse in search of his brother who had murdered a white man.
- Holdenville, Okla.: On December 5, an unidentified Negro, charged with an attack on a white woman, was taken from jail by a mob of about fifty men and hanged. His body was riddled with bullets.

The *New York Times* of November 26 gave the following news, which is most unusual:

Fort Worth, Texas, Nov. 25: Robert Lowe, a Negro youth, charged with assaulting a ten-year-old white girl, was acquitted by a jury here at noon today. The Negro recently was rescued twice from a mob.

Haiti

The proceedings of the Naval Board of Inquiry have been closely followed by the National Office. The *New York Tribune* of December 2 carried a dispatch stating that a group of Haitian citizens had cabled to Secretary Daniels protesting against the conduct of the Naval Board of Inquiry in that the Board failed to investigate "numerous alleged cases of mistreatment and murders of Haitians by members of the United States Marine Corps."

The National Office immediately wired Secretary Daniels asking that the protest made by the Haitian citizens be published for the American people.

Secretary Daniels replied by sending us a copy of the telegram from the Haitian citizens as well as a copy of his order to Admiral Mayo to make a full investigation: The telegram was as follows:

Haitian people enter protest against the departure, suddenly of Naval Court without deciding on numerous cases of bad treatment and murder of Haitians by Marine Corps. The right to bring these facts to the knowledge of the magnanimous people of America. (Signed) Citizens of Port-au-Prince.

Secretary Daniels cabled this telegram to Rear Admiral Harry S. Knapp who is now in Haiti and added:

Department understands Court of Inquiry has left on Niagara. Please ascertain who above citizens of Port-au-Prince are and take up such matters as they may desire to present in connection with the protest stated above along the lines of your general investigation.

The National Secretary has written several times to a dozen of the leading Haitian citizens to [stir] them to united action in the present crisis of their country. He has received a resolution adopted and signed by fifty-five prominent Haitians pledging themselves to such action. He has also received numerous letters from Haitians thanking him for efforts made in behalf of Haitian independence.

An article on Haiti written by the Secretary appeared in the *Christian Herald* for November 6.

Reduction of Southern Representation

As a response to the telegram which was sent to Congressman Siegel by the last meeting of the Board of Directors urging a reapportionment of representation in accordance with the terms of the Fourteenth Amendment, Mr. Siegel wrote that our telegram would be submitted to the Census Committee. He asked whether we desired to be heard before the Committee to which we replied in the affirmative.

On December 3 the Secretary, the Assistant Secretary, and Mr. Seligmann had a conference with Mr. Siegel in New York in which Mr. Siegel said he was to introduce a bill which would bring up the whole question of southern representation.

The press of December 6 carried the news that on December 5 Congressman George H. Tinkham of Massachusetts had announced that he had prepared a resolution for introduction the following day "directing the House Census Committee to make an inquiry into the extent of disfranchisement of Negroes in the South and to recommend cutting down the representation of those states accordingly." Mr. Tinkham insists that the representation of the southern States in the

House and in the electoral college should be reduced unless Negroes are allowed to vote.

On December 5 the National Office sent a telegram to Mr. Tinkham endorsing his demand and offering to place evidence at his disposal.

Arkansas Situation

A telegram received from Attorney Scipio A. Jones, December 6 stated that the Arkansas State Supreme Court had reversed the verdict in the six cases pending before it. Mr. Jones has been asked to wire us the details. It is assumed that these cases are those of the men whose cases were remanded for a new trial. The men were retried and resentenced to death in the Phillips County Circuit Court.

In connection with the Arkansas cases—a press dispatch was received at the National Office stating that the Helena, Arkansas, Branch of the American Legion had passed a resolution asking that the Governor exercise no clemency in behalf of the convicted men but that the men be electrocuted. The National Office sent a telegram of protest against the misuse of the functions of the American Legion, to Colonel F. W. Galbrath, Jr. National Commander, and asked if it is the intention of the American Legion not only to exclude colored veterans of the World War from membership but to publicly urge the execution of the colored men whose cases are before the courts.

Ku Klux Klan

The Ku Klux Klan, the revival of which began in 1919, has now branches in nine states: Alabama, Arkansas, Florida, Georgia, North Carolina, South Carolina, Tennessee, Texas, and Virginia. Its Headquarters are at Atlanta, Ga.

The National Office has issued a statement to the press warning against the acceptance of statements from "Col." William J. Simmons, "Imperial Wizard" of the Ku Klux Klan to the effect that his organization stands for Americanism, and pointing out that on the contrary the Ku Klux Klan exists to enforce the violation of the United States Constitution by terrorizing Negroes out of their vote.

Governor Bickett of North Carolina has condemned the organization and methods of the Ku Klux Klan, branding it as a "wicked appeal to race prejudice."

Louisville Bond Issue

For some time previous to election day the Louisville Branch had been fighting a Bond Issue proposed for the University of Louisville, a white institution in which no colored persons are allowed to enter. The Bond issue was to tax all citizens alike for this school and the Branch fought it on the ground of taxation without representation. Due to the activity of the Branch in getting out literature and securing speakers against the Bond issue, it was defeated on election day.

Civil Rights

The first civil rights case brought by a Negro to engage the attention of the California Court of Appeals was fought and won by Attorney E. Burton Ceruti, member of the Board of Directors of the N.A.A.C.P. The decision affirms the right to damages of a colored boy who was obliged to sit in a segregated section of a motion picture theatre in Fresno, California. It is expected that the case will be referred to as a precedent in other states where civil rights laws similar to the one in California are in force.

Publicity

Since the last report to the Board the following press stories have been sent out:

Civil Rights, 1
American Legion, 1
Justin Elie (Haitian Pianist), 1
Florida Election Riots, 1
Anti-Lynching Legislation, 1
Lynching, 1
Ku Klux Klan, 1
National Secretary, 2
Brooklyn meeting, 2
Haiti, 3
Reduction of Southern Representation, 4

Publications

A single sheet entitled, "Done in 1920," has been published for distribution at meetings. This gives the outstanding accomplishments for the year 1920.

Literature Sent Out

During the past month, 9,091 pieces of literature have been sent out. These included 1,394 pieces of organization literature (used by branches); 5,711 "Why All Americans," 135 "Legal Aspects of the Negro Question," and 114 "The Negro Question?" also 319 "Appeal to the Conscience of the Civilized World."

James Weldon Johnson, Secretary
December 8, 1920

Report of the Secretary for the
Board Meeting of March 1921

Anti-Lynching

In keeping with the suggestion made at the annual meeting of the Anti-Lynching Committee, influential and wealthy persons are being written to with a view to interesting them in the fight the Association is making against lynching, to the extent of making a substantial contribution to this work.

New Jersey Legislature

On February 16 a letter was received from Dr. W. G. Alexander, member of the House of Assembly of New Jersey, requesting that the Association prepare for him immediately the kind of Memorial or Resolutions it would like to have passed in the New Jersey Legislature asking Congress to make lynching a federal crime. The following resolutions were drawn and sent to Dr. Alexander:

Whereas, sixty-five persons were lynched in the United States in 1920, one of the victims of mob murder being a woman and eight being burned at stake.

Whereas, twelve persons were lynched in the United States between January 1 and February 18, 1921, of whom two were publicly burned at stake with degenerate cruelty.

Whereas, lynchings are not only unopposed by state and local officers but are for the most part carried out with impunity by the mob whose members are rarely ever prosecuted.

Be it therefore resolved, that in the name of the humanity for which America stands, the United States Congress be and hereby is asked to enact into law H.R. 14097, introduced in the 66th Congress, second session, by Representative Leonidas C. Dyer of Missouri, "to assure to persons within the jurisdiction of every state the equal protection of the laws, and to punish the crime of lynching" or such other legislation as the Congress may devise.

In addition the National Office sent to each member of the New Jersey House of Assembly copies of "An American Lynching" and "A Ten-Year Fight Against Lynching."

Since the last report to the Board the following lynchings have occurred:

• Wauchula, Fla.: February 10. Ben Campbell, a Negro, was taken from jail by a mob of 200 to 300 men, strung up to a telephone pole and his body riddled with bullets. The lynching followed the identification of Campbell by a young white girl whom he was alleged to have attacked earlier in the day.

- Ocala, Fla.: February 12. A mob broke into the county jail, and seized a Negro who had been arrested on a charge of attacking an aged white woman, took him to the scene of the alleged crime and hanged him. Though most of the papers carried the story as the usual case of "assault," the *New York Telegram* carried the headline, "Florida Mob Lynches Negro who Hit White Woman."
- Odena, Ala.: February 12. A Negro charged with cutting a Talladega policeman to death with a razor was taken from a train by a mob which boarded the train four miles above Odena, where the sheriff was expected to board the train with his prisoner in an effort to take him to Birmingham for safekeeping. Just as the sheriff started to board the train the mob swarmed out and took the Negro from the officer.
- Athens, Ga.: February 16. A mob of 5,000 stormed the Clarks County Jail and after forcibly taking John Lee Eberhardt, a Negro charged with the murder of Mrs. Walter Lee of Oconee County, from the jail, burned him at the stake.

State and county authorities have started an investigation into the Athens lynching and rewards totalling $4,500 have been offered for the arrest and conviction of members of the mob. $3,000 of this was offered by Governor Dorsey and the remainder by the board of county commissioners.

Arkansas Cases

The Arkansas situation to date is as follows: The Association has paid in the Arkansas cases and the Robert L. Hill extradition case $5,000 in attorneys fees and $3,499.39 in court costs, stenographic services, etc., making a total of $8,499.39. In addition, the Citizens Defense Fund Commission has expended the sum of $10,000 for court costs and attorneys' fees in connection with these cases.

The total expenditures to date for attorneys' fees are $11,100, $5,000 of which has been paid by the National Association and $6,100 by the Citizens Defense Fund Commission. The Association is further obligated to pay additional fees of $3,000. When this latter amount shall have been paid, the total expenditures of these cases will be $21,499.39, $11,499.39 of which will have been paid by the N.A.A.C.P.

On February 21, Scipio A. Jones wrote requesting that the Association authorize the employment of Colonel Brundidge of Searcy, Ark., to assist in the trial of the cases, succeeding the late Colonel Murphy. Mr. Jones stated that Colonel Brundidge's services could probably be secured for $2,500 although he had set a price of $5,000. On February 26 this letter was answered and the Association informed Mr. Jones of the payment of the amounts listed above and asked that Colonel Brundidge be employed but that his fee be paid from the balance of $3,000 which the Association has yet to pay.

Delegation to Senator Harding

Through correspondence the Secretary arranged for a delegation of citizens from Jacksonville, Fla., to have an interview with Senator Harding while he was at St. Augustine. The delegation consisted of Bishop Hurst, Dr. J. Seth Hills, Mr. N. K. McGill, and Captain James W. Floyd. They called on Senator Harding on February 22 and report having had a very satisfactory conference with Mr. Harding. They were informed that men of color would receive appointments through the South. The committee was also given assurance that wherever trouble was started in the South, the matter would be investigated.

National Woman's Party

Some weeks prior to the Convention of the National Woman's Party in Washington, February 15–18, Miss Ovington opened correspondence with officers and members of the Advisory Council of the Woman's Party requesting that a representative colored woman be invited to address the Convention. The persistent and heroic work of the Woman's Party in securing the passage of the Nineteenth Amendment made it reasonable to suppose that it would fight for the protection of the rights of the women in the South, both white and colored. Members of the Advisory Council warmly advocated Miss Ovington's proposition only to be met with refusal by Miss Alice Paul, President of the National Woman's Party, on the ground that representation in the Convention was limited to organizations which had undertaken a definite legislative program for women. Efforts to prove to her that the N.A.A.C.P. came under this head were futile. Mrs. W. Spencer Murray was very active in assisting the Association to gain recognition in the Convention. As a last resort the National Association called upon a number of representative organizations of colored women urging them to send delegates to Washington for a hearing by Miss Paul just prior to the Convention. The call met with an enthusiastic response from all over the country. Sixty women came from fourteen states and the District of Columbia, representative of the best thought and interests of colored women. Mrs. Mary Church Terrell was chosen spokesman for the delegation. Miss Paul showed no interest whatever. Immediately after this interview the colored women formed the Anthony League with Dr. Winifred S. Brown of the District of Columbia as President. The first work of the League was to make the National Woman's Party Convention go on record on the question of disfranchised women.

Mrs. Hunton acted for the National Office in organizing the delegation of colored women which appeared before the Convention. A full report of what was accomplished in Washington will be given by Mrs. Hunton at the Board meeting.

Haitian Mission

Pursuant to the recommendation made at the February meeting of the Board, the Secretary wrote Mr. Storey regarding his acting as counsel for the Haitian Mission.

Mr. Storey has expressed his willingness to act with Mr. [Arthur] Spingarn as far as advising and consulting with him are concerned, but he does not feel that his business will allow him to go before committees in Washington, examine witnesses, etc.

The three members of the Haitian Mission, now in this country, are keeping in close touch with National Office and have already had several interviews with the Secretary.

Publications

During the month reprints have been made of the pamphlets, "An American Lynching," and "A Ten-Year Fight Against Lynching." These are being used as Drive Literature. Reprints have also been made of a portion of the February Bulletin for use in the Drive.

Publicity

Since the last report to the Board the following press stories have been sent out:

"An American Lynching" has been sent to the entire white and colored press of the United States and to a selected list of papers in Europe, Japan, and South America. "A Ten-Year Fight Against Lynching" has been sent to the Colored Press of the United States.

Literature Sent Out

During the month 23,765 pieces of literature have been sent out. This does not include instructions sent to branches on the Drive which consisted of forty pages of mimeographed material.

Spingarn Medal Award

Bishop John Hurst, Chairman of the Committee of Award of the Spingarn Medal, has called a meeting of the Committee for April 13 or 14 at the office of the Association. A press release asking for recommendations has been sent to the white and colored press, and it is asked that all recommendations be in the hands of the Committee by April 1.

James Weldon Johnson, Secretary
March 5, 1921

Report of the Secretary for the
Board Meeting of June 1921

Anti-Lynching

Since the last report to the Board the following lynchings have occurred:

- April 25: Pearl River County, Miss.: An anonymous letter from Pica-yune, Miss., states that a Negro was lynched on the charge of having assaulted a white girl.
- April 26: Picayune, Miss: A Negro whose name could not be learned was hanged to a telegraph pole and his body riddled with bullets, after a mob had taken him from the sheriff and justice of the peace. He had been accused of assaulting the wife of a white man near Ozone, Miss.
- April 29: Bowling Green, Mo.: Roy Hammonds, nineteen years old, awaiting transportation to the penitentiary on a charge of attempted assault on a fourteen-year-old white girl, was seized by a mob which overpowered the sheriff and hanged [him] to a telegraph pole.
- May 7: Berry Bolling, white, an alleged "mountain bad man," was lynched by a mob of fifty armed men who gained entrance to the Scott County jail, removed him and hanged him to a tree. He had been arrested on a charge of murdering a white woman.
- May 8: Starke, Fla.: Sam Ballinger, who shot and killed a deputy sher-iff, was taken from the Bradford County jail and lynched. The mob worked so quietly that the lynching was not discovered until morning when the body was found hanging to a tree.

Tulsa, Oklahoma, Riots

On June 1 the City Editor of the *New York Evening Post* telephoned the National Office asking if it had any statement to make regarding the riot taking place in Tulsa, Okla. At that time the National Office had no knowledge of the affair. The *Evening Post* editor read over the telephone dispatches which had just come into his office stating that there had been about seventy-five fatalities and a half dozen blocks burned in the colored section.

The Secretary gave the *Post* a statement to the effect that, judging from the meager details, the riot was one of the worst that had taken place in recent years. This statement was also sent to the City News Association.

The Executive staff decided that an investigation should be made as to the real causes of the riot and the Assistant Secretary was sent to Oklahoma for that purpose, leaving within six hours after the news had been received.

The Secretary telegraphed the Governor of Oklahoma asking that he use the powers of his office to stop the disorders and offering the full cooperation of the N.A.A.C.P. He also wired President Harding asking for an utterance on the riots.

On June 2, eight colored people from Oklahoma came to the National Office asserting that they had been victims of peonage in and near the town of Okmulgee, which is about thirty miles from Tulsa, and that colored people in that section had received warnings weeks ago to leave the state or suffer the consequences. Before their flight the house of one of these persons had been set on fire three times in one night.

A story regarding these refugees was given to the press.

Relief Fund

The National Office has established a relief fund to be applied to aiding the colored victims of the riot.

The Assistant Secretary is expected to return before the meeting of the Board when a full report of his investigation will be given. So far we have only the statements regarding the riot made in the daily press.

Arkansas Situation

Mr. Scipio A. Jones writes under date of May 30:

> I have reason to believe that Judge Jackson will pass on the petition for change of venue Wednesday, June 1, and entertain some hope that the Governor will postpone indefinitely the electrocution of the other six men until after the trials of the six men who have been granted new trials.
>
> We have prepared our petition for habeas corpus proceedings in the event the Governor refuses to postpone the execution in these cases. If Judge Jackson grants the change of venue and sends it to Woodruff County, the cases will not likely be tried until some time in August, and I have planned to file petition to the courts of this city (Little Rock) asking that the six men awaiting trials will be granted bail. I have also planned to have all of the five-year men apply for parole the first of August. If this is granted, it will only leave the twenty-one-year men in the penitentiary.

It is hoped that a further report can be made on this matter at the meeting of the Board.

Jasper County Peonage Cases

Clyde Manning, who was implicated in the murder of eleven Negroes on the plantation of John S. Williams, has been sentenced to life imprisonment. As stated in the last report, Williams was convicted of murder in the first degree with a recommendation for mercy. This automatically sentenced him to life imprisonment.

Other Peonage Cases

As a result of the investigation being carried on by the Department of Justice arrests and convictions for peonage have been made in Florida, Georgia, Mississippi, and Tennessee. One of the cases in Florida was that of ex-Governor Sidney J. Catts who was charged with forcing Negroes whom he as Governor had pardoned to work on his farm. He was arrested on May 21 in Georgia and released on $2,500 bail, to appear June 13.

Anti-Lynching Measures

Since President Harding's message to Congress many anti-lynching measures have been introduced and the National Office has made an effort to impress upon the President and upon various Congressmen who seem anxious to see something done to stop lynching, that the colored people are looking to Congress to provide a remedy for lynching and not merely to provide for the investigation of lynching, as suggested by some of the bills introduced.

Dyer Bill

While in Washington (May 22–25) the Secretary saw Congressman Dyer who is sanguine that his anti-lynching bill will be reported out and that he will get a rule on it. He feels confident that no further hearings on the bill are necessary.

The Secretary saw Senator Curtis and told him that the Association had decided to support an anti-lynching bill rather than a resolution asking for an investigation of lynching. Senator Curtis said that he would be glad to give the bill his support.

The Secretary also saw Senator Capper and Congressmen Madden and Miller. Mr. Madden stated that he would exert all his strength toward securing the passage of the Dyer Bill. Mr. Madden is on the House Steering Committee and is able to help greatly in pushing the bill.

Congressman Martin Ansorge, who has also introduced an anti-lynching bill which calls for little more than an investigation, assured the Secretary that his bill would be entirely subordinated to the Dyer Bill. He said he was not pushing his bill at all but would labor to help the Dyer Bill; but that in case the Dyer Bill failed, he felt that the only remedy would be a bill calling for an investigation with the hope that the result would be to arouse national public opinion.

The Secretary believes that the present state of the Dyer Bill is good. Not only does Mr. Dyer feel confident of the bill, but it appeared to be the consensus of opinion among all the members of Congress with whom the Secretary talked that the Dyer Bill stood the best chance of any piece of anti-lynching legislation yet drawn of being passed. Senator McCormick expressed himself as in favor of Congressional investigation of lynching.

Inter-racial Commission

While in Washington the Secretary talked with Senator Spencer who has introduced what is up to this time the best bill on an Inter-racial Commission. The Senator seemed extremely well satisfied with his bill. The Secretary pointed out several features of the bill and suggested changes which had been discussed by the Association's staff, but the Senator feels that his bill is about as good as it can be made. One of the points to which attention was called was the proportion of colored members on the commission, named in the bill. It was suggested that the commission be composed of four white persons, four colored persons and the Chairman. Senator Spencer felt that the bill stood a much better chance of becoming a law as it was drawn, with six white and three colored members. He stated to the Secretary that he was working to have the bill reported out but that Senator Overman, one of the three members of the sub-committee on the Judiciary, who had the bill in charge, was opposed to it.

Later the Secretary saw Senator Overman and talked with him regarding the matter of an Inter-racial Commission. Senator Overman stated that his opposition was not merely to a commission on the race question, but that he was opposed to all commissions; that he opposed them because he was an old state's righter and did not believe in federal commissions interfering in the affairs of the states. He said another objection was that they were expensive and he did not feel like voting salaries and expenses for a commission to ride around the country and write a report nobody would read. (It must not be gathered from these statements that Senator Overman was curt or discourteous in this interview. On the contrary, he was extremely courteous and cordial.) The Secretary endeavored to impress upon the Senator the points in favor of a commission which are well known to the members of the Association's Board.

The Secretary endeavored to see Senator Ernst who is Chairman of the Sub-Committee on the Judiciary, which has the Inter-Racial Commission Bill in charge. Senator Ernst could not be seen in the three days that the Secretary was in Washington because of the presence of several delegations of Kentucky office-seekers in the city. However, the Secretary saw Mr. Robinson, the Senator's secretary, who assured him that the Inter-Racial Commission bills had not yet received any consideration and that it was not likely that Senator Ernst would be able to get to them before the lapse of two or three weeks. He said that the Senator had received all the communications sent from the National Office to the various senators regarding these bills, as they had been referred to him; and that he had sent them with other memoranda to President Harding. Mr. Robinson promised to keep the National Office informed as to the progress of these bills.

While in Washington the Secretary gathered that none of the Commission bills now drawn will be seriously considered but that the administration will have a bill drafted to carry out the ideas which President Harding has on the matter. The Secretary has taken up the matter with President Harding.

Committee on the Census

The Secretary saw Congressman Siegel, Chairman of the Committee on the Census, while in Washington, and talked with him regarding the hearing on the apportionment bill. Mr. Siegel said that he was not sure that there would be a hearing but that we would be notified in the event there was.

Haiti

The Secretary had a talk with Senator McCormick on the subject of Haiti. Senator McCormick is in favor of drastic reformation in Haiti but feels that the United States should remain there in a civil capacity for some time to come. He said that he had recently talked with Secretary Denby of the Navy and that Mr. Denby was no longer inclined to regard the Haitian charges as "mere rot." He said Mr. Denby expressed himself as in favor of abolishing military occupation.

Jim Crow

The Secretary talked with Congressman Madden regarding the Jim Crow Bill which he has introduced. Mr. Madden did not seem to be decidedly hopeful about his measure.

Washington Correspondent

Mr. Harold B. Allen, secretary to Congressman Miller of Washington, is acting as the Association's Washington correspondent. Mr. Allen declines to accept any remuneration for this service. He is deeply interested in the race question and is exceedingly well informed on men and affairs in Washington. The Secretary talked with Mr. Allen over the general situation with regard to measures in which the Association is interested

Frank A. Linney

During the last Presidential campaign Frank A. Linney of North Carolina, who is now seeking appointment as United States Attorney for the Western District of that state, made the following statement, as chairman of the Republican State Committee:

> The Republican Party has not made any effort to organize the Negroes in this campaign, men or women, nor will it openly, secretly or other-

wise connive at any such political strategy. I pledge to the women of North Carolina that if we carry the state in this election, you will have a strictly white government, honorable and efficient; and I further assure the good women of the state that in the future the Republican Party's policy will be to let the Negro stay out of politics. If the Democratic organization will meet us half way we are in a fair position by agreement between us to eliminate any possibility of the Negro question in this or any subsequent campaign.

Now the colored citizens of North Carolina are opposing Mr. Linney's appointment and the National Office is aiding them in every possible way. In the beginning of their fight the Secretary placed in Mr. Milholland's hand a copy of their petition to President Harding who took immediate steps to block the appointment. The Secretary also urged the Ohio Branches to send protests to the Attorney General who comes from that state.

During his trip to Washington the Secretary called on Senator Overman and talked with him regarding Mr. Linney and his sentiments as expressed above. Linney's appointment is in the hands of a subcommittee of which Senator Overman is a member, and his appointment would have been turned down absolutely had not Senator Overman asked for a reconsideration of the case.

The hearing on the Linney case is set for June 8 at which time citizens from North Carolina will appear.

"Birth of a Nation"

In the report for May it was mentioned that preparations were being made for picketing "The Birth of a Nation" which was being shown at the Capitol Theatre in New York City.

On May 6 a number of overseas veterans in their uniforms and three women who had done Y.W.C.A. work overseas, walked quietly up and down before the theatre and distributed leaflets descriptive of the activities of the Ku Klux Klan. There was no disturbance, and people seemed eager to receive the leaflets, none of them being thrown upon the streets. This method of protesting against the film after appeals to the manager of the theatre and to the city authorities had failed.

Notwithstanding the fact that there was absolutely no disorder five of the pickets, three of them women, were arrested. On May 12, in the West Side Court, Magistrate Ten Eyck offered to dismiss the charges against them if they would promise not to picket the Capitol Theatre again. Through their attorneys, Aiken C. Pope and James C. Thomas, retained by the Association, the pickets replied that they would not make any such promise, preferring to make this a test case. Accordingly, Magistrate Ten Eyck found them guilty and suspended sentence. The case is now on appeal.

Boston

The Boston Branch, together with other organizations, including a colored post of the American Legion, the Knights of Columbus, the Colored Veterans of All Wars, the National Colored Pythian Organization, the National Equal Rights League, was successful in preventing the showing of the film ["Birth of A Nation"] in that city. Mayor Peters suspended the license of the Shubert Theatre, acting upon the recommendation of the Board of Censors which had received protests from the organizations mentioned.

The fight made in New York did not succeed as in Boston because in New York there are no censors with the authority conferred on the censors in Boston. The Mayor and Police Commissioner of New York, to whom protests were carried, declared their lack of legal authority to interfere with the showing of the film.

Publicity

The Colored Press is most generous in space given to the news releases sent out from the National Office, which are very often given front page display.

Editorial mention in the white press is frequent. Exceptional success was had with the publicity concerning the Tulsa race riot. The *Evening Post* of June 1 published a front page interview with Dr. Du Bois and on the following day an interview with the refugees from Oklahoma. This interview also appeared at some length in the *Globe* and on the following morning in the *Times*, the *Tribune* and other newspapers, including the *World*, which displayed it on the front page. The *Call* published on June 2 a front page interview with the Secretary. The City News Association was given the text of the telegram sent President Harding in regard to the riot and this appeared in a number of newspapers.

The *New York Evening Post* of June 8 also carried a special story by the Assistant Secretary (sent up from Oklahoma) on the Tulsa riot.

Publications

In the *New York Age* of May 7 the Secretary commented on Governor Dorsey's booklet, "The Negro in Georgia." This statement has been reprinted in a four-page leaflet which is being distributed.

Reprints of several other pamphlets have been made during the month.

Literature Sent Out

During the month 30,488 pieces of literature have been sent out. These included:

A Ten-Year Fight Against Lynching	1,759
An American Lynching	1,415

The American Congo   970
The NAACP vs. the KKK   1,909
Done in 1920–Program for 1921   18,184

James Weldon Johnson, Secretary
June 9, 1921

Report of the Secretary for the Board Meeting August 1921

Anti-Lynching

Since the last report to the Board the following lynchings have occurred:

- July 23. Hattiesburg, Miss.: Casey Jones (white) convicted of the murder and sentenced to be hanged July 18, but whose case was pending before the Supreme Court, was taken from the County jail and hanged in the courthouse yard by a mob of about seventy-five masked men.
- August 3: Lawrenceville, Va.: One of two Negroes arrested August 2 in connection with the murder of a white man on August 1 was lynched. The other Negro was not molested.

Tulsa Riot Case

In response to a communication from the N.A.A.C.P. Committee in Oklahoma regarding the handling of the cases of the victims of the Tulsa Riot, in conjuction with the Tulsa Colored Citizens Relief Committee, the Secretary made it clear to our Committee that the National Office would not be responsible for the payment of any amount beyond what may be collected in the Tulsa Relief and Defense Fund. This letter stated:

> The National Office cannot enter into any agreement for the employment of counsel whereby it becomes responsible for sums which may exceed the receipts in the funds being collected for this specific purpose. The National Office can only take the position of giving assistance in this matter and that assistance will be all that is possible to give and will be limited only by the amount of money we are able to collect into the Tulsa Relief and Defense Fund. The Association must avoid placing itself in a position where it may have shouldered upon it a greater share of the responsibility than was its original intention to undertake.

Arkansas Situation

In the cases of the six men whose death sentences were affirmed by the State Supreme Court, a motion for a writ of error to the United States Supreme Court was filed and heard on August 4.

On August 4 the National Office received the following telegram from Scipio A. Jones:

Justice Holmes denied our petition for writ of error.

According to previous correspondence with Mr. Jones, the step to be taken in the event that the above action was taken by the United States Supreme Court would be the filing of a motion for a writ of habeas corpus in the Federal Court of the Eastern District of Arkansas. It is hoped that by this means the execution of these men can be delayed until after October when the other six cases will be re-tried in the Lee County Court.

According to a letter received from Dr. I. Garland Penn, who has recently been in Arkansas, the feeling is general in the state that the men will be eventually acquitted, and it is his opinion that the cases are being handled in a very intelligent manner by our lawyers.

Ray Extradition Case

Since September, 1920, the Detroit Branch of the Association and the National Office have been fighting to prevent the return of Thomas Ray, a colored man, to Wilkinson County, Ga., where he was wanted on a charge of murder. Ray's statement made under oath and amply borne out by the testimony, was that he shot and killed DeWitt Falkner, a white man of poor reputation in that community, when Falkner had without provocation, while intoxicated, attempted to kill Ray. Falkner seems to have gone on a wild rampage against colored people.

Ray escaped to Canada, later going to Detroit, where he was arrested.

The Association won a great victory when on the night of August 1, Governor Alexander J. Grossbeck revoked the writ of extradition which had been granted to the Georgia authorities by Albert Sleeper, Governor Grossbeck's predecessor in office. Following the granting of the original writ, a writ of habeas corpus was applied for by Ray's attorneys and granted. Ray was immediately re-arrested on the indictment which had been sent on from Georgia, the original arrest having been made on a warrant. Another writ of habeas corpus was applied for to the State Supreme Court, which affirmed the verdict of the Wayne County Circuit Court on July 20. Then a further appeal was made to Governor Grossbeck who held in abeyance the writ of extradition pending an investigation into the charge made by Ray's attorneys that plans had been made to lynch Ray.

On August 1 a telegram was received from W. Hayes McKinney, President of the Detroit Branch as follows:

Michigan's greatest Governor revokes warrant in Ray Case. Revocation of warrant ends case. Ray is free and released. If desired will send Governor's opinion. Most wonderful I ever heard. Also cuts of Governor and attorneys for September *Crisis*.

The National Office immediately wired its sincere and hearty thanks to Governor Grossbeck.

The attorneys in the case were Messrs. Willis and Hinton, employed by Ray's father, and the Detroit Branch associated with these lawyers its President, W. Hayes McKinney who is also a lawyer. The National Office rendered valuable assistance in this case, twice sending the Assistant Secretary to Michigan to testify, once before the Governor and once at the time of the motion for the second writ of habeas corpus.

Maurice Mays Case

The Knoxville (Tenn.) *Journal* of August 8 reported two cases of attacks upon white women, which tend to corroborate Mays' assertion that he is innocent of the crime attributed to him. In one of these cases the man, said to be a dark white man, told his victim that if she screamed he would murder her as he had killed Bertie Lindsey (the woman Mays is said to have murdered). Both of these alleged attacks occurred after Mays had been placed in prison.

The National Office has given wide publicity to this latest information, and has urged that the public give Mays all possible aid in his defense.

Colored Railway Trainmen

At the request of the Association of Colored Railway Trainmen the N.A.A.C.P., during the latter part of 1919, took up with the Railroad Administration the question of discrimination against colored trainmen under General Order #27 issued by Mr. McAdoo, at that time Director General of Railroads. This order granted equal pay for the same work done by all classes of employees.

In order to avoid paying colored trainmen in Southern States, particularly of the Illinois Central and the Yazoo and Mississippi Valley Railroads, colored trainmen who were doing and have done the work of baggage men, switchmen, brakemen and conductors, were classed as porters and given only the pay of porters.

In January, 1920, the Assistant Secretary appeared, with representatives of the Association of Colored Railway Trainmen, before a special board at Washington to argue the case. This effort proving of no avail, an appeal was taken to the Board of Wages and Working Conditions, with the result that colored men were granted an increase amounting to $1,225 monthly and back pay amounting to more than $125,000.

Following this victory white trainmen in Mississippi, Arkansas, Tennessee and surrounding states adopted Ku Klux Klan methods of getting rid of the colored trainmen. This situation became more acute with the industrial depression. Early in 1921 anonymous posters appeared and anonymous letters were sent to colored men threatening them with death unless they quit their jobs. When the colored men refused to be intimidated, a number of trains were halted and colored trainmen dragged from them, in some cases being severely beaten and in others killed. Appeals to state, county, and municipal authorities produced no results.

The matter was then taken up with the Interstate Commerce Commission under Section 1, Paragraph 23, of the Interstate Commerce Act which provided that during the continuance of the war any person who hampered or interfered with the passage of interstate commerce freight was guilty of an offense against the federal government.

The matter was also referred to the Department of Justice. The Interstate Commerce Commission claimed that it had no authority to take action. The Department of Justice declared that only one case came under the Act referred to above and that was the case of Howard Hurd, a colored man who was killed prior to the passage by Congress and the approval by the President of the Joint Resolution of March 3, 1921, which provided that all war-time acts of Congress should be construed as if the war had terminated March 3, 1921.

The Association immediately requested the Department of Justice to investigate the case of Howard Hurd hoping that it would result in an exposé of conditions which had caused the deaths of other trainmen.

On August 1 the *New York World* told of the arrest of two white men at Water Valley, Miss., on a charge of ambushing a colored trainman, stating that one of these men had been re-arrested by federal officers after he had made bond on the state charge. According to announcements of officials of the Illinois Central Railroad, special agents employed by them had discovered that a price of $300 had been placed on the head of every colored trainman. The Superintendent of the Illinois Central declared that colored trainmen would be protected at all costs. The National office is in receipt of a letter [from] J. H. Eiland, President of the Association of Colored Railway Trainmen, expressing hearty appreciation to the Association for its efforts.

Dyer Anti-Lynching Bill

While in Washington, July 25–28, the Secretary saw Mr. Dyer and talked with him regarding the anti-lynching bill. Mr. Dyer appeared to be more sanguine than ever regarding the ultimate passage of the bill. He stated that at a recent hearing at which Mr. Goff, the Assistant Attorney General appeared, Mr. Goff endorsed the constitutionality of the measure. The Secretary also talked with Mr. Moores who is the actual author of the Dyer Bill. Mr. Moores is also confident about the ultimate passage of the bill. He was at the time at work on a supplementary brief to be printed together with Mr. Goff's testimony before the Committee.

Note: Mr. Goff's testimony together with Mr. Moores' brief has been printed and copies have been secured by the National Office for distribution. (Copy enclosed.)

Mr. Dyer stated that he did not wish to have the bill reported out until after the recess which Congress would take probably about the middle of August, for a period of perhaps six weeks. He said his reasons were that the men in Congress were in bad temper on account of the hot weather and the large amount of work to be done, and that therefore definite action on the bill should not be risked at this time.

Inter-racial Commission Bill

The Secretary also talked at length with Senator Ernst regarding the Inter-racial Commission Bill. Mr. Ernst declared himsef in favor of such legislation. He stated that only Senator Overman of the sub-committee was opposed. Mr. Ernst stated also that he had taken the matter up with the President. He said that he had taken the Spencer Bill, which provides for a commission to study the race problem, and combined it with the McCormick Bill, which provides for the investigation of lynching, both bills being in the hands of his Committee.

The Secretary pointed out to Senator Ernst the probable danger of handicapping the Inter-racial Commission bill by joining it with the anti-lynching idea. He also called the Senator's attention to the status of the Dyer anti-lynching bill in the House. The Senator said he would cut out the lynching feature of the bill if it endangered the whole measure. He also stated that the only question which the majority of the subcommittee were hesitating on was the ultimate effect of this legislation. The Secretary feels the need of making very clear to Senator Ernst the Association's idea of an Inter-racial Commission Bill.

Colored Men in the Navy

Before leaving Washington the Secretary called on Colonel Theodore Roosevelt, the Assistant Secretary of the Navy, and brought to his attention the matter of the ratings of colored men in the Navy. The Secretary reminded Mr. Roosevelt that ten years or so ago colored men held high ratings in the Navy. He reminded him that at the Battle of Manila the first gun was fired by a colored gunner's mate. He then told Mr. Roosevelt that during the last few years colored men were unable even to enlist in the Navy except as mess boys, in other words, as servants, and that they were not permitted to hold the non-commissioned ratings which had previously been held by colored men.

Mr. Roosevelt expressed surprise at this condition. He made a memorandum and said he would look the matter up. The Secretary, however, will continue to press the matter through correspondence.

Haiti

A Senate Investigating Committee has been appointed in accordance with Senator McCormick's resolution, passed by Congress which provides "that a committee of five senators inquire into the occupation and administration of the territories of the Republic of Haiti and of the Dominican Republic by the forces of the United States.

At the meeting of the Conference of Executives on July 28 the matter was discussed. The Chairman was asked to attend a conference to be held at the office of the *Nation* on July 29, and it was voted that the Association send Mr. Seligmann to Washington to have charge of the publicity regarding the hearings before the Senate Investigation Committee and that the Association would approporiate $200 for immediate use in connection with the investigation.

At the Conference which the Chairman attended Mr. Ernest Angell was chosen as the lawyer to handle the Haitian matter.

On August 2 the Secretary attended a meeting held at the office of the *Nation* at which the Society for the Independence of Haiti and Santo Domingo was formed. This society [is] to begin work at once in connection with the hearings to be held before the Senate Investigating Committee. The temporary officers elected were: President, Moorfield Storey; Vice President, James Weldon Johnson; Secretary, Mrs. Helena Hill Weed; Treasurer, Robert Herrick; Executive Committee: Dr. Ernest H. Gruening, Herbert J. Seligmann, and Albert De Silver.

Pan African Congress

Dr. Du Bois and Mr. White, the Assistant Secretary, sailed for Europe on August 6 for the Pan African Congress. A program of the Congress is enclosed.

Case of Arthur K. Bird

(Colored Soldier) Upon the solicitation of a recruiting sergeant at Providence, R.I., Arthur K. Bird re-enlisted in the army after having been honorably discharged from the 156th Depot Brigade, a colored organization. Mr. Bird called the attention of the clerk to the fact that he had been erroneously listed as a white man. The clerk changed the designation under the heading "Race" to "colored." Mr. Bird is of such fair complexion that he may be easily mistaken for a white man. In spite of the correction made, Mr. Bird was sent to the Fifty-eighth Infantry at Camp Lewis, Washington. Upon arrival at the camp he found that the Fifty-eighth Infantry was a white organization and notified his Commanding Officer that he was not a white man. He was thereupon assigned to special duty.

Later Mr. Bird was dishonorably discharged, the reason being assigned as "fraudulent enlistment." In April this case was referrred to the National Office which took up the matter immediately with the War Department, demanding a thorough investigation and a correction of the injustice done Mr. Bird. The investigation proved him to be right in his contention. A letter to the National Office from the Adjutant General states "a certificate showing that he (Mr. Bird) is entitled to be regarded as having been honorably discharged from the military service has been prepared and forwarded to him."

Moorestown, N.J., Case

With regard to the case of the colored man arrested at Moorestown, N.J., reported at the last meeting of the Board by Dr. Sinclair, the National Office has written to the President of the Camden, N.J. Branch asking that the matter be investigated.

Harlem Hospital

In view of the number of complaints made by colored citizens of New York City in regard to treatment received at the Harlem Hospital, the National Office wrote a letter to Mayro Hylan asking that at least two colored members be appointed to the governing board of the Hospital. This letter followed the filing of a brief by Aiken A. Pope, a colored lawyer representing the Harlem Medical, Dental and Pharmaceutical Society, charging discrimination against and mistreatment of colored citizens.

Following the letter to Mayor Hilan the matter was referred to Commissioner of Public Welfare Bird S. Coler who requested the Assistant Secretary to call at this office and go over the matter personally with him. Mr. Coler stated that since 1902, when the management of Bellevue and Allied Hospitals was taken from under the direction of the Commissioner of Public Welfare, Harlem Hospital had been controlled by the medical schools of Columbia, Cornell, and New York Universities, and that the City of New York had little power towards the appointment of men to the various hospitals. The Assistant Secretary pointed out to the Commissioner that it was not only the privilege but the duty of the Mayor, where the welfare of the hospital system was concerned so acutely as in the case of Harlem Hospital, to appoint men who would correct the evils in the system. After asking the Assistant Secretary to furnish him with a list of the names of qualified colored physicians, the Commissioner tentatively promised to urge the appoinment of colored men at a meeting of the Board of Trustees of which he is a member.

Publicity

White Press: *The Globe* and *Evening Post* published long accounts of Mr. Aiken A. Pope's brief re: the Harlem Hospital, the latter on the front page; also the *World* and the *Times* carried references to the letter to Mayor Hylan. The *Call* also mentioned the Harlem Hospital matter. The *New York Call* on July 25 published on the front page an interview with the Secretary regarding the Ku Klux Klan and on August 1 an interview on the Haitian inquiry by the Senate Investigating Committee.

Colored Press

Extraordinary success was had with the matter sent out on the Dyer Anti-Lynching Bill, several newspapers giving it the major part of their first page, and many reprinting an editiorial which was sent out from the National Office with the story.

Publicity

Since the last report to the Board the following press stories have been sent out:

Anti-Lynching Bill, 4
Lynching, 3
Detroit Conference, 2
"Birth of a Nation," 1
Ku Klux Klan, 1
Tulsa Riot, 1
Harlem Hospital, 1
Ray Extradition Case, 1
Pan-African Congress, 1
Maurice Mays Case, 1

James Weldon Johnson, Secretary
August 15, 1921

Report of the Secretary for the Board Meeting of February 1922

Dyer Anti-Lynching Bill

Immediately after the Board meeting on January 9 the Secretary left for Washington.

On Tuesday, January 10, the Bill was taken up in the House but the debate was not continued on Wednesday, nor for several days thereafter, on account of the Post Office Appropriation Bill. During this time the Secretary had a number of conferences regarding the measure with leaders in Congress. He spent much time in looking up references and data to aid Senator Burton of Ohio in getting together material for his argument in favor of the Bill. Senator Burton requested the Secretary to assist him also by looking up and verifying certain legal references which he required for his speech. This the Secretary in turn requested Mr. James A. Cobb to do. Mr. Cobb kindly consented and gave a great deal of his time to the work. Mr. Cobb and the Secretary went to Senator's Burton's home, at his request, on Sunday night, January 15, and conferred with him about two hours.

On January 17 debate on the Bill was resumed, and Mr. Burton made a strong argument for the constitutionality of the measure, during which he got a great deal of valuable material into the Congressional Record.

On January 18, Calendar Wednesday, business under the Calendar rule was dispensed with, and the debate on the Dyer Bill was continued. The Democrats throughout the debate continued their filibuster to prevent consideration of the measure. The debate on Wednesday was another test of the strength of the Bill, as it took a two-thirds vote to suspend Calendar Wednesday.

On both days, the debate was very bitter. The most effective opposition, however, came not from Southern Democrats but from certain Republicans, notably Mr. Hersey of Maine and Mr. Reavis of Nebraska. Speeches of Southern Democrats were bitter in terms but absurd in their reasoning. The bulk of their argument consisted in repeating the exploded canard about rape being the cause of lynching and in denunciation of the Negro.

After January 18 the Bill was not taken up again until January 25. During this interval the Secretary returned to the National Office, but was in Washington again on Tuesday morning, January 24.

Immediately upon reaching the capital on the morning of the 24th, the Secretary saw and talked with Mr. Mondell, floor leader of the House. Mr. Mondell stated that the Bill would not come up on the 24th on account of the fact that the Independent Offices Appropriation Bill was not yet disposed of; that he was not sure the Dyer Bill would be continued on Wednesday; that he himself was in favor of disposing of it during the week, but that many of the leaders had expressed a desire for a little more time on it; and that as he felt the full agreement of the leaders was necesssary to put the Bill through, it might be best to leave it until Monday, January 30, and then keep it up until passed. He said he had called a meeting of Republican leaders in the Speaker's room to discuss the matter. In fact, Mr. Mondell was on his way to this meeting when the Secretary entered his office.

The Secretary did not see Mr. Mondell when he came out of this meeting, but while he was seated in the gallery during the roll call Mr. Mondell beckoned to him from the floor to meet him in the lobby. There Mr. Mondell stated to the Secretary that the Bill would come up on Wednesday whether the Appropriations Bill was finished or not.

On Wednesday, January 25, the House voted by a two-thirds vote to suspend Calendar Wednesday and proceed with the debate on the Anti-Lynching Bill. As the debate went on it grew more bitter. Speeches of the most truculent character were made by Representatives Sisson of Mississipppi and Blanton of Texas. Both of these speakers spoke not only actually in favor of mob rule but in utter defiance of anything that the Federal Government might propose to do. Mr. Blanton virtually said, "You can pass this law if you want to, but whenever we find it necessary we will lynch Negroes just the same."

From the opening of the debate the whole situation was quite tense, and this tenseness was greatly magnified by the presence of large numbers of colored people in the galleries. In fact, every available niche in the galleries was crowded with representative colored citizens of Washington, members of the Branch having turned out in large numbers. It could be seen that this tenseness had great effect upon the members of Congress. When Mr. Mondell, Republican leader, rose to speak, his voice was trembling with suppressed emotion. He made one of the

best speeches that [was] made on the Bill. The pent-up feelings, both of the men on the floor and the people in the galleries, broke loose during the colloquy which took place between Mr. Sisson of Mississippi and Mr. Cooper of Wisconsin. Mr. Sisson, in closing his speech, declared that lynching will never stop until "black rascals" keep their hands off white women and children. Representative Cooper retorted that it was the first time he had heard lynch law justified on the floor of the House. The rest of Mr. Cooper's speech was lost in the confusion but Mr. Sisson shouted, "I dare you to say that again in any other place."

The colored people in the galleries rose and cheered. Southern Democrats shouted from the floor, "Sit down, niggers," to which some voice replied, "We are not niggers, you liar!"

For several minutes the entire chamber was in an uproar despite strenuous efforts of Chairman Campbell of Kansas, speaker pro tem, to restore order.

On Thursday morning before Congress convened, Mr. Mondell talked with the Secretary and said that he was not sure a vote could be forced on that day but that they hoped to put the Bill through not later than Friday.

When Congress convened on Thursday, January 26, the debate was resumed. The Democrats continued their filibuster, but this seemed merely to solidify the great majority of Republicans. The Republican leaders pressed the matter and by parliamentary strategy cut off the delaying tactics of the Democrats. The Bill, therefore, reached a vote much earlier than anyone had expected. The roll call on the final vote began at 3:02 in the afternoon and at 3:30 the Speaker declared the bill passed by a vote of 230 to 119.

One of the most effective speeches on the Bill was made by Mr. W. Bourke Cockran, Democratic member from New York. Mr. Cockran's speech was very adroit and, the Secretary believes, was chiefly responsible for the Northern Democratic votes which the Bill received.

After the passage of the Bill by the House, the Secretary began a survey of the situation in the Senate. This survey he continued on Friday up to three o'clock in the afternoon, when he left Washington for New York.

The Secretary saw and talked with Senators Capper, Curtis, and Ernst. Senator Ernst is the only senator that he saw who is a member of the Senate Committee on the Judiciary, the committee to which the Bill has been referred in the Senate.

The fight in the Senate will not be an easy one. In the first place, the Senate Committee on the Judiciary is composed of men who are not sensitive to colored votes, that is, with the exception of Senator Ernst of Kentucky. The Republican members of the Committee are: Senators Knute Nelson, Minnesota, Chairman of the Committee; Cummmings, Iowa, a very influential member; Brandegee, Connecticut, also a very influential member; and Norris, Kansas. Senator Borah, who is a power, but at the same time not particularly interested in colored people, is from Iowa. Other Republicans on the Committee are Senators Dillingham, Vermont; Colt, Rhode Island; and Shortridge, California.

Among the Democrats the only man approachable would be Senator Reed of Missouri.

The Secretary talked with one of the Republican leaders who told him confidentially that the night before he had been in a conference at the White House at which were present the Republican leaders in the Senate. The question of the Anti-Lynching Bill came up and several of these Republican senators declared that they were hesitant about bringing up in the Senate any question which would cause dissension.

The Secretary is at once taking steps to bring all possible pressure upon members of the Senate Committee on the Judiciary, to promptly consider and report the Bill. This is being done both through communications to the Branches in the states from which these particular senators come, and through letters to prominent individuals.

Letters have also been sent from the National Office to certain "key senators" impressing upon them the fact that colored people of the country are disappointed and dissatisfied with the Republican administration thus far and that the passage of the Anti-Lynching Bill would go farther to abolish this state of mind and reassure the colored people than anything else which the administration might do.

The Secretary has also written directly to the members of the Senate Committee on the Judiciary requesting early and favorable action upon the Bill.

The following memorial to the United States Senate has been prepared and is being sent, with the request that it be signed, to various groups all over the country, including presidents of colleges, Catholic and Episcopal bishops, state governors, clergymen of evangelical churches, and other prominent individuals:

> The killing and burning alive of human beings by mob in the United States is a reproach upon our country throughout the civilized world and threatens organized government in the nation. Since 1889 there have been 3,443 known mob murders, some sixty of the victims being women. In only a few instances has prosecution of lynchers been even attempted. American mobs murdered sixty-four persons in 1921, of whom four were publicly burned at stake. The House of Representatives on January 26, 1922, in a response to insistent country-wide demand, passed the Dyer Anti-Lynching Bill, which invokes the power of the federal government to end the infamy of American mob murder. The Bill is now in the hands of the United States Senate. The undersigned United States citizens earnestly urge its prompt enactment.

In addition, lettters have been sent to the signers of the Address to the Nation, which was the result of the Anti-Lynching Conference (1919), asking them to use their influence upon members of the Committee on the Judiciary and other senators for the passage of the measure.

The Secretary is still of the opinion that Senator Curtis, who three years ago introduced an anti-lynching resolution for the Association, is the best possible man we can get in the Senate to lead the fight for us. We are greatly handicapped in that we have no man on the Judiciary Committee who can lead the fight in the Senate as Mr. Volstead, Chairman of the House Judiciary Committee, led the fight in the House. The Secretary, however, feels that there is a trump card which can be played in the Senate which was not used in the fight in the House—and that will be the influence of the President.

Arrangements are being made to hold a mass meeting in New York at the Town Hall. It is the aim of the Association that this meeting shall have national importance. Among the speakers who have been invited are Representative Dyer, Senator Calder, and Mrs. Corrine Roosevelt Robinson.

The memorial to the United States Senate to which signatures are now being secured will be read at this meeting and adopted. It is hoped that the largest degree of publicity possible will be secured.

Lynching

Since the last report to the Board, the following lynchings have taken place:

- January 8: Williamsburg, S.C.: Two unknown men were lynched by a mob of whites. One of the men had been accused of having improper relations with a white woman. He and a friend tried to elude the mob which came to the woman's home while he was there, but they were overtaken and shot to death.
- January 10: Eufaula, Ala.: Willie Jenkins, alleged to have insulted a white woman and to have threatened her husband was shot to death. County authorities have begun an investigation.
- January 14: Oklahoma City, Okla.: Jake Brooke, a packing house employee, was kidnapped from his home and hanged from a tree, near Oklahoma City. To date six of the lynchers have been sentenced to life imprisonment.
- January 17: Mayo, Fla.: A mob of overpowering officials seized a Negro who was alleged to have killed a white man, and lynched him on the outskirts of the town, hanging him and riddling his body with bullets.
- January 28: Bollinger, Ala.: An unidentified white man was found burned to death. Later the body was identified as that of Drew Conner.
- January 29: Pontotoc, Miss.: Will Bell, charged with having attacked a young white woman, was taken from officers by a number of unidentified men as he was being transferred to Jackson, Miss., for safekeeping, and was shot to death.
- February 1. Crystal Springs, Miss.: Will Thrasher, accused of attempting to attack a white school teacher, was hanged.
- February 2. Malvern, Ark.: Harry Harrison was taken from the sheriff of Hot Springs County and two deputies at the door of a train by a party of 200 masked men and riddled with bullets.

The Bullock Extradition Case

The National Office has played an important part in preventing the extradition of Matthew Bullock from Canada to North Carolina.

In January, 1921, Bullock's brother became involved in an altercation with a white clerk over the price of apples. The result of the altercation was a race riot in which Plummer Bullock and another colored man were lynched. Matthew Bullock fled to Canada where he has proved himself a good citizen and has worked every day since being there.

About January 15 North Carolina authorities learned of Bullock's presence in Canada and telegraphed the chief of police at Hamilton asking for his arrest on charges of "inciting to riot and shooting a white man."

Deportation proceedings were immediately begun and the immigration board in Hamilton ordered Bullock's deportation on the ground that he had entered Canada with forty-one dollars instead of the $250 required by law. The Inspector of Immigration of Hamilton, however, requested Bullock's counsel to appeal the decision to the Canadian government at Ottawa, which he did.

On January 19 the Buffalo Branch requested by telegram and long distance telephone that the Assistant Secretary be sent, at their expense, to Canada in the case. The Assistant Secretary left the same night for Buffalo where he held conference with the Branch officers, and in company with Mr. Talbert, called upon the chief of police and the assistant chief of Buffalo, and secured their promise, after explaining the case, to arrest Bullock on a technical charge, if he was deported, and to hold him on suspicion until the Association could bring pressure to bear on Governor Miller to deny Bullock's extradition to North Carolina, or to institute habeas corpus proceedings in the event that Governor Miller refused to comply with the Association's request.

The Assistant Secretary then left Hamilton where he had conference with F. F. Treleaven, attorney for Bullock, and the Rev. J. D. Howell, who was leading the fight for Bullock. From them he learned that the principal task to be performed was the securing of adequate publicity for the arousing of public sentiment strong enough to cause Canada to refuse extradition or deportation. The Assistant Secretary immediately got in touch with representatives of the two local papers in Hamilton and with the Toronto and Montreal papers, as well as with the Associated Press. Because of the splendid attitude of these papers a large amount of very excellent publicity was secured.

After making arrangements with Messrs. Treleaven and Howell to keep the National Office advised of developments that we might be prepared to act, in the event of deportation, the Assistant Secretary returned to New York.

On February 1 the National Office received from Mr. Howell the following telegram: "Bullock is free." This, of course, meant that the Canadian government declined to deport Bullock.

School Histories

The attention of the National Office was called by one of the teachers in the New York Public Schools to the hearings which were being held, before Commissioner of Accounts, David Hirshfield, on the subject of the patriotism of American histories.

Mr. Pickens, Field Secretary, represented the National Office at the hearing on February 3 and made a plea for the inclusion in American histories of the part played by Negroes. Mr. Pickens' report follows:

After listening to the other speakers I saw that this was the finest possible opportunity to present the case of the Negro, and proceeded to do so. They had all spoken mainly of "Pro-British" histories, although one man spoke of anti-Jewish attitudes.

I endeavored to show that the Negro suffers greatly from "omissions" in American history, even where he has been the agent of outstanding achievement; that this is the foundation of the "race problem," by either prejudicing the mind of the young or failing to fortify the young mind against active prejudice. I cited abundant instances from American history.

Commissioner Hirshfield stated to me at the close that the Association will be at liberty to present any written matter February 20, if we desire, for his records.

About one hundred people, members of the city government, of the school board, principals, teachers, authors, and reporters, were present. Most of them asked for the exact name and address of the N.A.A.C.P.

The Field Secretary will seek data from colored teachers. The Field Secretary's remarks were carried fully by the daily papers.

Publicity

The Association's press releases are carried each week by almost all of the important colored papers. During the last month several papers have carried as many as four and five Association stories at one time. Since the last report to the Board the following press stories have been sent out:

Dyer Anti-Lynching Bill, 13
Bullock Case, 3
Discrimination in Capitol Restaurant, 1
Charge by *Negro World*, 1
Discrimination in motion picture films in South Carolina, 1

James Weldon Johnson, Secretary
February 1922

Report of the Secretary for the
Board Meeting of October 1923

Annual Conference

At the Fourteenth Annual Conference of the Association held at Kansas City, Kansas, August 29–September 4, the following report of the Committee on Recommendations to the National Body was adopted:

We, your Committee on Recommendations to the National Body, after due diligence and faithful consideration of the many suggestions placed before us, beg leave to submit the following report:

1. To further the work of the Association and to give greater stimulus to weak branches, we recommend that state organizations be formed, but that the character and the manner of the same be left to the discretion and the direction of the National Body. We urge early action on the matter, however.

2. That the work of the Association may be augmented and its principles more surely perpetuated, we recommend that the organization of Juvenile and College Chapters be materially stressed from now on.

3. That as rapidly as possible Executive Secretaries be appointed for the larger branches.

4. We recommend that all memberships received directly from individuals by the National Office be immediately reported to the Branch in whose territory the membership is located and that the Branch Secretary report to the National Office all memberships actually paid into the Branch treasury.

5. We recommend a discontinuance of the free distribution of certificate buttons and that certificate members receive the annual report of the Association in lieu of the button.

6. We recommend that all solicitations for membership in communities where active branches are in existence be recognized and regarded as the duty and special property of said branch. We further urge that in any contingency when the National Office finds it imperative to call for funds, the request be made through the branches adjacent to the territory solicited.

7. We give hearty recommendation to the suggestion that the National Office encourage branches to use what shall be known as "Liberty Banks" whereby each member shall be pledged to contribute one cent per day to the work of the Association and that the funds so acquired be known as an "Anniversary Fund" to be remitted to the National Office on the twelfth day of February of each year.

8. We recommend that the programs at our annual conferences, both for business and mass meetings, be hereafter shortened and, that there might be no misunderstanding, that the time allotted to each speaker be printed on the program.
   Respectfully submitted.

The Committee on Recommendations to the National Body upon the recommendation of the committee on time and place, Philadelphia was selected as the place of meeting of the Fifteenth Annual Conference, during the last week in June, 1924.

Twenty-fourth Infantry

The National Office has worked out and set in motion a comprehensive plan for a nation-wide campaign to free the fifty-four members of the Twenty-fourth Infantry now in Leavenworth Prison.

Following the visit to the prison during the Kansas City Conference, with the great interest aroused in these cases as a result of that visit, the National Office felt that this campaign should be inaugurated immediately. In mapping it out great care was taken to make it as economical as possible, and it is felt that the plans outlined below will enable us to secure pardon for the men from President Coolidge at an extraordinarily low cost. The following steps have been taken:

A personal letter has been written to each of the colored newspaper editors of the country asking cooperation. A large number of the most influential newspapers have replied expressing in every instance very cordial cooperation and full support of the Association's efforts. In order to keep down the cost, the National Office is not printing the petitions itself but has drafted and had printed a model petition (copy enclosed). From this a mat was made which was sent on September 29 to a selected list of newspapers and magazines together with a second personal letter and summary of the facts in the Houston riot cases.

A letter was written to each branch of the Association asking (1) cooperation in printing the petition and securing signatures thereto, and (2) that each branch send the names of all colored and friendly white ministers, heads of lodges, clubs, women's organizations, etc., in its city. These names are coming in rapidly.

A letter was sent also to the Bishops of the various branches of the Methodist Church, and to the heads of the Baptist Church asking that they enlist the support of the ministers and churches of their denominations. A similar letter was sent to the heads of the fraternal orders of the country.

On September 29 an Open Letter to the Christian Ministers of America was released through the Colored Press asking their cooperation and, as in the case of the heads of the various denominations, requesting that Sunday, November 11, be set aside as Houston Martyrs Day. It is felt by the National Office that through these meetings at least 100,000 signatures to the petition may be secured which should result in executive clemency by President Coolidge.

Johnstown, Pa.

On August 31 at Rosedale, a suburb of Johnstown, Pa., a colored man, Robert A. Young, said to have been crazed by liquor or dope, ran amuck and killed a policeman who attempted to arrest him A riot call was sent in and before Young, who had barricaded himself in a house in the neighborhood, was killed he shot five policemen, killing two of them. Investigation by the Chief of Police of Johnstown resulted in a public statement that only one colored man was involved and that he had been slain. Johnstown, thereupon, became quiet again except for the burning of crosses by the local Ku Klux Klan. A week later Mayor Joseph Cauffiel of Johnstown returned to the city and issued an arbitrary order that all Negroes and Mexicans who had not been residents of Johnstown for at least seven years must get out of town immediately. A number left, though investigation showed that not nearly so many left as were reported.

On receiving reports of Mayor Cauffiel's order the Secretary wired Governor Pinchot as follows:

> Today's New York newspapers report that because of the killing of two policemen and the wounding of four others, crimes alleged to have been committed by Negroes of Johnstown, Pa., more than two thousand Negroes have left Johnstown because of order issued by Mayor Joseph Cauffiel that only Negroes resident in city for seven years would be allowed to remain. National Association for the Advancement of Colored People with four hundred and fifty branches and membership of one hundred thousand, composed of members of both races, herewith registers its protest against this high-handed injustice through such wholesale deportation by the Mayor of Johnstown of men, regardless of innocence or guilt, solely because their skins are black. It is so obvious as to make it a superfluous statement that the only action which should have been taken by the Mayor and other authorities of Johnstown would have been to seek out and punish those guilty. This Association respectfully requests you to use all authority vested in your high office to correct this grievous injustice if the facts stated above are found to be true and to protect the colored citizens of Johnstown against the Ku Klux Klan methods of Mayor Cauffiel.

At the same time Mayor Cauffiel was wired as follows:

> Press dispatches in today's newspaper report that more than two thousand Negroes have left Johnstown as a result of your order that only Negroes resident in the city for seven years would be allowed to remain because of the shooting of two policemen and the wounding of four others, these crimes alleged to have been committed by Negroes. If the facts as reported above are correct, National Association for the Advancement of Colored People, with four hundred and fifty branches and membership of one hundred thousand, composed of members of both races, vigorously protests against this high-handed injustice in such wholesale deportation. It appears to us that you have totally exceeded authority vested in you.
>
> It is the duty of the Mayor and the other authorities of Johnstown to seek out and punish the guilty instead of punishing men whose only offense is that their skins are black. We respectfully urge that the hounding of colored citizens be stopped and that the City of Johnstown cease making itself a tool for carrying out the threats of the Ku Klux Klan.

The National Office also secured the services of Attorney George H. White, Jr. of Pittsburgh, who went to Johnstown to investigate the situation. On September 18 Governor Pinchot wired the Secretary as follows:

Your telegram received. On return to Milford wired Mayor Cauffiel asking him for full statement of facts and reason for action taken. The whole power of this commonwealth will be used if necessary to maintain constitutional rights.

This unequivocal statement by the Governor was made public and was published widely throughout the country, most of the newspapers carrying the story on their front pages.

Mayor Cauffiel then attempted to modify his former belligerent attitude, declaring that instead of ordering Negroes and Mexicans out of the city he had merely "advised" them to leave. He became still more apologetic when the Mexican Government on September 19 added its protest to that of the N.A.A.C.P.

On September 18 a primary election was held in Johnstown in which Mayor Cauffiel was a candidate for election. He, however, ran fifth in a field of seven, receiving, according to newspaper reports, less than fifty votes, indicating that his arbitrary action was not endorsed by the citizens of Johnstown. The New York white press headed the account of the Mayor's defeat "Mayor's Negro Ban Costs Him His Job," giving the N.A.A.C.P. credit for the victory. This splendid victory won by the Association is one of the most striking in its history.

McCoy Rendition Case

On September 17 the *Pittsburgh Courier* wired the National Office for information relative to the proper procedure in fighting a case of interstate rendition. The National Office immediately wired instructions advising that lawyers should be secured and a writ of habeas corpus applied for in the event the Governor signed the writ of rendition. On the following day a telegram was received from Attorney Frank R. Stewart, President of our Pittsburgh Branch, giving the facts in the case as follows:

One Dock McCoy, a colored resident of Pittsburgh for two years, had in 1921 been accused of killing a white man in North Carolina and fled to Pittsburgh when a mob sought to lynch him. McCoy, on the other hand, produced evidence to prove that he was several miles from the scene at the time when the crime was committed and further declared that he was certain he would be lynched if sent back to North Carolina.

The National Office forwarded full data on lynching, together with the history of procedure in the Tom Ray, Matthew Bullock, and Robert L. Hill cases. Mr. Stewart wrote to the National Office a letter of warm appreciation for the assistance rendered and requested that we secure, if possible, data from North Carolina regarding the case. The National Office wrote to a number of individuals in North Carolina asking for this information.

Upon the recommendation of the National Office a continuance of the case to October 2 was secured to allow the gathering of additional information.

Spruce Pine, N.C., Deportation

Upon receipt of information that an armed mob of two hundred whites was rounding up colored citizens of Spruce Pine, N.C., and deporting them on freight trains the National Office on September 28 sent the following telegram to Governor Cameron Morrison:

> Press dispatches report that an armed mob of two hundred citizens of Spruce Pince, N.C., is today rounding up all male citizens in Spruce Pine, N.C., and vicinity and deporting them on freight trains because of alleged attack by a Negro upon an aged white woman. National Association for Advancement of Colored People is requesting of you information regarding correctness of this report and is also asking that you as Governor of the state use all powers at your command to protect the civil and constitutional rights of colored citizens who are being taken from their homes and jobs regardless of their innocence or guilt.

On the same date the Governor replied as follows:

> My actions in matter referred to by you are being given to Associated Press as quickly as can be done and prevent action of state being prematurely made known to the lawless from whom we seek to protect the state. You can get information through the news source as the rest of the public acquire it.

Publicity

Since the last report to the Board the following news releases have been sent out:

Conference, 2
Twenty-fourth Infantry, 2
Book Chat, 2
Johnstown, 4
Spruce Pine, N.C. Deportation, 1
Dock McCoy Rendition Case, 1
Lynching, 1
Dyer Bill, 1
Migration, 1

James Weldon Johnson, Secretary
October 2, 1923

Report of the Secretary for the
Board Meeting of October 1924

Residential Segregation

At the last meeting of the Board Mr. James A. Cobb of the Legal Committee stated that besides the Washington Segregation Case there were five similar cases pending in various parts of the United States.

Washington Segregation Case

As suggested by Mr. Cobb at the last meeting of the Board the National Office sent out in September a press release giving detailed information regarding the Washington Segregation Case. This release was in the main a statement by Mr. Cobb in which he stressed the importance of securing if possible from the United States Supreme Court a favorable decision, since this bar against colored people, if sustained, would have the practical effect of nullifying the victory won in the Louisville Segregation Case.

On Saturday morning, October 4, a conference on the Washington Segregation Cases with Mr. Louis Marshall was held at his office. Present at the conference were Mr. Marshall, Mr. Arthur B. Spingarn, Mr. Cobb, Mr. Stockton, and the Secretary.

The case was discussed in all of its important phases. Mr. Marshall made suggestions growing out of his study of the brief and the record. He advised that as promptly as possible an application for a writ of certiorari be made in order that the case might be brought before the Court in all of its phases in the event of the Court's ruling that the case as brought up on appeal was not before it. Mr. Cobb stated that he would take immediate steps to make the application. Mr. Marshall expressed the opinion that the case should not rest entirely upon constitutional grounds but should include the broad question of policy. He also expressed his willingness to give his aid in arguing the case before the Supreme Court.

Louisiana Segregation Law

The Louisiana State Legislature has enacted a measure, which has been signed by the Governor, providing for the segregation of colored and white people in communities having a population of 25,000 or more. The new law was reported by Dr. George W. Lucas, President of the New Orleans Branch, who stated that the bill was evidently prompted by protests against certain colored people who are purchasing property in districts heretofore known as white.

During the month of September, Mr. Bagnall, Director of Branches, visited New Orleans and reported as follows on the segregating law:

It is expected that the desrire for re-election and the approval of their white constituency will cause the judges in the civil courts, the court of appeals and the state supreme court to give adverse decisions even though it is clear that the United States Supreme Court has already in the Louisville case declared this act unconstitutional.

In a later message from Mr. Bagnall he states that the feeling in New Orleans is tense; that a joint committee of Creoles and Americans has been organized to fight a test case; that Negroes living in white blocks have been threatened as a result of the new law.

School Segregation

Cases of segregation in public schools have been reported to the National Office from Indianapolis, Ind., Dayton, Oh.; Boynton and Muskogee, Okla.; Coffeyville and Arma, Kan.; and Imperial, California.

The Indianapolis School Case was reported to the September meeting of the Board. In reply to our letter asking him to review the documents in this case and give us his opinion, Senator Beveridge wrote regretting that pressure of business prevented his giving attention to this matter; whereupon the National Office wrote to Mr. W. S. Henry, Attorney for the local Branch, asking him to submit a list of influential attorneys from which associate counsel might be *chosen*; also to advise as to probable expense so that the National Office may determine what part of the expense it will bear.

Dayton: On September 8 the National Office received a telegram from a representative of the Parents Protective Association of Dayton, Ohio, stating that Dayton had started a fight on segregation in public schools.

The National Office at once wired that in its opinion this case was a very important one and offered to send a National officer to Dayton. Subsequently Mr. Bagnall was sent to Dayton and he reported that great interest was being manifested in the fight; that at a joint meeting of the Branch Executive Committee and that of the Parents Protective Association at which he was present, it was agreed that the Branch should enter the fight as an organization, the two organizations fighting the matter together.

Mr. Bagnall reports that the case is not an easy one and will probably be lost in the lower courts.

Young Women's Christian Association

(Case of Miss Lydia Gardine): On July 24 Miss Helen McKinstry, Director of the Central School of Hygiene and Physical Education of the Y.W.C.A., wrote Miss Lydia Gardine of East Orange, N.J., "I see no reason why you are not eligible for admission to the Central School . . . Attend to the matter of registration as soon as possible." On August 5 Miss McKinstry again wrote Miss Gardine: "If you had only mentioned this fact (that Miss Gardine is an American Negro) on your eligibility estimate blank the matter would not have been carried this far . . . We are by the terms of our arrangement with Central not allowed to admit colored girls to the school . . ."

Miss Gardine referred the case to the National Office and a letter was sent to the Chairman of the National Board asking an official statement as to (1) if Miss McKinstry's action is officially approved, and authorized by the National Board; (2) if not, what action will be taken in this specific instance toward Miss McKinstry, and what action will be taken in similar cases in the future.

No reply having been received to this letter, the National Office wrote on September 3 asking for a statement on the case. To date no statement has been received, but on October 7 a letter was received from the Chairman of the National Board stating that this matter will come up before the Board at its first fall meeting.

Rochester Dental Clinic

(Case of Dr. F. Irving Gray): On September 4 Dr. F. Irving Gray reported that he was being discriminated against at the Rochester Dental Clinic in that he could not secure admittance to carry on his practice work as required after graduation.

The matter was referred to Dr. Franklin Book of Rochester who had been working with the Rochester Branch in case of discrimination by the Eastman Theatre there. Dr. Book referred the case to Drs. Levy and Lunsford who gave the National Office valuable advice regarding conditions in Rochester.

Case of Samuel A. Browne

Samuel A. Browne, a mail carrier, purchased a house on Fairview Avenue, West Brighton, Staten Island. The purchase was made on February 2 but Mr. Browne did not move into the house until July 4. In the meantime, about March 15, he was offered $9,000 for the house, which offer he refused (the purchase price was $8,500). It developed that their neighbor, a white man, had made the offer indirectly and that he had remarked that if the Brownes moved into the house they would make it so uncomfortable for them they would be glad to leave. On May 26 a letter was received by Mr. Browne marked "KKK" notifying him that if he moved into the house it would be the worst day's work he ever did. This letter was taken to the head of the Detective Bureau who said he did not believe the letter was of Klan origin. However, Mr. Browne was given permission to carry a gun.

On July 28 the National Office wrote Lieutenant James Gegan of the Police Department asking protection for Mr. Browne and the request was complied with. After the Brownes had moved into their new home a series of meetings were held by residents of the community. Fire insurance in two companies was withdrawn. Another purchase offer was made, this time $9,500; this also was traced to Mr. Browne's white neighbor. Mr. Browne succeeded in having insurance placed with another company, whereupon the Building and Loan Association compelled him to secure $1,000 additional fire insurance.

On August 31 at three o'clock in the morning the front windows of Mr. Browne's house were broken out with rocks. On September 3 another offer was made to buy the house for $10,000, which Mr. Browne refused. A mass meeting of the whites was held that night.

The National Office referred this case to the New York Department of Justice and also to the Federal Department of Justice at Washington. On October 6 a letter was received from the Federal Department of Justice stating that "After consideration of the carefully prepared statement of facts submitted with your letter, the Department does not feel that a prosecution could be successfully maintained under Section 19, 211 as amended, 212 of the Criminal Code."

Mrs. Browne telephoned on October 7 that her fire insurance had again been cancelled.

William Pickron Rape Case

On September 19 a letter was received from the President of the Wilmington, Del., Branch asking advice in a case where rape had been committed upon Miss Rosie Deputy, colored, by her white employer, William Pickron. When Miss Deputy and her mother went to testify against Pickron they were told that the case had been settled and were not permitted to testify.

The National Office wired Governor Denney of Delaware requesting an investigtion of the case. Governor Denney immediately got in touch with the officers responsible in the case and sent to the National Office a detailed report from the Attorney General to the effect that there was no evidence of assault and that Pickron had not confessed to the crime. A committee of colored citizens wrote letters of protest to the officers in charge and finally Pickron was again arrested but on a lesser charge, that of attempted assault. He is now being held in $6,000 bond awaiting trial before the Grand Jury.

Louise Thomas

The press has carried full reports of the case of Louise Thomas in Pennsylvania who has been sentenced to death for murder.

The National Office wired Governor Pinchot asking executive clemency, and the Governor has replied that he can take no action unless the case is referred to him by the Board of Pardons.

Mamie Pratt Case

The case of Mamie Pratt who was assaulted by Roy Sullivan, a white man, at Baxter Springs, Kansas, has been reported upon at various meetings of the Board. News has been received at the National Office that the date for the trial of Sullivan has been changed to October 6. A later wire (received October 8) states that the trial has been postponed until the December Court.

The Elias Ridge Case

In the report to the April meeting of the Board a detailed account was given of the case of Elias Ridge, a thirteen-year-old colored boy, accused of murder and sentenced to be hanged.

On August 1, in accordance with the vote of the Board, the National Office sent a check of $100 to W. H. Twine of Muskogee, Okla., the attorney in the case. Mr. Twine acknowledged receipt of the check and promised to send the brief and a full report of the case. These have not yet been received. In his letter Mr. Twine states that Ridge's life would be saved. He has again been written to for a full report on the case.

Ellis Island Case

Dr. D. Butler Pratt, Dean of Religion, Howard University, asked the assistance of the N.A.A.C.P. in the case of R. S. Lindsay being detained on Ellis Island. The National Office took the matter up with the New York officials and succeeded in having Mr. Lindsay admitted to the United States under bond.

Lonnie Hunter, et al.

In February at Raymond, Hinds County, Miss., four Negroes were sentenced to death for the alleged murder of a white woman. The principal witness for the state was a small colored boy, scarcely above an idiot, who is said to have been induced to pretend to turn state's evidence.

Inasmuch as mob violence was threatened, the defendants were tried and convicted within a week of the commission of the alleged crime.

The case was appealed to the Supreme Court of the State by Attorneys Teat and Broom in an effort to secure a reversal, in which event there would be a change of venue and a separate trial for each of the four defendants.

On May 9 Mr. Teat wrote the National Office asking financial assistance in the case, stating that he believed the defendants to be innocent. The National Office referred the matter to Mr. [Arthur] Spingarn, Chairman of the Legal Committee, who suggested that some trusted person be aked to give Mr. Teat's standing and the merits of the case. Dr. Redmond of Jackson, Miss., was asked for this information and he sent a complete history of the case, stating that when the Judge saw that Attorney Broome was getting at the bottom of the case, he took Mr. Broome off and appointed other counsel for the defense of the half-wit; that the blood exhibited in the court room was found to be rabbit's blood. Mr. Redmond stated that the people of Mississippi were afraid to take any interest in the case but that Mr. Teat would take the cases for $2,000; that he believed the attorneys conscientious; that if the Association could not pay $2,000 it might make a small contribution inasmuch as four men, absolutely innocent, are being held for murder. The National Office wrote Mr. Redmond that the fee of $2,000 was entirely too high but that it would be interested in hearing from the attorneys if they had anything further to say.

On August 26 Attorney Broome wrote that the hearing would be held on September 22 and that he believed the cases would be won if there was money enough to fight them.

The latest information is that the cases are to be argued on October 27 or November 24, and Mr. Broome states that the attorneys are proceeding to the best of their ability at great cost and sacrifice of professional prestige. He still hopes that the N.A.A.C.P. will cooperate in the case.

Oteen Veterans Hospital

It was reported at the May meeting of the Board that while the Secretary was at Asheville, N.C., in April a delegation of colored patients at the Veterans Hospital there called on him and laid before him the complaint that certain elements among the white patients at the hospital were seeking to have them removed and sent to the Veterans Hospital at Tuskegee. Upon investigation by the Association it was found:

1. That Ku Klux Klan agitation at Oteen had produced a threat against one of the colored war veterans and a position asking for the removal of twenty-nine of them to the government hospital at Tuskegee;
2. That twenty-six colored patients were segregated in one ward where there was bad overcrowding;
3. That the attitude of Dr. Archie McAllister, white, associate medical officer of the Oteen Hospital, had been intolerable and that he had let it be known that he wanted to get rid of all colored patients;
4. That Dr. McAllister had forced patients to pay for signing insurance blanks, which is contrary to government regulations, and that he had accepted pay from colored patients in the government hospital, threatening them to keep them silent; and
5. That Dr. McAllister charged a patient for the signing of sick blanks and threatened the patient for reporting the matter.

Upon completion of the N.A.A.C.P. investigation the Association's report, supported by affidavits and other documents, was forwarded to General Frank T. Hinos, Director of the Veterans Bureau at Washington. The report was acknowledged by E. A. Shepard, Chief of the Inspection Division of the Veterans Bureau, in a letter dated May 28, in which Mr. Shepard said:

It is believed that the information contained in your letter and in the affidavits submitted will be of much assistance in correcting any irregularities which may exist.

The outcome of the report of the Association and of the investigation by the Veterans Bureau is reported as follows in the *Asheville Citizen* for October 8, in a special dispatch from Washington:

A letter from Dr. James Miller, Medical Officer-in-Charge at Oteen, advised Dr. McAllister that the central office at Washington had directed a discontinuance of his services after giving careful consideration to a report of an investigation made of his case.

The dispatch further reports that Senators Simmons and Overman of North Carolina have been asked by southern whites to intercede for the dismissed doctor.

Senator Capper and the Ku Klux Klan

At the September meeting of the Board it was voted that Senator Capper be again written to and asked that he give attention to the Association's former communication requesting a statement from him requesting his attitude on the Ku Klux Klan.

The Secretary wrote to Senator Capper and received the following reply, dated September 13:

My dear Mr. Johnson:

Your letter of September 9 reached me here on the day of my return from an eastern vacation trip.

If the Klan endorsed me for United States Senator I knew nothing about it. I received a majority of 118,000, and probably a large part of the Klan voted for me, but if they voted for me they did so of their own accord, and without any promise of any kind or character. The Klan was not an issue so far as the Senatorial candidacy was concerned, and I do not believe it should be an issue. In this city about nine-tenths of the voters, regardless of creed or color, supported me.

I am not a Klansman. I do not know who their leaders are in this state. I have never talked with any Klansmen. I am absolutely under no obligations whatever to this or any other organization. I might add that I am opposed to all forms of religious intolerance and race prejudices. Ever since I became interested in public affairs one of the things I have always made a fight for was to guarantee to every American citizen, regardless of creed or color, his rights under the constitution of the United States.

Please regard this letter as a reply to Mr. White's letter of August 19 as well as your letter of September 9.

With kindest regards, I am
Very respectfully,

(Signed) Arthur Capper

Race Riot, Bridgewater (Va.)

The press of October 3 carried dispatches telling of a race riot which had been raging for several days at Bridgewater, Va., as a result of an automobile containing colored people colliding with another car. One white boy was reported to have been shot and many white and colored people injured.

The National Office wired to Governor E. Lee Trinkle asking that state troops be used if necessary to stop the riot and protest the colored people who, according to press accounts, had been ordered off the streets. The Governor replied that immediately upon receipt of our wire he had telephoned to Bridgewater; that he had not known of the disturbance before the receipt of our telegram; that he found all quiet at Bridgewater; that he aimed to protect all citizens.

Publicity

Since the last report to the Board the following press releases have been sent out:

Ku Klux Klan, 4
Twenty-fourth Infantry, 1
Haiti, 2
Washington Segregation Cases, 1
Dayton School Segregation, 1
Migration, 1
Discrimination, 1
Politics, 2
Crime, 7
Book Chat, 2
Contributions, 2
Walker Scholarships, 1
Spingarn Medal, 1
Race Riot, 1
Miscellaneous, 10

James Weldon Johnson, Secretary
October 9, 1924

Report of the Secretary for the
Board Meeting of July 1925

Annual Conference

The Sixteenth Annual Conference held at Denver, Colorado, June 24–30, was by far the greatest and most successful conference yet held by the Association. The local arrangements by the Denver Branch were perfect, every detail being looked after and carried through without a single hitch. Not only were the sessions and the mass meetings all that could be desired, but so were the entertainments.

Thirty states and seventy-five cities were represented at the Conference, by 215 delegates.

At the opening session the following message from the [U.S.] President was read:

My dear Mr. Johnson:

I have your request for a message of greeting to the Annual Conference of the National Association for the Advancement of Colored People, to be held in Denver, the last week of the present month.

The request is one with which it is a pleasure to comply, because of my strong conviction that this organization has had an important part in bringing about the manifest advancement in the fortunes of the colored people, which has taken place in recent years. The evidences of that advancement are so numerous that a mere recital of them would require a voluminous document. Many factors have contributed to bringing about this change for the better, and I join in your own feeling of confidence that the improvement will continue under the wise leadership of the real friends of the colored race, and because of the sincere efforts of the colored people themselves in accomplishing the results which they so earnestly desire.

Messages were read also from Mr. Storey, Miss Ovington, and Mr. J. E. Spingarn.

The Sunday mass meeting was preceded by the largest parade of colored people ever held in Denver. Fifteen hundred were in line, including veterans of the Spanish-American War and the World War, as well as uniformed members of fraternal and other organizations, business and professional men.

On Sunday morning the pulpits of the sixteen leading churches of Denver were filled by National and Branch officers of the Association.

On June 22 delegates to the Conference from the East, passing through Chicago, were entertained at dinner by Miss Jane Addams, at the Chicago City Club; and on July 2, on the way back, they were entertained at dinner in Chicago at the Appomattox Club.

The resolutions adopted by the Conference included an "Annual Address to the Public" and "Special Resolutions," on the attempt of General Robert Lee Bullard "to defame and discredit the men of the Ninety-second Division of the American Expeditionary Forces in France," declaring it "a hostile gesture, most improper in any army officer, from the element in the South that is still unenlightened and still cave-dwelling, and a gross, wanton insult to ten per cent of the people that pay General Bullard his wages and whose servant he is"; on Haiti, requesting "that American troops be withdrawn from Haiti at once and the country restored to such of its people as survive"; and on the commemoration of the birthdays and public services of "the leaders of the great Abolition movement that freed this country from the terrible blight and ineffable shame of slavery."

The resolutions in full will appear in the August Number of the *Crisis*.

Recommendations to the National Board: Following is the report of the Committee on Recommendations to the National Board:

We, your Committee on Recommendations to the National Board, submit the following recommendations:

1. That the National Association continue to hold annual conferences;
2. That the minimum annual membership remain $1.00;
3. That a condensed report of the doings of the annual conference be furnished local branches with the view of stimulating them to greater activity;
4. That due cognizance be given Congressman Dyer's recommendation of support of Senators favoring change of Senate rules; and also that the attitude of candidates for public office be ascertained, through questionnaires, and published with a view of supporting man and measures rather than party or politics;
5. That greater prominence be given the work of the young people by the local and National organizations, by giving them a place on the annual program;
6. That the National Association through the National Office and local branches secure and encourage the presentation of scholarships to worthy young people for higher education;
7. That local branches be encouraged to maintain permanent headquarters;
8. That the National Office encourage through school boards the placing of Negro Literature and History on the supplementary reading lists of public schools, and in public libraries;
9. That in order to secure greater efficiency in branch activities, and extend branch organization, another field secretary be appointed;
10. That in order to facilitate the organization of branches for regional conferences, and establish relationships between all branches, the National Office compile and send to each branch after the annual elections a directory containing the names and addresses of officers for each branch;
11. That in order to supplement the work of the field secretaries a voluntary Speakers' Bureau be organized; and
12. That Junior Branches be given a representative on the National Staff, in order to create larger interest and stimulate young people to greater activity.

The Seventeenth Annual Conference

The Committee on Time and Place reported that invitations for the Seventeenth Annual Conference had been received from Indianapolis and Chicago, and that the invitation from Chicago had been accepted.

General Bullard's Slander

A slanderous article by General Robert Lee Bullard, maintaining that the Negro soldiers of the Ninety-second Division were cowards and could not be made to fight, that they had been guilty of rape, and that they showed the Negro generally to be inferior and incapable of soldierly qualities, was published in the *New York Herald-Tribune* of June 9.

The Secretary replied to General Bullard's article, his letter appearing in the *Herald-Tribune* of June 10.

The National Office also communicated with Colonel William Hayward, Major Hamilton Fish, and Dr. Emmett J. Scott, requesting them to write to the *Herald-Tribune* in protest against General Bullard's article; also to Doubleday, Page & Co., who are to publish a book containing General Bullard's article, calling their attention to the libel upon Negro soldiers and the Negro race and asking that those chapters be amended before the book is published.

Letters were written to the *Herald-Tribune* as requested, but no satisfactory reply was received from Doubleday, Page & Co.

Military Training Camps

The following reply has been received to the Secretary's letter to the War Department making inquiries as to what provision had been made with regard to the training of colored men for military services:

My dear Mr. Johnson:

The organization of the Citizens Military Training Camps is not based upon communities but on Corps Areas, each of which comprises several states. For example, the First Corps Area includes the States of Maine, New Hampshire, Vermont, Massachusetts, Rhode Island, and Connecticut. Neither white nor colored units are constituted at Corps Area C.M.T. Camps if the enrollment one month prior to the date for such camp indicates an attendance of less than fifty qualified eligible men. Camps authorized on the above basis are held, however, even though the number actually reporting falls below that number.

In the event of less than fifty applications being received by a Corps Area Commander for any particular type or unit, candidates may, provided no additional expense accrues to the Government, be assigned to a regularly constituted unit of such type in another Corps Area, or candidates may be enrolled for such units outside of Corps Areas in which they reside by signifying their willingness to pay the extra expense involved. This policy pertains to both white and colored applicants.

Yours very truly,
(Signed) "Dwight F. Davis
Acting Secretary of War"

Twenty-fourth Infantry

Ben Cecil, another of the men of the Twenty-fourth Infantry, was released on July 2, on home parole under the supervision of Mr. W. Hayes McKinney of Detroit,

Michigan, former President of the Detroit Branch of the N.A.A.C.P., and now member of the Legal Committee of the Branch. This brings the total number of men released since the petition was presented to President Coolidge to thirty.

The Luther Collins Case

Luther Collins, charged with criminal assault upon a white woman, whose case has been pending since January, 1922, has been granted a third trial, through the efforts of the Houston, Texas, Branch. Collins' first trial resulted in the death penalty. Upon the presentation of additional evidence as to his innocence by the Houston Branch a new trial was secured which resulted in a mis-trial and dismissal of the jury which could not agree. Collins was tried again on a change of venue and was sentenced to ninety-nine years in the penitentiary. The Houston Branch took an appeal from this decision to the Court of Criminal Appeals, which court rendered a decision in June, 1925, reversing the conviction and remanding the case for re-trial because of errors in the admission of certain testimony. This Court held that the trial court erred in permitting a police officer to testify that he arrested the defendant because he answered the description of the Negro which the officers had orders to pick up for the offense charged.

This reversal carries the case until the fall of 1925, and it is felt that Collins will be freed either upon being brought to trial or through failure of the state to continue prosecution.

The magnificent defense for Collins by the Houston Branch has had a profound effect upon the court authorities of Texas. At no time has the Branch called upon the National Office for aid in this case.

The Elmer Williams Case

Another case which has been successfully handled by the Houston Branch is that of Elmer Williams, who has been saved from death after making a full confession of the murder of a white woman. After a number of Negroes had been arrested and had provided alibis and the woman's husband also had been arrested for the crime, Elmer Williams was arrested in Ohio and offered to plead guilty if the State would give him a life term. This the District Attorney refused to do.

The Houston Branch entered the case and brought Mr. Sidwell, Superintendent of the Nebraska State Insane Asylum, to Houston. Mr. Sidwell proved that on the night the woman was murdered Williams was incarcerated in the Nebraska Asylum under his care and was not released until twelve days after the murder.

Williams was released and the Houston Branch is taking the necessary steps to have him committed to the Texas State Asylum.

"Birth of a Nation"

The "Birth of a Nation" film has been barred a second time from the State of Ohio by a decision just rendered by the Ohio Supreme Court sustaining Vernon

M. Reigel, State Director for Education, in his contention that the film is not moral, educational, or amusing. Mayor Davis of Cleveland has ordered the film seized at the opera house where it was to be shown. Upon appeal by the Griffith interests to the Federal Court, the right to show the film was granted but the State Supreme Court now bars it.

Publicity

Since the last report to the Board the following press releases have been sent out:

Annual Conference, 16
Twenty-fourth Infantry, 3
Military Training Camps, 1
General Bullard's Slander, 2
Ku Klux Klan, 3
"Birth of a Nation," 1
Anti-Intermarriage Laws, 1
Revision of Senate Rules, 1
Branch Work, 5
Book Chat, 2

James Weldon Johnson, Secretary
July 13, 1925

Report of the Secretary
for the Board Meeting of February 1926

Washington Segregation Case

On January 8 the Washington Segregation Case was argued before the Supreme Court of the United States. Argument was made by Mr. Storey and Mr. Marshall. The other attorneys representing the Association were also present: Messrs. Spingarn, Stockton, Cobb, Davis, Lewis, and Schick.

Defense Fund

The American Fund for Public Service at its meeting on January 6 received the report of the Association's Secretary on the Defense Fund and voted not only to pay over to the N.A.A.C.P. the $15,000 it had originally agreed to give if the Association raised $30,000 but an additional sum of $6,552.79, this latter sum being a gift of one dollar for each two dollars raised above $30,000 up to noon, January 6.

The full accounting of the Defense Fund, to February 1 is as follows:

Total contributions from individuals and organizations	$ 42, 391.36
Original contribution from the American Fund	5,000.00
Additional contribution on the raising of $30,000	15,000.00
Further additional contribution from the American Fund	6,552.79
Contribution to be received from Mr. Rosenwald contingent upon raising the second $24,000	1,000.00
Amount raised by the Detroit Branch and disbursed locally for the Sweet Case	6,137.64
TOTAL	$ 76,081.79

Dyer Anti-Lynching Bill

Congressman Dyer is planning to arrange a joint hearing of the Senate and House Committee, on the Dyer Anti-Lynching Bill. Mr. Stockton and the secretary are planning to be present at the hearing. There will be a Senate hearing on anti-lynching legislation on February 16 which the Secretary will attend.

Anti-Intermarriage Bill

(District of Columbia): On January 5 Senator Caraway of Arkansas introduced in the United States Senate a bill (S.2160) prohibiting "the intermarriage of the Negro and Caucasian races" in the District of Columbia. The bill further provides that it shall be unlawful for any person so married to reside in the District of Columbia; that persons so married and now resident in the District of Columbia shall, if they remove from the District, be prohibited from returning for the purpose of re-establishing a residence; that any person performing a marriage ceremony between a person of Negro blood and a white person shall be guilty of a felony; and that the penalty for violation of any provision of the act shall be a fine of not more than $1,000 and imprisonment for a period of not less than one year nor more than five years.

The Secretary has written the Association's branches requesting that each branch communicate with the senators from its state urging that they vigorously oppose the bill; also that the members of the branch be urged to send individual letters or telegrams to these senators; that they ask prominent and influential persons, both white and colored to do likewise; that they interview editors of local newspapers urging them to write editorials against the bill; and that churches, lodges, fraternal organizations be asked to pass resolutions against the bill, such resolutions to be forwarded to their respective senators.

Disfranchisement

On reading dispatches in the New York newspapers telling of the arrest of Mrs. Elizabeth Little in Birmingham, Ala., for endeavoring to procure registration of Negroes qualified to vote in the coming election, the National Office took occasion to wire President Coolidge asking that the federal government use its full power to end the disfranchisement of colored voters in Alabama.

The President's secretary replied that the Association's telegram had been referred to the Attorney General.

Ku Klux Klan (New York)

On January 12 the Court of Appeals, the highest court of the State of New York, upheld the constitutionality of the Walker Anti-Klan law, declaring that the law does not constitute an unreasonable and arbitrary exercise of the legislative authority. The Walker law, whose enactment was backed at a legislative hearing by the N.A.A.C.P., requires secret societies to file lists of their members and other information with the Secretary of State.

Lynching

Since the last report to the Board the following lynching has taken place:

Ocala, Fla.: January 12: A band of masked men took Nick Williams from two officers, bundled him into an automobile and lynched him at a lonely spot eighteen miles from Ocala. Williams had been jailed on suspicion in connection with an attack on a white woman. When seized he was being taken to a hospital to be identified by the woman.

The *New York Evening World* of January 27 carried a dispatch to the effect that Assemblyman Louis A. Cuvillier from New York City had advocated the invocation of lynch law as a means of stopping crime in New York State.

The National Office issued a statement denouncing Mr. Cuvillier's appeal.

The National Office has noted with pleasure the determined effort on the part of Governor Fields of Kentucky to preserve order during the trial of Ed Harris, Negro, said to have confessed to attacking a white woman, murdering her husband and two children. However, the National Office has not communicated with the Governor, feeling that he would be more likely to accomplish his aims if no outside interference was offered.

Detroit Mob Violence

On February 2, in a conversation with Mr. Clarence Darrow, the Secretary and the Assistant Secretary were informed that Mr. Darrow had heard recently from

Mr. Robert M. Toms, Prosecutor of Wayne County, Michigan, that the Sweet Case would come to trial again between the 5th and 10th of March; that probably Henry Sweet would be put on trial first. It was Mr. Darrow's opinion that the State would not succeed in securing a conviction of Henry Sweet and that Mr. Toms will not try more than one or two in case the first tried is acquitted. Mr. Darrow requested that the Assistant Secretary meet him in Detroit some time in February when the matter of counsel can be settled.

Oswald Durant Case

Oswald Durant, the Meharry medical student sentenced to life imprisonment for alleged assault upon a white girl in Nashville, Tenn., and later given a new trial, is still out on bond. The case has been set several times for a re-hearing but as yet has never come to trial. The attorney in charge of the case is of the opinion that it will never come to trial.

Attack on Fourteen-Year-Old Colored Girl

On February 2 the attention of the National Office was called to the case of a fourteen-year-old colored girl who was detained against her will in a deserted barn, in the Bronx, New York City, and criminally assaulted by ten men. When the ten men were arraigned on January 29 they pleaded not guilty to the charges and were held in $5,000 bail each.

The case was scheduled to come up in the Eighth District Court on February 2 but because of the girl's condition was postponed until she is able to appear in court.

The National Office immediately got in touch with the Children's Society and was informed that the Society would push the case to the limit. The Society advised, however, that as a result of her experience, the girl developed double pneumonia and is in a very critical condition at Metropolitan Hospital on Welfare Island; that the girl's mother lives in Virginia and because she has a number of very young children cannot come to New York; that the girl is destitute, and that if the Association could do anything in a social welfare way it would be appreciated.

The National Office has retained Alan L. Dingle, a capable young attorney, who has been instructed to follow the case through for the N.A.A.C.P. both the legal side and the welfare end, and to take such steps as are advisable. He has also been instructed to visit the girl, to talk with the hospital authorities, and to secure the girl's statement to be used in the event of her death.

Case of the Rev. W. A. Price

The Rev. W. A. Price of Alexandria, Va., after having numerous advertisements of a cruise to the Holy Land, published in the *Christian Herald*, to which he has been a subscriber for ten years, made arrangements to take the trip on Steamship Republic, sailing from New York on January 21. On January 6 Mr. Price received a letter from Mr. James W. Boring, manager of the cruise, stating that he feared Mr. Price would "feel out of place and embarrassed" as he was the only member of his race booked for the cruise. He advised Mr. Price to postpone the trip until next summer when a party including Negroes would go to the Holy Land. Mr. Price replied that he did not wish to withdraw or postpone his trip, stating, "I am sure there could not be any more embarrassment than to have to withdraw after having perfected all arrangements." After a representative of the *Christian Herald* Tour had called upon Mr. Price at Alexandria and failed to persuade him to forego the trip, the following telegram from Mr. Boring arrived at Mr. Price's home after he had left for New York:

> We find it advisable cancel your reservation for transportation on Steamship Republic Mediterranean Cruise as per general conditions set forth on page 30 of cruise booklet in which right is reserved to decline to accept or retain any person as member of cruise at any time. Certified check covering amount deposited by you for reservation and passport visas also cost of your passport will be mailed you tomorrow.

Mr. Price upon his arrival in New York claimed his passage. When it was refused he applied for help from the National Office where he was assured he could have legal assistance if he wanted to bring suit. A conference was arranged with Mr. Arthur B. Spingarn, Chairman of the Legal Committee, who advised a conference with Mr. Graham Patterson, publisher of the *Christian Herald*. Mr. Patterson declared the *Herald* was helpless in the matter and advised that Mr. Price forego the trip. Suit in the case, however, was not pressed because of the acceptance of Mr. Price of a settlement of $150.00 from the *Christian Herald* Tour director for his loss in time, railroad fare and the trouble he had sustained.

Publicity

During the month of January the following press releases were sent out:

Defense Fund, 8
Sweet Case, 2
Segregation Case, 4
Anti-Lynching Legislation, 1
Anti-Intermarriage Bill, 1
Disfranchisement, 1
Ku Klux Klan, 1
Who's Who in the N.A.A.C.P., 3
Discrimination, 1
Meetings, 3

Book Chat, 1
Miscellaneous, 8

James Weldon Johnson, Secretary
February 3, 1926

Report of the Secretary for the
Board Meeting of May 1926

Anti-Lynching Legislation

The Dyer Anti-Lynching Bill is still in the hands of the Senate Committee on the Judiciary. The National Office is doing everything possible to have the bill reported favorably. Senators Ernst of Kentucky, Harreld of Oklahoma, and Cummins of Iowa, all members of the Senate Committee on the Judiciary, are candidates for reelection to the Senate; therefore, the National Office has requested the branches in these states to bring all pressure possible on them to have a favorable action on the Bill.

Congressman Berger's Bill: On April 16 an Anti-Lynching Bill was introduced in the House of Representatives by Representative Victor Berger. Newspaper dispatches state that in a statement Representative Berger assailed the Republican Party for failing to carry out its 1924 platform pledge to enact an anti-lynching law.

Louisiana Segregation Case

On April 26 a letter was received at the National Office from Dr. Lucas, President of the New Orleans Branch, that the Hon. Loys Charbonnett, chief counsel in the segregation case handled by the Branch, left New Orleans on April 25 for Washington to file the case in the United States Supreme Court. While in Washington Mr. Charbonnett consulted with Mr. James A. Cobb, who went over the case with him and aided him in having it properly docketed.

Kansas City, Mo., Segregation Case

Mr. Roy Wilkins, News Editor of the *Kansas City Call*, has written the National Office that a case identical in every respect with the Curtis Case has arisen in Kansas City, Mo., and is now in the Circuit Court. He states that a lone signer of a restriction covenant is seeking an injunction against the moving in of a colored family; that if the injunction is granted it will affect about thirty families who have purchased and moved into, or who contemplate moving into, the district.

The district attorney in this case, Elmer E. Hall, Esq., requested a copy of the Association's brief in the Curtis case, which has been sent him.

Reprint of Decision in Louisville Segregation Case

Because of the large number of segregation cases arising in various parts of the country, the National Office has had reprinted the Decision in the Louisville Segregation Case rendered by the United States Supreme Court in 1917 and will supply copies to those wishing to know the exact text of the Decision.

Ku Klux Klan (Imperial, Pa.)

Communications were received from two sources in Imperial, Pa., that on April 13 the Ku Klux Klan had attacked in their home a number of colored families who had been brought to Imperial by the Pittscoal Company to work in their mines. The colored people defended themselves and in the affray the superintendent of the mines was wounded. Though a number of the colored men were jailed on a riot charge no arrests were made among the whites.

The National Office referred this matter at once to the Pittsburgh Branch.

Mob Violence at Carteret (N.J.)

New York papers of Monday evening, April 26, and Tuesday morning, April 27, carried dispatches stating that as the result of the murder of a white man by Negroes a colored church at Carteret, N.J., had been burned and hundreds of colored people had been driven out of town.

On April 27 the National Office got in touch by telephone with Dr. W. G. Alexander of Orange and the Rev. Louis Berry, President of the Newark Branch, who promised to keep in close touch with Carteret and report to the National Office. Also the following telegram was sent to Governor A. Harry Moore:

> Newspaper dispatches from Carteret, N.J., state that as the result of some trouble a mob burned down a colored church in or near that town and drove out one hundred colored families. The National Association for the Advancement of Colored People respectfully urges that you use all of the means and powers at your command to see that the innocent colored people concerned have the full protection of the laws of the State of New Jersey and that those who are guilty of the outrages which have been perpetrated shall be apprehended and punished in accordance with the law.

The Director of Publicity went to Carteret on the morning of April 27 and called on Mayor Mulvihill of whom he asked full police protection for the colored citizens of the town. Mr. Seligmann reported that upwards of one hundred colored people were driven out and that of those who remained many stayed all night in the Armour and Liebig fertilizer plants where they were employed, or barricaded themselves in their homes.

In the afternoon of April 28 Mr. Berry telephoned the National Office that crowds were milling around in Carteret and the indication was that there would be further mob violence. Mr. Berry said that a delegation from Newark and the Oranges, headed by himself as President of the Newark Branch, planned to call upon the Governor that night and urge protection for the colored people of Carteret.

The same afternoon the following letter was received from Governor Moore:

Dear Mr. Johnson:

You may be sure that I would be glad to do all in my power to assist you in the matter referred to in your telegram.

Thanking you for your interest, I am

Very truly yours,
A. Harry Moore, Governor.

It being plainly evident that the Governor either had not read the telegram from the National Office, or had misunderstood it, a second telegram was sent him immediately, as follows:

Your letter received acknowledged receipt my telegram. I judge from it my message did not reach you personally or you did not understand it. I telegraphed urging in the name of the National Association for the Advancement of Colored People that you use all means and powers at your command to protect innocent Negroes of Carteret against further mob violence. Communications within the hour from Carteret indicate probability of riotous demonstration tonight. We call upon you to take steps to avert such an outcome by military guard if necessary.

Mr. Berry reported to the National Office that just as the delegation was arranging to go to Trenton on April 28 to call upon the Governor, it was learned that the Governor was in Atlantic City.

On May 4 a dispatch in the *New York Times* stated that many of the families who left Carteret had returned to their homes; that the Chief of Police had assured the colored people that they would receive every protection at work and in their homes.

Poteau (Okla.) Schools

On March 27 the National Office received from citizens of Poteau and Talihima, Okla., a petition complaining about the inferior school conditions for colored children in these two towns. The National Office at once sent the petition to Oklahoma

City Branch asking whether or not the Branch could take any action in the matter. On April 20 a letter was received from Dr. S. C. Snelson, President of the Oklahoma City Branch, stating that the petition was taken to the State School Commissioner at the Capitol and by the Commissioner taken up with the proper authorities of Le Flore County. Dr. Snelson said the Oklahoma Branch would do everything possible to help in the case and that the people of Poteau and Talihima had been advised to make their case a campaign issue in the coming election with those running for office as County Commissioners.

Death of Dr. William A. Sinclair

Dr. William A. Sinclair, member of the Board of Directors of the N.A.A.C.P. since 1912, died on April 20. However, the National Office did not receive news of his death until Saturday afternoon, April 24.

The Secretary telegraphed Mr. Isadore Martin, Philadelphia member of the Board, requesting that he select an appropriate wreath as a tribute from the National Board of Directors. The funeral was on Sunday, April 25.

Dr. Sinclair was stricken while on his way to the April meeting of the Board. He telephoned the National Office on Thursday, April 15, that he had gotten as far as Newark, N.J., and then had been obliged to leave the train.

Lynching

Since the last report to the Board the following lynchings have occurred:

- Picayune, Miss., April 22: Harold Jackson, white, was taken from jail at Poplarville, Miss., and removed to Picayune where a rope was place around his neck and he was forced to jump from a bridge, hanging himself. Jackson was awaiting action by a grand jury on charges that he had played a part in the slaying of two federal entomologists. He was also under indictment in connection with the murder of a white woman in 1924.
- Albuquerque, N.M., April 26: The body of Santiago Platero, Navajo Indian, charged with the murder of a government cattle inspector, was found hanging from a tree near the scene of the murder. A coroner's jury found he had come to his death "by hanging by parties unknown."

Detroit Mob Violence Case

The second trial of the Sweet Case began on April 19. (It will be remembered that in the first trial the eleven defendants were tried jointly and that the trial resulted in a hung jury.) A jury was secured on Saturday, April 24, and the State began putting in its evidence on Monday, the 26th. Clarence Darrow, chief counsel, stated to the Assistant Secretary at the close of the first week that he felt the defense's case was very much further advanced than at a corresponding period of the first trial. This opinion was based upon the facts: (1) that the full and fair publicity during the first trial had definitely swung sentiment towards the defendants' case; (2) that many of the prosecution witnesses had forgotten the testimony they gave at the first trial and obvious lying was therefore more definitely shown; and (3) that separate trials in many ways were proving advantageous.

The first defendant to be tried is Henry Sweet. In a statement to the police on the night of the shooting Henry Sweet admitted that he had fired from a front window. It was learned subsequently that he was not in the room at the time of the shooting but had sought in this way to take the blame upon himself because his brother, having a wife and child, could less afford punishment.

Lester Moll, Assistant Prosecutor, stated to the Assistant Secretary on April 30 that the prosecution expected to finish putting in its case during the week of May 3. It is felt that all evidence will be in and arguments to the jury completed during the week of May 10. There is general feeling in Detroit that the case will end either in another mistrial or acquittal.

Mr. Julian Perry has accepted a fee of $1,000.

Indianapolis Segregation Ordinance

In the campaign organized by the Indianapolis Branch against the residential segregation ordinance passed by the City Council on March 16, $5,400 has been raised and more than 1,200 members secured. The law firm of Miller, Bailey and Thompson has been retained and will be assisted by Attorneys R. L. Brokenburr, W. S. Henry and F. B. Ransom, the latter serving without compensation. The entire state of Indiana is being organized in preparation for similar ordinances. The National Office has written the Indianapolis Branch commending it upon this splendid campaign and at the same time suggesting that they proceed with the most rigid economy in the prosecution of the suit, bearing in mind the fact that the Indianapolis ordinance falls into the same category as the Louisville Ordinance upon which the Supreme Court rendered decision in 1917, and that therefore the major part of the work of drawing briefs has already been done.

Cornelia Harris (Tennessee "Incest" Case)

Word has come to the National Office that the Nashville Branch has retained Attorney Jeff McCarn to prosecute the case of Mrs. Cornelia Harris who was given a term of two years for marrying and living with a mulatto who it was charged, was white. Mr. McCarn is the lawyer who handled the case of Oswald Durant, the Meharry Medical student. Letters have been received from Mrs. Harris and Judge B. D. Bell, her attorney, claiming that Judge Bell had not been advised of the change in attorneys and that, therefore, he had been treated discourteously by the Nashville Branch. The National Office made clear its position, informing Judge Bell, Mrs. Harris, and Dr. F. A. Stewart of the Nashville Branch that it is not familiar with the details of the retention of Mr. McCarn but hopes

there will be no handicap through two attorneys who may be working at cross purposes.

Case of Mrs. Purnell

The case of Mrs. Belva Purnell, who was attacked by a white automobile inspector at Seaford, Delaware, was heard at Milford, Del., one month after the act was committed and then only after the National Office had taken up the matter with the Governor and the Attorney General of the State. The President of the Wilmington Branch reports that out of a long list of witnesses for the defense, not even the doctor was called to testify for Mrs. Purnell but that a white doctor testified that he had treated her for headache; that testimony of Mr. and Mrs. Purnell was unshaken even under severe cross-examination; that everybody believed the woman's story but nobody admitted it. The case was dismissed upon insufficient evidence.

Case of Miss Espanola Holliday

The National Office has received a reply to its letter to the Sisters of Charity regarding the case of Miss Espanola Holliday, the young colored woman who was refused entrance to Providence Hospital, Washington, D.C. This reply states:

> We sent a letter of acceptance not knowing that she was a Negro— never even suspecting such a thing, as we had never had an application from one. When she arrived and we found her to be a Negress we were just as much distressed as was the young woman. We did all in our power about the matter at once—tried to get her in at Freedmens' Hospital, but they could not take her until September.

The report further states that Miss Holliday accepted their offer to get her at Bellevue Hospital; that they gave her dinner, put her in a taxicab, and offered her money, which she refused. They state that they returned to Miss Holliday all her papers for use in entering Bellevue, but Miss Holliday claims that her application blank on which was written the word "Negro" was never returned to her. Miss Holliday feels that her railroad fare from Colorado to Washington should be refunded to her. The Assistant Secretary has sent the report from the Sisters of Charity to Miss Holliday for further action.

Seventeenth Annual Conference

The Seventeenth Annual Conference will be held at Chicago, June 23–29.

Under the Presidency of Dr. Herbert A. Turner, the Chicago Branch is making very rapid strides towards completion of plans for the meeting. Dr. Turner has appointed as heads of the various committees a number of the most active and influential citizens of Chicago. In April the Assistant Secretary spent five days in Chicago helping to complete the plans and speaking at various meetings. Not only is Chicago planning a great meeting, but interest among the branches in the approaching Conference appears greater than in any previous year. To date (May 4) delegates have been reported from eleven states. Among the speakers who have already accepted are Bishop Archibald J. Carey of the A.M.E. Church; Clarence Darrow, Countee Cullen, Dr. John Haynes Holmes, Dr. John Hope, Mrs. Addie W. Hunton, Miss Ovington.

Publicity

Since the last report to the Board the following press releases have been sent out:

Dyer Anti-Lynching Bill, 1
Segregation, 4
Sweet Case, 2
Mob Violence, 2
Ruby Edmonds Case, 1
Negro Soldiers' Monument, 1
Haiti, 1
Meetings, 3
Conference, 6
Contributions, 1
Weeks Editorial, 4
Book Chat, 2
Contests, 2
Annual Report, 1
Who's Who in the N.A.A.C.P., 4
Miscellaneous, 6

James Weldon Johnson, Secretary
May 4, 1926

Report of the Secretary for the Board Meeting of November 1926

Washington Segregation Cases

On November 2 the National Office received from Mr. George E. C. Hayes the following statement:

Judge Cobb has suggested that I call your attention to the action of the Court, Mr. Justice Bailey, is passing upon a recent segregation case, in which a preliminary injunction was being sought.

The case was that of Ida K. Miller, et. al. vs. Harry A. McGowan, et. al., Equity No. 46,116. Our office represented the colored defendants, Elias T. Whitlock and Laura A. Whitlock, his wife. The covenant in question had only to do with occupancy by Negroes and was worded as follows:

> Subject to the covenant that the said land any part thereof, or any improvements thereon, shall not be occupied by any person of the Negro race or having Negro blood.

The suit attempted to restrain a pending sale. The white defendant, Harry A. McGowan, through his attorney, demurred to the Petition, setting forth that the covenant did not purport to restrain sale but rather simply occupancy and that there was nothing to keep a white person from selling to a Negro. The Court sustained the demurrer. The attempt was also made, through an application for a preliminary injunction, to restrain the Negroes from moving into the premises pending the hearing of the case on its merits. The Court denied this injunction.

We feel the case important because our Courts here have recently refused to make Negroes move out of premises covered by such covenants upon application for preliminary injunctions on the ground that there was no such emergency as required same, but had not, until this case, refused to enjoin Negroes from occupying *pendente lite* where they were not yet in possession of same.

We also consider important the fact that the Justice in refusing the preliminary injunction, by way of comment, stated that it was his belief that any such covenant which was permanent in its character and fixed no limit of time was invalid.

As against the colored defendants, the case is still pending for hearing on its merits. Counsel for the plaintiffs has indicated that the case is to be dismissed, but to date that has not been done.

LaBelle, Fla., Lynching Investigation

Mr. H. A. Rider, County Prosecuting Attorney of LaBelle, Fla., has written that the court at which the lynching of Henry Patterson (May 11) will be investigated by a grand jury, was to convene at Fort Myers, Lee County, Fla., on November 2, but that he had secured a promise from the state Attorney, provided it meets with the approval of the Judge, that the investigation will not be taken until November 29.

Check for sixty-one dollars ($61.00), the amount received through Bishop Hurst, has been sent by the National Office to Mr. Rider.

Louisville Libel Case

Messrs. William Warley and I. Willis Cole, editors of the *Louisville News* and *Louisville Leader*, respectively, who were under indictment for libel—the charge growing out of strong protests imprinted against farcical trials of colored men accused of crime in Kentucky—appeared for trial October 6 at Madisonville, Ky. Briefs in the case were submitted and a decision is expected some time in November. Messrs. Warley and Cole state that if the decision is against them they will carry the case to the Kentucky Court of Appeals and, if necessary, to the United States Supreme Court.

With the approval of the Chairman of the Legal Committee, the National Office has sent to the Louisville Branch check for five-hundred dollars ($500.00) to cover attorneys' fees in connection with the case, up to and through the Kentucky Court of Appeals if necessary.

Ray Vaughn and the United States Naval Academy Football Team

On October 27 the National Office received a telegram from the *Baltimore Afro-American* stating that the United States Naval Academy football team had refused to play Colgate University unless Ray Vaughn, colored member of the Colgate team, was kept on the bench. The National Office at once sent a telegram to Secretary of the Navy protesting against such "unsportsmanlike, undemocratic and un-American action." The Superintendent of the Navy instituted an investigation and on October 28, the following telegram was received from the Bureau of Navigation:

> Referring your telegram October 26 . . . it is believed that you are misinformed on the subject as Superintendent Naval Academy reports they did not refuse to play under circumstances aforementioned. And further information is that Ray Vaughn did not come to Naval Academy with the University team. Will be pleased to consider any information you have in this matter.

A telegram to Ray Vaughn from the National Office brought the following reply:

> The Navy did not officially protest my playing against them as a member of Colgate team. Knowing that the Navy was an institution in the South, the athletic officials here at Colgate talked the matter over with me and we decided it was best that I not accompany the team.

The *Baltimore Afro-American* has also been in communication with Naval Academy authorities, and it is felt that in [the] future they will hesitate to take any such position as indicated in the Annapolis–Colgate game.

The Sweet Case

On October 29 the National Office received a letter from Mr. Julian Perry, colored attorney in the case of Dr. Ossian H. Sweet, et al, Detroit, stating that Judge Murphy had advised him that he had been spoken to by Mr. Toms, Prosecutor, regarding the possibility of trying Dr Sweet; that Judge Murphy explained, however, that a conference was to be had before a definite decision was made.

The Secretary and the Assistant Secretary had a conference with Mr. Darrow, in New York, on October 30, when Mr. Darrow said he was not apprehensive about any such step being taken but that he would be in Detroit on Thanksgiving Day and would see both Judge Murphy and Mr. Toms and talk with them about the matter.

Dyer Anti-Lynching Bill

Congressman Dyer has written the National Office suggesting that a conference be called in Washington, between November 15 and December 1, for the purpose of discussing the subject of federal legislation against lynching and seeing how best we can work in the coming session of Congress toward having the Anti-Lynching Bill enacted into law. Mr. Dyer suggested that the N.A.A.C.P. is the organization to call this conference.

The National Office feels that Mr. Dyer's suggestion is an excellent one, but that not only would it give us more time but might be more effective, if the conference is held as soon as possible after, rather than before, Congress convenes.

Before actually settling on any program, the Secretary will go to Washington and have a conference with Mr. Dyer on this matter.

Samuel A. Browne Case

On October 26 Mr. Samuel A. Browne and Mr. William A. Morris, President of the Staten Island, New York Branch, called at the National Office and reported that the arguments for dismissal of the indictment in the criminal action against Musco M. Robertson had been heard in the Supreme Court, Part I, Brooklyn, on October 26.

Briefs for both sides were to be filed by November 3. The civil action filed by Mr. Browne is still pending.

New York University Discrimination

This is the case in which Thomas W. Young and Miss Reba McLain were discriminated against because of race prejudice and in which Mr. Young was denied admission to one of the dormitories and Miss McLain was asked to withdraw from her class in Physical Education.

Since this case was reported the Assistant Secretary has received a letter from Mr. Voohis, Assistant to the Chancellor, stating in part:

I am persuaded, from your letter of the 6th, that further discussion by letter of the matters to which you refer would be unfruitful. It is difficult to strike the common point of view. May I suggest, therefore, that if you are inclined to carry the discussion further, you give me . . . and yourself, I should hope . . . the benefit of personal conference, at your convenience, at this office . . .

The Assistant Secretary has made arrangements with the Chairman of the Legal Committee to confer with Mr. Voohis on this case.

The Aiken (S.C.) Lynching

At 3:00 a.m. on October 8, a mob took from the Aiken, S.C. Jail two colored boys and a colored woman, Demon Lowman, age 22, Clarence Lowman, age 15, and Bertha Lowman, age 27, carried them a mile and a half from Aiken and shot them to death. The Assistant Secretary, going as a special correspondent of the *New York World*, went to South Carolina, visiting in Spartanburg, Columbia, Aiken, Warrenville, Graniteville, and other towns, and made a full investigation of the lynching. The complete story of the case is given in a press story sent to the colored press on October 29, copy of which was sent to the members of the Board.

The Aiken lynchings offer undoubtedly the most convincing testimony we have ever secured of the inability of the states to prevent lynching. The Assistant Secretary was able to get in touch with certain responsible white and colored people of South Carolina who were in possession of definite facts. These facts were carefully investigated and on his return to New York City, the Assistant Secretary wrote a seven-page letter to Governor McLeod giving him the names of twenty-two members of the mob and of some spectators which included the sheriff, his two deputies, policemen for the city of Aiken, three cousins of Governor McLeod, two members of the Grand Jury which is investigating the lynching, and other persons equally prominent; gave the Governor the name of the lawyer in whose office the Klansmen met and planned the lynching, and furnished him with detailed information regarding each one of the participants in the murder.

It will be remembered that the victims were charged with the murder of Sheriff H. H. Howard who on receipt of an anonymous letter, had gone with three deputies all dressed in civilian clothes and not wearing badges, to arrest the Lowmans on a charge of selling liquor. Demon Lowman having been called from his home at night two weeks before by a group of Klansmen and severely beaten, the Lowmans were apprehensive and rushed into the house. The four white men ran towards the house drawing guns and in the melee, Mrs. Annie Lowman, 55, was killed by Deputy Sheriff (later sheriff) Nolle Robinson. Bertha and Clarence Lowman were very dangerously wounded and Demon Lowman was shot. They were tried and convicted in a farcical trial and their cases appealed to the State Supreme Court which reversed the convictions and remanded the case for trial. On retrial, the State's case fell down so completely that the presiding judge granted a motion for a directed verdict in the case of one of the three defendants and it seemed probable the other two would go free also. It was at this point that the mob stepped in and lynched the three.

At the time of the writing of this report, Governor McLeod has not replied to the Assistant Secretary's letter.

The *New York World* has sent its star man, Oliver H. P. Garrett, to South Carolina to go into the situation fully and Mr. Louis Marshall has sent Mr. Ochs of the *Times* a copy of the letter to Governor McLeod. A story has been sent to the colored press and it was carried very widely and has been commented upon editorially most favorably.

A copy of the letter to Governor McLeod is being sent to the newspapers which opposed the lynching. Some of the newspapers have denounced the lynching most vigorously.

Publicity

Since the last report to the Board the following press releases have been sent out:

Legal Defense, 1
Miami Disaster, 2
Lynching 2
Michigan Civil Rights Case, 1
Intercolonial Conference, 1
Meetings, 3
Pittsburgh Courier, 2
Crisis Prize Contest, 1
Dr. Du Bois in Europe
Contributions, 1
Book Chat, 1
Week's Editorial, 7
Miscellaneous, 5

James Weldon Johnson, Secretary
November 3, 1926

Report of the Secretary for the Board Meeting of September 1927

Maurice Mays Case

In August, 1919, Maurice Mays, a young colored man, was arrested in Knoxville, Tennessee, charged with the murder of Mrs. Bertie Lindsey, a white woman. Although the trial resulted in a verdict of murder in the first degree, the general opinion among both white and colored in Knoxville was that Mays was not guilty, and the Knoxville Branch of the N.A.A.C.P. undertook to have the case investigated in an effort to save him from the chair. The investigation brought out evidence to show that at the time of the murder, Mays was at his own home asleep more than a mile from the scene of the crime. The National Office called upon the other Tennessee branches to cooperate with the Knoxville Branch and more than $600 was raised as a defense fund. Notwithstanding these efforts, Mays was finally executed.

A dispatch from Norton, Virginia, dated August 20, 1927, states that Mrs. Sadie Mandil has confessed to the crime for which Maurice Mays was put to death; that she killed Mrs. Lindsey because a few nights previous she had trailed her husband to the Lindsey home and had seen her husband and Mrs. Lindsey together on the street.

The dispatch states also that the Chief of Police of Norton, Virginia, had been advised by the office of the Knoxville Chief of Police that Maurice Mays had paid the death penalty for the crime and that records there show no charge against Mrs. Mandil. Thereupon, Mrs. Mandil was released from custody.

Los Angeles Bathing Beach Segregation Case

On July 17 four men, Dr. H. G. Hudson, President of the Los Angeles Branch; and Messrs. Romulus Johnson, James Conley, and John McCaskill, were arrested while bathing in the tide waters off the beach front at Manhattan, California. The men were represented by Attorney Hugh E. Macbeth who succeeded in bringing out the fact that the public pier and all of the beach front is owned by the city of Manhattan but is leased to a private individual, Oscar Bassonnette. Mr. Bassonnette testified that he had given police officers instructions to arrest or eject "undesirable characters" trespassing upon the property which he had leased. The two policemen who made the arrest testified that they had been instructed by Mr. Bassonnette to arrest any colored person who went in bathing on his property. The charge brought against the four colored men was that of resisting an officer and the Magistrate found them guilty as charged, giving each a fine $100 or twenty days in jail. Attorney Macbeth gave notice of appeal and the men were released on property bonds of $500.

On August 20 the following telegram was received from Dr. Hudson:

> Manhattan Beach fight won. Only forty-five days from the first intimidation of colored citizens in Manhattan to complete victory by Los Angeles Branch. Attorney Hugh E. Macbeth of Legal Committee conducted case on broad Americanism with vigorous legal fight and thorough propaganda. Manhattan arrested judgment and cancelled lease.

Pan African Congress

The Fourth Pan African Congress was held in New York City, August 21–24. The Congress was called by the Circle for Peace and Foreign Relations, of which Mrs.

Addie W. Hunton, former Field Secretary of the N.A.A.C.P., is Chairman; and it was presided over by Dr. Du Bois.

Two members of the staff of the N.A.A.C.P. attended as delegates from the Association—the Director of Branches and the Field Secretary.

There were 158 delegates, from twenty-eight states and eleven foreign countries.

The addresses and discussions were of the usual high order and exceedingly informative. Much interest was awakened by the statements of Chief Amoah III, concerning conditions in Africa, and those of M. Dantes Bellgardes, former Haitian Minister to France, concerning conditions in his country resulting from American invasion. Members of the Association's staff delivering addresses were Dr. Du Bois, Mr. Bagnall, and Mr. Pickens.

A committee was formed to call a conference in 1928 at which time it is planned to perfect the machinery of a permanent organization.

A prominent feature of the Congress was a very large series of maps and charts depicting almost every phase of the problem discussed. These were prepared under the direction of Dr. Du Bois.

The speeches and discussions indicated a serious understanding of the problems involved and a deep appreciation of international relations.

San Diego Hospital Discrimination

On September 7 the following telegram was received from the San Diego, California, Branch of the Association:

> The San Diego Branch of the National Association for the Advancement of Colored People was victorious in its fight for admittance of colored girls as nurses in the San Diego County Hospital, beginning September 5.

Publicity

A development of considerable importance during the month was the arrival of Mr. J. R. Steelman, a graduate student of the University of North Carolina, who spent upwards of two weeks at the National Office gathering material for a book on mob violence and lynching. The Director of Publicity spent much time with Mr. Steelman supplying him with matter from the files and conferring with him on his book. Mr. Steelman gave assurance that full credit for the material he obtained and the help given him would be given the N.A.A.C.P. in the book. Coming as it will from the South, such an acknowledgment ought to form a vital step in our peaceful penetration.

Another significant event of the month was the publication by the *New York Times* on August 18 of an editorial commending the pamphlet by the Secretary on "African Races and Culture" and specifically mentioning the Association by name. This editorial has been widely reprinted by both white and colored newspapers and has resulted in a demand for the pamphlet by teachers, libraries, etc. Among the white dailies reprinting the editorial are the Beaumont, Texas, *Enterprise;* the *Des Moines News;* the *Amsterdam* and the *New York Recorder.*

The *Nation* in an editorial of August 24 quoted from the N.A.A.C.P. lynching statistics.

An evidence of the impression made by the Annual Spring Conference in Indianapolis was furnished by an article written by the art critic of the *Indianapolis Star,* referring to the Conference and urging that its good effect be followed up by support of colored artists. The work of two young colored painters of Indianapolis was then exhaustively dealt with by the *Star's* critic.

James Weldon Johnson, Secretary
September 8, 1927

Report of the Secretary for the Board Meeting of October 1927

Extradition Case

During the past month the attention of the National Office has been called to three cases in which Southern states are seeking to have returned to their jurisdiction for trial colored men charged with crime. In two of these cases the National Office has aided. The third case was handled by the District of Columbia Branch.

The Edward Glass Case

At the September meeting of the Board the Secretary reported regarding the efforts being made by the San Francisco and Northern California Branches to prevent the extradition of Edward Glass to Sapulpa, Oklahoma. This case is still pending. At the request of Mr. Edward D. Mabson, attorney in the case, the National Office wired Governor C. C. Young of California, on September 7, urging that he grant a delay of thirty days in the proceedings in order to permit the presentation of facts and arguments. The National Office also sent data regarding lynchings in the United States and a sworn affidavit regarding lynching in the State of Oklahoma since 1889. These were used at a hearing on the case held September 26. The Court ruled against receiving evidence of mob violence at the time Glass left Oklahoma.

It being felt that a decision in the case would hinge upon present day conditions in Sapulpa, the National Office was requested to send a confidential man to Sapulpa to secure information which would show whether or not Glass would have a chance of a fair trial. The National Office was fortunate in securing Dr. A. Baxter Whitby, former President of the Oklahoma City Branch, to make this investigation. Dr. Whitby's report has not yet been received.

In the meantime a telegram has been received from Mr. Mabson stating that adverse judgment has been rendered, order to show cause discharged, and petition denied; whereupon appeal to the United States Circuit Court has been filed and perfected. The case will probably be heard at the February term.

Mrs. H. E. De Hart, Secretary of the Northern California Branch, has written the National Office that the Executive Committee accepted with thanks the appropriation of $250 made at the September meeting of the Board, that the Branches have raised more than $600.

The Samuel Kennedy Case

Samuel Kennedy, charged with having "slapped" a white man in Georgia and with having escaped after a chaingang sentence of eighteen months, was found by the Georgia sheriff in Chicago where he was taken in custody. Kennedy denied ever having lived in Georgia, declared he knew nothing of the crime and said he could furnish a clear alibi as to his whereabouts at the time the crime was said to have been committed.

The case was taken up by the Chicago Branch, represented by Attorney Harold M. Tyler.

After a hard fight in Chicago, Kennedy was remanded to the Georgia sheriff who secretly left the city by motor. The sheriff missed train connections at Terre Haute, Indiana, and he turned Kennedy over to the local sheriff for safekeeping overnight, thereby losing temporary custody of his prisoner. The Terre Haute Branch of the N.A.A.C.P. secured a writ of habeas corpus and $500 was pledged for carrying the case to the Indiana Supreme Court.

At the request of the Chicago Branch the National Office requested Attorney R. L. Bailey of Indianapolis to assist Attorney Tyler in the case.

Mr. Morris Lewis of the Chicago Branch reports that the Circuit Court of Indiana has taken charge of the matter with a continuance granted, and that he feels sure of ultimate victory.

On October 3 a wire was received from Mr. Bailey stating that the Governor of Indiana had refused to issue the warrant.

James Blevins Case

James Blevins, now living in Washington, D.C., was wanted in Birmingham, Alabama, for assaulting white men (in self-defense). Blevins was a prosperous carpenter and paper-hanger in Birmingham and had incurred the enmity of certain white people. He was warned to leave town and when he refused to do so was called upon by two white men who demanded $100 and the deed to his home. On being refused they opened fire to which Blevins replied with a single shot from a shot gun. He was afterwards brutally beaten over the head with pistols, kicked and then left unconscious. Afterward Blevins was treated by a physician and when he became able and got an opportunity to do so he drove in his automobile from Birmingham to Washington.

The authorities in Birmingham obtained from the Governor of Alabama a writ for Blevins's return. The case came to the notice of Mr. Neval H. Thomas, President of the District of Columbia Branch who referred it to the Branch's attorney, Mr. Sylvester L. McLaurin. McLaurin associated himself in the case with Professor William H. Richards. The attorneys instituted habeas corpus proceedings and had the extradition writ quashed, and Blevins was released. Within twenty minutes he was rearrested and another writ of habeas corpus was obtained from another Branch of the Supreme Court of the District of Columbia, from whose ruling appeal has now been taken to the District of Columbia of Appeals where argument is to be had soon.

While both lawyers feel that the facts in the case will justify a reversal and release of the prisoner by the Court of Appeals, they are considering details incident to appealing the case to the Supreme Court of the United States if such further proceedings become necessary.

Gary (Indiana) School Desegregation

Press dispatches stated that on Monday, September 26, 1,400 students of the Emerson High School at Gary, Indiana, walked out because twenty-four Negro students appeared at the school for enrollment.

The National Office at once telegraphed the officers of the Gary Branch requesting a report on the school situation and urging prompt action on the part of the Branch. The National Office also telegraphed Mr. Morris Lewis of the Chicago Branch requesting him to go to Gary at the expense of the National Office to investigate the school situation there.

The first reports, both from Mr. Lewis and from the officers of the Gary Branch seemed to show that the matter would be amicably settled, but later it developed that the school authorities acceded to the demands of the student strikers and that the Gary City Council passed to final reading an ordinance providing for a separate school for the colored students; that a temporary school will be erected at once for which the ordinance appropriated $15,000.

In view of this later development the Secretary called Attorney R. L. Bailey of Indianapolis on the long distance telephone asking whether he could go to Gary to ascertain for the National Office just what the conditions were. Mr. Bailey agreed to go to Gary and did so on September 30. He reports that he first met with the colored lawyers of Gary, eleven in number. This meeting was called to consider the school law. He also attended several mass meetings of colored people, and finally, with a committee, had interview with the Mayor of Gary and Superintendent of Schools William A. Wirt.

Mr. Bailey reports that both the Mayor and the Superintendent of Schools are firm in their stand that colored students shall be segregated in accordance with the demands of the striking white students.

Coffeyville (Kansas) Riot Cases

Regarding the Coffeyville (Kansas) Riot Cases, Mr. Elisha Scott, attorney representing the N.A.A.C.P., reports as follows:

> Since the State of Kansas lost the case of the State of Kansas vs. Ira Kennedy and Julia Mooney, the sentiment against Anderson and Ford, who were charged with inciting the riot, changed materially in their favor. Through the work of the N.A.A.C.P., and the best class of the other group, sufficient pressure was brought on the County Attorney that he made a motion to dismiss the Anderson and Ford cases, and the same was sustained. That closed the Coffeyville Riot Cases, in so far as our organization is concerned, as I understand it.
>
> There is yet pending, however, a case of the City of Coffeyville against Napoleon Anderson for discharging firearms in the City of Coffeyville, on the night of the riot. As you will appreciate, the City will file that case and obtain a conviction in the lower Court in order that they may help out their civil cases, in which Anderson is suing the City for the sum of $10,000.

Mr. Scott reports that he will assist in the defense of this latter case at the insistence of the local Branch.

The Anderson Case (Port Huron, Mich.)

On September 15 the National Office sent the transcript of record in the case of William Anderson, Port Huron, Michigan (on trial for murder) to Mr. Oscar W. Baker of Bay City, Michigan, with the request that Mr. Baker review the evidence in the case. Mr. Baker reviewed the case and gave as his opinion that the record presents justification of the verdict of the jury since there appears to be no appeal to race prejudice. Mr. Baker thinks, however, that since the Port Huron Branch had taken part in the trial it would be best to go through with the motion for a new trial and appeal to the Michigan Supreme Court. He states that the entire action, including expense and attorney's fees, should be within $500.

The National Office has written the Port Huron Branch requesting a definite estimate of the total expense of the case, including attorneys' fees.

The National Legal Committee is considering the case in the light of Mr. Baker's opinion.

The Abe Washington Case (Jacksonville, Fla.)

In accordance with the vote of the Board at the September meeting, the transcript of record in the case of Abe Washington, convicted of murder and sentenced to be hanged, was submitted to Mr. Louis Marshall, for his opinion. Mr. Marshall expressed his willingness to prepare a brief in the case but felt that he needed more time than was indicated. The National Office therefore communicated with Mr. S. D. McGill, attorney in the case, suggesting that he try for an extension of time. Mr. McGill has replied that he will file the original brief on October 8; that the State will then have twenty days in which to file its brief. Mr. McGill will file his reply brief ten days later, which will be November 8, and he feels sure that if Mr. Marshall does not have his brief ready by that time an extension of time can be secured.

Mr. Marshall writes the National Office that as soon as he receives the copy of Mr. McGill's brief and that of the State he will prepare a reply in time to be filed in the Florida State Supreme Court.

Peonage Investigation

Miss Helen Boardman left New York on September 24 for the purpose of making the peonage investigation, in accordance with the vote of the Board at the September meeting. No report has as yet come from Miss Boardman.

Segregation in Government Departments

The matter of Segregation in Government Department at Washington has been taken up by the District of Columbia Branch under the leadership of its President, Mr. Neval H. Thomas. Vigorous protest has been made to Secretary of the Interior, Hubert Work.

Results are already evident. Mr. Thomas reports that two Negro clerks were ordered on October 1 to report in white sections as pension examiners. This carries promotions in salaries, breaks down part of the segregation system, and gives them a much higher grade of work.

Roswell Hamilton Case

The Oklahoma City Branch brought to the attention of the National Office the case of Roswell Hamilton who was convicted of murder and sentenced to death for the killing of deputy sheriff and a night policeman at Wetumka, Oklahoma, on April 10, 1926. The Branch reported that the Criminal Court of Appeals had reversed the decision of the lower court and had ordered that Hamilton be given a new trial on the ground that the prosecution's argument was an appeal to race prejudice.

The Oklahoma City Branch has not assumed a specified financial obligation in the case but has decided to give whatever moral and financial support it is able.

On September 21 the National Office received a telegram from the Oklahoma City Branch stating that the case was unexpectedly docketed for October 3 and asking for the loan of $100 for three months, which would aid the Branch in relocating witnesses and preparing the case. Check for $100 was forwarded.

Discrimination by Siasconsett (Mass.) Bus Line

The American Civil Liberties Union brought to the attention of the National Office a complaint that the Siasconsett (Mass.) Bus Line was discriminating against colored people. The matter was referred to Mr. Butler R. Wilson for investigation.

Publicity

The number of press releases issued during September was forty-two.

At the end of the month the Committee of Executives decided to entrust the *Crisis* notes of the Association's activities to the Director of Publicity. The title of the notes has been changed to "The N.A.A.C.P. Battle Front," and they will appear in the *Crisis* each month under the new title and editorship.

Additional reprints of the *New York Times* editorial commenting on "African Races and Cuture" published by the Slater Fund have been noted in the Montgomery, Alabama, *Advertiser;* the Charlotte, N.C. *Observer;* and the Des Moines, Iowa, *Capital.*

A letter sent out by the Association calling attention to the Association's fight against the Ku Klux Klan and pointing to conditions in Indiana and Alabama as justifying opposition to the Klan has been printed on the editorial pages of the Springfield, Mass. *Republican,* the *Union* of the same city, and Boston *Herald.*

Conspicuous display was given the Association's protest on the attempt to segregate colored students in Gary, Indiana. The *New York Times* published the N.A.A.C.P. protest on the center of the first page and the *New York Herald-Tribune* published a second story on September 20.

The Director of Publicity has outlined and begun work on a booklet to be issued in the Twentieth Anniversary year of the N.A.A.C.P. setting forth the Association's history and the significance of its work and major achievement.

James Weldon Johnson, Secretary
October 5, 1927

Report of the Secretary for the Board Meeting of March 1929

Richmond (Va.) Segregation Ordinance

Newspapers of February 15 carried a dispatch to the effect that a Residential Segregation Ordinance had passed the Board of Alderman of the City of Richmond, Virginia, and was before the Mayor for his signature.

The resolution proposing this ordinance was presented to the City Council of Richmond in November by Alderman Henry Woody, and as soon as the matter was brought to the attention of the National Office the Richmond Branch of the N.A.A.C.P. was advised how to fight against the adoption of the ordinance. A special Citizens' Committee was formed which appeared before the City Ordinance Committee and protested against the ordinances. However, the ordinance was passed.

Upon receipt of information that the ordinance was before the Mayor for his signature the National Office wired the Mayor calling his attention to the decisions of the United States Supreme Court in the Louisville and New Orleans Segregation and suggesting "that the City of Richmond may be saved money through your refusal to sign what appears obviously to be an unconstitutional ordinance." The Mayor was further advised in this telegram that "we will consider it incumbent upon us, should the ordinance be signed by you, to take such legal action as will nullify this latest attempt to do that which the highest court in the land has said is unconstitutional:

Mayor Bright replied at once, by telegram:

The racial segregation ordinance will be approved by this office. The ordinance is drawn in the interest of both races. Those who oppose it are entirely within their rights in having the courts pass upon its constitutionality.

To this telegram the National Office replied that "courts have already held such ordinances unconstitutional and enactment of same is flouting of fundamental law of land as laid down by United States Court."

A second telegram was received from the Mayor stating that the communications from the National Office had confirmed his "conviction that the principle involved in the segregation ordinance is highly desirable for the peace and social good order of our people."

At the same time the National Office was in touch by telegraph with the President of the Richmond Branch, Mr. C. V. Kelly, and Mr. Kelly, and Mr. J. B. Pollard, representing the Citizens' Committee, and offered its services and the cooperation of the National Legal Committee in combating the ordinance. The National Office also offered to send to Richmond a member of the Executive Staff to confer with the Citizens' Committee and with the attorneys. The request came that a representative from the National Office be sent for a conference February 26, and the Assistant Secretary went to Richmond for this conference.

The Assistant Secretary found the Citizens' Committee well organized and composed of some of the most progressive citizens of Richmond and that it has, apparently, the unqualified support of the ministers of the city. Unfortunately, the Richmond Branch of the N.A.A.C.P. has been inactive for several months and for this reason action against the ordinance is being taken by this special Citizens' Committee instead of by the Branch.

The Committee has tentatively retained Mr. J. B. Pollard, a colored attorney, who was of counsel of the United States Supreme Court in the Louisville Case and who is also working now in conjunction with the National Office in the matter of the Virginia White Primary Law. On Mr. Pollard's recommendation, the Committee employed Mr. Alfred E. Cohen, a white attorney of Richmond. Mr. Cohen was also of counsel in the first Richmond segregation case.

The Assistant Secretary made it clear to individuals and at a lengthy session of the Citizens' Executive Committee that the N.A.A.C.P., while it had no desire to control the case or to take complete charge of it, was interested in keeping unbroken the record of success against segregation ordinances which it had been fighting for upwards of fifteen years; that the National Office volunteered its advice in seeing that the records were properly prepared so that there would be no chance of a reversal of the Louisville decision through a faulty record.

The Assistant Secretary emphasized the fact that the colored people of Richmond could and should raise the three or four thousand dollars necessary to win this case.

After considerable discussion it was voted unanimously by the executive committee that the proffered legal aid and advice from the National Office be accepted with deep appreciation and that the interest of the N.A.A.C.P. in sending the Assistant Secretary to Richmond be acknowledged with thanks.

District of Columbia Appropriations Bill

During the month of February a delegation of colored people of the District of Columbia appeared before the Senate Committeee on Appropriations to protest against certain features in the new school bill—cutting down allotments for new buildings and grounds for colored children, and the elimination of a $175,000 addition to the Lovejoy School, recommended by the Director of the Budget. The elimination was alleged to have been made at the insistance of white property owners, leaving the colored children on part-time schedule.

The Committee consisted of Mr. Pickens, Field Secretary; Messrs. Neval H. Thomas and A. S. Pinkett for the District of Columbia Branch; Messrs. Thomas A. Johnson, Kelly Miller, and Mrs. Anna Murray.

Charleston Public Library Discrimination Case

On February 12, Order of the Circuit Court of Kanawha (W.Va.) County was entered carrying into effect the decision of the Supreme Court of Appeals of West Virginia by granting a Peremptory Writ ordering the Board of Education to admit colored people of Charleston to the Charleston Public Library without discrimination.

On January 22 Judge Maxwell rendered a Concurrent Opinion on a petition for a re-hearing filed by the Board of Education on January 3. This opinion is very specific in defining the power held by a subordinate governmental agency, declaring that such agency has no police power.

Roy Freeman Case

The National Office, on Feburary 15, contributed $250.00 towards the defense of Roy Freeman who is charged with murdering Police Officer William G. Horn in Dayton, Ohio.

At a previous trial Freeman had been convicted of murder in the first degree, but on appeal the conviction had been set aside and the case remanded for a new trial. The Dayton Branch is interested in the case and appealed to the National Office for financial aid. The case is now set for trial on March 11.

Robert Bell and Grady Swain

Mr. W. J. Lanier, Attorney of Record in the Robert Bell and Grady Swain cases, has informed the National Office that March 5 has been set as the date for trial, at Cotton Plant, Arkansas. The previous conviction of these defendants was set aside and the cases remanded for a new trial. For this new trial Mr. Lanier secured a change of venue.

The National Office has sent its check of $250.00 as a contribution towards the expenses in the second trial.

Edward Glass Case

Mr. W. E. McMurray, President of the Oklahoma City Branch, has informed the National Office that a jury returned a verdict of "guilty of murder" in the case of the State of Oklahoma vs. Edward Glass. The defendant was sentenced to life imprisonment.

Mr. Francis Willis Rivers Admitted to New York Bar

On February 13 Mr. Francis Willis Rivers was elected to membership of the Association of the Bar for the City of New York. Mr. Rivers is the first Negro lawyer to be elected to membership in this organization. Mr. Louis Marshall proposed Mr. Rivers for membership and Mr. Arthur B. Spingarn was one of his endorsers. Mr. Rivers was an exceptionally fine candidate to test hitherto unbroken rule against the admission of Negro lawyers. He is a graduate of Yale University where he was elected to Phi Beta Kappa, and also a graduate of the Columbia Law School. He has been practicing in New York for about six years.

Smoker for Clarence Darrow

For some time the National Office has sought ways of interesting the thinking and well-to-do men of Harlem more largely in the work of the N.A.A.C.P. It was decided that one way of doing this and of crystallizing general approval of the

National Association in Harlem would be through a Buffet Smoker for Clarence Darrow. Accordingly a group of approximately one hundred and twenty-five men was invited to a smoker at the nominal tax of $1.50 per man.

The Smoker was held at the Witaka Club on February 18. There were present 115 men, most of them from Harlem, some coming from Brooklyn and New Jersey. Mr. Darrow's address aroused great enthusiasm and the evening, besides being a most pleasant one, resulted in a more cordial interest in the Association.

On March 1 an organization meeting was held at which with great enthusiasm a Men's Committee of Greater New York was formed. It is felt that not only will this move result in greater direct support for the N.A.A.C.P. but that through the holding of three or four smokers each year the men of Harlem may learn to know more of the outstanding men of the country and these men in turn will have the advantage of meeting some of the representative colored men of New York.

Lynching

The first lynching recorded for the year 1929 occurred at Brooksville, Florida, where the body of "Buster" Allen was found hanging from a tree, on February 20. Allen had been arrested charged with attacking a white girl and had been taken to jail in Tampa for safekeeping. He was released to two men who presented a letter purporting to be an order from the Sheriff of Hernando County, which letter was later found to be a forgery.

Publicity

Gratifying results were had from the letter written by Senator Capper and sent out to the white press announcing the Lincoln's Birthday anniversary of the N.A.A.C.P. The letter was published in upwards of twenty-five leading newspapers in New York and throughout the country and elicited a warm editorial from the *St. Louis Globe Democrat*.

Announcement of the campaign for $200,000, together with the Twentieth Anniversary Call written by Mr. Villard, was featured in many colored newspapers.

An article on the Twentieth Anniversary by the Secretary will appear in *The Crescent*, organ of the Phi Beta Sigma Fraternity.

On Lincoln's Birthday three of the executives spoke over the radio: the Secretary from Station WEAF, the Assistant Secretary from Station WOV, and the Director of Publications and Research from Station WEVD. On February 19 the Director of Publicity spoke from Station WOV, and the Chairman of the Board and Dr Louis T. Wright have spoken from the same station since that date. In fact, a series of addresses regarding the work of the Association will be delivered over Station WOV on Tuesdays at 2:45. Other speakers scheduled are Mr. John E. Nail and Mr. William T. Andrews.

Releases on the Richmond segregation ordinance and the Association's oppositon to it were published in white dailies of the South and were featured in the colored press.

During the month the Association has received clippings of its releases from a magazine published in England and from a German newspaper, the *Weser Zeitung*, published in Bremen.

The Director of Publicity prepared a full-page advertisement for the *Crisis* calling attention to the $200,000 Twentieth Anniversary Campaign.

James Weldon Johnson, Secretary
March 7, 1929

Report of the Secretary for the Board Meeting of October 1929

Expulsion of Negro Members of Brooklyn (N.Y.) Protestant Episcopal Church

Newspapers of September 17 quoted the Reverend William Blackshear, Rector of the Protestant Episcopal Church of St. Matthews, Brooklyn, New York, as having announced from his pulpit on the previous Sunday that Negro members would no longer be permitted in that church.

The National Office at once took up this matter by addressing a letter to the Vestry of St. Matthew's Church asking that they disavow and repudiate the action taken by Mr. Blackshear; also a letter was sent to Bishop Ernest M. Stires of the Long Island Diocese, asking that he "take such steps as may be proper to disavow, in behalf of the Prostestant Episcopal Church, the utterance and acts of the Rev. Mr. Blackshear and such of the Vestry as condone them." No reply has been received from the Vestry of St. Matthew's, but on September 23, a letter was received from Bishop Stires setting forth at length his personal attitude and that of the Prostestant Episcopal Church on the action of Mr. Blackshear. In his letter Bishop Stires said, "In my opinion such an announcement is indefensible. The Rev. Mr. Blackshear knows that this is the Bishop's firm conviction." The letter, which has gone to members of the Board in the Association's press releases, constituted virtually a repudiation of the position taken by Mr. Blackshear and his vestry, which on September 23 issued a statement supporting Mr. Blackshear. This statement, published in New York newspapers, read:

Due to the general misunderstanding of the real views of the Rev. Mr. Blackshear as to his parochial policy, with which this vestry is in harmony, it is deemed advisable to make no further statement.

In this case the N.A.A.C.P. has won a victory before the court of public opinion. From its inception the issue had prominent space in metropolitan dailies, not only in New York but in other cities; clergymen have been delivering sermons upon it; newspaper offices have been deluged with letters, many of which were published, concurring in the stand taken by the Association. Forty-two Protestant clergymen have signed and published a statement condemning the attitude of the rector and the vestry of St. Matthew's. On the whole, the press publicity in connection with this incident is unprecedented. For thirteen consecutive days, beginning September 17, the N.A.A.C.P. was featured in the press, stories being telegraphed throughout the country and eighteen editorials appearing, including four days' discussion of the matter by Heywood Broun in his syndicated column. The news magazine, *Time*, summarized the incident, with a reference to the leadership of the N.A.A.C.P.

The *New York World* of September 30 carried a statement to the effect that the House of Bishops of the Protestant Episcopal Church in the United States, in session at Atlantic City, New Jersey, that "the question of expelling Negro members from his (Mr. Blackshear's) congregation is one concerning himself alone."

The National Office, on the same date, addressed a telegram to Bishop John Gardner Murray, Presiding Bishop of the Protestant Episcopal Church in this country, making inquiry as to whether the House of Bishops had been correctly quoted.

In reply, the following telegram was received from Bishop Murray:

Report in error. House of Bishops not yet in session.

Shooting of Lincoln University Student by Brooklyn (N.Y.) Policeman

Ralph Baker, a student at Lincoln University (Pennsylvania), about to enter upon his senior year, was shot, on September 9, at the Troy Avenue Station of the Fulton Street Elevated in Brooklyn, by Patrolman Walter G. Lowe, #4073, of the 80th Precinct, New York.

News of this incident was published in the papers of September 10.

The National Office promptly dispatched a telegram to Commissioner of Police Grover T. Whalen requesting immediate suspension of Lowe and a thorough impartial investigation into the shooting. Lowe was suspended within a few hours after the dispatch of the Association's telegram.

The next step taken was to address a communication to Judge Charles Dodge, Prosecuting Attorney of Kings County, requesting action by the Prosecutor's Office against Lowe. Judge Dodd himself telephoned the National Office welcoming a conference with N.A.A.C.P. representatives.

Following personal investigation of the affair by the Association's Special Legal Assistant, in which valuable aid was given by Dr. Henry H. Proctor of Brooklyn and Dr. George E. Haynes of the Federal Council of Churches, a conference was arranged with District Attorney Dodd. At the conference, attended by the Special Legal Assistant, the Assistant Secretary, and the Director of Publicity, eyewitnesses gave statements to Assistant District Attorney Barshay, who was placed in charge of the case by Judge Dodd.

Following this conference, the Special Legal Assistant, with Assistant Prosecutor Barshay, appeared before City Magistrate Folwell on September 17 to demand a summons for Patrolman Lowe. The summons was issued returnable October 1.

Patrolman Lowe claimed that Baker and his companion, William Fontaine, had offended his woman companion and himself while on an elevated train. The Patrolman was off duty. He claims that he left the train at the Troy Avenue Station to place the boys under arrest, when one of them struck him; that thereupon, he drew his revolver and shot at one of the boys to prevent their escape.

According to the statements made to the District Attorney's Office by eye-witnesses to the shooting, who had been secured through the efforts of the National Office, the situation was different.

Two persons who were passengers in the same car with Lowe and his companion stated that they distinctly remembered seeing them as well as two colored boys in the car, but that these two boys do not answer to the description of Baker and Fontaine. Miss Gladys Brehagen, one of these witnesses, says that just as the train was drawing into the Troy Avenue Station she arose to leave the car, and she remembers both boys approaching the door of the car for the same purpose. She also recalls seeing two colored boys running in the direction of the train and that they passed her. The next thing she recalls is the report of two shots and seeing Lowe following one of the boys with his gun in his hand. These facts, of course, show that Baker, the man who was shot, was not one of the men on the train by whom Patrolman Lowe claims to have been annoyed, but that he had not yet boarded the train.

Mrs. and Miss Thurber at whose home (located within three minutes' walking distance of the Troy Avenue Station) Fontaine and Baker had been visiting, testified that the young men had left the Thurber home only long enough to have reached the Troy Avenue Station. Their testimony showed conclusively that Baker and Fontaine were not the two men with whom Lowe had the altercation.

Louisiana Murder Case

One of the two white men sentenced to prison in connection with the murder of two colored women and the wounding of a third, has accepted his conviction and sentence without further appeal, and has begun to serve his term of life imprisonment.

It will be recalled that the shooting of these women occurred on Christmas Day, 1928, at Eros, Louisiana.

The National Office on September 4 sent its final check of $50.00 for this case, making a total of $300.

Florida White Primary Case

Mr. F. W. Marsh of Pensacola, Florida, attorney in charge of the Florida White Primary Case, has advised the National Office that the case will be heard in the Florida State Supreme Court on October 11.

Suit is being brought by a colored citizen, Mr. H. D. Goods, for $5,000 damages against election clerks who denied him a vote in the primary election in April of this year. This action will test the attempt to evade the decision of the United States Supreme Court in the Texas White Primary Case.

Asbury Park (N.J.) Case

Dr. William J. Parks, President of the Association's Branch in Asbury Park, New Jersey, has informed the National Office that Mr. E. Louis Moore, attorney for the Branch, is about to file papers in the Beach Segregation Case. The Branch is contesting segregation on beach property owned by the city and leased to private parties. Comprised in this case will be actions arising out of assault alleged to have been committed by lifeguards against colored people.

Gary (Indiana) School Case

Brief in the Gary School Case was filed in the Indiana State Supreme Court on August 19. This case is being conducted by Messrs. R. L. Bailey of Indianapolis and Edward McKinley Bacoyn of Gary, to each of whom is being paid the sum of $150.00 for the appeal. To date, $75.00 has been sent each of these attorneys.

Arkansas White Primary Case

The National Office has been asked by Attorneys John A. Ribbler and Booker & Booker of Little Rock, Arkansas, for financial aid in appealing a White Primary Case (Robinson et al. vs. Holman et al.) to the State Supreme Court.

Suit in this case was filed in the Pulaski (County) Chancery Court on November 22, 1928, by Dr. J. M. Robinson and others, asking the Court to restrain the Election Commissioners and others of the City of Little Rock from interfering with them or any other colored persons properly qualified in their effort to vote in the City Democratic Primary. The petition was heard by Judge R. M. Mann, acting for the Chancellor who was out of the state; and the order was granted.

On December 11, 1928, attorneys for the Plaintiffs filed an amended petition, making the State Chairman and Secretary of the Arkansas Democratic State Central Committee parties defendant to the suit, together with their successor in office, so that should the order become permanent it would be state-wide.

Hearing on the matter of making the injunction permanent was delayed until August 29, 1929, when Chancellor Dodge decided in favor of the defendants, dismissing the petition and dissolving the temporary restraining order granted by Judge Mann. Chancellor Dodge did not render a written opinion, neither did he pass on any of the issues other than to hold that the petition be dismissed for want of equality.

In their letter to the National Office, attorneys for the plaintiffs estimate the cost of the appeal at $650.00 and state that the Little Rock Branch has guaranteed $150.00 of this amount.

The Legal Committee has considered this case and the application for financial assistance and feels that except in the form the action takes, it involves no principle not covered by the Association's White Primary Case now pending in Texas. However, the matter of making a small contribution toward the expenses of the case will be brought up at the October meeting of the Board.

Turley Wright Rape Case

Newspapers of August 15 and several days thereafter carried dispatches regarding the sentencing to ten years imprisonment of Turley Wright, at Centerville, Tenn., charged with attacking a white woman, Mrs. Zora Johnson Lynn. A significant statement in the first news item was that "The State had asked for the death sentence until it was revealed that Mrs. Lynn had falsely sworn against the Negro."

The trial of Wright ended suddenly after two members of the State's staff withdrew from the case because of their announced belief that Wright had been "framed" and after two granddaughters of Mrs. Lynn admitted they testified falsely that Wright had cowed them with a pistol during the attack. His attorneys asked for a new trial.

On August 15 the National Office wrote to Bishop I. B. Scott, President of the Nashville, Tenn., Branch, asking whether Wright had adequate legal counsel for his new trial, and stating that the National Office was willing to aid in any way that it could. Bishop Scott wired at once that the general opinion was that nothing would come of the case and that Wright would have been acquitted at once had it not been unsafe to do so in the face of the attending excitement.

In the meantime, on August 17, the National Office communicated with Mr. W. L. Pinkerton, attorney for the defense appointed by the court. Correspondence with Mr. Pinkerton has been of a confidential nature but he has repeatedly expressed his confidence in the innocence of Wright and his determination to see that he is acquitted.

The *Nashville Banner* of September 29 states that the motion for a new trial for Wright was sustained, September 28, by Judge J. C. Robbs, who presided at the earlier trial.

The news item stated that in addition to the motion, which was in written form and contained reasons for the plea, "Mr. Pinkerton produced various documents purporting to bear upon the illegality of the conviction. One of these was a sworn statement, secured from several members of the trial jury, that doubt of guilt had existed in their minds at the time of the verdict. These jurors, according to the statement, had administered the minimum penalty of ten years rather than subject the Negro to mob violence.

The dispatch states further that "Judge Hobbs, in setting aside the verdict and granting a new trial, stated that he could not sanction a penitentiary sentence in the light of the evidence produced in court at Centerville."

Lynching

Since the last report to the Board the following lynchings have occurred:

- Calvert, Texas: September 1, a mob of whites, alleged to have been led by the town marshal, riddled the body of Cleveland Williams with bullets. The dying man's body was tied to the back of an automobile and dragged through the streets. He had been accused of writing several notes to a white man.
- Gastonia, N.C.: September 14, Mrs. Ella May Wiggins was killed by a shot fired by a mob.

Death of Mr. Louis Marshall

Mr. Louis Marshall, valuable member of the Board of Directors and member of the National Legal Committee, died at Zurich, Switzerland, on September 11th. His funeral was held in New York City, at Temple Emanuel, on September 24. The Association's Secretary was among the honorary pallbearers.

Mr. Marshall first became interested in the N.A.A.C.P. through the victory in the Arkansas Cases, which he hailed as of primary importance, pointing out that he had tried without success to procure such a decision in the Leo Frank Case. From that time he continued to interest himself in the work of the Association, and as is well known, gave unstintingly of his services.

Will of Mr. Alfred M. Heinsheimer

The will of the late Alfred M. Heinsheimer of New York provides the sum of two thousand five hundred dollars ($2,500) for the N.A.A.C.P. The Chairman of the Legal Committee will attend to all details in connection with procuring payment of the same.

Publicity

The Association's achievement in publicity regarding the matter of the expulsion of members of St. Matthew's Protestant Episcopal Church of Brooklyn, New York, has already been mentioned in this report. During the thirteen consecutive days in which items regarding this affair appeared in the press, on some days the N.A.A.C.P. was featured in an additional story, the participation of representatives of the Association in the funeral services of Mr. Louis Marshall being widely noticed.

In addition, the following items appeared:

Letter in the *New York Times* calling attention to the fact that Paul Robeson is not the first colored man to play "Othello"; letter of thanks to the Editor of the *New York Evening Post* for an editorial on the Blackshear incident; press releases published in New York and Brooklyn papers on the Association's action in the case of the shooting of Ralph Baker, young Lincoln University student; stories and photographs of the laying of a wreath at Lincoln's statue in Union Square under the auspices of the N.A.A.C.P.

Emergency Fund

In February, 1925, the Board of Directors voted that the sum of Two Hundred and Fifty Dollars ($250.00) be placed in the hands of the Secretary for emergency purposes, and that such amounts be added from time to time as might be necessary to keep the fund at the original amount.

In the same month the Secretary opened an account with the Central Mercantile Bank (now the Bank of the United States), placing in the account the sum of $250.00, which fund has been used in accordance with the vote of the Board, additions being made as provided for.

On September 27, 1929, prior to leaving the office for his year's leave of absence, the Secretary transferred the amount of two-hundred and fifty dollars ($250.00) from the Bank of the United States to the Association's account (General Fund) at the Corn Exchange Bank.

Institute of Pacific Relations

In accordance with the vote of the Board at the September meeting, the Secretary leaves New York on September 30, to attend the Institute of Pacific Relations holding its Third Biennial Conference in Kyoto, Japan, October 28–November 9. He sails from Seattle on the SS President Pierce October 5.

James Weldon Johnson, Secretary
September 30, 1929

Speeches, Essays, and Articles, 1920–1937

Editor's Note

Atlanta University's male students founded the Phi Kappa Society in 1878. The society sponsored debates and other programs on topics of current interest. When James Weldon Johnson entered Atlanta University as a freshman in 1890, he joined the Phi Kappa Society. Elected president of the society in 1893, he became one of the best debaters in the university. During his student years at Atlanta, he was the recipient of numerous awards for his oratory skills, creative writing, and polemic essays. Johnson would ply his talent as a writer again on a regular basis as editor of the *New York Age*. Beginning in 1914, for nearly ten years he wrote a weekly column for the *Age*, the oldest of the New York black papers and one of the most influential in the nation. In the pages of the *Age*, he was exemplar as an agitator, a philosopher, a literary critic, and a mentor to aspiring creative artists. For seven years he was concurrently an editorial writer for the *Age* and an NAACP official. As an NAACP official he wrote for a number of publications, including the *Crisis, American Mercury*, the *Nation, Harper's Magazine*, the *New York Herald Tribune*, and the *Amsterdam News*. In the following selection of speeches, essays, and articles, Johnson consistently attempted to educate Americans in general, and black Americans in particular—as an essential for generating public opinion, which was indispensable for building the early civil rights movement.

The N.A.A.C.P.'s Fight Against Lynching

Johnson in this address recounts the NAACP's efforts to abolish lynching. He discusses the Association's eight-year systematic, tenacious, and organized actions to wipe out the heinous act. The NAACP relied heavily
upon publicity to educate the public on the issue of lynching. Consequently,
there was some appreciable effect, and out of that grew Federal legislation.
This address was given at the NAACP's Annual Meeting on January 3, 1923.

I shall not take any time to go over all the various steps in the fight against
lynching, especially in these recent months. Nevertheless, there is a good deal to
be learned from the results and from the benefits which have come from that fight.

There has been a fight against lynching going on for some time in this country.
The first that I remember was protest made a number of years ago against the
burning of Sam Hose, and there was one voice which rang out stirring against it
in almost scathing indictment of American civilization, and that voice was the
voice of a man whom perhaps America thinks of generally as an infidel; but his
was one of the greatest brains and one of the biggest hearts that America ever
knew. That man was Robert Ingersol.

In that day when Robert Ingersol spoke and spoke as he did about the lynching
of Sam Hose, it took some bravery to do it. When ministers of the gospel were
silent this so-called atheist spoke out. In years following there were sporadic and
individual voices here and there, but the recognized, systematic fight against
lynching began with the work of the National Association for the Advancement
of Colored People.

The National Association for the Advancement of Colored People began its
concentrated effort to abolish lynching with the raising of an anti-lynching fund
of ten thousand dollars. That was a little more than eight years ago. It then began
a systematic, persistent, organized effort to abolish lynching. We began through
agitation. Of course, a great many people decry the agitator, but the agitator has
his uses. A great deal of that agitation was done through the *Crisis*. We attempted
through the *Crisis*, to put this horrible thing before the American people, and we
did. It was then new. Many of us have grown used to it now. People used to say
in those years gone by, "I do not like to read the *Crisis*, it depresses me; it makes
me sick." That was exactly our aim. We meant to make America sick of its sin,
and so we put up to the American people the raw, naked, ugly, brutal facts. We
attempted to hold the mirror of America as it was before the nation's eyes that it
might see itself a sinner among the nations of the world.

And so we agitated, and held public meetings, and called conferences, and sent
investigators into the South, and learned the actual facts about the individual
cases of lynching. These investigators came back and these reports were published

in such newspapers and such periodicals as would print them; they were printed in pamphlets and circulated in this country and in Europe. And so gradually, year after year, we worked on public opinion, awakening it, quickening it, until there was some perceptible effect.

Out of those efforts grew federal legislation. Mark you, federal legislation, even the thought of it, was not possible ten years ago, or eight years ago, or six years ago, or four years ago. It was this continual stirring, stirring, by the National Association for the Advancement of Colored People which made it possible to have a bill introduced in the Congress which gained any notice whatever. The Dyer Anti-Lynching Bill is not the first anti-lynching bill which was introduced in Congress, but you never heard of any other, and you never heard of any other for the simple reason that American public opinion was not prepared for such a thing. That preparation was mainly made by the National Association for the Advancement of Colored People particularly. Of course, other agencies have helped, but the principal work, the initiative, the propelling force behind the fight against lynching, has been the work of the National Association.

You can measure the growth of this public opinion if you will just think of this country as it was ten years ago. Ten years ago there were very few newspapers which dared to speak out against lynching. On the other hand, there were newspapers not only in the South but throughout the North, which apologized for it, which condoned it. There were ministers of the gospel all over the South—which gospel I do not know—but there were ministers who rose up in their pulpits and declared they would lead a mob. Only five or six years ago the Governor of a Southern state declared from the executive mansion that he would come down and lead a mob to lynch a Negro.

Today in the North no newspaper would dare apologize for lynching, and all over the South we have newspapers condemning lynching—the *Atlanta Constitution*, the *Macon Telegraph*, the *San Antonio Express*. We have individual men speaking out who were not brave enough to speak out before; and we have the most encouraging sign of all—the white women of the South speaking out far more strongly than a man ever dared to speak, saying, "We condemn lynching": in other words, "We do not thank you for covering it up by any excuses that you are doing it to protect womanhood; we do not want our womanhood protected that way." These things mark a great change.

That is the preliminary work. Then we got the Dyer Anti-Lynching Bill into Congress, and we put behind it such forces as had never exerted or never demonstrated before.

We say the Bill is defeated. Not entirely. Technically, the Bill is still in Congress. The Bill has been abandoned, but it is still in Congress and will not be officially dead until the fourth of March. The fate of the Bill is regrettable, of course. Nevertheless, the fight for the Dyer Bill was not a defeat; it was not a loss; a great deal has been accomplished. By putting that Bill into Congress and uniting as we did behind it, the preliminary work we have been doing all of these years was spread out before the whole nation. By the fight for the Dyer Anti-Lynching Bill we made lynching a national issue and we have made it also, what is more important, a great political issue. That was accomplishing a great deal.

I want to speak quite frankly and say that I do not believe we could have acted more wisely, more diplomatically, then we did act in pushing the Dyer Bill. The Bill was brought to this final issue and even though it failed to pass, nevertheless, it was well worth the effort, because for once the colored people have shown and demonstrated a power which they did not before realize, and not only the colored people, but they have brought to their support and in cooperation with them white people who would not have otherwise been attracted.

The fate of the Dyer Bill was brought about for two reasons; the determined antagonism of the Southern Democrats and equally by the lukewarmness, the apathy and the cowardice of the Republicans; and between you and me, I have greater admiration for the determination and the courage of the Southern Democrats than I have for the Republicans in their cowardice.

We who were interested in the Bill did all we could to urge the Republicans to stand firm, and believe that public opinion would have made the position of the filibusterers untenable. Being on the ground, I saw that the Republicans felt it sufficient to allow the Democrats to assume responsibility for the defeat of the Bill and that thereby they would be safe. Of course, there were exceptions. There were a scant dozen who were willing and ready to keep up the fight until the fourth of March if necessary; but the leaders did not have the interest of the Bill at heart, because they felt just what some of our own men are feeling—that no matter what happens, we must stick to the Grand Old Party. And so they could but believe that no matter what happened, we were irrevocably bound to vote the Republican ticket purely upon and for historical reasons.

Now, what is before us? Of course, we are not going to give up the fight. We have just begun to fight. Yet, we must fight along several lines. We must keep up public education by the sort of intelligent agitation which we have been carrying on for the past ten years. We have got to realize—and realize it almost painfully that that education is not for white people alone; a great deal of it must be among our own people. We must educate the people of our own group to the vital importance of the fight we are making.

If the National Association for the Advancement of Colored People does not have a single concrete achievement to its credit, the mere fact that it carries on a continuous effort to keep alive in the breasts of Negroes the realization that they must have equal citizenship rights with every other American citizen and to keep alive the determination that they must have these rights—so long as we can keep alive that spirit there can be no ultimate defeat. But if for once the Negro himself acquiesces and accepts what the dominant majority wishes to put upon him, a permanent secondary status in this country, then God Himself will not be able to save us.

And so we must keep up the fight for education of white people and of black people as well, and we must not forget also the exercise of our own inherent power.

There are states in this country where we have political power. We only need the common sense to exercise it. When we do that we will be respected. We must make ourselves respected as a political element before we can get what we expect through political channels.

I can prove that we have political power. We demonstrated it in a small degree in the last election. There was not a wide enough demonstration to accomplish all that we desired, but today the Republican leaders who failed us are worried.

There are those among us who will say, "Let us not say anything which sounds like apostasy to the Grand Old Party." My advice is that even though we cannot at present outline a definite and conclusive line of action, for the present we will let the Grand Old Party simmer in its own fat and we will let them worry for a while.

The National Association will formulate what we will consider to be a wise and a sound policy, and when we have done so, have done before, give us your heartiest and most heartfelt cooperation.

Is the Negro a Danger to White Culture?

In the following article Johnson reponds to John Powell, whose article raising issues of Anglo-Saxon superiority had appeared in the *New York World*. Johnson states here that the Ku Klux Klan is the extreme result of Anglo-Saxon superiority propaganda. He further explains that the concept of Anglo-Saxon superiority is built on lies by shallow-pated dogmatists who spread their dubious theories of race inferiority. This article was written in December 1923.

Is the Negro dangerous to white culture and to the white race? Is it true that "Anglo-Saxon culture" is threatened by aliens? Is it true that "Anglo-Saxons" are the only group fit for leadership, cultural and political, in America?

Yes, seems to be the answer to these questions by the "Anglo-Saxon Clubs" of which Mr. John Powell of Virginia wrote in the *World* of December 2. To the specific questions raised by Mr. Powell and the "Anglo-Saxon Clubs" I am glad in response to the request of the editor of the *World*, to make reply, as Secretary of the National Association for the Advancement of Colored People, as a Negro, and, primarily, as an American.

For the attitude exemplified by Mr. Powell is a common one. At its extreme, it results in the formation of the Ku Klux Klan and its alleged protection of Anglo-Saxondom. At its mildest it issues in such a program as the one Mr. Powell outlines, maintaining virtually the same creed as the Klan, minus the violence. This attitude is grounded on assumptions about what makes an American, what is dangerous to an American, what American culture is and who created it. Before discussing the program, it will be necessary to examine those assumptions. Let me take them one by one:

1. "The rapid submergence of the original American stock in many parts of the country." The original American stock, the American Indian, is almost extinct. The white original stock includes settlers from almost every part of Europe, including Hessians, Scotch, Irish, English, Dutch, French, and Spanish. Furthermore

the Negro must be included among the original stock because he came to the American continent in 1525 with the Spaniards to what afterwards became Jamestown. His first coming to the English was in 1619, one year before the Mayflower landed at Plymouth. The Negro continued coming, or being brought forcibly and against his will, until the early part of the nineteenth century. None have come in any quantity since then. The Negro is certainly part of the original American stock, whether Mr. Powell likes it or not.

2. "Anglo-Saxon Civilization." Mr. Powell says there is no doubt in anyone's mind what Anglo-Saxon civilization is, although he concedes there never was an Anglo-Saxon race. I submit there never was an Anglo-Saxon culture and defy anyone to point to any culture in the world's history except possibly that of the Australian bushmen and the Tasmanian aborigines which was not the product of fertilization of different races and bloods, different kinds of civilization, brought together through commerce, race mixture, the arts. Many of the best things in America have been created here or brought by people whom Mr. Powell and the "Anglo-Saxon Club" group would doubtless look upon as aliens. The mythical Anglo-Saxon—and by the term I assume Mr. Powell means people of English descent, they are among the late comers to America, later than French, Spanish, and Negro. This leads me to question Mr. Powell's idea of culture. What is culture anyhow? Is it something that belongs to someone like an automobile? Is it the color of your hair, the price of family tradition? Is being elected to office a sign of culture? It seems to me Mr. Powell and his group of Anglo-Saxons have things badly mixed.

3. "The Traditional American Virtues and Principles." If Mr. Powell wants to go back far enough to Puritan days in New England, for example, one of the traditional American virtues was a willingness to take part in the burning of witches, men and women, and other American virtues and principles included such intolerance as made the settlers fine, flog and imprison people for being members of the Society of Friends, better known as Quakers; as drove out Roger Williams from Massachusetts. Those virtues were perhaps understandable in those days, in which a rigid social organization was necessary to meet frontier conditions. No one but a maniac would maintain that they were suited to the years in which we live. In fact, the ideals of the founders of this country, such as they were, are more often misstated and misrepresented than almost anything else in America. The founders made some pretty clear and definite statements about these ideals and principles in the two documents on which the American state and American civilization are supposed to be founded. But the "Anglo-Saxon" element, which most loudly proclaims its fealty to the principles and virtues of the founders of the nation, at the same time most flagrantly disregards both the letter and the spirit of the Constitution and the Declaration of Independence.

Let me not be understood as claiming that culture lies alone in the political field, with which these two documents mainly are concerned. On the contrary, with the change of America from a frontier and border land, to a producing and then to a manufacturing land, and lastly to the richest and most powerful country in the world, great changes have come in our conception of culture. We can afford, and we have, things that the founders of the country never dreamed of, in the way of science, of painting, theater, music, literature. Those gifts are the gifts of Europe and Asia to America; and it would be short-sighted indeed to deprive ourselves of them, at the time when the world is looking to America not only for help in the political and economic fields, but to receive and guard the art of the world which, owing to the terrible disorganization in Europe seems threatened with extinction.

The greatest gifts in those fields have been made in America by people not of English descent. It is not necessary for me, though I am ready to do so if challenged, to illustrate with names. I will confirm myself to the Negro who, in his native state in Africa, produced sculpture which is the wonder of people who have taken the trouble to look at it. Some of this work was exhibited in the Brooklyn Museum last year. In music and poetry it is almost superfluous to speak of the Negro's achievements. If the Negro has not produced a composer of world rank on American soil, neither has the white English-descended group. But the Negro has given to America her only true folk-song. And the Negro provided Joel Chandler Harris with the material for the only true American folk lore yet written. Possibly there are many people who do not know of the achievements of the Negro poet, Paul Laurence Dunbar, of the many other Negro poets who have enriched the American heritage. If any of these people pride themselves on being "Anglo-Saxon" they had better look, not to their program, but to the state of their own education and culture. And there is of course Du Bois's *Souls of Black Folk*, and the more recent *Darkwater*, not to mention the fiction of Chesnutt and others, as part of the Nergro's contribution to American culture.

In fact, in any field in which the "Anglo-Saxon" cares to challenge him, whether in wars on American soil—in every one of which, as well as in France the Negro took honorable part—whether in industry, invention and science—as for example the work of Professor Carver of Tuskegee awarded this year's Spingarn Medal—in business and the professions—in any honorable field of human endeavor the Negro has rendered more than his share despite the overwhelming obstacles against which he has had to contend in America.

The Negro's case is not so dissimilar from that of other aliens, in so far as culture is concerned. Mr. Powell deplores the "polyglot boarding house" aspect of America with its foreign-language newspapers, its racial and national traditions maintained by immigrants. I say it is better to encourage these people to bring here their cultural heritages, to give us in America the benefit of their songs and dances and literature and customs, then to try to force them to conform to some "Anglo-Saxon idea of what is American. Think of Steinmetz in the field of science; of Carl Schurz in politics; of Ernest Bloch in music; they and thousands of others benefit us not by making themselves over into lifeless effigies conforming to English traditions, but by giving us most freely the best in themselves. Hardly any human being but will respond with enthusiasm to an opportunity to give of his best. But tell him what he must and must not be . . . , and you produce social and individual death.

4. "Our present national incoherence." Everyone will agree with Mr. Powell that there is national incoherence. But they will differ about the way of changing it to union in culture. Mr. Powell and the members of the "Anglo-Saxon Clubs"

believe in organization. Just what their organization will accomplish seems doubt-ful. Their stress seems to be not on providing people with opportunity, but on telling them what they must not do. That is, of course, in a sense very American. Certain types of Americans conceive of the supreme mission of Americans as telling other Americans what they must not do. Liberty means liberty for the other fellow if he does what I tell him. If he doesn't, he must be whipped into some idea of what liberty means. That is some people's conception of "liberty." Better have none of it and have one king, than several hundred thousand would-be kings.

Of course, what worries Mr. Powell and his "Anglo-Saxons"—let us not forget that there is no such thing as an "Anglo-Saxon"—what worries them most is intermarriage between persons of Negro and of white descent. Here again, it is necessary to examine the assumption which is the basis of a fear that, in many parts of the country is hysterical and can therefore be used for every sort of political and propaganda purpose.

5. "No race even slightly admixed with Negro blood has failed to decay cul-turally." There it is. It is untrue. It is supported with ignorance of history, with fake science, with dogmatic insistence. The Negro is inferior, say the Madison Grant—Lothrop Stoddard Kindergarten of Writers; and the professional upholder of the Anglo-Saxon myth cries out loud hurrahs. Let me quote another one of Mr. Powell's statements, as a sample of the large slices of knowledge he deals in: "History, ethnology and biology all bear out the Anglo-Saxon instinctive conviction in favor of racial integrity." But there is no such conviction. Do the three million Americans of part Negro-part white complexion represent this "instinctive con-viction." Why did some twenty-nine or so states have to enact laws against inter-marriage if this instinctive conviction was on the job? The answer is obvious. Mr. Powell's statement is not only unsupported, it is directly controverted by the state-ments of our foremost anthropologists like Professor Franz Boas of Columbia Uni-versity, Dr. Robert H. Lewis and Dr. Alexander Goldenweiser, among many others. Here is a case in which "Anglo-Saxon culture" seems to have been inadequate to the demands placed upon it, for its defenders have not taken the trouble to find out if what they were saying was true.

Biologically, the evidence is not that the Negro is inferior. Neither is the eth-nological evidence in this direction. And as for history, the Mediterranean races, among whom there has always been a strong admixture of darker races, have produced some of the most magnificent achievements of the human spirit, polit-ically, in literature, in the plastic arts. As for the decay of culture—how about Europe of today? Mr. Powell is not claiming that the collapse is due to Negro blood is he? Culture seems to be in the greatest peril, just now, in the very regions where the predominance of light-haired, light-skinned races is most unquestioned. But I would not adopt Mr. Powell's method of blaming it on a race. Rather I would ascribe part of Europe's frightful state, to such poisonous nonsense and untruth as shallow-pated dogmatists spread about race inferiority. As for the Negro race, intermixture was forced on him by the American white man. The Negro did not desire it any more than he originally desired to come to America. There is certainly no widespread ambition among Negroes to marry white persons, such as the hysterical proponents of the Anglo-Saxon myth like to imagine. And the difficulties in the way of both parties to such mixed marriage are enough to deter most persons from entering upon them. "But on racial grounds," as Mr. Herbert J. Seligmann says in "The Negro Faces America," "no prohibition of intermarriage has as yet been justified." The worst way to attempt to justify such a prohibition is with lies about what "science" or history have to tell.

To Mr. Powell's conception of an America run by people who talk about "Anglo-Saxon" culture and Anglo-Saxons without knowing what they mean, I should like to oppose the conception of a young writer who has been dead a few short years but who will be remembered when the "Anglo-Saxon" enthusiasts will have passed to well-merited oblivion. That writer was Randolph Bourne. Bourne, in an essay entitled "Trans-National America," conceived this country as the world's first experiment in the cooperation of people of various nationalities and races, an experiment grown up unawares on American soil. He saw Americans as being Americans in spirit, because of their love for the American ideal, and not because they could measure up to any narrow social or racial conceptions. He felt that the hope of the world lay in making this experiment possible, in giving vital people everywhere the opportunity to contribute toward it in their own way. It is this warm, and generous, and truly American attitude of welcome and expectancy that I should like to oppose to the narrow doctrine of Mr. Powell. The "Anglo-Saxon" acts as if he had something to fear. He behaves like a coward. The American does not have to. He can receive the contribution of any spirit, any nation and any race. If he cannot, then he had better say so. He had better stop twaddling about democracy, liberty, and what-not. Let him then come out boldly and say: that is a country for people who call themselves Anglo-Saxons without knowing what they mean; people who intend to make America their own cozy little club where everyone else can exist on sufferance only. I cannot conceive that his doctrine, with its false assumptions and its spurious talk about fake "science" will find any general acceptance among my fellow citizens.

Presiding at Annual Mass Meeting Speech

In this speech Johnson reviews the NAACP's work during the preceding year, 1923. He states that one of the NAACP's objectives is to take stock of what has been gained so that the Association's staff will move forward with the strength and confidence of hindsight. This address was given at the Annual Mass Meeting of the NAACP in New York City on January 6, 1924.

Ladies and Gentlemen:

We are met together today for two purposes—first, to take stock of what the past twelve months show for us and to reassemble, as it were, our lines of battle for the continuance of the struggle that is before us. It is a very usual thing, after having put forth great effort, to feel a desire for realization, and not only that, but generally after putting forth great effort we experience a sense of discouragement, especially when we see how much there is to be accomplished in comparison with the little that has been done.

And yet the year 1928 does show for us a great many things which should bring us satisfaction. We ought not to be discouraged even when we look at all that is yet to be accomplished; and I do not think that we are, because we are learning more and more fully that the fight which is before us is one which will not bring victory by any sudden spurt however brilliant it may be, but it means constant pressure all along the line.

But it is well to look back and take stock of what has been accomplished in order to go forward with greater confidence and greater faith; and the year 1923 has a good deal to show.

In the field of the struggle for fundamental human rights we can look to the great decrease in lynchings. The year 1923 shows twenty lynchings against sixty-one in 1922. These figures are more significant when we remember that there have been as many as 226 lynchings in the United States in a single year. But while they do show encouragement, it means that we must keep up the fight. Those figures—that great decrease in lynchings are largely due to the fact that we were able to use Congress as a forum in which to tell the truth about lynching, the most effective force in the world.

Yet, we cannot stop. Twenty-eight lynchings, as small as the figure may appear in comparison with 226, put upon us the obligation to continue this fight against lawlessness as long as a single person accused of any crime, whether black or white, is deprived of life in this country without due process of law in a duly constituted court. In this fight, although the vast majority of the victims are black, nevertheless we are fighting upon this platform of Americanism. We fight against the lynching of white men as well as against the lynching of black men. And yet, too, in this field of the fight for justice, for trial by due process of law, by orderly processes, we can look back to the fact that the year 1923 saw the saving of the lives of twelve men who for four years, in Arkansas, have had their lives in jeopardy—since 1919. Twelve men have been saved from the electric chair. Six of them have gone entirely free and the other six soon will be. Of the sixty-seven men in that same state, victims of conspiracy, who were put into the penitentiary, fifty-nine of them are today out and free men.

1923 also shows the great movement put in motion for releasing the martyrs of the Houston Riots, the men of the Twenty-fourth Infantry. In the office of the N.A.A.C.P. we have petititons already signed by 115,000 American citizens asking for the release of these men, to be presented to President Coolidge, and we shall have more before these petitions are presented.

Not only these fields, but we can take even wider scope. In the fields of economics and industry we have achieved a great deal. This migration northward, bringing our people northward, placing them in the industrial centers, making of them industrial factors, opening up a new vista of life and hope and activity for the whole race, is doubly advantageous. It is seldom that things are doubly advantageous, but here is a thing which works a benefit for those who come and often a benefit for those who remain in the South. It works good both ways.

And then, too, we may look over the field of science and art. The year 1923 shows a Negro scientist, Professor George W. Carver of Tuskegee Institute, winner of the Spingarn Medal, and thereby gives the country a knowledge of what he had accomplished, a thing the country had not known before.

We have seen Roland Hayes, perfect and matchless singer of the songs of the world and especially the beautiful songs of his people—soloist for the great Boston Symphony Orchestra—we have seen him charm and captivate audiences and critics of New York City.

Then, too, although he does not live and work among us, yet he was born here, a son of a late Bishop of the A.M.E. Church, we have Henry O. Tanner, dean of American artists, decorated with the ribbon of an officer of the Legion of Honor by the Government of France.

These are a few of the things. If I stood here and cataloged them I would not have a chance to perform the duties which are now at hand.

Looking back over 1923, perhaps the thing most to be content about is the general awakening of the whole race, a consciousness and vivifying, a looking out and up, a vision, a sense of responsibility, a sense of our own responsibility.

And now, last but not least, among the things that 1923 means to us is that we have retained and we have also gained friends, sincere friends, from the opposite race—I do not like the word opposite—and some of those friends are with us today. They are on the platform. They are here because they are interested in our cause; they are here because they are willing to fight side by side with us in that cause. Have you ever thought that among the things that we ought to be thankful for is the quality of our friends among the white people. If we should write the names of the friends of the American Negro among the American white people from the beginning of our history in this country we should have the honor roll of the nation.

[Introducing Theodore Roosevelt]

This man I need not introduce. I need only to present him to you. You know who he is and you know what he stands for. He is our friend, and I am very proud to be able to say that he is my friend individually. I am proud to say that it is one of my boasts that his great father before him—I was able to count myself a friend of his. So we have with us a man who is our friend by inheritance and by tradition.

I will say to you, Colonel, that we look to the name of Roosevelt to mean a great deal to us now and much more in the years to come.

Our friends are not so many but their quality is high and you, sir, you stand in a place among the high places in this country and you can do much for us, and we hope and believe you will.

Ladies and gentlemen, I have the great honor and privilege of presenting to you the worthy son of a great father, Colonel Theodore Roosevelt.

Haiti and Our Latin-American Policy

In this address Johnson raises the question, "Why is America in Haiti?" He discusses America's sinister and insidious reasons for occupying the island country. He further condemns America for its weak and insincere rationalization of the seizure of Haiti. This address was delivered at the "World Tomorrow Dinner" in New York City on March 31, 1924.

I could begin to talk on the subject assigned to me first by rehearsing something of Haiti's history for the one hundred and ten years of her independence; how through the valor and heroism of her own people she abolished slavery, threw off the French yoke and made herself the second in point of time of all the independent republics in the western world; how, due entirely to her aid and assistance, Bolivar was able to set up the first republic on the South American continent and how she asked nothing in return for her help except that the great liberator of South America should abolish slavery forever. I could summarize Haiti's long struggle to maintain her independence in the face of the intrigue of European powers and the utter lack of sympathy of the United States. This lack of sympathy on the part of the United States is easily explained by the fact that the black slaves of Haiti in rising up and chopping off the heads of their masters had set a dangerous example. How she maintained her independence in spite of isolation by language and race, and in spite of the most malicious, cruel, and, on the whole, most misleading propaganda ever aimed at a weak and uneffective nation.

Secondly, I could trace the steps by which the United States, a year before she took Haiti by force of arms, tried through diplomatic and economic pressure to acquire a suzerainity over the black republic, and how she went in by force because an opportunity was offered, at the very time when diplomatic negotiations for a treaty that would accord her certain rights of overlordship were pending. I could follow this with a recital of atrocities committed by American Marines after the military seizure that are actually true, even if unbelievable.

But I shall not review the history of Haiti, fascinatingly interesting as it is, because there is not time to do so.

And I shall not recite the atrocities, because—Oh, what's the use? The American people are used to too many atrocities at home to shudder at atrocities committed on an island in the Caribbean Sea; not having a very clear idea as to where either the island or the sea is located. When the great American public can pick up its daily newspaper and read of a thousand American men, women and children—women holding their babies up to see the sight—gathering around and looking at a fellow American, though black, tortured with red-hot irons, then baptized with gasoline and set afire, why should it regard anything done to the black natives of "some way off semi-barbarous island" as sensational news?

Atrocities—what else could be expected under the conditions? Given the military domination of any people whatever by any foreign power whatsoever, and atrocities follow as naturally, as necessarily, as water follows from a combination of two parts of hydrogen and one of oxygen.

What I propose to do in my limited time is merely to point out briefly the real reasons for our being in Haiti, and to comment upon the manner in which this government rationalizes its Haitian policy into an act of political necessity, of true benevolence and of unadulterated altruism.

Let me take up the latter first. I want to get rid of it because it makes me hotter than anything in the whole Haitian situation. If this government came out and frankly said why we were in Haiti, two-thirds of the iniquity of the whole matter would be cleared away at once. But, of course, if the government did such a thing we wouldn't be in Haiti; in fact, would never have gone into Haiti.

The first point in governmental rationalization was that the seizure of Haiti was a political necessity; that there was danger that it would be seized by some European power, the implication being that that European power was Germany. When we remember that we seized Haiti in August, 1915, and how busy at that particular time Germany was with other matters, we wonder how an intelligent State Department or even an unintelligent one, for that matter, could offer such a reason. Of course, at that time Germans were in a dominating position in Haiti; but they were not German soldiers; they were German merchants. And as soon as we seized Haiti, those German merchants came under the Alien Property Act, just as German citizens in the United States did.

A second point in governmental nationalization and in the deluding of the American people was that there was a state of anarchy in Haiti; that the people had retrograded into barbarism; that they had even gone back to cannibalism.

Our State Department, shortly after the exposé of conditions under American military occupation, seriously brought forward the charge of cannibalism in defense, or at least in extenuation, of our policy in Haiti. The State Department solemnly sat for the testimony of someone who had heard someone say that Haitians had caught an American marine, cut out his heart, liver, kidneys and other vital organs, and eaten them raw. A tough meal—I should say.

When I was in Haiti I made special effort to see if I could find any evidence of cannibalism—it is an old charge against Haiti. I could find no evidence. But after all, I thought, which is worse, to eat a human without cooking him—as is alleged to be the custom in Haiti—or to cook him without eating him—as is known to be the custom in Mississippi? I concluded that the utilitarian purpose involved in the Haitian custom renders it the less reprehensible.

There was, too, the charge of graft among Haitian governmental officials that we had to put a stop to. I hope no American newspapers are reaching Port-au-Prince, for there is likelihood that the poor, picking, heathen Haitian grafter will drop dead of astonishment, or laugh himself to death.

Then, of course, there was and still is the pious pose and talk about our altruistic purpose. Our sole desire is to do the Haitians good; and the Haitians declare that we have pretty nearly done it. We have built several good military roads over which we can quickly transport our troops from one end of the island to the other, and we have introduced a few sanitary improvements. But we have built no new schoolhouses nor conferred any other vital benefits. We have been in Haiti nearly ten years, and it can be truly said that although the Haitians may be wiser, they are no better off and no happier.

Our Department of Commerce lays great stress on the increase in figures of import and export, as though the doubling and tripling of export values went into the pockets of the poor devils who raise the crops.

Porto Rico under our benevolent rule has increased her trade figures until they are, roughly, four times as much as lagging Haiti's. Since Porto Rico's population is about one-half of Haiti's, her trade per capita may be said to be eight times as much. Now, according to the Department of Commerce philosophy, the natives of Porto Rico ought to be eight times better off and eight times happier than the natives of Haiti. I don't believe the Department of Commerce would claim that.

Our real reason for being in Haiti is a matter of dollars and cents—dollars and cents for American pockets.

Achievements and Aims of the N.A.A.C.P.

The Chicago Defender, a black weekly newspaper, asked Johnson to restate the aims and purposes of the NAACP after its sixteen-year history. In 1925 Johnson eagerly accepted this opportunity, and in the following article he answers the question, "What has the NAACP done?"

In spite of sixteen years history of the National Association for the Advancement of Colored People, together with what it has accomplished, and the clear statement of its purpose, there are still people who ask "What has the N.A.A.C.P. done?" These questions may spring from ignorance or from intentional blindness. I therefore eagerly seize the opportunity given by the *Chicago Defender*, to restate for the great public reached by this newspaper, not only the aims and purposes of the N.A.A.C.P. but to call to mind a few of the achievements which justify the enormous labor which has been and is being expended in the work of the Association. I think it only necessary to state the aims of the N.A.A.C.P. to make it clear that it is absolutely necessary for every Negro in America that those aims be realized. What are those aims and how have we thus far realized them?

The N.A.A.C.P. set out to establish, safeguard, and fortify the fundamental citizenship rights of every colored man, woman and child in America. It demands justice in the courts, equal opportunity for education of colored with white children, and equal and fair deal for the colored workman on the job. In any public place the N.A.A.C.P. demands that the Negro shall have exactly the same accommodation and courtesy accorded to any other American citizens. It wants the Negro respected as men and women, his gifts and achievements acknowledged, to the end that the United States Constitution may be made something more than a scrap of paper and there be in America democracy in fact as well as in name. How has the National Association for the Advancement of Colored People gone about realizing its program?

It began by opposing lynching, the bestial degeneracy and cruelty of the mob. The N.A.A.C.P. has spent more than $50,000 in the first and only organized, persistent, intensive campaign of fact and education against lynching in America. In that campaign it has held upwards of 4,000 mass meetings and distributed millions of pieces of literature. It investigated lynchings, published the only authentic statistical study on lynching, "Thirty Years of Lynching"; held the first National Anti-Lynching Conference in New York in 1919, reached upwards of 5,000,000 white Americans through newspapers, advertisements stating the ugly facts. Moreover the N.A.A.C.P. made of the United States Congress a trumpet through which the facts on lynching were broadcast to the country and to the world.

What was the result of this nation-wide, this international campaign? A reduction in the number of lynchings to their lowest figure, sixteen in the year 1924. The espousal of this cause by other bodies such as the Federal Council of Churches. A growing determination throughout the nation that lynching must end.

But lynching is not the only form of violence relentlessly fought by the N.A.A.C.P. Practically every important race riot of recent years has seen an investigator of the N.A.A.C.P. on the spot either while the riot was still going on, or immediately afterward. What happened after the Arkansas riots of 1919 is, or should be, familiar to every colored person in America. The N.A.A.C.P. not only was the first to get and publish the truth about the peonage conditions prevalent in Arkansas; it successfully defended the colored farmers, until now, of those originally sentenced to death and long prison terms, not one has been executed or remains in jail.

In the case of the 24th Infantrymen, involved in a race riot after they had been maltreated while wearing the United States uniform in Houston, Texas, the N.A.A.C.P. has fought their battle from the day of the riot in 1917, until the present time, when less than half of those sentenced to jail remain in prison and those remaining are soon to be released.

These are the more spectacular cases. Year in and year out the N.A.A.C.P. reached down into the heart of the south, has uncovered abuses, has helped those in need of help, has prevented the extradition of colored men to southern states when it was evident they would not be given a fair trial there. Hundreds of appeals have come to the N.A.A.C.P. every year and so far as the energy of its officers and the funds at its disposal have availed, the N.A.A.C.P. has given help.

It has done more. It has fought for the Negro's right to vote where he is being fraudulently and illegally deprived of it. It has insisted upon the Negro's right to choose where he shall live unmolested by ruffians or mobs, winning the Louisville Segregation case before the United States Supreme Court in 1917, and carrying to that same tribunal the question of segregation by property owners' agreement, a case that will probably be argued this fall. In Staten Island, in Detroit, throughout the country, it has backed up and is defending colored men who have resisted the mob's demand to vacate their homes.

Against the Negro's enemies, and they are many, the N.A.A.C.P. has fought untiringly. It began the campaign to show up the revived Ku Klux Klan and has fought the Klan ever since then, as it has fought other manifestations of criminal intolerance. It has challenged every utterance of newspaper editors or other public men that have come to its attention slurring the Negro or his achievements. It has carried not only into the white and colored press of America, but into the newspapers of England, France, Germany and even South America, Africa, and India the cause of the American Negro. The National Association for the Advancement of Colored People is known throughout the civilized world and is respected as one of the most formidable agencies working for justice to the black man that the world has ever known.

Finally, it has encouraged and continues to encourage Negro artists and writers. The annual award of the Spingarn Medal calls Negro achievement to the attention of the civilized world.

These are only a few of the activities of the National Association for the Advancement of Colored People. They are activities which are carried on daily, week by week and year by year. They affect every colored man, woman and child in America whether they know it or not. Every Negro has a stake in the fight the N.A.A.C.P. is making against terrific odds. But at many points the fight has been victorious. The extent of the eventual success of the program undertaken depends upon colored Americans. Will they rally to those who are fighting their battle? If they do, an organization speaking for eleven million people cannot be ignored. Already, the N.A.A.C.P is listened to in Congress, in the White House.

The Negro must save himself. He must save himself or destroy America. He is striving for the basic principles upon which the American democracy was built. If those principles are allowed to rot and wither away, if they perish, then American democracy must fail.

The N.A.A.C.P is carrying on the Negro's struggle, not alone in behalf of the Negro, but for the sake of the future of America as a whole. Its effectiveness depends primarily upon the loyal, unstinted and united support of American Negroes.

The Militant N.A.A.C.P

Johnson, in this essay, discusses the NAACP's role in abolishing lynching. He also points out that while lynching is the most sensational work of the Association, there are numerous other accomplishments. He makes the specific point that there is undoubtedly no phase of race relations that the NAACP has not profoundly affected. This essay was written in 1929.

It seems hard to believe that the National Association for the Advancement of Colored People has been in existence nearly twenty years. This spring it is to have its Nineteenth Annual Conference.

When it was begun, as a small committee, in New York, following the terrible race riots in Springfield, Illinois, where Abraham Lincoln had lived, it faced a very different condition in this country from what now prevails. Discrimination, disfranchisement, lawless attacks upon the Negro were at their height, and few if any voices were raised in protest. Lynching was not only condoned but defended even by ministers of the gospel and men in public office. And, on the affirmative side of the Negro's participation in American life, little of the development had occurred which has since then made Negro writers and poets familiar to white readers, Negro singers and musicians to concert-going audiences, and Negro skilled workers, business men, scientists, part of the productive power of the nation.

Joining with the forces of the Niagara movement, in which Dr. W. E. B. Du Bois had been a leader, the N.A.A.C.P. at once struck out upon a militant program. It undertook to find out many of the disputed facts of race relations and publish them to the world. It determined to agitate until the grosser forms of oppression and discrimination were made a matter of common knowledge and public shame. And it set out to foster in every possible way the creative and productive abilities of the American Negro.

The fact that there are now a number of other groups doing similar work, such as the Commission on Interracial Relations and the Federal Council of Churches, testifies to the energy and determination with which the N.A.A.C.P. brought its campaign to public attention. Undeterred by the small numbers with which it came into being, it set energetically to work.

Its major attack was on the ghastly crime of lynching, the public murder— often with most horrible tortures—of human beings while other human beings, men, women, and children, looked on. Investigators were sent by the N.A.A.C.P. to the scenes of lynchings. Every scrap of available information, including photographs of the lynching scenes, they accumulated and brought to the New York Offices. The investigators worked at the risk of their lives. But they got the facts. And those facts were published to the world. They were published to the world in newspapers, in magazines, and in our own publication, the standard compilation on the subject: "Thirty Years of Lynching in the United States" with yearly supplements to date. Old newspapers, and particularly the records of the *Chicago Tribune* were gone over carefully, and every lynching recorded was carefully noted and tabulated.

From the work on lynching done by the N.A.A.C.P. and its investigators, several facts emerged. First, that lynching did not occur only as vengeance on the "usual crime" of rape. It was proved that less than one in five of the victims of lynchings mobs had even been accused of this crime; and that men and women of dark skin had been murdered on any and every pretext which might occur to people determined to terrorize them.

These facts were carried before the American public in the most dramatic way. They were published to the nation in debates on the floor of the House of Representatives in Washington. There, Representative Leonidas G. Dyer of Missouri, became champion of the Federal Anti-Lynching Bill which has become known by his name as the Dyer Anti-Lynching Bill. The N.A.A.C.P. sponsored this measure and backed it to the limit. People in every part of the United States were roused to write to their Representatives and urge its enactment. In speeches before crowded mass meetings, in newspaper and magazine articles and editorials, the question was agitated. The N.A.A.C.P. even raised money for a full page advertisement setting forth "The Shame of America" which appeared in leading newspapers throughout the country during the fight in Congress. The Dyer Anti-Lynching Bill was passed in the House of Representatives in 1922 by a vote of 230 to 119. And though the Senate blocked it by a filibuster which threatened to tie up the nation's business, and refused even to allow debate on the Bill, much, enormously much, had been accomplished.

After this terrific campaign of the N.A.A.C.P. few people in the country were ignorant of the major facts about lynching. And the ancient Bogey of "the usual crime" had been scotched once and for all. A course of national education in one of the elementary phases of race relations had been completed. The pioneering of the N.A.A.C.P. was paid generous tribute lately by Dr. Charles S. MacFarland, General Secretary of the Federal Council of Churches of Christ in America, in an article published by a number of newspapers:

> The arousing of public opinion against lynching and the consequent decrease of the practise can be largely traced to a campaign of public education participated in by social agencies, the white and Negro newspapers, and our organised church forces of the country. The first organization active in combating the evil was the National Association for the Advancement of Colored People which more than ten years ago began a thorough research into the history of the evil, secured the support of hundreds of prominent citizens in appeals against mob murder and began an active campaign for Federal legislation against it. Largely through the stimulation of that organization, successive bills were introduced by Congressman Dyer and the public discussion of these appeals was a large factor in focusing public attention.

In the course of this fight the N.A.A.C.P. presented to the United States Senate, urging enactment of the Dyer Bill, the petition being signed by twenty-four state governors, thirty-nine mayors of cities, forty-seven judges and lawyers, eighty-eight Bishops and church men, including three Archbishops, twenty-nine college presidents and professors, thirty editors and many other prominent citizens. Congressman Theodore Burton of Ohio, who has had a long and distinguished political career, told me that that petition was one of the most impressive if not the most impressive such appeal he had ever seen.

The Association's struggle against lynching, while the most spectacular, is by no means the only or even the most important part of the work it has accomplished. I think it is fair to say that there is no phase of race relations in America which the Association has not profoundly affected.

By way of contrast to the anti-lynching campaign, consider the effect on public opinion in America of the Spingarn Medal. This medal is given annually through the generosity of the Association's Treasurer, Mr. J. E. Spingarn, to the colored man or woman of African descent and American citizenship who is deemed by the Committee on Award to have most highly distinguished himself or herself in some honorable field of human endeavor. When I name of a few of the recipients of the medal—Dr. Carver of Tuskegee, Roland Hayes, William Stanley Braithwaite,

Dr. W. E. B. Du Bois, Anthony Overton, Dr. Ernest Just,—you will see what a wide field the awards have already covered. Moreover, it has called public attention as perhaps no other single event each year, to the existence of outstanding and or creative ability among colored Americans. The awards are published in the newspapers all over the world. And they are recorded in such compendiums as the *World Almanac*.

But the major work of the N.A.A.C.P. of course has been one of affirmation and defense of the Negro's fundamental citizenship and human rights. For this purpose the N.A.A.C.P. has had often to step into the courts and invoke their aid. Many of the Association's cases have gone before the United States Supreme Court on appeal. And it is here that final and decisive victories have been won which cannot be wiped off the slate. These victories stand to be made use of by colored people whenever the rights involved may be challenged or infringed.

For example, in 1917, the Association's President, Moorfield Storey of Boston, who began his distinguished career in championing the Negro as private secretary to Senator Charles Sumner in reconstruction days,—Mr. Storey, went before the United States Supreme Court in a case arising out of a residential segregation ordinance enacted in Louisville, Kentucky. And he obtained a decision from the highest tribunal in the land forever outlawing residential segregation by state or municipal enactment. Does anyone doubt that if the N.A.A.C.P. had lost that case, such laws would have been soon on the books of most of the cities of the country? The Association's next victory was won against segregation by mob eviction in Detroit, where the celebrated criminal lawyer, Clarence Darrow, upheld the right of Dr. Ossian H. Sweet and his family and friends to defend his house against mob attack.

The third phase of residential segregation, by agreement among white property owners, is now being attacked by the N.A.A.C.P., and under the direction of perhaps the foremost authority on constitutional law in America, Mr. Louis Marshall, a member of the N.A.A.C.P. Board of Directors and of its National Legal Committee, a case involving this issue is being prepared for submission to the United States Supreme Court.

During 1927, when the N.A.A.C.P. within a space of two weeks obtained two favorable decisions from the United States Supreme Court, one of these decisions, was in the Texas White Primary Case which, prohibited any state from passing a law to prohibit Negroes voting in primary election. And this year, in three states, Negroes were commencing court proceedings to defend their voting rights, based on this decision. The second Supreme Court decision won in 1927, reaffirmed the victory won in the Louisville Segregation Case in 1917, by declaring unconstitutional a segregation ordinance enacted in New Orleans.

I have mentioned several cases of lawyers in this summary of the N.A.A.C.P. work. Moorfield Storey, the National President, has been president of the American Bar Association. Clarence Darrow is perhaps the foremost criminal lawyer in the United States. Louis Marshall is an authority on constitutional law second to none living. These men, and others, like Arthur B. Spingarn, Charles H. Studin, James A. Cobb, Herbert Stockton, have repeatedly given their time and genius to the legal problems confronting the N.A.A.C.P. because of the interest its cause has held for them. Had we been compelled to pay them even a fraction of what they can command for their services, the N.A.A.C.P. annual budget would have been more than exhausted on a single case.

One more of the Association's legal victories I should like to mention, because it reversed a principle previously enunciated by the United States Supreme Court. This occurred in the so-called Arkansas Peonage cases. You may recall that in 1919, the country was informed of a Negro "plot to massacre Whites." Scores of Negroes were killed in the Arkansas cane brakes. After a farcical trial, eighteen were sentenced to death and sixty-seven were condemned to life imprisonment and long prison terms. The story is too long to tell here. But an investigator for the N.A.A.C.P. went to Arkansas. He found that peonage was at the root of the trouble and the Negroes, instead of "plotting" to "massacre" their landlords, had merely attempted to organize and employ a lawyer in the effort to obtain a statement of account and settlement from their landlords. The cases of these poor Negro farmers were carried to the highest courts in Arkansas and before the United States Supreme Court where Moorfield Storey won a decisive victory. The Supreme Court in its decision stated emphatically that the men had been denied their constitutional rights in that, though they had been tried in a duly constituted court, that court had been paralyzed by mob domination. Today all of the men, the twelve sentenced to death and the sixty-seven others sentenced to prison are free.

Now I could take up many more pages with the achievements of the N.A.A.C.P. In many instances, it has prevented extradition of colored men to Southern states where there was reason to suppose fair trial would not be given. It has investigated race riots and published its findings. It has given aid and legal counsel in innumerable small cases arising out of race injustice and prejudice. It sponsored and its attorneys drew up the Civil Rights Act of the State of New York which has been used as a model in many other states. It has prevented the enactment in northern states of bills which would prohibit the marriage of persons of white and Negro ancestry, mainly on the ground that such bills struck a blow at colored women. The N.A.A.C.P. was the first in this country to proclaim the Ku Klux Klan a public and national menace; and facts obtained by the N.A.A.C.P. helped start the New York World on its exposé of the Klan. The N.A.A.C.P. from the time of the Houston, Texas, riot espoused the cause of the 24th Infantrymen who had been insulted, harassed, provoked, and threatened into defending themselves from mob violence. It procured commutation from sentence of execution of a number of these men, and by petitions, in one case numbering 135,000 signatures, presented to successive Presidents of the United States, it has procured review of the cases and releases on parole, until now only one of the "Houston martyrs" remains in jail.

The list of achievements of the N.A.A.C.P. is too long for detailed or even for summary recital here. But I trust the main principles which have guided and continue to guide it in its work are clear. It is determined the Negro shall have not favor but opportunity. It wants him physically free from peonage, socially free from insult, mentally free from ignorance; and it will fight for his citizenship rights until he is fully, in the complete sense of the word in America, a man.

The work of the N.A.A.C.P. is conducted on a ludicrously small budget, eighty per cent of which is made up of small contributions and membership fees from one to five dollars paid in by Negroes. The white people who are taking part in its work do so, not merely to benefit and advance the Negro, but because they realize it is a work essential to the principles and the life itself of American democracy.

Address Before the Twentieth Annual Meeting of the N.A.A.C.P.

In the following address, Johnson speaks to the Twenty-first Annual Meeting of the Association in 1931. As he retires from the NAACP he pronounces the organization and its aims and its achievements as now part of American history. Johnson further discusses the numerous hurdles the NAACP has overcome and some disadvantages that continue to plague the organization. In his new role as Vice-President and member of the Board, he reaffirms his commitment to the work of the NAACP.

Madam Chairman, Ladies and Gentlemen:

I must speak to you briefly, because of the hour for one thing. I know that in speaking of the work of the N.A.A.C.P I cannot trust myself to speak briefly, and for that reason I am going to confine myself more or less to some notes which I have jotted down.

In the first place, the work of this Association of ours has already been set forth so well and so fully that there is very little that can be added. Indeed, there ought to be no need of rehearsing the work of this organization to an audience such as this, for, as our President has just said, its aims and its achievements are a part of our national history. It is a very obvious fact now that this organization has proven itself to be one of the revolutionary movements in America and American life. Its platform when it was first announced, was regarded as radical and visionary and even dangerous. Many white people who were friendly to the Negro looked upon the new organization with apprehension, and a great many colored people were doubtful and timid. I think timid is too mild a word; they were actually scared. The platform had that effect because it did not compromise with principles. It did not begin by saying that colored Americans were entitled to so much of this and so much of that. It did not begin by saying that the Negro might at once claim certain rights of citizenship but that he ought to wait a century or two before laying claim to certain others. The N.A.A.C.P. began its fight with its feet squarely and firmly placed upon the eternal principles of common justice and common rights and in standing there it immediately claimed for the Negro every right of citizenship under the same terms they were granted to all other citizens, every right that would be accorded any citizen in accordance with the fitness he had through character, intelligence and culture. Such a program was indeed revolutionary. It frightened off a great many white people who were more or less friendly to the Negro and by a curious alignment of circumstances threw masses of colored people into an opposing camp.

Today it is easy for white people, even for liberal southern white people, to think well of the N.A.A.C.P. But in those early days it took real courage; and so the white men and the white women who stood with this organization during those perilous years and who still stand with it have gone through every test that can be demanded of its friends. Of course, the Negro who is too timid to stand with this Association today simply brands himself as craven.

At the present time if there is criticism of the Association's program it is not that it is radical but rather that it is conservative. The Association has beyond question achieved and succeeded, but as much as has been done, there remains still more to do. As great as has been the success, it ought to be greater. The Association has wielded great power, but there exist opportunities and resources sufficient to increase that power ten-fold, fifty-fold, a hundred-fold; and the fact that it is not increased is a reflection upon the intelligence and the seriousness with which the American Negro is meeting the greatest problem that confronts him. And that brings me to the main thought that I wish to give you.

Negroes in this country ought to regard the National Association for the Advancement of Colored People not merely as an organization but as a movement. They ought to regard its principles as a religion; a religion of common sense and common safety, but more than that, a religion that looks far into the future and seeks to gain for generations yet to come fuller freedom, brighter opportunity and a chance for a richer life than we ourselves possess. Is not this a religion to fire and inspire every heart beneath a dark skin that beats in these United States; and I believe that if our churches are going to justify the full share of the sacrifice and money that they cost, they will join this religion of the world here together with the religion of the world hereafter.

The Association is not merely cramped through ignorance and indifference. It frequently has to withstand direct attempts to curtail it, to hamstring it. Enemies on the outside we can deal with because we meet them face to face; but there are also enemies on the inside who strike in the dark. Only a few days ago a Negro newspaper published in Harlem carried a story stating that I was resigning from the secretaryship because of dissension within the Association—because I was disgruntled over the election of J. E. Spingarn to the presidency. Now, almost any other name than that of J. E. Spingarn would have made that story less absurd. About fourteen years ago—Mr. Spingarn alluded to it slightly; I will tell it a little more fully, a little over fourteen years ago Mr. Spingarn and I were brought closely together. During the summer of 1916 he organized the Amenia Conference, so named because it met at his beautiful country place at Amenia, New York, where we were entertained. Now, the Amenia Conference takes its place, a historical place, among the meetings in the United States called to consider the race question. I was invited to that conference and I attended it, and it was there that J. E. Spingarn, then chairman of our Association's Board, decided in his mind that I ought to become an official worker in this organization. He spoke to Dr. Du Bois about it and Dr. Du Bois agreed with him, but it was due to J. E. Spingarn that I became the Association's field secretary, a position that was created for me, and later its secretary. Moreover, at the Amenia Conference there began between him and me a friendship which is stronger and deeper today than ever. I say this and I say it not only in rebuttal of the insinuations of this article I have been speaking of; I say it regardless of that—that if there is any man better suited for the presidency of the National Association for the Advancement of Colored People than J. E. Spingarn I do not know him. I need not tell you anything about him. You know him fully as well if not better than you know me. But he has not been so much before us in recent years; and those of you who do not know him quite so well, you have this afternoon got the sight of the man's soul, you have got a breadth of that sincerity of his which will never cease so long as there is wrong and injustice to be overcome.

But this newspaper story, which went into details about a stormy board meeting which, in fact, was never held, was not concerned about the truth, and the truth could easily have been learned. It was concerned with injecting into the ranks of the Association a poison. It was concerned with driving a wedge that could have no other effect than to weaken it. This leads me to speak a word of warning against a danger that is not visionary—the danger of the cultivation of a sort of racial chauvinism, the very sort of thing in the white race that we are constantly opposing. There is a laudable race pride that we need to possess, but this racial chauvinism is race pride run amuck. In the hands of a demagogue it can be a dangerous force, a force that we must guard against; and this will be true for yet many years. We need every brave and sincere friend that we can hold and that we can make. We have too few of them now, and it is certainly not for us to bring about that day when we have no more Storeys, nor more Spingarns, or Oswald Garrison Villards, or Ovingtons, or Kelleys, or Darrows. That will be a sad day for us.

With regard to my retirement from the secretaryship; some very complimentary things have been said about me by those with whom I have been associated in this work—things that would embarrass me if I did not feel and know that they were said in deep sincerity. Now, I throw aside false modesty, and I am saying that during these fourteen years of service I have striven to do my very best. I am saying that I have never stinted my efforts, my abilities or my strength; but I must also say that whatever I have been able to do I have not been able to do alone. I have had all through these years a Board of Directors whose counsel and faithfulness and support have never failed me. I have had a wonderful staff of colleagues, a staff not outmatched in any similar organization in this whole country. I have had the loyal cooperation of that staff. I have had the cooperation of Walter White, Robert W. Bagnall, William Pickens, Herbert J. Seligmann and William T. Andrews; and moreover, I have had the benefit of the intelligence, skill and seemingly unlimited capacity for work of Miss Randolph. As my secretary she was, in fact, my right hand. And, too, I could always count upon the reliability and fidelity of Mr. Turner, our Accountant, in point of service the oldest of us all. Now, I learned to look upon this staff as a gifted family, each member possessing his own unique and individual talent, and if there is anything in this connection that I might boast of it is that I had enough wisdom to recognize those talents and to seek to draw from the possessor the full play of all his powers. And finally, neither I, nor the Board, nor the staff could have accomplished what has been done in these past years except for the zeal and devotion of the men and women active in our branches all over the country and the support that has been generally and generously given by the Negro press.

I am retiring from the secretaryship but I am not retiring from the Association. I am relinquishing these duties in order to devote my time more fully to writing than the administration of the office allows, and in doing that I feel that I shall be serving the cause in a somewhat different way but with no less endeavor and no less faith. As I said in my letter of resignation, I might have experienced an insuperable hesitancy in taking this step had it not been for the splendid work of the Association and the magnificent way in which it has been carried on during this past year under the leadership of Walter White. I spoke just now about being lucky enough to have enough wisdom to recognize the talents of this gifted family of colleagues. Perhaps I ought to pat myself on the back that I had perception enough to see the talents in this young man when was just a boy. That is another story which might be told at another time.

Now, furthermore, I am not only not retiring from the Association. I see now I am receiving honorary duties. I am glad of it and that in my new relation to the work as a Vice-president and a member of the Board I shall be active in the work. This work, as it has been, will always remain for me a part of my life, a greater part of my hopes, and in a still higher degree, my religion.

Leadership and the Times

As a speaker at the NAACP Annual Conference in Detroit, Michigan, in January 1937, Johnson offers a speech on leadership in which he argues that business leadership, political leadership, educational leadership, social leadership, and spiritual leadership are being called into question. The complexities and characteristics of leadership are numerous, he asserts, especially since with each generation the demands for changing leadership are imperative. He pays tribute to the effective leadership of NAACP Secretary Walter White, who is the recipient of the Twenty-third Annual NAACP Spingarn Medal.

I am going to talk to you for a few moments about leadership. But in these turbulent times, in this age when fundamental ideas of civilization, of society, and of life are shifting so rapidly, a discussion of leadership in traditional terms is archaic. Who in this day rises on a platform or stands on a street corner to talk about leadership, except to criticize, discredit, and deride it? Indeed, the discrediting of leaders has become a popular pastime, and no individual is too lacking in wisdom or experience or even in ordinary common sense to indulge in it.

Business leadership, industrial leadership, political leadership, educational leadership, social leadership, spiritual leadership—all are under fire. The temper of the times is to put no faith in any leadership. This is a result that has naturally followed loss of faith in business integrity, political sincerity, in the aims and objectives of education, in the efficacy of religion, in the capacity of democracy—in a word, loss of faith in the whole social scheme.

Now, I shall not begin this talk by turning the tables and denouncing the denouncers in like terms. I know and I recognize that there are reasons for the present attitude toward leadership. Leaders in each of the fields I have just mentioned have fallen short. But in this day when civilization appears to be making one of its epochal shifts, it is only human for them to have fallen short; in many instances to have failed.

I want to repeat here a remark I have often made, and it is this: The critic can always function 100 percent. Probably there is no individual so dumb that he cannot point to failings in the execution of a plan that somebody else is trying to carry out.

The doer never has and never will function 100 percent. If he registers fifty percent he ought not feel discouraged. If he rises to sixty per cent or more, he should feel that he has been successful. If he makes a perfect score above ninety percent, he should at once be transported to celestial regions and forthwith given his crown, his robe, his slippers, and his harp. Leaders are only human, so it is foolish and wrong to demand of them the attributes of omniscience and omnipotence. When the critic turns his hand or his head to doing, he finds himself face to face with these truths of reality.

A thought I wish to impress upon you at this point is that despite all the talk about lack of leadership, there are still leaders. There always have been leaders, and there always must be leaders. Humanity is so ordered that it cannot function as society without leadership. Without leadership there would be stagnation or chaos. Social schemes are not automatically created and do not automatically carry themselves through. They must be formulated, made articulate, put into action, and given force. That is the office of leadership. And remember that leadership of this kind comprehends a wide scope, ranging from systems of philosophy and of morals, born of the world's supreme intellects and greatest souls, down to the influences that spread from the lives of innumerable men and women wholly unknown to fame.

Society is never without leadership. Leadership may be high, it may be low. It may become absolutely bad or it may degenerate into the leadership that leads merely to confusion. But be it good, bad or indifferent, there is always leadership. Bear this in mind, humanity can follow bad leadership just as it can follow good leadership.

The next thought I wish to bring to you is that there is never an age without good leadership. In the midst of all the turmoil there are today those who like one crying in the wilderness are calling out words of wisdom, but the crowd does not hear them or, if it hears, it does not heed. Eventually, sooner or later, they will be heard. In all the ups and downs of human history these voices crying in the wilderness are finally heard, then it [the crowd] turns and listens again. If this were not so, what we call civilization would long ago have vanished.

Now, you and I realize that I should not be making the most of this opportunity if I stood here and continued to talk about leadership in general terms. What you have the right to expect of me is that I apply the general to the specific. And the specific in this instance involves the aims and objectives of this Association and the purposes that are uppermost in your minds as you gather here tonight.

We, like America at large, have followed the trend, and lambasting our leaders has become a popular indoor and outdoor sport; without doubt, since leaders are human, there are many things wrong with them—just as there are with followers—and, as every group of people has, we have the right of openly criticizing the words and actions of those who stand as leaders. But the criticisms should be based on knowledge, it should be sound, it should be fair.

In fact, leadership cannot afford to be free of criticism; and the leadership that cannot tolerate just criticism isn't worth very much. Leadership needs criticism. Free of criticism it is prone to go to the head like an intoxicating liquor. Whenever it has the power to silence criticism it becomes a dangerous thing. The world has before it now the terrifying examples of Mussolini, of Hitler, and of Stalin.

I have just said that criticism of leadership ought to be based on knowledge; that it should be sound and fair. Such criticism calls for weighing the question as to whether or not the ways and means advocated are the most adequate that can be used at the time and under the circumstances. With this criterion in mind we can correctly estimate whatever has been advocated by leadership throughout our whole history. This criterion will reveal the juvenile quality of much of the criticism that we hear about leadership in former generations.

There was time when wise leadership called on the courage and faith that would sustain swift feet. This was the leadership that had its highest example in the great Harriet Tubman. The fleeing slave, hiding by day and running by night, set his course by the North Star, and pressed on till he set foot on soil beyond the Ohio River and the State of Maryland, or perished in the attempt. Now, it would be absurd to criticize the runaway slaves for running instead of making a stand and fighting it out.

Losing sight of this criterion has led to most of the criticism of what the present generation rather contemptuously calls, "old leadership." The first fact to be ascertained about the leadership of any period is whether the ways and means it advocated were the most adequate that could be used at the time and under the circumstance.

Now, a corollary to what I have just said is: leadership that might have been fairly adequate for a former generation is not to be condemned because it does not apply to the present situation. Another corollary is: new ideas in leadership must constantly be developed to keep pace with the ever changing situation.

The situation that we call the Race Problem is not static. It is not like a problem in mathematics; that is, one involving fixed factors and given rules with which it is to be worked out to an invariable result. The situation is steadily shifting. New factors continue to enter and the rules are subject to change. So the crux of the problem constantly shifts. It is not what it was a hundred years ago, or fifty or twenty or even ten years ago. And each shift implies a higher issue. It is from this fact that we can always draw fresh hope, deeper faith, and higher courage. In the most perplexing, disheartening moment of the present we can glance back over the shifting scenes of three centuries and see how far we have come. And we can feel with certainty that the way can be no rougher in the future than it has been in the past, and therefore no power this side of God's heaven can keep us from pressing forward.

Today we are witnessing a major shift, a major shift not merely in our particular situation but in the whole national scene. We are, in fact, witnessing a silent revolution—and not too silent at that—which involves far-reaching political, economic, and social changes.

In the political sphere we see the breaking up of old political alignments and the formation of new ones. We see at present the possibility of the formation of a political party that will be directly responsible and responsive to the worker. We have in the past two or three years seen on our part a complete abandonment of an age-old tradition that kept us a one-party group. And we have seen the effect which this action has already had and will still further have on the one-party system of the Deep South. It is this side of prophecy to say that this action will eventually lead to the abolishment of the one-party system of the Deep South; and that, in turn, will lead not only to the political enfranchisement of the black man but also of the white man in the South. For under the present system the latter has practically no more actual political freedom and independence than the former.

The leadership of the N.A.A.C.P. has long envisaged this outcome, and persistently labored for its realization. I distinctly remember that as secretary of the organization, and addressing the annual conference that met in Indianapolis in 1927, ten years ago, I urged that the Negro should vote independently and in disregard of the tradition that he owed eternal allegiance to the party of Abraham Lincoln. Notwithstanding the fact that neither Abraham Lincoln nor any one resembling him was running on the Republican ticket. My remarks were received in a somewhat painful silence. Those remarks today would be commonplace.

In the sphere of labor, industry, business, commerce, and social well-being we are witnessing a still more vital shift. A fairer economic share for labor, definite limitations upon "rugged individualism" and predatory interests, workers' security, unemployment insurance, old age pensions, national socialization of health and welfare, state or collective control of basic utilities—such concepts as these, which a generation ago America had hardly heard of, are today a part of the conscious thinking of the masses. The emphasis of life today is not so much upon humanitarian appeals as it is upon economic demands.

It is evident that the type of leadership of a former day could not cope with or be expected to cope with the present situation. New knowledge and new techniques are required. Present day leadership must perfect itself in that new knowledge and those new techniques. That is the task now before leadership all over the world. Our own leadership needs to be one able to steer the Negro into these fresh political, economic and social currents, or we shall be left stranded on the shore.

Our leadership must keep progressive. It must keep pace with the rapidly shifting situations in the world of realities. One of its chief tasks must be to make the overwhelming masses of the Negro an integral part of the present day workers' movement. Now, this is something easier said than done; nevertheless, it is a task in which Negro leadership must not fail.

There is an old idea of leadership to which most of us still cling: the idea of a single leader who combines within himself all the elements of leadership necessary for our guidance and salvation, of a Moses who will certainly deliver us out of the hands of the Egyptians. The day for that type of leadership is past. The present situation requires a diversified leadership. The leadership of many minds united on a common objective. The situation requires leadership on all the fronts of the single battle in which we are engaged. We must have leaders in the fight for civil equality, for industrial equality, for political equality, for educational equality, and for social equality.

The term "social equality" is quite generally taboo even among us. Perhaps I had better define what I mean by "social equality." I mean by it personally that I do not consider anybody or know of anybody too good to associate with me. The term "social equality" needs to be defined, for the general meaning has been stretched to absurd limits. In some sections of the country it embraces everything from intermarriage to breathing the air in the same public park. A definition of social equality which I believe every self-respecting colored person and white person can stand on is:

There should be nothing in law or public opinion to prevent persons of like interests and congenial tastes from associating together if they mutually desire to do so.

If I were discussing the race problem as a whole I would attempt to show how vital and far-reaching is social equality as one of the factors in the problem. I shall epitomize by saying that we cannot possibly attain actual equality in any principal phase of national life so long as we constitute a caste of pariahs, so long as we are commonly regarded as a class of untouchables. Yes, we must have leadership on all these fronts, and social equality, within the definition I have given, is one of the fronts.

I have said that the present situation is so new, so complex that it requires the abandonment of the old idea of an individual leader, of a Moses; that it requires diversified leadership. But the essential thing to be achieved in this diversified leadership is coordination. All too often leadership on one front has fallen into the error of feeling that it was fighting the whole battle single-handed, and winning it alone. Such a feeling has at times run so high that it has set itself to fight leadership on other fronts harder than it fought the foe. It is essential that all the fronts should know and feel that they are fighting for a common victory.

The question of leaders naturally brings up the question of followers. There can be no leaders unless there are followers. Followers have obligations and responsibilities as well as leaders. As followers, we need to have intelligence, a sense of loyalty, and sense of honor.

We need to have enough intelligence to weigh and estimate men so that we can recognize real leadership when we see it, whether it is in high or lowly position, and to detect the spurious from the genuine; enough intelligence to stimulate and help real leadership both by approval when it is merited and by criticism when it is deserved; enough intelligence not to be swept away by the winds of doctrine issuing from every loud-mouthed demagogue or smooth-tongued charlatan who comes along. We need a sense of loyalty that will impel us to give unstinted support whenever we find leadership that is capable and trustworthy, and to bear with it in its human weaknesses. And we need a sense of honor that will deem it an unworthy thing to seek to destroy a leader because of personal animosities or to crucify him merely to make a Roman holiday.

Unless we can be followers of this kind, we have no reason or right to look for great leaders.

Let me add another thought. The term "leader" has been accommodatingly stretched, but great leaders are not and never were numerous. Leaders of the first magnitude are among the rarest of humans; God makes one only every so many centuries. We, as every other group, have on hand a large supply of self-set-up leaders. But real leadership is not a distinction to be assumed; it is an office to be achieved. Of the real leader the people some day become aware, and say: This man serves well, let us follow him.

The subject on which I have based these remarks seem a fitting one because the occasion of this gathering is to pay tribute to real leadership; to progressive, intelligent, courageous leadership; to leadership that has kept pace with the fast shifting situation. I am especially proud to take part in these exercises tonight because of my close relations with the man we are here to honor.

I look at Walter White and my mind goes back through the years to 1917, when I was in Atlanta to organize a branch of the Association. It was then that I first saw him. He was just a stripling. He may have boasted a mustache; if so, it was of such low visibility as to be scarcely discernible, and I did not note it. But I was quick enough and wise enough to note that his was the moving spirit in getting together the local group that I met with and formed into the Atlanta Branch. One of the most satisfying incidents in my life is the one of recognizing on first sight the capabilities and possibilities of Walter White; for that belongs to the kind of feat in perspicacity which is not often accomplished.

From that time I have watched his career as I would that of a younger brother. And I have felt a justifiable pride and enjoyed a vicarious honor in watching him grow; in seeing him develop from an unknown youngster into a man of national distinction; and, finally, in knowing him to be the one to take upon his shoulders the great responsibility and the great burden of being the executive officer of this organization. How well he has carried the responsibility and burden we all know.

Tonight, we are here to see him awarded the highest badge of distinction a Negro American may win. He is still a young man, and has many years of service before him. Walter, may God bless you in all your efforts, and keep you humble in your achievements.

PART II

THE SELECTED WRITINGS OF
WALTER WHITE,
1929–1955

Walter White, circa late
1940s. From the collection of
Jane White Viazzi

Walter White and family, circa 1932. From the collection of Jane White Viazzi

Walter White
(July 1, 1893–March 21, 1955)

A Chronology

1893   Born to George and Madeline Harrison White on July 1 in Atlanta, Georgia.

1905   Witnesses the Atlanta race riot at the age of twelve. Helping to defend his home and family against a mob of bloodthirsty whites, he realizes his identity as an African American.

1912   Enters Atlanta University's freshman class.

1916   Graduates from Atlanta University and works as an insurance agent for Standard Insurance Company in Atlanta. Helps to form the Atlanta branch of the NAACP and spearheads the campaign against the mounting racial discrimination as practiced by the Atlanta Board of Education.

1917   Meets James Weldon Johnson in Atlanta. Johnson persuades him to join the staff of the national office of the NAACP.

1918   Joins the staff of the NAACP in New York City on January 31. His major areas of responsibility include helping to coordinate the legal program.

1919   Volunteers to undertake the dangerous task of investigating some of the most sinister crimes of lynching in the south. Because of his blue eyes, blond hair, and overall Caucasian appearance, is able to "pass." The NAACP uses his findings as data for their publication *Thirty Years of Lynching*. This work, the first statistical analysis of lynching, is published by the Association.

1920   James Weldon Johnson becomes chief executive officer (secretary) of the NAACP and White is the Association's assistant secretary. The advent of Johnson and White as a leadership team marks the beginning of black decision-making power among the highest ranks of the NAACP.

1921   With W. E. B. Du Bois, attends the Second Pan African Congress (London, Brussels, and Paris) as a delegate.

1922   Marries Leah Gladys Powell of Philadelphia. Daughter, Jane, is born on October 30.

1924   Publishes *The Fire in the Flint*, a novel about lynchings.

1926   Publishes *Flight*, a novel about the issue of "passing."

1927   Son, Walter Carl Darrow, is born on June 8. Travels to France with family for one year on a Guggenheim Fellowship to write third novel; instead writes *Rope and Faggot: The Biography of Judge Lynch*, a nonfictional account of lynching, which is published this year.

1929   Becomes acting secretary of the NAACP during James Weldon Johnson's leave of absence.

1930   Leads one of the NAACP's most successful campaigns, against the confirmation of Judge John J. Parker for a seat on the U.S. Supreme Court (an accomplishment he considered to be one of his most important during his NAACP tenure). As the Depression sets in and membership declines, confirms his remarkable leadership and interpersonal skills in keeping the NAACP solvent by raising funds from white philanthropists. James Weldon Johnson resigns as secretary on December 17.

1931   Becomes secretary of the NAACP. Persuades the board of directors to hire Roy Wilkins, a reporter for the *Kansas City Call*, as Assistant Secretary.

1933   Helps to establish the Joint Committee on National Recovery to fight discrimination in President Roosevelt's New Deal programs. Attends the Second Amenia Conference at the Estate of J. E. Spingarn in Amenia, New York.

1934   W. E. B. Du Bois publishes an editorial in the *Crisis* on "nondiscriminatory segregation," contradicting the Association's fundamental ideology of integration, and causing a fiery debate between Du Bois and White, which ends in Du Bois's resignation. White takes over the *Crisis* and appoints Roy Wilkins as acting editor.

1935   Secures a foundation grant and hires Charles Hamilton Houston as head of the newly established NAACP Legal Department.

1937   Accepts the Twenty-third Spingarn Medal for investigating lynchings and for his efforts in trying to secure a federal anti-lynching bill.

1945   Serves as consultant to the U.S. delegation at the San Francisco Conference which organizes the United Nations. Publishes *A Rising*

Wind, based on his personal observations as a war correspondent in the the European, Mediterranean, Middle East, and Pacific war zones.

1946   Leads delegation of the National Emergency Committee against violence to the White House for an audience with President Truman to brief him on the turmoil in Columbia, Tennessee.

1947   Suffers a severe heart attack while vacationing in St. Croix. Takes a leave of absence from the NAACP.

1948   Serves as consultant to U.S. delegation at the United Nations General Assembly in Paris.

1949   Takes leave of absence from the NAACP and participates in the Round the World Air Town Meeting, visiting European countries, Israel, Egypt, and India. Publishes autobiography, *A Man Called White*.

1951   Returns from leave of absence but is still in delicate health.

1954   As White's efforts in building the NAACP's legal structure pay off, the Association enjoys a string of legal achievements, including the victorious *Brown* decision. Takes another leave of absence due to heart problems.

1955   Publishes *How Far the Promised Land?* a volume dealing mainly with his NAACP work. Dies on March 21 of a heart attack, at home in New York City. Funeral is held at St. Martin's Episcopal Church in Harlem. Is cremated and interred in Ferncliff Cemetery in Hartsdale, New York.

Selected Reports of the NAACP Secretary to the Board of Directors, 1932–1954

Editor's Note

Walter White stopped in at the NAACP offices on the afternoon of March 21, 1955. He had just returned from a one-month vacation in the Caribbean where he had been recovering from a second heart attack. Appearing to be in top form and delighted to be back in the thick of things, he decided to return to work before the planned date of April 1. Unfortunately, this would be his last day at the NAACP. Three hours after he left his office, he died of a heart attack at home in New York City. Roy Wilkins wrote that it was so typical of him to stop by the office before going home to die. Only an act of God could stop White, the relentless civil rights crusader.[1]

When White joined the staff of the NAACP in 1918 as assistant secretary, he volunteered to undertake a dangerous assignment. He used his deceptive appearance to pass for white in order to gain information for the NAACP in its quest to publicize the facts of the reprehensible crime of lynching. As NAACP investigator, White often mingled with the perpetrators of the crime. Talking with them as a white man, he often cheered their heinous acts to appear sincere. Hearing these executioners boasting about riddling "nigger wenches" with bullets until they stopped moaning, or witnessing the charred body parts of lynching victims passed around for souvenirs, he would become nauseated.

When these murderers became suspicious of him, he was forced to flee these southern villages, escaping within inches of his life. White became invaluable to the NAACP for his investigations of forty lynchings and eight race riots. He gathered information for the NAACP's publicity machine that no discernible black man could have attained.

White was no stranger to mob violence. At the age of thirteen his family home became a target for an angry mob of racists during the Atlanta riot of 1905. This experience marked a turning point in his life. He realized what it meant to be a black person in America. Years later, in his autobiography, he wrote about the experience:

In the quiet that followed I put my gun aside and tried to relax. But a tension different from anything I had ever known possessed me. I was gripped by the knowledge of my identity, and in the depths of my soul I was vaguely aware that I was glad of it. I was sick with loathing for the hatred which had flared before me that night and come so close to making me a killer; but I was glad I was not one of those who hated; I was glad I was not one of those whose story is in the history of the world, a record of bloodshed, rapine, and pillage. I was glad my mind and spirit were part of the races that had not fully awakened, and who therefore had still before them the opportunity to write a record of virtue as a memorandum to Armageddon.[2]

In 1931, when White succeeded Johnson as secretary, the Association had been in existence for 22 years. Under his leadership, emphasis began to shift away from racial brutalities, because lynchings had begun to decline drastically. At this time the Association's resources concentrated mainly on battling the white primaries, restrictive housing covenants, segregation in transportation and places of recreation, and the inequities in education from the primary level to graduate school.

Like Johnson had been, White was plagued by charges of a white-controlled NAACP. Although Johnson is credited with the advent of the black bureaucracy in the organization, White must be credited with solidifying the NAACP's black hierarchy and base of power.

Although the Association was in the forefront in regard to discriminatory economic policies that plagued President Franklin Roosevelt's Administration, young black intellectuals like Abram Harris and Ralph Bunche condemned the NAACP for being markedly influenced by certain white board members. These critics further challenged the organization to take up causes like the unionization of black workers. Walter White answered these critics by setting up a Committee on Future Plan and Program, chaired by Abram Harris. As a result of this committee, branches began to receive more decision-making power in electing board members. In the midst of these criticisms, NAACP board chairman J. E. Spingarn resigned. White seized this opportunity to further empower his role as secretary, and to satisfy African Americans who were eager to see a black board chairman. In 1935 he championed the distinguished African-American physician Louis T. Wright for the job of chairman of the board. White used his personal friendship with Wright to make his own appointments to the board of directors.

In that same year, White would institute another important change. Before 1934 the legal cases for the Association had been generally handled by white attorneys such as Moorfield Storey, Arthur Spingarn, Clarence Darrow, Louis Marshall, Arthur Garfield Hays, and others, all of whom donated their services to the Association. Lawyers of this high caliber were crucial to the work of the NAACP because it was difficult for black attorneys to receive even-handed treatment from the hostile judicial system. White was under pressure from black lawyers to take over the legal work, and he knew that if black lawyers were handling the Association's well-publicized cases, black memberships would increase.

Charles Hamilton Houston, a Harvard Law School graduate and dean of Howard University's School of Law, had been serving as a part-time lawyer for the NAACP. He had already gained a national reputation for making Howard's Law School one that produced highly skilled and activist black attorneys who were trained in civil rights litigation.[3] In 1935 White secured a grant to create a legal department and hired Houston to head it. This selection of Houston signaled an affirmation by the NAACP of his desire to place emphasis on educational disparities.[4] Houston would become the chief strategist of the long-range struggle against educational discrimination that climaxed nearly twenty years after he joined the staff and four years after his death. His vision of using the law as a tool to fight racial inequities was consummated in the celebrated *Brown* decision of 1954.

White had deftly laid a solid organizational structure, beginning in the 1930s, that set the NAACP on a path of legal victories generating a civil rights revolution that changed the course of America.

During his 24 years as secretary, White used his skills as publicist, writer, orator, investigator, administrator, and fund-raiser to continue to strengthen the NAACP.

The following selections of his monthly reports to the board reveal his penchant for detail, his enthusiasm for the work, his enterprising mind, and the nature of the work he presided over as secretary.

Report of the Secretary for the
Board Meeting of February 1932

The Scottsboro Cases

[On March 25, 1931, nine African-American boys, aged 14 to 20, were charged with raping two white girls. The incident allegedly occurred while the boys were traveling on a freight train at Pain Rock, Alabama. Subsequently, eight of the youths were convicted and sentenced to death. The 14-year-old received life imprisonment. The defendants were initially represented by the NAACP's legal team. The Communist Party intervened through the International Labor Defense (ILD). The NAACP wanted no association with the Communist Party; therefore, the NAACP withdrew from the case.]

In accordance with the resolution passed at the January meeting of the Board, that resolution by which the N.A.A.C.P. withdrew from the Scottsboro Cases was sent to the parents and guardians of the defendants and to the press of the country. Since the passage of the resolution, letters have been received from two of the defendants asking that the Association remain in the cases, or at least take their individual cases; and on January 13 the following telegram was received from the Chattanooga Ministers Alliance:

> The Interdenominational Ministers Alliance understand by press report that the National Association for the Advancement of Colored People has withdrawn from the Scottsboro Case their legal aid in the defense of nine Negro boys. In view of the fact that the I.L.D. Legal force has all but gone to pieces because of questionable tactics and other developments and that the boys might be brought into court without legal aid, we beg you to prevail with your Board that the N.A.A.C.P. re-enter the case.

To this telegram the Secretary replied, enclosing the statement made public regarding the Association's withdrawal from the case, and setting forth in detail the reasons for this action. In his letter the Secretary stated that the only way in which the Association could re-enter the case would be upon the request of the defendants and their parents or guardians, with exclusive control of the case in its hands.

Upon receipt of information regarding the action of the Board, Mr. Roderick Beddow of the firm of Fort, Beddow and Ray wrote the National Office, as follows:

> The formal resolution of your Board clearly and unqualifiedly sets forth your Association's views as to its future policy concerning the eight Scottsboro boys. Your statement to the effect that the I.L.D. has accepted

responsibility should ring with profound solemnity in the ears of everyone seeking to advance the interest of an organization of that kind. They have accepted the responsibility. They ruthlessly waved aside the proffered assistance of a great and intellectual man. Unfortunately, for the eight Scottsboro boys, I am fearful that the I.L.D. in a very short period of time will hear the sad news that unquestionably will be delivered in the form of an opinion in the Supreme Court. People in this country are not going to tolerate militant tactics. . . . In view of the conduct and activities of the I.L.D. and their representatives, my views coincide with those of Mr. Darrow and Mr. Hays, and that is the only dignified thing left for you to do was to withdraw with the declaration that "the responsibility is yours."

Dr. George Fort Milton, editor of the *Chattanooga News*, has been very much interested in the part the N.A.A.C.P. has played in the Scottsboro Cases. On January 15 the National Office received from Mr. Milton a letter in which he told of a debate published in *The Forum* for December, 1926, in which the affirmative was taken by George W. Chamlee who is the attorney for the I.L.D. in the Scottsboro Cases. The subject of the debate was "Is Lynching Ever Defensible?" It so happens that Mr. James Weldon Johnson, then Secretary of the N.A.A.C.P., wrote a stinging reply to Mr. Chamlee which was published in *The Forum* for February, 1927.

On January 15 the National Office wrote to the International Labor Defense letting them know that this information was in the files of the N.A.A.C.P. and offering to send copy of same to the I.L.D. This letter was sent by registered mail and to date no reply other than the return receipt card has been received.

The *Chattanooga News* for January 22 carries a story of the trials in the Scottsboro Cases which began on January 21. Here the trials are referred to as "an invisible but powerful effort to so prejudice the people and even the courts of Alabama against the eight Negroes . . . to the extent that there will be no possible way of saving them from the electric chair." The story goes on to say that "those familiar with the case sensed a feeling that a certain element interested in the case had been gradually building up sentiment against the Negroes in order to insure that they would be made martyrs to the cause of Communism."

It will be probably thirty days or more before the final decree of the Supreme Court is announced.

All of the press, with but few exceptions, expresses the opinion that the Association followed the only proper course of withdrawing from the cases when it did. Dr. Will W. Alexander of the Interracial Commission has written the National Office: "You have gone the second mile and I feel that you have nothing to regret. . . . The dignified withdrawal of your Association seems to have left a good impression." Mr. P. B. Young, editor of the Norfolk, Va., *Journal and Guide*, writes: "I think the Association would be wise in leaving the Scottsboro Case to the I.L.D. and let that organization take responsibility for what follows."

The Texas Primary Case

On January 7 the United States Supreme Court heard argument on the case of *Nixon vs. Condon* made by Mr. James Marshall of the N.A.A.C.P. National Legal Committee. Mr. Arthur B. Spingarn, Chairman of the Legal Committee, was present in court.

The State of Texas announced that it would not argue the case but would only submit a brief and therefore the N.A.A.C.P. was limited to one attorney of argument.

On January 18 word was received from the Clerk of the Supreme Court that the Court had ordered a reargument of the case, the time to be set by the Court. The State of Texas applied for permission to file a brief after the time set had elapsed, and in granting this permission the reargument was ordered.

The Case of Robert Bell and Grady Swain

The National Office has been assured that latest developments in the case of Robert Bell and Grady Swain show that there is no chance of clemency before March or April. Governor Parnell has promised that he will see to it that the parole board acts favorably at its spring meeting. The Governor has been much impressed with the way in which the case has been presented by Messrs. Booker of Little Rock and has interviewed the judge who handed down the opinion in this case.

The Gary (Indiana) School Case

On January 5 the Supreme Court of Indiana overruled the petition of the Association's attorneys for a re-hearing in the Gary School, thus upholding the ruling of the Porter Circuit Court that Alberta Cheeks, a colored girl, had no right to demand that she be allowed to attend a school for white children.

"The Birth of a Nation"

Upon representation to the city council of Portland, Oregon, by the N.A.A.C.P. local Branch and the Council of Churches that the film contained objectionable scenes which might stir up race hatred, the film was barred. Mayor Baker took a firm stand that the film should not be shown. This is the fourth time that application for permits to show the picture have been denied.

Judge James Baldwin

Because he imposed a savagely severe death sentence upon a colored man who had thrown himself upon the mercy of the courts, colored people and their friends opposed the appointment as a federal judge of Judge James Baldwin of Decatur, Illinois.

At the request of the Decatur Branch the National Office began quiet and intensive work on Judge Baldwin's nomination when it was revealed that he had been recommended for the federal judgeship, wiring the Department of Justice requesting that the appointment be held up pending completion of an investigation into Judge Baldwin's attitude toward Negroes. This inquiry revealed that "a number of colored citizens of Decatur say that they would as soon trust their legal rights to a court in Georgia as to this judge" and that Judge Baldwin had a conspicuous record of reversals of his decision by higher courts.

The result of the Association's efforts was that Judge Baldwin failed to receive the appointment. President Hoover has appointed Charles G. Briggle as Federal Judge for the Southern Illinois District.

Senator LaFollette's Unemployment Bill

Senator Robert M. La Follette has introduced into the United States Senate a bill providing for a federal appropriations in conjunction with the states for the relief of the unemployed. The bill, known as S. 3045, authorizes the appropriation of $375,000,000 to be immediately available, $125,000,000 of which shall be expended in the fiscal year ending June, 1932, and the balance in the fiscal year from that date to July 1, 1933. Forty per cent of this sum is to be matched by the various states. A Federal Emergency Relief Board is to be created for the administration of the fund, which Board shall consist of the Chief of the Children's Bureau in the Department of Labor, the Director of Extension Work in the Department of Agriculture, the chief of the Vocational Rehabilitation Service of the Federal Board for Vocational Education, and two members to be appointed by the President. The bill provides also for Advisory Boards.

In the opinion of the National Office the bill as now drafted does not provide for sufficient safeguard against discrimination on account of color. In a conference with Senator La Follette in Washington on January 29 the Secretary pointed out this insufficiency. Senator La Follette said he recognized this but that opposition to the bill is already so great that he feels we would create a practically insuperable barrier against its passage if we tried to have it amended. He is of the opinion that since Miss Grace Abbot of the Children's Bureau will be the Chief Administrative Officer, and since the state expenditures are subject to approval by Miss Abbot and other officials in charge, in its present form there is ample machinery provided in the bill for checking any discrimination.

On January 30 the National Office wrote the Association's branches in fourteen northern and western states urging that they bring pressure to bear upon their respective senators for their vote in favor of the measure, since this legislation is of great importance to the Negro who suffers from unemployment more than any other racial group. The branches were urged to try to influence other organizations to bring similar pressure upon senators.

Senator La Follette plans to bring the bill upon the floor of the Senate during the present week.

The Villa Lewaro

On January 11 Mrs. Julia Mitchell, New York representative of the Mme. C. J. Walker Company of Indianapolis, telephoned the National Office asking that an option be signed permitting the sale of the Villa Lewaro, a purchaser having been found willing pay the sum of $47,500 for the property.

The matter was referred to the Chairman of the Legal Committee who advised that the Association could not sign the option but could only sign a consent to the option insofar as it had the right under the will of the late Mme. C. J. Walker; that it could include in the consent an agreement to execute a quit claim deed under the option, and would deliver the same upon payment of $5,000.

This information was transmitted at once to Mr. F. B. Ransom of Indianapolis, attorney for the Mme. C. J. Walker Company, and to Mrs. Mitchell; and on January 14 the consent to the option was signed.

On January 15 letter was received from Messrs. Brandeis, Hirschberger and Stilwell stating that copy of the option had been sent to Mr. Ransom, duly signed by the purchaser, and that they were awaiting word from the purchaser as to the exact date when she desires to sign the formal contract. The National Office is to be notified upon receipt of such word.

The Daniel H. Williams Will

On January 11 the Chairman of the Legal Committee attended a conference in Chicago at the offices of Messrs. Heth, Lister, and Collins, attorneys for the Executor and Trustees of the Estate of Dr. Daniel H. Williams. He reports that the contestants of the will agreed to withdraw their contest upon the payment of $10,000 and that this offer was immediately rejected by the representatives of the various beneficiaries under the will. The Chairman of the Legal Committee offered to give the contestants five per cent of such sum as the Association might actually receive, to be paid as and when received, doing so not because he believed the contestants had a valid claim but because he believed the "nuisance" value was at least that amount. He reported further that the amount of the rest is problematical.

Before leaving Chicago the Chairman of the Legal Committee retained Mr. William H. Holly to represent the N.A.A.C.P. He reports that if the will is admitted to probate and Mrs. Blanche Williams Zaratt, niece of Dr. Williams, receives one-half of the trust estate as provided in the codicil, none of the specific legacies can be paid in full and will be subject to abatement; that there will be no residuary estate unless some new assets are discovered.

Under date of January 27, the Chairman of the Legal Committee received the following letter from Mr. Holly:

Mr. Bates tells me that his clients have finally concluded to accept your offer of 5% and has arranged with the attorneys for Mrs. Zaratt for the payment of 10%. He wishes the settlement to take the form of an assignment by the institutions we represent of 5% of the funds received by them under the Will, the assignment to be made to Mr. Bates and his clients, one-quarter to him and the balance to be divided between the clients. Is that method of settlement satisfactory to you?

The Chairman of the Legal Committee asks that the Board pass upon this matter at the February meeting.

The Cutter House, Princeville, Illinois

Mr. C. F. Cutter who is now in England has communicated with the National Office offering to give the Association a house which he owns in Princeville, Illinois, known as The Cutter House. Mr. Cutter says the house was a station on the Underground Railroad. The communication came in the form of a post card bearing a picture of the house, sent to *The Crisis*, with the request, "Please find out what best use the N.A.A.C.P. would make of this place if I were to give it to them, and let me know."

This offer was considered by the Committee on Administration and it was decided that the Secretary should write to Mr. Cutter that the ideal arrangement would be to make The Cutter House a shrine in the form of a memorial or museum; but that due to the financial situation now as it affects the Association, the only thing which could be done, should Mr. Cutter be generous enough to give the House to the N.A.A.C.P., would be to get the best price possible for it and devote the money to the work of the Association.

Annual Conference

The Secretary conferred on January 8 with officers of the District of Columbia Branch regarding plans for the Annual Conference.

Invitations to speak have been extended to President Hoover, Dr. R. R. Moton, Senator Arthur Capper, Senator Robert M. La Follette, Jr., Prof. John Dewey, Dr. Harry Emerson Fosdick, Mr. Walter Lippman, and Mr. Stuart Chase. Senators Capper and La Follette have accepted. Dr. Moton has not answered definitely but has said he wants very much to accept. A letter from Mr. Theodore G. Joslin, Secretary to President Hoover, states that indications now are that it will be impossible for the President to accept our invitation; however, he suggests that we get in touch with him again on April 15.

Committee on Negro Work

The Chairman of the Legal Committee, Mr. Nathan R. Margold, Mr. Morris L. Ernst, and the Secretary met at Mr. Ernst's office on January 21 to consider the matter of the appropriation from the American Fund for Public Service.

There was discussion as to whether or not the Association should consent to the cutting down of the appropriation with the understanding that the money would be paid over a short time, or whether it should stand out for the eventual payment of all or as nearly the full amount as possible of the original appropriation.

It was agreed that for the time being we should hold out for the full amount.

The Tom Carraway Case

Due to the fact that Mr. S. Redmond of Jackson, Mississippi, with whom the National Office first dealt in connection with the case of Tom Carraway, insisted on a much larger fee than the $250 which could be devoted to the case, the National Office has requested that he go no further in the case. It also developed that Mr. Redmond had made some misrepresentations to the National Office as to work actually done by him in this case. Reliable information has come to the National Office that the stay of execution in the case was secured not by Mr. Redmond but by Attorney James Cowan of Gulfport, Miss. Bishop H. E. Jones and others of the Interracial Commission are watching the case for the Association.

The National Office has already sent Mr. Redmond a fee of $125.00. Mr. Cowan agreed to handle the case to completion for $250.00 The Interracial Commission offered to pay $125.00 of this, provided the remaining $125.00 allotted by the N.A.A.C.P. could be transferred to Mr. Cowan. On January 16 the National Office sent to Bishop Jones [a] check of $125.00 to be turned over to Mr. Cowan.

Lieutenant-Governor Bidwell Adam of Mississippi, Bishop Jones reported, seemed favorably disposed in the case and wanted to help all he could. However, Mr. Adam's term of office expired on January 19, and now the Association is awaiting word from Bishop Jones as to what has been done on the case since the check was sent him on January 16. It is hoped that Mr. Adam has used what influence he could with the Governor.

United States Supreme Court

Upon the resignation of Mr. Justice Oliver Wendell Holmes from the United States Supreme Court the National Office began to check carefully the records as to their attitudes toward the Negro of all those named as probable successors to Mr. Justice Holmes. Enthusiastic cooperation in the Association's efforts to keep posted is being given by the branches and by lawyers, editors, and others all over the country.

The Case of Ernest Herring

Recent press reports told of the case of Ernest Herring who has been convicted of the murder of a postmaster of Kerr, N.C., and sentenced to death by electrocution. Immediately upon reading of the case the National Office wired a correspondent at Wilmington, N.C., asking for facts and the status of the case which are:

Chevis Herring, brother of Ernest, was convicted and electrocuted for the same crime. Both judges who presided at the trials of Chevis and Ernest in their instructions to the jury stated that had it not been for the testimony of Chevis there would not have been sufficient evidence for the case to go to the Grand Jury. Chevis Herring was a mental defective and in the opinion of the mental expert who testified for the state was not capable of making any statement that would have weight in deciding any matter.

Mr. Bagnall who was in North Carolina at the time the case came to the attention of the National Office was asked to make an investigation. He went to Raleigh, N.C., and talked with Ernest Herring in the death house, who declared he knew nothing of the murder. Mr. Bagnall then went to Clinton, N.C., where he talked with Messrs. Butler and Butler, the attorneys appointed by the court to defend Herring. At Mr. Bagnall's request Messrs. Butler and Butler have written the National Office expressing their sincere interest in the case and their confidence in Herring's innocence. They have already spent several hundred dollars on the case and are desirous of carrying it through. This they offer to do for any sum the Association is willing to pay. They are now making efforts for executive clemency and if they fail in this they intend to make a motion for a new trial at the next term of the Superior Court which begins on February 8.

The date set for Herring's execution was January 15 but the Governor was prevailed upon to make a personal visit to the prison, where he interviewed Herring, following which a sixty day reprieve was ordered.

Lynching

The only lynching recorded thus far in 1932 by the N.A.A.C.P. is that of Joseph Kahahawai of Hawaii, on January 8. He with four other men was accused of an attack upon Mrs. Thomas H. Massie, wife of Lieutenant Massie, U.S.N. He was kidnapped and shot to death.

The story of this whole affair has been carried in detail in the public daily press.

The National Office felt called upon to protest to the Secretary of the Navy against the defense of "lynch law" by Admiral William V. Pratt, Chief of Naval Operations. In his statement, which was made public, Admiral Pratt declared that "American men will not stand for the violation of their women under any circumstances and have taken the law into their own hands repeatedly when they have felt the law has failed to do justice." The Secretary of the Navy has replied denying that Admiral Pratt advocated lynch law and claiming that the statement made by him was rather a "warning intended to prevent the application of that law."

On January 26, Mrs. Granville Fortescue, mother of Mrs. Massie, Lieutenant Massie, and two naval enlisted men, Edward J. Lord and Albert O. Jones, were indicted for second degree murder.

Lewisburg, West Virginia: In his report to the December meeting of the Board the Secretary told of the double lynching at Lewisburg, West Virginia, and of the investigation being instituted by Governor Conley of that State. In a communication under date of December 1 Governor Conley wrote the National Office: "There will be no let-up. Race, color, or religion must not be permitted to interfere with bringing to justice the persons guilty of this deplorable crime, which under the laws of this state is classed as murder."

Five members of the mob were arrested. However, a letter received from Mr. T. G. Nutter on February 1 states:

> The Grand Jury at Lewisburg refused to indict the lynchers, although, in my judgment, they had sufficient evidence before them to do so. The jury was so influenced as to prevent it from bringing indictments. Doctor W. E. Myles, a brother of the constable who was killed, was indicted for attempting to place "biased" jurors on the Grand Jury. He pleaded guilty and was fined $100.
>
> We have not given up hope in getting indictments. I am expecting a report today from a party who has been making some investigations and Mr. W. W. Sanders and myself are planning to take the matter up with the Governor and insist that the evidence be re-submitted to the next Grand Jury that meets in Greenbrier County.

Haiti

On January 15 the National Office sent to Senator Reed Smoot, Chairman of the Senate Finance Committee, a memorandum asking a full and searching probe of Haitian loans floated and held in this country, with particular reference to the operations of the National City Bank of New York. The memorandum challenged statements by President Hoover concerning the 1922 loan which he said was "desired by Haiti," claiming this was a "misstatement of fact."

This memorandum was made public and it was also sent to each member of the Senate Finance Committee and other members of the Senate whom the National Office felt would be interested in the subject.

Many senators have replied that they will do whatever is possible to aid in having the Senate Finance Committee act favorably upon the request of the Association.

A special dispatch in the *New York Times* of January 27 stated that Senator William H. King of Utah had announced that he would press for an investigation of the loans forced upon Haiti. The National Office wired Senator King that colored people throughout the nation will follow the investigation with deep interest, and offered all information in possession of the Association.

Rosenwald Offer

Much of the time of the Secretary has been spent in an effort to secure contributors who would help meet Mr. William Rosenwald's second offer: to contribute to the N.A.A.C.P. $500 a year for three years provided $4,500 in contributions of

$1.000 and $500 for the same period could be secured. The Secretary in addition to personal appeals and appeals by letter in New York City, has spent several days in Philadelphia interviewing prospective contributors. Thus far the following contributions have been secured:

Mr. Noel Sullivan, San Francisco, $500.00
Mr. John H. Hammond, Jr., New York, $500.00
Mrs. Fannie T. Cochran, Philadelphia, $500.00
An Anonymous Contributor, $500.00

Publicity

A number of stories were featured in the white press during the month. The report of the Annual Meeting was published in the *Times* and the *New York American*. The lynching figures of the Association were not only widely published but received editorial comment in papers as distant as the Lewistown, Idaho, *Tribune* and in Georgia, the *Jefferson Herald* and the *Brunswick News*. A release concerning the Einstein message to Negroes, published in *The Crisis*, was featured in the *New York Times*.

The supplement memorandum to the Senate Finance Committee on Haiti was the subject of a release distributed by the Associated Press and received more than a third of a column of space in the *Philadelphia Bulletin*. A request to the Associated Press by the Director of Publicity that the N.A.A.C.P. be mentioned in connection with the story on the Texas White Primary Case argument in Washington brought specific mention of the Association in the Associated Press dispatches.

During the month the Director of Publicity completely re-wrote the Annual Report to drastically condense it in accordance with the suggestion of the President, Mr. J. E. Spingarn.

A translation by the Director of Publicity of a letter to the *Herald Tribune* by the Haitian Minister was published in that newspaper, January 31.

Walter White, Secretary
February 2, 1932

Report of the Secretary for the
Board Meeting of March 1933

The Wagner Resolution

Senator Wagner's resolution for a Senate investigation of conditions on the Mississippi Flood Control project was passed in the Senate on February 22.

Mr. Rifkind, secretary to Senator Wagner telephoned the National Office on February 23 that unanimous consent of the Senate is necessary to secure consideration of a resolution; that Senator Wagner had been waiting until all of the possible opponents of the resolution would be absent from the floor of the Senate; that a number had indicated that they would object to unanimous consent, that on February 22 Senator Wagner found his opportunity when he noted that no opponent of the resolution was on the floor. He promptly asked for unanimous consent, which was gained, and then the resolution was passed unanimously, no debate being allowed on unanimous consent.

The time for formal reconsideration of the resolution expired on March 3 in the closing hours of Congress, and a telegram from Mr. Rifkind stated that the special committee provided for in the resolution would undoubtedly be appointed on that date. However, the committee was not appointed; the following telegram regarding this was received from Senator Wagner on March 3:

> Committee response to Senate Resolution 300 will not be appointed until opening next session of Congress. This will permit two Democrats to serve on Committee.

This means that the investigation will certainly take place. The resolution as amended and passed provides for a special committee of three senators to investigate all the charges which have been made by the N.A.A.C.P. The appropriation was cut from $10,000 to $1,000 by the audit committee. It is expected that this amount will be increased after the investigation gets under way. The National Office is preparing a list of witnesses who will testify as to conditions.

The Public Affairs Committee of the National Young Women's Christian Association is giving the Wagner Resolution its support. The New York headquarters of the committee has placed the facts on the levee conditions before the various state committees and these in turn have written and wired senators urging favorable action on the resolution.

The *Women's Press*, official organ of the Y.W.C.A., carried in its March issue an editorial urging support of the resolution.

The Harlem Hospital Inquiry

The committee of Inquiry into the Harlem Hospital situation has engaged Dr. E. L. W. Corwin of the New York Academy of Medicine and Dr. Gertrude E. Sturges to make the inquiry under the direction of the committee. Drs. Sturges and Corwin began their work on February 26.

The National Office and the committee are putting forth strenuous efforts to raise the sum of $2,500 required to defray the expenses of the inquiry, this to be the maximum cost. One of the members of the committee, Dr. William Darrach, has taken up the matter with Dr. Kappel of the Carnegie Corporation and the application is now being considered by the Corporation. Letters of appeal have also been sent to a number of individuals suggested by Dr. Niles, chairman of the committee; and Mrs. Dwight W. Morrow has made the first contribution of one hundred dollars.

No publicity is to be given to the work of the committee until the inquiry is completed and no statements whatsoever are to be made except through the chairman of the committee.

The Joseph Crawford Extradition Case

On February 18 Governor Ely of Massachusetts signed the warrant for rendition of Joseph Crawford, accused of the murder of Mrs. Agnes B. Ilsley of Middleburg, Virginia, to the state of Virginia. Quick work by Mr. Butler R. Wilson who, with former Attorney General J. Weston Allen, has defended Crawford in his fight against extradition, secured a petition for a writ of habeas corpus. A hearing on the merits of the writ will be held in Boston on March 24, when Mr. Wilson and Mr. Allen will submit their arguments. They will concentrate largely on the fact that Negroes are not allowed to sit on juries in Virginia. The National Office has aided in securing affidavits from citizens of Virginia to this effect. Check for twenty-five dollars was sent from the National Office to cover the cost of the writ of habeas corpus, since the Boston Branch has exhausted its treasury and it is not thought wise to make a public appeal for funds for the case at this time.

For three days the National Office carried in the *New York Times* personal column an advertisement seeking to locate a Virginia white woman, now a resident of New York, who wrote an anonymous letter last year to the *Amsterdam News* in which she made sensational charges that Crawford did not commit the murders of Mrs. Ilsley and her maid but would be made the "goat" for someone else. No word has been received from this woman but on March 7 there came to the National Office Mr. John K. Boeing, brother of Mrs. Ilsley, he having read the advertisement. The Secretary discussed at length the evidence which Mr. Boeing and other members of his family have gathered, which in their minds, establishes at least a reasonable presumption that the murders were committed by Crawford. The Secretary explained to Mr. Boeing that the reasons of the Association for opposing rendition of Crawford to Virginia are based upon our belief in Crawford's statements and those of the witnesses appearing at the hearing before the Attorney General, who declared that Crawford was in Boston at the time the murders were committed. Mr. Boeing is getting for the National Office statements from certain individuals bearing upon the points discussed.

At Mr. Wilson's request that the National Office get a competent attorney to examine the venire that indicted Crawford and to see if the Judge, in calling a special venire, followed the Virginia code, the National Office wrote to Mr. Charles H. Houston of Washington, member of the N.A.A.C.P. National Legal Committee, and Mr. Houston has undertaken this task, going to Virginia on March 9.

The Scottsboro Cases

In response to a request from Mr. Roger N. Baldwin of the American Civil Liberties Union, who telephoned that an emergency had arisen in the pre-trial conference on the Scottsboro Cases necessitating the immediate presence of a New York conference in Chattanooga, the National Office upon the advice of the Chairman of the Legal Committee contributed thirty-five dollars ($35.00) towards the expenses of the trip. Mr. Baldwin reported that this conference arose out of the fact that Ruby Bates, one of the two white girls in the case, voluntarily requested it, announcing that she had a statement to make. The total cost of the trip was estimated at one hundred and twenty-five dollars ($125.00).

The Beaver County (Pa.) Deportation Cases

The latest advice to the National Office in the Beaver County, Pennsylvania, deportation cases (the expelling of fifty Negroes from Industry, Pa. in January) comes from Attorney General William Schnader in a letter dated March 2nd in which he states that in accordance with the state law he has written to the Judge of the District Court in Beaver County suggesting that the Judge request an investigation by the Attorney General's Office. If this suggestion is carried out it will enable the Attorney General's Office to invest the powers of special assistant attorney general in an attorney of Beaver County appointed by the Judge. The Judge has not as yet replied to Mr. Schnader.

The Lebanon, Tennessee, Mob Violence Cases

Mr. Albert E. Barnett who has been handling the matter of the Lebanon Mob Violence Cases and who had been in constant communication with the National Office writes that the matter of appeal from the sentences of life imprisonment for two of the colored men involved and of twenty-five years in the penitentiary for a third was taken up by him with the defense attorney; that the defense attorney feels there is ample ground for an appeal and that the only hindrance is a financial one.

A small group of persons assembled at a meeting in Nashville under the auspices of the Fellowship of Reconciliation raised a total of $50.00 to add to the contribution of $100 already made by the National Office toward this case. The defense attorney has indicated that he would go on with the case for $200; that above this amount he himself will bear the expenses. Mr. Barnett feels confident that the remaining $50.00 can be raised in Nashville.

Mr. James Weldon Johnson has been cooperating with Mr. Barnett in this matter.

The Doris Weaver Case

Hearing on the mandamus proceedings in the case of Miss Doris Weaver who was refused admission to the home management practice cottage of Ohio State University was had on February 17. Miss Weaver was represented by Messrs. Charles W. White and Claybourne George of Cleveland, and the granting of the writ of mandamus was opposed by attachés from the Attorney General's Office.

Decision in the case has not yet been announced by the Supreme Court, although the case has now been under consideration by the Court for more than two weeks. Attorneys for Miss Weaver are firmly of the opinion that the decision will be one favorable to Miss Weaver.

Efforts are being made to raise in the State of Ohio, through the Ohio State Conference of N.A.A.C.P. Branches, funds to cover the expenses in this case.

University of North Carolina Discrimination Case

The colored citizens of North Carolina, represented by Messrs. Cecil A. McCoy and Conrad O. Pearson of Durham, are planning to bring a suit to test the constitutionality of the practice of excluding Negroes from the professional schools of the University of North Carolina. It is the opinion of the National Legal Committee and of the Committee on Administration that if the people of North Carolina are willing to go through with the case, the National Office should give possible aid. At the opportune time one of the North Carolina attorneys is to come to New York for a conference with Mr. Margold and the Legal committee regarding the suit.

The Theodore Jordan Case

After the Association had saved the life of Theodore Jordan who was scheduled to hang on February 3 for the murder of a white dining car steward at Klamath Falls, Oregon, in June, 1923, news came from the Portland Branch under date of February 22 that Jordan had authorized the formation of a Jordan Defense Committee, and that he has criticized the action of the N.A.A.C.P. Mr. C. E. Ivey, President of the Portland Branch, stated that a committee from the I.L.D. called upon him and demanded that they be allowed to participate in the case and that a group of the I.L.D. had attended a Branch meeting and attempted to break it up.

The National Office has written to Jordan asking for a signed statement of his wishes in the case, as to whether he wishes the Association to continue in it, and in the meantime it has advised the Portland Branch to take no further steps until a reply is received from Jordan.

The Will Sanders Case

The National Office interested itself in the case of Will Sanders, a sixteen-year-old youth in South Carolina condemned to die for the murder of a white woman. Upon reading in the daily press that Sanders had been sentenced in seventy-seven minutes, the National Office communicated with Mr. N. J. Frederick of Columbia, S.C., member of the National Legal Committee, asking him what could be done in the case. Following Mr. Frederick's reply that the trial had been regular in every way, the National Office inquired of him if move for commutation of sentence could not be initiated. Upon Mr. Frederick's advice, the National Office wrote to Bishop Kirkman Finley of Columbia asking if he would head a movement among influential persons for commutation of sentence. Bishop Finley replied that he had examined the case in detail and did not feel that he could intervene. On March 1 the National Office telegraphed Governor Ibra Blackwood urging commutation; and on March 2, at the insistence of Mr. Isadore Pulier, a young white lawyer of New York City who formerly lived in South Carolina, the National Office telephoned Mr. Frederick asking that he file petition for a writ of habeas corpus in the federal court on the ground that Sanders was without adequate legal protection at the trial and at the time when his appeal should have been made. Mr. Frederick stated that it was impossible to frame a petition for this writ which would hold water; that the federal judges in South Carolina were thoroughly familiar with the Sanders case and were not disposed to upset the State machinery. Sanders was electrocuted on March 3.

A news dispatch on February 11 reported that Solicitor W. Gist Finley of York, S.C., proposed to exhibit Sanders' dead body on the courthouse steps after his electrocution. The Association sent a sharp telegram of protest against this "Middle Age barbarism" to Governor Blackwood. The proposal was not carried out.

The Jess [Jesse] Hollins Case

Jess Hollins is still being held in jail although at Okmulgee, Oklahoma, on February 27, Judge Mark L. Bozarth sustained a demurrer filed by Hollins' attorney charging that the original information on which Hollins was convicted and sentenced to death was faulty. The demurrer charged the information was defective on three points: (1) that said information does not substantially conform to the requirements of the statutes in charging the defendant with the crime of rape; (2) that more than one offense is charged in the information; and (3) that the facts stated in the said information do not constitute a public offense.

As soon as the judge sustained the demurrer Samuel Cunningham, Assistant County Attorney, asked permission to amend the information. Hollins' attorney disputed the jurisdiction of the court to grant such permission, holding that with the sustaining of the demurrer there ceased to be anything before the court over which it had any jurisdiction. The Judge remarked that perhaps he had jurisdiction but at any rate would give the County Attorney on April 2 an opportunity to submit a brief on the court's jurisdiction.

However, on March 7 Mr. Cunningham returned to Okmulgee from Sapulpa and voluntarily asked Judge Bozarth to dismiss the information which he on February 27 had asked permission to amend. As the case now stands, there is no charge in any court against Hollins. It is possible, however, that new information will be filed in Creek County against the prisoner, but his lawyers are confident that they will defeat any future moves to hold him.

Hollins was arrested, tried and convicted in Sapulpa, Oklahoma, in December, 1931, on charge of criminal assault upon a white woman. He was saved from death on August 17, 1932, by the intervention of the Oklahoma branches of the N.A.A.C.P. The National Office contributed $100.00 toward the defense fund.

Flogging at Clearwater, Florida

The National Office has had further correspondence from the office of Governor David Sholtz on the matter of the flogging of M. B. Harvey and W. D. Williams in Clearwater, Florida, on November 4, 1932. Mr. J. P. Newell, Secretary to Governor Sholtz, sent to the National Office a letter from the sheriff of Pinellas County, Florida, which states that many persons have been interrogated on the flogging at the insistence of the Governor's office, but that no definite information as to the identity of the floggers could be secured. The letter also stated that the Negroes of Clearwater did not seem to be fearful of their safety and that the sheriff would like to interrogate W. D. Williams whose whereabouts is unknown to him. The Governor's secretary stated that Williams and his family would be guaranteed every protection as a matter of course. The National Office has communicated with Mr. Williams' brother at Tampa asking whether Mr. Williams will consent to go back to Clearwater and tell his story. To date no reply has been received.

"The Green Pastures"

The final word on the jim-crow showing of "The Green Pastures" in Washington, D.C., on February 26 was received from Mr. A. S. Pinkett, secretary of the District of Columbia Branch, on February 28. Mr. Pinkett reported that few of the influential citizens of Washington attended the special showing for colored people only, estimating the attendance at 500.

When the order of Elks refused to sponsor the separate showing, the National Theatre itself took over the project. Mr. Pinkett reports that the discussion incident to this whole matter and the barring of Negroes from the National Theatre on other occasions has aroused public opinion in Washington to resist jim-crowism in every form. It has built up a new consciousness of the effect of segregation and of the necessity of resistance.

"Run Little Chillun Benefit"

In accordance with the vote of the Board at the February meeting, the National Office handled for the second performance of "Run Little Chillun," on March 2, three hundred tickets, one hundred orchestra seats, one hundred first balcony, and one hundred second balcony. The result of the sales, for which the National Office was to receive twenty-five per cent on each ticket sold was as follows:

    102 tickets @ $2.00
     36 tickets @ 1.50
     39 tickets @ 1.00
     28 tickets @   .50

A ten per cent tax was collected on each ticket sold, the whole amount of the tax being turned over.

Check for $264.35 was sent Mr. E. L. Rockmore, the producer, on March 3.

Committee to Call upon President Roosevelt

In accordance with the vote of the Board at the November meeting—that the Chairman of the Board, the Secretary and another member of the Board seek a personal interview with Mr. Roosevelt, President-elect, for the purpose of establishing contact with him on the race question and to arrange with him for a representative delegation to call upon him at the White House to present the colored man's point of view—a telegram was sent on January 4 to Mr. Roosevelt at his New York City address requesting the interview. (It seemed best to wait and get in touch with Mr. Roosevelt in New York City.) On January 13 Mr. Marvin McIntyre, secretary to Mr. Roosevelt, telephoned the Secretary at the National Office acknowledging receipt of the telegram and apologizing for the delay. He said Mr. Roosevelt had been trying to squeeze in time for the interview but had not been able to do so; that Mr. Roosevelt was anxious to talk with the committee and wanted to do so as soon as he returned from the South. Mr. McIntyre asked the Secretary to get in touch with him on Mr. Roosevelt's return in order to arrange the time and place for the appointment.

On February 18 the Secretary telephoned Mr. McIntyre's office and was told that since the request was made there had been several changes in the President's program; that, however, Mr. Roosevelt was anxious to grant the interview and that he would let the Secretary know within a week just what could be done.

On February 22 the following telegram was received from Mr. McIntyre:

"Due to pressure of work regret impossible to arrange requested."

Mr. Harold Ickes, Secretary of the Interior

Upon noting that Mr. Harold Ickes of Chicago, formerly President of the Chicago Branch of the N.A.A.C.P., had been appointed Secretary of the Interior in President Roosevelt's cabinet, the National Office sent Mr. Ickes a telegram of congratulations. Mr. Ickes replied:

I especially appreciate the cordial and friendly telegram received from you under date of February 25. While I am at the head of the Department of the Interior I hope that every citizen, regardless of race or creed, will feel that he is getting a square deal. I shall welcome help and suggestions from you at any time.

Publicity

In addition to the regular weekly releases during the month of February the Publicity Department on February 1, 9, and 15, and on March 1 released special stories to the New York City dailies and press associations on the exclusion of Negroes from "The Green Pastures" in Washington; on the protest against the deportation of Negroes from Industry, Pennsylvania; and on the plea for commutation to life imprisonment of the death sentence of Will Sanders, sixteen-year-old Negro youth of York, South Carolina.

Literature and information was mailed to three correspondents seeking material for college essays and theses on the Negro; and office interviews were granted to three students seeking information and pamphlets for papers to be submitted to their New York University classes.

Our clippings service shows that interest continued unabated in the George Crawford extradition case and in the Association's campaign to have labor conditions on the Mississippi Flood Control project investigated. These two topics received wide mention in the daily press. One of the most popular stories released to the Negro press, judging by its almost universal carriage in the news columns, was the item telling that the Atlanta Branch program for 1933 called for the establishment of a school for voters. An equally popular item was the account of the Association's fight in behalf of Miss Doris Weaver for admission to the practice home management cottage at Ohio University.

As a means of stimulating activity in the branches a mimeographed news sheet containing items telling of the activities of branches in various parts of the country was prepared and sent out on March 1. It is planned to issue this kind of intra-organization publicity about once a month.

The Secretary had an article in the February 25 number of *Friends Intelligencer*, which number was devoted to race relations. The Secretary also spoke during the month over the Radio Station WLWL on the Catholic Interracial Hour on the topic, "Negro Citizenship." This speech was reprinted in the *Interracial Review*, a Catholic monthly published in St. Louis.

The Field Secretary spoke during the month over Radio Station WEVD on the work of the Association, particularly on the Mississippi Flood Control Project.

Walter White, Secretary
March 1933

Report of the Secretary for the Board Meeting of January 1934

Overview

Today we inaugurate a new and, we hope, a more satisfactory method of reporting to the Annual Meeting on the past year's activities. Instead of a long and detailed account of the wide variety of cases, issues, procedures, and the like, the Secretary gives only a terse statement of the highlights of the year's work. Most of you who attend these annual meetings have closely followed the work during the year and are already familiar with most of the cases reported. We attempt, therefore, to spare you the necessity of listening to an over-long account. Full details will be given in the printed annual report which we hope this year to be able to have in your hands by the middle of February or as soon as the auditor shall have been able to make his annual examination of our books.

Despite the fact that 1933 marked the fourth year of the depression; that appeals to the Association more than tripled as the economics clash became more acute, especially along the color line; and in spite of the greatly reduced staff and fund for work; 1933 marked one of the most successful years in the history of the Association. More cases were handled and more success was gained in this struggle than in almost any year since the organization of the N.A.A.C.P. This more frequently than not has meant a seven-day week for executives and not infrequently working days of from twelve to twenty hours. Despite this, however, the staffs, both executive and clerical, have worked faithfully, efficiently, and without complaint. One of the chief duties of the Secretary during the year has been to restrain his associates from working too hard rather than to urge to do more work. Never before has the esprit de corps of the Association been so excellent.

It will be noted in the Treasurer's report that despite the financial situation there was raised during the year for all purposes, $60,257.81, which is only a little more than $6,000 less than the total raised for all purposes ($66,536.65) in 1932. The 1933 income included $34,000 plus general income and $15,000 plus from legacies, the balance being for legal defense, life memberships, the Harlem investigation and for the Scottsboro cases.

Mississippi Flood Control Project

A struggle for nearly two years, beginning with an investigation made by Miss Helen Boardman in July 1931, culminated during 1933 in the passage of the Wagner Resolution for a Senate investigation which in turn led to the signing of an agreement by the Public Works Administration and the War Department that unskilled workers not only on the Flood Control project but on all projects financed by the government in the South will receive forty cents an hour for a thirty-hour week. Some 30,000 Negro workers under this agreement are receiving now a maximum of $12.00 a week for a thirty-hour week in contrast with $8.00 for a working week of from sixty to eighty hours as was previously the case.

The N.R.A.

A considerable portion of the efforts of the Association during 1933, both as an organization and in conjunction with other organizations which pooled their efforts for economic justice in the Joint Committee on National Recovery, have been devoted to the struggle to prevent the victimizing of Negroes under the new deal. Most of you know how disastrous has been the effect in many parts of the country of some of the codes which have resulted in the displacement of Negroes by white workers. The Association has incessantly and in every way possible demanded the appointment of qualified Negroes as members of boards, committees, and commissions having to do with the whole program of National Recovery. It has interested itself in all of the codes which directly or indirectly affected Negro workers such as the cotton textile, laundry, coal mining, contractors, steel, and other codes. It has vigorously and with a fair measure of success protested against discrimination and against instances of violence where Negroes have been victimized. A striking instance of the latter was the driving from his home and pastorate of the Rev. E. D. Hughes of Selma, Alabama, by leading citizens of the town who included a bank president, a prominent manufacturer, the chief of police and the head of the Chamber of Commerce because he refused to endorse a code providing for a wage differential not only in Selma and in Alabama but in the entire country.

The Association has been particularly active in opposing the attempts, some of them by colored people, for Jim Crow homestead subsistence regions, because of the danger of having the federal government establish an official precedent for the separation of Negroes into segregated communities which, despite the best of intentions, will invariably result in inferior conditions.

Work must be done during 1934 in this same direction, especially in seeing that Negroes gain their rightful share of employment upon projects financed by state as well as by the federal government. Activity in the former connection of significance is the passage of bills drafted and supported by the N.A.A.C.P. branches and the National Office by the legislatures of Indiana, Illinois, and New Jersey prohibiting discrimination on account of race or color on projects financed by the state.

Continued efforts have been made against discrimination in employment on Boulder Dam. A detailed investigation was made by Mr. Leland S. Hawkins, President of the San Francisco Branch, at the request of the National Office, and his report is now being acted upon by the Department of the Interior which has promised correction of the gross discrimination against Negroes on this federal-financed project.

Legal Defense

This outstanding example of successful legal defense during 1933 was in the famous George Crawford case. The question of the unconstitutionality exclusion of Negroes from juries in southern states was raised in this case, due chiefly to the vision and ability of Dean Charles H. Houston of Washington, for the first time in the history of American law. The N.A.A.C.P. attorneys contended that a state which violated one section of the federal constitution by illegal exclusion of Negroes from juries should not under the law have the right to appeal to another part of the same constitution for the return of a Negro fugitive for trial, which would be illegal. The late Judge James A. Lowell's decision granting writ of habeas corpus asked by the N.A.A.C.P. lawyers created a nation-wide and world-wide sensation. Since Judge Lowell's decision five southern states have placed Negroes on juries for the first time, and a prominent southern editor has stated to the Association's Secretary that the Crawford case marks the end of the illegal barring of Negroes from juries.

The Circuit Court of Appeals reversed Judge Lowell's decision and the United States Supreme Court denied a review of the Circuit Court of Appeals' decision, but the moral effect of Judge Lowell's decision has been enormous. Incidentally, the *Yale Law Review* will publish this month an article contending that Judge Lowell's decision was correct.

Crawford was returned to Virginia and a trial was held which established a new standard in many respects for such trials. The Association retained to defend Crawford four brilliant young colored attorneys—Messrs. Charles H. Houston, Leon A. Ransom, Edward P. Lovett, and James Tyson. The brilliant defense afforded Crawford by these attorneys has had a most profound effect in Virginia and throughout the country. An entirely new concept of the ability of the Negro lawyer has been created. It was discovered just before going to trial that the defendant had not told the truth about his being in Boston at the time the two murders were committed. This circumstance, however, enhanced the importance of the subsequent developments, for here was a case where a Negro was guilty by his own admission of a murder, of not only one white woman but two, in the South, tried and defended in the South by colored counsel, and saved from the electric chair. The brilliance of the defense brought forth most sincere and almost extravagant expressions of admiration from the judge, the prosecution, and the press. New history, legal and racial, has been made by this case and the effect of it will be felt for many years to come. The State of Virginia, through Governor Pollard and other officials, the press of the State, and citizens both white and colored, joined in remarkable fashion in assuring the absence of mob violence and a fair trial. Although the Court ruled against defense counsel in its motion to quash the indictment and dismiss the petit jury panel because of illegal exclusion of Negroes from the grand and petit juries, it is certain that the way in which the case was handled will result in Negroes being placed on both grand and petit juries throughout the State in [the] future. As a matter of fact, this has already been done in various parts of Virginia.

Among other legal cases of great significance which have been handled by the branches and the National Office are the following:

The Willie Peterson Case in Alabama
The Jesse Hollins Case in Oklahoma
The Beaver County Deportation Cases in Pennsylvania
The Daniel Bush Case in Michigan
The Wilford Hall, Jesse Williams, Tom Carraway Cases in Mississippi
The Claude Peoples and Charles Simpson Cases in North Dakota
The Robert Bell and Grady Swain Cases in Arkansas
The Case of Oscar Gordon and son in Georgia

and many others to tell of which would unduly lengthen this report.

Education

In 1933 the Association began in North Carolina a determined assault upon the gross discrimination in teachers' salaries and in educational opportunities for colored children. It is proceeding upon the theory that the most effective attack upon segregation and Jim Crowism, to which it is irrevocably opposed, is to exhaust every legal recourse to secure absolutely identical accommodations for white and colored pupils in all the states where there are separate schools. In this fashion it is felt that in time the dual educational system of the South will be made so expensive that the states which practice such separation will realize that the dual system is too expensive for continuance.

In North Carolina a suit was brought for a writ of mandamus to compel one of the professional schools of the University of North Carolina to admit a qualified Negro. This writ was denied when a Negro educator, president of a state-supported school for Negroes, refused to give the applicant a letter of clearance, which was required for submission with the application. Denial of the writ on this technicality, however, has stirred North Carolina, both white and colored, to a realization never known before of the extent of the insecurities.

This suit, followed by an attack upon the twenty-two per cent differential between salaries of white and colored teachers, has stirred the state from end to end. A younger, more determined and more militant group of leaders, both white and colored, have been heartened by this struggle and they are rapidly displacing the selfish, more timorous, older leaders. The effect has spread to other states and under the appropriation from the American Fund for Public Service this struggle will be vigorously continued during 1934.

Special mention must be made of the brilliant work done by William H. Hastie of Washington, young colored attorney recently appointed assistant to the Solicitor of the Department of the Interior; Messrs. Cecil McCoy and Conrad O. Pearson, colored attorneys of Durham; and others.

Developments in these cases are all the more significant in that they marked during 1933 the emergence of a fine group of young lawyers, both white and colored, who have given unselfishly and without stint of their energies to the Association. Among those who should be especially mentioned are Charles H. Houston, chief counsel in the George Crawford case and active also in the Willie Peterson and other cases as well as in the general program of the Association; Willliam H. Hastie; Messrs. Leon A. Ransom, Edward P. Lovett, James G. Tyson of Washington, and Louis L. Redding of Wilmington, Delaware, who on his own initiative made a personal investigation of the Princess Anne, Maryland, lynching; Homer S. Brown, President of the Pittsburgh Branch; Professor Karl Llewellyn of the Columbia University Law School who aided in drafting the Costigan-Wagner Anti-Lynching Bill; Abram Sepenuk, a young white attorney of New Jersey who had ably and successfully handled without cost to the Association a number of cases in New Jersey; Harry E. Davis of Cleveland, member of the Association's Board of Directors; Charles W. White and Claybourne George of Cleveland; Irvin C. Mollison of Chicago.

Lynching

One of the most discouraging aspects of the Association's work in 1933 was the alarming increase in lynchings, twenty-eight having occurred as against ten in

1932. In the printed annual report will be given a detailed account of the Association's activities in regard to lynching including investigations made of the lynching of Norris Dendy of Clinton, S.C., and of George Armwood of Princess Anne, Md., as well as of other mob murders.

Costigan-Wagner Anti-Lynching Bill

When it was seen that state action, as in California with the outrageous statement of Governor Rolfe and on the eastern shore of Maryland, was not enough to suppress mob action, the National Office secured the cooperation of the National Legal Committee, especially Mr. Herbert K. Stockton and Mr. Arthur B. Spingarn aided by Professor Karl Llewellyn of the Columbia University Law School and others, in drafting a bill to make lynching a federal offense. Senators Edward P. Costigan of Colorado and Robert F. Wagner of New York introduced the bill in the Senate (S.1978) on January 4, 1934. The bill will shortly be introduced in the House, efforts being made to secure a southerner to introduce it in order to lessen the sectional issue which played so large a part in the defeat of the Dyer Anti-Lynching Bill. In order to remove as far as possible also the racial angle, the Association has asked and secured the unstinted cooperation of other organizations including the American Civil Liberties Union, the Public Affairs Committee of the Y.M.C.A., the Interracial Commission, the Women's International League for Peace and Freedom, the Federal Council of Churches, and other groups. A determined effort will be made to secure enactment of this bill into law.

The Association urged President Roosevelt to utter a public pronouncement against lynching and others made similar requests, which resulted in the most straightforward denunciation of lynching ever uttered by a President, delivered in the President's address on December 6 to the Federal Council of Churches. The Association also asked the President to include reference to lynching and to urge specific legislation against it in his address to the Congress. This also was done.

It is the general feeling in Washington that the Costigan-Wagner Bill will have at least the quiet support of the White House and perhaps its open advocacy.

The Writers' League against Lynching

To aid in the campaign against lynching and the stirring of public opinion against the rising tide of mob violence, the Association organized in November the Writers' League Against Lynching. Some of the most distinguished writers in America, including Sinclair Lewis, Fannie Hurst, Edna Ferber, Inez Haynes Irwin, Louis Bromfield, Harry Henson, Suzanne LaFollette, and many others. Though this will be an independent organization it is working in close cooperation with the N.A.A.C.P. in its opposition to lynching. The headquarters of the League are in the office of the N.A.A.C.P.

Harlem Hospital Committee

A committee numbering among its members some of the most distinguished medical authorities of America has at the invitation of the Association made a detailed study of the difficulties in Harlem Hospital, the only tax-supported institution in the country which has to so large an extent a mixed staff. The inquiry was broadened to include the whole field of medical opportunity for Negro doctors and nurses.

The committee's report of more than 80,000 words establishes a new yardstick in the matter of opportunity for service in tax-supported hospitals and in medical schools which, because of the distinction of the committee making the report, is of nation-wide significance. Two of the recommendations which will have most effect are for the ending of discrimination against Negroes in medical schools and of denial of opportunity to serve on the staffs of tax-supported hospitals throughout the country.

The Association hopes to be able to get sufficient funds to print the report in full for widespread distribution.

Cooperation

One of the most significant high points of the year has been the magnificent cooperation given the Association by other organizations, especially by the Young Women's Christian Association through the Woman's Press, by the Consumers League, the American Civil Liberties Union, the Federal Council of Churches, the Interracial Commission, the Young Men's Christian Association, and various other organizations and individuals. Many of the organizations mentioned and others are cooperating in the plans for the Twenty-fifth Anniversary of the Association in 1934.

Walter F. White, Secretary
January 8, 1934

Report of the Secretary for the
Board Meeting of February 1936

The Van Nuys Resolution

Following a number of conferences in Washington with Senator Costigan, Senator Frederick F. Van Nuys, and others, a new strategy with regard to getting a federal anti-lynching law passed by the present session of Congress has been decided upon:

On January 6 Senator Van Nuys, who was chairman of the subcommittee which conducted the hearings on the Costigan-Wagner Bill last spring and who is very friendly toward the measure, introduced a resolution providing for a Senate investigation of the lynchings which occurred in 1935 after the filibuster against the Costigan-Wagner Bill.

The investigation is based upon the statement made during the filibuster against the Costigan-Wagner Bill that federal legislation is unnecessary as the states can and will prevent lynchings and punish lynchers and upon the further fact that following the filibuster fourteen known lynchings took place, in 1935. It is proposed to focus attention on the fallacy of the statement made by the filibusterers and utilize this sentiment for passage of the Costigan-Wagner Bill.

The resolution is still in committee but is expected to be reported favorably any moment. Senator Van Nuys' office advises that the report has been delayed due to the fact that it has not been possible to secure a quorum of the Judiciary Committee.

The Association's branches and organizations cooperating on the Costigan-Wagner Bill have been urged to communicate with Senator Henry F. Ashurst, chairman of the Senate Committee on the Judiciary, urging a favorable and speedy report on the Van Nuys resolution.

Word has come to the National Office that there is some reluctance on the part of some members of the Senate to appropriate sufficient money to make thorough investigation of the fourteen lynchings, and pressure is being brought by the National Office and by the branches and cooperating organizations, pointing out that Congress has appropriated large sums for other investigations and should not be reluctant to appropriate money for the investigation of lynching.

It is expected that among those to be subpoenaed by the Senate Committee will be County Attorney O. P. Moore of Colorado County, Texas, who stated he would take no action with regard to the lynching of two boys, fifteen and sixteen years old, because the lynchings were "the expression of the will of the people"; also Governor J. C. B. Ehringhaus and Solicitor Bickett of North Carolina, who were unable to effect arrests of the lynchers of Goven Ward, an insane man, even after the N.A.A.C.P. had placed in their hands the names of nine of the lynchers, with evidence against each of them.

The Secretary has conferred, in Washington, with Dr. Will W. Alexander and Mr. Arthur Raper of the Interracial Commission which made investigations of most of the lynchings of 1935. Mr. Raper is cooperating in the preparation of background material for the use of the Senate Committee and in the compilation of the witnesses to be subpoenaed to testify.

The National Office has asked the branches in the vicinity of each of the lynchings to gather and send to the National Office as much specific information as they can secure; and it has also asked the cooperating organizations to do the same.

Negotiations are now under way by means of which it is hoped that at least a part of the hearings will be broadcast, particularly the testimony of prominent witnesses like Governor Ehringhaus of North Carolina.

Senator Borah and Anti-Lynching Legislation

In accordance with the vote of the Board at its December meeting, the National Office arranged for the picketing of a mass meeting at which Senator William E. Borah spoke on January 28, in Brooklyn, New York City.

When Senator Borah arrived for this meeting, which marked the opening of his campaign for nomination for President of the United States, he was greeted by fifty pickets carrying signs criticizing his stand on the Costigan-Wagner Anti-Lynching Bill. (Correspondence which the National Office has had with Senator Borah on this matter was quoted in the Secretary's report for the December meeting of the Board.)

Although the weather on the night of January 28 was below-freezing, with a biting wind, the pickets, consisting of members of the New York Branch and the Brooklyn Junior Branch of the N.A.A.C.P., the Youth Council of the Abyssinian Baptist Church in New York City and members of the Holy Trinity Baptist Church of Brooklyn, remained in front of Kismet Temple for an hour or more awaiting Mr. Borah's arrival. They also distributed some 2,500 of the enclosed leaflet addressed to Senator Borah.

Mr. Borah devoted a considerable portion of his speech to a defense of his stand against the Costigan-Wagner Bill. He was, however, considerably less assured in his stand in his letter to the Association's Secretary of November 23. At the Brooklyn meeting Senator Borah confined himself to a statement that if someone presented him with a bill which he believed to be constitutional he would support it and, in the face of vigorous heckling asked, "Is William E. Borah the only culprit? Why don't you take your questions to Cleveland and Philadelphia and get an answer there?"

Among those who have made direct inquiry of Senator Borah as to his determined stand on the unconstitutionality of any federal anti-lynching law is Professor Karl N. Llewellyn, member of the Association's National Legal committee. In his letter of December 12 Professor Llewellyn said:

> There is one point on which I hope you will find time to enlighten me. It has to do with a lawyer-legislator's responsibility on points of constitutionality . . . The problem becomes pressing to me, Sir, because of your definite views on the Costigan-Wagner Anti-Lynching Bill . . . If lawyers as honest and able as Wagner and Costigan feel the bill to be sound not only on policy but on constitutionality, should the discussion not proceed on the basis of the policy considerations involved, leaving the admitted doubt on constitutionality to be settled by the constitutional arbiter, the Supreme Court?

Following the picketing of the Brooklyn Mass Meeting, the National Office wrote Senator Borah pointing out that his speech in its references to anti-lynching legislation was wholly inadequate and also asking that the Senator reply to the Association's letter of November 25 in which it was asked that he state, if he honestly believed the federal government can act against lynching only through a constitutional amendment, why in the twenty-nine years he has been a member of the Senate he has never introduced such a constitutional amendment; although during that period 1,356 lynchings have taken place. Senator Borah has not replied to this letter. In his letter the Secretary made it clear that opposition to Senator Borah's stand should not in any way be considered as approval by the N.A.A.C.P. of reactionary Republicans, candidates of elements.

Conference with President Roosevelt

On January 2 the Secretary held a conference with President Roosevelt, at the White House. The appointment for the Secretary was arranged in answer to a request made on November 13, following the lynching of two boys in Texas, that the President received a small delegation to discuss with him the lynching situation and the general plight of the Negro.

The Secretary left with the President a memorandum on issues which are of great importance and concern to American Negroes—Lynching; Discrimination in Relief and Public Works; the Post Office and Civil Service; White Primaries; Army and Navy; [and the] Department of Justice.

The President was exceedingly cordial but equally non-committal. He seemed to favor a Senate investigation of the lynchings of 1935 after the filibuster as provided in the Van Nuys resolution. He requested to talk with Attorney General Homer N. Cummings regarding a bill to authorize the Department of Justice to investigate all cases of improper interference with the courts.

The Secretary did confer with the Attorney General, on January 15, after having discussed the proposed bill with the Chairman of the Association's Legal Committee and with other executives of the Association. It was the consensus of opinion, however, that no particular advantage would be gained through such a measure, nor would it be wise for the Association to sponsor it. This decision has been transmitted to the President, with the statement that the Association preferred to concentrate its efforts in the Van Nuys resolution and the Costigan-Wagner Bill.

Governor Eugene Talmadge (Georgia)

Just prior to the convening of the Southern Committee to Uphold the Constitution at Macon, Georgia, on January 29, the National Office wired Governor Eugene Talmadge asking that he state publicly his position on certain points; the telegram was addressed jointly to Mr. Talmadge and to John Henry Kirby, permanent chairman of the convention, and stated:

> Disfranchisement, gross discrimination against Negro citizens in apportionment of public moneys for education, violation of constitutional guarantees against illegal search and seizure and suppression of right of free speech, free assembly, and free press, lynching, mob violence,

and other denials of constitutional rights, are the rule and not the exception so far as eight million Negroes are concerned and many white Americans. Unless the Southern Committee to Uphold the Constitution takes an unequivocal stand on behalf of all these constitutional rights and vigorously works to enforce these constitutional guarantees, intelligent Americans of all races will rightly consider the Southern Committee to Uphold the Constitution a laughing stock.

No reply to this telegram has been received, but it is interesting to note that newspapers of January 30 in reporting the meeting stated that white-haired Thomas Dixon of South Carolina, who wrote "The Klansman," hit at Walter White, secretary of the National Association for the Advancement of Colored People, who had wired the convention demanding a stand for all individual rights guaranteed in the Constitution. Mr. Dixon is quoted as saying:

We do not lower ourselves to reply to any such organization because today it is the rottenest Communist organization in America. With its lobby in Washington it suggested the rotten Costigan-Wagner anti-lynching bill to bring back force law in the South.

American Federation of Labor

On January 17 the National Office sent a telegram to William Green, President of the American Federation of Labor, meeting in convention at Miami, Florida, urging that the A.F. of L. support a constitutional amendment providing for the safeguard of human rights and liberties. The telegram was sent after it had been noted in the press that the executive council of the A.F. of L. had decided to ask [for] an amendment to the federal constitution giving Congress the power to enact legislation establishing minimum wages and maximum working hours. Also, the National Office wired President John L. Lewis of the United Mine Workers asking that his organization support the amendment suggested by the N.A.A.C.P. Other labor groups including the International Ladies' Garment Workers Union, the Amalgamated Clothing Workers, and The Brotherhood of Sleeping Car Porters, were asked to join in the Association's request.

On January 21 President Green replied:

I will give the suggestion you make in your telegram careful thought and consideration.

The Executive Council has not yet decided upon the character and form of the constitutional amendment which would be acceptable to Labor. As you well know, the consideration of such an important subject involves a careful analysis of the scope, meaning and interpretation which might be placed upon any constitutional amendment drafted and favored by the American Federation of Labor.

Scottsboro Defense Committee

In the absence of the Special Counsel from the city, the Assistant Secretary has been attending the meetings of the Scottsboro Defense Committee, representing the N.A.A.C.P.

Since the special meeting of the Board on January 18, when it was voted that the N.A.A.C.P. borrow from the Amalgamated Bank $1,000 of the $3,000 necessary to place sufficient funds in the hands of Mr. Liebowitz to assure his leaving for Alabama on January 20, two meetings of the Scottsboro Defense Committee have been held, one on January 23 and the other on January 24.

The committee was hurriedly summoned together on January 23 upon receipt of a rumor that someone was planning to have the boys plead guilty and accept a prison sentence. By long distance telephone to Mr. Watts in Alabama this rumor was thoroughly discredited, and the committee issued a statement on the conviction of Haywood Patterson and the sentencing of Patterson to seventy-five years in the penitentiary, calling it a "challenge to the conscience of the nation" and asking financial support.

The meeting of January 24 was another hasty assembling of the members of the committee on receipt of the news of the shooting of Ozie Powell, one of the defendants, by the sheriff. Another statement was issued by the committee.

On Sunday, January 26, the Assistant Secretary was one of the speakers at a mass meeting in New York City at which $515.00 was raised for the Scottsboro Defense Fund. On the same date N.A.A.C.P. branches in Detroit; Pittsburgh; Newark, New Jersey; and New Orleans held joint mass meetings with representatives of the other groups in the Scottsboro Defense Committee.

The Assistant Secretary also spoke at a Scottsboro mass meeting in Corona, New York, on January 31, and at still another in Harlem, New York City, on February 4.

The Field Secretary has been conferring with a Brooklyn group which is planning a mass meeting there around February 20.

The Scottsboro Defense Committee has requested the National Office of the N.A.A.C.P., because of its facilities, to act as a clearing house for the publicity on these cases, in the committee's names; and news releases have been going to the newspapers from this office in the name of the committee. The Assistant Secretary has also collaborated on the writing of a comprehensive pamphlet on the Scottsboro Cases, for wide distribution.

On January 31 the Secretary attended a meeting of the Scottsboro Defense Committee to decide upon sending Dr. Allen Knight Chalmers, Chairman of the Committee, to Alabama, to help organize an impartial committee to investigate and ascertain the truth regarding the shooting of Ozie Powell. It was decided that Dr. Chalmers should go and that preferably the committee should be made up as largely as possible of distinguished Alabamans, though with some membership from outside the state. Dr. Chalmers' departure, however, has been held up because of engagements he could not break and because of communications from certain individuals in Alabama asking for a conference with a committee of the Scottsboro

Defense Committee to consider the possible procedure in the future handling of the cases, in which Alabamans would assume a larger responsibility for the defense.

Brown, Ellington, and Shields (Kemper County, Miss.)

Argument on the appeal of Brown, Ellington, and Shields to the United States Supreme Court was made on January 10 by Earl Brewer, Esq., of Jackson, Miss., the counsel engaged for the three sharecroppers accused of murdering a white tenant farmer in Kemper County, Mississippi, in 1934.

Observers in the courtroom have written the Association that Mr. Brewer made a very effective appeal and that the members of the Supreme Court were visibly shocked at the story of the way the confessions were extorted from the three men. The so-called confessions are the only evidence against them

The decision of the Supreme Court has not been handed down at this date.

Mr. Brewer has written that the entire balance now due him is $69.86, which he asks that we send at our earliest convenience. Of course, if the cases are remanded for a new trial there will be much additional expense.

Amendment to the Lindbergh Kidnapping Law

The National Office has drafted an amendment to the Lindbergh Kidnapping Law, including specifically kidnapping for purposes of injuring or killing the victims as well as for ransom and reward.

Introduction of the amendment was held at the suggestion of Mr. William F. Illig and others, pending decision of the United States Supreme Court in the case of Arthur Gooch who, with a companion, kidnapped two officers in Texas and transported them into Oklahoma to prevent the officers' arresting Gooch and his companion. Gooch appealed the death sentence to the United States Supreme Court on the ground that this was not a proper use of the Lindbergh law since no question of monetary reward was involved. The United States Supreme Court on February 3 ruled unanimously, Mr. Justice McReynolds delivered the opinion of the court, that there was no impropriety in the conviction of Gooch, and his death sentence was affirmed.

The Association's Legal Committee and the Special Counsel are studying the decision, and it appears it will be desirable to introduce the amendment, but specific action is being held up pending completion of study of the decision.

On February 4 the National Office wired the Attorney General and also President Roosevelt, in light of the decision in the Arthur Gooch case, urging that the Department of Justice proceed against the kidnappers of Claude Neal who, in 1934, was seized in Alabama and transported across the state line to Marianna, Florida, where he was lynched.

University of Maryland Case

On January 15 the Maryland Court of Appeals affirmed the decision of the trial court that Donald Gaines Murray was entitled to mandamus to compel his admission to the School of Law of the University of Maryland. The decision was unanimous and remarkably frank, considering the various currents of public opinion in Maryland. This decision is a land-mark for all future attacks on discrimination in professional education. The National Office distributed mimeographed copies of the decision to the Negro press and several papers have commented editorially on it.

University of Missouri

On January 24 suit was filed by Lloyd Gaines of St. Louis, Missouri, to compel the registrar of the University of Missouri to act on his application for admission to the School of Law.

On the legal side, this case is made easy by the decision in the University of Maryland case; but on the other hand, the situation is more difficult to handle because Columbia, Missouri, where the University is located, is a small town, whereas the School of Law for the University of Maryland is in Baltimore. Besides, Baltimore has never had a race riot, whereas an innocent Negro was lynched in Columbia about twelve years ago, with students from the University of Missouri taking a leading part. The National Office is now at work trying to build up a favorable sentiment and respect for law among the university constituency in Missouri.

"Medical Opportunities for Negroes"

The proof of the manuscript of "Medical Opportunities for Negroes" (Harlem Hospital Report) has been corrected and returned to Scribner's. This will be published in the spring.

Christmas Seals

The total received to date for Christmas seals is $1,867.37.

Governor Lehman's Offer

Govenor Herbert H. Lehman has recently renewed his generous offer to give $1,000, a year for three years providing the Association can secure four similar contributions. In his letter of January 9, Governor Lehman says:

> Although I am simply swamped with requests and find the greatest
> difficulty in caring for pledges already made, I am so much interested

in the work of the Association that providing you can secure four similar contributions, I shall be glad to renew my previous contribution to the Association of $1,000 a year for three years. My contribution, however, must be entirely contingent upon your receiving four similar contributions for the same period of time.

The National Office is making strenuous efforts to meet Governor Lehman's offer. Suggestions from members of the Board as to persons who might be approached would be deeply appreciated.

National Office Lease

The lease on the National Office has been renewed for two years at a rental of $2,200 per year. The renewal of the lease includes the re-decorating of the offices.

Miss Nannie H. Burroughs, one of the Association's Vice-Presidents, had offered to raise funds and be responsible for the re-decorating, but since the landlord has been induced to do this, the National Office has written Miss Burroughs asking what her plans are now, since she had also in mind some rearrangement of the offices.

N.A.A.C.P. Birthday Celebration

The Special Assistant to the Secretary is planning a country-wide celebration of the Association's Birthday which falls on February 12. Branches have been asked to arrange a celebration to fall on any date during the month of February, the form of the celebration—dinner or dance, etc.—to be left to the decision of the branch. To date forty (40) branches have responded. The real purpose of the celebration is to raise funds to help wipe out the Association's end-of-the-year deficit of $7,000.

Monthly Mass Meetings

With the Annual Mass Meeting of the Association held on Sunday, January 5, a series of monthly mass meetings in New York City was instituted, to be held under the joint auspices of the National Office and the New York Branch. The chief speaker at the annual mass meeting was Angelo Herndon, who spoke on the Scottsboro Cases. The Secretary spoke on the Association's work.

The second meeting in this series was held on Sunday, February 2 at the Mother A.M.E. Zion Church, and the principal speaker was Mr. Victor Ridder, W.P.A. Administrator for New York City. Another speaker was Mr. Howard Kester, prime mover in the Southern Tenant Farmer's Union. The Assistant Secretary represented the National Office in this program.

The third meeting will be held on Sunday, March 8, when the speakers will be Mr. Oswald Garrison Villard and Mr. James Marshall. The general theme for this meeting will be the school conditions in Harlem. The Special Counsel will talk on the Association's legal work.

Publicity

During January the Association received a great deal of publicity on (1) the winning of the University of Maryland cases; (2) the questioning and picketing of Senator William E. Borah on his stand on the anti-lynching bill.

Walter White, Secretary
February 6, 1936

Report of the Secretary for the Board Meeting of August 1940

Annual Conference

The Association's Thirty-first Annual Conference was held at Philadelphia, Pennsylvania, June 18–23. There were in attendance four hundred delegates from thirty-three states and the District of Columbia, representing the Association's Senior Branches. Also, Youth Councils and College Chapters were well represented.

Delegates showed a keen interest in the various topics discussed at the business sessions, as many as time allowed taking part in the discussions.

The keynote speech of the Conference was delivered by the Association's President, Mr. Arthur B. Spingarn, at the opening session on Tuesday evening, June 18. Mr. Spingarn followed Mr. John L. Lewis, Chairman of the Congress of Industrial Organizations. Other speakers at the evening sessions were: Mr. Earl B. Dickerson, Chicago, Illinois; Dr. Russell L. Cecil, New York City, who made the presentation of the Spingarn Medal; Mr. Herbert E. Millen, Philadelphia; Dean William H. Hastie, chairman of the Association's National Legal Committee; Mr. Aubrey Williams, Administrator of the National Youth Administration; and the Assistant Secretary. On Sunday afternoon the speakers were Hon. Fiorello H. La Guardia, Mayor of the City of New York; and the Association's Secretary.

Spingarn Medal Night

On Wednesday evening, June 19, Dr. Russell L. Cecil presented to Mrs. Louis T. Wright, in the absence of Dr. Wright, the twenty-fifth Spingarn Medal. Dr. Cecil took for his subject, "Public Health and Medical Service." In accepting the Medal Mrs. Wright read a statement which had been prepared by Dr. Wright, in which he said: "To be a Spingarn Medalist puts one in excellent company. My predecessors in this respect comprise a group of men and women of the best caliber. They have made distinguished records for themselves in their chosen professions and have used their best energies to help in the advancement of their race. . . . May I thank everyone concerned for the trust they have placed in me and the honor they have done me by awarding me the Spingarn Medal, which will prove to be an inspiration for greater service."

Sunday Afternoon

The closing session of the Conference was held on Sunday afternoon, June 23, at the Metropolitan Opera House, with a seating capacity of 5,000. The hall was well filled with those who had come to hear Mayor La Guardia and the Association's Secretary. In his speech Mayor La Guardia stressed the need of national unity which "we can bring about through the process of democracy."

Party Platform

During the Conference the N.A.A.C.P. presented to the Platform Committee of the National Republican Convention meeting in Philadelphia suggested planks touching upon problems affecting the Negro. These planks urged inclusion of the Negro in the armed services; passage of the federal anti-lynching bill; legislation abolishing the poll tax and white primaries; abolition of the color line in employment in all tax-financed projects; equitable distribution of federal funds to states for education, housing, health, relief, farm aid, etc.; extension of social security to agricultural, domestic and casual labor; abolition of the color line in federal government posts; and enforcement of civil rights laws in all sections of the United States.

The Conference voted to present identical planks to the Democratic National Convention. (The presentation was made to the Democratic National Convention meeting at Chicago, on July 12, by a committee headed by the Secretary, the other members being Mr. Roscoe Dunjee, member of the National Board of Directors; Mr. Irvin C. Mollinson, member of the National Legal Committee; and Prof. W. Robert Ming of the Howard University Law School.)

Resolutions

Members of the Board have received copies of the resolutions adopted at the Conference. The resolutions expressed the stand of the N.A.A.C.P. regarding: National Defense; Mob Violence; Political Action; Governmental Appointments; Education; Public Health and Medical Services; Labor Unions; Enforcement of Civil Rights; Discrimination in the W.P.A.; Housing; Wages and Labor; Youth Needs; Textbooks; Sharecroppers and Tenant Farmers; and extended sympathy of the Association to the peoples of Norway, Denmark, France, Holland, Belgium, Finland, Estonia, Lithuania, and Latvia, "who today are being subjugated by the totalitarian governments of the world; and to the Ethiopians, Czecho-Slovakians, and Poles who have been enslaved in the labor armies of Germany and Italy whose governments are functioning on the basis of a master race."

Merit Scrolls

At the Sunday afternoon meeting Merit Scrolls for outstanding work done through N.A.A.C.P. were presented by President Arthur B. Spingarn to: Dr. Leon A. Hansom, Washington, D.C.; Mrs. Sarah Merriwether Nutter, Charleston, West Virginia; Mrs. Zella M. Taylor, Los Angeles, California; Mr. George C. Gordon, Springfield, Massachusetts; Rev. E. C. Estell, Dallas, Texas; and Mr. Withas M. Gayle, Newark, New Jersey. All of the recipients, with the exception of Mrs. Taylor, were present to receive their scrolls in person.

Life Membership Medals

Also [at the] Sunday afternoon meeting Life Membership Medals were presented to: Miss Marian Anderson, Philadelphia; Mrs. Ellen Ford Brooks, Swiftwater, Pennsylvania; and Mr. Delvin J. Johnson, Cleveland, Ohio. Miss Anderson's Medal was received by her sister, Miss Alyce Anderson; Mrs. Brooks was present; while Mr. Johnson's Medal was sent to him by mail.

Youth Section

The Fifth Annual Meeting of the Youth Section of the Annual Conference drew an attendance of 135 registered delegates and twenty-five registered observers. The delegates were representative of twenty-two states and thirty-five cities, which gave an excellent cross-section of the Association's Youth work.

Republican and Democratic Platforms on the Negro

Each of the major political parties included in its platform a plank on the Negro dealing with some of the points presented to the platform committees by the N.A.A.C.P.

The Republican plank, adopted at Philadelphia, reads:

> We pledge that our American citizens of Negro descent shall be given a square deal in the economic and political life of this nation. Discrimination in the civil service, the Army and Navy and all other branches of the government must cease. To enjoy the full benefits of life, liberty, and pursuit of happiness universal suffrage must be made effective for the Negro citizen. Mob violence shocks the conscience of the nation and legislation to curb this evil should be enacted.

The Democratic plank, adopted at Chicago, reads:

> Our Negro citizens have participated actively in the economic and social advances launched by this Administration, including fair labor stan-

dards, social security benefits, health protection, work relief projects, decent housing, aid to education, and the rehabilitation of low-income farm families. We have aided more than half a million Negro youths in vocational training education and employment.

We shall continue to strive for complete legislative safeguards against discrimination in government services and benefits, and in the national defense forces. We pledge to uphold due process and the equal protection of the laws for every citizen, regardless of race, creed, or color.

Mob Violence and Lynching at Brownsville, Tennessee

One of the most flagrant cases of violation of the rights of Negro citizens anywhere in the United States has occurred at Brownsville, Tennessee. The outrages here began on June 3 when Mr. J. Emmett Ballard, a colored attorney, was prevented from arguing a case in the local courthouse and run out of town. Mr. Ballard had gone to Brownsville to argue a case for his client, Solomon Bailey, who had been charged with felonious assault upon a white man.

Without any warning a mob of whites entered the courtroom, threatened Mr. Ballard, and attempted to do him bodily harm, being restrained only by the judge hearing the case. The mob finally drove him out of the courtroom and he was escorted by the sheriff to the city limits with the mob at his heels.

It was believed that not only did the whites object to having a Negro lawyer appear in the courthouse, this being the first time for such an occurrence, but also that the recent decision of Negroes of Brownsville to make a strong fight for the ballot had incensed the whites. This latter belief was proved true when on Sunday morning, June 16, Elisha Davis was aroused from sleep by a mob of whites and told to prepare to leave home. He was hustled into an automobile and carried to the "river bottom" six miles away. Here he was questioned about the purpose of the N.A.A.C.P., a branch of which had been organized in Brownsville in July, 1939. He was also told to name the members of the organization in Brownsville in July 1939. Davis told members of the mob that one of the purposes of the N.A.A.C.P. was to urge Negro citizens to "vote if we want to and not to vote if we don't want to and make better citizens." When he was threatened with death unless he told the names of all those who intended to vote, he gave the names of several persons whom the mob knew of. He was then taken to the edge of the town and told never to return on pain of death. He walked eight or nine miles and finally arrived at Jackson, Tennessee, where he is still staying for safety.

On June 22 the body of Elbert Williams was found in the Hatchis river swamp. Williams disappeared from his home on June 20 after he had helped to organize Negro citizens of Brownsville in a "register-and-vote" drive preparatory to the 1940 Presidential election. Immediately after the lynching a reign of terror was instituted in which a number of other Negroes were run out of Brownsville.

Among those forced to leave Brownsville was the Reverend Buster Walker who appeared before the Association's Thirty-first Annual Conference in Philadelphia and gave a vivid account of the treatment Negroes in Brownsville had received.

The Association's Secretary spent three days in Tennessee making an investigation of the outrages perpetrated upon colored citizens of Brownsville, and immediately thereafter the National Office placed in the hands of President Roosevelt and the Department of Justice the Secretary's report which listed the names of leaders of the mob. These included two bank officials, several police officers, a state highway commissioner, and several merchants. The report was also sent to United States District Attorney McClananhan at Memphis, Tennessee.

On July 10 Assistant Attorney General O. John Rogge wrote the National Office:

> Reference is made to your letter to me dated July 1, 1940, and your letter of the same date to the President, which has been forwarded from the White House.
>
> You will be glad to know that the Federal Bureau of Investigation has been requested to make a thorough investigation of violations of civil liberties of Negroes in Brownsville, Tennessee.

Accompanied by Dean William H. Hastie, Chairman of the Association's National Legal Committee; and Dr. Leon A. Ransom, member of the National Legal Committee; the Reverend Buster Walker conferred with the Department of Justice at Washington, and promise was made to institute a full investigation and to prosecute the offenders if the facts warranted. Dean Hastie is keeping a day by day check on whether or not the Department means to live up to its promise.

Following the Reverend Buster Walker's speech at the Philadelphia Conference, the delegates and visitors present contributed $156.00 toward his expenses during his enforced absence from Brownsville, his home for the past fifty-five years.

On July 8 the National Office of the NA.A.C.P. made a nationwide appeal for funds to aid Elisha Davis now in Jackson, Tennessee, away from his wife and seven children (Check for $25.00 was sent to Mr. Davis on July 22.)

Lynching

The lynching of Elbert Williams at Brownsville, Tennessee, is the only lynching officially recorded by the Association since the last report to the Board, though two or three reported cases are being investigated.

Because Tuskegee Institute reported that during the first six months of 1940 there had been no lynchings, the National Office, on July 3, sent the following telegram to Dr. F. D. Patterson, President of Tuskegee.

> We are inexpressibly shocked by Tuskegee's statement that no lynchings occurred during the first six months of 1940. On March 2 Sarah Rawls and Benton Ford were flogged to death by a mob at Atlanta, Georgia. Five days later Ike Gaston was beaten to death by a mob in the same city. On June 22 Elbert Williams, Negro, was lynched at Brownsville, Tennessee, for attempting to exercise his constitutional rights to register in order to vote in the 1940 Presidential election. Such inaccurate statements by Tuskegee Institute do irreparable harm by causing public vig-

ilance against mob murder to relax and by giving enemies of the Anti-Lynching Bill ammunition for sabotage of such legislation.

On July 13 Dr. Patterson acknowledged the telegram saying:

I have given this matter quite a bit of thought and have discussed it several times with our own Department of Research and Records. I feel that the matter has reached the point where, for many reasons, it is desirable that those agencies making reports get together in an effort to make a clean-cut statement as to what properly constitutes a lynching.

The National Office has expressed agreement that these organizations should get together and has asked Dr. Patterson what date in September for such a meeting would best suit his convenience.

The Anti-Lynching Bill

In transmitting to President Roosevelt the Secretary's report on his investigation of the Brownsville, Tennessee, situation, the National Office wrote the President urging that he "publicly and uncompromisingly insist on action by the Senate on the Anti-Lynching Bill." This request was made of the President mainly because Senator Alben W. Barkley, Majority Leader of the Senate, had written the National Office that because he did not believe cloture could be invoked on the Anti-Lynching Bill he did not propose to make any effort to get the bill to a vote.

At the Democratic National Convention in Chicago Senator Barkley assured the Negro delegates that "the Anti-Lynching Bill will be voted upon before Congress adjourns." On July 23 the National Office wrote Senator Barkley expressing gratification of the colored people of the country at this statement and asking to be advised of the approximate date when the bill will be called before the Senate for debate and vote.

Chicago Exposition

The N.A.A.C.P. has an exhibit booth as one of the features of the American Exposition which opened on July 4 in Chicago, to run until September 4. The booth contains panels illustrating the work of the Association and also displays and information about *The Crisis*. Literature is passed out to those interested.

Federal Housing Authority Discrimination

Information has come to the National Office that in a real estate development scheme in Dover, Massachusetts, the F.H.A. has proposed a "protective covenant," reading:

No person of any race other than the———shall use or occupy any building or any lot, except that this covenant shall not prevent occupancy by domestic servants of a different race domiciled with an owner or tenant.

The National Office has written to F.H.A. Administrator Stuart McDonald condemning this policy on the part of the F.H.A. and pointing out that "this type of racial discrimination and segregation is not only unreasonable and unjust but is also unlawful use of federal funds." The Association's letter further insisted that "the Federal Housing Administration in Washington take a firm stand and issue specific instructions to all local F.H.A. units that there shall be no discrimination or segregation, either spoken or approved, by the Federal Housing Administration."

Negroes in the Armed Forces

The National Office has written to Secretary of War Henry L. Stimson and to the Secretary of the Navy Frank Knox urging them to take the steps necessary to prevent any discrimination against Negroes in the new defense program and to remove the old types of discrimination now existing in the armed forces, to the end that Negroes will be integrated into the armed forces without discrimination because of race or color.

The Ku Klux Klan

Request has been made of Chairman of the House Committee on Un-American Activities, Congressman Martin L. Dies, to investigate the activities of the Ku Klux Klan, the request being based upon the proposed joint meeting of the Ku Klux Klan and the German-American Bund at Andover, New Jersey, on August 18. This is but one of many requests to Congressman Dies over a long period for investigation of the Klan. In view of the statement by Congressman Dies that he was investigating the German-American Bund, the N.A.A.C.P. charged that the proposed merger demonstrated the similarity of the program of the two groups.

Norfolk, Virginia, Teachers' Salary Case

As soon as the mandate in the Alston Case (reported at the July meeting of the Board) was received by the local federal court in Norfolk, N.A.A.C.P. attorneys applied for an early hearing on the merits. The School Board of the City of Norfolk has notified the N.A.A.C.P. that it plans to apply to the United States Supreme Court for certiorari. The Association's attorneys are insisting that unless a bond be posted by the City of Norfolk to stay execution of the mandate the case be immediately set for hearing on the merits.

Wilmington, Ohio, School Segregation Case

Attorneys Theodore Berry and William A. McClain of Cincinnati, assisted by Mr. Hubert T. Delany and the Special Counsel (Mr. Marshall) on the brief, handled for the Association a case of school segregation in Wilmington, Ohio. The case involved the establishment of a segregated school. The opinion of the State Supreme Court held that the question of segregation by the school board had not been established by the facts in the record. The decision was based entirely upon the narrow ground that the burden was upon the Negro plaintiff to clearly establish segregation. By so doing the court avoided the broad question of the right of a school district to segregate children in the absence of express statutory provision authorizing such segregation. Because of this narrow point of decision it is doubtful whether there are grounds for applying to the United States Supreme Court for certiorari. The decision has been sent to members of the National Legal Committee for their consideration and advice.

Texas Primary Case

The new case to test illegality of the refusal to permit Negroes to vote in the Texas Democratic primary is being prepared. The records of the Texas Legislature are being checked from the time of the beginning of the primary system in Texas, along with research by the National Office.

Walter White, Secretary
August 1, 1940

Report of the Secretary for the
Board Meeting of February 1942

National Defense

The National Office is becoming increasingly busy in its effort to see that the Negro is not discriminated against in the many phases of the National Defense program.

The American Red Cross

Much time during the past month has been devoted to efforts to have the American Red Cross accept Negroes as blood donors for wounded sailors and soldiers. In a letter to Dr. E. H. Alexander of New York City under date of December 30, S. Sloan Colt, Director of the Red Cross War Drive, stated, "The Red Cross is now able to obtain from white donors enough blood to keep all the processing plants fully occupied so that the total amount of blood plasma available to the armed forces is not lessened by our inability to accept Negro donors."

Dr. Alexander referred to the National Office this communication which was in answer to a protest made by Dr. Alexander.

On December 30 the National Office wrote to the Secretaries of War and the Navy, regarding the refusal of the American Red Cross to accept Negro blood, pointing out the statement of the Director of the Blood Donor Service: "the American Red Cross is acting pursuant to the requests and instructions of the Army and Navy." Appeal was made that the present policy be discontinued and that the American Red Cross be instructed to "Accept the blood of all donors, regardless of race, providing all other requirements are met."

On January 15 Rear Admiral Ross T. McIntire, Surgeon General of the Navy, wrote the National Office; "So far as the Navy is concerned . . . it has never requested the American Red Cross to refuse to take blood from Negro donors." Immediately upon receipt of this letter the National Office wrote to Norman I. Davis, President of the American Red Cross, informing him of the Navy's denial and asking him to explain the contradictions to the American public. No reply has as yet been received from Mr. Davis.

Although Secretary of War Stimson has been urged by telegram to answer the Association's letter of December 30, to date no reply has been received.

On January 16 the Association's Treasurer wrote to Mr. Colt, Director of the American Red Cross War Drive, protesting against this discrimination. Copy of her letter was sent to several of the more important daily newspapers and magazines in New York City.

In New York City it was learned that it was the intention of the Red Cross to set up offices in the Department of Welfare to receive blood donations and that Negro employees of the Department had been told that their blood was not wanted. Thereupon the National Office made the request of Mayor Fiorello H. La Guardia that as long as the Red Cross practiced its discrimination against Negroes they be not allowed to set up such offices in City departments, thus making the City of New York a party to this discrimination.

Under date of January 16 the National Office wrote to Commissioner William Hodson of the New York City Department of Welfare urging that the Red Cross be not permitted to set up this proposed blood donor center where there are hundreds of Negro workers on complete equality with their white fellow workers. Immediately upon receipt of the Association's protest, Commissioner Hodson telephoned that he had just issued an order that there should be no blood-bank stations in the Department of Welfare until all who wished to donate their blood were permitted to do so without discrimination.

Through reliable newspaper and magazine correspondents the Association has been informed, confidentially, that the Red Cross while refusing the blood of Negroes has accepted the blood of Chinese, Filipinos, and even Japanese after Pearl Harbor. It was also learned that Red Cross Headquarters in Washington have been so swamped with letters regarding this subject, many of them from white as well as Negro Americans, protesting the ban on Negro blood, that according to one of the Red Cross officials. "We haven't had time to file all of them, much less read them."

It is also reliably reported that the Red Cross, the Army, and the Navy have agreed on a new policy, to accept Negro blood but to segregate it, though within the last fortnight the Red Cross announced that segregation of Negro blood would be both prohibitively expensive and impossible of accomplishment.

Proposal of Volunteer Negro-White Division

On December 22 the National Office proposed to General George G. Marshall, Army Chief of Staff, that there be created a volunteer division of the U.S. Army open to all men of any race, creed, color, or national origin. The suggestion was not an original one with the N.A.A.C.P., since it was made by Mr. Claude A. Barnett, Director of the Associated Negro Press, at a conference of Negro editors with General Marshall and other War Department officials in Washington early in December. The Association's proposal was backed up by a number of editors of prominent weeklies throughout the country. It has also been endorsed by white southerners, including Dr. Frank P. Graham, President of the University of North Carolina; Mr. Mark Ethridge, Editor of the *Louisville Courier-Journal* and Chairman of the President's Committee on Fair Employment Practice; and Mr. Howard Kester, General Secretary of the Fellowship of Southern Churchmen.

From a confidential government source in Washington the National Office has been advised that "if several hundred young white people who are in Class I would write to the Adjutant General or to the Secretary of War stating their willingness to serve in the same organization with Negro soldiers, the effect upon the thinking of the War Department might be considerable." The National Office has transmitted this information to several organizations which it believes would be sympathetic toward the proposal, asking them to do what they can to have such letters written.

On January 15 Mr. Gerald White, young New Yorker, was inducted into the United States Marine Corps. Mr. White made the request that he be put into the proposed Volunteer Division.

The daily press of January 17 carried announcement of a plan "reported today to be under discussion in Administration circles in Washington" to recruit a Liberty Legion. It stated: "Proponents of the plan said that such a legion would tend to nullify Axis appeals to racial groups within the United States by bringing all nationalities into the war effort and by emphasizing that the war is essentially an international civil war."

Distribution of Leaflets at Joe Louis Fight

To emphasize the Negro's protest against discrimination by the Navy the National Office distributed at the fight at Madison Square Garden, New York City, between

Joe Louis and Buddy Baer, for the Navy Relief Fund, leaflets carrying the following:

> The U.S. Navy refuses even to enlist Negroes except as messmen. Negroes are given no training in navigation, gunnery nor anything else; in spite of this, a Negro messman distinguished himself in defense of his country and his ship. Why does the Navy appeal for more men when it won't take thousands of willing Negroes? Is this the democracy we are fighting for? If the safety of your country means anything to you, write your Senators, Congressmen, the President and Secretary of the Navy Frank Knox.

This was made the more impressive by having appeared on the same sheet reproduction of a story in the *New York Times* of December 22nd telling of the heroism of a Negro messman at Pearl Harbor, on December 7. The leaflet bore the slogan, "Heroism Knows No Colorline."

Negro Hero at Pearl Harbor

The National Office submitted to President Roosevelt the suggestion that the Negro mess attendant who manned a machine gun against the Japanese planes at Pearl Harbor on December 7 be given the distinguished service cross or some other appropriate recognition. It was pointed out that this heroism is especially noteworthy in view of the fact that Negro volunteers are accepted only as mess attendants by the Navy and are thus not given training in the use of arms. A similar communication was sent to Secretary Frank Knox of the Navy.

Under date of December 31 Secretary Knox wrote the National Office; "Please be assured that an investigation will be made relative to the reported heroic action of the Negro mess attendant. The Navy Department will certainly recommend proper recognition for any such heroic action." A similar reply was received from Lieutenant Commander Paul C. Smith, Press Relations Officer for the Navy Department, to whom President Roosevelt referred the Association's letter.

Army Death Penalty Withdrawn

The National Office on December 22 sent to Secretary of War Henry L. Stimson protest against an order issued by Lieutenant Lewis A. Bonifay of the Seventy-Seventh Coast Artillery asking for the death penalty for "relations between white and colored males and females whether voluntary or not." The order was issued allegedly "because reports have been received that white women in the vicinity have been accosted by colored soldiers." The N.A.A.C.P. asked that Lieutenant Bonifay be removed if the order was found in excess of his authority.

The War Department reported to the National Office that "the order was found to be contrary to the support of verbal orders of the regimental commander who has caused the order to be withdrawn."

Posters, Murals, etc., Re: Defense and Stamps

A large number of complaints have been received at the National Office regarding the omission from posters, murals, and other visual aids to the sale of Defense Bonds and Stamps of Negro faces, which would indicate that Negroes, too, are a part of America. A letter from the National Office to Mr. Harold Graves of the Treasury Department, under date of December 30, brought a reply from Mr. S. D. Mahan, Associate Director of Information, Defense Savings Staff, showing complaint was with regard to the mural in Grand Central Station, New York City. Mr. Graves explained that the mural was an actual photograph of migrant workers in California and was not posed for the purpose for which it was used. He stated: "In billboard posters which have been designed and in material which we are preparing Negroes are included as part of the group."

Subsequent to this correspondence the National Office received several complaints regarding a poster used which purports to show children of all races which make up America. However, no Negro face is included. Regarding this the National Office has written Secretary of the Treasury Henry Morgenthau.

Proposed Cuts in Non-Defense Expenditures

The first report of the Joint Congressional Committee on Non-Defense Expenditures recommended abolition of the National Youth Administration, the Civilian Conservation Corps, the National Defense Training activities of the Office of Education, the Farm Tenant Program, and the Farm Securities Administration. The report also recommended curtailments virtually equivalent to abolishment of defense training courses operated by the Works Progress Administration.

Because these curtailments, if effected, would seriously affect Negroes who, in spite of the President's executive order, are still discriminated against in employment in defense industries[.] [T]he National Office has urged individuals to write their senators and congressmen protesting against this move; and on September 29 the National Office addressed a letter to all United States senators and congressmen appealing to them to do all in their power to preserve the gains made under these agencies.

Some seventy senators and representatives have replied to the Association's letter and an encouraging number of these have indicated that they will favor the continuance of some of the phases of these programs.

Farm Security Administration Loans for Poll Taxes

The National office received information during January that the Farm Security Administration had issued instructions that there be included in the search of records of white clients a search as to whether or not their poll taxes had been paid; that if they had not, an amount sufficient to cover this payment might be included in Farm Security Administration loans. However, Negroes are not included in this provision.

The Association's Special Counsel held a conference in Washington with C. B. Baldwin, Administrator of the Farm Security Administration, and other officials of the agency, at which time Mr. Baldwin stated that he would not issue instructions that Negroes be included now or in [the] future; he would stand behind the statement of E. S. Morgan, Director for the Southeastern Region of the agency, that "the Farm Security Agency has not and never will do anything contrary to local custom and regulations."

Speakers Bureau

The National Office is compiling a list of persons to form a Speakers Bureau. This Bureau is mainly for the use of the Association's branches, it being understood that the volunteer speakers will speak at branch meetings as often as their time will permit. Branches will be expected to pay travelling expenses and for entertainment. When individual speakers can give sufficient time, it is hoped it will be possible to arrange hours of several branches, which will reduce the cost of travel to each branch.

The Secretary's California Trip

On February 10 the Secretary will leave for California. On February 12 he is speaking at Mid-Year Convocation of the University of California, at Berkeley. This is reported to be the first time in the history of the University that a Negro has been invited to address the entire student body or to have the problem of color presented under such conditions.

Additional speaking engagements to be filled by the Secretary in the Bay Area include: the Commonwealth Club, when his speech will be broadcast; International House of the University; the Concordia Club; the League of Women Voters; the Alameda County and San Francisco Branches of the N.A.A.C.P.; and other appointments, including labor groups.

From Berkeley the Secretary goes to Los Angeles and Hollywood. Arrangements are being made for Mr. Wendell Willkie and the Secretary to speak to the Motion Picture Producers Association; the Academy of Arts and Sciences; and to other groups and individuals, regarding the harmful effect of the limitation of Negroes in the cinema to roles of menials and comics.

Following these engagements and after speaking for the Los Angeles Branch, the Secretary will fill speaking engagements for Texas Branches of the N.A.A.C.P. at El Paso, Austin, San Antonio, Corpus Christi, Houston, Galveston, Bomar, Tyler, Texarkana, Dallas, and Fort Worth.

The tour will cover a month, the Secretary returning to New York on March 9.

Lynching

On January 25, at Sikeston, Missouri, Cleo Wright, thirty-year-old Negro, was lynched. Wright was taken from jail following his arrest on being suspected of an attempted attack on a white woman. He was dragged through the Negro district of town, after which his body was set afire.

The National Office immediately urged upon President Roosevelt that he request Congress "to enact without delay legislation which will give authority to the federal government to proceed against lynchers and lynching." In the Association's telegram to the President it was pointed out that Japanese propagandists would cite this lynching as evidence of what colored races of the Far East may suffer if the democracies win the war.

University Cases—University of Missouri (Bluford vs. Canada)

The new complaint on behalf of Miss Lucile Bluford against S. W. Canada, registrar of the University of Missouri, was filed in the United States District Court for the Western District of Missouri, Central Division, at Jefferson City on Wednesday, January 7. This new complaint combines Miss Bluford's action for personal damages against the registrar for his refusal to permit her to register for graduate courses in Journalism, with an action for a declaratory judgment and permanent injunction declaring the policy and practice dictating said refusal to be unconstitutional and enjoining its continuation.

Meanwhile, ground has been broken for a school of journalism at Lincoln University, the State-maintained university for Negroes at Jefferson City, and it is intended that this school will be ready by February 1, the beginning of the second semester; a faculty of Negro journalists has been hired and other plans, all designed to forestall Miss Bluford's suit, have been made. It is Miss Bluford's intention to make careful comparison of the facilities to be offered at Lincoln and those offered at defendant university and if the former is found lacking she will proceed with her suit.

University of Tennessee Cases

Dr. L. A. Ransom, member of the National Legal Committee and chief counsel in these cases, wrote to Chancellor A. E. Mitchell of the Knox County Chancery Court, pointing out that it had been a year since oral argument in this case, yet no decision had been rendered. On December 4, the Chancellor renderd an opinion as follows:

By virtue of Chapter 43 of the Public Acts of 1941 and Section 5, Chapter 87 of the Public Acts of 1941, the questions involved in this litigation have become moot. An order will be prepared dismissing this suit at the cost of the respondents.

The implication of the decision is that since Tennessee has adopted statutory measures looking towards professional education of Negroes, the issue in the case has become moot and the Negro relators have no standing in court.

An appeal has been noted and Dr. Ransom will confer with other members of the National Legal Committee, as well as with Messrs. Carl A. Cowan and Z. A. Looby, Tennessee counsel directly responsible for the conduct of the case, as to the form the appeal shall take.

Teachers' Salary Cases

On January 21 the Special Counsel conferred witht A. P. Tursaud, local counsel in this case, and other interested parties with respect, among other things, to the failure thus far of Judge Wayne G. Borah, before whom the case was heard in November, to render a decision. On February 2 Judge Borah decided in favor of the plaintiff, McKelpin. His decision dismissing in the plea made by defendants, questioning the jurisdiction of the court, means that the defendant must now plead on the merits of the case.

Birmingham, Alabama

Following the filing of a petition for equalization with the local school board in November, the board promised the Negro teachers an early conference for discussion of the matter. Arthur D. Shores, local counsel representing the teachers, reports that the county Superintendent of Education "has virtually assured us that it will equalize salaries without any court action."

Atlanta, Georgia
(William H. Reeves/School Board)

Early in December, 1941, Atlanta City Attorney J. C. Savage, in reponse to a request from the Atlanta Board of Education, rendered an opinion on the petition filed by William H. Reeves, local Negro teacher, for salary equalization, stating that in his estimation the petition was without merit and "In accordance with your further request, I advise you that the Board of Education is authorized to discharge any permanent teacher for the good of the service, to be finally and exclusively judged and determined by the Board."

Attorney A. T. Walden, member of the National Legal Committee and local counsel in this case, indicated that the local Citizens' Board was adopting this opinion as its official reaction to Reeves' petition and that according to plan "we should proceed to file the action as soon as a definite and final answer is received from the Board of Eduction."

The Special Counsel conferred with Attorney Walden and the Citizens' Committee on January 23, and in anticipation of an unfavorable answer from the Board proceeded to draft the complaint for filing in the proper federal court.

Richmond, Virginia
(Antoinette E. Bowler vs. School Board)

On December 24, Attorney Oliver W. Hill, local counsel in this case, filed suit on behalf of Miss Antoinette E. Bowler, local Negro teacher, against the school board for salary equalization. This action followed the school board's having taken, during the previous week, the position that it could not accept the plan for equalization over a five-year period as contended for by the teachers.

Thereafter, on December 27, the school board by vote of four to three determined to reverse itself and accept the five-year plan on condition the teachers would withdraw their suit. The teachers, on January 9, voted to leave the matter in the hands of their attorneys and on January 26 the Special Counsel and Attorney Hill conferred with the Richmond City Attorney with reference to terms of settlement. No further details are available at this time.

Newport News, Virginia (Dorothy Roles vs.
School Board)

Early in December, a petition for equalization was filed with the Newport News School Board on behalf of Miss Dorothy Roles and the Newport News Negro Teachers' Association. On December 27 Dr. J. H. Saunders, Newport News Superintendent of Schools, proposed a five-year equalization plan. Notwithstanding Dr. Saunders' proposal, the school board on January 3 voted to withold action on Miss Roles' petition pending a report from a committee representing the Negro Teachers' Association, which committee, the board alleged, had promised to consider a verbal proposal for re-equalization made to it by the school board in 1940.

On January 21, the Newport News Negro Teachers' Association formally rejected proposal made to its committee by the school board and informed the board that all subsequent negotiations must be carried on through its attorney.

Palm Beach County, Fla.
Stebbins vs. Board of Public Instruction

The defendant in this case having moved to dismiss the complaint filed on behalf of Charles Stebbins, Negro teacher of Palm Beach County, for equalization of salaries paid him and other Negro teachers and principals with those paid white teachers and principals, the case came on for hearing before Judge Holland in the Federal District Court at Miami on January 17. At this hearing, a lawyer representing the Florida Education Association (white teachers) asked for leave to intervene in the case on the ground that they had an interest in the outcome of this case. Their position was that if a decree is granted it would either raise the salaries of the Negro teachers or lower those of white teachers, and they, therefore had an interest. S. D. McGill of Jacksonville, local counsel in this case, and the Special Counsel argued that no pleadings had been filed by the Florida Education Association and that they must file a motion to intervene, although this entire move was only for the purpose of delay and the hearing should proceed on the original motion to dismiss.

The lawyer for the school board made a motion to have the case transferred to Tampa where another and similar case was pending. Judge Holland, however, continued the case until February 7, at which time he will hear both the motion to intervene and the motion to dismiss.

Hillsborough County, Fla.
(Hilda T. Turner vs. Board of Public Instruction)

Suit for equalization in Hillsborough County was filed on behalf of Hilda Turner in November and soon thereafter a motion to dismiss was filed by defendant school board. Argument of this motion has been set for February 3, before Judge Barker in the Federal District at Tampa, Florida. S. D. McGill of Jacksonville and the Special Counsel will represent the teachers.

Duval County, Fla.
(Mary White Blocker vs. Board of Public Instruction)

The defendant board of public instruction in ths case filed a motion to dismiss the complaint filed in November on behalf of Mary White Blocker, Negro teacher in the Duval County public schools, for equalization of salaries paid Negro and white teachers. Argument on this motion is to be heard on February 4 by Judge Strum in the Federal District Court at Jacksonville. S. D. McGill and the Special Counsel will appear for the teachers.

Marion County, Fla.
(Stark versus Board of Public Instruction)

On January 9 suit was filed by George H. Stark and the Marion County Teachers' Association for equalization of salaries that are paid Negro and white teachers in Marion County. Subsequently, the school board filed the usual motion to dismiss and inasmuch as this action comes within the jurisdiction of the same court in which the Stebbins case (Palm Beach County) is to be argued on February 7, an effort is being made to have this case set down for argument on that date.

Walter White, Secretary
February 5, 1942

Report of the Secretary for the
Board Meeting of September 1945

The Full Employment Act

The National Office and the Washington Bureau have watched carefully the Full Employment Bill which was introduced on January 22 by Senators Robert F. Wagner, James E. Murray, Elbert Thomas, and Joseph C. O'Mahoney. On June 10 the National Office sent to each of these senators the resolution adopted by the N.A.A.C.P. Board of Directors at the June meeting. The resolution gave the Association's endorsement to the bill and urged its immediate enactment by the Congress. In his acknowledgement Senator Murray wrote: "It is exceedingly encouraging to know that your group is so actively aware of the necessity for affirmative federal action to assure sustained employment opportunities after the war for all who are willing and able to work." Senator Wagner wrote: "As sponsor of this legislation I will do my best to have the bill enacted in the near future."

Upon invitation from Senator Murray the Administrative Assistant of the Washington Bureau, on July 26, met with 103 House Co-Sponsors of the Bill to work out plans for nation-wide support of the measure.

During hearings on the bill, the Association's Secretary appeared (on August 29) before the Senate Banking and Currency Committee on behalf of the N.A.A.C.P. The Secretary opened his statement by saying, "Full employment is so fundamental to the well-being and development of this nation and every community that the N.A.A.C.P. considers an adequate program of full employment in the post-war period as one of its major interests. . . . Our support of this legislation is based on the following statement in the bill: 'All Americans able to work and seeking work have the right to useful, remunerative, regular and full-time employment, and it is the policy of the United States to assure the existence at all times of sufficient employment opportunities to enable all Americans who have finished their schooling and who do not have full-time housekeeping responsibilities freely to exercise this right.' "

The Secretary then pointed out statistics on Negro labor which have caused a major economic change during the past five years of war and stressed the fact that the Negro is anxious to retain what gains he has made, and to continue to improve his status.

While his appearance before the Senate Banking Committtee was for the Full Employment Bill, the Secretary urged also enactment of measures establishing a permanent Fair Employment Practice Commission; a national housing policy; amendment to give assistance to veterans without discrimination; enactment of the Kilgore-Forand Employment Compensation Bill, the Pepper Amendment to the Wage-Hour Act (to provide a minimum wage to an increased number of workers, including particularly agricultural and domestic workers), and the Wagner-Murray-Dingell Bill (for broadening of the old-age retirement pensions and other benefits); and enactment of federal legislation against lynching and the poll tax.

The Fair Employment Practice Commission

Senators Joseph Ball of Minnesota and Harold H. Burton of Ohio have stated that they and other senators will insist that the legislature create a permanent Fair Employment Practice Commission to be called up and considered early in the autumn, following the recess of the Congress. In a joint statement, made public on August 7, Senators Ball and Burton said: "One of the most significant bills apparently left completely out of the Democratic program is that to establish a permanent F.E.P.C. . . . We shall insist that the F.E.P.C. bill, which has been on the Senate calendar for several months, be given early consideration in the fall."

In a letter to Senator Alben W. Barkley, Majority Leader of the Senate, the Assistant Secretary pointed out that the filibuster by Senators Bilbo and Eastland to prevent action on the matter of a permanent Fair Employment Practice Commission was being generally interpreted among colored people as the official attitude of the Democratic Party. Senator Barkley replied:

> This part of your letter is most inaccurate. You may recall that the Democratic Party in its platform in 1944 endorsed the principle of the F.E.P.C., and President Truman has, in a special message to Congress, endorsed it and asked for its establishment as a permanent agency. . . . Neither the Democratic Party nor the Democratic membership of the Senate can be held responsible for the attitude of any single Senator.

In a second letter the Assistant Secretary pointed out to Senator Barkley that

> despite your personal attitude, and despite the forthright pronouncements on this issue by President Truman, colored people in the end must judge the Democratic party attitude not by the statements of one or two leaders, but by what the party is actually able to deliver in the way of legislation affecting their interest.

On August 23 the National Office wired President Truman that mounting racial tension in sixteen key states due to uncertainty as to a fair chance for employment in the postwar period was indicated. The Association's telegram urged that the present F.E.P.C. Committee be continued "so that it may contribute its experience to the solution of vexing problems already upon and may at the same time reassure Negro citizens that the government has not abandoned them and that the democracy their soldiers fought for is at work on the home front."

The Pan-African Congress

Following discussion of the proposed Pan-African Congress at the July meeting of the Committee on Administration, the Secretary, while in Washington July 30–31, talked with Mr. John Dickey, Chief of the Bureau of Public Information of the State Department; and with Judge Robert P. Patterson, Under Secretary of War.

Mr. Dickey informed the Secretary that when the Association's program for the Pan-African Congress is definitely arranged and definite dates for beginning and adjournment of the Congress are set, he will accompany the Secretary to see the Chief of the Passport Division of the State Department and give whatever assistance is necessary for the securing of passports. Mr. Dickey will then arrange an appointment with the Transportation Division of the State Department.

When asked how many will attend the Congress, the Secretary set a tentative number of from eight to twelve. Mr. Dickey pointed out that unless delegates can obtain a high official priority it is exceedingly doubtful if any of them can return to the United States under four months, because of the heavy redeployment of troops.

Judge Patterson assured the Secretary that if the State Department will give its vigorous approval of the congress, the War Department will provide round trip air transportation; but that if the State Department gives only general approval, transportation by water will be provided. The Secretary made an effort to talk with Mr. Stettinius, Secretary of State, but he had left the city to be gone for a week or more.

In a memorandum to the Secretary dated August 15 Dr. Du Bois stated that the convening committee of England, appointed by colored members of the Trade Union Congress, have called a Pan-African Congress with an eight-day program, to meet immediately after the conclusion of the World Trades Union Congress. Dr. Du Bois submitted a list of organizations which he suggested should be invited to join with the N.A.A.C.P. in participating. The Secretary pointed out in a memorandum to Dr. Du Bois that he felt this should be considered by the Committee appointed by the Board; because unless this is to be a Congress properly worked up along the lines set forth at the meeting of the sub-committee of the Pan African Congress Committee which was held in Washington on July 16, with proper representation and proper program, it is questionable whether or not we should participate; but in the event of non-participation we should let the French Government know that this is not the Congress that government granted us permission to hold.

Efforts have been made to find out when the Washington members of the Pan-African Congress Committee—Messrs. Hastie, Bunche, and Logan—can come to New York for a meeting of the Committee, this meeting to be fitted in with the vacation schedules of the New York members of the Committee. It is hoped that this meeting can be arranged prior to the September meeting of the Board.

National Public Housing Conference

On August 2 the Secretary was present at a meeting of the National Public Housing Conference held in Chicago. Two issues of direct concern to the N.A.A.C.P. were on the agenda, one of them at the request of the Secretary—the decision of Judge Thomas Maher in the Hamtramck, Michigan, case. Facts in the case were given as related in a telegram from the National Office Legal Department to the Secretary. When request was made of the Secretary for suggestions as to possible action, he suggested that action be held in abeyance pending the outcome for the study being made by the N.A.A.C.P. Legal Committee. Mr. Lee Johnson, Executive Vice-President of N.P.H.C., stated that a study was also being made by attorneys for N.P.H.C. and requested that the N.A.A.C.P. Legal Committee inform N.P.H.C. of its findings and recommendations so that N.P.H.C. and the N.A.A.C.P. might work in conjunction with each other. The Secretary promised that this would be done.

The second issue had to do with restrictive covenants. A memorandum from Charles Abrams of New York City was read, the gist of which is that the N.P.H.C. should take no action on such covenants as they are "a private matter." The Secretary vigorously opposed a motion that Mr. Abrams' recommendation be adopted as the official position of the N.P.H.C., and as a result of this and other protests the recommendation was tabled. A committee on which the Secretary is to serve is to draft a new recommendation for presentation at the next meeting of the N.P.H.C. Board. The Secretary has requested of Mr. Johnson the full text of Mr. Abrams' recommendation, upon receipt of which the Legal Department will draft a new resolution for submission to the N.P.H.C. committee.

National Housing Agency

On March 5, 1945, a suit was filed against John B. Blandford, Administrator of the National Housing Agency, and the National Housing Agency to enjoin the defendants from excluding qualified Negro war workers from public housing in New Boston, Texas. The Government filed a motion to dismiss the suit.

On August 5 attorneys for the N.A.A.C.P. filed with the District Court of the District of Columbia, where the suit is pending, Points and Authorities in Opposition to the Motion to Dismiss. Counsel for the N.A.A.C.P. were Judge William H. Hastie, the Special Counsel and the Administrative Assistant of the Washington Bureau.

Delmo (Missouri) Farm Homes

The National Office has made request of the Department of Agriculture for extension of the time during which bids may be received on the Delmo farm homes in Southeast Missouri.

The Delmo homes, in accordance with a recent act of Congress, are to be sold by the Farm Security Administration. These homes were built in 1939 at a cost of more than $500,000, following the eviction of over 1,500 sharecropper families from cotton plantations. Farm families moved in and have occupied the homes up to the present time but certain influences in the area have been agitating to have the government sell the homes and thus place the sharecroppers at the mercy of the plantation owners on their pre-1939 basis. The farm workers petitioned the government to delay the sale with the idea that, if given time, they may be able to raise sufficient funds to purchase the homes themselves.

A bill introduced in Congress prior to its recess in July did not reach the floor.

Office of Defense Transportation

During July the National Office wrote to President Truman pointing out that failure to hire Negroes in the face of an urgent demand from the War Manpower Commission was chiefly responsible for the transportation crisis. It was pointed out that the critical situation in the movement of troops was a direct result of the refusal of the Stacey Committee, created in January, 1944, to make recommendations based upon an F.E.P.C. report on discriminatory practices of fourteen railroads and seven unions. The Association requested immediate employment of Negroes.

The Washington Bureau

In addition to matters on which the Washington Bureau worked with the National Office, already mentioned in this report, the Bureau reports the following for the period July 1–August 15:

> Conference with Senator Capehart: A Conference was had with Senator Homer Capehart of Illinois to urge him to vote for cloture in case of filibustering against F.E.P.C. and the Anti-Poll Tax Bill. He indicated that he was favorably disposed toward both measures and to vote for cloture. His commitment to support the Wagner-Murray Social Security Bill, the Full Employment Bill, the Federal Aid to Education Bill, and conversion bills was sought. He stated unequivocally that he would support the Social Security Bill and would give the others study.

School Lunch Bill: H.R 3370

A bill to appropriate fifty million dollars to provide school lunches for children attending public and non-public schools was reported out of the House Agriculture Committee without a non-discrimination clause. The original bill, which the Committee re-wrote, contained specific provisions prohibiting discrimination because of race, creed, and color in states maintaining separate schools. These provisions were deliberately stricken out. Efforts are being made to have the non-descrimination clause restored when the bill comes before the House.

Senator Eastland's Attack on the Negro Soldier

The Bureau urged Senator James Mead of New York to refute the attacks made by Senator Eastland of Mississippi on the Negro soldier. The Bureau also supplied Senator Mead with material, part of which he incorporated in his statement made on the floor of the Senate on July 18.

Voting Records of Senators and Congressmen

The voting records of senators and congressmen on matters affecting the Negro during the first seven months of the Seventy-ninth Congress were compiled by the Washington Bureau. An analysis was made of the issues involved and this analysis will appear in the September *Bulletin*.

Veterans' Discrimination

On July 11, discrimination by the Military Order of the Purple Heart against Negroes was exposed and protested. The Mount Vernon Chapter of the Order had rejected the membership application of Private Samuel H. Dinkins who won a citation in October, 1944, in the Philippines.

Congressman Rankin

A conference was had with Mr. Walter Davenport of *Collier's* to help block out an article he proposes going to expose Congressman John E. Rankin who, by means of his chairmanship of the House Veterans Committee of World War I, is a virtual czar of legislation affecting veterans of World War II.

"Stay Out of Harlem" Order

In Danton Walker's column in the *New York Daily News* of July 23 appeared the statement: "New York police are warning all whites that they enter Harlem after dark at their own risk."

The National Office wrote to Commissioner Lewis J. Valentine requesting an explanation and asking if the directive was based on the idea that the proportion of crime in Harlem is greater than in other sections of New York City. The Association's letter pointed out that "an assertion of this type does great harm to the 500,00 Negro citizens of New York, and does particular harm to the 300,000 residents of the Harlem area, the vast majority of whom are law-abiding citizens."

In reply to the Association's inquiry Commissioner Valentine wrote:

No orders have been issued or will be issued while I am Police Commissioner relative to whom shall be prohibited from entering any part of the City of New York. There was absolutely no foundation or justification for any such statement.

Work of the Membership Secretary

Beginning with January, 1945, Miss Lucille Black has worked as Membership Secretary. Since the Director of Branches was without a secretary for several weeks early in the year, there was a delay in transferring to another worker the numerous tasks Miss Black had performed as assistant to the Director of Branches.

In an effort to secure renewal of memberships expiring early in the year, a letter was sent in February to 7,500 persons whose names were being removed from the *Bulletin* mailing list asking that they renew either through their local branches or by sending their membership fees to the National Office. No noticeable increase in memberships sent to the National Office was shown, so that whether or not the time and expense involved was warranted cannot be determined until a follow-up can be made by branches using lists furnished them at the conclusion of the Nation-Wide Membership Campaign.

The Membership Secretary has assisted in the planning of field work itineraries and in arranging tours and speaking engagements for other members of the staff; cooperated with the Director of Branches in preparations for leadership training conferences at Cleveland, Indianapolis, Kansas City, Atlanta, and New York City; has addressed several meetings in New York and vicinity; assisted in organizing the campaign of the Newark, New Jersey Branch; and also participated in a clinic on branch problems at the meeting of the Maryland State Conference of Branches at which 225 branch officers and delegates were present.

All correspondence dealing with memberships has been handled by the Membership Secretary. She has also supervised the preparation of membership certificates and the *Bulletin* files. During the heaviest periods an average mailing of 10,000 certificates has been made. The *Bulletin* run for July was 373,800. This does not indicate the Association's present membership since the list does not include soldier memberships and thousands of members whose correct addresses have not been sent to the National Office.

Since early March the Membership Secretary has devoted full-time to the promotion of the Nation-Wide Membership Campaign. Four hundred and sixty-eight branches indicated participation in the campaign, which was conducted by more than three hundred campaign chairmen and approximately two thousand workers throughout the country. An effort was made also to enlist volunteer workers from the membership-at-large, through a notice carried in the *Bulletin*. Special kits were prepared and sent to these workers. The Membership Secretary supervised the distribution of all campaign material and furnished publicity matter for press releases and the *Bulletin*.

Walter White, Secretary
September 5, 1945

Report of the Secretary for the
Board Meeting of November 1947

Report of the President's Committee on Civil Rights

The President's Committee on Civil Rights presented its report to the President on October 29. This Committee was appointed by the President as a result of the conference arranged at the White House by the N.A.A.C.P. and participated in by the Secretary, who acted as spokesman for the delegation: Dr. Frederick E. Ressig representing the Federal Council of Churches of Christ in America, James Carey of the C.I.O., Boris Shishkin of the A.F.L., and Dr. Channing H. Tobias.

After reading copy of the report, the Secretary wired President Truman as follows:

> May I on behalf of the National Association for the Advancement of Colored People express to you our profound admiration for the report of the President's Committee on Civil Rights. It is beyond all question the most forthright governmental pronouncement of a practical program for assurance of civil rights not only to minorities but to all Americans which has yet been drafted. The Committee has charted a course for the executive and legislative branches of government, both national and state, and for the people which if followed will make real our principles of human freedom.

A wire was also sent to Charles E. Wilson, Chairman of the Committee and a letter to each member of the Committee expressing our thanks and appreciation for the magnificent job which they did.

The Special Counsel issued a statement pledging support of the recommendations made by the President's Committee and asking all groups interested in first-class citizenship for all Americans to redouble their efforts to bring the Committee's proposals into reality. The full text of the statement appeared in the October 3 press releases.

The National Office has purchased 2,000 reprints of the report which was published on a special supplement to *PM* and is sending them to branches, youth councils, and college chapters. Copies of the report as published by the U.S. Government Printing Office have been ordered and a copy will be sent to each member of the Board. The report has been published by Simon and Schuster at $1.00 per copy. Branches and all friends of the Association are being urged to distribute the report as widely as possible among ministers, radio commentators, public officials, officers of labor organizations and women's clubs, civic groups, and other molders of public opinion.

Mr. Wilson, as chairman of the Committee, has been asked to select a date when a luncheon or dinner in honor of the Committee can be given both to pay tribute to the Committee and to mobilize public opinion for implementation of the

Committee's recommendations. It is proposed that responsible organizations and individuals will be asked to join in sponsoring the event.

Petition to the United Nations

On October 23 the Association presented to the United Nations at Lake Success its petition on the denial of human rights to minorities in the case of citizens of Negro descent in the United States. The petition was presented by the Director of Special Research to M. Laugier, Assistant Secretary for Social Affairs of the U.N., and John P. Humphrey, Director of the Division of Human Affairs.

In introducing the Director of Special Research, the Secretary stated that "no lasting cure of the causes of war can be found until discrimination based on race or skin color is wiped out in the United States and throughout the world."

The Director of Special Research stated that our petition "is a frank and earnest appeal to all the world for elemental justice against the treatment which the United States has visited upon us for three centuries—we, who are an integral part of this land and ever as loyal as any other group of its citizens."

The petition consists of chapters by Dr. Du Bois, Earl B. Dickerson, Chicago attorney, Milton R. Konvitz of Cornell University, W. Robert Ming, Jr., of the University of Chicago, Leslie S. Perry of the N.A.A.C.P. Washington Bureau and Dr. Rayford W. Logan of Howard University, and [it] was compiled under the editorship of Dr. Du Bois.

Probe of Alleged Communists in Hollywood

In a wire to J. Parnell Thomas, Chairman of the House Committee on Un-American Activities, the Secretary urged that the Committee "guard most carefully against penalizing any producer, writer, director, actor, actress, who has worked to change the dangerous stereotyped treatment of minorities in films, particularly of the Negro." The Secretary stated further that it is "important that responsible public officials should not fall into the dangerous error of labeling 'subversive' honest American doctrine of freedom, justice, and equality."

Voting Record of Congressmen Published in *Bulletin*

The voting record of Congressmen on legislation affecting the Negro was published in the October issue of the *Bulletin*. Among the issues included were the poll tax, Taft-Hartley law, rent control, school lunch appropriation, the Rees' Federal Employee Loyalty Bill, admission of Hawaii as the 49th state, portal-to-portal pay bill, votes on the seating of Bilbo, increasing subsistence allowances for veterans, and the confirmation of David Lilienthal as chairman of the Atomic Energy Commission. Listed also are the names of all congressmen who have signed Discharge Petition #9 to bring the Case Anti-Lynching Bill, HR-3488, up for vote in the House.

N.A.A.C.P. Sends Greetings to C.I.O. A.F.L. Conventions

In a wire to C.I.O. President Philip Murray on the occasion of the annual convention of the C.I.O. in Boston, the Secretary stated:

> Because we know there is no difference between assaults upon the rights of labor and the various forms of discrimination which oppresses minorities, we stand with you in your fight to erase this legislation from the law books of the land. Our National Convention in June unanimously agreed that the Association's Labor Department should work for the repeal of the Taft-Hartley Law. . . .

The Secretary wired President William Green at the convention of the A.F.L. in San Francisco urging that:

> As you meet in this historic year, may the delegates have a new determination to war against segregation and discrimination in all of the communities of the nation. . . . Our organization recognizes that we have a common fight for justice. We join with you in a pledge to keep the torch of freedom held high and brightly burning.

Forrestal Asked to Abolish Jim Crow

On October 9 the Secretary wrote to James Forrestal congratulating him on his new post as Secretary of Defense and upon his treatment of Negro enlisted men while he served in the capacity of Secretary of the Navy."

The Secretary urged that he issue a directive establishing a uniform "policy for the three arms of America's defense consistent with the policy presently effective in the United States Navy."

President Urged to Consider Eight-Point Medical Program

In a letter to President Truman the Secretary pointed out that the shortage of trained men and women in scientific fields, as emphasized by the U.S. Scientific Research Board, is nowhere more acute than in the area of health and medical education for Negroes. The Secretary outlined an eight-point program as well as a National Science Foundation which "if enacted into law, would carry provisions for fellowships for promising students as a nationwide coordinating scientific educational program and under no circumstances must any action be taken at the present time that would place Negro citizens under this Foundation in a separate or Jim Crow group." The Secretary enclosed with his letter a copy of Dr. W. Montague Cobb's pamphlet, "Medical Care and the Plight of the Negro," urging the President to read it in its entirety.

Article by Secretary in *Saturday Review of Literature*

An article by the Secretary, "Why I Remain a Negro" which appeared in the *Saturday Review of Literature* of October 11 has been reprinted by the Committee of 100 for use in an appeal to raise funds for the NAACP Legal Defense and Educational Fund, Inc. Fifty thousand copies have been reprinted. The Article will also be reprinted in January issue of the *Reader's Digest*.

Article by Secretary in *Collier's*

Another article by the Secretary, "Will the Negro Elect the Next President?" will appear in the November 22 issue of the *Collier's Magazine*. It emphasized the N.A.A.C.P.'s position of non-partisanship and the result of the N.A.A.C.P.'s campaign urging political independence and the careful scrutiny of the records of candidates for public office.

Walter White, Secretary
November 1947

Report of the Secretary for the Board Meeting of April 1951

Annual Convention

The Forty-second Annual Convention of the Association will be held in Atlanta, Georgia, June 16 through July 1. Sessions will be held in the Municipal Auditorium with the exception of the Friday evening and the Sunday mass meetings. The mass meeting on Sunday will be held at Herndon Stadium.

Speakers

It is hoped to have Mr. Charles E. Wilson speak at the Tuesday mass meeting, along with the Administrator who will give the keynote address. Dr. Benjamin Mays and Senator Irving Ives have been invited to speak on Wednesday evening; the Special Counsel and two youth speakers—one Negro and one white—will speak on Thursday evening; Senator Hubert Humphrey has been asked to speak on Friday evening along with the recipient of the Spingarn Medal. Miss Josephine Baker has canceled certain of her engagements in order to be with us on Saturday evening, June 30. Dr. Ralph Bunche and the Secretary will speak at the Sunday mass meeting.

Coverage

The Secretary has written Mr. John Johnson and Mr. Allen Morrison of *Ebony* suggesting that they do a feature story illustrated with color photography on our Annual Convention.

Washington Conference on Civil Rights

At the April meeting of the Board of Directors, a resolution was adopted calling for a civil rights conference in Washington, D.C. in May to formulate a coordinated plan of action in the fight for civil rights. The nation's leading church, labor, fraternal, and civic organizations are being asked to participate. The conference will discuss the apparent trend toward appeasement of the Dixiecrats and other reactionaries as exemplified by the appointment of white supremacy advocates Millard Frank Caldwell and Robert Ramspeck as Federal Civil Defense Administrator and Chairman of the Civil Service Commission respectively. Also to be discussed at this meeting will be amendments of the Senate cloture rule, the long delay in issuance of an emergency F.E.P.C. order, the Army's failure to proceed with the integration of Negro and white servicemen and the continuation of segregation policies in Washington, D.C. May 20 has also been designated as "oust-Caldwell" day which will be observed by mass meetings under the auspices of N.A.A.C.P. branches throughout the country.

In accordance with this action of the Board, the Secretary wrote to some fifty national organizations expressing the hope that each would be able to join the N.A.A.C.P. in this conference "so that we may together develop an effective program and better coordinate our efforts." Organizations were asked to send two to three of their top executives to this conference to be held May 22–23, in All Souls Unitarian Church. To date the following organizations have accepted our invitation to be participants: The American Civil Liberties Union, Anti-Defamation League of B'nai B'rith, American Jewish Congress, American Jewish Committee, Congress of Racial Equality, N.N.P.A., National Urban League, Hotel, Restaurant and Bartenders International Union of America, National Dental Association, Japanese American Citizens League, National Alliance of Postal Employees, National Bar Association, National Community Relations Advisory Council, National Baptist Convention, Inc., Scottish Rite Free and Accepted Masons of North America, A.D.A., A.F.L., A.V.C., Brotherhood of Sleeping Car Porters, C.I.O., and U.A.W.-C.I.O.

In further efforts to organize this civil rights meeting, the Secretary, Administrator, Public Relations Director, Earl B. Dickerson and W. Robert Ming met in Chicago, April 21, with representatives of the N.N.P.A. to develop plans for joint action and furthering this fight. Following the meeting, on May 3, 1951, a letter was sent to publishers of all Negro newspapers asking their cooperation in the campaign against Caldwell. The letter was signed by the Secretary and Mr. Dowdal Davis, the President of N.N.P.A.

State Conferences of Branches have been invited to send no more than ten delegates to this meeting, and representatives who were present at the White

House Conference in February have been asked to come to Washington on the 22nd of May in order to formulate plans for the program.

The Secretary is attempting to arrange for [a] May 23 conference with the Democratic and Republican leaders of both houses of Congress.

Winstead Amendment

N.A.A.C.P. branches in eleven key states sent forty-four representatives to Washington in an all-out lobbying effort to defeat the Winstead segregation amendment to the Draft-UMT bill. These delegates also worked to gain support for the amendment sponsored by Congressman Frank Havenner (D. Calif.) which makes it a federal offense to assault or murder a member of the armed services. The work done by Clarence Mitchell and activities of the delegates contributed considerably to elimination of the Winstead Amendment from the Barden Bill which the representative of North Carolina had offered as a substitute for the administration-sponsored draft bill. The vote was 178 to 126.

Subsequently by a vote of 138 to 123, the House eliminated the segregation amendment to the draft bill. The vote to eliminate the Winstead amendment followed an effective plea by representatives William Dawson, Democrat of Illinois, and Adam Clayton Powell, Jr., Democrat of New York. The N.A.A.C.P.-sponsored amendment to protect servicemen against assault by local police officers and civilians was defeated by a vote of 63 to 46. The administration opposed enactment of this amendment and the vote was taken when most of the supporters of the amendment were absent from the floor.

Eighth Orientation Conference

From April 8 to 16, the Secretary participated in an orientation conference conducted by the Department of Defense for civilian leaders. The conference was in the nature of a tour in which seventy-five civilian leaders participated and included two and a half days in the pentagon and field trips to U.S. Marine Bases at Quantico, Virginia; USAF Base at Eglin, Florida; U.S. Naval Base at Pensacola, Florida; and U.S. Army Infantry School at Fort Benning, Georgia.

There was marked increase in the willingness to accept the principle and practice of racial integration in the Armed Services. At Eglin Field and at the Pensacola Naval Base, the Secretary reports, there was remarkable integration although the percentage of Negroes serving or being trained as officers was small. Three Negroes had been graduated from the Pensacola Naval School as advisors. The Secretary saw no Negroes at Quantico but was told that several were being trained at another Marine Base. At Fort Benning the Secretary was told that twelve per cent of the military personnel is colored and that integration is moving along quite well. The method of integration was not specified. Subsequently the Secretary wrote to Major General John H. Church asking him to advise what methods were being used.

No Negroes participated in the demonstrations that the Secretary witnessed, and he saw no colored officers at officers' mess. However, he did note that there were [a] number of Negroes in the beginners' class of the Paratroop School at Fort Benning.

Conference with Finletter

On March 31, Thomas K. Finletter, Secretary of the Air Force, telephoned that the integration program of the Air Force had encouraged a serious snag in a demand of seventeen southern states forced by Senator Allen J. Ellender of Louisiana that all training of Air Force personnel at Southern schools would be subject to the segregation laws of the Southern state.

Mr. Finletter explained that certain subjects were not provided for in Air Force installations, which necessitated sending of trainees for these particular courses to schools close to the Air Force bases. Mr. Finletter informed the Secretary that a proposal had been made that each trainee thus sent to an outside school be given the option of refusing to go to a segregated school, in which event he would be sent to one in a non-segregated state. In a letter dated April 6 the secretary strongly opposed any surrender by the Air Force because yielding on any significant point might prove to be the opening wedge in stopping integration. Since these schools claim that their enrollment and income were dropping to such an extent as to put them in jeopardy and since they would be paid generously by the Government for such training, it was urged that they be told they could not secure such contracts unless they were willing to train all on an equal basis. In the event of refusal by the schools, it was urged that trainees either be sent to schools outside the segregated field or that facilities be established on the air force bases for such training.

Mr. Finletter informed the Secretary on April 30 in Washington that the latter course had been decided upon and that training schools in all necessary subjects will be established by September 1.

F.E.P.C.

On April 4, a letter signed by A. Philip Randolph and the Secretary was sent to President Truman pointedly asking when an F.E.P.C. executive order would be issued. The letter reviewed the many steps taken by Negro leaders and organizations in an effort to secure an executive order. Despite repeated assurance that action would be taken, nothing had been done, the letter said. The letter concluded, "We of the Nation have waited patiently and in daily anticipation for the establishment of an F.E.P.C. with authority to implement the policy you have so consistently advocated. We feel constrained now, Mr. President, to ask when we may expect such an executive order." No reply has been received.

Conferences with Secretary of State Acheson
and Mr. Charles Wilson

On April 13, conferences were held with Secretary of State Dean Acheson and Charles E. Wilson, Director of Defense Mobilization. A sub-committee of the original White House group met with these officials. At the conference with Mr. Wilson, Dr. Arthur Flemming of his staff was present. He is manpower expert with the office of Defense Mobilization and was formerly chairman of the U.S. Civil Service Commission. Mr. Wilson expressed general agreement with the requests of the group and stated that he would appoint a Negro assistant to him to deal with the general policy questions of his office and to be solely limited to questions of policy relative to Negroes. Mr. Wilson said Dr. Flemming would be available to work with the sub-committee on specific problems raised with regard to efforts to integrate Negroes into every phase of the Nation's defense mobilization efforts.

Later the same day, the subcommittee met with Secretary of State Acheson who expressed a sympathetic attitude toward the statement submitted by the group and promised to look into the general problems raised by it. Although he indicated he would not make any recommendation for an Assistant Secretary of State along ethnic consideration he did request that the committee consult with Mr. Haywood T. Martin, Director of Personnel of the State Department on policies of the Department in integrating Negroes in the domestic and foreign services.

Subsequently on the 19th of April, a conference was held with Mr. Martin by some members of the group, Mr. Clarence Mitchell representing the N.A.A.C.P., and as a result the following is indicated:

1. Mr. Martin would welcome a list of recommendations from our full committee of a qualified Negro to work in his office and be responsible to him on general personnel problems of the State Department. Pending this appointment, he would accept recommendations from the full committee of a qualified Negro in an advisory or consultant capacity to aid him on the general personnel of his department, specifically related to the issue discussed at the meeting with the group.

2. He would welcome recommendations from the full committee of a list of persons whom the committee believes are qualified for specialized service in the State Department, both in the administrative field and the foreign service. He would accept recommendations by the committee of promising persons for the Internship Program of the State Department.

3. He would welcome helpful suggestions from the full committee in the procedure presently being used by his department as it might affect the employment of Negro citizens.

American Jewish Congress Award to
N.A.A.C.P.

The N.A.A.C.P. received a check for $1,000 representing the Stephen Wise Memorial Award. The Association was cited for "distinguished public service during 1950." Presentation was made by Rabbi Irving Miller, President of A.J.C., at a dinner at the Hotel Plaza. The Special Counsel accepted the Award on behalf of the Association.

Kappa Alpha Psi Contribution

On Sunday, May 6, the Secretary spoke at a meeting of Kappa Chapters in Brooklyn, N.Y., after which he was presented with a $1,000 check representing a contribution from the Kappa Alpha Psi fraternity.

Levittown

In response to a letter from the Secretary which pointed out the refusal of Levitt and Sons, Inc. to sell or lease homes to Negroes, Senator Irving Ives (R., N.Y.) replied stating that he had supported every effort to place in federal housing legislation a prohibition against segregation or discrimination because of race, religion, color, national origin, or ancestry. He said his reason for commendation of the housing developments built by Levitt and Sons at Levittown, L.I., did not carry with it approval of the policies pursued by the Levitts with respect to occupancy. His commendation applied solely to the production of housing and to nothing else.

Contribution to Inc. Fund—Ike Williams

Following a visit to Pompton Lakes, N.J., by the Secretary and the Director of Public Relations, Ike Williams has agreed to give a contribution to the Legal Defense and Education Fund. This is in lieu of a benefit which was at first considered (see report of Director of Public Relations).

Charges against Miss Loretto Chappell

In accordance with the decision of the Board at its April meeting, the Secretary wrote to Mrs. M. E. Tilly and three other responsible persons in Atlanta for advice as to the best course of action to follow in order to lend our support to Miss Loretto Chappell in the matter of the recent investigation of her loyalty by a Georgia state legislative investigating committee. He has been advised that the "Chappel affair is another one of Talmadge's schemes to intimidate Negroes and liberal whites." The Secretary suggests that because of the facts as given by Mrs.

Tilly and others, the N.A.A.C.P. and the Inc. Fund should not be involved in the publicity surrounding the case. However, he suggests that some way be found to make a contribution since the basis of the fight is anti-Negro prejudice by Talmadge. The Secretary also feels that the facts should be placed before the *New York Times* or the *Herald Tribune* in an effort to secure an exposé of what a responsible white person in Atlanta calls "a sinister Fascist threat" and material has been submitted to Mr. Edwin L. James of the *Times* with the request that a top flight reporter be sent to Atlanta to make an investigation and write a series tying it in with the recent meeting in Charleston called by Governor Byrnes and in which Herman Talmadge and Fielding Wright participated along with himself.

Ford Foundation

The committee appointed by the Board to draft, with the Secretary, an application to the Ford Foundation has had two lengthy meetings. The final draft of the application is expected to be finished by May 16 when it will be submitted to the committee for whatever revisions need to be made. It is believed that this will be the most comprehensive program yet drafted for attack on the present and future phases of the problem of race both as an American and as a world question.

Mrs. Thornburg Cowles has been appointed by the chairman of the Board as a member of this committee and has worked faithfully with the committee.

The Secretary requested Judge William H. Hastie and Dr. Ralph J. Bunche to accompany him in making the formal presentation either in Pasadena or in New York and discussing the report and answering such questions as the directors of the Ford Foundation may see fit to ask. However, because Dr. Bunche has accepted membership on the Ford Foundation Committee on Advancement of Education, he cannot properly join in an application to a Board of which he is a member. But Dr. Bunche has authorized the Secretary to inform the Ford Foundation that had he not accepted membership on that committee, he would have joined in making the application.

Segregated Hospitals

As noted in previous reports, H.R. 314, which is Congressman Rankin's Bill setting up a Jim Crow Veterans Hospital at the Booker T. Washington birthplace in Virginia, was denied passage on the unanimous consent calendar twice. However, Congressman Rankin has succeeded in getting the Rules Committee to clear his bill and it is now on the union calendar of the House. This means that it can be brought up at a time when Mr. Rankin feels he can get it passed.

We are working against this proposal and have numerous pledges of support. However, it will require a process of patient watching to catch it when it is brought up for a vote and also it will require considerable cooperation on the part of the Congressmen in order that they will be available when needed to vote against it.

Electoral College Resolution

H.J. Res. 19, which is Congressman Gossett's Resolution to change the electoral college system in a manner which would give greater advantage to southern states in national elections, is again troubling us. It will be recalled that this Resolution was defeated when brought to the House floor by Congressman Gossett in the Eighty-first Congress. A subcommittee of the House Judiciary Committee has the matter under consideration. We have been advised confidentially that the subcommittee intends to approve H.J. Res. 19, although the chairman of the subcommittee has indicated that no final action has been taken. We are working with members of the sub-committee and the full Judiciary Committee in the hope that we may halt this measure there.

Apprentice Training Legislation

In the Eighty-first Congress, several attempts were made to nullify a favorable decision of the Federal Fair Employment Board. This decision has enabled colored veterans to take apprentice training as plate printers in the Bureau of Engraving. The attempts in the Eighty-first Congress on the part of those who sought to cancel out the Board's decision were unsuccessful. However, these same interests have persuaded Congressman Robert Ramsay of West Virginia to introduce H.R. 1507 and H.R. 290. These bills have the same purpose as those introduced in the Eighty-first Congress. We are urging West Virginia N.A.A.C.P. leaders to ask Congressman Ramsay to abandon these bills.

Florida and North Carolina Elections

We have requested Chairman Guy Gillette of the Senate Subcommittee on Privileges and Elections for an opportunity to make a plea for an investigation of the 1950 senatorial elections in North Carolina and Florida. We have been advised by Senator Gillette that an effort will be made to grant our request.

Segregation in the Armed Services

The Washington Bureau has been holding a number of meetings with representatives of the Department of Defense on certain critical problems bearing on segregation and other difficulties in the Armed Services. The Department of Defense has been gathering data on N.A.A.C.P. suggestions that (1) racial designations be eliminated on forms and records; (2) draftees and volunteers be housed and fed on Government installations in areas where local businesses refuse to accommodate them on a non-segregated basis; and (3) that additional colored people be assigned to integrated national guard units as those units are called into active duty. A report on how these proposals will be handled has been promised us.

The Bureau was advised in a meeting on May 1 that segregated swimming arrangements at Fort Custer in Michigan have been ordered discontinued following the Association's protest, and similar complaints we filed about segregation in other forts or camps are being processed.

So many individuals and organizations protested about segregation at Fort Dix, New Jersey, that it is certain that many people will claim credit for ending the unfair practices there. The Washington Bureau notes for the record that Fort Dix was among the installations that the N.A.A.C.P. complained about in the meeting with Assistant Secretary of the Army Karl D. Johnson on November 10, 1950. He promised correction at the time.

Atomic Energy Commission

In previous reports, we have discussed the Atomic Energy projects at Paducah, Kentucky, and Aiken, South Carolina. As a result of information received from a reliable source the Washington Bureau has filed charges against the Atomic Energy Commission on behalf of Mrs. Barbara Banks and Miss Evelyn Mills of Paducah. We charged that A.E.C. officials violated Executive Order 9980 by refusing to interview these applicants when they sought jobs as clerical workers. We are continuing a broad program affecting both of these areas. This requires action on specific complaints on the overall hiring practices.

We recently received a letter of appreciation from South Carolina for work done by Mr. Fisher on a housing project in that area. We were advised that plans were under way to make this project available to whites only. Mr. Fisher's action in Washington with the A.E.C. officials halted these plans. Meanwhile, we have received a new report from South Carolina stating that colored carpenters seeking work were told "no colored needed today."

Investigation of Baltimore Employment Service

In line with action mentioned on the A.E.C., the Washington Bureau has had numerous requests for investigations of various types of employment discrimination. One such request from Baltimore has revealed a terrible pattern of discrimination in the local employment service. The investigation of this discrimination is still under way. However, some of the preliminary results show that during the months of August, September, and October in 1950, 502 white people were placed in government jobs but only 46 colored people were placed. Under the clerical and professional placements, it is shown that during September 1950, 1,009 white people were referred while only 15 non-white people were referred. During November 1950, 1,335 white people were referred and only 42 non-white people were referred. These figures undoubtedly could be duplicated in a number of other offices of the employment services around the country. They serve to warn against optimistic statements about the large number of jobs colored people are getting and rosy presentations of the decline of discrimination in employment because of the abundance of defense contracts, etc.

Mob Action Against Florida Residents

Mr. James Gallon and his son, James, Jr., came to the Washington Bureau last month from Greensboro, Florida. They stated that they had been beaten with ax handles during an argument with a white store owner in their own home town of Greensboro. The store owner was assisted by a mob of white persons and the Gallons were forced to flee from the local community. They have stated that they are unwilling to return to Florida. Unfortunately, the Department of Justice advised that it had no grounds for acting in this case. Hence, we have assisted the men in getting employment in Washington. The facts on their case have been sent to the Florida State Conference of N.A.A.C.P. Branches for the present campaign to get an anti-lynching bill passed in Florida.

Important Specific Cases

Special attention is directed to the following matters which are among the things being handled by Mr. Fisher:

1. Elmer N. Fassett, a veteran, sought assistance of the N.A.A.C.P. for himself and other men who were denied the right to continue any kind of training under the G.I. Bill. Mr. Fassett and other men were dropped from a plumbing course in Baltimore, Maryland, following an alleged disorder in class. Mr. Fisher worked with representatives of the Baltimore Branch and the Veterans Administration on this case. On April 4, the V.A. announced that Mr. Fassett and other veterans similarly barred from training because of the incident would be reinstated to full benefits of the law.
2. Mr. Fisher represented William H. Howard, an employee dropped by the Federal Security Agency, at a hearing on April 12. This case is significant because it appears that Mr. Howard was released by a supervisor who objected to his efforts to eliminate racial discrimination in the section where he was employed.
3. The Research Assistant met with Charles H. McGuire, Director of National Shipping Authority, to discuss the problem of employment of colored officers. Mr. McGuire stated that he would see what could be done on an informal basis to gain employment for these men. A letter has been sent to Mr. McGuire urging action on his part to see that the non-discrimination clauses are enforced in the General Agency Agreements in order that the colored officers might have an opportunity to work.

Respectfully submitted,
Walter White, Secretary
May 14, 1951

Report of the Secretary for the
Board Meeting of June 1951

Annual Convention

The number of delegates to the Forty-second Annual Convention of the N.A.A.C.P. is expected to exceed 1,000.

Sessions of the Convention will be held in the Atlantic City Auditorium of the Friday night meeting to be held at the Wheat Street Baptist Church and the Sunday meeting to be held at Herndon Stadium.

At the direction of the Board, the Secretary invited Walter Reuther to address the opening session of the convention on Tuesday evening along with the Administrator who is delivering the keynote address. Mr. Reuther was unable to accept because of previous commitments. The Secretary has written Edward Barrett, Assistant Secretary of State in charge of Public Affairs, inviting him to speak at the opening session.

Other speakers scheduled to address the convention are Dr. Benjamin Mays and Philip Willkie on Wednesday, the Special Counsel on Thursday, Dr. Ralph J. Bunche and the Secretary on Sunday. On Friday evening, the Spingarn Medal will be presented to Mrs. Mabel Keaton Staupers by Lillian Smith for "spearheading the successful movement to integrate Negro nurses into the profession and professional societies and into American life as equals."

The July meeting of the Board will, as usual, be held during the Annual Convention. It will be a dinner meeting on Thursday. The place of the meeting has not yet been determined but will be announced at the convention.

Miss Josephine Baker agreed to give up two lucrative engagements to perform on Saturday, June 30. However, as a condition she stated she and her company must stay at a downtown hotel. The Secretary wired the three leading hotels in Atlanta—the Atlanta Biltmore, the Georgian Terrace, whose owner Joseph Gatlin is a Frenchman, and the Henry Grady requesting reservations for Miss Baker, her husband and members of her company. The Biltmore replied they were filled to capacity. The other two hotels said simply they could not give the requested reservations.

The Secretary thereupon wired Secretary of State Acheson urging that he do what he could to see that Miss Baker was given the reservation requested. Receiving no reply, he again wired the Secretary of State requesting an appointment for a group of distinguished American citizens to discuss the matter with him. Francis Russell, Assistant Secretary of State, telephoned the Secretary on Saturday, June 2, and said that Mr. Acheson was devoting his entire time and attention to the senatorial hearings on firing of General MacArthur. He asked what action we wished taken. We urged the State Department to communicate with the Atlanta Hotels to point out that refusal to give accomodations to Miss Baker and other members of her party who were French citizens, as well as to the Americans, would create world-wide criticism not only of Georgia but of the entire United States. He agreed to do what he could.

The Secretary has pointed out to Miss Baker that although this discrimination is stupid, he felt it was more important for her to appear before 5,000 persons in an unsegregated city auditorium than to stay at a white hotel. Miss Baker remains adamant in her refusal to appear unless given the reservation requested in a white hotel. The Atlanta Branch has advised the Secretary that a committee is to meet with the Biltmore hotel in a further effort to secure a reservation for Miss Baker.

Washington Conference

At the call of the N.A.A.C.P., thirty-one national organizations sent sixty-seven representatives to Washington on May 22–23 to confer and map out a program to secure action on civil rights legislation.

In his opening remarks, the Secretary pointed out the apparent cessation of active support for civil rights legislation by the President and his appointment of men like Millard Frank Caldwell and Robert Ramspeck. He also pointed out that it was the vote of racial and religious minorities and organized labor which in the final analysis elected Mr. Truman, and the Democrats would not today be the majority party had it not been for Mr. Truman's stand on civil rights.

On Tuesday, May 22, the delegates assembled, approved and signed a letter to 315 congressmen urging defeat of the Rankin bill, H.R. 314, providing for a segregated veterans hospital for Negroes at the birthplace of Booker T. Washington in Franklin County, Va. The letter pointed out, "It would be irony for wounded veterans of the Air Force and the Navy who served and fought without segregation in their units to be separated according to race and color for treatment and rehabilitation in veterans hospitals set up by their own country." The letter also pointed out that the area proposed for the hospital was inaccessible and far from important centers of population and from any recognized medical center.

The delegates also agreed on the following points to receive priority in conferences with the majority leader of the Senate and the minority leaders of the House and Senate:

Request full-dress hearings on the Lehman, Morse, Ives, and Humphrey resolutions dealing with change in Senate rules with due notice to all interested persons and adequate time to be heard, as well as on the Sabath resolution in the House.

Request that F.E.P.C. bills in Senate and House be reported out.

Comprehensive civil rights bill.

Legislation to provide federal protection against assault by civilians on Army, Navy, and Marine personnel, now given to Coast Guard.

Anti poll tax.

Anti-lynching bill.

Conflict of interest statute be waived for members of the Nimitz Commission, its members and its staff.

Approval of Kefauver–Taft bill which would give to citizens of the District of Columbia the right to vote.

In the conference with Representative Joseph Martin and Senator Kenneth Wherry, Senator Wherry agreed to present the group's request for hearings on the rules change to the committee which was meeting immediately thereafter. Later, while the group was conferring with Senate Majority Leader McFarland, Senator Wherry returned to announce dramatically the decision of the Senate Rules Committee to take up again and hold hearings on the changing of the Senate Rules in order to make it easier to break filibusters.

Although Senator Wherry agreed to take up with the committee the matter of hearings on the rules change, he nevertheless defended the Wherry compromise rule which he sponsored with Senator Carl Hayden, saying that it was workable and "all that is necessary is to get the votes." He said he could get thirty-eight and possibly forty Republican votes for cloture and all that was necessary was to get the Democrats to deliver twenty-six of their fifty votes. Senator McFarland was unable to say how many votes his party could deliver for cloture nor would he make a commitment on holding around-the-clock sessions to break the inevitable filibuster against revision of the Senate rules.

The Secretary has written to all participants in the conference requesting that they submit the names of persons who can be asked to testify at the hearings on change in the rules.

At the conclusion of the conference, the delegates agreed to the release of the following statement:

For the past two days, we, the representatives of thirty-one democratically constituted organizations representing more than twenty-three millions of loyal Americans, have met to examine the status of the rights of minorities and the reforms which three and a half years ago the President's Committee on Civil Rights said required action then.

Since that time there has been no congressional action on this program and very little executive implementation.

This inaction by the Congress on the repeated recommendations of the President stems from the cynical irresponsibility of both political parties and the open operation of a reactionary bi-partisan coalition whose response is to the forces of bigotry and special privilege.

We renew the request that has been made so often to President Truman since the Communist attack on South Korea, that he issue an executive order establishing an F.E.P.C. in defense employment, and that he obtain the same integration in the Army that is being established in the Air Corps, Navy, Marine Corps, Coast Guard, in veterans hospital and in military cemeteries around the world.

We call upon the Congress to assume its responsibility to the American people through enactment of urgently needed legislation upholding the basic rights of all the people. To this end we have urged upon the leadership of both parties the following minimum program.

[The delegates list the following] three demands:

1. Revision of the Senate rule on cloture to facilitate breaking of filibusters. We have asked for open hearings on resolutions providing for this change as introduced by Senators Lehman, Lodge, Ives, Morse, and Humphrey. This reform must be made to free the American people from rule by veto of a minority of one-third plus one of the Senate.
2. Immediate committee action on pending F.E.P.C. legislation with a view of enactment of such a law with enforcement powers during this session of the Congress.
3. Enactment of legislation to provide protection for members of the U.S. Army, Navy, and Marine Corps from physical assault by civilians. This is essential for protection of servicemen of all races as is evidenced by the killing of two unarmed handcuffed paratroopers by the chief of police of Hawkinsville, Georgia, on May 17.

We have presented this program to the leadership of both parties of both houses. We have been given assurance that it will be considered.

We take nothing for granted. We will return to the people we represent and call for unceasing insistence upon the performance of this program.

N.N.P.A.–N.A.A.C.P. Conference–Cocktail Party

A meeting between the committee appointed by the Negro Newspaper Publishers Association to represent them, and the committee appointed by the N.A.A.C.P. Board to work out a plan of cooperation between the two groups is scheduled to be held on Thursday, June 14, at 4 P.M. in the secretary's office.

In accordance with a previous vote of the Board of Directors, the N.A.A.C.P. will entertain the N.N.P.A. on Friday, June 15 at a party to be held in the Willkie Building from 5 to 7 P.M. It is hoped that all members of the Board who are able to attend will do so.

Public Housing

The resolution of the Board of Directors, passed at its May 14 meeting, condemning the action of the House of Representatives in limiting to 5,000 the number of housing units to be developed under the public housing program was sent out in the Association's press releases of May 17. Subsequently, the figure of 5,000 units was raised to 50,000.

Bill to Protect Servicemen

The Secretary sent identical telegrams to the Secretary of Defense, Attorney General J. Howard McGrath, and Senator Richard B. Russell, chairman of the Senate

Armed Services Committee, recalling the Association's demand for legislation to protect servicemen and urging passage of the bill (H.R. 4301) proposed by Congressman Havenner of California to extend to all servicemen the protection now given to marshals, judges, the Coast Guard, and certain other federal employees. The Secretary cited the recent slaying by Police Chief Thomas Bragg of two unarmed servicemen while they were handcuffed and in the custody of the police officer.

Secretary's Statement re: MacArthur

Following General MacArthur's disavowal of responsibility for segregation of Negro troops under his command in the Far East as reported by the *Courier*, the Secretary issued the following statement:

> There is nothing in my experience with General MacArthur to justify or warrant any charge that he is a "white supremacist." On the contrary, he was exceedingly cordial and frank when I talked with him in the Philippines in 1945 and in Tokyo in 1949. On both occasions we discussed the possibility and necessity of abolition of racial segregation in the armed services. It will be remembered that the 93rd Division had been sent to the Pacific after being trained as a combat unit. But on arrival in the Pacific it was split up, scattered widely and used as port battalions, trucking companies, engineering companies and other service units. At the request of the then Secretary of War, Robert P. Patterson, I discussed the re-assembling of the Division and refresher training in combat. General MacArthur promised to do this and kept his promise.
>
> But on the matter of actual steps towards integration of the troops under his command I cannot agree with General MacArthur. In 1946 President Truman issued his executive order to abolish racial discrimination in the armed services. This order has been obeyed by the Navy and the Air Force. But when I was in Japan in 1949 I saw little evidence of any compliance with the integration order. I saw a few instances of integration in housing of officers and some in a service club at Yokahama. But the pattern of segregation otherwise was as rigid as ever.
>
> Thurgood Marshall found the same to be true in Tokyo and Korea in 1951.
>
> Thus, General MacArthur cannot escape responsibility for the continuation of the pattern of segregation among the troops under his command which led among other unfortunate consequences to the disproportionate number of *court martials* which have occurred in the Far East command.

Ford Foundation Application

The first draft of an application for a grant of two million from the Ford Foundation has been completed and sent to members of the committee appointed by the Board to assist in preparation of this document, with the request that they send to Harold Gram who prepared the draft, their criticisms and suggestions. It is hoped that Judge Hastie will be able to join the Secretary in presenting the application in New York or Pasadena. The Secretary has also requested that Senator William Benton, who has been most helpful in making contact with persons connected with the Foundation and who is a member of the Committee working on the application, join in making the presentation if it is possible for him to do so. Dr. Ralph Bunche who has accepted membership on the Committee for Advancement in Education of the Foundation is unable to join in making the formal presentation because of his acceptance of membership on this committee. However he has authorized the Secretary to say he is willing and available to answer any questions in connection with the application and would have joined in signing it had he not accepted membership on this committee.

Committee to Defend Dr. Du Bois

An ad in the *Afro American* calling for dropping the charges against Dr. Du Bois and other Peace Information officials and requesting contributions for his legal defense contained statements by a number of individuals and the resolution of the N.A.A.C.P. in connection with the indictment. The ad also carried a picture of Dr. Du Bois under which appeared "Director, Special Research, National Association for the Advancement of Colored People." A letter was subsequently received from Alice Citron, Secretary of the Committee to Defend Dr. Du Bois and Associates in the Peace Information Center, regretting the error appearing under the picture of Dr. Du Bois and stating:

> Our original copy, of course, did not contain the statement. We believe it was an inadvertent error caused in all probability by the use of a photograph that contained such information on the back of the picture.
> We are sorry for the completely unforeseen mistake.

Violence against Negroes

On April 30 the Secretary received a wire from officers of the branch in Tampa, Florida, calling attention to acts of violence against Negroes. Specifically, the officers called attention to the killing of two Negroes and the beating of two others "by unknown hoodlums" in Winter Garden, and the deliberate and willful burning of Dr. and Mrs. Ralph B. Wimbish's home in Tampa because they purchased in a so-called white neighborhood.

The Secretary has requested that the officers send us further details and all available information so these incidents can be taken up with the Department of Justice.

Appointment of Negro to Military Court of Appeals

In January of 1951 the secretary wired President Truman as follows:

> In view of the disproportionate number of cases involving Negro members of the Armed Forces, the National Association for the Advancement of Colored People urges you to appoint a qualified Negro civilian to the position of Judge of the Court of Military Appeals pursuant to the power vested in you [under] Public Law 506, Article 67, Title 50, U.S.G.A. 654. Such an appointment in our view would be clear evidence to the world of your determination to afford to all members of the Armed Forces, regardless of race, creed and color, equality of treatment.

The Secretary only received a perfunctory reply.

In April, 1951 the Secretary sent a copy of the wire to Messrs. Herbert Lehman, Paul Douglas, Henry Cabot Lodge, Jr., and William Benton urging that they personally join in this request. He sent each of these persons copy of the Report on Korea by the Special Counsel which points out the need for the appointment of a qualified Negro on this court.

Senator Lodge received a letter from Matthew Connelly after having written the President, acknowledging his letter and stating the President "appreciates your interest in writing to him and asks me to assure you that he is giving careful consideration to all of the recommendations which are coming to him relative to these pending appointments."

Subsequently the President nominated the following three persons, none of whom is a Negro, to compose a tribunal to pass on court martial judgments imposed on members of the Armed Services:

> Paul W. Boraman, Dean of Law at Tulane University, New Orleans, for a five-year term expiring May 1, 1956.

> George W. Latimer, member of the Supreme Court of Utah, Salt Lake City, for the ten-year term expiring May 1, 1961.

> Robert Emmett Quinn, West Warwick, R. I., Judge of the Rhode Island Superior Court, for the fifteen-year term expiring May 1, 1966.

Walter White
June 1951

Report of the Secretary for the
Board Meetings of December 1951 and January 1952

Leadership Conference on Civil Rights, 1952

The Leadership conference will be held in Washington, D.C., on February 17–18. Registration of delegates will be held in [the] Statler Ballroom. Delegates will be required to pay a $3.00 registration fee.

Briefing sessions for delegates on the Senate filibuster rule, organization of state delegations and interviews with senators and congressmen will be held from 2 to 5 P.M. Sunday afternoon in the Ballroom. An informal dinner will be held in the Statler at $4.00 per plate on Sunday at 7 P.M. There will be speeches by Senators Lehman, Humphrey, Benton, and the Secretary at 8:15 P.M. in the Ballroom on the civil rights program.

On Monday morning, there will be a brief meeting in the Caucus Room of the Capitol prior to meetings with congressmen and senators. Reports on the interviews with congressmen will be given on Monday afternoon at the All Souls Unitarian Church, 16 and Harvard Streets, N.W. The closing meeting will be held in the Church on Monday evening and will be addressed by Walter Reuther of the U.A.W.W.–C.I.O., and A. Philip Randolph of the Brotherhood of Sleeping Car Porters. A. Powell Davies will preside.

Madison Square Garden Benefit

Plans for the benefit are going well. To date over 10,000 tickets are in circulation. Twenty-six of the forty-two boxes are sold at the price of $100 per box. Over twenty stars have agreed to appear, among them Tallulah Bankhead, Canada Lee, Muriel Rahn, Camilla Williams, Barry Gray, and Jimmy Durante.

Dick Campbell will produce and direct the entire show including the dramatic presentation, "Toll the Liberty Bell." An active ticket committee of nearby branches, individuals and organizations is working diligently to make the night a success. Indications are that the Garden will have a most representative group in attendance.

Death of Senator Capper

Senator Arthur Capper who served as a vice-president of the N.A.A.C.P. for more than thirty-five years died during December.

In a letter dated December 20, the Secretary extended the deepest sympathy of the Association to Mrs. A. L. Eustice, sister of the late Senator. Lauding him for his work, the Secretary said "the world has lost a noble man and a great humanitarian and we in the struggle for human rights have lost a devoted friend."

Bombing and Death of Mr. and Mrs. Harry Moore

On Christmas night Harry T. Moore, state coordinator of N.A.A.C.P. branches, was killed as a result of a blast from a bomb which wrecked his home and subsequently killed Mrs. Moore. Attorney General J. Howard McGrath was immediately asked to make a thorough investigation of the matter and similar action was demanded of Governor Warren of Florida. The Department of Justice was asked to receive a delegation of national and Florida organizations "to discuss steps which must be taken to end these outrages."

The Board of Directors voted to contribute $1,000 to the family for the restoration of the home and other expenses and an appeal was sent out to the Association's branches asking for contributions and calling upon them to hold immediately a service for Mr. Moore.

The Secretary issued a statement reiterating his former charge that Governor Warren has consistently refused to take any steps to uphold law and order in that state.

The Secretary, Administrator, and Special Counsel spoke at a mass meeting in New York City held at the Mount Olivet Baptist Church on January 6. Other speakers included Shat Polier of the American Jewish Congress, Charles Zimmerman of Local 22, I.L.G.W.U., A.F.L., and Holbert Warner, vice-president of the National Maritime Union, C.I.O., at which time funds were raised for the defense and other expenses involved in the case.

In a letter signed by Arthur B. Spingarn, President, and Louis T. Wright, Chairman of the Board of Directors, the President of the United States was called upon to "invoke all the powers of the Federal Government to the end that Harry T. Moore may vindicate in death those principles and practices he sought in life." The letter reviewed the events leading up to the assassination of Mr. Moore and cited the fact that no one in our nation can proceed with safety on the basis of democratic living if bombs and terror be permitted to supplant the Constitution and laws of free America.

On January 8, the Secretary and representatives of sixteen organizations consulted with the Attorney General and asked for an investigation. The Attorney General was also urged to call immediately a federal grand jury to investigate the crimes in Florida. In response to these requests the Attorney General revealed that he had given authority to J. Edgar Hoover of the F.B.I. for a complete and unlimited investigation of the incidents that have occurred and any further ones that might occur. He also instructed the F.B.I. to let the determination of jurisdiction await the detection of all guilty persons which he said is "of first importance."

At a meeting held in Jacksonville, Florida, on January 19 and 20, 200 delegates from branches in twelve southern states conferred and action was taken on the terror in Florida. An official declaration was adopted which included plans to push registration and voting of Negroes throughout the South. A committee composed of the State Presidents of the N.A.A.C.P. was formed to carry out active political education and action campaigns.

In the absence of the Secretary because of illness, the Administrator was the official speaker at the Jacksonville meeting.

Committee on Government Contract Compliance

The Committee on Government Contract Compliance created on December 3, 1951, by executive order consists of the following persons: Mr. Dwight Palmer, President of General Cable Corporation, Chairman; James Carey, Secretary-Treasurer, C.I.O. and President of I.E.U.–C.I.O.; Irving Engel, of the American Jewish Committee; Oliver Hill, former Richmond, Va., City Councilman and a member of the National N.A.A.C.P. Legal Committee; Dowdal Davis, Editor of the *Kansas City Call*; George Meany, Secretary-Treasurer of the A.F.L.; Russell Forbes, Deputy Administrator, General Services Administration; Michael J. Galvin, Under Secretary of Labor; Everett L. Hollis, General Counsel, Atomic Energy Commission; John D. Small, Chairman, Munitions Board, Department of Defense.

Changes in Field Staff

Assistant Field Secretary Lester Bailey has resigned from the staff effective February 15. Miss Gertrude Gorman joined the field staff on January 2.

Talmadge Demands Purge of Negroes on T.V.

Protesting against the demand of Herman Talmadge of Georgia that Negro performers be barred from TV, the Secretary wired a statement adopted by the members present at the Forty-third Annual Meeting to the presidents of all the leading networks appealing to them to meet the un-American, impudent and unreasonable demand of Governor Herman Talmadge by the use of more qualified colored Americans.

Stuyvesant Town Evictions Withdrawn

After conferences with the officials of the Metropolitan Life Insurance Company, the latter withdrew the eviction notices which had been issued to nineteen families in the insurance company's project. The Administrator was a member of the group who conferred with officials of the company and as a result of this meeting, the evictions were halted and announcement was subsequently made they would be withdrawn.

N.A.A.C.P. Annual Meeting

On January 7, 1953, the Association's annual meeting was held in the Willkie Memorial Building. Reports for the year 1951 were given by the Secretary, Administrator, Assistant Special Counsel Robert Carter and other departmental heads.

Ballots for sixteen vacancies on the Board of Directors were counted and the new directors' names were announced.

Names and number of votes of each new director appears in the minutes of the January Board meeting.

Freedom of Choice Movement

Recently the Association's attention was called to a "Freedom of Choice" movement sponsored by a California organization known as America Plus, Inc. The movement's first objective is a referendum in the state of California to eliminate the state's civil rights laws. These laws would be replaced with a movement which would permit proprietors of places of public accommodation to select their own patrons on a discriminatory basis. It would also permit the establishment of exclusive neighborhoods on the basis of race, color creed, or national origin and would grant employers the right to reject applicants because of race, religion, or nationality and therefore it is patent that this organization's purposes are openly designed to restrict citizenship rights and privileges of Jews and Negroes and other minorities. The group is headed by State Senator Jack B. Tenny who is also on California's Little "Dies Committee." It has announced that it will extend its activities throughout the nation in an effort to wipe civil rights statutes off the books of every state.

The Secretary denounced the movement and stated that the Association will rally every possible resource to head it off. The Secretary announced that a plan of action to secure funds to fight the movement has been organized; civic groups, religious organizations, Jewish associations, and organized labor, and Negro organizations will be asked to participate.

Cost of Segregation

In letters dated December 3 to the governors of New York, New Jersey, Connecticut, Pennsylvania, Indiana, Ohio, Illinois, Massachusetts, the Secretary urged them to use their influence with their respective congressional delegations to prevent southerners sharing in the use of federal grants to support racial segregation, pointing out that the eight states referred to above paid more than fifty per cent of the federal tax revenue during the fiscal year ending June 30, 1951. Ten southern states carried only nine per cent of the tax burden. He stated that the people in these respective northern states are carrying an added tax burden because of segregation in the south and accordingly asked that they take official notice of the federal programs for housing, schools, and other benefits. While southern states need financial help, the Secretary said, such help should be given on the condition of not wasting money on segregation. He asked that the governors urge members of Congress from other states to give full support to language forbidding expenditures of federal money for segregated facilities. Such language should be included in all bills for housing, schools, hospitals, and other proposals for giving assistance to the states.

Stork Club

The so-called final report of the Mayor's Committee on Unity in the Josephine Baker Stork Club case was termed "inexplicable and fantastic" in a letter to Chairman of the Committee Arthur W. Wallender. The report released by the Mayor's office found "nothing to substantiate a charge of racial discrimination." The Secretary expressed amazement that the committee which on November 23 deplored the "deep and sinister" implications of the case, a month later asked that it be considered closed. The Secretary asked the reasons for this amazing change.

Through her attorney, Arthur Garfield Hays, Miss Baker has filed a $400,000 libel suit against Walter Winchell, and his publishers.

The Secretary wrote Governor Thomas E. Dewey in January enclosing a clipping from the *New York Post* which described Sherman Billingsley as having violated and been convicted of violation of the Volstead Act. He pointed out that it was the N.A.A.C.P.'s understanding that no person with a criminal record, particularly if the charge is violation of the Volstead Act, is eligible under the State Liquor Act for a liquor license. The Governor was urged to investigate the charges and upon proof of their validity have the license of the Stork Club revoked.

Death of Bishop Gordon

Bishop Buford Gordon of North Carolina, head of the Seventh Episcopal District of the A.M.E. Church, died recently. Bishop Gordon was a long-time friend and loyal worker for the Association and was one of the principle speakers at the Association's Forty-first Annual Convention in Boston in 1950. The Secretary wired Mrs. Gordon expressing the Association's sympathy and calling the Bishop "not only a great leader of the church but also an eloquent and uncompromising advocate of justice and the practice of Christianity in everyday life."

Death of Judge Patterson

Judge Robert P. Patterson, former Secretary of War and staunch friend of the Association, was killed in an airplane crash January 22 at Elizabeth, N.J. The Secretary wired condolences. Judge Patterson was not only a long-time supporter of the Association, but he also served as chairman of the N.A.A.C.P. Testimonial Dinner to Dr. Ralph J. Bunche in January 1951.

Senate Rules Change Inadequate

The resolution approved on January 2, 1952, by the Senate Rules Committee to permit cloture to cut off a filibuster on a vote of two-thirds of the Senators present and voting was attacked as inadequate by the Administrator. He pointed out that the resolution will not aid attempts to pass civil rights legislation. The change does not alter section 3 which prohibits a cloture vote on motions to take up a measure. He further asserted that the resolution is the same as the 1949 rule, in that debate is still in no way limited on a motion to take up civil rights or other measures. The Association is interested in having the Senate adopt a rule which will permit cloture by a majority vote.

Loyalty of Philleo Nash

The loyalty of White House Aide Philleo Nash, who was attacked on the floor of the Senate by Senator Joseph B. McCarthy, Republican from Wisconsin, was upheld by the Secretary. In a telegram to the Senator, it was pointed out that Mr. Nash had worked closely in his position as White House Aide with the N.A.A.C.P. and that organization was deeply impressed with his sincerity and devotion to the nation's highest ideals of justice. The wire further pointed out that we were shocked and distressed to learn of the serious charges which had been made.

Death of Harold Ickes

On learning of the death of Harold L. Ickes, former Secretary of the Interior, and one-time president of the Chicago Branch, N.A.A.C.P., the Secretary wired Mrs. Ickes expressing the Association's sympathy and praising her husband for being the first to abolish racial segregation in the Department of the Interior, thereby setting an example to other governmental agencies. He recalled the occasion in 1939 when Constitution Hall refused permission to Marian Anderson to sing there and Mr. Ickes placed the facilities of the government at her disposal.

Judge William H. Hastie acted as an honorary pallbearer at Mr. Ickes' funeral. Judge Hastie and Mr. Clarence Mitchell represented the Association at the funeral.

Walter White, Secretary
January 1952

Report of the Secretary for the Board Meeting of May 1954

Philip Murray Award

On May 12 the Philip Murray Memorial Foundation presented the Association a grant for $75,000 in a ceremony held at the Carnegie Foundation for International Peace. Formal presentation of the award was made by Walter Reuther, president of the C.I.O.. The check was accepted by Arthur B. Spingarn, president of the

N.A.A.C.P. Other speakers were Mr. Arthur Goldberg, Mrs. Eleanor Roosevelt, Mr. W. Averell Harriman, and Mr. Willard Townsend.

The Grant was made to aid in development, through educational means, of a climate of opinion receptive to eradication of racial discrimination and segregation. It will be set aside in a separate fund for financing such projects as films, literature, and community action programs.

Virgin Island Bill

The Association opposed a proposed bill to amend the Organic Act for the Virgin Islands on the ground that it would constitute a "backward step" for the people of the islands and would do "irreparable harm to America's reputation and prestige."

The principal point in the Association's objection is that the proposed bill takes away from the local legislature the right to participate in reorganization of the existing departments, bureaus, or agencies of the executive branch of the territorial government. This power the legislature has had during the past eighteen years under the 1936 Organic Act and there is no existing basis for depriving the legislature of this democratic function in a bill which will in all probability serve as the law of the territory for the next fifteen to twenty years. The House bill, HR 5181, has been removed from the consent calendar by Chairman Miller of the Insular Affairs Committee and sent to the Rules Committee. This procedure will give all factions an opportunity to present their case before the full House prior to passage.

Supreme Court Decision in School Cases

In accordance with the vote of the Board at its March meeting, a special meeting of the Committee on Administration was called to consider the decision in the school segregation cases as soon as the decision was announced and a statement issued for the press as follows:

> The National Association for the Advancement of Colored People regards the unanimous decision handed down today by the United States Supreme Court as a highly significant step in the forward progress of American democracy. In overruling the "separate but equal" doctrine laid down by *Plessy* vs. *Ferguson* in 1896, the Court reinforced the faith of all Americans in the basic justice of our system.
>
> This ruling further vindicates the forty-five-year fight of the N.A.A.C.P. to establish the principles that to segregate is to discriminate and, accordingly, violates our Constitution and the American democracy is decadent and that Negroes or other minorities cannot obtain justice through the democratic process.
>
> In accordance with the Court's decision, the N.A.A.C.P. is fully prepared to present further argument for the formulation of decrees and

will exert every effort to win full community compliance with this historic decision.

We have high regard for the integrity, intelligence, and understanding of the American people, North and South, and their respect for law. We are confident that the people of the South, Negro and white, will get together on the basis of the Court's decision and jointly formulate plans to carry it out at the local level. Our units in the South stand ready to share responsibility in complying with the new ruling.

In hailing this vital decision, we are acutely aware that much remains to be done to extend the frontiers of human freedom. The N.A.A.C.P. will not be content until every form of racial discrimination and segregation is eliminated from American life.

The Board heartily congratulates its legal staff, headed by Thurgood Marshall, and extends thanks to that great host of lawyers, historians, social scientists, and others who volunteered their services to assist our legal staff in the preparation of the briefs and arguments for these cases. Especially are we grateful to our membership and to the host of other Americans of both races who have supplied the necessary funds for this epochal struggle.

Following the decision, the Association received excellent publicity in the press, radio and television. The Secretary, Special Counsel, and other members of the staff gave numerous interviews, appeared on a number of television and radio programs, and the Secretary gave an interview to *U.S. News and World Report* which appeared in the May 28 issue of the *U.S. News*, copy of which was mailed to members of the Board and officers of the Association. The Secretary and Special Counsel jointly did a program for the Voice of America for overseas consumption.

Hundreds of letters and wires of congratulations have been received by the Association from all parts of the country and some from other parts of the world.

Atlanta Conference

On the weekend following the decision in the school cases, a conference was held in Atlanta, Ga., of state conference, regional and some branch officers. Representatives from seventeen southern and border states and the District of Columbia assembled there and issued the following statement:

We, as representatives of the National Association for the Advancement of Colored People from seventeen southern and border states and the District of Columbia, have assembled here in Atlanta, Georgia, May 22–23, for the purpose of collectively developing a program to meet the vital and urgent issues arising out of the historic United States Supreme Court decision of May 17 banning segregation in public schools.

All Americans are now relieved to have the law of the land declare in the clearest language: ". . . in the field of public education the doctrine of 'separate but equal' has no place. Separate educational facilities are inherently unequal." Segregation in public education is now not only unlawful: it is un-American; true Americans are grateful for this decision. Now that the law is made clear, we look to the future. Having canvassed the situation in each of our states, we approach the future with the utmost confidence. This confidence is based upon many factors including the pledges of support and compliance by governors, attorneys general, mayors, and education officials; and by enlightened guidance of newspapers, radio, television and other organs of public communication and comment.

We stand ready to work with other law abiding citizens who are anxious to translate this decision into a program of action to eradicate racial segregation in public education as speedily as possible.

We are instructing all of our branches in every affected area to petition their local school boards to abolish segregation without delay and to assist these agencies in working out ways and means of implementing the Court's ruling. The total resources of the N.A.A.C.P. will be made available to facilitate this great project of ending the artificial separation of America's children on the irrelevant basis of race and color.

While we recognize that school officials will have certain administrative problems in transferring from a segregated to a non-segregated system, we will resist the use of any tactics contrived for the sole purpose of delaying desegregation.

In pursuit of our objective, we will accelerate our community action program to win public acceptance of the Court's desegregation order from all segments of the population. To this end, we are confident of the support of teachers, parents, labor, church, civic, fraternal, social, business, and professional organizations.

We insist that there should be integration at all levels including the assignment of teacher-personnel on a non-discriminatory basis. The fullest resources of the Association, including the legal staff, the research staff and educational specialists on the staff, will be utilized to insure that there will be no discrimination against teachers as a result of integration.

We are aware that our region has been overburdened in its effort to provide education for all children—in part because of the dual system—and accordingly, we strongly support federal aid to assist our states in the building of new schools and the expansion of educational facilities for all our children, provided that any such legislation contains the necessary safeguards to insure the distribution of funds in accordance with the requirements of the court's decision.

We look upon this memorable decision not as a victory for Negroes alone, but for the whole American people and as a vindication of America's leadership of the free world.

Lest there be any misunderstanding of our position, we here rededicate ourselves to the removal of all racial segregation in public education and reiterate our determination to achieve this goal without compromise of principle.

At a press conference following the two-day conference, Carl Johnson, member of the National Board, read the statements to the press, radio, and television commentators. During the press conference the Special Counsel reported that the Association would press forward immediately with the campaign of submitting petitions to local school officials to desegregate as soon as possible. The Secretary stated that the ruling of the Supreme Court would be greatly strengthened by the expansion of the Negro vote on which the Association is now working.

Loyalty Investigation of Dr. Bunche

On May 26 the newspapers reported that Dr. Ralph Bunche was being interrogated by the International Organizations Employee Loyalty Board. Immediately upon publication of the news, the Secretary issued the following statement:

> Any question of the loyalty of Dr. Ralph J. Bunche or of his devotion to his country and the democratic process is shocking.
>
> As one who has steadfastly opposed communism and every other form of dictatorship throughout my entire life I gladly stake whatever reputation I may possess on Dr. Bunche's unqualified loyalty and integrity.
>
> Dr. Bunche is not only a great and distinguished American but a great and distinguished citizen of the world whose entire career has been dedicated to the preservation and enlargement of human liberty. To achieve that status he has had to overcome, because of race, great handicaps.
>
> I have learned at first-hand in Asia, Africa, Latin America, the Middle East, and Europe as well as in the United States that Dr. Bunche is one of the truly great symbols of Americanism at its best. This has been particularly true among the two-thirds of the peoples of the world who are nonwhite. They, because of his example, have been encouraged to refuse to follow communist propaganda and to continue to have faith in democracy.
>
> Millions of Americans of every race, creed, color, and national origin will join in urging swift and unequivocal action to end this unseemly farce.

He also requested permission to appear before the Board to testify in behalf of Dr. Bunche on the basis of their twenty-five years of friendship and working together. The Secretary did appear and did testify. Many others including Dr. Channing H. Tobias, Chairman of the Board, and Mrs. Eleanor Roosevelt requested opportunity to be heard but the Board after hearing Dr. Bunche and after reported interrogation of his two ex-communist accusers, issued a public statement at the office of the U.S. Delegation to the United Nations completely clearing Dr. Bunche, as follows:

> As a matter of justice to the individuals concerned, the International Organizations Employees Loyalty Board does not disclose any informa-

tion concerning its proceedings. However, since the Board was unable to prevent public disclosure of the fact that it was holding hearings concerning Dr. Ralph J. Bunche it has decided to depart from its policy in his case and to make a prompt and public disclosure of its decision.

The full board had its second meeting with Dr. Bunche yesterday following which it unanimously reached the conclusion that there is no doubt as to the loyalty of Dr. Bunche to the government of the United States.

This conclusion has been forwarded to the Secretary of State for transmittal to the Secretary General of the U.N. At the same time it has been informally transmitted to Dr. Bunche.

Annual Convention

Speakers—persons scheduled to address the Annual Convention evening meetings are Channing H. Tobias, who will deliver the keynote address on Tuesday, June 29; Mr. James B. Carey of the C.I.O., the Special Counsel. Dr. Theodore K. Lawless of Chicago, famed dermatologist, will receive the Spingarn Medal. Dr. Charles H. Mayo of Mayo Clinic, Rochester, Minn., has been invited to make [the] presentation.

The Sunday mass meeting will be addressed by Dr. Ralph Bunche and the Secretary.

Walter White, Secretary
June 12, 1954

Speeches, Essays, and Articles, 1929–1955

Editor's Note

In addition to his work as assistant secretary of the NAACP, Walter White contributed articles and essays to numerous journals and newspapers. He also wrote a syndicated column for the *New York Herald Tribune*.

The following are selected writings by White during his tenure as acting secretary and secretary of the NAACP. They include NAACP Convention and Annual Conference speeches, articles from his *New York Herald Tribune* column; and essays written for *Harper's* and the *Nation*. In general, the writings presented here are thematically consistent with his NAACP work.

I Investigate Lynchings

When Walter White joined the staff of the NAACP he became a zealous crusader against lynching. His novel *Fire in the Flint*, published in 1925, is one of the most compelling on the subject. His nonfiction *Rope and Faggot: A Biography of Judge Lynch*, published in 1927 and written on a Guggenheim fellowship, became the first significant work on the phenomenon of lynching. The following essay is an account of White's personal investigations of lynching. This article was written in 1929.

Nothing contributes so much to the continued life of an investigator of lynchings and his tranquil possession of all his limbs as the obtuseness of the lynchers themselves. Like most boastful people who practice direct action when it involves no personal risk, they just can't help but talk about their deeds to any person who manifests even the slightest interest in them.

Most lynchings take place in a small towns and rural regions where the natives know practically nothing of what is going on outside their immediate neighborhoods. Newspapers, books, magazines, theaters, visitors, and other vehicles for the transmission of information and ideas are usually as strange among them as drypoint etchings. But those who live in so sterile an atmosphere usually esteem their own perspicacity in about the same degree as they are isolated from the world of ideas. They gabble on *ad infinitum*, apparently unable to keep from talking.

In any American village, North or South, East or West, there is no problem which cannot be solved in half an hour by the morons who lounge about the village store. World peace, or the lack of it, the tariff, sex, religion, the settlement of the war debts, short skirts, Prohibition, the carrying-on of the younger generations, the superior moral rectitude of country people over city dwellers (with a wistful eye on urban sins)—all these controversial subjects are disposed of quickly and finally by the bucolic wise men. When to their isolation is added an emotional fixation such as the rural South has on the Negro, one can sense the atmosphere from which spring the Heflins, the Ku Klux Klaners, the two-gun Bible-beaters, the lynchers, and the anti-evolutionists. And one can see why no great amount of cleverness or courage is needed to acquire information in such a forlorn place about the latest lynching.

Professor Earle Fiske Young of the University of Southern California recently analyzed the lynching returns from fourteen Southern States for thirty years. He found that in counties of less than 10,000 people there was a lynching rate of 3.2 per 100,000 of population; that in those of from 10,000 to 20,000 the rate dropped to 2.4; that in those of from 20,000 to 30,000, it was 2.1 per cent; that in those of from 30,00 to 40,000, it was 1.7, and that thereafter it kept on going down until in counties with from 300,000 to 800,000 population it was only 0.05.

Of the forty-one lynchings and eight race riots I have investigated for the National Association for the Advancement of Colored People during the past ten years all of the lynchings and seven of the riots occurred in rural or semi-rural communities. The towns ranged in population from around one hundred to ten thousand or so. The lynchings were not difficult to inquire into because of the fact already noted that those who perpetrated them were in nearly every instance simple-minded and easily fooled individuals. On but three occasions were suspicions aroused by my too definite questions or by informers who had seen me in other places. These three times I found it rather desirable to disappear slightly in advance of reception committees imbued with the desire to make an addition to the lynching record. One other time the possession of a light skin and blue eyes (though I consider myself a colored man) almost cost me my life when (it was during the Chicago race riots in 1919) a Negro shot at me thinking me to be a white man.

II

In 1918 a Negro woman, about to give birth to a child, was lynched with almost unmentionable brutality along with ten men in Georgia. I reached the scene shortly after the butchery and while excitement yet ran high. It was a prosperous community. Forests of pine trees gave rich returns in turpentine, tar, and pitch. The small towns where the farmers and turpentine hands traded were fat and rich. The main stores were well stocked. The white inhabitants belonged to the class of Georgia crackers—lanky, slow of movement and of speech, long-necked, with small eyes set close together and skins tanned by the hot sun to a reddish-yellow hue.

As I was born in Georgia and spent twenty years of my life there, my accent is sufficiently Southern to enable me to talk with Southerners and not arouse their suspicion that I am an outsider. (In rural South hatred of Yankees is not much less than hatred of Negroes.) On the morning of my arrival in the town I casually dropped into the store of one of the general merchants who, I had been informed, had been one of the leaders of the mobs. After making a small purchase I engaged the merchant in conversation. There was, at the time, no other customer in the store. We spoke of the weather, the possibility of good crops in the Fall, the political situation; the latest news from the war in Europe. As his manner became more and more friendly I ventured to mention guardedly the recent lynching.

Instantly he became cautious—until I hinted that I had great admiration for the manly spirit the men of the town had exhibited. I mentioned the newspaper accounts I had read and confessed that I had never been so fortunate as to see a lynching. My words or tone seemed to disarm his suspicion. He offered me a box on which to sit, drew up another one for himself, and gave me a bottle of Coca-Cola.

"You'll pardon me, Mister," he began, "for seeming suspicious but we have to be careful. In ordinary times we wouldn't have anything to worry about, but with the war there's been some talk of the federal government looking into lynchings.

It seems there's some sort of law during wartime making it treason to lower the man power of the country."

"In that case, I don't blame you for being careful," I assured him. "But couldn't the federal government do something if it wanted to when a lynching takes place, even if no war is going on at the moment?"

"Naw," he said, confidently, obviously proud of the opportunity of displaying his store of information to one whom he assumed knew nothing whatever about the subject. "There's no such law, in spite of all the agitation by a lot of fools who don't know the niggers as we do. States' rights won't permit Congress to meddle in lynching in peace time."

"But what about your State government—your Governor, your sheriff, your police officers?"

"Humph! Them? We elected them to office, didn't we? And the niggers, we've got them disfranchised, ain't we? Sheriffs and police and Governors and prose-cuting attorneys have got too much sense to mix in lynching-bees. If they do, they know they might as well give up all idea of running for office any more—if something worse don't happen to them—" This last with a tightening of the lips and a hard look in the eyes.

I sought to lead the conversation into less dangerous channels. "Who was the white man who was killed—whose killing caused the lynchings?" I asked.

"Oh, he was a hard one, all right. Never paid his debts to white men or niggers and wasn't liked much around here. He was a mean 'un, all right, all right."

"Why, then, did you lynch the niggers for killing such a man?"

"It 's a matter of safety—we gotta show niggers that they mustn't touch a white man, no matter how low-down and ornery he is."

Little by little he revealed the whole story. When he told of the manner in which the pregnant woman had been killed he chuckled and slapped his thigh and declared it to be "the best show, Mister, I ever did see. You ought to have heard the wench howl when we strung her up."

Covering the nausea the story caused me as best I could, I slowly gained the whole story, with the names of the other participants. Among them were pros-perous farmers, business men, bankers, newspaper reporters and editors, and sev-eral law enforcement officers.

My several days of discreet inquiry began to arouse suspicions in the town. On the third day of my stay I went once more into the store of the man with whom I had first talked. He asked me to wait until he had finished serving the sole customer. When she had gone he came from behind the counter and with secretive manner and lowered voice he asked, "You're a government man, ain't you?" (An agent of the Federal Department of Justice was what he meant.)

"Who said so?" I countered.

"Never mind who told me, I know one when I see him," he replied, with a shrewd harshness in his face and voice.

Ignorant of what might have taken place since last I had talked with him, I thought it wise to learn all I could and say nothing which might commit me, "Don't you tell anyone I am a government man; if I am one, you're the only one in town who knows it," I told him cryptically. I knew that within an hour everybody in town would share his "information."

An hour or so later I went at nightfall to the little but not uncomfortable hotel where I was staying. As I was about to enter, a Negro approached me and, with an air of great mystery, told me that he had just heard a group of white men discussing me and declaring that if I remained in the town overnight "something would happen" to me.

The thought raced through my mind before I replied that it was hardly likely that, following so terrible a series of lynchings, a Negro would voluntarily approach a supposedly white man whom he did not know and deliver such a message. He had been sent, and no doubt the persons who sent him were white and for some reason did not dare tackle me themselves. Had they dared there would have been no warning in advance—simply an attack. Though I had no weapon with me, it occurred to me that there was no reason why two should not play at the game of bluffing. I looked straight into my informant's eyes and said, in as convincing a tone as I could muster: "You go back to the ones who sent you and tell them this: that I have a damned good automatic and I know how to use it. If anybody attempts to molest me tonight or any other time, somebody is going to get hurt."

That night I did not take off my clothes nor did I sleep. Ordinarily in such small Southern towns everyone is snoring by nine o'clock. That night, however, there was much passing and re-passing of the hotel. I learned afterward that the merchant had, as I expected, told generally that I was an agent of the Department of Justice, and my empty threat had served to reinforce his assertion. The Negro had been sent to me in the hope that I might be frightened enough to leave before I had secured evidence against the members of the mob. I remained in the town two more days. My every movement was watched, but I was not molested. But when, later, it became known that not only was I not an agent of the Department of Justice but a Negro, the fury of the inhabitants of the region was unlimited—particularly when it was found that evidence I gathered had been placed in the hands of the Governor of Georgia. It happened that he was a man genuinely eager to stop lynching—but restrictive laws against which he had appealed in vain effectively prevented him from acting upon the evidence. And the Federal government declared itself unable to proceed against the lynchers.

III

In 1926 I went to a Southern State for a New York newspaper to inquire into the lynching of two colored boys and a colored woman. Shortly after reaching the town I learned that a certain lawyer knew something about the lynchers. He proved to be the only specimen I have ever encountered, in much traveling in the South, of the Southern gentleman so beloved by fiction writers of the older school. He had heard of the lynching before it occurred and, fruitlessly, had warned the judge and the prosecutor. He talked frankly about the affair and gave me the names of certain men who knew more about it than he did. Several of them lived in a small town nearby where the only industry was a large cotton mill. When I asked him if he would go with me to call on these people he peered out of the window at the descending sun and said, somewhat anxiously, I thought, "I will go with you if you will promise to get back to town before sundown."

I asked why there was need of such haste. "No one would harm a respectable and well-known person like yourself, would they?" I asked him.

"Those mill hands out there would harm anybody," he answered.

I promised him we would be back before sundown—a promise that was not hard to make for if they would harm this man I could imagine what they would do to a stranger!

When we reached the little mill town we passed through it and, ascending a steep hill, our car stopped in front of a house perched perilously on the side of the hill. In the yard stood a man with iron gray hair and eyes which seemed strong enough to bore through concrete. The old lawyer introduced me and we were invited into the house. As it was a cold afternoon in late Autumn the gray-haired man called a boy to build a fire.

I told him frankly I was seeking information about the lynching. He said nothing, but left the room. Perhaps two minutes later, hearing a sound at the door through which he had gone, I looked up and there stood a figure clad in the full regalia of the Ku Klux Klan. I looked at the figure and the figure looked at me. The hood was then removed and, as I suspected, it was the owner of the house.

"I show you this," he told me, "so you will know that what I tell you is true."

This man, I learned, had been the organizer and leader of the local Klan. He had been quite honest in his activities as a Kluxer, for corrupt officials and widespread criminal activities had caused him and other local men to believe that the only cure rested in a secret extra legal organization. But he had not long been engaged in promoting the plan before he had the experience of other believers in Klan methods. The very people whose misdeeds the organization was designed to correct gained control of it. The man then resigned and ever since had been living in fear of his life. He took me into an adjoining room after removing his Klan robe and there showed me a considerable collection of revolvers, shotguns, rifles, and ammunition.

When we sat down I listened to as hair-raising a tale of Nordic moral endeavor as it has ever been my lot to hear. Among the choice bits were stories such as this: This sheriff of an adjoining county the year before had been a candidate for reelection. A certain man of considerable wealth had contributed largely to his campaign fund, providing the margin by which he was reelected. Shortly afterwards a married woman with whom the sheriff's supporter had been intimate quarreled one night with her husband. When the cuckold charged his wife with infidelity, the gentle creature waited until he was asleep, got a large butcher knife, and then artistically carved him up. Bleeding more profusely than a pig in the stock yards, the man dragged himself to the home of a neighbor several hundred yards distant and there died on the door-step. The facts were notorious, but the sheriff effectively blocked even interrogation of the widow!

I spent some days in the region and found that the three Negroes who had been lynched were about as guilty of the murder of which they were charged as I was. Convicted in a court thronged with armed Klansmen and sentenced to death, their case had been appealed to the State Supreme Court, which promptly reversed the conviction, remanded the appellants for new trials, and severely criticized the judge before whom they had been tried. At the new trial the evidence against one of the defendants so clearly showed his innocence that the judge granted a motion to dismiss, and the other two defendants were obviously as little guilty as he. But as soon as the motion to dismiss was granted the defendant was rearrested on a trivial charge and once again lodged in jail. That night the mob took the prisoners to the outskirts of the town, and told them to run, and as they set out pumped bullets into their backs. The two boys died instantly. The woman was shot in several places, but was not immediately killed. One of the lynchers afterwards laughingly told me that "we had to waste fifty bullets on the wench before one of them stopped her howling."

Evidence in affidavit form indicated rather clearly that various law enforcement officials, including the sheriff, his deputies, various jailers and policemen, three relatives of the then Governor of the State, a member of the State Legislature and sundry individuals prominent in business, political and social life of the vicinity, were members of the mob.

The revelation of these findings after I had returned to New York did not add to my popularity in the lynching region. Public sentiment in the State itself, stirred up by several courageous newspapers, began to make it uncomfortable for the lynchers. When the sheriff found things getting a bit too unpleasant he announced that he was going to ask the grand jury to indict me for "bribery and passing for white." It developed that the person I was supposed to have paid money to for execution of an affidavit was a man I had never seen in the flesh, the affidavit having been secured by the reporter of a New York newspaper.

An amusing tale is connected with the charge of passing. Many years ago a bill was introduced in the Legislature of that State defining legally as a Negro any person who had one drop or more of Negro blood. Acrimonious debate in the lower house did not prevent passage of the measure, and the same result seemed likely in the State Senate. One of the Senators, a man destined eventually to go to the United States Senate on a campaign of vilification of the Negro, rose at a strategic point to speak on the bill. As the story goes, his climax was "If you go on with this bill you will bathe every country in blood before nightfall. And, what's more, there won't be enough white people left in the State to pass it."

When the sheriff threatened me with an indictment for passing as white, a white man in the State with whom I had talked wrote me a long letter asking me if it were true that I had Negro blood. "You did not tell me nor anyone else in my presence," he wrote, "that you were not white except as to your name. I had on amber-colored glasses and did not take the trouble to scrutinize your color, but I really did take you for a white man and, according to the laws of———, you may be." My informant urged me to sit down and figure out mathematically the exact percentage of Negro blood that I possessed and, if it proved to be less than one-eighth, to sue for libel those who had charged me with passing.

This man wrote of the frantic efforts of the whites of his State to keep themselves thought of as white. He quoted an old law to the effect that "it was not slander to call one a Negro because everybody could see that he was not; but it was slanderous to call him a mulatto."

IV

On another occasion a serious riot occurred in Tulsa, Okla., a bustling town of 100,000 inhabitants. In the early days Tulsa had been a lifeless and unimportant village of not more than five thousand people, and its Negro residents had been forced to live in what was considered the least desirable section of the village, down near the railroad. Then oil was discovered nearby and almost overnight the village grew into a prosperous town. The Negroes prospered along with the whites, and began to erect comfortable homes, business establishments, a hotel, two cinemas and other enterprises, all of these springing up in the section to which they had been relegated. This was, as I have said, down near the railroad tracks. The swift growth of the town made this hitherto disregarded land of great value for business purposes. Efforts to purchase the land from the Negro owners at prices far below its value were unavailing. Having built up the neighborhood and knowing its value, the owners refused to be victimized.

One afternoon in 1921 a Negro messenger boy went to deliver a package in an office building on the main street of Tulsa. His errand done, he rang the bell for the elevator in order that he might descend. The operator, a young white girl, on finding that she had been summoned by a Negro, opened the door of the car ungraciously. Two versions there are of what happened then. The boy declared that she started the car on its downward plunge when he was only halfway in, and that to save himself from being killed he had to throw himself into the car, stepping on the girl's foot in doing so. The girl, on the other hand, asserted that the boy attempted to rape her in the elevator. The latter story, at best, seemed highly dubious—that an attempted criminal assault would be made by any person in an open elevator of a crowded office building on the main street of a town of 100,00 inhabitants—and in open daylight!

Whatever the truth, the local press, with scant investigation, published lurid accounts of the alleged assault. That night a mob started to the jail to lynch the Negro boy. A group of Negroes offered their services to the jailer and sheriff in protecting the prisoner. The offer was declined, and when the Negroes started to leave the sheriff's office a clash occurred between them and the mob. Instantly the mob swung into action.

The Negroes, outnumbered, were forced back to their own neighborhood. Rapidly the news spread of the clash and the numbers of mobbers grew hourly. By daybreak of the following day the mob numbered around five thousand, and was armed with machine guns, dynamite, rifles, revolvers, and shotguns, cans of gasoline and kerosene, and—such are the blessings for invention!—airplanes. Surrounding the Negro section, it attacked, led by men who had been officers in the American army in France. Outnumbered and out-equipped, the plight of the Negroes was a hopeless one from the beginning. Driven further and further back, many of them were killed or wounded, among them an aged man and his wife, who were slain as they knelt at prayer for deliverance. Forty-four blocks of property were burned after homes and stores had been pillaged.

I arrived in Tulsa while the excitement was at its peak. Within a few hours I met a commercial photographer who had worked for five years on a New York newspaper and he welcomed me with open arms when he found that I represented a New York paper. From him I learned that special deputy sheriffs were being sworn in to guard the town from a rumored counter attack by the Negroes. It occurred to me that I could get myself sworn in as one of these deputies.

It was even easier to do this than I had expected. That evening in the City Hall I had to answer only three questions—name, age, and address. I might have been a thug, a murderer, an escaped convict, a member of the mob itself which had laid waste a large area of the city—none of these mattered; my skin was apparently white, and that was enough. After we—some fifty or sixty of us—had been sworn in, solemnly declaring we would do our utmost to uphold the laws and constitutions of the United States and the State of Oklahoma, a villainous-looking man next [to] me turned and remarked casually, even with a note of happiness in his voice: "Now you can go out and shoot any nigger you see and the law'll be behind you."

As we stood in the wide marble corridor of the not unimposing City Hall waiting to be assigned to automobiles which were to patrol the city during the night, I noticed a man, clad in the uniform of a captain of the United States Army, watching me closely. I imagined I saw in his very swarthy face (he was much darker than I, but was classed as a white man while I am deemed a Negro) mingled inquiry and hostility. I kept my eye on him without appearing to do so. Tulsa would not have been a very healthy place for me that night had my race or my previous investigations of other race riots been known there. At last the man seemed certain he knew me and started toward me.

He drew me aside into a deserted corner on the excuse that he had something he wished to ask me, and I noticed that four other men with whom he had been talking detached themselves from the crowd and followed us.

Without further introduction or apology my dark-skinned newly made acquaintance, putting his face close to mine and looking into my eyes with a steely, unfriendly glance, demanded challengingly:

"You say that your name is White?"

I answered affirmatively.

"You say you're a newspaper man?"

"Yes, I represent the New York———. Would you care to see my credentials?"

"No, but I want to tell you something. There's an organization in the South that doesn't love niggers. It has branches everywhere. You needn't ask me the name—I can't tell you. But it has come back into existence to fight this damned nigger Advancement Association. We watch every movement of the officers of this nigger society and we're out to get them for putting notions of equality into the heads of our niggers down South here."

There could be no question that he referred to the Ku Klux Klan on the one hand and the National Association for the Advancement of Colored People on the other. As coolly as I could, the circumstances being what they were, I took a cigarette from my case and lighted it, trying to keep my hand from betraying my nervousness. When he finished speaking I asked him:

"All this is very interesting, but what, if anything, has it to do with the story of the race riot here which I've come to get?"

For a full minute we looked straight into each other's eyes, his four companions meanwhile crowding close about us. At length his eyes fell. With a shrug of his shoulders and a half-apologetic smile, he replied as he turned away, "Oh, nothing except I wanted you to know what's back of the trouble here."

It is hardly necessary to add that all that night, assigned to the same car with this man and his four companions, I maintained a considerable vigilance. When the news stories I wrote about the riot (the boy accused of attempted assault was acquitted in the magistrate's court after nearly one million dollars of property and a number of lives had been destroyed) revealed my identity—that I was a Negro and an officer of the Advancement Society—more than a hundred anonymous letters threatening my life came to me. I was also threatened with a suit for criminal libel by a local paper, but nothing came of it after my willingness to defend it was indicated.

V

A narrower escape came during an investigation of an alleged plot by Negroes in Arkansas to "massacre" all the white people of the State. It later developed that the Negroes had simply organized a cooperative society to combat their economic exploitation by landlords, merchants, and bankers, many of whom openly practiced peonage. I went as a representative of a Chicago newspaper to get the facts. Going first to the capital of the state, Little Rock, I interviewed the Governor and other officials and then proceeded to the scene of the trouble: Phillips county, in the heart of the cotton-raising area close to the Mississippi.

As I stepped from the train at Elaine the county seat, I was closely watched by a crowd of men. Within half an hour of my arrival I had been asked by two shopkeepers, a restaurant waiter, and a ticket agent why I had come to Elaine, what my business was, and what I thought of the recent riot. The tension relaxed somewhat when I implied I was in sympathy with the mob. Little by little suspicion was lessened and then, the people being eager to have a metropolitan newspaper give their side of the story, I was shown "evidence" that the story of the massacre plot was well-founded, and not very clever attempts were made to guide me away from the truth.

Suspicion was given new birth when I pressed my inquiries too insistently concerning the share-cropping and tenant-farming system, which works somewhat as follows: Negro farmers enter into agreements to till specified plots of land, they do receive usually half of the crop for their labor. Should they be too poor to buy food, seed, clothing, and other supplies, they are supplied those commodities by their landlords at designated stores. When the crop is gathered the land-owner takes it and sells it. By declaring that he has sold it at a figure far below the market price and by refusing to give itemized accounts of the supplies purchased during the year by the tenant, a landlord can (and in that region almost always does) so arrange it that the bill for supplies always exceeds the tenant's share of the crop. Individual Negroes who had protested against such thievery had been lynched. The new organization was simply a union to secure relief through the courts, which relief those who profited from the system meant to prevent. Thus the story of a "massacre" plot.

Suspicion of me took definite form when word was sent to Phillips County from Little Rock that it had been discovered that I was a Negro, though I knew nothing about the message at the time. I walked down West Cherry Street, the main thoroughfare of Elaine, one day on my way to the jail, where I had an appointment with the sheriff, who was going to permit me to interview some of the Negro prisoners who were charged with being implicated in the alleged plot. A tall heavy-set Negro passed me, and *sotto voce*, told me as he passed that he had something important to tell me, and I should turn to the right at the next corner and follow him. Some inner sense bade me obey. When we had got out of sight of other persons the Negro told me not to go to the jail, that there was great hostility in the town against me and that they planned harming me. In the man's manner there was something which made me certain he was telling the truth. Making my way to the railroad station, since my interview with the prisoners (the sheriff and jailer being present) was unlikely to add anything to my story, I was able to board one of the two trains a day out of Elaine. When I explained to the conductor—he looked at me so inquiringly—that I had no ticket because delays in Elaine had given me no time to purchase one, he exclaimed, "Why, Mister, you're leaving just when the fun is going to start! There's a damned yaller nigger down here passing for white and the boys are going to have some fun with him."

I asked him the nature of the fun.

"Wall, when they get through with him," he explained grimly "he won't pass for white no more."

The Negro and the Supreme Court

President Hoover nominated Judge John J. Parker, a circuit court judge from North Carolina, to be an associate justice of the Supreme Court. Within one week Walter White had checked into Parker's record and learned that ten years before, when Parker was a candidate for governor of North Carolina, the *Greensboro Daily News* quoted him as saying, "The participation of the Negro in politics is a source of evil and danger to both races and is not desired by the wise men in either race or in the Republican Party of N.C." Walter White believed that any jurist who maintained such a viewpoint was not qualified to serve on the High Court. He further argued that

Parker was not fit to defend the Thirteenth, Fourteenth, or Fifteenth Amendments. White spearheaded the NAACP's campaign to defeat the nomination of Parker. Because of the NAACP's valiant fight, the Senate rejected the nominee. In the following essay, White writes about the Association's role in the defeat of Supreme Court nominee John J. Parker. This essay was published in *Harper's* in 1930.

Few events of recent years have stirred public interest so deeply or caused wider and more acrimonious discussion than the rejection by the United States Senate on May 7 of the nomination of John J. Parker as an associate justice of the United States Supreme Court. The narrow margin of defeat—forty-one to thirty-nine votes—and the circumstances that all of the remaining sixteen senators were paired attests the tenseness of the struggle to choose a successor to the late Mr. Justice Sanford. Acute as was the feeling at that time, one runs little risk in prophesying that the rejection of the North Carolinian holds for the future immense political significance. For, to quote the *Washington Post*, "Negro political consciousness, until the last year or so rather vague, has been much stirred by the Senate's rejection of Judge John J. Parker. . . . The potentialities of the Negro vote in northern states have been much enlarged by attributes of the recent struggle over the justiceship. At the same time the case may stimulate a revival in parts of the South of the race question as an acute political issue."

"There are in the effluvium of that result impressive evidence of a 'comeback' by the Negroes as a minority voting power," the Washington newspaper adds, "on a scale that may cause them to be reckoned with more seriously than at any time since southern reconstruction days. For Negro voters now easily can decide contests between the big parties in a half dozen or more large northern states. All they need are political mindedness, cohesion, and management. And in the result of the fight over Judge Parker there are makings for all those requirements."

It seems certain that all this and more is true. For the struggle against confirmation of the North Carolina jurist, so far as the Negro's part in that rejection is concerned, marked in startling fashion not only resentment by eleven million Negroes against a rapidly growing disregard of their political rights, but signalized as well that the Negro no longer intends supinely to permit the whittling down, little by little, of the constitutional rights which, theoretically, belong to him as an American citizen.

Because of the significance of that struggle it will perhaps be worth while here to record something of the manner in which Negroes made themselves felt. When the late Justice Sanford died it was generally understood that a southern jurist would be named as his successor. Negroes and especially the National Association for the Advancement of Colored People understandably were somewhat apprehensive as to what southerner would be chosen. There was no feeling against the possible nominee simply because he might be from the South, but there was deep concern as to whether he represented the old or the newer South—whether he was of the school which still agreed in theory and practice with the Dred Scott decision that a Negro possessed no rights which a white man was bound to respect.

With particular apprehension Negroes read of the possible choice by President Hoover of one of two men, one of them a member of the United States Senate, who are notorious Negrophobes. Judge Parker's nomination came from a clear sky as reports from Washington indicated that he stood little chance of having his name presented to the Senate. A hurry-up call for information from reputable North Carolina citizens, white and colored, revealed that in 1920 Judge Parker, as the Republican gubernatorial nominee of that year, had declared in his speech of acceptance of the nomination that "the Negro as a class does not desire to enter politics. The Republican Party of North Carolina does not desire him to do so. We recognize the fact that he has not yet reached that stage in his development when he can share the burdens and responsibilities of Government. . . . I say it deliberately, there is no more dangerous or contemptible enemy of the State than men who for personal or political advantage will attempt to kindle the flame of racial prejudice or hatred . . . the participation of the Negro in politics is a source of evil and danger to both races and is not desired by the wise men in either race or by the Republican Party of North Carolina."

The issue was clear-cut and unmistakable. Judge Parker seemed either unaware of or indifferent to the fact that the Federal Constitution forbade denial of the right to vote to any citizens on account of race, color, or previous condition of servitude. He made no distinctions between Negroes who possessed character, education, property, and intelligence and those who were without these attributes. Nevertheless, those Negroes and whites who disagreed with him wanted to be free from any taint of unfairness towards Judge Parker. The National Association for the Advancement of Colored People telegraphed him to ask if he had been correctly quoted by the newspapers of his own state, or, had he been correctly quoted if he held in 1930 the same views he had expressed a decade before. Inquiry of the telegraph company revealed that the telegram of inquiry had been delivered. When three days had passed and no reply was received, a formal protest against his confirmation by the Senate was filed with the Judiciary Committee.

No serious consideration was given at the time to the Negroes' protest. At the hearing of the sub-Committee of the Judiciary Committee, the committee and the press gave practically all their attention to the protests of organized labor who opposed confirmation on the basis of Judge Parker's decisions involving the so-called "yellow dog" labor contracts. The spokesman for the Negroes was heard only after all other protestants had been allowed to speak, and even his statement aroused only mild interest.

Soon, however, the Negro protests began to pour into Washington in a steadily mounting volume. Telegrams, long distance telephone calls, letters, petitions, and personal visits impressed upon various Senators, particularly from northern and border states where the Negro vote is potent, that their Negro constituents were very much in earnest in their opposition to confirmation of a judge who had brazenly repudiated the guarantees of the Fourteenth and Fifteenth Amendments to the Constitution in so far as Negroes were concerned. A few of the Senators were frankly skeptical of the protests, believing that they were ephemeral and would soon die down. Others resented the protests, being somewhat bewildered at the spectacle of the Negro stepping out of his traditional role of a meek, uncomplaining creature who submitted without question to whatever was put upon him. Others were alarmed at the extent of the movement and apprehensively thought of approaching elections. Soon they began beseeching the White House to withdraw the nomination and save them the choice of voting either against the Administration or the wishes of their constituents. To such requests the White House turned a deaf ear.

The National Association for the Advancement of Colored People headed up the movement, sided without reservation by the two hundred Negro newspapers of the country, by the National Association of Colored Women representing approximately 250,000 women, by fraternal organizations, churches and individuals. On no issue have Negroes ever worked so unitedly since the Civil War. Faced with what at times seemed insuperable odds and confronted with all the influence in Parker's behalf which the Administration could muster, the struggle went grimly on.

No button-holing of Senators at Washington was indulged in. Through friendly sources including Washington newspaper correspondents constant contact was maintained with developments at the Capitol. Exact information was had regularly on certain attractive offers which were made to Senators if they would only agree to cast their vote for confirmation. Equally exact were the reports of threats made against other members of the Senate if they did not stand by the nomination. Cajolery and blandishments were used on some of the newer Senators and knowledge was had of the recipients, the users and the kind of persuasive arguments which were used. Through this information the meager resources of the Negroes, who were desperately fighting to keep from the Supreme Court bench a man who was willing to disregard their rights as citizens, could be and were conserved.

It was no easy task. Many of the newspapers were fair in both their editorial and news columns but many others were not. The editor of a North Carolina daily in whose columns had appeared the direct quotations which Judge Parker was charged with making sent a telegram which was read into the Congressional Record denying that his paper had ever published such an item. The question of veracity having thus been raised, photostatic copies of the yellowed, ten-year-old clipping were, within twelve hours, placed by the Advancement Association in the hands of the President, of members of the Senate, and of the press. Thereafter no further charges of inaccuracy by Negroes on this point were raised.

On another occasion, supporters of the nominee pointed to a decision he had rendered in a case involving residential segregation of Negroes in Virginia as proof of Judge Parker's lack of prejudice against colored people. Within a few hours after the statement had been made it was pointed out that in the case in question the Federal District had first declared the Richmond Segregation Ordinance invalid on the basis of two unanimous United States Supreme Court decisions, which held arbitrary residential segregation by city ordinance or state law on the basis of color unconstitutional. Judge Parker, as one of three judges sitting in the Appellate Division to which appeal had been taken, had merely concurred in a *per curiam* decision with the two other judges.

During a tense moment of the fight when it seemed certain that confirmation or rejection would surely be by an uncomfortably narrow margin, it was learned that certain individuals were industriously working in behalf of Judge Parker by appealing to the sectional or racial prejudices of certain Southern Democratic Senators. Of them was being asked, "Are you going to let it be said that Negroes have beaten you too into line?" Obviously, appeal to certain of these Senators coming from states where Negroes are not allowed to vote and who thus were peculiarly amenable to racial prejudices would have been unwise if not disastrous. Yet, united support of Parker on a sectional basis would have insured his confirmation. Certain of these Senators, especially some who are notoriously addicted to Negro-baiting, were queried as to the truth of rumors that they intended "to vote for confirmation and thus help reward North Carolina for going Republican in 1928." Presented in this vivid fashion, these Senators remembered that the nominee's Republicanism had undoubtedly played a large part in gaining the nomination, that his elevation to the Supreme Court bench would unquestionably play a material part in subsequent elections. And there was as a result of the queries, little purely sectional support of Judge Parker.

Amusingly enough, strenuous efforts were made by flattery and other less pleasant means to induce Negroes of prominence to endorse Judge Parker and thus offset the welling tide of Negro opposition. One of the most distinguished Negro educators of the country was thus approached. He not only flatly refused to endorse Parker but registered effectively his strong opposition. Negro politicians, editors, business men, ministers, and others were sounded out with the same result. A few nonentities were cajoled into writing endorsements (or signing endorsements written for them) but to no avail. One of these endorsers in a North Carolina town was featured in the local white press as a man of influence among Negroes and a possible United States minister to the Republic of Haiti; on the same day appeared another news item telling of the same man's indictment by a Federal Grand Jury. Only one Negro of standing—an educator in North Carolina who is president of a school for Negroes supported almost in entirety by state funds—gave active support to Parker and his action brought down upon his head unequivocal condemnation from Negroes of all classes. In contrast with this man's attitude some 188 prominent Negroes of North Carolina signed affidavits which were sent to the Senate Judiciary Committee in which these men and women registered their strong opposition to confirmation and set forth the reasons for that disapproval of Judge Parker. When over-zealous friends of the jurist went so far as to make threats against Negroes who would not sign endorsements, even this intimidation proved unavailing. In New Jersey a prominent young Negro physician practically abandoned his practice, and almost literally lived for weeks in his motor car as he visited ministers, fraternal order leaders, officials of civic and welfare organizations, and other influential Negroes to stir them to action. This man's zeal was typical of the attitude of Negroes all over the United States. In Chicago, Cleveland, Detroit, Kansas City, Los Angeles, Philadelphia, Baltimore, St. Louis, and other cities where large numbers of Negroes reside mass meetings were held at which telegraph blanks were provided for the use of those who wished to write and pay for messages to their Senators. It was estimated that from Chicago alone on the Sunday before the vote on the nomination more than two thousand telegrams were sent to the Illinois Senators, many of these messages coming from churches, lodges, and other organized bodies. One message spoke for 84,000 Negro Republican women.

"The result," wrote Dr. W. Burghardt Du Bois, the distinguished Negro editor, "was a campaign conducted with a snap, determination and intelligence never surpassed in colored America and very seldom in white. It turned the languid, half-hearted protest of the American Federation of Labor into a formidable and triumphant protest. It fired the labored liberalism of the West into flame. It was ready to beat back the enemy at every turn. . . . So in every twist and turn of the enemy, the battle was pressed down to the last minute."

II

What does this demonstration, new in American political history, portend? Is it to be regarded as naught but an ephemeral outbreak of resentment by Negroes which will soon be forgotten? Predictions are always precarious ventures. But when one looks backward and realizes that the unyielding opposition to confirmation of one holding views such as Judge Parker held has been in the making for more than forty years, one can realize that the recent event at Washington may be one of the most portentous happenings of our time. The Negro did not beat nor could he have beaten Parker singlehandedly. Some of the Senators who voted against confirmation did so because of convictions that the Supreme Court was becoming far too conservative and was showing tendencies to lay greater emphasis on property than on human rights. Others were moved by the protests of organized labor speaking through the American Federation of Labor. Some of the southern members of the Senate unquestionably were motivated in their opposition to Parker by the understandable suspicion that choices of a North Carolina Republican was in a measure due to the desire to annex permanently that southern state to the Republican column.

Detached and non-partisan observers agree, however, that the determining factor in the rejection was the Negro, to whose influence they attribute no less than eleven adverse votes and perhaps more than that number. The seeds of that protest were sown four decades ago. Dissatisfaction with and rebellion against the treatment accorded him have constantly though imperceptibly grown throughout the last forty years. To understand this one needs only to consider the story of the Negro's climb, often thwarted, towards recognition as an integral part of American political life.

At the close of the Civil War there were two distinct schools of southern white thought on the Negro and on the most profitable course for the late Confederacy to pursue in reentering the Union. One school led by General Robert E. Lee was convinced that no other course was wise than to accept the verdict of armed conflict and, more, to understand that fundamentally the War of Rebellion had been a conflict between two diametrically opposed economic systems— between the agricultural, slave-holding South and the industrial North. The industrial revolution had outmoded the economy on which the South had relied and the only sensible thing to do, they argued, was to forget the glories of the past, most of which had never existed in reality, and to build a new scheme of things based on the new conditions. Unhappily, such wise counsel was not followed. Instead the South as a whole turned to the tragically ludicrous Ku Klux Klan, the White Camellias, and other such movements designed to re-enslave the freedman as far as was possible without bringing again the armed forces of the North.

Beginning in the 1890s, after federal troops had been removed from the South, various means were utilized to take the ballot away from the recently enfranchised freedman. Among the first widely used efforts at disfranchisement were the so-called Grandfather clauses. Various southern states passed constitutional amendments imposing educational requirements upon all voters and providing that no person should be allowed to vote unless he were able to read or write any section of the state constitution. Exemptions, however, were specifically granted to all those who, or whose ancestors, had the right to vote and had voted anywhere in the United States prior to January 1, 1866.

Among the states which passed such constitutional amendments was Oklahoma. A test case arose in that state which eventually reached the United States Supreme Court. The late distinguished authority on constitutional law, Moorfield Storey of Boston, submitted a brief in this case (*Guinn and Beall v. The United States*, 238 U.S. 347) on behalf of the National Association for the Advancement of Colored People of which he was President. In this brief Mr. Storey clearly pointed out the real purpose and nature of the exemption, especially as signified by the choice of January 1, 1866, as being clearly designed to disfranchise Negroes. "The effect of the amendment," declared Mr. Storey, "is to allow almost anybody to vote, whatever his education or extraction, unless he happens to be a Negro, for it is well known to the Court as it was to the framers of the amendment that practically all residents of the United States, other than Negroes, enjoyed the right to vote in 1866." The Supreme Court in its decision declared such constitutional amendments unconstitutional.

Later on there came into general practice the system of primary elections. This system offered another means of denying the ballot to Negroes in certain states. Various of these states passed laws prohibiting Negroes from voting in Democratic primaries. It is a well-known fact that in most of the states of the south, and especially of the lower south, the Democratic primary is the election. In the Texas Democratic primary in July, 1926, for example the six candidates for Governor received a total vote of 735,186; in the subsequent general election Dan Moody, Democratic gubernatorial candidate, was elected by 89,263 votes over the Republican candidate who received 11,354. The United States Supreme Court was asked to pass upon the issue involved in the Texas law and similar laws in the other southern states. The case involved a qualified Negro Democrat of El Paso, Texas, Dr. L. A. Nixon by name. Dr. Nixon, a property holder, a man of education and a citizen esteemed by both races, was refused under the terms of the law the right to vote in a Democratic primary. When the case reached the United States Supreme Court a unanimous decision ruled the Texas law unconstitutional, "because it seems to us hard to imagine a more direct and obvious infringement of the 14th Amendment."

Those who were determined that Negroes should not be allowed to vote in certain states were not, however, to be discouraged. The next step was the passage by various legislatures, among them Texas, Arkansas, Florida, and Virginia, of enabling acts giving to political parties the right to determine their own qualifications for membership. In other words these state legislatures said, in effect, that political parties should have the right and power to do that which the Supreme Court had said the states themselves could not do. Various test cases have arisen under these enabling acts. In a case arising in Virginia, that of *West v. Bliley*, Judge D. Lawrence Groner of the Federal District Court sitting at Richmond promptly declared this enabling act unconstitutional. Appeal was taken to the Appellate Division of the Federal court which affirmed Judge Croner's decision. Proponents of the measure did not take advantage of the right of appeal, permitting the time granted for such appeal to pass.

This long drawn out, difficult and expensive attempt to prevent violation of the Negro's constitutional rights has been carried on chiefly by Negroes and their friends as represented in the National Association for the Advancement of Colored People. Perhaps the chief value of this struggle has been in educative effect upon Negroes themselves in causing them to realize the importance of the ballot. Colored Americans do not imagine the vote in itself to be a panacea for all the ills from which they and others suffer. They do realize, however, that voteless people is a defenseless people. They know that when a man can be denied the right to say who shall govern him, who shall enforce the laws, and who shall have control over the expenditures of public funds, that the man so denied may more easily be made the victim of lynching, segregation, denial for industrial and educational opportunity and, in brief, kept in the position of a subject race.

The full impact of this restlessness and of this dissatisfaction with his lot in American life made the impact of Negro influence in the Parker case of considerable weight. It marked, according to general opinion, the major political demonstration by the Negro since the Civil War. The influence of that demonstration did not end when the Senate voted on the Parker nomination. In Kansas, for example, when Senator Henry J. Allen ran in the Republican primaries for reelection during the summer of 1930, he polled in Kansas in the Negro districts only twenty-seven per cent of the Negro vote where normally he would have received not less than seventy-five per cent of that vote, and probably a good deal more. In Ohio where Senator Roscoe C. McCulloch stood in 1930 for re-election to fill the unexpired term of the late Senator Theodore E. Burton, Negro voters of the state without regard to political affiliation or other circumstances united against Senator McCulloch because of his vote and speech for confirmation of Judge Parker. Ohio is normally a Republican state by a margin of 400,000 to 500,000 votes. Nomination by the Democrats of Robert Johns Bulkley, a distinguished lawyer, personally popular and a "wet," together with the inevitable reaction against the Administration because of unemployment cut down the normal Republican majority to the point where the 150,000 Negro voters of Ohio practically held the balance of power.

Never before has Ohio seen such a campaign, nor has there been in the history of the State so astounding a turn-over among Negro voters. In Cleveland in the election precincts predominantly peopled by Negroes, considerably more than half of the voters either supported McCulloch's Democratic opponent or refrained altogether from voting for a United States Senator. A well-informed lawyer declares that "there is no escaping the fact that in Cuyshogs County Negroes contributed substantially to McCulloch's defeat for without their support Bulkley's majority would have been considerably less."

In Negro precincts of Toledo, Bulkley polled slightly more than three times more votes than McCulloch. In Columbus the colored wards went to Bulkley by large majorities. In Akron two-thirds and more of the Negro voters supported McCulloch's opponent. In Canton eighty-six per cent of the Negro vote went to the Democratic senatorial nominee and only fourteen per cent to McCulloch, while large numbers of others abstained altogether from voting for a United States Senator. The same margins of Negro revolt obtained throughout the State. It can hardly be questioned that McCulloch's defeat was primarily due to economic depression and prohibition, but it is also equally true that the margin of defeat was in the main supplied by resentment of Negro voters against his support of Parker.

A similar revolt occurred in Kansas, a rock-ribbed Republican State. Negro voters supported, practically without exception, Senator Arthur Capper, Republican, and a member of the Board of Directors of the National Association for the Advancement of Colored People. The same voters swung against Senator Capper's Republican colleague, Henry J. Allen, helping materially wheat farmers and labor to defeat Allen. "Undoubtedly Allen would have won had he had every Negro vote as in previous years," is the verdict of a leading newspaper man of the State.

Though less successful, Negro voters in Rhode Island opposed Senator Jesse H. Metcalf and in Delaware, Daniel H. Hastings who, too, had voted to confirm Judge Parker. Though each of these Senators was reelected by exceedingly narrow margins, the effect of the breaking away from the Republican party of the colored voters of these States cannot be ignored. In Providence, according to reliable observation, less than fifty per cent of Negro voters cast their ballots for the Republican ticket. At least thirty per cent voted the Republican ticket but scratched Metcalf, while twenty percent and more voted a straight Democratic or a split ticket. In Newport Metcalf's Democratic opponent's plurality was increased eighty-seven per cent by the Negro vote.

Senators who voted against confirmation, such as Senators Capper of Kansas, Thomas J. Walsh of Montana and Thomas D. Schall of Minnesota, were loyally voted for reelection by the Negro voters of their respective States. Party lines have been cast aside. The psychology of victory has replaced that of defeatism. It is well within the range of possibilities that the part played by Negro voters in carrying on a sustained campaign for a high principle, which resulted in the rejection of Parker, may mean and unquestionably will mean the greatest step yet taken towards political emancipation of the Negro by the Negro himself.

Finally, one legitimately may ask, why should Negroes have been so stirred by a nomination to the Supreme Court bench? What though Parker held such views—he, if confirmed would have been but one of nine justices?

The answer lies in the fact that, whatever his fate in lower courts, Negroes have come to feel especially within recent years that in the Federal Supreme Court he stood his best chance of obtaining justice. In that court there have been won six notable decisions within the last fifteen years, each of them of far reaching effect on the Negro's constitutional rights. Three of those decisions outlawed the herding of Negroes in ghettos by means of city ordinance or state laws; another established the principle that trial of a person accused of crime in a court dominated by mob influence is not due process of law; while two others ended disfranchisement by means of Grandfather Clauses and through enactments preventing participation in Democratic primaries.

Negroes and their friends know too that within the next few years cases testing other forms of disfranchisement, cases challenging unequal apportionment as to race of public funds, state and federal, for education, issues of the "Jim Crow" car system and of segregation by means of private property holders' covenants will be carried for decision to the Supreme Court. Negroes have noted the considerable number of 5 to 4 decisions within recent years by that court. And they know that one vote by a justice holding Parker's anti-Negro views might easily mean an appreciable increment to their already heavy load. Emphasis has perhaps been laid too heavily upon the import to Negroes of the Parker rejection. Its possible effect upon the whole American scene may possibly be no less marked. The migration northward of a million and a half Negroes since 1916 has given the Negro the balance of political power in no less than eight states. Each of the last ten years has seen growth of emphasis by Negroes on men and issues and less on party. This rapidly increasing political independence and political mindedness have within them potentialities which may conceivably play a role of vast importance in the political life of the United States within the next decade.

Immediately, Parker's rejection means a number of things. It has given hope to Negro voters in demonstrating that intelligent, sustained struggle for a principle can be successful. It has created a new and wholesome respect for the Negro among informed, fair-minded whites. It has forcibly reminded Americans that the 14th and 15th Amendments to the Federal Constitution are not yet wholly dead. And it has served notice convincingly upon politicians that it is no longer wise to attempt to climb to high office on the backs of helpless blacks through violent Negrophobic attacks.

Reverberations of the Parker rejection may be heard for some years to come.

On Racist Textbooks

The NAACP became concerned about a New York City Board of Education textbook which was called to the attention of the Association. The book, *How the United States Became a World Power*, about black life during the Reconstruction era, is filled with inaccuracies and stereotypes. In the following essay, Walter White recommends to the NAACP Board of Directors that a representative from the Association evaluate the New York City Board of Education's textbooks, especially on history and civics. This essay was written in 1932.

The semi-annual monthly meeting of the Committee on Administration will be resumed on Monday, September 28.

Among other matters which should be considered at that time is one which has recently been brought to the attention of the National Office by Miss Josephine Wooten, a teacher in the New York Public Schools. After reading the following memorandum on this and my proposal of steps to be taken, will you not be good enough to communicate with me at once regarding it.

Miss Wooten has loaned the Secretary one of the text books now being issued in the New York Public Schools, the volume in question being *How the United States Became a World Power*, in the City History Series, by Helen F. Giles, published by Charles E. Merrill Company, New York. This volume is used in the second half of the sixth year. In discussion of the Reconstruction Era, such statements as the following are made:

> When they (Negroes) realized that they were free, many thought they must get away from the plantation where they had lived as slaves; though they had little idea of where to go or what to do. They had no homes and no money. They began to wander about, stealing and plundering. In one week in a Georgia town, one hundred fifty Negroes were arrested for thieving.
>
> Many ignorant Negroes thought that the property owned by their former masters was theirs now, and some even took possession of land and began building houses, and planting their farms. Often they were insulting to the white people. In some localities conditions were so bad that the white women were afraid to go outside their homes even in the day-time. Many of the white people slept with a gun within reach so that they could protect themselves in case they might be attacked by a Negro.
>
> By 1871 Congress had pardoned most of the white leaders of the War, and they were again allowed to vote and hold office. But it was almost impossible for white men to be elected in four of the states, because there were many more Negroes than white men in these states. So the white men decided to take other means to get the power back into their own hands. A secret society, known as the Ku Klux Klan, was organized, and its members set out to spread terror among the ignorant Negroes. Knowing that the Negroes were very much afraid of spirits, or ghosts, the members would dress in long white robes with hoods over their heads and grinning masks hiding their faces. Disguised in this way, they would visit the home of a Negro in the dead of night. When they had roused the trembling Negro from sleep, they would make all sorts of threats of horrible things that would happen to him if he dared vote in the next election. The Negroes were quite terrified and nothing could make them go to the polls after such a visit.

It is the Secretary's feeling that something should be done immediately regarding such statements being taught to the several million pupils in the New York City Public Schools.

Effort was made some months ago to get the New York Women's Auxiliary to appoint a committee to go over all the text books, especially history and civic text books, to compile material such as the above and to prepare therefrom an authoritative document as the basis for a protest to the Board of Education and to the Mayor.

No city in the country offers a more likely chance of successful elimination of such paragraphs than New York, and especially in view of the coming elections. The example set by New York would undoubtedly be followed by branches in other cities.

Aside from the good done, such a protest would be especially helpful right now when the N.A.A.C.P. Drive for Membership is on. Such action on our part would more directly touch the colored people in Harlem than even the Scottsboro Cases, for there are no people there who do not have children or friends with children in the public school.

The Secretary has been asked by Mr. Edgar N. Parks, who has been a most faithful worker for many years for the Association, to help find employment for his niece, Mrs. Eloise Walker Percival. Mrs. Percival is an honor graduate of New York University.

Miss Wooten is securing for us a list of text books approved by the New York Board of Education. She informs me that all these books are on file at the Board of Education Building at Fifty-ninth Street and Park Avenue.

The secretary would like to recommend that Mrs. Percival, or someone equally competent and who could be engaged for not more than $25.00 a week, be engaged to go to the Board of Education Building and go carefully through the textbooks on history, civics, etc., and make exact copies of all passages which may be objectionable. Such work ought not take more than two weeks. If this work were started immediately we could make public this study during the course of the Membership Drive which Mrs. Daisy Lampkin is preparing for in Harlem, the actual drive to occur during the first two weeks in October.

We could commence this work at once if the committee thinks well of it.

The Negro on the American Stage

Influenced greatly by James Weldon Johnson, Walter White developed a strong literary interest and ultimately became a successful writer of both fiction and nonfiction. An active participant in the Harlem Renaissance, he published two novels during the height of the literary movement. Like Johnson, he believed that African Americans have been abundantly endowed "with the stuff of which drama is made. . . ." In this essay, written in 1932, he offers an assessment of African Americans' influence and status on the American stage.

Of all the racial groups in American life, there is none whose history and experience on American soil is packed so tight with the stuff of which drama is made as that of the Negro. One might with complete safety go even further and assert that his role in the new world is, more than that of any other, richer in extremes of experience ranging from stark tragedy and poignant grief following in the wake of the lynching mob, the slave auctioneer's block, and the catastrophic pestilence of mob rule to the compensating buoyancy of spirit, often mistaken for shiftlessness and mental incapacity, by means of which the Negro has been able to keep alive in a hostile environment which might have crushed a less richly endowed people.

This wealth of experience and this spiritual endowment has nowhere found expression more abundantly than in its influence on the American stage. If presentation of the Negro or of black-face whites playing the part of Negroes has almost exclusively been such as to give a not altogether true picture of the real Negro, the Negro's influence has been felt just the same. Until the past decade or so, the Negro performer and the Negro theater [were] divided by necessity sharply into two classes. One of these was that of theatres in wholly Negro neighborhoods where the appearance of a white face in the audience would have been most unusual bringing with it a constraint none the less real because masked with great shrewdness. There the Negro performer, usually earning a mere pittance hardly sufficient to provide more than a most meager existence, could and did indulge in lusty and at time ribald humor, in penetrating and at times merciless satire at the foibles and shortcomings of himself, his fellow-performers, the audience and the Negro as a race. No member of the audience ever dreamed of taking offense even at the most cutting jibes. Instead, applause and laughter could invariably be measured by directness of the hit.

It is impossible to estimate fully and accurately the influence this genuinely Negro theater has had not only on the Negro but on America as well. It is certain that few forces which have directed Negro life have done more to debunk the Negro in his own estimation and to keep him free from the smugness and overweening self-esteem which afflicted and still does afflict white America. It is from this source that much of Negro secular music has sprung and in this atmosphere that the "blues" used so effectively by George Gershwin in his "Rhapsody in Blue" and by other song writers, Negro and white, were nourished and developed and given a hearing. So, too, from this environment came Negro actors and singers such as the late Charles Gilpin, Florence Mills, Frank Wilson of "Porgy" fame, Clarence Muse now appearing frequently in the cinema, Rose McClendon, Josephine Baker, and a host of others less well-known or entirely unknown to white audiences but who possessed, many of them, remarkable talent. I would not have the reader think that all these unknown and unsung performers were geniuses. As in every other venture there was the usual large percentage of mediocrities. But among them were those who emerged and many who never became known outside of the narrow orbits of grimy, drafty, ill-smelling little theaters who had genuine love for stage and a great skill for its exacting life.

For the pay was so meager and often non-existent, the life so hard that none could or would remain in it unless the smell of grease-paint were deep in their nostrils. I remember once talking with that strange genius, Charles Gilpin, about the time of the furors over his having been chosen by the Drama League as having given one of the outstanding performances of that season in Eugene O'Neill's "The Emperor Jones." If ever a man was born for the footlight Gilpin was that man. Year after year he played in obscure little playhouses in and near Memphis, New Orleans, Atlanta, and other southern towns. More often than not his wages were sufficient only to keep body and soul together, and it was far from uncommon for the show to go broke and pay him nothing. Then Gilpin would put aside the grease-paint and cork and return to waiting table or running as a Pullman porter, saving his tips and wages until the inevitable day when the call of the theater was too strong to resist, and he, cursing himself for an improvident idiot but with a strange happiness, would once again engage himself to some small Negro theatrical troupe. One does not wonder that in such a life he found forgetfulness in liquor which shortened his life and made him in days of fame and prosperity a trial to managers who were never sure he would appear for a scheduled performance until Gilpin hove into sight.

The other Negro theater is the one known to white audiences. It was first the world of the minstrel show performers, white and colored, working in burnt cork and all using Negro or pseudo-Negro themes and humor in usually highly exaggerated picturizations of Negro life. This phase was followed by the natural sequence—gifted comedians like Bert Williams, George Walker, Ernest Hogan, Miller and Lyles, and the famed extravaganzas presented by Cole and Johnson, by Williams and Walker, and their successors and imitators.

But despite these contributions and the influence they had, especially in solo and chorus dancing, on the theater as a whole, the Negro until very recent years was invariably presented on the stage to white audiences in a most limited number of fixed roles. There was, as has been seen, the slap-stick, broad-humored buffoon, usually in flamboyant clothing or with patches on his trousers and knees, who fed the vanity, fortunately, but often enough the Negro character in the theater and especially in the cinema was portrayed as a brutish creature, fresh from the jungle, swept by passion of lust and murder, and to be curbed only by the rope and faggot of the lyncher. A third role was that of a kindly, faithful servant of pre-Civil War vintage, who, twisted with rheumatism and tortured with lumbago hobbles on stage along towards the end of the third set, his white wool thatch glistening in the spotlight, to offer his handsome young master his lifetime savings hoarded in an old sock so that the young hero may clasp the beautiful and virginal heroine in his arms instead of going to jail.

Within the last decade these stereotypes have little by little begun to be discarded and retired to a well deserved rest, which one hopes will be eternal. Slowly there is coming in their stead a more veritable presentation of the Negro and of Negro life in its relations to the American scene. Certain vital changes were necessary to make this possible and these have subtly been taking place during the years since the World War. One of those changes is that of the attitude of white Americans toward the Negro, particularly in the discarding of fixed concepts of what a man should do, say and think under given stimuli if that man's skin happened to [be] black. The wartime migration northward of Negroes which came

about as a result of stoppage of immigration from Europe and of growing industrialization of the United States made the colored American a less infrequent and
slightly less unknown part of the American scene. Novels, poems, and songs by
and about Negroes have been published in great numbers which pictured an Af-
ramerican who did not always fit into the stencils of buffoon, criminal, or menial.
Awards such as the Spingarn Medal and the Harmon Foundation prizes directed
public attention to the existence and contributions of Negro scientists, business
men, singers, writers, educators, and others of distinguished ability. Such organizations as the Interracial Commission in the southern colleges and universities
and the National Association for the Advancement of Colored People made rapid
strides in causing at least the enlightened minority of the American mass mind
to recognize the absolute necessity of intelligent and less biased appraisal of the
Negro and the color question. This development was speeded by the emergence
of Japan and the Far East, of India through the widely publicized Gandhi, of Africa
and of other remote parts of the world whose exploitation had played so large a
role in the jealousies and quarrels which led to the late World War. It became
impossible to pick up a newspaper but that one encountered some item which
directed attention to some aspect of the problem of race. Try as one might, he
had great difficulty in avoiding impingement upon his consciousness, either pleasantly or otherwise, that there are colored peoples on the earth whose lives and
destinies were inextricably interwoven with the future of white peoples and of the
world.

It was inevitable that this growing consciousness should find expression on the
stage, seeking always as it does for legitimate exploitation of new themes and
fresh thrills. This delving into the drama of Negro life was concurrent with and
greatly aided by the rapidly developing preoccupation of American dramatists with
the American scene and creation of a native American drama. Pioneers in the
field of drama about Negro life began to be heard from, the number including
Ridgley Torrence, Eugene O'Neill, Paul Green, and others less well known who
began to write one-act and full length plays which found expression in countless
little theaters throughout the country as well as on Broadway. Of this material
O'Neill declared, "The possibilities are limitless and to a dramatist open up new
and intriguing opportunities: the gifts the Negro can and will bring to our native
drama are invaluable ones" while Ridgley Torrence expressed the opinion that
"The Negro, other things being equal, might produce the greatest, the most direct,
the most powerful drama in the world."

Naturally, though craftsmen of undoubted skill and experience in dramaturgy
began to write of Negro life, great plays in profusion sprang into being overnight
no more than was the case with Irish plays and the Abbey Theater or with other
folk material during the years immediately after first recognition of new sources
for play making. Negro writers who knew the life of their people had to learn the
technique of the theater; all too often their first attempts were too heavily laden
with sentimentalism or propaganda. White writers, most of them with the best
of intentions, either did not trouble themselves to learn at first hand or were
incapable of understanding and interpreting Negro psychology as formed by two
and a half centuries of slavery and sixty years of only nominal freedom. The

results to date have thus fallen short of success in attaining really great plays, but we have gone a long way on the road towards that goal.

For a variety of reasons, the plays of Negro life which have gained widest attention have been written by Eugene O'Neill, Paul Green, and Marc Connelly. Certain of these plays are significant not only in themselves but as signposts. "The Emperor Jones" is perhaps the best example of this dual role, combining as it does sound workmanship in its picturing of a strong human will disintegrating under the sledge hammer blows of fear and superstition and helplessness in the face of implacable destiny, with overtones of the particular problems which, being a Negro, the Emperor had to face. O'Neill's later play, "All God's Chillun," was infinitely less successful because he did not dare go logically to the inevitable conclusion of the theme with which he started. Even the great skill of Paul Robeson could inject no more than a semblance of life and verity into the play. Dealing as it did with miscegenation, success lay only in honest treatment. It will be remembered that the story dealt with a white girl, the cast-off mistress of [a] white prize-fighter, who finds protection and sustenance in marriage with an ambitious Negro law student. O'Neill sought to explain the marriage of convenience on the grounds of a loyalty felt by the student, Jim Harris, which dated back to the days when he and the girl were childhood neighbors and playmates. As a concession to white prejudice the playwright went to some pains to emphasize that there was no physical relationship between man and wife, and to even greater efforts in causing her to develop speedily into violent homicidal insanity. Spiritually and mentally far inferior to her husband, a finale is supplied by incarceration of the girl in an asylum. One wishes that the reputation of America's greatest dramatist were unmarred by this play or that he had not yielded unconsciously to an environment which at that time was even more hostile than now to honest treatment of a theme in life that is not as infrequent as Negrophobes maintain.

Paul Green in his Pulitzer prize-winning "In Abraham's Bosom" treated courageously and effectively of Negro life in the South which, he unlike most white Southerners, had studied with genuine understanding, free from superficiality and superiority. Though the play was one of defeat for the black man of ambition and training, yet there was shot through its terrible tragedy and hopelessness the spark of truth and conviction. Remarkably enough, it enjoyed a long run and several revivals and won in 1927 the accolade of the Pulitzer Prize.

"Porgy" from the novel of another distinguished and gifted Southerner, DuBose Heyward and his wife, Dorothy Heyward, was a remarkable folk tale from out of the deep South, in which the strands of tragedy, ecstasy both religious and carnal, and high drama were woven with considerable expertness and effectiveness. The play sloughed off towards its end but one will not soon forget that extraordinary finale to the first act where the wake over her murdered husband is being held in Serena's room. The mourners sang with a moving intensity and harmony seldom heard on Broadway or anywhere else and beat the time with striking effect as shadows were flung on the background from the rhythmic flinging of arms and hands and bodies upward and downward.

And who has not seen nor heard of "The Green Pastures"? It was in this unusual play, a sort of modern-day Miracle Play, that the Negro actor came into his own and demonstrated conclusively even to those who had been inclined to think of him as something of a passing fancy of the play-going public that he could transmit over the footlight delicate fantasy and the most subtle of emotions and never once falter. This was especially true of Richard B. Harrison, handsome in a patriarchal fashion and blessed with a voice of richness and power who played the exacting role of "De Lawd." Mr. Harrison had never been on the stage before he appeared in Marc Connelly's version of the concept of Biblical stories as envisioned by rural Negroes in the backwoods of Louisiana.

I had been invited to sit in on rehearsals and had been reluctant to do so for I had known Marc Connelly only as the author of shrewdly satirical plays such as "Beggar on Horseback," "Dulcy," "O the Ladies," and "The Wisdom Tooth." After offering various excuses I finally went to the theater one bitingly cold Sunday afternoon early in February, 1930. The theater was cold and draughty, there were no costumes or sets, the cast had reached that stage of rehearsing hated by managers and stage directors where pristine excitement had died down and the actors look ahead to the far-off opening night more or less as children do the coming Christmas. But for Marc Connelly there was no Santa Claus a long way off—for him Christmas was already here. His bald head glistening in the footlights he dashed about, giving a word of advice here, of encouragement or approval there, of instruction to this one or that. Between times he told in vivid snatches of descriptions of the sets Robert Edmund Jones had designed, of the costumes then in the making. And above all else there was a tenderness and respect in the relations between Mr. Connelly and Mr. Harrison that was not of the theater. It was as though the simplicity of the play and its characters had also filled the author and leading player of "The Green Pastures."

Later I heard from Mr. Connelly how true this was. He had been searching a long time, he explained, for something tangible in belief in a world of scoffing, of skepticism, and of doubt of everything and everybody. Time and time again he had believed his search ended only to find himself mistaken until he had by chance read Roark Bradford's "Ol' Man Adam and His Chillun," stories of the Bible as interpreted and believed by Negroes of the deep South. Connelly found in these sketches, when Bradford had been content simply to serve as amanuensis in recording what he had heard from the lips of the Negroes of his native Louisiana, "an attempt to present certain aspects of a living religion in the terms of its believers." Combined with this was humor and warm human understanding and high drama in the interpretations which grew out of the imagery of the ancient Hebrew prophets after it had passed through the minds and hearts of the southern Negro and gained enrichment and now beauty thereby.

But Connelly was not content to gain his material at second hand. He made two lengthy trips to the South. He gained the confidence of the Negroes of the bayou region of Louisiana without difficulty for his attitude was free from all suggestion of superiority and his manner was that of a friend. On one of his trips Connelly was told of the coming of a famed Negro evangelist to a little church across the river on the following Sunday. Despite a torrential downpour Connelly and Bradford set forth early that day, crossing the river in a flat-bottomed boat that required hard rowing to propel it through the swiftly flowing stream. On reaching the church the two found that the heavy rain had kept many away but the preacher seemed unaware of the fact that the little church was not crowded as would have been the case in fair weather. The two white members of the congregation, fearing their presence might make the preacher and his hearers self-conscious, took seats in the rear of the church. When the collection was taken the congregation one by one marched forward to place their coins on the table. Connelly and Bradford debated the wisdom of going forward also and making themselves too conspicuous or of remaining quietly in their seats. They determined on the latter course. The local minister, without appearing to do so, noticed that they, of all the assemblage, had not contributed. The ushers at a signal from the pastor passed through the audience with collection plates, each member of the congregation reaching into pocket or purse and depositing something in the baskets. With all solemnity the ushers passed by the empty benches which separated the two white visitors from the rest of the faithful and came to Connelly and his companion. The baskets were empty, the whole pantomime having been gone through with solemnity to save the visitors from embarrassment. Afterwards Connelly went home to dinner with the preacher and thus was formed a friendship which bore abundant fruit when "The Green Pastures" later was presented for two years on cynical, hard-boiled Broadway.

Ridgley Torrence's sweeping prediction, made at the time of the presentation of his superb one-act plays of Negro life in New York in 1917, that the Negro "might produce the greatest, the most direct, the most powerful drama in the world" may be too optimistic. One is safe in asserting, however, that out of the soil prepared by the plays mentioned and countless others less generally known which have been written and produced during the last few years, we may confidently expect significant contributions to a native American drama and even perhaps truly great plays. New York saw during the theatrical season of 1931–1932 a half dozen or more Negro plays. That no one of them could be called first-rate by the most kindly of critics is relatively unimportant. The mere production of so many plays of Negro life is evidence of a process of birth, of creative recognition of the inherent beauty and strength and power of this material. Thus any appraisal or description of the part played by the Negro on the American stage written at this time should not be thought of in terms of a rounded, fully developed movement. One must, instead, look upon it as being in the process of growth which, in some not distant day, may loom large in its influence upon our drama and our national life.

Discrimination in Federal Control Construction

In 1931 the American Federation of Labor discovered that the U.S. Army Corps of Engineers was paying black workers on the Mississippi Flood Control Project an average of ten cents an hour and was working these laborers twelve-hour days. The NAACP sent Helen Boardman, a researcher, to Mississippi to investigate conditions for black workers. Miss Boardman verified the American Federation of Labor's findings and also uncovered other atrocities. In the following essay Walter White discusses the action the Association will take up with the federal government to stop these inhumane labor conditions. This essay was written in 1932.

As reported to the Board of Directors at the June meeting, the National Office took advantage of the offer of Miss Helen Boardman, who was to be in the West on other business, to make an investigation of discrimination against Negroes in the construction of federal flood control along the Mississippi River.

Miss Boardman completed her investigation in July and made her report to the National Office. The report disclosed that:

1. Colored American citizens are being employed with the funds of the United States government at an average wage of ten cents an hour, and that they are being worked almost without exception on a twelve-hour day, with a seven-day week and no holidays and no pay for overtime; that those long hours are in force despite the fact that all the projects are from six weeks to six months ahead of schedule.
2. The wages for colored labor range from one dollar to three dollars for a twelve-hour day, with very few cases of a three-dollar wage. The average wage is ten cents an hour.
3. A commissary system is in effect in most camps, which insures that the contractor will not have to pay more than maintenance for his labor. In many instances Negro laborers pay out from fifty to seventy-five per cent of their wages in commissary charges or other items imposed by the contractors.
4. The attitude of many contractors toward their labor is reminiscent of slavery at its worst. Men are beaten on the slightest pretext and fired without pay on the slightest provocation.
5. Colored men work under most unsanitary living conditions, in crowded, floorless tents. No provision is made for the disposal of garbage; and disease is rampant.

A copy of Miss Boardman's detailed report was sent, on August 22nd, to President Hoover with the request that the machinery of the federal government be set in motion to correct the conditions cited. The report was sent also to Secretary of War Patrick J. Hurley and to Attorney General William DeWitt Mitchell; also to twenty-six United States senators. President Hoover referred the report to the War Department, and under date August 25, a letter was received from Major General Brown, which showed that he evidently was angered because of the revelations of this investigation made under the auspices of the N.A.A.C.P. General Brown did not deny the facts as set forth in the report but instead excused the low wages paid by stating that the government made it a policy to pay the wages paid customary in the region in which its projects are being worked. He excused the long hours by saying the flood control work was of an emergency nature but did not explain why the twelve hours double shifts were necessary when all the work is from six weeks to six months ahead of schedule. Also, General Brown attempted to belittle the reports of brutality by saying that no names and addresses of men beaten were given, and he made the preposterous suggestion that the men complaining take their cases to court. General Brown, a native of Tennessee, cannot help but know that it is worth any Negro's life to let it be known that he had told of conditions in these camps.

The National Office replied to General Brown's letter pointing out that "the tone of your reference to this report distinctly indicates an attitude of hostility which, to say the least, is most astounding in an employee of the United States government," and that the proper procedure was for the government "vigorously, swift, courageously, and without bias" to make a thorough investigation of the alleged conditions, to correct them and to follow up the correction by strict, periodic inspections to see that such conditions are not re-established.

Copy of General Brown's letter together with copy of the reply was sent to President Hoover, the National Office stating that "this Association takes very definite exception to the attitude of Major General Brown in his reception of this report." The request was made of the President that he instruct the War Department to investigate and correct the conditions reported, without bias.

Under date of August 31 the National Office received the following letter from Secretary of War Hurley, who had not up to this time acknowledged the report which had been sent directly to him:

My dear Mr. White:

Your letter of August 29 to the President has been handed to me by him personally.

Generally Brown's letter to you and yours to him have been carefully noted. I have noted no reason to be partial to General Brown, but must be just to him in that efforts to get fair and humane treatment to labor under this Department on the projects for river and harbor improvement under my direction and in his charge have been initiated and carried into execution by him.

I regret that General Brown did not assure you of a thorough, unbiased and fair investigation of your complaints. I will do so now. Accordingly, the President of the Mississippi River Commission has been directed to institute such an investigation. Should the results show that wrong in any way is being inflicted on the labor engaged on the Mississippi River project, appropriate action will be taken by me to apply the necessary remedies.

(Signed) Patrick J. Hurley
Secretary of War

In acknowledging Secretary Hurley's letter the National Office made the suggestion that since the contract system on the flood control work has necessitated two investigations of alleged abuses in less than a year, the system be abolished and the work taken over by army engineers.

Closely following the communication from the Secretary of War came a letter from Major General Brown, under date of September 1, asking for the name and address of the investigator for the N.A.A.C.P. so that arrangements might be made for this agent to testify at an inquiry being instituted by Secretary Hurley. The National Office promptly offered to produce the investigator at the time and place of the hearing. Under date of September 6 Major General Brown wrote that the investigation is being conducted by the President of the Mississippi River Commission at Vicksburg, Mississippi, adding:

> Should you desire the testimony of your investigator to be taken, I will transmit his name and address, with the desire, to the President, Mississippi River Commission, and he will make all arrangements for the testimony. If you do not desire that the testimony of your investigator be taken, or if you are indifferent in the matter, kindly consider my request for the necessary information.

Upon receipt of this latest communication from Major General Brown, the National Office wrote immediately to the Secretary of War telling him of the correspondence with Major General Brown and stating that the N.A.A.C.P.

"will decline to send any investigator connected with this Association to Vicksburg or to any other city in Mississippi for investigation. We do not believe that in the atmosphere which prevails in the State of Mississippi . . . any persons, white or colored, connected with this organization could be heard without intimidation or insult and possible bodily injury." The National Office offered to produce its agent in either Washington or New York and to have the testimony given orally or in the form of a deposition.

All the twenty-six Senators to whom copies of Miss Boardman's report were sent were absent from Washington for the summer, but the material was forwarded to some of them at their homes, and from these acknowledgments and comments have been received. Both Senator Arthur Capper and Senator Robert F. Wagner expressed the opinion that such conditions should not be allowed to continue.

On September 6 the Secretary and the Assistant Secretary called on Senator Wagner at his New York office for a conference which lasted about an hour. Senator Wagner was not deeply stirred by the revelations in this whole matter. The Secretary pointed out to him that we were convinced that unless the matter should be kept alive there would be the usual whitewashing with correction, perhaps, of the more patent and notorious evils, at least until after the elections; that the only hope for really correcting conditions was through a senatorial investigation. Senator Wagner agreed to the request that he not only introduce a resolution in the Senate when it reconvenes for such an investigation but that he announce now from his own office that he will introduce such a resolution.

It was pointed out to the Senator also that this was a part of the whole problem of Negroes getting jobs on government-financed projects such as the Hoover Dam, constructing of post offices and highways and other self liquidating projects as provided for in the Wagner Bill. The Assistant Secretary brought to the Senator's attention the situation in Mississippi where the only way in which federal moneys are to be expended is through the state highway projects, upon which no Negroes are employed, according to statements being published in the newspapers of Mississippi.

Senator Wagner promised not only to follow up the Mississippi Flood Control project but all other instances which we might bring to his attention of discrimination against Negroes in employment on projects financed wholly or in part by government funds.

Negro Citizenship

Walter White delivered a radio address in New York City at the invitation of the Catholic Interracial Hour. In the following speech, given on December 26, 1932, he discusses the inequities African Americans face particularly in the area of labor.

Of all the racial groups in America, none has been more directly affected than the Negro during this period of skepticism and doubt of physical, mental, and spiritual suffering. This trying period has caused the twelve million American Negroes, in common with other individuals and groups, to examine and re-examine with critical eye the life about him, the protestations as well as the acts of the Negro's fellow-citizens, and to delve more deeply than ever before into the causes—religious, economic, political, and social—of the present world distress.

I am grateful to my very good friend Father LaFarge for extending to me the invitation to speak on Negro citizenship on this Catholic Interracial Hour. The very word "Catholic" evokes for me memories and associations, most of which are warming and inspiring. It recalls to me the rare experience I had some years ago of talking for some hours with the late James Cardinal Gibbons. It recalls many pleasant and profitable conversations with my friend, Father LaFarge. It recalls the great humanitarian services to the Negro and to the American Indian of Mother Katharine and her associates, particularly Mother Mercedes, whom I have had the opportunity of meeting and knowing. And, finally, it evokes memories of my childhood in the deep South where, in Atlanta, Georgia, I never failed to marvel as a child that the only Christian church into which Negroes could enter for worship, other than exclusively Negro churches, was in the Catholic church there. When a few years back the infamous Ku Klux Klan was sweeping like a prairie fire throughout America, battening upon race and religious prejudice, it is not to be wondered that Negroes should have turned from some of the evangelical Protestant denominations in which the Klan had its greatest strength to the Catholic church, where race prejudice existed to a far lesser degree than in the Protestant denominations.

There is no one of my listeners, I am certain, who does not agree that the very last place in which race prejudice should exist is in the church. I wonder how many of those listeners, however, realize the suffering—the poignant agony which lies back of the poem by the brilliant young Negro poet, Countee Cullen, entitled, "For a Certain Lady I Know," which goes:

> She even thinks that up in heaven
> Her class lies late and snores
> While poor black cherubs rise at seven
> To do the celestial chores.

May I utilize the few minutes which remain to me to cite some of the conditions which the American Negro faces today. It matters not how intelligent, how well educated, how honest, how ambitious he may be. Great as is the suffering through unemployment in the country at large, that suffering is proportionately much smaller than that among Negroes. Prior to the world war, Negroes were generally barred from northern industries and the surplusage of Negro labor in the South caused that labor to be lightly regarded. The war stopped immigration from Europe and gave opportunity for the first time to Negroes to enter industry. Unfortunately, the period between the opening up of industry to Negroes and the present economic crisis was not long enough to permit the Negro as a whole to build up reserves to tide him over periods of unemployment, nor wholly to break down prejudice against him on the part of employers, labor unions, his fellow-workers, and the public at large. As a result, there is tragic truth in the statement that Negroes invariably are the last to be hired and the first to be fired.

Today, in the larger industrial centers like Chicago, Negroes form four per cent of the population but sixteen per cent of the unemployed. The same proportion, generally, applies to practically all of the industrial centers. The result is poverty so dire as almost to be incredible.

Even when special situations give the Negro an opportunity to work, he is robbed of the benefits. Let me cite the present enormous project, financed by the federal government and paid for out of the national treasury for which Negroes are taxed at the same rate as whites, to control the flow of the Mississippi River and to prevent repetitions of the disastrous floods which have occurred along that river. This is one of the greatest engineering feats of modern times, so enormous as almost to dwarf the imagination. The building of levees, spillways, and other means of controlling the river must of necessity be done under a broiling sun that carries a temperature at times as high as one hundred and twenty degrees. The work has to be done in swamp land where malaria and typhoid fever are common. The federal government, through the War Department, let this work to contractors. A recent investigation made by the National Association for the Advancement of Colored People, and a previous one made by the American Federation of Labor, have established beyond all doubt that inhuman treatment of labor is the rule on this project. The majority of the workers are Negroes, for only they can withstand the terrible working conditions, the long hours, and the excessive heat. These separate investigations have established that Negroes are forced to work twelve, fourteen, and sixteen hours a day, seven days a week. Though supposed to be paid at the rate of $1.26 a day they are [swindled] of even this meager wage by a trick commissary system under which workers are required in many of the cases to purchases at least $4.50 worth of goods each week. They are charged this sum whether they buy that much or not. Charges are made for ice water, for the rent of a tent, and in most instances no tents are supplied, for the hiring of cooks to prepare their meals, and for other items which absorb all their wages. Senator Robert F. Wagner of New York has introduced in the Senate a resolution for a Senate investigation of these conditions and of the heartless brutality to which Negro men and women are subjected by those who are exploiting them. May I urge my listeners to telegraph their senators urging their support of this resolution, known as Senate Resolution 500, in order that these terrible conditions may be exposed and corrected.

These are only two of the phases of life with which the Negro is faced in America. Lynchings have decreased in number, but they still take place, with little public outcry against them. In many states of the South the federal constitution is willfully and shamelessly violated in the disfranchisement of Negro citizens. In most states of the South, where Negro children are required to go to segregated schools, they are given enormously inferior equipment. There are even cases where for the education of each white child fifteen times as much is expended as for the education of each colored child, and all this money comes from public funds.

Is there any wonder that the Communists are concentrating on appeal to the Negro to help overthrow a government which permits such things to go on unchallenged and almost unnoticed? In closing, may I pay tribute to those of the Catholic church who are assiduously striving to increase the activities of the church among colored Americans? They are rendering a service which is far greater than that of benevolence towards an oppressed group. I am particularly happy to pay tribute to those who look upon Negro Catholics, not as wards and as objects of pity and benevolence, but who regard them as real brothers on a plane of equality and mutual respect. Race prejudice, like religious bigotry, is a cancer which can and will destroy all that is precious and beautiful. We of the National Association for the Advancement of Colored People, an organization numbering in its membership and its executive staff and its Boards of Directors persons of all races and creeds, will be happy to supply to those listeners who are interested [in] specific information on the problems upon which I have had time only to touch very lightly.

Memorandum from the Secretary
Re: The N.A.A.C.P. and *The Crisis*

In 1934 W. E. B. Du Bois shocked Walter White and many NAACP officials when he vowed to make segregation the subject of a year-long discussion in the *Crisis*. The Association had never really defined segregation with clarity; therefore, there was some ambiguity in its working policy of segregation. In fact the NAACP had supported segregation in certain situations such as the all-black veterans' hospital in Tuskegee, Alabama, and a separate training camp for black officers during World War I. Even in the face of this unclear policy, Walter White believed that the Association remained firmly devoted to abolishing all forms of segregation. Throughout 1934 White and Du Bois exchanged bitter editorials in the pages of the *Crisis*. The burning question for White was, "Why had Du Bois introduced the issue in such a public way?" And Du Bois consistently accused White of trying to censor him as editor of the *Crisis*. In the following memorandum White expresses his dismay over the financial troubles of the *Crisis* and also responds to the issue of segregation as it relates to NAACP policy.

No Secretary of the N.A.A.C.P. has ever been without complete control of the Board of Directors. Every important action and every matter of policy is either submitted to the Board at its regular meetings and passed upon by the Board or approved or disapproved at subsequent meetings of the Board. Regular reports of the Secretary and other officers in great detail are sent to members of the Board, as well as the minutes of all Board meetings. Since the resignation of Mr. Johnson the Committee on Administration appointed by the Board has met regularly each month, two weeks after each regular Board meeting.

As for the *Crisis*, during the years from its beginning up to the date of the incorporation of the *Crisis* Publishing Company, December, 1922, the Board of Directors of the N.A.A.C.P. has never yet passed upon the budget of the *Crisis*, the editor himself determining his own salary and the salaries of all other employees of the *Crisis*. The receipts and disbursements of the *Crisis* have been kept in a separate account and checks have been drawn by the Editor. The Budget Committee of the Association has never passed upon the budget of the *Crisis* except when the N.A.A.C.P. budget provided for moneys to the *Crisis*. Even then it did not pass on the *Crisis* fund but merely included provisions. No Secretary has ever signed Association checks. Persons signing Association checks are all non-salaried officers authorized to sign checks by Board resolutions.

Not one cent of *Crisis* profits, in the years when the *Crisis* was self-supporting and making such profits, was ever contributed to the N.A.A.C.P. It is our understanding that some of the profits of the *Crisis* went into publication of the Brownies' Book decision to publish which was made independently by Dr. Du Bois and Mr. Dill, then Business Manager of the *Crisis* and which was never passed upon by the Board of the N.A.A.C.P., nor approved by it. We understand also that some profits went into the publishing firm of Du Bois and Dill. We understand, however, that the books of the Brownies' Books and Du Bois and Dill, Publishers, are no longer in existence, so we do not know how much of the profits of the *Crisis*, if any, were used in either of these ventures.

In 1918 an agreement was made between John R. Shillady, then Secretary, and the *Crisis*, whereby the *Crisis* would allow the Association the regular agents' discount, or forty cents, on each subscription. As Association memberships of $2.50 and up included subscription to the *Crisis* and as most of these larger memberships came as the result of field work by N.A.A.C.P. officers, this allowance of the same commission given to regular *Crisis* agents served, according to the agreement, in lieu of the *Crisis* sending out field agents, since the N.A.A.C.P. officers were in effect working as field agents for the *Crisis*.

Certain members of the Board, including Charles Edward Russell and Carl Murphy, have for several years urged that publishing of the *Crisis* be suspended. The Board, however, has been loath to do this, contributing instead, since 1929, a total of $35, 409.38, as follows:

Trade accounts paid during 1932 and 1933 and		
balance due on account 1934		$11,274.22
Salary to Dr. Du Bois		
1930	$1,666.64	
1931	5,000.00	
1932	4,387.44	
1933	2,658.08	
1934 (Budget Item)	$1,200.00	14,910.16
Loans to the *Crisis*, unpaid		3,075.00
Salary to George Streator, 1934 Budget Item		1,200.00
Crisis Expenses, 1934 Budget Item		1,200.00
Contributions—one-half amount contributed		
by Julius Rosenwald Fund, 1930 to 1932		3,750.00
TOTAL		$35,409.38
Loans to the *Crisis*: July, 1929	$1,500.00	
August, 1929	1,500.00	
	$3,000,00	

During the incumbency of the present Secretary the Editor of the *Crisis* has never made one offer to help the N.A.A.C.P.

In May, 1932, the Editor of the *Crisis* agreed to do four weeks of field work for the Association, two in the spring and two in the fall. Mr. Bagnall, then Director of Branches, sought to arrange such a schedule but he was never able to arrange a schedule which met with Dr. Du Bois's approval. This work, therefore, was never done. (See memoranda between Mr. Bagnall and Dr. Du Bois.)

Instances have been reported to the National Office of Dr. Du Bois charging fees to the N.A.A.C.P. Branches for lectures. In order to preserve peace these complaints have not even been referred to Dr. Du Bois. They have, however, whatever the circumstances, created criticism and dissatisfaction.

Every year the Association has received complaints from contributors and subscribers to the *Crisis* relative to matter which has appeared in the *Crisis*. It has been the uniform practice not to say anything about these complaints other than to inform those complaining that the N.A.A.C.P. practiced as well as advocated free speech. There have been instances of contributors refusing to contribute further; but nothing has been said about this to Dr. Du Bois.

The motive of the Association and its attitude towards the *Crisis* have been persistently misinterpreted. When circulation or advertising or income dropped, it would seem reasonable that the Association on being asked to make up deficits should have the right to inquire why circulation and income declined. Unquestionably, the depression played its part, but attention is called to the fact that the *Crisis* felt it necessary to borrow $3,000.00 in the name of the Association, which sum the Association had to repay in July and August, 1929. It was the opinion of the Association that when a magazine, of any enterprise, begins to lose money, careful inquiry should be made into the reasons for failure of income to keep abreast of expenses. Revisions in business and editorial policy should be made after intelligent, unprejudiced analysis is made of policies when such policies are found to be either wrong or antiquated.

The Association's effort to take such action and at the same time with no offense to Dr. Du Bois have not met with the same spirit of cooperation as motivated the Association. Instead, these efforts were resented and it was made quite clear that the Editor of the *Crisis* would brook no interference under any circumstances and that he wished to maintain absolute control, wishing from the Association only money to make up whatever deficits occurred.

In this connection it needs to be pointed out that the Association has had to reduce drastically its staff, salaries, and budget. It has had to forego printing sorely needed literature for propaganda purposes and for carrying on the work of the Association, and frequently has been unable to meet its own obligations, due to the heavy drain upon its resources which payment of *Crisis* obligations has entailed.

On Segregation

Numerous requests have been made of the National Association for the Advancement of Colored People for a statement of the position of the Association on an editorial by Dr. Du Bois on "Segregation" in the January issue of the *Crisis*. It is fitting and proper that the statement of the Association's position should first appear in the *Crisis*, the official organ of the Association.

Various interpretations have been placed upon Dr. Du Bois's editorial, a number of them erroneous and especially the one which interprets the editorial as a statement of the position of the N.A.A.C.P. It may be stated definitely that the N.A.A.C.P. has from the date of its foundation been opposed to segregation in any form, without any reservation whatever. Dr. Du Bois's editorial is merely a personal expression on his part that the whole question of segregation should be examined and discussed anew. There can be no objection to frank and free discussion on any subject and the *Crisis* is the last place where censorship or restriction of freedom of speech should be attempted. I wish merely to call attention to the fact that the N.A.A.C.P. has never officially budged in its opposition to segregation and it is as strongly opposed to segregation as it ever was. Since Dr. Du Bois has expressed his personal opinion why this attitude might possibly have to be altered I should like to give my personal opinion why I believe we should continue to maintain the same attitude that we have for nearly a quarter of a century, but I repeat what I am about to say is merely my personal opinion just as Dr. Du Bois's editorial expressed his personal opinion.

Let us put aside for the moment the ethical and moral principles involved. It is my firm conviction, based upon observation and experience, that the truest statement in the editorial is:

> ... there is no doubt that numbers of white people, perhaps the majority of Americans, stand ready to take the most distinct advantage of voluntary segregation and cooperation among colored people. Just as soon as they get a group of black folk segregated, they use it as a point of attack and discrimination.

It is for this very reason that thoughtful colored people will be hesitant about following the advice that "groups of communities and farms inhabited by colored folk should be voluntarily formed" where they involve government-financed and approved arrangements like the Homestead Subsistence projects.

It is unfortunate that Dr. Du Bois's editorial is being used by certain government officials at Washington to hold up admission of Negroes to one of the government-financed relief projects. Protest had been made against exclusion of Negroes to Mrs. Roosevelt and others. Plans to admit Negroes as a result of the protest are being delayed with the editorial in question used as an excuse for such delay.

To accept the status of separateness, which almost invariably in the case of submerged, exploited and marginal groups means inferior accommodations and a distinctly inferior position in the national and communal life, means spiritual atrophy for the group segregated. When Negroes, Jews, Catholics, or Nordic white Americans voluntarily choose to live or attend church or engage in social activity together, that is their affair and no one else's. But Negroes and all other groups must without compromise and without cessation oppose in every possible fashion any attempt to impose from without the establishment of pales and ghettoes. Arbitrary segregation of this sort means almost without exception that less money will be expended for adequate sewerage, water, police and fire protection, and for building of a healthful community. It is because of this that the N.A.A.C.P. has resolutely fought such segregation, as in the case of city ordinances and state laws in the Louisville, New Orleans, and Richmond segregation cases; has opposed restrictive covenants written into deeds of property, and all other forms, legal and illegal, to restrict the areas in which Negroes may buy or rent and occupy property.

This principle is especially vital where attempts are made to establish separate areas which are financed by moneys from the federal and state governments for which black people are taxed at the same rate as whites. No self-respecting Negro can afford to accept without vigorous protest any such attempt to put the stamp of federal approval upon discrimination of this character. Though separate schools do exist in the South and though for the time being little can be done towards ending the expensive and wasteful dual educational system based upon caste and color prejudice, yet no Negro who respects himself and his race can accept without at least inward protest these segregated systems. It is admittedly a longer and more difficult road to full and unrestricted admission to schools, hospitals, and other public institutions, but the mere difficulty of the road should not and will not serve as a deterrent to either Negro or white people who are mindful not only of present conditions but of those to which we aspire. In a world where time and space are being demolished by science it is no longer possible to create or imagine separate racial, national, or other compartments of human thought and endeavor. The Negro must, without yielding, continue the grim struggle for integration and against segregation for his own physical, moral, and spiritual well-being and for that of white America and the world at large.

Reds vs. the Freedom Train

The NAACP, White argued, was one of the most concrete roadblocks in the Communist Party's path. It was typical of certain Communist forces to vilify the NAACP leadership through campaigns of falsehoods. The Association stood up to the Communists by empowering its board of directors and staff to revoke the charter of any NAACP branch that fell under the influence of the Communist Party. In the following *New York Herald Tribune* article, published in 1946, White discusses the Communists' order to its followers to discredit the Freedom Train.

The Communist Attack on the Freedom Train seemed so unbelievably silly when I first read it, I was certain that some enemy of Communism or some very smart Freedom Train publicist had concocted the diatribe.

Even after authenticity of the secret directive to Communist units signed by the chairman of the "National Educational Agitation and Publication Department" had been admitted by the Communist Party; I found it difficult to believe any person or group could make himself or itself so ridiculous.

Equally incredible is the paralyzing fear (among otherwise normal and sane Americans) of a minuscule political party whose brains are of such caliber as to issue or even to think of such a document.

It was singularly interesting to note that the same editions of newspapers reporting Communist instructions to its members to attack Freedom Train appearances throughout the country also published indignant demands that the "constitutional" rights of an alleged Communist labor union official be protected. The same demand, which is perfectly valid, has been made recently in behalf of Gerhart Eisler, Eugene Dennis, and other Communists that violation of the basic rights of a Communist leads inevitably to abridgment of the rights of every citizen however far to the other pole of political belief he may be.

But now the Communists order their members to sneer at and discredit, as far as lies within their power, the very document whose protection they seek and whose name they invoke whenever they become entangled with the law.

This observer happens to believe devoutly that it is not only as imperative to protect as zealously the rights of dissidents as those of the most securely entrenched and respectable elements in our society but that it is even more imperative for the simple reason that the former's rights are more likely to be trampled upon.

A banker or a chamber of commerce president has the money to hire lawyers to represent him if he runs afoul of the law. Most of his friends and class will rally to his defense if only for reasons of self-preservation. Moreover, he is less likely to be trod upon in the first place because of his prestige and position.

The poor or the politically dissident have none or, at best, very few of these weapons of defense. Their rights are certain to be the first to undergo assault and abridgment. This makes all the more inexplicable the Communist order to its followers that it discredit the Freedom Train.

Suppose it be granted, for the sake of argument, that the National Association of Manufacturers, the United States Chamber of Commerce, and Winthrop Aldrich have a demagogic purpose in being among the sponsors of this publicity campaign for the Bill of Rights, the Constitution, and the Emancipation Proclamation.

But what can that purpose be in attracting more people than have ever before in the years of the existence of the Constitution to see and read for the first time what their rights are under that document? A much more sinister "demagogic purpose" would be preventing the people from learning their rights and how to obtain them in actual everyday life.

The Freedom Train exhibit would have been even timelier and more valuable if it included contemporary freedom documents such as Executive Order 8802 prohibiting job discrimination because of race, creed, color, or national origin, or the Wagner Act. It is unfortunate they are not included.

But if the papers which mark the milestones of the struggle for freedom in America are made better known and respected, that will be a gain for democracy and certainly no advancement of any "demagogic purpose."

I can only conclude sadly that Communists have amply proved themselves capable of as great absurdity and downright stupidity as those who declared a year ago that if only price controls were abolished, prices would topple way down to "their natural level." A level of ninety-eight cents a dozen eggs and dollar a pound butter!

White Hails Film on Anti-Semitism

In the following article, Walter White praises producer Darryl Zanuck and his film company for its courage in presenting a sincere depiction of anti-Semitism on the screen. He expresses his desire to see African-American life portrayed in a more honest and positive light on the big screen. This article was written in 1947.

Wendell Willkie would be proud of the film company of whose board he was chairman for the courage it has shown in making "Gentleman's Agreement" the most forthright exposé of anti-Semitism yet to appear on the screen.

To Darryl Zanuck who personally produced the picture, Laura Hobson who wrote the novel, Gregory Peck who plays the leading role, and every other individual connected with the film, are due the gratitude of decent Americans.

Even so excellent a picture as "Crossfire" ducked some of the implications and manifestations of racial and religious bigotry in the United States, the most serious menace to the democratic process which exists. "Gentleman's Agreement" pulls not a single punch. Its most devastating effect is its exposé of the "nice" people who live in smug complacency in suburban Connecticut towns like Darien and New Canaan. These are the people who erroneously consider themselves "liberal" who twice a year denounce Bilbo and Gerald L. K. Smith and at the same time think nothing of dirty little dinner table stories about minorities.

If as many millions of Americans see this mature and courageous film as should see it, there ought to be at least a diminution of the embarrassed laughter which hereafter greets anti-Semitic, anti-Roosevelt, anti-Negro, and other smutty little jokes which have been so prevalent at dinner parties in recent years.

It is certainly hoped that "Gentleman's Agreement" will be a financial success to justify the courage it took to produce it and overcome the nameless fears which plague Hollywood.

Some of the writers and producers who have recently been pilloried by the House of Un-American Affairs Committee as "Communist" have been almost solely the individuals who have fought racial stereotypes in moving pictures.

Being anathema to the Communist, I do not know who is or is not a dues-paying, card-carrying member of the party. I, therefore, have no means of finding out if writers like Dalton Trumbo or Ring Lardner, Jr., are either Communists or fellow travelers.

What I do know is that Trumbo's speech to the World Writers' Congress in 1943 on what Hollywood has done to perpetuate and spread caricatures of the Negro is the ablest and most courageous of its kind with which I am familiar.

Ring Lardner's script for the U.A.W. (C.I.O.) based on "The Races of Mankind" is another example of the fight against bigotry made by too few persons in Hollywood.

It will be remembered that "The Races of Mankind" was used by the United States Army in its educational courses until the recently jailed Congressman Andrew J. May of Kentucky threatened to cut the War Department budget, even though we were then at war, unless the Army abandoned the use of this pamphlet on comparative racial mental abilities.

If "Gentleman's Agreement" is patronized as it deserves, there is hope that Hollywood will stop being afraid and will continue to tackle hitherto taboo subjects of this character. Perhaps in time it may even have the courage to do an honest picture about the Negro.

Moral Advance Seen in Report by Committee on Civil Rights

> Walter White called President Harry S. Truman's report by the Commission
> on Civil Rights the most uncompromising and forthright declaration by a
> government agency on racial bigotries to date. This committee was formed
> in response to the "bloody summer" of 1946, when lynchings and mob
> violence against African Americans escalated. In this article, White praises
> Truman for establishing the Committee on Civil Rights to address these
> atrocities. He wrote this article in 1947.

Today Americans who look to the future, Lloyd Morris asserts in his just published "Postscripts to Yesterday," display no serenity, are opposed with an increasing disenchantment with the social order and are plagued with a growing conviction of deterioration of the "moral atmosphere."

There is, unhappily, a tremendous volume of evidence to support Mr. Morris's pessimism. But there is also evidence that the moral conscience of America not only is not entirely moribund, but in some respects is more percipient and courageous than it was in 1896, the year to which Mr. Morris looks back with nostalgic reverence.

The most striking proof of this is the report of President Truman's Committee on Civil Rights. That document is notable in two respects. It is the most uncompromising and specific pronouncement by a governmental agency on the explosive issue of racial and religious bigotry which had ever been issued. It is equally remarkable in that, for the first time, distinguished representatives of industry have spoken out on the subject.

In this space from time to time there has been criticism of the lack of concern by industrialists with assaults on democracy. Conservatives who have most to conserve should be the first to act against denials of liberty. The bland assertion by several of the most potent organizations of business men that the preservation of civil liberties is not a matter of their concern has been appalling.

But Charles E. Wilson, president of the General Electric Company, and Charles Luckman, president of Lever Brothers, have set an example which merits the highest praise. It is no reflection upon the churchmen and labor leaders who served on the President's committee to say that their part in formulating this course of action is less significant than the participation of Mr. Wilson and Mr. Luckman. On the contrary, it is a tribute to the churches and to trade unionism that their spokesmen are expected to take such a stand.

But it took real courage for the industrialists. I do not know how many millions of dollars worth of General Electric products and of Lever Brothers soaps are sold in areas of the United States where bigotries are so deeply entrenched that economic reprisals might be threatened against the corporations which take the kind of decent stand the presidents of these two companies have.

I do not believe there will be any such reprisals, or that it would matter if they were attempted. If this prediction proves to be true, another of the nameless fears which hold conservatives will thereby be destroyed.

As one of those who suggested to Mr. Truman that a more direct approach to the menace of bigotry is necessary, I would like also to pay tribute to him. During the bloody summer of 1946 there was a succession of lynchings and other acts of mob violence against minorities. A National Committee Against Mob Violence was formed in the Willkie Memorial Building in New York to meet this situation, and a delegation from that committee, representing church, labor and civic groups, placed the facts before the President. But business groups declined to participate.

I shall never forget Mr. Truman's face as he listened to the details of the gouging out of the eyes of Isaac Woodard, a Negro War veteran, by the chief of police of a South Carolina town who not only admitted but boasted of his act. The President decided to take direct action, and the Committee on Civil Rights was the first step.

The choice of its personnel marks a distinctly new and tremendously important concern of every segment of the American people with the basic problem of human rights. The report puts Congress, and particularly the conservative Republican-Southern Democratic bloc, squarely on trial.

But the job is not one for Congress alone, as the report points out. State legislatures, private organizations, and each individual American have been told by the President's committee what needs to be done. Whether democracy survives depends in large measure upon what we do.

Abolition of Racial Segregation at Truman's Inaugural Praised

When Harry Truman became President in 1945, there was a great deal of uncertainty about him. A haberdasher from Klan country (Independence, Missouri), he had been a judge back in Kansas City, and one of the favorable things he did was to save a black boys' school that whites believed was too good for black youth. As a U.S. senator in 1935, he had backed the Costigan–Wagner Anti-Lynching Bill. His civil rights record was indeed viewed as moderate. As time passed, Walter White found Truman an ally on many issues concerning race. In the following *New York Herald Tribune* article, White writes that Truman has set a precedent by inviting blacks to every event of his inauguration. This article was published in 1949.

Although only a few commentators mentioned it a miracle occurred in Washington on January 20 almost as incredible as the spectacular re-election of President Truman. The miracle was that of total abolition of racial segregation.

The man from the Southern state of Missouri ordered done what had never been done before in American history. Negroes were invited to every event, from the inauguration itself to the reception at the National Art Gallery given by the President and Mrs. Truman, the Truman-Barkley dinner, the gala on inauguration eve, at which Dorothy Maynor and Lena Horne starred: the Shoreham Hotel cocktail party for the members of the Democratic National Committee, and innumerable lesser but well mannered guests, according to Bob Considine, were Negroes, while a distinguished American woman told me that the most beautiful and smartly gowned woman she had ever seen was a colored guest at the ball.

Probably nine out of ten white Americans would have been convinced on Jan. 19 that "it couldn't happen here." Dire predictions would have been uttered of fist fights, angry words or even race riots if the previous custom of a Jim Crow ball in a dingy and remote section of Washington were abandoned. Equally ominous fears of racial clashes would probably have been voiced about Negro guests at Washington's hotels—or of conspicuously empty seats at the inaugural itself, similar to the much photographed and publicized empty table of Governor Olin D. Johnston of South Carolina, at last year's Jackson Day Dinner in Washington, in protest against the Truman civil rights program.

What happened? Precisely nothing, except that this year's inauguration was better behaved than any in recent history. Americans rose, as they have a habit of rising, to emergency, to the challenge of ordinary human decency. In one of the choicer stands in the Capitol Plaza, directly in front of the spot where President Truman of Missouri and Vice-President Barkely, of Kentucky, were sworn in, one in ten of the guests was dark-skinned. When a Negro couple in their eagerness to see what was going on stepped in front of three white women with marked Southern accents there was no complaint by the latter, only a gracious acknowledgment for the apology of the colored couple when they recognized their discourtesy.

I have mentioned that this was the best behaved inaugural of many quadrennial. Perhaps that pleasant circumstance was due in part to the staying away from Washington of an element which has formed a sizable proportion of the crowd at previous inaugurations of Democratic administrations.

These were the "wool hat boys" who utilized the occasion to consume vast quantities of liquor, to rid their lungs of the rebel yell in the nation's capital in defiance of "damyankees," who found expression of their frustrations by using electric buzzers on unsuspecting and attractive women. They were the willing victims of salesmen of tawdry "souvenirs" at 500 per cent profit to the venders of fantastic quantities of unappetizing box lunches and hot dogs.

Unable to stomach the sight of the inauguration of the man they had attempted to desperately defeat because of his insistence that Americans of every creed and color were entitled to equal protection and opportunity, this boisterous element remained at home to the great delight of 1,000,000 visitors and 2,000,000 residents of Washington who are not amused by bad manners. As a result, a President re-entered the White House in an atmosphere of dignity and friendliness unusual in Democratic administrations.

The only evidence of a new atmosphere of human relations to be observed was the stony silence or the boos of spectators, many of them with Southern accents, as the automobiles of Governor J. Strom Thurmond of South Carolina and of Governor Herman Talmadge of Georgia passed by. One of the most conspicuous of these voices was Miss Tallulah Bankhead's from the President's reviewing stand.

May I add one post-inaugural note of developing democracy Washington? Marcus Helman's transformation of the National Theater, Washington's only outlet for the living theater, into a motion-picture house in lieu of abolition of the color line has been a dismal failure financially. White Washington, by their almost unanimous avoidance of the National Theater, are demonstrating to Mr. Helman that they, too, are growing up despite evidence that much remains to be done to make Washington what it should be.

Can it be that a segregationless inaugural and a boycott of a theater are proving that Americans are beginning to practice as well as talk about democracy? It could be.

Fate of Democrats in 1950 Seen Hinging on Stand on Civil Rights

In this article Walter White reminds Senate Democrats running for reelection in 1950 in states where the election will likely be close that labor, minority groups, and other voters will hold the balance of power. The candidates will be judged by their actions on civil rights. White expresses no confidence in the reactionary Republicans that they will bring about needed change.

The political complexion of the Senate in 1950 may possibly have been determined by a small meeting in New York on February 5. Representatives of twenty-two national organizations played a decisive role in giving Democrats control of both Senate and House of the Eighty-first Congress. These organizations bluntly served notice that "no other recourse will be given us except to give control of the Senate in 1950 to the Republicans" if the Democratic Senate leadership allows that party's civil rights pledges to be nullified by blustering Dixiecrats.

That such a threat can be fulfilled and is no idle boast is evident on examination of the politically powerful groups which spoke. Organized labor was represented by both the American Federation and the Congress of Industrial Organizations. Protestant, Catholic, Jewish, women's and Negro organizations were there. With the exception of the Americans for Democratic Action, none of the powerful bodies could be classified as "professional" political ones. They spoke for millions of independent voters who, during the last sixteen years, have taken away from political machines the deciding of national and local elections.

It would have been enlightening, and probably embarrassing, to the present Senate leadership to hear the discussion of their apparent surrender to the threats of Southern Senators to prevent action on any legislation in the Eighty-first Congress unless amendment of the Senate filibuster rules is shelved. Speaker after speaker commented sharply on the failure of the majority leadership to make any visible effort to bring up the issue.

Fears of a double-cross on the civil rights issue or, at best, timidity which would cause disastrous postponement were justified by subsequent revelation in Washington that a "gentlemen's agreement" had been entered into to postpone, until after February 28, consideration of amendment of the rules or any other important legislation. It is a deliberate attempt to weaken organized labor's support of civil rights legislation by refusing to take up rules amendment until the Taft-Hartley act is ready for Senate action.

Since it is estimated that from four to eight weeks will be devoted to debate on amendment of the Taft-Hartley act, this "deal" will permit [the] appropriations bill, particularly for natural defense and housing, to reach the Senate calendar and be ready for action when the Taft-Hartley vote is eventually taken. By this maneuvering the majority leadership hopes to avoid a showdown on civil rights.

More than a dozen Democratic Senators must stand for re-election two years hence in states where the margin between the two parties is normally slim and where labor, minority, and other voters whose representatives joined in the warning, unmistakably hold the balance of power. The statement reminded the Democrats that it is their party, and not its individual members, which is on trial. Double-crossing or reneging on its unequivocal pledges on civil rights will be the yardstick by which the party will be judged. Puerile political finagling to postpone action on amendment of the Senate rules until the Taft-Hartley act is ready for Senate action, as a means of taking away the support for labor for civil rights legislation, was roundly scored.

The conferees by no means gave a clean bill of health to the Republicans. It was recognized that with but a few exceptions the Republicans are equally guilty of chicanery on the issue. There were no illusions that turning over control of the Senate twenty-one months from now to reactionary Republicans would create much change.

But the responsibility lies squarely on the majority party. Just as the independent voters in pivotal states defeated Republicans in 1948 because of their failure as the majority party in the Eightieth Congress, so are the Democrats in line for the same treatment in 1950 if they fail to keep their pledges.

It seems to be in the cards that unless they reread the election returns and learn that President Truman, and not Strom Thurmond, won, much of the present Democratic leadership is in for rough sailing.

A Sign of Political Change in the South

In the following article Walter White praises Governor W. Kerr Scott of North Carolina for appointing Dr. Frank P. Graham as the new U.S. senator. White writes here that Graham's appointment adds to the growing number of southern congressmen who are able to think beyond selfish geographical lines.

The most dramatic, because of its unexpectedness, and the most heartening evidence of the political metamorphosis in the South is the appointment by Governor W. Kerr Scott of North Carolina of Dr. Frank P. Graham as the new United States Senator in North Carolina last week. I found the politicians stunned and the people jubilant. More than fifty persons had been urged upon Governor Scott for the appointment by various political factions. It would appear that none except Governor Scott and Senator Graham knew that North Carolina's most distinguished citizen was being considered for the post.

It has taken superlative courage and vision for the quiet and diminutive new Senator to carve the career he has made in any part of the United States and especially in the South. Dr. Graham has made the University of North Carolina one of the truly great appropriations for the university because of his belief that education should embrace all the knowledge available. At the same time, despite the fantastic charges of Senator Bricker, he has been made the target of attacks by Communists. It would be a mistake on the basis of these assaults from extreme Left and extreme Right to class Dr. Graham as a middle-of-the-roader. He is not a gradualist, especially on such explosive subjects as the race problem, although he believes that the educative process, both in classrooms and in life itself, is the most useful means of solving the problems which harass mankind.

The chief significance of the appointment lies in its addition to the small but growing number of members of the Congress from the South who are able to think beyond selfish sectional lines. Along with men like Claude Pepper, of Florida, and Estes Kefauver, of Tennessee, Senator Graham will help to increase courage on the part of numerous fellow Southerners.

Perhaps Senator Graham's appointment to the Senate and the kind of leadership he will give there may toughen the character and sharpen the intelligence of his fellow Southerners and of the Senate at large through demonstration of the fact that one can refuse to be a slave to bigotry and tradition and at the same time be successful in politics.

Fifty Years of Fighting

Perhaps one of the most valuable signs of progress in the NAACP struggle for civil rights was that little time was spent on the issue of lynching during 1950. This progress represented a true change in the pattern of race relations in America. In the following essay, White discusses the five major campaigns in the struggle for freedom in the first half of this century.

It is a fascinating, heartening, discouraging experience to celebrate the *Pittsburgh Courier's* fortieth birthday by looking back to compare the status of civil and human rights in the United States at the halfway mark of the Twentieth Century with that of the beginning of the century. American minorities yet have a long way to travel before they can leave their homes in the morning with assurance that the color of skin or slant of eyes or nose will not subject them to subtle or unsubtle denials of their right to walk in human dignity among their fellowmen. In their path still stands the mark of the ghetto to thwart ambition and create the inner bitterness which discrimination and segregation create.

But when one looks backward as I did when I tried to write about what I had known and experienced during thirty of those fifty years of struggle a satisfying experience bordering on elation rewarded me. Not that I was content, Instead, it was the comfort of knowing that the cause of human rights was moving from the defensive to the offensive in terms of battle. Where, a half century ago, governors like Cole Blease of South Carolina and other demagogues like Tillman, Vardaman, Hoke Smith, Tom Watson, Heflin and others so infamous [in recent] memory were rising to power unchallenged by any organization or individual forces of decency, today such characters are either loathed or laughed at.

At the turn of the century men like these openly and proudly defended lynching. Ministers of the gospel of Jesus of Nazareth brazenly praised lynchers. Southern legislatures enacted "Black Codes" to re-establish slavery legally up to the absolute limit of re-creation of military rule by the North. Segregation of Negroes in schools, transportation, employment, and housing as well as total disfranchisement was enacted to the tune of the rebel yell. Meanwhile the North was delighted to forget the carnage and bitterness of the late Civil War and turn its attention to building vast individual and corporate fortunes both in the great cities and in the newly opened land of the West through the Homestead Act.

Henry W. Grady's advice to young Southerners to go North and get jobs on Yankee newspapers, magazines, and book publishing firms to control thereby national thinking on the Negro and the south was being taken with devastating effect on the cause of civil rights and Negro emancipation.

Fear, guilt, greed, and humiliation rode implacably the unreconstructed South like the Four Horsemen at the Apocalypse or the resurgent Nazis of contemporary Germany. Writers like Thomas Dixon were broodingly stirring the sinister vials of hate to concoct novels like *The Clansman* from which a perverted genius of the films, David Wark Griffith, was later destined to make the greatest breeder of hatred, "The Birth of a Nation," which Hollywood could ever produce.

Although the Ku Klux Klan had been temporarily discredited and disbanded, the hate it had spawned continued to sweep not only the South, but its poison had spread to the entire nation and the world. Ruthless exploitations of dark people in Asia and Africa under colonialism to feed the insatiable demand for raw materials and manpower which the new world of science and industrial expansion in Europe and America demanded made convenient the spreading of theories of racial superiority which raped the Southern Bourbon pattern.

Against this tidal wave of bigotry and bitterness few voices were audible. In the North most of the Abolitionists had been silenced by death or age. Few of their descendants inherited the principles and passion of their fathers. Trotter in Boston and Max Barber in Philadelphia fought doggedly but feebly against white indifference and Negro apathy. At Tuskegee, Booker T. Washington reaped the rewards of his conciliatory and appeasement speech at Atlanta in 1895 and moved forward as cautiously as he dared to attract Northern philanthropy and avert Southern hostility.

But when the future seemed most hopeless a few rays of light began to break in the darkness. Du Bois's *Litany of Atlanta* after the Atlanta race riot of 1906, flashed like an angry meteor across the sky of white complacency and Negro timidity. On Lincoln's birthday, fifty-three men and women met in New York City in 1909 and formed the National Association for the Advancement of Colored People. The following years there were born the National Urban League and the *Pittsburgh Courier* which joined the *New York Age*, the *Chicago Defender*, the *Baltimore Afro-American*, the *Norfolk Journal and Guide*, and other papers in informing and stimulating discussion and action against the black-out of civil rights which was inundating the nation.

There is no space within 2,000 words to tell either the whole story or to elaborate on any one of the major phases of this half-century of struggle. Instead, one can only set forth the five major campaigns—three of them specific and the other two shifts in ideology—which highlight what in some respects is a bloodless revolution of attitude.

The first of these is the determined fight in both courts of law and of public opinion to force compliance with the guarantees of the Bill of Rights and especially the Fourteenth Amendment of the Constitution.

In twenty-four of twenty-six cases involving fundamental issues of human liberty carried to the United States Supreme Court the Negro has emerged victorious.

In innumerable other cases in lower courts similar victories have been won, frequently against odds which seemed insuperable. Within a few days there will be argued in the United States Supreme Court the twenty-seventh case in which the issue of whether or not there can be equality within the framework of segregation has been placed unequivocally before the court. Should the Negro emerge victorious in that case, the Herman Sweatt one from Texas, a profound alteration in the concept of what is segregation may be accomplished. Of that more later.

But important as have been achievements in inducing American courts to measure up to the full implications of the Constitution by requiring compliance with the law, equally if not more important is the educative effect of these cases on American public opinion. Gunnar Myrdal asserts that the existence of a Bill of Rights forces Americans at least to suffer from troubled consciences when they glibly extol a doctrine of freedom for all men, even though they render lip service only most of the time to that precept. Use of the courts and the Constitution by the Negro and his friends has served as an invaluable goad to the American conscience and thereby helped to narrow the gap between lip service and performance in assuring human rights to all.

The Sweatt case is the latest and most sharply etched example of the second important phase of this fifty-year battle. Until quite recent years nearly all white Americans and a majority of Negro Americans accepted the unwholesome doctrine that racial segregation would be a permanent or at least a long-lived reality.

Today not one intelligent person, even in the deepest South, believes that. Today even the Rankins and Talmadges know they are on the defensive and that the walls of segregation cannot be shored up much longer. For that very reason of their desperateness as well as the illogicality and uneconomic aspect of their struggle to maintain "white supremacy" they will fight all the more like cornered rats.

But the tide has been turned against them, primarily by the Negro himself in rejection of any and all appeasements in the form of larger appropriations for segregated institutions. That basic cleansing of his own thinking by the Negro and others is the most significant development of the Twentieth Century so far as civil rights and human rights are concerned.

The third front is the emancipation of the Negro from political chattel slavery. Mass migrations during and after World Wars I and II distributed the Negro population in such fashion as to make possible today's holding of the balance of power in several pivotal states. But [these] population shifts would have had little or no effect had not the Negro used his vote with increasing independence and intelligence. It is possible that when the definitive political history of the first half of the Twentieth Century is written one of the events of greatest impact upon American political history may prove to be the defeat of John J. Parker for the United States Supreme Court in 1930.

Not only did that event demonstrate the possession of power and the ability to use it effectively and successfully by the Negro voter for the first time in American history. It also marked one of the most decisive turning points of the Supreme Court in relation to the people of the United States in demonstrating that henceforth no President could nominate to the court any person who did not place human rights at least on a par with property rights.

It has been the recognized and growing political strength, acumen and recognition of the Negro voter during the two decades since the Parker fight which have marked the fourth phase of the civil rights struggle. This is the battle for legislation in Congress and state legislatures to implement civil rights and the less spectacular fight against vicious bills. Although Senate filibusters have stymied F.E.P.C., anti-lynching, anti-poll tax, and other bills the fight for such legislation has stirred, educated and unified Negro and white Americans. It has kept the searing searchlight of publicity on these evils and thereby steadily forced those who favored and practiced such discrimination more and more on the defensive.

It is possible and probable that even as you read these words, Senate Dixiecrats and reactionary Republicans may be again waging a filibuster against the F.E.P.C. But they will not be unaware of the nation-wide disgust they are incurring now or the political and moral consequences they may have to meet in 1950 and 1952.

Lynchings, meanwhile, have been materially reduced, the poll tax and employment discrimination increasingly unpopular and other denials of opportunity to minorities less and less approved as a direct result of the fight for legislation. Such a volume of public opinion cannot and will not be denied. Nor has any part of the struggle been in vain.

Fifth and finally, there is the emergence of the issue of human rights on the world stage as a direct consequence of two world wars, the revolt against colonialism and racism, the breaking forever of illusions of white moral or military superiority, and embarrassment to the United States in its new position of world leadership.

No longer can the United States get away with telling other peoples what they must do as long as denial of civil rights to its own citizens confront Americans in every international conference. Thus a new and immensely potent drive has been added to the battle for human justice to all Americans irrespective of race, creed, color, or national origin.

It is somewhat late for use of football analogies. But I can think of none better than to say that the first half of the Twentieth Century has been devoted to a struggle to move the ball from the shadow of one's own goal post up to the center of the field. The advocates of civil rights have certainly moved the ball at least to the fifty yard line.

I might be even more optimistic and say that it has been rushed even further into the enemy's territory. The fight during the second half of the century will be that of carrying the ball further down the field and across the goal line of the enemy. And that must mean not only full civil rights for American minorities but also for all oppressed peoples of the world. Either we must attain freedom for the whole world or there will be no world left for any of us.

Report on Civil Rights

The year 1951 was the year of the hate bomb. It had been most widely used in Florida. In a frantic attempt to stop the progress made by the NAACP and its allies, the hate bomb became a new instrument of terror. On Christmas night of 1951, NAACP Florida coordinator Harry T. Moore and his wife were murdered by a bomb planted beneath their house. Florida was not alone in this evil. Hate bombs exploded in Birmingham, Dallas, Atlanta, Nashville, and in California. Other forms of violence erupted in Cicero, Illinois, in Louisiana, and in other places. Despite the horrific atrocities, there were some important gains made this year, such as acquittal of four of the six men in the Trenton Six case, eradication of segregation in the army in Korea, and the slowing down of segregation in publicly financed institutions of higher education in the South. During this year the Legal Defense and Educational Fund handled 702 cases, 77 of which were brought to trial. With the catapulting of legal attack on segregated public elementary and secondary schools in Atlanta, Georgia; Clarendon County, South Carolina; Topeka, Kansas; and Wilmington, Delaware, the Legal Department opened a new phase in its quest for "equality under the law." In the following report, White discusses the gains and setbacks and the goals of the NAACP at the close of 1951.

Among gains made on the civil rights front during 1951 were the acquittal of four of the six men being retried for murder in the Trenton Six cases; the federal indictments returned against seven city officials of Cicero, Illinois; the abolition of segregation in the Army in Korea, and the continuing breakdown of segregation in publicly financed institutions of higher education in the South.

Despite these notable gains, there was ample evidence of enduring vitality of bigotry, intolerance and violence culminating in the Christmas night murder by bombing of Harry T. Moore at his home in Mims, Fla. Mr. Moore paid with his life for his devotion to the fight for equal rights for Negroes in his home state.

At times during the year, justice and human rights in America seemed to be standing still, even moving backward a few steps just when the world's jitters should have hammered home the need for cleaning up our Jim Crow backyard and strengthening our democracy as never before. Yet, ironically, we saw in our country a resurgence of violence—rioting, home burning, bombing, police brutality, and mockery of the revered American concept of "Equal Justice Under Law." Cicero, Martinsville, Groveland, Birmingham, Miami, and Mims, the horror names of 1951, drove home more strongly than ever the continuing and increasing need for the N.A.A.C.P.

Prompted by complaints of mistreatment by Negro GIs fighting in segregated units in Korea, the Association in January sent its special counsel, Thurgood Marshall, to the Far East to investigate circumstances surrounding the seemingly excessive number of court martial actions against Negro servicemen. After conferring with the men themselves and with top level Army personnel in Japan and Korea, including General of the Army Douglas MacArthur, Mr. Marshall uncovered facts revealing shocking discrimination against Negro soldiers. His documented report charged that the segregation policies prevalent in the Far East command lay behind the injustices, and led to the announcement that the all-Negro 24th Division would be liquidated and segregation terminated in the Far East Command. Legal action by the N.A.A.C.P. subsequently won reduced sentences for a number of the court-martialed men.

On the legislative front, the year looked gloomy from the start. After the Eighty-first Congress dissolved with a do-nothing record on civil rights, convening of the Eighty-second Congress offered no promise of improvement. The restoration of life-or-death power over legislation to the House Rules Committee, together with President Truman's appointment of former Governor Millard F. Caldwell of Florida as Director of Civil Defense, all seemed omens of appeasement of the Dixiecrats. The N.A.A.C.P. girded itself for a hard fight against reactionary forces in the new Congress, and met with a certain degree of success. It mobilized its branches and outside organizations for the ultimate defeat of the Winstead amendment, which would have permitted inductees to serve in segregated units if they so chose. It also called together a group of organizations for a civil rights meeting in Washington in May, and was able to bring about open hearings on a change in Senate rules to prevent filibusters. The N.A.A.C.P., of course, has been in the forefront of the campaign to do away with the filibuster, and was extremely active in the Washington hearings.

Education Battle Continues

In Education, where the greatest strides have been made in recent years by the Association, the picture again looked brighter than in any other field of N.A.A.C.P. endeavor. In February, the University of Maryland announced that the doors of all its colleges and schools would be opened to Negro students and that all its facilities would be available on an unsegregated basis. In March, an N.A.A.C.P. victory in the U.S. Court of Appeals, ending the ban against Negro students at the law school of the University of North Carolina, seemed to be a decisive development in the fight for educational equality—because if the court refused to uphold the "equality" of the best-equipped and longest-established segregation law school in the country, it seems unlikely that it would in the future uphold any hastily thrown-together makeshift Jim Crow institution of higher learning.

The focus has now shifted to the elementary and high school levels, with the launching of legal attacks against segregated public schools in Atlanta, Georgia; Clarendon, County, S.C.; Topeka, Kansas; and Wilmington, Delaware. It may well be that decisions affecting the ultimate outcome of segregation in public elementary and secondary schools will be handed down by the U.S. Supreme Court in 1952.

Groveland Tragedy

In April, the Association won what looked as though it might have been its most outstanding victory of the year, when the Supreme Court unanimously reversed the convictions of Samuel Shepherd and Walter Irvin in the infamous Groveland, Florida, "rape" case, and ordered a new trial. In a precedent-shattering concurring opinion, Justice Robert H. Jackson excoriated the role played by a biased and inflammatory press in influencing the jurors, and said that "These convictions, accompanied by such events, do not meet any civilized conception of due process of law."

But the victory was tragically short-lived, for on November 6, the eve of the re-trial ordered for Shepherd and Irvin by the highest court in the country, Sheriff Willis McCall shot the two defendants down in cold blood on a dark country road. Samuel Shepherd was killed outright; Walter Irvin, miraculously escaping instant death, stands trial now, although he was critically wounded. The slayer still holds the office of Sheriff of Lake County, and thus far nothing has been done to punish him for his defiance of the law and of the United States Supreme Court. N.A.A.C.P. attorneys are again defending Irvin, and branches are circulating petitions calling for justice in the case.

Appalling examples of "unequal justice" cropped up through the year. In February, seven Negroes were put to death in Martinsville, Va., after their conviction for rape—a crime for which no white person in the State pays with his life. In Cicero, Ill., a grand jury investigating the July rioting, precipitated when the Harvey E. Clark family tried to move into their new apartment in a white neighborhood, indicted—not the rioters—but the N.A.A.C.P. attorney and others who aided the Clarks after they suffered the complete ruin of their belongings at the hands of the mob. (The N.A.A.C.P. finally won the dismissal of the ridiculous charges against the attorney, George Leighton, but not until irreparable harm had been done by this miscarriage of justice.) Subsequently, after a number of conferences with N.A.A.C.P. officials, the Department of Justice moved in and impaneled a special federal grand jury and special prosecutor. Indictments were then returned against seven city officials for their role in preventing the Clarks from moving into their apartment.

In Yanceyville, N.C., in November, Mack Ingram went on trial for "looking" at a white girl from a distance of seventy-five feet—a "crime for which he had previously been convicted and sentenced to two years at hard labor. A hung jury resulted in a mistrial.

Victory in Trenton

Not all of the year's court cases brought grief to the cause of human rights, however. In one case on which the eyes of the world were centered—that of the Trenton Six—the N.A.A.C.P. defended two of the four men who were acquitted after the fifteen-week murder trial, the longest in New Jersey's history. All six of the defendants had previously been convicted and their convictions reversed by the N.J. Supreme Court. The Association is now participating with other organizations in an appeal for Collis English and Ralph Cooper, the two who were convicted.

Washington Bureau

The Washington Bureau of the Association continued to act as a watchdog over pending legislation and other happenings in the nation's capital which affected the program of the N.A.A.C.P. and the welfare of Negroes and other minority groups. Testimony was offered at congressional hearings on all such matters. One of the outstanding accomplishments of the Bureau during the year was the securing of a guarantee against employment [discrimination] and other discrimination at the giant new H-Bomb projects underway in Aiken, S.C., and elsewhere in the South.

In June, the Association held a history-making convention in Atlanta, Georgia, climaxed by the appearance of a police motorcycle escort to lead Dr. Ralph Bunche, speaker at the closing mass meeting, from the airport to the municipal auditorium. In addition to Dr. Bunche, the delegates were addressed by Dr. Benjamin Mays, president of Morehouse College; Philip Willkie, Indiana legislator and son of the late Wendell Willkie; Dr. Algeron Black, chairman of the board of leaders of the New York Society for Ethical Culture; and Albin Krebs, former editor of the student newspaper of the University of Mississippi. Mrs. Mabel K. Staupers was presented with the Spingarn Medal for her outstanding work in eliminating discrimination in the field of nursing. The 750 delegates were outspoken and unequivocal in their condemnation of segregation and discrimination, and left the convention with renewed dedication to the fight against these evils on every front.

From the convention came the Association's campaign to have the new "Amos 'n' Andy" television show removed from the air. Blasting the show for depicting the Negro in a derogatory manner, the delegates adopted a resolution calling upon branches and other individuals and organizations to protest the program and to use every means at their disposal to discourage sponsorship of this and similar shows.

As the year drew to a close, the need for intensifying the fight against discrimination was becoming more and more apparent. This need was dramatically reflected in an upward swing of N.A.A.C.P. membership figures in 1951. Despite a number of setbacks, the Association and its friends were anything but discouraged, and faced 1952 with hope and determination for attacking the job ahead.

N.A.A.C.P. Forty-second Annual Meeting Speech

NAACP branches across the country held memorial meetings to pay tribute to the martyred Harry T. Moore and his wife, and to reconfirm their commitment to the struggle to achieve the goal for which the Moores died. At a meeting in Jacksonville, Florida, NAACP branch officials representing fifteen southern states made plans for southwide action to eradicate terror and intimidation against black citizens. In the following address to the NAACP Annual Meeting in January 1952, Walter White asserts that the accomplishments gained by the NAACP have created a climate for hatemongers to react. The greatest task ahead for the Association, he proclaims, is to overcome ignorance, misinformation, and fear.

In no recent year have Negro Americans had to fight so hard to hold on to their faith in democracy as in 1951. The cold-blooded fiendish bomb slaying at Mims, Florida, on Christmas night of Mr. and Mrs. Harry T. Moore ended in shame and horror twelve months of almost totally unpunished mob violence in Florida, Illinois, Texas, Louisiana, Virginia, Alabama, and other states. The year produced attempted legal lynching for "rape at 75 feet" in North Carolina and equally fantastic intimidation efforts in courts of law, both North and South. It saw development of a new and sinister technique—efforts to bar N.A.A.C.P. and other lawyers in Florida, Missouri, and North Carolina from courts when they sought through proper judicial procedures to protect basic constitutional rights of minorities.

Mob violence spread during 1951 against Jews and Catholics in Florida and against labor unionists in other Southern states. Democratic and Republican politicians and officials like frightened rabbits studiously avoided the civil rights issue despite the ominous reports of shrinkage of the prestige of the United States in Asia and Africa because of reports of race terrorism here. At times during 1951 it almost appeared as though American bigots were on Stalin's payroll to supply a steady stream of material to turn the colored peoples of the world away from the democracies and towards communism.

But despite the disheartening setbacks, the N.A.A.C.P. fought on. Its investigators and staff members were promptly on the scene in Cicero, Mims, Dallas, and other places when violence flared. It gathered and turned over to federal and local authorities evidence against mobbists. It publicized the stark, bitter truth to awaken America to the peril to the security of all Americans of the rising tide of hate. It continued to expose fearlessly and effectively the criminal hypocrisy of those who talked glibly about democracy even as they denied it to fellow Americans of different color or creed. It continued its phenomenally successful appeal to the courts of law and public opinion. It rallied to the cause of human freedom and acted as coordinating agency and sparked a swiftly growing number of organizations and individuals to oppose bigotry. It did so because forty-three years of experience cause us to know that the majority of Americans want to deal justly with their fellow citizens. Our greatest task is to overcome ignorance, misinformation, and fear.

Our staff traveled 248,514 miles and spoke at 731 meetings. It wrote and published over 200 books, magazine articles, syndicated columns, and pamphlets to tell the truth about the race question in addition to weekly and spot news releases. Members of the Board and staff appeared on scores of radio and television programs. Thanks to a bequest, Dr. Algeron Black, leader of the Ethical Culture Society and a member of the N.A.A.C.P. Board, inaugurated a weekly news and opinion broadcast in New York City.

The N.A.A.C.P. sent its special counsel, Thurgood Marshall, to Korea and Japan to investigate and initiate corrective action on the ruthless courtmartialing of Negro soldiers. As a result this evil practice has been almost completely abolished, aided by the wiping out of racial segregation in the armed forces in Korea. A steady campaign to urge Negroes to register as voters which will be greatly intensified in this election year has resulted, along with the efforts of others, in more than one million colored voters in the South. That number will be at least doubled by November. It will materially deter Dixiecrats and like-minded violators of the Constitution. We can safely assert that there will be more Negro voters in the South in November than Governor James Byrnes and Herman Talmadge can persuade to join them in bolting. These colored voters by adding their power to that of Negroes in seventeen northern and border states where they have the balance of power may again as in 1948 decide who will be our next President.

We are fully aware of the fact that it is this growing political, economic, and moral strength which causes trigger happy sheriffs and resentful politicians whose power hitherto has been based on "keeping the Negro in his place" to resort as they did in 1951 to violence and chicanery. We accept their challenge. We are not afraid. We shall fight all the harder. Neither nitroglycerin bombs nor Senate filibusters can stop our upward climb.

We ask all Americans irrespective of race to join us. We ask it not for fifteen million Negroes alone but for their own sakes as well. Recent years have marked the ominous shrinkage of democracy all over the world. That decline has been most marked in areas where dark-skinned human beings live. The social revolution now sweeping Asia, Africa, and Latin America is only incidentally a Communist inspired movement. It is a revolt against white arrogance and colonial exploitation which would continue if Stalin and every other Communist in the world turned capitalist overnight.

For this and other reasons, the N.A.A.C.P.'s program of equal justice under the law within the framework of democracy for every American whatever the color of his skin is the most important one of all for the preservation of freedom. Because this is true, we ask the moral, financial, and active support of every American who is intelligent enough to rise above race prejudice.

N.A.A.C.P. Annual Convention Speech

The struggle against racial segregation and the push for an increased black vote were the issues that dominated the meetings of the 750 delegates from 37 states who attended the convention. The delegates committed the NAACP to an intense drive to end segregation in "all phases of American life." A panel of experts in the fields of anthropology, economics, psychology, education, housing, and law, under the direction of Special Counsel Thurgood Marshall, explained the characteristics of segregation and how it impacts upon the nation, the community, and the individual. Walter White offered the following address at the closing mass meeting of the convention in 1952.

Bishop [Spottswood], members of the Board of Directors, distinguished guests and ladies and gentlemen. It was warm enough when I came in, but after that introduction, virtually entombing me someplace by my friend Bishop Spottswood, makes it much warmer—in fact so warm that I think you will agree with me that people on the platform deserve to be as comfortable in the office—as you in the audience, you who are not burdened with coats. So, with your permission, I'm going to take my coat off and share—invite the people on the platform to do the same thing. It's just a little better. You may have noticed that I left the platform just as Roy was making that moving appeal. The reason I left was because Senator Humphrey called, and he told me to say hello to you, how happy he was to have been with us in spirit and almost in flesh, to tell you because of the crucial fights in the United States Senate and the House of Representatives now in beating back the attempts of the Dixiecrat Republican coalition to destroy human progress and social legislation that the Senate was in session until well past ten o'clock last night, and the last plane that would have put him here in time for this meeting left Washington last night at five-thirty P.M. daylight savings time. But he was delighted to hear me tell him how attentive you were and how you applauded and then stopped applauding suddenly, lest you miss a single one of his words.

And he told me to tell you that to the day of his death he will continue this struggle without compromise, until race prejudice is entirely abolished from the American scene.

We've come to the end of a very great convention. I want to pay special tribute to Jimmy Stewart and to the other officers and members of the Oklahoma City branch, and to the people of the city of Oklahoma City, both white and colored, who have made our stay here so pleasant and so profitable. And I want to pay tribute to you, you who have sat through sweltering heat from eight o'clock in the morning until past midnight sometimes at night in committee meetings, working to do the kind of job which has made this one of the greatest of conventions we have ever held. And I want to pay tribute also to my colleagues in the National Office and on the national staff scattered around the country, people who work so hard that I as executive secretary of the Association, am constantly worried lest some of them are going to destroy their health even more by the manner in which they work day and night, Saturdays, Sundays, and holidays, never for a moment being off of the job. I'd like to say of them that you owe them a great tribute, because of the great work which they have done so faithfully and so well.

And now I come to the part of the program where I shall attempt, with the aid of my associates and with your aid, to try to chart the course which lies ahead of us, and to judge what is coming and what we need to do in the light of what has gone on in the immediate and in the distant past. In a memorable and uncompromising commencement address at Howard University on June 13, which was affirmed in his magnificent message to this convention, President Truman listed some of the gains in human rights which have been won during the past decade. With justifiable pride he cited his own actions toward the goal, particularly his appointment in 1946 of the President's Commission on Civil Rights. He pointed with satisfaction to the presence of more than a thousand Negro students in the universities of ten Southern states, from which they had been hitherto barred, the reduction to five of poll tax states, the decline of old-fashioned lynchings, in which mobs of hundreds and sometimes even a thousand burned human beings, their fellow human beings, at the stake, of the abolition of segregation in the Air Force and the Navy, and its partial abolition in the Army, and of the progress which has been made in employment and in the housing of minorities. We of the N.A.A.C.P share the President's pride in what has been done today. We join in his grim warning that we are a long way from the goal of genuine justice for all Americans, whatever their race, creed, color. We are proud because it was the unremitting, the uncompromising battle of the N.A.A.C.P. for more than forty-three years, often against appalling odds, which is chiefly responsible for those gains which the President names. It was the long and expensive legal battle waged by the N.A.A.C.P. under the direction of Thurgood Marshall and Charles Schuster, and other brilliant lawyers both white and colored which was climaxed in and won the Universities of Oklahoma and Texas cases, that opened the doors to admit the thousand Negro students of whom the President spoke.

But ahead of us is the continuing struggle to abolish segregation at the grammar school and undergraduate levels. The next step in that battle will be the argument in the United States Supreme Court next October of the now famous

Clarendon County, South Carolina, and the Topeka, Kansas, cases. We will win that fight. It must be won. It must be won! We will win it despite the un-American, the incendiary threats of the Herman Talmadges and the Jimmy Byrneses to use physical violence if needed to defy the courts if they rule against segregation. [The government] in South Africa is waging an identical battle with that of Byrnes and Talmadge, a battle against freedom to the peril of democracy and to the peace of the world. Those struggles are of the same sort; they are identical in motivation.

Mr. Truman told with pride of the reduction of lynching. Again, the N.A.A.C.P. can review more than four decades of investigation and exposure of the bestial facts about lynching, of the long and oft-times disheartening campaign for federal anti-lynching legislation which focused public attention on that evil and created, even in the deepest South, revulsion against it, of standing almost alone until recent years in the struggle to wipe out the horrible crime of lynching. But here we need to warn America that we cannot relax for a single minute the fight against mob violence. Today a new, more cowardly and less-easy-to-detect method of mobism has taken the place of the ole-time lynching bee. It is the use of dynamite or nitroglycerin bombs, placed under the homes of men and women like Harry and Harriet Moore in Florida or thrown into synagogues or Catholic churches, or even into the homes of white, Protestant, native-born Southerners. These new weapons of terror endanger the lives of not only the intended victims but of whoever happens to be in the immediate vicinity. Such cowardly attacks increased in number during 1951 and thus far in 1952. Every such bombing is worth ten divisions of troops of ten atom bombs to Soviet Russia, because each of them gives propaganda ammunition to the enemies of democracy, ammunition of tragic effectiveness against the United States. Recently I talked about this violence with a distinguished but puzzled Scandinavian editor. He had just completed a five-month tour of the United States. "You Americans talk so much about freedom," he said, "but do little or nothing to stop those who continually violate and advocate violation of the laws and principles you claim to believe in. If a man went around your country," he went on to say, "went around your country poisoning your water supply, you would slap him in jail to stop him from killing people, but you permit poisoners of the mind to operate unchecked, even electing them upon occasion to high office. How can you expect us to believe you, when you tell us we must act democratically and be opposed to totalitarianism or else lose your favor!"

The present political campaign should force us to ask ourselves such questions soberly and thoughtfully. During recent months the callous political deals and the cold-blooded buying of delegates to the national Republican and Democratic conventions, as though these delegates were so many head of cattle bought for delivery to the Chicago stockyard, ought to make us wonder how long democracy can stand brazen tactics. Bought delegates from five Southern states to the Republican national convention may determine the choice of the next President of the United States. It is reliably reported that the price per delegate has reached the all-time high of $2,500 per head. Merchants of racial and sectional hate are using not only cost but every conceivable trick, however low, to put over at the Democratic convention either an anti–civil rights candidate and platform or, failing that, a compromise ticket and sell out. Let us here solemnly warn both political parties that if either one of them sells out on this most fundamental of principles, it will bring down upon itself the wrath of millions of independent voters. Not least among those independent voters and more determined on this issue than most, is the Negro vote, now nearing two million strong in the South and holding the potential balance of power in no less than seventeen Northern states, with 281 votes in the electoral college. I say this not as a threat—only as a simply, easily-verifiable statement of fact: the Negro vote of Ohio, Illinois, and California decided the 1948 Presidential election. Since then, the number of Negroes of voting age has grown by close to a million and a half. Many of these live in the seventeen states where the Negro vote is large enough already to make it impossible, except in a landslide, for either party to win without that Negro vote.

What choice does this crucial Negro voter have today? The Negro is owned by no political party. He believes in and wants an honest two-party system. The South since the Civil War has proved that a one-party system is bad for the country and bad for the South. On the plane of enlightened self-interest, the Negro voter knows that the political power of any disadvantaged minority is greatest when the two parties are fairly evenly divided. The Negro vote wishes to vote straight Republican as it was forced by circumstances to do prior to 1932. But the desire to vote for the best platform and candidate irrespective of party has again and again been thwarted by Republicans from William Howard Taft to Robert A. Taft. Quadrennially the G.O.P. pursues the illusive will-o-the-wisp of capturing the South. Republicans have been totally unable, except in a few instances like Wendell Willkie to understand that the only coalition the reactionary South will accept is one in which Republicans surrender completely all principles and all integrity on the racial and the civil rights issues.

Many voters of both parties waited eagerly to hear General Eisenhower's view on domestic issues on his return from Europe. Having talked with him overseas during the war, I had learned that his position on many problems was best described as quite moderate, but I found him an affable person, apparently willing to listen and to consider new ideas and new facts. I hope that the highly complex problems he had faced as Supreme Allied Commander during the war and after the war as head of NATO had demonstrated to him that modern science had ended forever the chances of peace unless nations were willing to subordinate national sovereignty to mutual cooperation and unity. Quite erroneously I believed, as I recently discovered, that General Eisenhower had learned that the spurious political doctrine of states' rights was as false and dangerous on the state level as on the world level. Equally unfounded was our belief that the success of racial integration in the Navy and Air Force and the ease with which General Ridgeway had abolished segregation in the Army in Korea had convinced General Eisenhower that he had been two timorous and skeptical of the inherent decency of white Americans when he had opposed in 1948 definite action to wipe out armed services segregation. If for no other reason, one would have thought General Eisenhower would have been impressed by the courage of General Ridgeway on armed services segregation as contrasted with lack of that virtue by General MacArthur—Eisenhower's bitter enemy. General MacArthur, who is keynoting the

Chicago convention and leading the fight against Eisenhower to capture the nomination either for Senator Taft or for himself. It has been a shock to listen to General Eisenhower's views on not only F.E.P.C. and segregation but on other issues which at present place him on the right of even Taft and Russell. Some say he has been badly advised to take up positions which appeal only to the most reactionary elements in the nation—to do so until after the convention, because he needs Southern delegates to get the nomination. One would think that he would know that no Republican today can be elected unless he wins the support of the great and growing independent vote, of which the Negro constitutes a measurable part. Neither Taft nor Eisenhower appears to be wise enough to know this obvious fact.

And what about the Democrats? The aging and embittered Governor Burns, the bombastic Herman Talmadge and Senator Alan Ellendar, are pulling their perennial bluff of threatening to bolt if the Democratic Party nominates a Presidential candidate favorable to human rights or includes a strong civil rights plank in the platform. We say to them and other Democrats what we said at Philadelphia in 1948: "Let them walk. Where can they go!" Where can they go! Nowhere except to political oblivion, and the sooner they go there, the better! It is about time for Northern politicians to stop shivering in their boots whenever a Dixicrat screams "bolt." Whatever else southern politicians may be, they are realistic about the majority party. Whatever happens, political realists like Russell of Georgia, Kerr of Oklahoma, Lister Hill of Alabama and the like are not going to give up the prestige and power they now enjoy. They know that Republicans like Taft would give the South only the crumbs from the patronage table. Precisely because they are realists. It is quite doubtful that either Russell or Kerr really believes he can be nominated and elected. They are playing a far shrewder game. They aim at either the Vice Presidency, which is only a single heartbeat away from the White House, or, failing that, they want to dictate who shall be the candidate and also the basic content of the platform. Intelligent Northern Democratic leaders who don't frighten easily and who place principle above expediency, like Senator Humphrey and Senator Herbert Lehman of New York, have awakened to the cheap poker game the conservative South has been playing. So too is the Negro awake, as well as many millions of other decent Americans. One thing is crystal clear: if the Democrats want to commit political hari-kari, let them nominate Richard Russell, Robert Kerr, or any other anti-civil rights candidate for either place on the ticket or pussyfoot on the platform plank on that issue. Let me say this with all of the solemnity and sincerity of which I am capable—and this is based upon conversations with thousands of you all over the country. But this is what I want to say on the basis of those conversations: should the Democrats nominate either a Southerner or a Northerner whose record is bad on civil rights, they can kiss the Negro vote goodbye. And I am equally convinced that they can kiss goodbye to a lot of other votes as well, particularly the voters who listen to men like Walter Reuther, whom you heard on Thursday night.

It is equally important in this crucial year of decision for members of the N.A.A.C.P. and all other enlightened voters to be as concerned with candidates for other offices as with who may be President and Vice President. It could be possibly more important. The most able and courageous President of either party would be virtually impotent if a reactionary Congress is elected along with him. We all know that the most dangerous handicap to decent government during the past decade has been the domination of Congress by the Dixicrat/reactionary-Republican coalition. Out of this evil combination has come the total blockade of civil rights, laws like the infamous McCarran–Walter Immigration Act, the defeat of amendments to prohibit housing and educational discrimination, the defeat of the Lehman Amendment to punish mob violence against members of the Armed services, the slaughter of the bills for statehood for Hawaii and Alaska, for anti-labor legislation and a host of other acts of omission or commission which hamstring and retard human progress. Read the records of your Senators and Congressmen in the October issue of *The Crisis*. Then vote accordingly, no matter what the party of the candidate for whom you vote.

Almost as important as who you send to Washington is who you elect as your governor, to your state legislature, your city council, your school board, your local housing board, and your sheriff's office. Frequently these less exalted elected officials effect immediately the lives and destinies of men and women like ourselves more directly than by what is done up in Washington by the President or the Congress. Take police brutality as an example. Some Americans—unfortunately, too many of them—have become so conditioned and so callous to crimes of violence against individuals that they fail to appreciate the awful significance even of the lynch mob. They fail to appreciate the significance of the pattern of police brutality which annually takes a frightful toll of maimed or murdered colored people, all too often arrested on minor charges and occasionally for crimes of which they are completely innocent. Statisticians looking at the decline of lynchings in the United States seem to believe that the old monster of mob violence is dead, yet in Birmingham, Alabama, alone twenty-eight colored people have been killed by policemen in the past five years, including one minister of the Gospel. In none of these cases were the persons killed charged with a crime that would have resulted in capital punishment if they had been tried and found guilty in a court of law. The assaults upon servicemen and the intimidation of colored citizens who seek to vote in the South are crimes that cry out for the passage of strong federal legislation against all forms of mob violence. The commendable work of the Department of Justice in prosecuting the Cicero, Illinois, officials who permitted the disgraceful rioting of last summer does not offset the fact that those responsible for the Florida killings and Alabama police brutality are still at large. In the 1952 election, there is no doubt that in some areas of the South, local election officials will seek to keep colored voters away from the polls by intimidation. This is a good time for us to let the Department of Justice know that its help is needed and we expect to get it to make certain that the fall voting in Dixie will be at least as fair as the elections under American supervision held in West Germany.

Or consider the acute housing problems of Negroes. The real estate lobby in Washington and real estate associations all over the nation cry out against any housing except that built by so-called private enterprise. How has the Negro fared under private housing enterprise? You heard Dr. Weaver on Friday night point out that between 1935 and 1950, more than 2,763,000 privately financed dwelling units were constructed in the United States, but of these only 100,000 or less than two percent went to those whose housing needs are most desperate—Negro citizens of the United States. As to housing financed or underwritten in whole or in part with public tax money, timidity or connivance by public housing officials in Washington with prejudiced real estate interests are forging a new, a nation-wide and more sinister pattern of segregation than ever existed before in the history of our nation. What the courts have forbidden state legislatures and city councils to do, and what the Ku Klux Klan has not been able to accomplish by intimidation and violence, the present federal housing policy is accomplishing through a monumental program of segregation in all aspects of housing which receive government aid. If there is complete segregation in housing the victories we have won on the job front, in the elimination of segregation in public educa-tion, and in creating interracial understanding will be almost completely nullified. The housing program of the Federal Government as currently administered in the entire South, all of the border states and in many Northern communities is one of the greatest single factors in underwriting segregation with tax money.

Or take the problem of being able to work at a job one is trained to do and which one wishes to do. During this period of full employment and prosperity, I don't know how long it lasts with the abolition or attempted abolition of price controls, but during this present prosperity and full employment, the memories of the wholesale firings of colored employees are not as vivid as they were during the 1930s. We also suffer from a false sense of security, because when jobs are available, a victim of discrimination can move on to a fairer-minded employer when he is turned down by a prejudiced one. But we cannot know, we do not know what the future holds on the employment front. We cannot afford the type of discrimination that takes place at the Lockheed Aircraft plant in Atlanta, Geor-gia, where out of more than 10,000 workers on the job, there are only 400 colored people employed, and every one of them is employed as a janitor. Whatever the future may hold, one thing is certain: we need, we must have an F.E.P.C. with enforcement powers in it. We shall never stop fighting until we obtain it. General Eisenhower says that he favors fair employment, but he would leave it to the states for their handling. Senator Taft favors a quote educational approach and end quote, because some areas of the country, in his opinion, would bitterly resent any other kind of program in this field. Senator Estes Kefauver says he favors an F.E.P.C. with enforcement power, if it is to be made a part of the Democratic world-wide responsibility. Senator Taft lashes out against Communists in government and corruption in high places. Senator Kefauver is a party champion of labor and of welfare legislation. All of these candidates may as well know now that where—whatever else they may be for, if they are not for an F.E.P.C. with enforcement powers, we are not for them.

These, then, are the victories we have won, these are the ones yet to be fought for and to be won. The future before us is neither cheerful nor devoid of cheer. Just as we have fought against heart-breaking odds before and won our battles, we shall fight again and win. The tides of history are on our side. Democracy can no more continue to deny us our right to freedom than it can stop the social revolution which sweeps through Asia today and which is beginning to sweep through Africa and Latin America. The have-nots of the world who have been kept in the bondage of poverty, hunger, and inferior status for many centuries are throwing off the yoke of their oppressors, and so are we! If democracy is wise and wants to survive itself, it will see that the wind is rising and will not be stayed. Abraham Lincoln once remarked that "God must have loved the common man because he made so many of them." I would like to say to the white world a paraphrase of Lincoln's statement, and to phrase it—paraphrase it—to read that God must have loved the colored man, because he made so many of them, twice as many as white men in this world of ours. By resolute action and by adamant opposition to the foes of democracy, we have measurably altered the pattern of American racial opinion and action. Unlike certain aspirants to the Presidency who shudder in simulated fear at laws which might make things worse instead of better, we know that you don't stop murderers from murdering by patting them tenderly on the wrist and saying, "Naughty, naughty," to them. We know that we may not win full equality tomorrow or even perhaps day after tomorrow, but we are going to continue fighting. We are going to continue fighting for democracy with every democratic weapon at our command, and we will never let up in that struggle. Let us never forget that it is far better to die on our feet than to live on our knees. To that end, as important to the survival of democracy as to our own survival, let us here today rededicate our lives, our fortune, and our sacred honor.

N.A.A.C.P. Forty-fourth Annual Meeting Speech

In 1953 the NAACP initiated its ten-year Fight for Freedom to eliminate all irrelevant racial distinctions in American life by January 1, 1963, the 100th anniversary of Abraham Lincoln's Emancipation Proclamation. The year 1953 was also the year in which the High Court asked for and heard re-arguments in five cases challenging the constitutionality of state-imposed segregation in elementary and secondary schools in South Carolina, Virginia, Delaware, Kansas, and the District of Columbia. In the following speech, White discusses the gains made by the NAACP during 1953, including the setbacks, as well as future plans of the Association. White gave this address in January 1954.

The year 1953 marked the nearest approach and witnessed the greatest gains of the N.A.A.C.P. towards the goals set by its founders in 1909. The most publicized and important phase was the legal attack on segregated education. But as basic to eventual victory of democracy over segregation was the degree and extent of coordination of administrative, legislative, and educational activities, especially at the grass roots level. Without the latter, court decisions and legislative decrees are virtually meaningless.

On the administrative level:

1. Creation of Committee on Contract Compliance.
2. Abolition of segregation on military posts. Norfolk, Charleston.

3. Policing railroad, bus, airport compliance with non-segregation decisions and orders.
4. Armed Services, steady and continuous N.A.A.C.P. action. Praise Eisenhower.

At the grass roots level:

1. N.A.A.C.P. calls on every church of every denomination or race, schools, newspapers, trade unions, parent–teachers' associations, educational organizations, and business groups to work incessantly for acceptance calmly of Supreme Court's decisions when handed down. Thereby—and only thereby—can violence be averted which demagogues are deliberately attempting to stir up. Commend such Southern papers as the *Atlanta Constitution* and the *St. Petersburg Times*.
3. Spontaneous nationwide reaction to Dr. Tobias' brilliant suggestion of F.F.F. Proud that Ambassador Dudley has agreed to direct and coordinate campaign.
4. Success of 1963 will benefit not only America's fifteen million Negroes. It will strengthen the free world by doing away with the costly burden of racial hatred and division and thereby win to our side two billion colored peoples of the world who now don't trust America and the white Western world.

N.A.A.C.P. is confident that we are now in a climate of opinion which makes America ready for calm acceptance of integration. We would disagree with Mr. Dooley's statement that "the Supreme Court has always followed the election returns." But history has proved that the Court has invariably reflected with accuracy the current temper of its time on social and related issues: *Dred Scott*, 1857; *Railroad Companies vs. Brown*, 1873; *Plessy vs. Ferguson*, 1896; [and] *Sweatt and McLaurin*, 1950.

Will enormous growth of American public opinion against bigotry, and pressures of world opinion be reflected by the Court in 1954 in pending cases? Am confident it will.

N.A.A.C.P. challenges America to repudiate those who would injure and discredit America by deliberately stirring up discord by predicting and promoting violence. They are fewer in number and lesser of influence than is realized. Newspapers are reflecting it. Unfortunate that television and radio are giving time to men like Talmadge and Byrnes to spew hatred and give millions an utterly false picture while not inviting better informed and more law-abiding authorities to tell the other side of the story.

There is a very important other side. Only the other day a white southern newspaperman and a white southern educator told me the story which I have found on numerous recent trips to the South to be true. The white South doesn't want segregation abolished but is resigned to it. [They believe the] staggering costs of actual equality utterly impossible to meet. The South doesn't want to spend its new wealth from industrialization that way. Its evangelical Protestant conscience is becoming increasingly bothered by the contradiction of Jim Crow. It doesn't dare come out for integration but wants someone else—the Supreme Court—to bell the cat. Then it can cleanse its house and say, "We have no other alternative since the Supreme Court has ruled out segregation."

Besides being clearly unconstitutional, such an evasion as abolishing public schools and subsidizing individual pupils would lead inevitably and swiftly to the most notorious scandals of American history. Educational quacks and racketeers would move in setting up their own debased standards. The states would be helpless to regulate these private schools or to establish any standards to protect the public investment or the school children, because to do so would be to exert state action which would be subject to the jurisdiction of the federal courts.

If the governors and legislators of these states do not realize what they are proposing, they will soon find out. They would do far better to join those enlightened southerners who already realize that segregation as a way of life is doomed. Just as we carried the fight against openly avowed segregation to the highest court in the land, so shall we fight any subtle forms of segregation or any attempts to evade a possible decision of the court outlawing Jim Crow.

Third, the growing political strength of southern liberals, particularly Negroes, is having its effect on the southern political scene. Well-founded reports [conclude] that even Herman Talmadge is making surreptitious overtures to Negro voters in Georgia. Older demagogues like Byrnes who are about to pass from the political stage are now the chief ones who continue to use race-baiting as their chief stock in trade.

Job Ahead

But as we record progress which has been made, we must consider and chart our campaign against the evils which yet remain. Victory in the school segregation cases, even if it be all we desire, will have but limited value at the grammar and high school levels as long as segregated housing continues. In that field we have made least gain because our own national government is using its funds, to which we help contribute, to expand and freeze segregation. One glaring example is Levittown in Bucks County, Pa., where William J. Levitt is using the resources of the F.H.A. to build 20,000 homes in that miracle of industrial development but bars Negroes. Your N.A.A.C.P. in cooperation with the Urban League, the A.F.S.G., the United Steelworkers Union, and the Bucks County Council is placing this issue before President Eisenhower who assured Messrs. Channing Tobias, Arthur Spingarn, Theodore Spaulding, and me he would never permit a penny of federal money to be spent for segregation or discrimination. The pity of it is that Levitt has brusquely dismissed the appeals of his co-religionists and others that he observe the Golden Rule and remember what bigotry has done and is doing to his own people.

Other examples: Beautiful, modern new housing developments encircling almost every American city and town, made possible only through federal, state, or municipal assistance from most of which Negroes are barred.

Task Ahead of Us in New Congress

Admirable though it be, [the] Committee on Government Contract is not a substitute for F.E.P.C. Anti-mob violence law [is needed] to protect members of Armed Services. Remember Harry Moore's murderers [are] still at large after two years and more.

Jobs—should there be a depression, recession, or whatever exercise in semantics may conjure up. Thanks to a somewhat less precarious position in industry the associations own efforts and those of most trade unions and a few enlightened employers, the percentage of Negroes first fired won't be quite as high as it would have been forty-five or even five years ago. But it will still be higher for Negroes as a whole in comparison with others.

Last June at our St. Louis convention, Harold Stassen, Mutual Security Administrator, declared that the N.A.A.C.P. could do more than any other organization in the U.S. to tell the truth about the race question in the U.S. and thereby answer the lies and distortions of the Communists and others who play up every example of injustice based on color in our country to two-thirds of the peoples of the world who are non-white. Only a few weeks ago an official who is quite high in the present government asked me what we were doing about Mr. Stassen's request. I told him we would be delighted to help our government but our government would not allow us to do what we could to tell the truth to the world of our progress in human and race relations under democracy.

I explained to him that contributions to the N.A.A.C.P. Legal Defense and Educational Fund were allowed tax exemptions for their contribution but those who gave to the N.A.A.C.P. were not granted that exemption. Because the Legal Defense Fund scrupulously operated in compliance with the requirements of the Internal Revenue Bureau, it has limited itself strictly to legal work even though educational work was included in both its title and authorized activities. Not being tax exempt, the N.A.A.C.P. has been unable to raise the sizable sums necessary to present the true story of race in the U.S. which Mr. Stassen and others feel needs desperately to be told.

An increasing activity of the N.A.A.C.P. is that of answering questions about race from visitors from all parts of the world brought here by the State Department, the Carnegie, and Ford Foundations, and other groups. Some remarkable results in the form of changed opinions when these visitors return home have been visible. But the time and expense of showing these visitors that America is not as evil or as incurably biased as she is painted has come out of individual pockets and the inadequate resources of the N.A.A.C.P.

America's survival, both in winning and holding the confidence of the peoples of Asia, Africa, and Latin America and in having continued access to the minerals and other essential raw material of its industrial production depends in considerable degree upon its telling the true story of American democracy to skeptical people all over the globe. As far as the N.A.A.C.P.'s funds and our government permit us to do so, we shall continue to tell the story both of victories over bigotry and of the job yet to be done. We know that that is the only story which will be effective—the truth.

It is gratifying to note that the Board of Education in Washington has recently dedicated a high school in honor of the late Joel E. Spingarn, donor of the Spingarn Medal and President of our Association from 1930 to his death in 1939. Previously he had served the Association with great distinction as Treasurer and Chairman of the Board of Directors. He dedicated his life to the goals of the Association.

The Joel E. Spingarn High School was opened for Negro students, but there are good grounds for hoping that before the end of 1954 this fine new school will serve the youth of all races in the nation's capital. This is as Joel would have had it—a democratic school in an integrated system of public education.

We look back with pride on a year of solid achievement. We look forward in 1954 with confidence which is based not only on the results of forty-five years of unremitting, uncompromising toil but also upon the receptivity of America, to change and correct evils which is possible only in a democracy. We call on Americans of every race, creed, class, and place of origin to join the battle for freedom with their efforts, their prayers, and their dollars. If enough of them do join with us, the centennial of the Emancipation Proclamation will truly see an America free of the corrosive poison of keeping another man down solely because of his race or color.

N.A.A.C.P. Forty-fifth Annual Meeting Speech

In 1954 the Supreme Court charted a new course for American schoolchildren—moving the nation away from the "separate but equal" pattern, toward the democratic goal of integration and equal opportunity. The historic unanimous decision handed down on May 17 concluded "that in the field of public education the doctrine of 'separate but equal' has no place." The Court declared that "separate educational facilities are inherently unequal." It held that "the plaintiffs and others similarly situated for whom the actions have been brought are, by reason of the segregation complained of, deprived of the equal protection of the laws guaranteed by the Fourteenth Amendment." In the following remarks, Walter White praises the attorneys, both living and dead, who brought about this legal victory. He discusses other accomplishments of the Association as well as the struggle ahead. White gave this address in January 1955.

The year 1954 marked one of the eight great epochs of the history of the Negro in America, in the unanimous decision of the United States Supreme Court outlawing segregation in tax-supported education. The eight epochs—some high, some low—began with the landing of the first Negro slaves in Jamestown, Va., in 1619; the signing of the Emancipation Proclamation by Lincoln in 1863; the Supreme Court decision in *Plessy* vs. *Ferguson* in 1896; the founding of the N.A.A.C.P. in 1909; the coming of age politically of the Negro in 1931 when organized Negro opinion played a major role in the rejection of a nominee for the U.S. Supreme Court who had advocated disfranchisement; the Report, in 1947, of the President's Committee on Civil Rights; and the anti-segregation decision of 1954.

The decision is in itself, of course, of great significance in that it, for the first time in American history, has put the law of the land unequivocally on the side of the guarantees of human rights which are written into every document which has made the United States the greatest democracy in history. For that victory we and the United States owe an eternal debt of gratitude to a number of great, courageous, and unselfish lawyers living and dead, who over the years have fought without compromise for unabridged citizenship for the Negro. That list includes such men as the late Moorfield Storey, Charles H. Houston, Arthur Garfield Hays, and Leon A. Ransom among those who are no longer with us. Among the living should be included Arthur B. Spingarn, William H. Hastie, Robert L. Carter, Loren Miller, and our own Thurgood Marshall.

But these and many more lawyers who could be named would be the first to say that court decisions, even those of the Supreme Court, have only token value unless backed by public opinion. Even the most optimistic in the N.A.A.C.P.—myself among them—had no idea how vigorous approval would be of the Supreme Court's decisions. Every major church, labor, and civil rights organization has hailed the decision. And other media of public opinion, including many in the South, have joined in that approval. Only a handful of noisy politicians has opposed the decision.

The major credit for this acceptance of the Court's decree goes to branches of the N.A.A.C.P.—during recent years joined by many other organizations—for their unremitting work which often, and even in Mississippi today has carried on in the face of violence and economic pressures. Today I want to pay tribute to the many thousands of unsung heroes and heroines who have done this job.

In addition to our successful court action in securing the anti-segregation ruling in public education, we have also made substantial contributions to the steady trend toward the final elimination of segregation in the armed services including schools on military posts; to the improvement of conditions for migrant farm workers in Pennsylvania and New York; and to the diminution of segregation in the District of Columbia.

We got off to a good start with our Freedom Fulfillment Conference in Washington on March 10 with President Eisenhower as the principal speaker to launch formally our Fight for Freedom drive. The President hailed our work, endorsed "the ideal of equality among all men" and again pledged the elimination of segregation wherever the federal authority extended.

You will hear in a few minutes the details of how in 1954 the N.A.A.C.P. has raised more money—not nearly enough of course—to finish the job. I want also to pay tribute here to all those who raised and sent to the National Office and to the N.A.A.C.P. Legal Defense and Educational Fund a total of $902,330.56, an increase over 1953 of $221,691.87 when $680,638.69 was received.

In this action, special praise should go to Kivie Kaplan and Benjamin E. Mays as co-chairmen of the life membership committee, who during 1954 secured 115 life memberships of $500 each paid in full and 340 on which initial payments were made. It is our hope that during 1955 even that record will be surpassed by a wide margin.

But it is not the N.A.A.C.P. alone which has benefited from the fact that during 1954 America turned the corner from partial towards full freedom for all its citizens. The pressures of world opinion have lessened because our own household is being cleansed. The burdened conscience of America has been eased by the fact that we are no longer as hypocritical a nation when we talk to the rest of the world about human freedom even as we deny it here. For its unanimous and unequivocal decision on this basic moral issue, unqualified praise should go to the United States Supreme Court. So, too, do we owe a debt of gratitude to President Eisenhower for his firm stand against racial segregation in Washington and the armed forces. However, that praise extends to very few of his party. We hope that both he and the Republican Party will recognize the need for a Federal fair employment practices law with enforcement powers, for the inclusion in all appropriations bills of amendments to prohibit expenditure of any Federal funds for segregation or discrimination, for drastic revision of the McCarran Immigration Act and especially of its infamous national origins provision, for legislation against Jim Crow in travel and more vigorous action against the bigots of such organizations as the White Citizens Councils now being formed in states like Mississippi and Alabama to put economic and other pressures upon Negroes who want full citizenship.

We also should insist upon the Democratic Party putting aside its present wooing of the South by surrendering on major moral principles. There are those like the *Wall Street Journal* who assert that the Negro voter will remain in the Democratic Party no matter what Eisenhower does about civil rights. Such persons don't know what they are talking about. In the crucial election year of 1956, the Negro voter in pivotal states where he holds the balance of power is going to vote for that party which is most honest on issues like civil rights, job security, and assurance to every American irrespective of race, creed, or color of the guarantees of the Federal Constitution.

What of the road ahead? It is superfluous for me to say that our biggest job is presenting to the Supreme Court within the next few weeks the most effective arguments possible for the termination of all segregation in all tax-supported education at a specific and early date. But with that purely legal job goes an equally important one outside the Court. That job is to use every instrument of orderly constitutional government to stop the efforts of organized bigots who from Milford, Delaware, to rural Mississippi are engaged in treasonable acts to flout the decrees of the Supreme Court. Spokesmen for such organizations as the White Citizens Council, which is a form of neo-Ku Kluxims, assert for public consumption that they are opposed to mob violence. But the inevitable effect of their action can and possibly will be violence which will do us incalculable harm both here at home and throughout the world.

There is one aspect of the attempt at evasion of the Supreme Court by the legislatures of South Carolina, Georgia, and Mississippi and of other groups which has been little noticed. It is well known that the schools of the South are the poorest in the nation. Even the wealthiest states are finding it impossible adequately to educate their children because of the rising costs of education and the tremendous increase of pupils. A report published by the National Citizens Commission for the Public Schools indicates that 50,000 new school rooms are constructed each year but the school population is increasing with such rapidity that 67,000 new classrooms are needed annually. Failure to keep abreast of the need in the past has created a present immediate need of 370,000 new elementary and secondary class rooms which will cost at least Eleven Billion Dollars. During the school years of 1952–55, 700,000 school children were on double or triple sessions; 840,000 went to school in make-shift accommodations such as barracks with inadequate heating, ventilation, and sanitation, while 400,00 more went to school in garages, church buildings, vacant stores and whatever other make-shift facilities could be found. The Commission also reports that at least sixteen per cent of all elementary and secondary pupils are housed in disease-breeding fire traps which do not meet even the minimum standards of safety. Where is the money coming from to meet these simple physical needs, to say nothing of higher salaries and other job security which must be supplied if the present trend away from teaching is to [be] slowed up? It is imperative that the Federal Government make available funds to meet this burden.

When such funds are voted, are Southern reactionaries willing to pay and to make their helpless children pay so great a price for their prejudices? I do not believe decent forces in the South and the nation will permit this.

But we do not have to speculate on the future. The states have received sizable Federal funds for education. According to the latest reports of the U.S. Department of Health, Education and Welfare, a total was contributed by the Federal Government for the year 1952–53 to seventeen southern states of $219, 959,097.63. This sum included support of land grant colleges, aid to vocational education and vocational rehabilitation, assistance to Federally affected areas, including school survey, maintenance and construction, public health education grants and transfers of real property and personal property to educational institutions, agriculture experiment stations, cooperative agriculture extension service and the school lunch program, cash and commodities. The figures by states from the Department of Health, Welfare and Education and of Agriculture are:

Alabama	$14,674,160.17
Arkansas	10,657,485.62
Delaware	1,013,305.50
Florida	10,433,234.65
Georgia	21,943,471.51
Kentucky	10,824,357.08
Louisiana	10,825,066.74
Maryland	11,186,707.83
Mississippi	9,536,095.96
Missouri	11,881,060.11
North Carolina	15,732,234.81
Oklahoma	11,570,463.95
South Carolina	12,725,670.22

Tennessee	12,409,359.56
Texas	28,306,471.64
Virginia	20,596,952.80
West Virginia	5,622,789.89
	$219,938,888.04

I can assure you that our Washington Bureau, under the brilliant direction of Clarence Mitchell, and your National Office will be on the lookout to prevent any penny of Federal Funds to be given to any state which violates the law of the land which has been laid down by the Supreme Court.

States like South Carolina and Mississippi and possibly others will try to establish "private" schools or to "subsidize" individual pupils by selling state bonds or other securities such as Georgia's "school revenue certificate." The Banking Commissioner of Ohio has recently declared as "ineligible investment" for Ohio banks the "offering of Georgia school revenue certificates." Branches of the N.A.A.C.P. should be constantly vigilant to see that their own state authorities do not permit floatation of securities which are in direct violation of the law. We must see to it that regulatory agencies such as the Securities Exchange Commission, the Federal Reserve Bank, State Banking Commissions, the New York and other bond and stock exchanges abstain from assistance to states to help them pay for deliberate violations of the law. Even in Mississippi, law-abiding and intelligent officials and individuals fear that taxpayers' suits may be filed to restrain the state from spending money for separate schools in violation of the Supreme Court's decision. We must not and we will not disappoint them.

And what are the prospects in the Eighty-fourth Congress? Through no merit of their own, southern Democrats will be chairmen of most of the important Senate and House committees through the seniority rule. It is reported by a national news weekly that the new Majority Leader, Lyndon Johnson of Texas, was able to keep the Democratic ranks unbroken in the recent McCarthy censor debate by promising Senator Eastland of Mississippi the chairmanship of the Senate subcommittee on Internal Security. This is irony raised to the nth degree. Senator Eastland has made it clear throughout his career that anyone who believes in the Fourteenth Amendment or more recently anyone who believes that the May 17 decision of the Supreme Court should be obeyed, is a "subversive."

But there are courageous men and women of both parties in the new Congress. Between now and the Presidential election of 1956, we can look to them for a vigorous and uncompromising fight for legislation which is absolutely essential to complete the task of wiping out racial bigotry in the United States.. The effectiveness of the N.A.A.C.P.'s effort for such legislation will in very large measure depend on what you, the branches, do in increasing the membership and doing the even bigger job of rallying the forces of decency in our country.

PART III

THE SELECTED WRITINGS OF ROY WILKINS, 1955–1977

Roy Wilkins, circa late 1960s. From the collection of Mildred Bond Roxborough

From left to right, Judge William Hastie, William J. Trent, Jr., Mrs. Roy Wilkins, Roy Wilkins, John A. Morsell, Mildred B. Roxborough, and Justice Thurgood Marshall at Roy Wilkins's seventieth birthday celebration, 1971. From the collection of Mildred Bond Roxborough

Roy Wilkins

(August 30, 1901–September 6, 1981)

A Chronology

1901   Born to William and Mayfield Edmundson Wilkins on August 30 in St. Louis, Missouri.

1906   Upon his mother's death, moves to St. Paul, Minnesota, to live with his uncle and aunt, Samuel and Elizabeth Edmundson Williams. Enters Whittier Grammar School.

1915   Graduates from the eighth grade. Enters the Mechanical Arts High School.

1918   Becomes the editor of the *Logwheel*, the high school newspaper.

1919   Graduates high school as salutatorian. Enters the University of Minnesota in the Department of Journalism.

1920   During college sophomore year, joins the staff of the *Minnesota Daily*, becoming the newspaper's first black reporter.

1921   Helps to form a chapter of Omega Psi Phi on the campus of University of Minnesota. (This national black fraternity had been founded at Howard University.)

1922   Becomes the editor of the *Minnesota Appeal*. Joins the St. Paul branch of the NAACP. Graduates from the University of Minnesota with honors.

1923   Joins the staff of the *Kansas Call*. As a reporter, attends NAACP Midwestern Race Relations Conference, where he first meets James Weldon Johnson and Walter White. He is immensely impressed by their leadership skills and intellectual acumen.

1926   Meets his future wife, St. Louis native and social worker Aminda (Minnie) Badeau.

1929   Marries Aminda Badeau.

1930   Is invited by Walter White to join the national staff of the NAACP.

1931   Moves to New York City and joins the NAACP as assistant secretary on August 15. His duties include writing, lecturing, organizing new branches, fund-raising, and reviewing legal cases.

1932   With journalist-writer George Schuyler, both disguised as laborers, investigates black labor conditions on the Mississippi Flood Control Project.

1933   Participates in organizing the Second Amenia Conference at "Troutbeck," the estate of J. E. Spingarn, in Amenia, New York.

1934   Is made acting editor of the *Crisis* after the resignation of W. E. B. Du Bois from the NAACP. Is arrested for picketing the Justice Department's National Conference in Crime being held at Constitution Hall, over the issue that America needs a federal anti-lynching law.

1937   Is named editor of the *Crisis*.

1941   Attends a conference of black editors and newspapermen on how black manpower would be best put to use if war came.

1945   Lectures in Berlin, London, and Paris under the auspices of the State Department.

1946   Enters Post Graduate Hospital in New York for an operation to remove a cancerous intestinal tumor.

1949   Becomes acting secretary of the NAACP. Steps down as editor of the *Crisis*.

1950   Chairs the National Emergency Civil Rights Mobilization, which convenes in Washington in January to lobby for fair employment and other civil rights measures.

1955   Becomes executive secretary of the NAACP on April 11.

1963   Participates in organizing the "March on Washington." Gives speech, "We Want Freedom Now."

1964   Receives the Spingarn Medal at the Fifty-fifth Annual Convention on June 23. Stands with President Lyndon Johnson while Johnson signs the Civil Rights Act, a bill for whose enactment Wilkins and other NAACP officials are credited.

1965   Reads message from President Johnson to an enthusiastic crowd in Berlin.

1966   Makes an attack against "black power" as a philosophy for African Americans. Characterizes the term "black power" as anti-white—a reverse Mississippi, a reverse Hitler, a reverse Ku Klux Klan.

1967   Receives the Annual Freedom House Award for furthering the cause of human liberty. Receives death threats from a black extremist group.

1970   Suffers another bout with intestinal cancer. Undergoes a successful operation.

1971   Heads the U.S. delegation to Monrovia, Liberia, to attend the funeral of President William Tubman. Receives New York City Bronze Medallion from Mayor John Lindsay, "for never losing faith in his country." Accompanied by his wife, makes another trip to Italy and Germany to determine how equal opportunity is working in the military.

1975   Is invited to the Lyndon Baines Johnson Ranch as a guest to attend a symposium on civil rights at the Johnson Library in Austin.

1976   Spends most of the year traveling to cities where NAACP branches host testimonial dinners in his honor.

1977   After forty-six years of service, retires from NAACP in the midst of a "great flood of nostalgia and affection."

1981   Dies at home in New York City on September 6.

1982   Autobiography, *Standing Fast*, is published posthumously. (The manuscript was completed a few weeks before his death.)

Selected Reports of the Secretary to the Board of Directors, 1955–1973

Editor's Note

When a New York City district attorney informed Roy Wilkins that he was a target of an alleged assassination plot by a black extremist group known as Revolutionary Action Movement (RAM), he wasn't at all phased by the news. He refused police protection and continued to take the subway to the NAACP offices each morning alone.[1] This attitude was so typical of Roy Wilkins because he disliked fuss and fanfare. As secretary, his frugality with NAACP funds was legend among staff. He was concerned for those who had sacrificed to pay the two-dollar membership fee because it was these dues-paying members who kept the NAACP solvent.

When he joined the staff of the NAACP in 1931, America was in the tight grip of the "separate but equal" doctrine. Lynchings were rampant across the South and in some border states. Jim Crow ruled in movie theaters, public accommodations, restaurants, hotels, and public transportation. By the time he became secretary in 1955, the doctrine "separate but equal" had been overturned, and lynchings had ceased across the South. At this time the NAACP had an impressive record, but it still faced the tasks of implementing school desegregation, abolishing the poll tax, acquiring federal protection for voting rights, and ending discrimination in public accommodations, housing, and jobs.

As secretary, Wilkins was chief executive officer, fund-raiser, propagandist, and orator. By the turbulent 1960s, one of his major challenges was to coordinate the Association's direction with that of other civil rights organizations which had also begun to speak for black America. To achieve this task, Wilkins pursued a more militant and activist stance for the NAACP, joining demonstrations such as the 1963 March on Washington, the Selma March in 1965, and the Meredith March Against Fear in 1966. His counterparts in these marches were such giants as Martin Luther King, Jr., Whitney Young, A. Philip Randolph, and James Farmer.

James Weldon Johnson, after joining the staff of the NAACP in 1916, endured criticisms from black leaders about the tightly-controlled white board of directors and the Association's predominately white administrative staff. During Walter White's tenure as secretary, the NAACP was questioned by a young group of blacks for its white board chairman and its white attorneys.

During Roy Wilkins's tenure as secretary, the NAACP came under attack for its white cooperation. The issue of interraciality in black movements in contrast to a racially self-reliant movement has been debated since before the founding of the NAACP in 1909. However in the mid-1960s the question heated up and it has not been settled to date. Wilkins explained the need for white cooperation in the civil rights movement in the following:

> I did not believe that integration was phony or that white people should be excluded from participating in the civil rights movement. They had created and maintained the problem of white racism, they owed it to themselves and the nation to help rectify the wrong.[2]

After the 1954 *Brown* decision, Wilkins had to contend with certain factions within the black community who wanted to "go it alone" because the process of school desegregation was moving too slowly. These factions argued that black children needed to be in all-black settings in order to gain race pride. And he had to contend with whites who were determined not to follow the High Court's decree on school desegregation. Segregationists were inserting road blocks to the Court's order through their state legislatures and by rampant acts of violence. And there was the insurgence of the impulsive black power movement led by Stokely Carmichael and later by H. Rap Brown. These young radicals criticized the NAACP leadership for its interracial cooperation and for its lack of militancy.

During this atmosphere, it was becoming increasingly difficult for Wilkins to keep the NAACP's working policy of full integration on track. He was spending more and more of his time and efforts explaining to both white and black America why the NAACP's policy of integration was the right course for a united America. It was also becoming more difficult for him to convince the impatient black college students and other youth why they should pledge themselves to the objective of the NAACP. Gifted orators like Carmichael and Brown attracted a massive following among young black Americans. Carmichael and Brown began to espouse the concept that the suffering of blacks in America had united them with the Third World nations. This concept reintroduced prominent nationalists like Marcus Garvey and the recently deceased Malcolm X. Although, as Wilkins contends, the young militants seemed to have forgotten that when Malcolm X returned from Mecca, he had moved from being an inflexible separatist to finding a peaceful coexistence with like-minded white people.[3]

The NAACP had been adamant since its inception in 1909 that segregation in all phases of American life must be eradicated. The Association maintained its policy of full integration from its earliest days, when it was branded as radical and irresponsible, into the 1960s and 1970s when many believed that it lagged behind the times and had outlived its usefulness.

Roy Wilkins, a consistent, thoughtful, and insightful man, was never going to back away from the NAACP's policy that segregation must go. He was never going to entertain the notion of separatism. In the following quote, he writes about those who condemned the NAACP to die:

> I want to point out that the school cases were a legal victory, a fitting reward for the N.A.A.C.P.'s faith in the basic institutions of the court and for its patient strategy of correcting injustices by taking them to the courts. . . . Many impatient folks would find it easy to criticize the N.A.A.C.P. for that very faith. I can still hear their epithets—from "babe in the woods" to "Uncle Tom"—ringing in my ears. No matter what was said later, the real point is that without the N.A.A.C.P there would have been no fight against lynching, no victory for restrictive covenants, no triumph over Jim Crow in the military, no liberating action for the school. The N.A.A.C.P. has been fighting the good fight for a very long time. It cleared the underbrush and opened the way for the civil rights movement in the fifties and sixties. Nat Turner or Mahatma Ghandi may have provided some new models as the years went on, but the N.A.A.C.P. was the granddaddy of us all.[4]

The following reports offer a characterization of Wilkins's work during his tenure as secretary of the NAACP, especially a critical understanding of his role in the black struggle in the modern civil rights movement. These reports reflect his leadership role in the enactments of the Civil Rights Acts of 1957, 1960, 1964, and 1965.

Report of the Secretary
for the Board Meeting of May 1955

Annual Conference

Some 800 delegates are expected to attend the Forty-sixth Annual Convention to be held in Atlantic City, N.J., June 21–26. Sessions will be held in the Atlantic City High School, Albany and Atlantic Avenues.

The opening mass meeting on Tuesday evening, June 21, will be a Walter White Memorial meeting with the President of the New Jersey State Conference, presiding, and with remarks by the President of the Association, Arthur B. Spingarn; the Executive Secretary, Roy Wilkins; Vice President Miss L. Pearl Mitchell, and Channing H. Tobias, Chairman of the Board of Directors. There will be a dramatic presentation on Wednesday evening at 8 P.M. The mass meeting that night will be addressed by Secretary-Treasurer of the A.F.L. William Schitzler, and Special Counsel Thurgood Marshall. On Thursday evening delegates from some forty states will submit their semi-annual reports on funds raised to accelerate the campaign for complete emancipation by 1963, at the Freedom Fund Dinner. The Honorable Robert B. Mayner, Governor of New Jersey, will speak on Friday evening. The Executive Secretary will speak at the closing mass meeting Sunday afternoon.

Day sessions of the convention will consist of workshops on Political Action, the Role of Youth in Securing Full Integration. Branch Action for Integration, Use of Publicity Techniques, Membership and Fund Raising, Organizing Labor and the N.A.A.C.P., Housing Problems, the Role of the Church in Desegregating the Community, Political Action in the South, and Program Activities for N.A.A.C.P. Youth Groups.

Annual Convention Board Meeting

The July meeting of the Board of Directors will be held during the Annual Convention in Atlantic City on Wednesday, June 22 at 5:30 P.M. at the Fox Manor Hotel, 2707 Pacific Avenue, and will be a dinner meeting. It will be the last regular meeting of the Board until September 12.

Bandung Conference

In accordance with the vote of the Board, the Secretary sent a message to the Asian-African conference in April in which he expressed the "hope that deliberations of the delegates will result in an opportunity of peoples to work out their destiny free of political, economic, or military pressures exerted by either eastern or western imperialist powers."

A reply received from Russian Abdulgan, conference secretary-general, advised that the conference had unanimously adopted a report expressing the delegates [goals].

Supreme Court Decision of May 21— Statement

At a special meeting of as many Board members in New York as could be present on short notice, the following statement was issued on behalf of the Board and officers of the Association on May 31, on the Supreme Court decree.

We are gratified that as to the counties and states directly involved in the litigation, today's opinion makes a clear-cut determination that the Negro school children must be given their rights "as soon as practicable on a non-discriminatory basis."

This is followed by language which limits delay to necessary administrative details of adjustment while at the same time making it clear that delay cannot be sanctioned simply because of disagreement with the decision. Today's decision directed lower federal courts to see to it that local school boards "make a prompt and reasonable start toward full compliance" with last year's historic decision. We are noting in the language of the opinion which sustains the view of some Southern states that delay in compliance may be of indefinite length.

Other areas of the South not directly involved in this litigation have been given clear notice that "all provisions of federal, state, or local law requiring or permitting such discrimination must yield to this principle" (of [the] May 17 decision). By force of this language counties and states which have held up their desegregation programs because of the continued existence of state laws requiring segregated schools are now free to desegregate their schools. We are confident that the affected school districts and others, including whole states which were awaiting this word, will proceed without delay on programs of desegregation. We are equally confident that the whole American people will support this historic decision to open up new avenues of democracy for all the children of our nation.

Our Association and our local chapters stand ready to cooperate with all officials on such programs.

Immediately following the May 31 decision, an emergency conference of some fifty-five N.A.A.C.P. leaders from sixteen southern states and the District of Columbia was held in Atlanta, Ga., June 4, to consider a program of action to make full use of the decisions of the Supreme Court of May 17 and May 31. The emergency conference heard an analysis of the Court's ruling of May 31, and action proposals by the Executive Secretary.

An eight-point program was adopted by the conference and sent as a directive to all N.A.A.C.P. branches. The program agreed upon is as follows:

1. File at once a petition with each school board, calling attention to the May 31 decision; requesting that the school board act in accordance with the decision and offering support of the branch to help the board in solving this problem.

2. Follow up the petition with periodic inquiries of the board to determine what steps it is making to comply with the Supreme Court decision.

3. All during June, July, August, and September, and thereafter, through meetings, forums, debates, conferences, etc., use every opportunity to explain what the May 31 decision means, and be sure to emphasize that the ultimate determination as to the length of time it will take for desegregation to become a fact in the community is not in the hands of the politicians or the school board officials but in the hands of the federal courts.

4. Organize the parents in the community so that as many as possible will be familiar with the procedure when and if law suits are begun in behalf of plaintiffs and parents.

5. Seek the support of individuals and community groups, particularly in the white community through churches, labor organizations, civic organizations, and personal contact.

6. When announcement is made of the plans adopted by the school boards get the exact text of the school board's pronouncements and notify the State Conference and the National Office at once so that you will have the benefit of their views as to whether the plan is one which will provide for effective desegregation. It is very important that branches not proceed at this stage without consultation with State and National Offices.

7. If no plans are announced or no steps towards desegregation taken by the time school begins this fall, 1955, the time for a law suit has arrived. At this stage court action is essential because only in this way does the mandate of the Supreme Court that a prompt and reasonable start towards full compliance become fully operative on the school boards in question.

8. At this stage the matter will be turned over to the legal department and it will precede with the matter in court.

Celebration of May 17, 1954, Decision—
Freedom Day

The first anniversary of the Supreme Court decision of May 17, 1954, banning public school segregation was observed by all units of the Association on May 17. Many other groups joined the Association in this celebration. On the preceding Sunday, May 15, the Secretary was heard on the University of Chicago Round Table radio program over the NBC network in a discussion of public school segregation. Daily and weekly newspapers all over the country published stories based upon an N.A.A.C.P. survey summarizing developments in school desegregation during the year. In many churches, sermons were delivered on desegregation on Sunday.

In New York City, Mayor Robert F. Wagner proclaimed the period May 15–21 as N.A.A.C.P. week.

On May 17, a dinner was held at the Plaza Hotel in observance of this anniversary, at which Adlai Stevenson, who had arrived only a few hours before from Africa, was an unscheduled speaker. Other speakers were Jacob Javits, New York State Attorney General, Dr. Channing H. Tobias, the Secretary and Special Counsel. Dr. Ralph Bunche and Dr. Buell Gallagher were co-chairmen of the dinner.

Killing of Rev. G. W. Lee of Belzoni, Miss.

The Secretary spoke to 400 persons at a memorial meeting for Rev. G. W. Lee of Belzoni, Miss., on May 2, killed on May 7 "because he thought he ought to vote just like other Americans." Rev. Lee had been threatened and told to withdraw his name from the registration lists but he refused to do this.

The Secretary wrote Attorney General Herbert Brownell requesting a conference to discus "developments in Mississippi since last fall" including plans "designed to prevent Negroes from registering and voting in elections held there."

A report from Southeastern Regional Secretary Ruby Hurley shows that at one time there were 400 persons registered in Belzoni (Humphreys County) and that threats and acts of intimidation reduced the number to ninety-one.

In his letter the Secretary charged that the killing of Rev. Lee was "an act to deprive Negroes of their constitutional right to vote as citizens of the United States and that the inactivity of the local law enforcement officers suggests toleration of this deprivation bordering on approval of murder as a weapon." The Secretary asked Mr. Brownell for a full investigation to determine the most effective means of bringing the murder or murderers of Rev. Lee to justice.

Mr. Warren Olney of the Department of Justice has written the Secretary acknowledging his letter and stating that the department is investigating all aspects of the matter and will be glad to confer upon completion of the pending investigation.

Request Change in A.A.A.S. Convention Site

In accordance with the vote of the Board of Directors at its May meeting, the Secretary wired Dr. Dale Wolfe, Administrative Secretary of the American Association for the Advancement of Science, protesting a plan to hold the December 1955 meeting of A.A.A.S. in Atlanta, Ga., because all facilities and conveniences customarily available to convention delegates will not be available to Negro delegates.

The Secretary stated:

It seems incredible that in 1955 when the trend is in the opposite direction, an Association of scientists, of all people, should hold a convention in the capital city of a state whose officials have proclaimed unalterable allegiance to the scientific myth of racial superiority and inferiority—or that such a convention of scientists would subject a section of its membership to the barbaric practices exemplifying this untenable position.

The Secretary requested that this protest be brought before the Board of Directors of A.A.A.S. at its meeting June 11–12 for consideration and action taken to shift the meeting to a site where no delegates will be humiliated on the irrelevant basis of skin color.

Humphrey-Daniel Resolution

The Executive Secretary has written branches of the Association in key states urging them to write their senators to vote against the Humphrey-Daniel resolution when it comes to the floor for action. The bill would divide each state's votes for President and Vice-President in the Electoral College in proportion to the popular vote received by the respective candidates. It was reported out of committee on May 19. Former Representative E. Gossett (D., Texas), an original sponsor of this resolution, defeated in a previous Congress, announced that its purpose was to curb the voting power of Negroes and other minorities in the more populous northern and western states.

Retention of Anti-Bias Ban in Army Bill

Following reports of efforts to eliminate the anti-segregation provision in the new National Guard reserve plan, the Secretary wired House majority leader John McCormack and minority leader Charles Halleck urging retention of the amendment. The amendment introduced by Congressman Adam Clayton Powell (D., N.Y.) barred assignment of military reservists to segregated units of the National Guard or the Air National Guard. The amendment was passed on May 18 by the House by a vote of 120 to 87 and immediately thereafter there was a movement to strike from the bill the section dealing with assignment of such personnel to guard units. The 1,300 local units of the Association have been called upon by the Secretary to urge their congressmen to support Mr. Powell's amendment.

Death of Mrs. Bethune

Mrs. Mary McLeod Bethune, vice-president of the Association, died on May 18 at her home in Daytona Beach, Fla. Wires of condolence were sent to Richard Moore, president of Bethune Cookman College in Daytona Beach, by the Chairman of the Board and Secretary.

Change in Convention Site by American Psychiatric Association

The Secretary wrote to Dr. R. Finley Gayle, Jr., president of the American Psychiatric Association, congratulating the organization upon its decision to move its

1956 convention from Dallas, Tex., to Chicago, Ill., because of discriminatory racial policies prevailing in Dallas.

Eastland Resolution to Investigate Supreme Court

The Executive Secretary wired Senators Kilgore and William Langer of the Judiciary Committee urging that the resolution to investigate the United States Supreme Court because of its ruling in the school segregation cases, introduced May 25 by Senator James O. Eastland of Mississippi, is unconstitutional on its face and that no action should be taken by the Judiciary Committee. The Secretary stated, "Senator Eastland's understanding of and regard for the United States Constitution can be measured by his almost 100 per cent anti-Negro campaign of last summer for re-election, by the fact that a Negro minister was murdered in his state May 7, 1955, for wanting to vote, and by the fact that the political system in Mississippi operated by the Democratic party through trickery, threats, and violence prevents 407,000 Negro citizens of voting age from casting their ballots in elections held there."

Senator Langer replied giving assurance that he will oppose the resolution introduced by Senator Eastland.

Roy Wilkins, Secretary
June 13, 1955

Report of the Secretary for the Board Meeting of April 1963

Birmingham, Ala.

In protest against the arrest of the Rev. Martin Luther King, Jr., and others who have been fighting discrimination in the State of Alabama, the Secretary, on April 15, wired Attorney General Robert F. Kennedy, urging Federal intercession and citing a specific law—in U.S. Code 242—which "makes it a crime under Federal law to deprive any U.S. citizen of constitutional rights under *color of state* law."

The Association also joined other organizations in protesting racial policies of several chain stores in Birmingham with demonstrations in major cities throughout the country. Picket lines were set up on Saturday, April 20, in front of Woolworth, Kress, Green and Newberry stores in New York, Philadelphia, San Francisco, Los Angeles, Flint, Detroit, and thirty-five other cities. Other organizations joined the picket lines in some few cities including the Transport Workers Union, UAW, Brotherhood of Sleeping Car Porters, CORE, ACWA, Negro American Labor Council, ILGWU, and the Retail Warehouse Department Store Union.

On April 25, the Secretary addressed the twenty-fourth nightly rally of Birmingham citizens working and marching against discrimination. In his remarks the Secretary praised the citizens who defied police dogs and other intimidation to protest segregation and predicted that today's Negro generation is the last that will endure any modicum of compulsory segregation. The Association is barred from operating in Alabama by state injunction (presently on appeal). However, the Secretary was in the state to speak for the John A. Andrew Clinical Society at Tuskegee and stopped off in Birmingham to pay his respects to Rev. King, Rev. Abernathy, Rev. Shuttlesworth, and the others.

On May 3 the Secretary again wired the President protesting the indiscriminate use of dogs, fire hoses, and night sticks by Birmingham police not only against demonstrators but against any and all dark-skinned onlookers. These actions, the Secretary said, "indicate police-imposed reign of terror designed to stifle all efforts by Negroes of that city to exercise constitutional rights of free speech and assembly. When coupled with arbitrary arrest of Freedom Walkers at Alabama State line, evidence is complete that there is no effective authority in Alabama which can be invoked for protection of basic constitutional guarantees to American citizens. In such circumstances there is no alternative to [an] urgent request that you speak directly both to Alabama authorities and to the nation as a whole calling for an end to these injustices and for commitment of that state to the rule of law. We urge that the full offices of the Government of the United States be employed to this end. Violence breeds violence and lawlessness encourages lawlessness. They must not be allowed to dictate the course of future events in Alabama." The Secretary also wired the Attorney General urging that the Justice Department promptly "extend Federal protection to Birmingham's Negro citizens who seek to exercise their constitutional rights in the face of constitutionally illegal restrictions and denials by Municipal authorities. . . ."

The Secretary also wired some 100 branches of the Association urging them to wire the President and the Department of Justice seeking them to intercede using the power of the Federal Government to restore sanity and order and to protect those who seek to exercise their constitutional rights in Alabama.

Reply to Congressman Powell

Attacks on the N.A.A.C.P. for including white persons among its officers and board members by Congressman Adam Clayton Powell have been refuted in a pamphlet, "The N.A.A.C.P. and Adam Clayton Powell." In it the Association answered point by point, with evidence, Mr. Powell's statement about the N.A.A.C.P. made on three different occasions.

The pamphlet has been mailed to all branch presidents and secretaries, members of the Board of Directors, organizations in the Leadership Conference on Civil Rights, and others.

Clarksdale, Miss.

On May 9 the Secretary is scheduled to speak in Clarksdale, Miss., at the branch's Freedom Fund dinner. It was felt that it would be well to utilize this occasion to demonstrate the Association's support of our workers in Mississippi and to pledge our Mississippi branches' national support for the anti-segregation drive now under way in Mississippi. In addition to the Secretary, therefore, the Chairman of the Board, the President of the Association, its Treasurer and Board members H. Claude Hudson, Margaret Bush Wilson, Leonard Burns, and C. R. Darden, will accompany the Secretary and will speak briefly at the banquet.

Clarksdale is the home city of Aaron Henry, Mississippi State Conference President, whose residence was bombed on April 22. It is hoped that the presence of top officers of the Association in this city serve to encourage Mississippi workers in their voter registration campaign and in their efforts to desegregate schools and other public facilities.

Firing of Dick Gregory

On May 1 the Secretary wired Frank Krulik of the Galaxy Supper Club in St. Albans, L. I., protesting the cancellation of Dick Gregory's contract. A spokesman for the club said that Mr. Gregory was late for several performances. The cancellation came after Mr. Gregory had announced that he was sending all of his salary to Mississippi to continue the fight there.

Freedom Walkers

The Secretary on May 2 wired the President and Attorney General urging that the Justice Department ensure protection for the Freedom Walkers—"American citizens who seek only free use of public highways." Ten persons, five white and five Negro, undertook to finish the protest march initiated by William Moore, a white postal clerk who was murdered for his belief while marching through Alabama.

The Association dispatched a mobile canteen truck from Chattanooga, Tenn., to escort the Walkers and supply food. The truck was driven by disabled Korean War veteran Lawrence Curry, 27. Mr. Curry has an outstanding N.A.A.C.P. record as a voter registration worker with the Chattanooga branch.

The Association also dispatched N.A.A.C.P. field secretary Vernon Jordan from Atlanta, Ga., to work with N.A.A.C.P. units along the way in preparing their communities for the Walkers.

Interview with *U.S. News and World Report*

U.S. News and World Report features a seven-page interview with the Executive Secretary in its April 22 issue. The Secretary, in answer to a series of questions, sets forth the goals of Negro Americans today and their mood of impatience with the speed with which the Negro is coming into the status of full citizenship.

Speaking Engagements

During the month of April the Secretary [was] in Louisville, Ky., for the Southern Police Institute Conference on Police Responsibility in Race Tension and Conflict. The conference was held at the University of Louisville. He also spoke April 18 for the New York City Branch; April 19 in Des Moines; and April 20 in Denver, Col.; April 30 for the American Jewish Congress Civil Rights Forum in the Bronx; April 24 for the John A. Andrews Clinical Society in Tuskegee Institute, Ala.; April 25 in Birmingham, Ala. at the twenty-fourth nightly rally of Birmingham citizens working and marching against discrimination; attended luncheon April 13 sponsored by the New York Chapter of the Links, Inc., honoring General Counsel Robert Carter; participated in the 1963 national conference of the American Society for Public Administration in Washington, D.C., April 5.

Death of Mrs. A. Philip Randolph

On April 15 the Secretary sent a wire to N.A.A.C.P. Vice President A. Philip Randolph expressing, on behalf of the members and officers of the Association, deepest sympathy on the death of his wife, Mrs. Randolph [who] died on April 14 after a long illness.

Roy Wilkins, Secretary
April 1963

Report of the Executive Secretary for the Board Meeting May and June, 1963

Jackson, Miss.

On Friday, May 31, the Secretary arrived in Jackson, Miss., to address a mass meeting and to assure the community of full support of the drive for desegregation of public facilities. On Saturday, June 1, while picketing in front of Woolworth's he was arrested along with Medgar Evers and Mrs. Helen Wilcher. All three were later released on $1,000 bail each.

The stepped-up movement for immediate desegregation of public facilities and an end to discriminatory practice in stores and other businesses was initiated at a meeting of the Mississippi State Conference on May 12. The demands were made in a resolution adopted at the executive board meeting.

The Mayor at first refused to meet with any committee representing the Negro community and specifically barred N.A.A.C.P. members in his announcement over two television stations May 19. Inasmuch as he criticized the N.A.A.C.P., Medgar Evers asked for equal time to reply. In a seventeen-minute address via television, May 20, Mr. Evers set forth the legitimate complaints of the Negro community, pointing out that the N.A.A.C.P. has been in Mississippi since 1918 and that he was a native of the state and a veteran of World War II. He appealed to the conscience of the white community.

Thereafter, at a mass meeting sponsored by the N.A.A.C.P. May 21, fourteen persons were elected to represent the Negro community on a bi-racial committee to work with city officials in efforts to desegregate places of public accommodation throughout the city. The Mayor accepted four of the representatives but added ten persons of his own choosing. Medgar Evers, one of those elected by the community, was rejected by the Mayor.

The Negro community rejected this committee after learning of the Mayor's selections and the four who had been selected by the community and accepted by the Mayor promptly resigned. In a wire to the Mayor they stated: "in view of the fact that the majority of the committee named was not democratically selected by the Negro community as their representatives, we feel that any meeting of this committee with you, under these circumstances, will serve no useful purpose." Although resigning from the committee, they expressed the "hope that some immediate and constructive steps will be taken by our city officers and leaders of both races that will spare our city from the impending crisis with which we are now faced."

The resignations apparently took the Mayor by surprise and after a delay he agreed to meet with all the committee members elected at the mass meeting, but he did add a very few men of his own.

At his meeting with them he is reported by all of them to have made the following promises: immediate acceptance of Negro applications for policemen and school crossing guards; declaration that all public facilities would be opened to all citizens on an equal basis, to be effective May 29; removal of all Jim Crow signs from gas stations and public buildings; and city officials would address Negro citizens with courtesy titles.

When the committee reported this to the mass meeting, the Mayor immediately denied he had made any such promises, declaring that he had promised only to receive applications for policemen and school crossing guards. He added that since the committee had misrepresented him, he would "take back" his promise on policemen and crossing guards.

As a result of the Mayor's reversal, sit-in demonstrations, picketing, and other forms of demonstrations got under way. Three members of the Youth Division and Professor Salter, adviser to the Tougaloo Chapter, sat in at the local Woolworth store. Professor Salter and Memphis Norman, student at Tougaloo, were attacked and Norman was hospitalized as a result of a severe beating and stomping, a photograph of which was carried in papers coast to coast. Police officials stood by passively.

The Attorney General was asked to order immediately an FBI investigation of the "unjustified arrests and refusal of police protection."

The Justice Department was also called upon to make a thorough investigation into a bomb having been thrown early on the morning of May 29 into the yard of Medgar Evers.

The N.A.A.C.P. State Office in Jackson at 1972 Lynch Street has become the nerve center of the demonstrations. Another telephone line has been installed and an adjacent room rented.

Gloster B. Current, national director of branches, is the top staff man in charge, assisting and counseling State Secretary Medgar Evers. Willie Ludden, regional youth secretary from the Atlanta office, is working with the young people. Mrs. Wright has been brought from Savannah, Ga., to help in the formation of women's committees. The newspaper, radio, and television men were numerous enough to require special attention and Jesse DeVore was brought down from Mr. Moon's office to help. Also, Mrs. Ferguson, Mr. Current's secretary, in order to help the overworked office secretary, Mrs. Ruby Hurley, came over from her Atlanta office to assist Mr. Current.

June 3, outside legal help began to arrive to give assistance to our Jackson attorney, Jack Young. General Counsel Robert L. Carter and his assistant, Miss Barbara Morris were joined by Jack Greenberg and Frank D. Reeves on June 4. On June 5, William B. Ming arrived from Chicago. The attorneys were planning affirmative legal action, not defensive moves.

By the weekend of June 1–2, 570 persons had been arrested, including several hundred under the age of eighteen. Up to June 5, a total of $64,000.00 in bail bond money had been sent by the National Office to Jackson. This sum just took care of releases pending trial. Additional bond money will have to be put up for appeals from convictions if the charges are not dropped. Children were released to the parents on the promise that they would be kept off the streets in demonstrations. Most bonds were for $100.00, a few for $500.00, since the charges were picketing, parading, blocking the sidewalk, etc.

The charge against Messrs. Evers and Wilkins and Mrs. Wilcher was conspiring to obstruct trade, an 1892 Mississippi law. The maximum fine upon conviction is $10,000.

N.A.A.C.P. personages who have been arrested and/or assaulted, in addition to those named include: Miss Pearlina Lewis of the N.A.A.C.P. North Jackson Youth Council; Miss Doris Allison, president of the Jackson N.A.A.C.P. Branch; and Mr. Ludden, who was severely beaten May 31.

The Jackson operation was undertaken after a report of the resolution of the Mississippi State Conference at the regular meeting of the Executive Committee of the Board on May 13 and the secretary was authorized

> to secure from whatever sources available the necessary sums to take care of the costs that may arise in connection with aiding the current selective buying campaign of our North Jackson Youth Council and the general drive toward the objective of putting an end to all forms of racial discrimination and segregation in Jackson.

Clarksdale, Miss.

Plans are under way to extend the Association's desegregation drive to Clarksdale, Miss. Aaron Henry, Mississippi State Conference president who resides in Clarksdale, heads a fifteen-man committee which has asked city officials and local businessmen for a conference to plan steps toward immediate desegregation of all public facilities. A communication to city officials May 24 remained unanswered as of May 31. The local newspaper, The *Clarksdale Press-Register*, editorially called upon the white community to ignore the N.A.A.C.P. and to refuse to confer with a representative committee of Negro citizens. Mrs. Ruby Hurley, Southern regional secretary, is assisting the Clarksdale community in developing its plans.

A series of mailings have been sent to branches of the Association alerting them to be prepared to act in protests and otherwise in support of the Jackson, Miss., effort. Subsequent mailings have been sent to keep the branches up to date on development.

Appeals for funds have also been made to help meet the cost of bail, medical bills, and other costs.

A memorandum giving background information on the desegregation drive in Jackson was sent to the full press release list and to Washington correspondents.

Birmingham, Ala.

Although unable to function officially in Alabama because of the injunction against the Association in that state, the Secretary on May 7, wired some 100 of the top branches across the country urging them to stage demonstrations in support of the Birmingham struggle around city halls and state houses and to inform local authorities of the outrage of citizens over the barbarity in Alabama. He also asked branches to appeal to President Kennedy to intervene.

On May 18 after Federal troops had been stationed outside Birmingham, the Secretary urged the President to maintain Federal troops in Alabama until Birmingham's hard-won agreement is safe to effect. The Secretary noted that "Alabama state troopers are doing their best to provoke Negro reaction in Birmingham and thus provide an excuse for extreme repressive action . . . in these conditions any withdrawal of Federal forces would be an invitation to white supremacy leadership to destroy any and all interracial agreements for predictable future."

Supreme Court Anti-Segregation Ruling

On May 20 the Supreme Court ruled in six sit-ins and other anti-segregation demonstration cases that a state cannot constitutionally require segregation or use its police to enforce separation of the races. The case originated in Alabama, Georgia, Louisiana, North and South Carolina.

Following the decision, the Executive Secretary wired thirty-four major corporations—hotel, restaurant, variety and drug store and theater—operating chain establishments throughout the country calling upon them to order an immediate end to racial discrimination in service and employment in all their local outlets.

Prince Edward County

On May 17, following announcement by the Department of Justice that "some remedial education program will be sponsored by the Federal Government," in Prince Edward County, the Secretary transmitted to the President a petition signed by some 700 Negro citizens of Prince Edward County which asked for a survey on the size and nature of the educational problems involved in re-establishing public schools, and for a comprehensive program designed to help children prepare for the reopening of schools. The Secretary noted that America "has sent specialists to distant lands to help distressed people. . . . The children of Prince Edward County need a program which will match in purpose, scope and quality, the best social and technical assistance project which our government has done anywhere in the world."

Durham, N.C.

On May 23 the Executive Secretary spoke at a mass meeting attended by some 2,600 persons in Durham, N.C., organized by youth and college chapters in Durham, N.C., under the direction of Attorney Floyd McKissick, adviser to the youth units.

The Secretary urged the Negro community not to give up demonstrations until an honorable agreement with city officials on desegregation of public facilities was reached.

Durham's Mayor Wence Graberek was present at the meeting and welcomed the Secretary to the city. He assured the Secretary and the audience that the city would work out its problems with fairness and justice.

Discrimination in Federal Employment

In a wire to President Kennedy on May 29, the secretary urged a "nation-wide survey of Federal employment patterns in key cities." The results would reveal, the Secretary said, "in some areas the employment pattern of Federal agencies is practically lily-white and these localities are not confined to the South."

The full text of the wire is as follows:

National Association for the Advancement of Colored People suggests that part of the basis for unrest and resentment among Negro citizens is the belief that Federal government employment is not freely open to them as to others. In some areas the employment pattern in Federal agencies is practically lily white and these localities are not confined to the South. In view of the fact that the unemployment rate among Negro workers is now more than twice that among whites, a nationwide survey of Federal employment patterns in key cities would be revealing and, shocking. Appropriate corrective action in expanded notification of civil service examinations and in recruitment, together with appointments of successful candidates free of suspicion of racial bias will be one positive step Federal Government could take in present situation.

A reply was received from Lee C. White, Assistant Special Counsel to the President, under date of June 1 and stated:

> As I am sure you know, the President's Committee on Equal Employment Opportunity has undertaken aggressive measures to insure that Negroes receive a fair break in their efforts to secure employment with the Federal Government. Particular stress has been placed on opportunities for promotion of Negro employees within the Federal service.
>
> Certainly there are many specific localities within the country where much more remains to be done, and you may be assured that attention has been given to this problem at the very highest levels of government. We hope that even the impressive record of the past two and one-half years will be improved drastically.

Philadelphia Jim Crow Union

In a wire to Philadelphia Branch President Cecil Moore, the Secretary commended the branch for its forthright attack upon Jim Crow in building trade unions. An N.A.A.C.P. picket line was formed after union contractors failed to keep an agreement to hire four Negroes to do plumbing, steamfitting, and electrical work on a school construction project, before work on the project began. After some days of hectic picketing during which both pickets and police suffered injuries, the N.A.A.C.P. won its point and signed an agreement on hiring. The full text of the wire is as follows:

> Entire National Association for Advancement of Colored People fully supports your forthright assault upon Jim Crow in building trades unions. The Philadelphia Branch's tactic of mass picketing of construction jobs will certainly be used by our branches in other cities confronted with this problem. Negro workers and their families are being strangled and starved by discrimination in employment with the result that their unemployment rate is more than twice that of white workers. Inasmuch as discrimination on public works in Philadelphia is in violation of contracts with the city, we are asking our lawyers to explore the possibility of a suit to stop all payments for work done in [this] violation of that contract. Our best wishes for early and complete victory in important campaign.

> Roy Wilkins, Secretary
> June 1963

Report of the Secretary for the
Board Meeting of September 1963

Beating of N.A.A.C.P. Official—Shreveport, La.

Following the brutal beating of Rev. Harry Blake, president of the Shreveport, La., Branch on September 22, by police, the Secretary on September 24, wired the Attorney General urging "immediate and adequate Federal presence in Shreveport and full support of legislative authority of the Attorney General of the United States to protect American citizens. . . ." Law enforcement officials, including the Commissioner of Public Safety, invaded the Thirteenth District Auditorium where a memorial meeting for the victim of the Birmingham September 15 bombing had been held.

Police harassed several persons in the neighborhood and effectively prevented them from attending the meeting. One teacher was struck on the porch of his own home.

To avert further violence, the Association temporarily suspended night meetings and demonstrations.

Birmingham, Ala., Church Bombing

The Executive Secretary attended and spoke at the funeral of three of the four young girls killed in the Sunday, September 15 bombing of the 16th Street Baptist Church.

The Secretary also wired the President on September 15 urging the "fullest use of Federal anti-bombing statute for complete intervention of the Department of Justice. . . ." The Secretary wired that "anything less than a strongly reinforced civil rights bill (will be) confessing that the Federal Government is willing to occupy a spectator role in the life and death struggle a beleaguered minority is waging for freedom from persecution and killing."

In a brief press interview September 18 at National Airport while enroute to Birmingham for the funeral, the Secretary urged that "every nickel" of Federal aid to Alabama, starting with the closing of Maxwell Air Force Base near the state capital of Montgomery, be discontinued. He noted that the Federal Government puts $100 million a year into Alabama.

In a long telegram expressing their shock and grief, ten Negro and white leaders of the March on Washington urged the President to "bring the full weight of your authority and influence to bear in guarantees that the atrocity of September 15 shall never be repeated. . . . When people cannot look to their government to defend them, they will take steps to defend themselves. . . ."

Challenge to Two Southern Governors

In similar wires to Governors Ross Barnett of Mississippi and George Wallace of Alabama, the Executive Secretary, on September 26, challenged them to open the doors of universities in their respective states to advocates of civil rights and integration.

The Secretary stated that the N.A.A.C.P. "has voiced no opposition" to their respective appearances at Princeton and Brown Universities. "We do object to the fact that under your administration the member institutions of your university system have not been permitted to invite speakers to advocate the abolition of racial segregation."

Strengthened Version of Rights Bill

In a wire to Congressman Emanuel Celler, chairman of the House Judiciary Committee, and to other members of the committee, the Secretary expressed appreciation for the strengthened version of the civil rights bill approved by the subcommittee which is drafting the final bill. The Subcommittee draft approved September 25 expands and strengthens the Administration's bill to include an F.E.P.C. section, authorization for the Attorney General to institute suits in cases of civil rights violation, and permanent status for the U.S. Civil Rights Commission. It also expands coverage for the public accommodations section of the bill to cover business operating under state authority, license, or permission.

Wires of appreciation were also sent to Representatives Peter W. Rodino, Jr., of New Jersey, who introduced and worked for inclusion of the F.E.P.C. provision, and Byron G. Rogers of Colorado, for his vital rule in pressing for the section authorizing the Department of Justice to take civil injunctive action in all cases where constitutional rights are abridged or denied.

Inequitable Death Sentence Protested

In a letter to Governor J. Millard Tawes of Maryland dated September 27, the Executive Secretary protested "the excessive and inequitable sentence imposed upon three young Negroes convicted and sentenced to death in the alleged rape of a sixteen-year-old white girl." The Secretary cited [a] six-month sentence meted out to a white man in Maryland who killed a Negro woman.

Christmas-Buying Boycott

A telegram was received September 23 from Louis E. Lomax on behalf of the Writers and Artists for Justice proposing that the N.A.A.C.P. endorse a nationwide Christmas-buying strike by Negroes and their sympathizers.

On October 1 the Secretary wrote Mr. Lomax as follows:

This will acknowledge the telegram of September 23 from the Writers and Artists for Justice proposing that the N.A.A.C.P. endorse a nation-wide Christmas-buying strike by Negroes and their sympathizers.

The leadership of the March on Washington, including the N.A.A.C.P., the Southern Christian Leadership Conference, the Congress of Racial Equality, the Student Non-Violent Coordinating Committee, the Negro American Labor Council and the National Urban League, at a meeting in Washington this week, gave careful thought to the problems of such a consumer strike.

All of us believe that there should be selective-buying campaigns in every local community, in which businesses with fair employment policies should be patronized and businesses with unfair policies should be passed by. The N.A.A.C.P. has staged many such selective buying campaigns successfully in localities where targets could be reached and sufficient consumer buying power was present. The N.A.A.C.P. will continue to stage such campaigns.

Perhaps grown-ups should restrain from costly presents to other grown-ups, and instead turn the money over to the civil rights cause. It seemed to those in the meeting that it would be unfortunate to further deprive Negro children, already brutalized by segregation, by denying them the annual joys of a Christmas tree and toys.

Since a general consumer buying strike would not have any effect directly on the Birmingham situation, it was decided to find out just what kinds of selective buying would have such effects. No consumer buys from U.S. Steel Company, for example, and U.S. Steel is the biggest employer in Birmingham. Research is proceeding on consumer products. All agreed that a boycott (which requires [a] tremendous amount of time, effort, and money to carry out) should have some clear cut purpose and some reasonable chance of being effective; otherwise, it is better not to start it.

It was pointed out also a 'shotgun' boycott against merchants everywhere, in addition to being ineffective in many localities, would be unfair to many persons who cannot have any effect on the situation in Alabama or the South generally.

The shock and anger and sorrow of the Birmingham bomb murders of four little girls in church, and of two lads shot to death in wake of the bombing are upon all of us. The deed will remain fresh in the hearts of all decent people of whatever race or station. We feel that each person should decide how best he can react effectively, but that organizationally we cannot sponsor a nation-wide Christmas boycott.

Speaking Engagements, Radio, T.V., Etc.

During the month of September the Secretary attended the Asilomar Conference at Pacific Grove, Calif., and spoke to some 750 delegates at a meeting on September 21. He spoke on Thursday, September 26, in Richmond, Va., at the convention of S.C.L.C.; appeared on A.B.C. network television in a one-half hour program,

"Youth Wants to Know" on Sunday, September 29; and was guest on a twenty-minute television interview with radio station K.P.R.G. in Honolulu on September 11; did a taping for German T.V. on September 27 and spoke at the Methodist Church Rally, September 29.

Roy Wilkins, Secretary
October 1963

Report of the Secretary for the Board Meeting of December 1963

Assassination of President Kennedy

On Friday, November 22, the Executive Secretary sent a wire to Mrs. Jacqueline Kennedy on behalf of the Association, expressing deepest sorrow on the tragic death of President John F. Kennedy. The Secretary also wired President Johnson following his oath of office ceremony.

Following the assassination, radio, television, and newspaper reporters began calling for comment by the Secretary on the impact of the tragedy on the anti-bias drive.

He [the Secretary] issued the following statement at the time:

The assassination of President Kennedy is a grim tragedy reminding us anew of the depth of hatred that some Americans are capable of harboring. The President's consistent commitment to and espousal of basic human rights for all earned the undying enmity of fanatic and loathesome bigots . . .

The shocking and terrible death of Mr. Kennedy deprives the nation and the world of stalwart and consecrated leadership in the ageless struggle for human advancement. Peoples everywhere who value humanity, liberty, and justice mourn his passing.

President's Message to Congress

Following the President's message to Congress on Wednesday, November 27, in which he called for the "earliest possible passage of the civil rights bill" for which President Kennedy fought, the secretary issued the following comment:

Millions will agree with President Johnson that early passage of the civil rights bill would be a fitting memorial to President Kennedy. Certainly the message of our new President left no doubt as to his recognition of the urgency of the civil rights issue or of his commitment to full support of the cause of equal rights for all Americans.

He was straight-forward on all the major domestic and international problems facing the nation and was ringing in his rallying cry against bigotry and hate and violence.

The whole message had a strong tone affirming basic Americanism. It cannot but assure all our citizens that our country will move forward and that President Johnson is ready to lead the Congress and the people in any action in the national interest.

The Secretary also telegraphed approval of the message to President Johnson immediately after the speech.

The Conference with President Johnson

At the new President's invitation, the Secretary conferred with President Lyndon B. Johnson at the White House for forty-five minutes on Friday, November 29, after which, in a statement to the press, he said he was convinced Mr. Johnson would push for enactment of the Kennedy civil rights package because of his "own conviction that it was essential and because of the political necessity" of it. The Secretary was the first civil rights official invited to the White House by Mr. Johnson.

Civil Rights Legislation

Continuing our effort to get passage of a strong civil rights bill, on November 22, the Secretary wrote all local units of the Association asking them to see their congressmen while they are home for the Thanksgiving holiday, asking their congressmen to speak to their House leadership of both parties and urge that the civil rights bill be brought out of the Rules Committee to the floor for debate and vote.

Speaking Engagements

During the months of October and November, the secretary filled an unusually large number of speaking requests from branches and other groups, as well as radio and television requests.

On October 30, he addressed the Harvard Business Club (New York City unit) composed of some 2,000 graduates of the University's school of business, which includes some of the most influential business leaders in the New York area.

On October 31, he spoke at a testimonial dinner sponsored by the Williamsbridge (N.Y.C.) Branch honoring Mrs. Wilkins. Seven-hundred persons were at the Freedom Fund dinner. On November 3 he delivered the closing address of the Mississippi State Conference in Biloxi, Miss. He addressed the Eastern conference of the American Association of Advertising Agencies on November 8. On November 7 he joined with the trustees of the Eleanor Roosevelt Memorial Foundation and some 200 friends in paying tribute to Mrs. Eleanor Roosevelt at Hyde Park at noon on the first anniversary of her death and spoke at the luncheon there following ground-breaking ceremonies for a new library wing; at night spoke at a dinner in Princeton, N.J., for a Western Electric group; November 10 spoke to one-day civil rights conference of the three branches of Judaism at [the] Ambassador Hotel in Los Angeles; on November 13, addressed a packed rally of some 2,000 persons in Orangeburg, S.C.; spoke to a group of representatives to the U.N. on November 14; November 18 addressed the St. Louis, Mo., Bar Association, participating on the program with John C. Satterfield of Yazoo, Miss., past president of the American Bar Association and adviser to Mississippi's Governor Ross Barnett. In his remarks, the Secretary stated that the civil rights crisis of today was brought about by "open defiance" of the 1954 Supreme Court ruling on school segregation. Resistance to the decision was generated in Mississippi and spread to other Southern states.

On November 17, the Secretary spoke to an overflow audience at the Sharp Street Memorial Church in Baltimore, sponsored by the branch. Over $6,000 was received at this meeting in cash and pledges. On November 20 he spoke at the University of Miami (Fla.) and on November 21 at Oberlin College in Ohio. Because of the tragic death of President Kennedy, engagements scheduled for November 23, 24, and 25, in Missouri, Washington, Chicago, Ill. and Atlanta, Ga., were canceled. The Secretary spoke November 26 at the annual Freedom House Awards Dinner.

Roy Wilkins, Secretary
December 1963

Report of the Secretary for the
Board Meeting of April 1964

Civil Rights Bill

"Letter To Senators" Campaign—As a result of the Association's campaign for letters to Senators in support of the civil rights bill, New York Senators Keating and Javits have reported a reversal in the trend of mail they have received. Last month these two Senators reported receiving mail 10–7 against the bill. On April 1, they reported that during the last week in March they received a total of 3,450 letters in favor of the bill, but 1,398 opposing it, better than two to one in favor of the bill.

The Executive Secretary had sent letters to all branches of the Association urging them to write their Senators and get their friends to do so urging passage of the civil rights bill.

Strategy Meeting of Leadership Conference

On April 1 an all-day strategy meeting of the Leadership Conference on Civil Rights was held in Washington, D.C., at the close of which the Executive Secretary, who is also chairman of the Leadership Conference, announced the following five-point activity program:

1. A one-day conference to be held in Washington of chairmen of voter registration committees from 190 Northern and Western units of the N.A.A.C.P. for progress reports and visits to Senators.
2. A student assembly, April 27-May 2, to hear addresses and participate in discussion on each of the bill's eleven titles.
3. A "Wire for Rights Day" on April 6 by women of B'nai B'rith, who will urge their 200,000 members and others to send telegrams to their Senators in support of the bill.
4. An interfaith meeting, April 28, at Georgetown University, followed by daily prayer services at the Church of the Reformation near the Capitol.
5. A steady stream of regular visits to Senators by delegations of their constituents representing various LCCR [Leadership Conference on Civil Rights] organizations.

Some sixty-two of the eighty national civil rights organizations participated in the conference. Seven Senators also participated.

Dirksen Amendments

The Leadership Conference on Civil Rights has sent a memorandum to all cooperating organizations calling for defeat of the amendment to the civil rights bill proposed by Senator Dirksen. Most of these amendments, the memorandum stated, perpetuate the worst defects of the original proposals and are designed to put as many obstacles as possible in the path of a working man who has suffered discrimination and is seeking redress. Particular attention was called to the present section on fair employment practices in the bill. "It cannot be strengthened," particularly, members of the conference were urged to write and express surprise and dismay that Senator Dirksen, as minority leader, would propose weakening a provision in the bill that Republicans helped write and fought for in the House.

On April 11, the Secretary spoke to some one thousand persons attending a dinner meeting of the Midwest Regional Conference of the N.A.A.C.P. in Indianapolis, Ind. On that occasion he reminded voters preparing to cast their ballots in the May 5 primary that one of the candidates, Governor George Wallace of Alabama, is head of a "child-murder state." On April 16 the Secretary addressed a meeting of the American Society of Newspaper Editors in Washington, D.C.; on April 21–22 he gave two major addresses in Pasadena, Calif., at the California Institute of Technology and the Y.M.C.A. The Secretary pointed out on that occasion that continuing opposition to full civil rights for Negroes contributes to the development of such faulty and ill-chosen tactics as the stall-in at the World's Fair. He pointed particularly to the California referendum on the fair housing law—one cause of the stall-in. "The stall-in is a smash at the American ghetto of housing discrimination—at all doors that hem the Negro in." On April 29, he spoke in Gary, Ind., at the first annual Freedom Fund banquet of the branch.

New Field Worker

During the month of April, Mr. Thomas H. Allen was appointed as field secretary for the New England region. Mr. Allen, a Howard University graduate, was formerly assistant to the Director of Special Services of the New York City Department of Welfare.

Russian Magazine Article by Executive Secretary

A recent issue of a magazine published in the Russian language by U.S. Information Agency features a lengthy article by the Executive Secretary, strictly for Russian consumption. In the article, the Secretary reviews what five presidents of the United States have done on civil rights: Presidents Roosevelt, Truman, Eisenhower, Kennedy, and Johnson. The Secretary also discussed the United States Supreme Court decision of 1954, which he termed "equivalent to a second Emancipation Proclamation."

Wallace in Indiana Primary

As was done by the Secretary last month in connection with support of Governor Wallace of Alabama in the Wisconsin primary, the Secretary again wrote letters to the editors of leading daily newspapers, this time in Indiana. He pointed out that support of Wallace means: bombing little girls to death in Sunday school; preventing Negro students from entering tax-supported state colleges and universities by "standing in the doorway"; closing high schools to prevent Negro children from entering; denying the vote to Negro citizens; black listing white citizens who differ with his white supremacy doctrine; using clubs, electric cattle prods, dogs, and guns on peaceful Negro protest demonstrators. This, the Secretary pointed out, is the real Governor Wallace who wants Indiana voters to designate him, "not for local sheriff, but for President of all the 186 million people of the United States.

Roy Wilkins, Secretary
April 1964

Report of the Secretary for the
Board May and June 1964

Civil Rights Bill

For the first time in history, the Senate on June 10 voted to limit debate on a civil rights measure. It voted 71–29, four more than the necessary two-thirds required for cloture, thus ending a seventy-five day filibuster.

The following Senators voted for cloture in a tense and exciting roll call at 11 A.M., June 10.

Democrats for—(44)

Anderson, N. M.	Mansfield, Mont.
Bartlett, Alaska	McCarthy, Minn.
Bayh, Ind.	McGee, Wyo.
Brewster, Md.	McGovern, S. Dak.
Burdick, N. Dak	McIntyre, N. H.
Cannon, Nev.	McNamara, Mich.
Church, Idaho	Metcalf, Mich.
Clark, Pa.	Monroney, Okla.
Dodd, Conn.	Morse, Oreg.
Douglas, Ill.	Moss, Utah
Edmonson, Okla.	Muskie, Me.
Engle, Calif.	Nelson, Wis.
Gruening, Alaska	Neuberger, Oreg.
Hart, Mich.	Pastors, R. I.
Hartke, Ind.	Pell, R. I.
Humphrey, Minn.	Proxmire, Wis.
Inouye, Hawaii	Randolph, W. Va.
Jackson, Wash.	Ribicoff, Conn.
Kennedy, Mass.	Symington, Mo.
Lausche, Ohio	Williams, N. J.
Long, Mo.	Yarborough, Tex.
Magnuson, Wash.	Young, Ohio

Republicans for—(27)

Aiken, Vt.	Javits, N. Y.
Allott, Colo.	Jordan, Idaho
Beall, Md.	Keating, N. Y.
Boggs, Del.	Kuchef, Calif.
Carlson, Kans.	Miller, Iowa
Case, N. J.	Morton, Ky.
Cooper, Ky.	Mundt, S. Dak.
Cotton, N. H.	Pearson, Kan.
Curtis, Neb.	Prouty, Vt.

Dirksen, Ill.   Saltonstall, Mass.
Dominick, Colo.   Scott, Pa.
Fong, Hawaii   Smith, Pa.
Hickenlooper, Iowa   Williams, Del.
Hruska, Neb.

The night before the cloture vote Senator Robert Byrd (D., W.Va.) spoke all night against the bill and Clarence Mitchell sat up in the gallery throughout the speech. Mr. Mitchell headed up the workers of the civil rights organization just as he did in the House campaign and all of them worked nights, days, weekends. Regular weekly meetings of the legislative agents were held Wednesday and every man reported on the Senators assigned to him. Reports from the home front were received and delegations from the states were guided to personal conferences with their Senators. Strategy meetings were held daily with Senate floor leaders and representatives of the executive branch. Mr. Mitchell was the generalissimo of the entire operation.

During the month of May, the Association had continued its efforts in behalf of passage of a strong bill without weakening amendments. On June 8th, the Secretary had wired President Lyndon B. Johnson, Senators Hubert Humphrey and Thomas Kuchel, as well as Senators in all states except Alabama, Florida, Georgia, North Carolina, South Carolina, Virginia, Mississippi, Arkansas, Louisiana, and Senator Tower of Texas, pointing out that the three amendments offered by Senator Hickenlooper and sponsored also by Senators Morton and Cotton would so restrict the effectiveness of the civil rights bill as to open it to charges of being minimal. He urged them to work against these and any other weakening amendments and to vote for cloture. Branches of the Association were also asked to get in touch with their Senators and urge defeat of the amendments and a vote for cloture.

The following statement commenting on the cloture vote was released by the Secretary on June 11:

The United States Senate's vote, on June 10, to close debate on the civil rights bill is a historic legislative achievement, both in the unexpectedly decisive margin of the victory and in being the first time that cloture has ever been effected on a civil rights measure. Southern Senators, with some Northern help, have successfully exercised minority tyranny over the legislative process; on June 10, 1964, seventy-one Senators concluded that the time had come to end this perversion of democracy and to ensure that the Senate should be able to work its will.

Negro citizens, keenly aware that the bill is no panacea and still leaves much to be done, will nonetheless rejoice at the clearing of the way to its enactment. They know how much it has cost them, in toil, tears, and substance, to develop the climate in which far-reaching legislation of this kind now becomes a probability. They know, too, how great a debt they and all other Americans of good will owe to the Senators of both parties whose vote made this history. The Senate's bipartisan leadership deserves our thanks and our congratulations, and it is noted with particular gratification that twenty-seven of the thirty-three Republican Senators voted in favor of cloture.

The N.A.A.C.P. will pursue without relaxation its work in behalf of speedy enactment of H.R. 7152. Achievement of the cloture victory does not reduce the need for continued effort by all the groups to whose labors over the past year much of yesterday's result must be credited.

Conference with Former President Eisenhower

On Saturday, May 2, the Executive Secretary, together with Sterling Tucker of the National Urban League, discussed at great length the pending civil rights bill with Former President Dwight D. Eisenhower at his Gettysburg, Pa., office.

In a statement of Republican principles published in a copyrighted article in the *New York Herald Tribune* May 25, Mr. Eisenhower stated that civil rights is the nation's most critical domestic challenge. The nation has "a profound moral obligation to each of its citizens, requiring that we not only improve our behavior but also strengthen our laws in a determined effort to see that each American enjoys the full benefits of citizenship."

May 17 Celebration

Branches throughout the country observed the tenth anniversary of the U.S. Supreme Court decision on public school desegregation on May 17 in a variety of events: Commemorative religious services, prayer marches, and public meetings.

Chief among the celebrations was the Association's "Freedom Spectacular" of May 14 closed circuit telecast.

In a statement to the press the Executive Secretary noted that ten years after the 1954 decision "over ninety per cent of Negro children in Southern and Border states still attended all-Negro schools." Meanwhile de facto segregation in non-Southern areas has increased. Nevertheless,

> the decision has been of pivotal importance in the developing civil rights crisis. It was the first sweeping affirmation by a branch of the Federal Government of the inherent illegality of compulsory segregation. Its impact has been extended far beyond the schoolhouse—to public accommodations, to recreational and health facilities, to transportation and housing, and to voting. It stimulated the upsurge of Negro militancy of the 1960s. It awakened the conscience of white America to the immorality and injustice of segregation. And it has provided a firm, constitutional basis for the continuing and accelerated struggle to rid the nation of the cancer of racism.

Also in observance of the anniversary, the Executive Secretary appeared on a number of radio programs and on three television programs: On May 13 with

Attorney General Robert F. Kennedy and Governor Carl E. Sanders of Georgia on C.B.S. T.V. network news special; on May 10 he was interviewed by a panel of newsmen on W.C.B.S. T.V. "Newsmakers" a half-hour program, and on Sunday, May 17, in a panel discussion from four to five p.m. on W.A.B.C. T.V. under the title, "Ten Years With All Deliberate Speed."

Tribute to Cardinal Spellman

The Secretary joined other distinguished Americans in paying tribute to Francis Cardinal Spellman on the occasion of his seventy-fifth birthday and his twenty-fifth anniversary as Archbishop of New York. A printed tribute to the Cardinal was published with messages from President Johnson; Richard Cardinal Cushing of Boston; Dr. Franklin Clark Ery, Chairman of World Council of Churches; Mrs. Clare Booth Luce, playwright; and Rabbi Louis Finkelstein, head of Jewish Theological Seminary.

Goldwater Rights Stand

Following the May 12 speech of Senator Barry Goldwater at Madison Square Garden in which he stated that election of the Republican party to power would "cool the fires of racial strife," the Secretary on May 13, wired him as follows:

> Your declaration in New York speech May 12 election of your party to power would cool the fires of racial strife ignores that strife has grown out of the refusal of certain states to initiate corrective measures themselves or to permit the Federal Government to protect the constitutional rights of United States citizens residing within their boundaries.
>
> The history of this issue is clear and is written in blood, all the way from Civil War to the assassination of Medgar Evers in Jackson, Miss., last June 12. Your record is clear also. You have stated repeatedly that you believe in leaving civil rights matters to the states.
>
> Regardless of how you rationalize your position you grant immunity to, if you do not affirmatively support, the use of the cattle prods and shotguns of Alabama state troopers, the armored tank and fire hoses of Birmingham police, the bomb murderers of little children in church in Alabama and the assassins in Mississippi. Your position is part of the cotton batting comfort accorded this regime of blood and death by those senators now blocking even a vote on a civil rights bill.
>
> There is no bill pending in any legislature which, to use your completely misleading language, seeks to force anyone to like anyone else. The pending civil rights bill seeks to secure the elementary rights to which every American citizen is entitled whether anyone loves him or not.
>
> You and your supporters can continue to play politics with this question in which is wrapped literally the psychological and physical life and death of twenty millions of Americans who for more than three hun-

dred years have given their country their life's blood. In return they have had their manhood rights doled out by the teaspoon. The time has arrived for the ending of all that. The root causes are known. The preachers of patience and paternalism are known. The machinery of oppression, such as the Senate filibuster, is nakedly exposed. Negro citizens will not return to this 1900 life in 1964.

If their pleas continue to be met with sophistry and antebellum oratory, there will certainly be violence in the streets and elsewhere. There is nothing left. There is no place to turn. Such persons as may want to see government move are blocked by the ignorant, the cunning, and the stubborn. Thus the Negro is forced back upon his own resources. In such a struggle he knows that he will be at a numerical disadvantage, but he reasons that he is already losing and being spat upon to boot.

We can agree with only one part of one sentence in your entire Madison Square Garden speech "that every American, regardless of his race or creed, will come to his senses in time to restore some common sense and decency to this situation." That common sense would include, of course, having the Federal Government act in Alabama, Mississippi, and similar states as well as in Viet Nam. Those of your party members in the Senate who have been hair-splitting and fence-sitting might well join Representative William McCulloch and the 137 other House Republicans who voted for the civil rights bill and thus help other Republican Senators who are providing leadership toward the responsibility and common sense you say you covet.

No reply has been received from Senator Goldwater.

N.A.A.C.P. Telecast

The Association's "Freedom Spectacular" (its first closed circuit telecast) was carried on May 14 in theaters and auditoriums in forty-six cities—sixteen of them in the Deep South. It marked the Tenth Anniversary of the U.S. Supreme Court decision of 1954 outlawing segregation in the public schools, and it was seen by integrated audiences in such Deep South cities as Jackson, Miss., New Orleans, La., Columbia, S.C., Chattanooga, Tenn. Some 12,000 persons saw the show in Madison Square Garden in New York City. Appearing on the show were such stars as Harry Belafonte, Richard Burton, Elizabeth Taylor, Sammy Davis, Jr., Burt Lancaster, Frederic March, Sidney Poitier, Lena Horne, Robert Preston, and others.

Also appearing in the production were Duke Ellington and his orchestra, Godfrey Cambridge, Gloria Foster, Ossie Davis and Ruby Dee, Jack Gilford, Piper Laurie, Roddy McDowell, Ed Begley, Agnes Moorhead, Edmond O'Brien, Edward G. Robinson, the Lon Fontaine Dancers, Bill Cosby, James Darren, Carolyn Jones, Gene Kelly, Keely Smith, Richard Widmark, Nat King Cole, Tony Bennett, Cannonball Adderly Jazz Sextet and Barbara McNair.

The First Freedom Bell Award was presented by the Executive Secretary to Federal Judge Thurgood Marshall "in grateful appreciation of his vital leadership role as N.A.A.C.P. Counsel in securing that epochal decision . . . made possible by his creative genius, perceptive insight . . . and profound knowledge of constitutional law."

In accepting the Award, Judge Marshall paid tribute to "all those laborers in the legal vineyard who joined with me," and to the "freedom loving Americans who brought the suits, often at grave risk, and who, when the suits were won, saw to it that they were put into effect."

The branches have been extremely slow, despite urgings, to send in reports complete enough for us to get a clear financial picture. We know that the show was an artistic success, but we discovered that it is difficult to sell tickets to a T.V. spectacular. Efforts are being made to secure permission from the participants to allow us to seek to sell the spectacular to a commercial network and to the British Broadcasting Company which has expressed an interest in showing it.

Medgar Evers Memorial Day

In a letter to all branches of the Association, the Secretary has urged observance of the anniversary of the death of Medgar Evers. The Secretary asked for additional memberships and contributions needed to undergird the Association's program in Mississippi. We noted the small but significant gains in Mississippi since Mr. Evers' death but said that Negroes are still faced with police measures ordered by the State Legislature to prevent them from obtaining their constitutional rights.

New York City Subway Rampage

The following is the full text of a statement issued through the Association's press releases of June 1 by the Executive Secretary on the rampages of juvenile hoodlums in the subways of New York City and elsewhere:

> The reports of weekend rampages on subways and elsewhere by juvenile hoodlums have shocked and dismayed us all. The fact that the persons responsible for the outrages were Negro and their victims reportedly white introduce an element that can be, and unfortunately has been, interpreted by many as indicating purely racial motivations for the assaults and vandalism. The National Association for the Advancement of Colored People deplores and condemns this behavior, but urges at the same time it be seen and judged in proper context.
>
> Most immediately, this is a police problem. Above and beyond any other considerations, the safety and security of law-abiding citizens, both white and colored, are menaced by such actions, and we call for an increase in the city's police forces sufficient to provide the needed protection.
>
> Beyond this, it is clear, from reports of savage teen-age terrorists in English resort cities and elsewhere abroad, as well as from such incidents as the attack by white teen-agers on Negro boys at Rockaway

Beach just a week ago, that our communities have as yet failed to find the solution to widespread teen-age restlessness and hostilities toward society. Everyone of us has a clear responsibility to do what needs to be done to bring into play the massive private and governmental resources which alone can be effective.

It needs also to be said that part of the context in which these Negro delinquents are bred is the deep bitterness and frustration which all Negroes feel at the continued denial of equal opportunity everywhere and at the unpunished beatings and killings of Negroes which continue to feature the civil rights scene in the Deep South. These nation-wide denials of justice do not justify teen-age criminal violence by even this handful of Negroes, and the overwhelmingly law-abiding Negro community does not condone it. Rather, they are determined that the frustrations engendered by racial injustices shall be channeled into constructive action to end the injustice.

At the same time, Negroes generally, while continuing to do their best to raise their families properly under great hardships, believe that the entire community must join them in assuming the burdens and responsibilities of creating the conditions in which such outbreaks will no longer take place.

Death of Prime Minister Nehru

On June 1 the Executive Secretary cabled Mrs. Indira Gandhi, daughter of Prime Minister Pandit Jawaharlal Nehru, New Delhi, that the N.A.A.C.P. joins the world in mourning the loss of her father, "a great leader, statesman, and humanitarian."

The Prime Minister was a life member of the Association, the life membership having been purchased for him by the *Pittsburgh Courier* in 1949 and presented to him by Mrs. Jessie Vann, Board member and then president and treasurer of the *Courier*.

Roy Wilkins, Secretary
June 1964

Report of the Secretary for the
Board Meeting July and August 1964

Speaking Engagements

During the months of July and August the Secretary continued to fill speaking engagements, make appearances on television and radio, and prepared articles for various publications; in addition to his administrative duties.

On July 2, he attended the White House ceremony at which the President signed the Civil Rights Act of 1964; spoke in Detroit July 4 at the Japanese-

American Citizens League's convention; attended the Republican National Convention in San Francisco, Calif., where he appeared before the Platform Committee, and made appearances on the three major networks; spoke July 13 in Long Beach, Calif., for the American Newspaper Guild Forum on Human Rights, at its annual convention, and in Flint, Mich., July 26, at a branch voter registration rally; on July 27 attended a White House dinner in honor of President and Mrs. Philibert Pairanana of Malagasy; on August 4, spoke at the National Medical Association convention in Washington, D.C., where he was presented with a Scroll of Honor; on August 7, taped a program for CBS Radio's "Let's Find Out," to be broadcast August 9; spoke for the Martha's Vineyard, Mass., branch on August 9; taped a program for WHN's "New York Speaks Out," on August 12; did taped interview for Oral History Project of John F. Kennedy Library; spoke in Boston, Mass., August 15 for the National Catholic Social Action Conference; August 18 at the Harvard University International Seminar sponsored by the Summer School of Arts, Sciences, and Education; appeared before the Committee on Platform and Resolutions of the Democratic National Convention in Washington, D.C., on August 19; and spoke that evening for Omega Psi Phi at its Forty-ninth Anniversary Founders' Banquet in Denver, Colo., and received the "Citizen of the Year" Award; attended the Democratic National Convention in Atlantic City, beginning August 21.

In addition to the above speaking engagements, the Secretary wrote articles for the *Saturday Review*, to be used in the early Fall; for the *New York Times* Magazine, which appeared on August 16; article on what Mrs. Eleanor Roosevelt meant to Negro Americans to be used in a special commemorative feature in the October *Ebony*; article for magazine to be distributed to some 10,000 lay leaders of the Catholic Church, to be distributed at the November convention of the National Association of Catholic Women; article for *McCalls* Magazine to be published in the November issue.

Republican and Democratic Conventions

On July 7 the Executive Secretary appeared before the Resolutions Committee of the Republican National Convention, in San Francisco, Calif., and urged the Republican Party to adopt a strong civil rights plank in its 1964 platform.

The Secretary appeared for the N.A.A.C.P. as well as the Leadership Conference of Civil Rights. He noted the support of Republicans in both houses of Congress for the Civil Rights Act of 1964 which could not have been passed, he said, without Republican support, and he urged the party to affirm the constitutionality of the Act and call for its vigorous enforcement, adequate appropriations to insure an effective and dedicated staff and provide for the expansion of the civil rights division of the Department of Justice.

The Secretary also noted the exclusion of Negroes from the Mississippi and other Southern state delegations for the first time in many Republican conventions and urged the convention to make unequivocally clear that the Republican party in every state must be open to all and that the party will refuse to recognize or to seat any state delegation chosen under a system of racial exclusion.

The Secretary's pleas for a strong civil rights plank were met by a very mild plank adopted by the convention, with no mention of Federal action.

As he did before the Republican Convention Platform committee, the Secretary called for "affirmation of the right of arrested civil rights demonstrators to trial in Federal courts and reasonable bail pending trial"; enactment of a law making "state, county, and city governments jointly liable in damages for misconduct of their officers"; establishment of "uniform standards for criminal defense . . . in state courts"; and abolition of "senatorial courtesy" as a device for denying Senate approval of appointment of "upright jurists, dedicated to the Federal protestations," to the Federal bench.

The Secretary urged that the Federal Government move at an accelerated pace on programs designed to broaden opportunities for the deprived segments of our population (the anti-poverty program), provide re-education, training in vocational skills, public works and health programs, slum clearance and improvement in the quality of schools.

He urged both parties to pledge action at the opening of the 89th Congress to assure:

1. A majority cloture rule in the Senate;
2. The twenty-one day rule and seven-day conference rule to overcome veto power of the House Rules Committee; and
3. Abolition of seniority as the sole qualification for committee chairmanships.

In addition, the Secretary called the attention of the Resolutions and Platform Committee of the Democratic Convention to the disfranchisement of some 900,000 Negro citizens in the State of Mississippi constituting approximately forty-three percent of the population, and in view of the fact that they have been denied participation in the process by which delegates to the National Convention are chosen, the Secretary urged that the delegates chosen by the Mississippi Freedom Party be seated. He also urged that the convention apply to all states a rule that hereafter the roster of the Democratic Party shall be open to all persons who subscribe to its principles, and that exclusion of such person will constitute a reason for denying seats to the offending delegation.

Hospital Aid to Mississippi Victims

In a wire to President Johnson on July 8, the Secretary joined with others in urging that the United States Government guarantee emergency treatment for civil rights workers who may suffer injury from Mississippi racists. The Secretary noted the shooting on July 6 of an eighteen-year-old girl attending a meeting in Moss Point, Miss., and the apprehension concerning expanded violence and risk of personal injury to civil rights workers in the state, and the likelihood that persons injured would not receive adequate medical attention. He asked that all available Federal medical facilities be made available to civil rights workers for emergency medical treatment.

On July 20, the Secretary received a letter from Lee C. White, Associate Special Counsel to the President, stating that "I have checked with the appropriate departments and agencies and am pleased to advise that under the existing policies of those Federal agencies which operate medical facilities treatment is available for emergency patients."

Pre-Convention Rally, Atlantic City, N.J.

On Sunday afternoon, August 23, just prior to the opening of the Democratic Convention, the N.A.A.C.P. held a parade and rally in Atlantic City on the grounds of Westside Memorial Building. Mayor Joseph Altman of Atlantic City welcomed the group. Speakers included the Executive Secretary, Representatives Roberts Nix of Philadelphia, and Adam Clayton Powell, New York City, Senator Harrison Williams of New Jersey, John Lewis of S.N.C.C., A. Philip Randolph, Rev. Ralph Abernathy, Aaron Henry, and Floyd McKissick of C.O.R.E.

Voter Registration

Intensifying the campaign to get out the vote, the Secretary has brought Miss Althea Simmons from the West Coast sub-regional office in Los Angeles, Calif. to serve as national coordinator of registration and voting for the period until Election Day in November and the follow-up required.

In addition, the Secretary on July 31 sent a memorandum to New York City branches calling attention to another Annual Convention resolution to oppose the candidacy of Senator Barry Goldwater for President. He urged branches to step up their registration campaign at once, making use of the New York City firehouses which have been made available for registration.

On August 12, following the finding of the bodies of the three civil rights workers in Mississippi, the Secretary wrote all branches and youth groups urging the greatest registration of Negro voters in history as the answer to the kind of action "that the states' rights candidate for the Presidency and his supporters would leave to the states, without any Federal action." "If the Federal Bureau of Investigation had not acted, these bodies would never have been found," he stated. ... "The Mississippi murderers must get an answer at the ballot box next November," the Secretary wrote.

Call to Major Civil Rights Organizations

On Wednesday, July 22, the Executive Secretary sent the following wire to the leaders of five major civil rights organizations, namely, Messrs. Martin Luther King, Jr., Southern Christian Leadership Conference; James L. Farmer, Congress of Racial Equality; Whitney M. Young, Jr., National Urban League; A. Philip Randolph, Negro American Labor Council; and John Lewis, Student Nonviolent Coordinating Committee:

Nothing could be plainer than that battle won imposes new challenges until final victory is achieved. The events of the past seventy-two hours, including the tragic violence in Harlem and the end of the Wallace candidacy for President, hard on the heels of the Goldwater nomination, are all linked together in ways that may produce the sternest challenge we have yet seen. The promise of the Civil Rights Act 1964 could well be diminished or nullified and a decade of increasingly violent and futile disorder ushered in if we do not play our hand coolly and intelligently. There is no safety in assumption that Goldwater cannot win the election. He can win it and he can be helped to win it if enough wrong moves are made. It is of the highest importance we take council at earliest moment to ensure that without modifying any essential position we do nothing to produce votes for Goldwater. None of us will knowingly jeopardize the prospects we have gained by such massive sacrifices and we can best ensure against such dangers by close and precise agreement among our organizations. I will call you within next three days to clear mutually acceptable date and place. . . .

The date of July 24 was agreed upon and this group met in the Willkie Building, N.A.A.C.P. headquarters, and four organizations agreed upon a program calling for increased political action, curtailment of mass demonstrations, and "justice and equality as well as law and order" in racially tense situations. The signees were Mr. Randolph, Rev. King, Mr. Young, and the Secretary. C.O.R.E. and S.N.C.C. said they could not sign.

In addition to those persons listed above, the conference was attended by Jack Greenberg of the N.A.A.C.P. Legal Defense and Educational Fund, Inc.; Bayard Rustin, deputy director of the March on Washington, and Cleveland Robinson, secretary-treasurer, District 65, Retail, Wholesale and Department Store Employee Union.

Immediately following the conference, a packed press conference was held in the Assembly Room of the Willkie Building, attended by all members of the group except Mr. Farmer, who had to leave before meeting the press.

The following statements were read to the press gathering by the Executive Secretary. Messrs. Farmer and Lewis refrained from signing these statements on the ground that such action required approval of the governing boards of the organizations they represent. Reporters of press, radio and television queried the leaders at length. The full texts of the two statements follow:

Political Action

We believe that developments since July 2, the date President Johnson signed the Civil Rights Act of 1964, warrant analysis by the organized civil rights groups and by all thoughtful unaffiliated civil rights advocates.

We call upon our members and supporters to utilize the months ahead to enlist voters, to expand the enforcement of the new Civil Rights Act, and to win new friends and new supporters for the civil rights cause which is not alone our cause, but the cause of America. Without the freedoms inherent in this cause neither we nor our country will be free.

Our own estimate of the present situation is that it presents such a serious threat to the implementation of the Civil Rights Act and to subsequent expansion of civil rights gains that we recommend a voluntary, temporary alteration in strategy and procedure.

Now we propose a temporary change of emphasis and tactic, because we sincerely believe that the major energy of the civil rights forces should be used to encourage the Negro people, North and South, to register and to vote. The greatest need in this period is for political action.

We, therefore, propose, and call upon our members voluntarily to observe a broad curtailment, if not total, moratorium of all mass marches, mass picketing and mass demonstrations until their election day, next November 3.

Such a move is not without precedent, since each of our organizations, at one time or another, in one local struggle or another, has voluntarily agreed to call off demonstrations for varying periods of time in order to make progress toward a goal.

In our view the election contest which is shaping up is a more imperative reason for a moratorium on demonstrations than any local or state condition that has confronted our forces heretofore.

The platform adopted under the Goldwater forces at the Republican convention in San Francisco is a states' rights platform, chosen at the very time Mississippi was exhibiting to a shocked nation the callous repression, the violence and death which mark the operation of the states' rights theory in the human rights field.

The proponents of liberalizing the civil rights plank of the platform to include specific mention of the obligation of the Federal Government were hooted down.

The platform as adopted called for "maximum restraint" of Federal "intrusions into matters more productively left to the individual."

We believe racism has been injected into the campaign by the Goldwater forces. The Senator himself maintains his position that civil rights matters should be left to the states—clear enough language for any Negro American.

Racial Conflicts

We wish to register our serious concern with the recent riots which have taken place in several urban areas. We would like to once again go on record as strongly opposing looting, vandalism, or any type of criminal activity and urge the cooperation and support of local leaders toward the elimination of this type of activity which damages both the community and the civil rights movement.

On the other hand we wish to draw a sharp distinction between the above named activity and legitimate protest effort by denied and desperate citizens seeking relief.

In meeting these situations we call for more socially sensitive police action, for machinery, for continuing communication, and local civilian review.

We suggest that leadership must seek in these situations justice and equality as well as law and order. Responsible Negro leadership needs desperately responsive white leadership as it relates to jobs, improved housing, and educational opportunities.

The established civil rights organization has by word, deed and constitution consistently rejected the participation of extremist groups such as communists.

Board Members Study Mississippi Conditions

In accordance with action of the Board of Directors at its June meeting in Washington, D.C., a seven-man committee under the chairmanship of D. H. Claude Hudson of Los Angeles, Calif., made a four-day tour of trouble spots in the state of Mississippi, beginning July 6.

Other members of the committee were: Alfred Baker Lewis, Greenwich, Conn.; John F. Davis, East Orange, N.J.; Chester I. Lewis, Wichita, Kan.; Kivie Kaplan, Boston, Mass.; L. Joseph Overton, New York City; and Dr. Eugene T. Reed, Amityville, L.I., N.Y.

On arrival in Jackson, Miss., Sunday evening, July 5, the committee issued a statement setting forth the purpose for its visit, namely, to observe and learn at first hand the exact status of the constitutional and human rights of Negro citizens in the state in regard to their right to vote, their personal and physical security from violence, from private citizens and the police, and in other respects as well.

The committee's statement expressed particular concern about breakdown of law enforcement in the Philadelphia area; the mysterious disappearance of the three young civil rights workers, and the unpunished beatings and assaults upon law-abiding citizens throughout the state, as well as the wanton destruction of property.

Armed with the new Civil Rights Act, the committee members broke the color bar at two Jackson hotels, a motel and a restaurant, checking into the Sun-N-Sand Motel, the King Edward Hotel, and the Heidelberg Hotel.

However, a prepared statement was read by Chester I. Lewis, Esq., of Wichita, Kan., in the first floor lobby of the Capitol in Jackson, Miss.

As a result of the committee's investigation, a wire was sent to Dr. John A. Hannah, Chairman of the U.S. Commission on Civil Rights July 8 urging that hearings be held in Mississippi on the denial of constitutional rights to Negro citizens in the state.

A news conference marking the conclusion of the tour was held on July 9 at the airport in Memphis, Tenn., at which time a five-point program proposed by the committee was announced, and recommended to the President and the Congress of the United States, as follows:

1. That the Federal Government take over the administration of the State of Mississippi under provisions of Article IV, Section 4, of the U.S. Constitution;
2. That the U.S. Commission on Civil Rights immediately start hearings in Mississippi on the breakdown of law and order and deprivation of the basic civil rights of Negro citizens:

3. That the Department of Justice act promptly on the many complaints of civil rights violations to that Department;

4. That the government dispatch to Mississippi a sufficient number of Federal representatives—FBI agents, marshals, and others—to protect the safety and lives of potential victims of the state's racism.

A conference was held with the Attorney General Robert F. Kennedy at which time the committee presented its findings and recommendations.

National Office staff members Gloster B. Current, Maurice White, and Robert L. Carter accompanied the Board committee on its tour.

Signing of Civil Rights Bill

On July 2 the Executive Secretary issued the following statement through the Association's press releases after joining with others at the White House ceremony at which the President signed the bill:

"The signing of the Civil Rights Act of 1964 by President Johnson represents the culmination of decades of efforts by the N.A.A.C.P. and many other organizations and individuals to secure congressional recognition of and action in behalf of the Negro's basic citizenship rights. It is both an end and a beginning; an end to the Federal Government's hands-off policy; a beginning of an era of Federally-protected rights for all citizen."

At our Fifty-ninth Annual Conference in Washington last week, we developed an implementation plan involving conferences with local officials and businessmen, an educational program and testing. The resolution adopted by our 2,180 delegates directed our 1,845 local units in forty-nine states to move immediately to seek compliance with the new law, particularly in those states for which the provisions of the law are new, such as public accommodations.

As important as is this Magna Carta of Human Rights, it does not mean that the struggle for full freedom is over. No law, or court decision, is self-implementing. We in the National Association for the Advancement of Colored People hope for widespread voluntary compliance. We know, however, that there will be hard core resistance in some communities. Our Association is prepared to meet this test and to press for implementation even in the face of stubborn resistance.

The Civil Rights Act of 1964 is the product of the joint efforts of many dedicated persons and of the inexorable forces of history. Many individuals, private citizens as well as public officials, Republican and Democrats alike, contributed to this historic day. Foremost among these have been Presidents John F. Kennedy and Lyndon Baines Johnson; and the Senate and House leadership: Senators Mike Mansfield, Everett McKinley Dirksen, Hubert Humphrey, Thomas Kuchel, and Congressmen John McCormack, Carl Albert, Charles Halleck, Emanuel Celler, William M. McCulloch, Clarence J. Brown, and Richard Bolling.

There was also the active, effective and dependable support of organized religion involving the three major faiths; of the A.F.L.-C.I.O. and its constituent unions; of many women's organizations, fraternal orders and civic associations, all working to achieve today's triumph.

Thanks for Cloture

On June 11 the Secretary wrote to the seventy-one senators—twenty-seven Republican and forty-four Democratic—who voted June 10 to invoke cloture, thereby ending the seventy-four day Senate debate on the civil rights bill.

Death of Senator Clair Engle

On July 31 the Secretary wired Mrs. Claire Engle on behalf of the officers and members of the Association, extending deep sympathy in the death of her husband. The Secretary stated:

> He will be remembered for countless service and evidences of personal integrity, but for none more so than his personal appearances in June 1964 to vote for cloture on the civil rights bill and then to vote for the bill itself. These were acts of courage and determination in the highest tradition of service to mankind in a crucial and historic hour. Senator Engle could have remained away on both questions and had his view point prevail, but in characteristic fashion he chose to record his convictions for history in a personal appearance despite his illness . . .

Roy Wilkins, Secretary
August 1964

Report of the Executive Director for the Board Meeting of October 1964

Immediately following a tour of West Coast branches (see September report), on October 2, the Executive Director* left the same day for a two-week vacation, returning to the office on October 16.

Speaking Engagements

On returning to the office he filled engagements as follows: October 16, Camden, N.J., for the Camden Branch in connection with its membership drive; October 18 in Orangeburg, S.C., at the South Carolina State Conference closing mass meeting; October 20 in Purchase, N.Y., for Manhattanville College of the Sacred Heart where he was cited as a "Leader, patriot, and man of faith," and where he received an honorary degree of Doctor of Laws; Detroit, Mich., October 21, to confer with the branch officers on financial problems; October 24, Washington, Pa., at the

---

*Title Secretary was changed in September 1964 to Executive Director.

Freedom Fund Dinner of the state conference during its Thirtieth Annual Meeting; October 25, Dillard in New Orleans, La., where he addressed the Founders Day observance; October 28, Fall Festival of the Bridgeport, Stratford, Conn., Branch; October 29, Newark, N.J., at the Freedom Fund Dinner celebrating the branch's Fiftieth year; October 31, Birmingham, Ala., reorganization rally for city and county representatives to re-launch N.A.A.C.P. in Alabama after eight years of silence under an injunction; November 1 at the Third Annual Freedom Fund Dinner of the St. Louis Branch, celebrating the branch's Fiftieth Anniversary, and the bi-centennial of St. Louis.

"Moral Decay" Film

On October 21 the Executive Director wired Robert W. Sarnoff, Chairman of the Board of NBC, expressing the dismay of the N.A.A.C.P. over the purchase of air time by the Goldwater-Miller Citizens Committee to show a "moral decay" film some parts of which were included to arouse anti-Negro feeling. Copy of the wire was also sent to Dean Burch, chairman of the Republican National Committee.

The text of the wire follows:

Published reports whose accuracy is acknowledged by citizens for Goldwater-Miller make it plain that "moral decay" film scheduled for NBC showing tomorrow is unprincipled attempt to arouse anti-Negro feeling and to play upon anxieties of some white people regarding alleged criminality and irresponsibility of Negro citizens. This film wraps up in a bundle entire Goldwater strategy in this area, namely, to depict Negroes as threat to community and, by catering to fear and ignorance and prejudice to win votes on lowest possible level. We are shocked and dismayed that National Broadcasting Company would lend itself to spread this kind of poison. Result can only be to increase racial tensions and to make more difficult the business of achieving racial justice.

The Executive Director also wired approximately one hundred branches of the Association calling attention to the broadcast and urging them to monitor their local N.B.C. outlet for this broadcast and make known their outrage "at this attempt to step up racial unrest." At the last minute the film was withdrawn from network showing, but was sent to local committees to use on local TV stations.

On October 27 the Director received a letter from Robert D. Kasmire, vice president of NBC, setting forth the NBC point of view in the matter, as follows:

In the interest of free and unobstructed political expression and discussion N.B.C. does not censor material presented by the campaign organizations in behalf of their candidates. We do, however, reserve the right to question material that might be defamatory or morally improper for family viewing, and in that connection we insisted that certain material we judged to be unduly suggestive be edited from *Choice* when it was presented for broadcast on our facilities. The sponsoring organization agreed to these excisions, but, then, as you know, on its own initiative decided to withdraw the film before broadcast.

Congratulations to Dr. King

On October 14, upon announcement of the selection of Dr. Martin Luther King [Jr.] as recipient of the Nobel Peace Prize, a wire was sent on behalf of the Association of congratulations to Dr. King and stating in part, "All Americans, irrespective of race, religion, or region of residence can justly take pride in the international recognition accorded your dedication and fruitful efforts to achieve racial harmony rooted in equal justice for all Americans."

Urge Clemency for Condemned South Africans

On October 14, a wire was sent to Secretary of State Dean Rusk in the name of the Executive Director respectfully urging that the U.S. Government bring to bear its influence in behalf of clemency for three Africans, namely, Vuysile Mini, Zinakele Kaba, and Wilson Khayingo, under death sentence in the Union of South Africa. "The weight of evidence against them (is) questionable under that country's repressive system and in any case their execution could serve no purpose other than cruel vengeance," the Director wrote.

A reply dated October 23 from Henry J. Tasca, Acting Assistant Secretary of State for African Affairs, re-affirmed the government's opposition to apartheid, to repressive legislation and political trials, and said that "the government has endeavored to use the influence of the United States, wherever possible, to moderate these practices." Mr. Tasca added that these three men "were charged and found guilty among other things, of murder of a state witness. Because any expression by us in a case such as this could be interpreted by South Africa as interference in that country's internal judicial processes, the Department must abstain from taking any action which might weaken its position and its efforts to moderate policies of apartheid."

Keating–Kennedy Campaign

On October 26, the Executive Director sent a letter to all New York State branch presidents clarifying the N.A.A.C.P.'s position on the New York State senatorial campaign.

The Secretary noted that (1) the New York State Conference in convention declined to endorse either Senator Keating or former Attorney General Robert Kennedy, (2) that the newly-elected president of the New York State Conference has endorsed Senator Keating but stated it as his personal choice, and (3) that Charles Evers, state secretary of the N.A.A.C.P. in Mississippi has published a written endorsement of Robert Kennedy, urging his election. Despite these endorsements by Messrs. Booth and Evers, the Director noted these do not represent official N.A.A.C.P. policy.

The Director set forth the long and excellent record of Senator Keating in support of civil rights legislation, as well as the activity on behalf of the civil rights particularly in the matter of Negro voting rights, and in the drafting of the Civil Rights Act of 1964, of former Attorney General Robert Kennedy, and stated that New York State Negro voters must make up their own minds how they will vote on these two men "Both of whom have excellent records on the civil rights issue. . . ."

Support of Candidates Who Voted for Civil Rights Bill

In response to appeals from Congressmen who had voted for the Civil Rights Bill and who wanted their districts reminded of their action, the Director sent letters to the districts of Rep. Milton J. Glenn in New Jersey and Rep. William McCulloch in Ohio. In Rep. McCulloch's case, the letter lauded his key role as floor manager of the Republican side for the bill and his strong testimony for it before the Judiciary Committee. Rep. McCulloch was re-elected, Rep. Glenn did not make it.

Roy Wilkins, Executive Director
November 8, 1964

Report of the Executive Director for the Board Meeting of March 1965

Speaking Engagements

During the month of March, the Executive Director continued to fill speaking engagements, and appear on radio and television, as follows:

On March 1, he testified before the Senate Rules Committee in Washington, D.C., on revision of Rule 22; on March 2, also in Washington, D.C., conferred with President Lyndon B. Johnson on voting legislation, with Vice President Humphrey and Attorney General Katzenback on the same subject, and on March 3 with Secretary of State Rusk with reference to the United States' policy on Africa. On March 6, spoke in Danbury, Conn., at a branch fund-raising affair; on March 7, he accepted the Guardian's (N.Y.C. Police) Ninth Annual Achievement Award in Brooklyn, N.Y.; on March 12 spoke for the Dayton, Ohio, Branch banquet; on March 14, spoke at the invitation of our branch president's at the city's memorial service in Casper, Wyo., for Rev. James J. Reeb; Unitarian minister fatally beaten in Selma, Ala.; attended funeral services for Board member Mrs. Daisy Lampkin in Pittsburgh on March 15; was present in Washington, D.C., on March 15 (night) for the President's message on voting rights to the Joint Houses of Congress; spoke at a rally March 18 under the auspices of the Brooklyn, N.Y., branch to raise funds for the defense of George Whitmore; on March 20, presided at a luncheon meeting for African diplomats in Washington, D.C., of the American Negro Leadership Conference on Civil Rights in connection with the voting rights bill in the afternoon and attended the Gridiron Club reception in the evening; on March 23 spoke at the Advertising and Publishing Lunch-O-Ree, Boy Scouts of America, at the Waldorf, in New York City, and on March 24 testified before the sub-committee of the House Judiciary Committee in Washington, D.C., on the voting rights bill; spoke March 25, in Montgomery, Ala., at the meeting on the State Capitol at the conclusion of the Selma-to-Montgomery March; spoke March 27 at Notre Dame University Law School, participating in their symposium on the topic of "Violence in the Streets" in 1964; taped a program for Victor Riesel's WEVD show on March 29; attended the Mayor's luncheon for astronauts Virgil Grissom and John Young, at the Waldorf-Astoria on March 29; attended funeral services for Mrs. Viola Liuzzo in Detroit, Mich., on March 30.

Alabama Voting Drive—March 7 Brutality

On March 7, Negro citizens in Selma, Alabama, engaged in a peaceful and orderly march to protest denial of their rights to vote, were set upon by Alabama State Troopers and a sheriff's mounted posse, using tear gas and clubs, and beaten brutally. The march and the attack were televised.

At its meeting on March 8, the Executive Committee considered the matter and passed the following resolution:

Like millions of other Americans, white and black, the members of the Executive Committee of the National Board of Directors of the N.A.A.C.P. are outraged at the Gestapo-like brutality of Alabama State Troopers, on Sunday, March 7, 1965, acting on orders of Governor George C. Wallace. The vicious misuse of state forces to prevent peaceable assembly and exercise of the right to petition for a redress of grievances by American citizens, was plainly in violation of both Federal and State law.

No responsible Federal official has indicated any intention on the part of the United States Government to enforce the plain provisions of Title 18, Sections 241 & 242 of the United States Code which provide for a fine or imprisonment or both for any action or conspiracy to deprive United States citizens of rights protected by laws of the United States. The right of peaceable assembly and other rights that have been protected by the Constitution of the United States since the founding of this republic. It is difficult to conceive of more patent violation of Section 214 & 242 than that which took place on that bloody Sunday in Selma, March 7.

Under these circumstances, we are as appalled by the fact that the Federal Government failed to take action against the Governor, State

Police, the Sheriffs, and deputies of Selma, as we are at the senseless violation which these officials perpetrated. It is ironic that the report of these carefully planned attacks on the Negro citizens should share the spotlight with the landing of the of the U.S. Marines in Viet Nam, sent to protect the Vietnamese against Communist aggression.

For more than a half-century the N.A.A.C.P. and other organizations have adhered to the position that the guarantees of individual liberties and rights could be provided and secured through the democratic process and within the United States legal and political system. Even when detractors of the American system both at home and abroad, either of the left or the right, were urging the contrary, thoughtful and responsible leadership in the N.A.A.C.P. defended the American system and exerted every effort in the courts, the polls, before the Congress, and before state legislatures and in the arena of public opinion—in short, making use of all the lawful means available to free citizens of a democracy to secure for the Negroes their inalienable rights.

It was demonstrated in Selma, on Sunday, March 7, 1965, that in the State of Alabama these devices will not work without the intervention of the Federal Government. If Federal authority will not avail because justice will not convict, then the rights of Selma Negroes must be protected by the Federal troops. If Federal troops are not made available to protect the rights of Negroes, then the American people are faced with terrible alternatives. Like the citizens of Nazi-occupied France, Holland, Belgium, Denmark, and Norway, Negroes must either submit to the heels of their oppressors or they must organize, underground, to protect themselves from the oppression of Governor Wallace and his storm troopers.

The Executive Committee of the Board calls upon the President of the United States to direct the responsible officers of government to take appropriate action so that there shall be no repetition of that bloody Sunday, in Selma, Alabama.

Immediately after the meeting, the Executive Director held a press conference since all media had been seeking comments on Selma. All three television networks, N.B.C., A.B.C., and C.B.S., many radio reporters with tape recorders, both wire services and most New York dailies, plus W.P.I.X., the Daily News T.V. station, were present. The Executive Director stressed the N.A.A.C.P.'s outrage over the attack by the troopers in Selma upon the peaceful men, women, and children marchers. He underscored the declaration of the resolution that if the Federal Government did not protect Negro citizens, self-protection would be devised, "underground or aboveground." Letters, telegrams, telephone calls, and newspaper clippings arriving later indicated this to be one of the most effective and overwhelmingly approved press conferences held since the one last July to announce a moratorium on demonstrations during the election campaign.

In accordance with action of the Executive Committee, wires were sent to the President and to the Attorney General calling for Federal Intervention and the dispatch of Federal troops to Selma, in the name of the Chairman of the Board.

A wire was also sent to Alabama Attorney General Richmond H. Flowers calling upon him "to invoke state criminal sanctions against those guilty of violating the rights of Negro citizens."

Citizens of Selma petitioned the Federal District Court for a temporary restraining order to prevent Governor Wallace and his deputies from interfering with their right to march.

However, on March 9, Judge Frank M. Johnson, Jr., denied the motion for a restraining order and issued a temporary injunction against marches until a hearing on the matter was held. He set the hearing for March 11.

The Executive Director issued the following statement with reference to the temporary injunction:

The order this morning of Federal Judge Frank Johnson restraining the Negro plaintiffs from marching today from Selma to Montgomery, Ala., placed the President of the United States in an untenable political position.

In effect, the court order gives the support of the Federal Government and its law officers to the edict of Governor George C. Wallace of Alabama that the marchers shall not march.

Under the order, Federal Marshals would be ranged shoulder to shoulder with the blue-helmeted Wallace troopers and would be compelled to join them in halting the march.

Judge Johnson followed the classic pattern of restraining the Negroes who seek their rights instead of the state which has moved brutally to deprive them.

The significant difference here in applying this time-worn formula is that the Federal Government has been made a partner—even if temporarily—of the Wallace storm trooper machine.

The Executive Director also made statements for Mutual Broadcasting Company, did a question-and-answer interview for W.O.R. radio, and an interview for W.M.C.A. with reference to the injunction.

Selma-to-Montgomery, Ala.

Following five days of hearings, Federal District Judge Frank M. Johnson, Jr., issued an injunction ordering Governor Wallace and other Alabama officials to refrain from "harassing or threatening" the protest marchers and to extend to them full police protection from hostile whites. He approved in full the plan for the march which was presented to court.

The March from Selma to Montgomery began on Sunday, March 21, and ended at the State Capitol in mass rally on March 25. The Executive Director was present and marched the final four miles from St. Judes, on the outskirts of Montgomery, to the State Capitol rally where an estimated 10,000 persons were gathered. He addressed the marchers along with others including Dr. Bunche, A. Philip Randolph, Whitney Young, James Farmer and Dr. King.

The marchers were protected on the fifty-mile trip from Selma to Montgomery by the Alabama National Guard, which had been federalized and by troops from the 720 M.P. Battalion from Ft. Hood, Texas, the 503 M.P. Battalion from Ft. Bragg, N.C., and 1,000 men standing by at Fort Benning, Ga.

Death of Jimmie Lee Jackson, Rev. James Reeb, and Mrs. Viola Liuzzo

On March 3 the Executive Director wired Mrs. Viola Jackson, mother of Jimmie Lee Jackson, slain in Dallas County, Ala., by an Alabama State trooper, expressing sympathy and condolences on behalf of the Association in the tragic loss of her son. The Director attended and delivered a eulogy at memorial services for Rev. James Reeb, Unitarian minister fatally beaten in Selma, Ala., held in his home town of Casper, Wyoming, March 14. On March 26, the Director wired Mr. Anthony Liuzzo expressing the Association's sympathy in the slaying of his wife, shot to death while driving her car along the highway between Selma and Montgomery. Mrs. Liuzzo, who had participated in the march earlier, was transporting marchers back to Selma. The Director also attended funeral services for Mrs. Liuzzo on March 30 in Detroit. She was [a] member of the Detroit branch.

Voting Rights Bill—President's Message to Congress

On March 16 the Executive Director wired President Lyndon B. Johnson thanking him for his speech delivered to a joint session of Congress and the nation via television and radio on Monday night, March 15:

> Thank you for your eloquent and history—making message of last night. It was a plea to your fellow Americans to vindicate their personal and their country's ideals. It will rank as momentous at the summit in the life of our nation and in the interpretation by a President of our high national purpose. We salute your reiterated pledge to use your chance as president to eradicate the condition pictured in your warm and moving lines: "And somehow you never forget what poverty and hatred can do when you see its scars on the hopeful face of a young child." The National Association for the Advancement of Colored People continues its dedication to the task of making those scars but a haunting memory and offers its full support to the President in this endeavor.

At a press conference held March 16 at National Office Headquarters the Executive Director again praised the President for his message and expressed confidence in his sincerity with respect to passage of the voting rights bill.

Wire to Sponsors of Bill

The Executive Director wired Senators Paul H. Douglas (D.Ill.) and Clifford Case (R.N.J.), who introduced a voting rights bill, expressing appreciation of the introduction of a bipartisan bill in line with the President's message. He expressed the hope that the legislation "which emerges will reflect in detail the President's and your own concern that obstacles to the participation of every voter in elections be demolished speedily through a simplified and effective remedy in law for the ills that now beset the prospective Negro voter."

Testimony Before Sub-Committee of House
Judiciary Committee

On March 24 the Executive Director testified for the N.A.A.C.P. and the Leadership Conference on Civil Rights, of which he is chairman, before the sub-committee of the House Judiciary Committee, and urged a stronger voting rights bill than the bill presently before the Congress.

The present bill needs to be strengthened by provisions requiring:

Total elimination of the poll tax as a requirement for voting in state and local elections as well as in Federal elections;

Deletion of the present bill's requirement that a prospective registrant apply to a state official before going to a Federal registrar or examiner to register;

Extended coverage of the registrar or examiner provisions of [the] bill to include all persons wrongfully denied the right to vote, regardless of location; and

Maximum protection for registered voters and prospective registrants against economic and physical intimidation and coercion.

The Executive Director noted that Republicans in both houses of Congress and outside of Congress have urged strong legislation to correct voting discrimination.

Roy Wilkins, Executive Director
March 1965

Report of the Executive Director for the
Board Meeting of June, July, and August 1965

Due to absence from the office on vacation of several National Office staff members, much of the time of the Executive Director was of necessity spent handling mail, administrative details, and other work usually handled by other staff.

Weekend Conference in Birmingham

During the summer months plans went forward for the special weekend conference scheduled for September 11–12 in Birmingham, Ala., culminating the summer voter-registration project.

In accordance with action of the Board of its Denver, Colo., meeting, the program has been expanded and includes pre-conference registration of delegates on Friday, September 10, and a meeting of the National Youth Work Committee with members of the Board and staff.

On Saturday, September 11, registration of delegates will continue and there will be a plenary session in the morning, workshops scheduled for the afternoon, and a Human Rights Dinner and Youth Dinner and Dance in the evening.

The mass rally is scheduled for Sunday afternoon, presided over by the Chairman of the Board and addressed by U.N. Undersecretary Ralph Bunche.

The September meeting of the Board is scheduled for 9 A.M. on Monday, September 13.

Communications have gone to all Board members and vice-presidents and to all units of the Association urging that delegates attend. Headquarters for the conference will be the L. R. Hall Auditorium. The Board of Directors will meet at the Parliament House Motor Hotel.

Visit of British Parliamentary Delegation

Seven members of the British Parliament visited the Executive Director at the National Office on June 23 at which time the Director, with other members of the staff, explained the work of the N.A.A.C.P. and discussed the civil rights issue, in which they expressed considerable interest, including the effectiveness of fair employment and public accommodations legislation, the role of the Congress in assuring equal opportunity, the significance of the Black Muslims, and prospects for the future.

Memorial Service for Ambassador Stevenson

On July 19 the Director attended memorial services for Ambassador Adlai Stevenson in the General Assembly Hall of the U.N.

Meeting with President Johnson

On August 3, the Director attended a meeting with President Johnson, the first in a series of discussions with civil rights leaders the President will have leading up to a White House Conference on civil rights some time this fall.

During the conference, the Director called attention to the fact that there are only nine Negroes among 4,000 midshipmen enrolled at the U.S. Naval Academy at Annapolis, Md.

The President thereafter directed Defense Department officials to look into the matter and make a report to him.

Personnel Changes

Former Field Secretary Leonard Carter has taken over his duties as West Coast Regional Director of the N.A.A.C.P., following Mrs. Pittman's appointment as West Coast fundraiser for the N.A.A.C.P. Special Contribution Fund.

Mr. Eugene Hampton, Jr., formerly of Davenport, Iowa, has been appointed as Director of Youth Programs, to fill the vacancy left when Mr. Laplois Ashford resigned to become Deputy Commissioner of Public Safety in Rochester, N.Y.

Mr. Hampton, who has done work toward his Masters Degree at the Universities of Iowa and Washington, has been active in the Davenport Branch and youth council and has a broad background in the civil rights movement. He is a graduate civil engineer from Tennessee A. & I. College.

U.S. Policy in Vietnam

On July 30, the Executive Director sent a memorandum to all local units of the Association warning that "organized units of the N.A.A.C.P. have no authority" for participating in the assembly of Underrepresented People called for Washington, D.C., August 6–9. While the call includes certain civil rights issues, the main emphasis is on demonstrating in opposition to U.S. policy in Vietnam.

The memorandum requested that N.A.A.C.P. leaders, "mindful that it is difficult for the public to disassociate them from the organization," heed this advice. He noted that the N.A.A.C.P. has not passed any resolution opposing U.S. policy in Vietnam nor has it ever called for crashing the White House or taking over the Capitol.

The full text of the memorandum was released to the press through N.A.A.C.P. releases of August 4, 1965.

Death of Judge Walden

A wire expressing the sympathy of the Association at the death of Judge A. T. Walden on July 2, 1965, was sent to his widow by the Executive Director. Judge Walden had served as a member of the Board of Directors of the Association and at the time of his death was a vice president and member of the National Legal Committee.

The Director cited Judge Walden as a "stalwart over the decades in the ongoing effort for human rights. He was an outstanding practitioner of his profession of the law and aided mightily in winning the legal definitions that improved the status of his people. . . . Throughout a long lifetime of service to his people, to his city and state and to his country, he earned the respect and affection he so richly deserved."

The Director of Public Relations represented the Association at the funeral services for Judge Walden at Wheat Street Baptist Church in Atlanta on July 7.

Convention Greetings

On July 20, the Executive Director sent greetings and assurance of continued cooperation to the National Urban League's 1968 Annual Conference at Miami Beach, Florida. The Director, in a letter to Whitney Young, Jr., stated: "In the difficult and demanding tasks of using the new legislative tools now available, of sharpening the preparation necessary to occupy the new openings which have been won and of stabilizing Negro family life, the N.A.A.C.P. looks forward to mutual and complementary activity toward the attainment of our common goals."

On August 6, the Executive Director sent greetings and best wishes for a fruitful convention to the Southern Christian Leadership Conference holding its ninth annual convention in Birmingham, Alabama, "the site of your massive and portentous assault upon the citadel of segregation in 1963."

Los Angeles Riot

During the five days of rioting in Los Angeles [that] erupted on Wednesday evening, August 11, the Executive Director was widely interviewed and quoted.

He was quoted by the New York dailies, by AP, and UPI. Three New York radio stations, the national television networks of A.B.C., N.B.C., and C.B.S. carried statements by the Director. He also made a direct broadcast over long distance telephone from his home to the C.B.S. radio station in Los Angeles which was carried live on the spot from his home.

In his statements the Director recognized the just grievance of Negro citizens in Los Angeles, the deep problems existing which have been given only superficial attention, and the unsympathetic police chief and department under Chief William Parker. He called for establishment of a bi-racial, non-partisan, uninfluenced commission to make a frank and fearless study of the causes that led to the outbreak and to make recommendations to prevent a recurrence.

However, rioting and looting must be put down with whatever is necessary as the first necessity toward any resolution of the problem, he said: "The civil rights cause does not, cannot, and will not condone, or in any fashion approve, rioting and looting as a weapon to secure citizenship rights."

The Director also wired Dick Gregory on August 19 quoting the statement attributed to him and stating that "because it is inconceivable to us that you could have made any such flatly untrue statements about the N.A.A.C.P., please let us hear from you immediately."

Mr. Gregory telephoned that his remarks over the telephone to Mr. Pearson had been misinterpreted. Mr. Pearson wrote that he knew of the N.A.A.C.P.'s work and reputation from his contacts with the late Walter White, but he was just quoting Mr. Gregory.

Roy Wilkins, Executive Director
August 1965

Report of the Executive Director for the Board Meeting of January–March 1971

Speaking and Other Engagements

On January 3, the Executive Director installed officers of the New York (Harlem) Branch; taped a five-minute statement on Martin Luther King, Jr. for WFAS Radio station on January 5; taped "Black Experience" in St. Louis; attended St. Louis Branch Founders Day Luncheon January 16; presented life membership plaque to Rt. Rev. F. J. Mugavero, Bishop of Brooklyn, at his office in Brooklyn on January 18; addressed session of the National Baptist Convention in Hot Springs, Ark. on January 20; attended annual meeting of Leadership Conference on Civil Rights in Washington, D.C., January 25; met with Secretary Romney of H.U.D. on January 28; and on January 31, spoke at dedication of new building which houses Southeast Regional Office in Atlanta, Ga.

During the month of February the Executive Director spoke for the Roosevelt, Long Island, Public Schools Parents Association on February 2; attended press conference re: jailing of Rev. Jesse Jackson of Operation Breadbasket for A&P boycott on February 5; main speaker at Lansing, Mich. Branch Freedom Fund Dinner, February 7; spoke at Education Conference at the University of North Carolina, Chapel Hill, N.C., under the auspices of N.A.A.C.P. College Chapter and others, on February 13; conferred with Mrs. Vincent Astor and Associates on possible foundation aid to Special Contribution Fund on February 19; and on February 23, conferred with the Carnegie Foundation on same subject. On February 24, with other Negro leaders attended White House meeting with Secretary Romney on revenue-sharing; spoke at meeting of the New Bedford, Mass. Branch on February 28.

The Executive Director filled the following engagements in March; Visiting Committee of Vanderbilt University School of Law in Nashville, Tenn., March 5–6; reception for Dr. Benjamin Mays in honor of his book *Born to Rebel* on March 12 in New York City; Gridiron Dinner in Washington, D.C., March 13; main speaker at Founders' Dinner of Oranges-Maplewood, N.J., Branch in Newark, N.J. on March 14; chaired meeting of Interracial Colloquy on March 15; on March 17; met with David Newsom and Beverly Carter, Assistant Secretary and Deputy Assistant Secretary of state for Africa, respectively, at luncheon arranged by Phelps-Stokes Fund; Executive Committee meeting of the Leadership Conference for Civil Rights in New York City on March 23; attended press conference held at National Office on March 25 disclosing suit Association has filed against the Town of Oyster Bay for its restrictive zoning policy; addressed Bay Area against the Town of Oyster Bay for its restrictive zoning policy; addressed Bay Area Life Membership Dinner in Oakland, Calif., on March 27; spoke for Tacoma, Wash., Branch on March 29; spoke at Breakfast sponsored by the Tacoma Chapter of Links, Inc., on March 30.

Angela Davis

The Association released the text of a resolution calling for a fair trial for Miss Angela Davis, adopted at the Board's quarterly meeting on January 11. (The full text of the resolution appears in the minutes of that meeting.)

Dwight D. Folsom

The Association called upon Governor Nelson A. Rockefeller to refuse to permit a seventeen-year-old Negro to be extradited to the State of Mississippi. In a letter to Governor Rockefeller dated February 2, the Executive Director cited a number of irregularities in the case and asked that the Governor consider revocation of the warrant for Dwight D. Folsom's arrest. The alleged crime took place last April. The Association urged:

> that the circumstances attending the youth's arrest and detainment without bail, the procedural irregularities which have occurred in the New York Court, the shameful and improper conduct of the Mississippi authorities, and the certain fate which this black youth faces upon his extradition be carefully considered and that this state refuse to extradite Dwight Folsom under these circumstances.

White House Briefings on Revenue-Sharing

The Executive Director was one of seven leaders attending a two-hour briefing on President Nixon's proposal for revenue-sharing. The briefing was chaired by Secretary George Romney, with discussion by John Ehrlichman, aide to the President, and a fifteen minute visit by the President. The Executive Director advised that the President's proposal for revenue-sharing deserves careful study by Negro voters, even though they have been burned many times by the funneling of unrestricted Federal funds to the States. There must be safeguards, he said, to see that the unrestricted billions of dollars go fairly, in each state, to all citizens without discrimination.

Others attending the White House Conference were Whitney M. Young, Jr., Executive Director, National Urban League, Miss Dorothy Height, President, N.C.N.W., Berkely Burrell, President, National Business League, Mrs. Cernoria Johnson, Urban League's District of Columbia office, and Mayors Richard G. Hatcher of Gary, Indiana, and Robert Blackwell of Highland Park, Michigan.

Radio Corporation of America

The Executive Director announced the Association's support of efforts to force a delay in the proposed removal of the corporate headquarters of Radio Corporation of America from New York City and Camden, New Jersey, to New Canaan, Conn.

The original complaint, which the N.A.A.C.P. is supporting, was filed by the Suburban Action Institute of White Plains, New York, with the Federal Equal Employment Opportunity Commission. The Executive Director said the N.A.A.C.P. believes that R.C.A. must secure irrevocable commitments from New Canaan officials that the town will rezone sufficient land for housing to be used by lower-income families presently living in the area. Housing must be provided also to accommodate the needs of R.C.A.'s black and other minority group employees affected by the proposed move.

In a related action, to oppose and eliminate "forced integration" in white suburbs, the executive Director also announced the Association's support of a package of bills being introduced in the New York State Legislature by Assemblyman Franz S. Leichter.

Death of Whitney M. Young, Jr.

The Executive Director issued the following statement on the death of Whitney M. Young, Jr.:

> The tragic and untimely death of Whitney M. Young, Jr., removes from the front ranks of the nation's freedom fighters one of the most dynamic and effective leaders in this struggle for human dignity. As Executive Director of the National Urban League, Whitney Young infused that 61-year-old organization with a new sense of urgency in the struggle and created a new image of vigor for an organization which had a traditional image. He brought to the crusade dedication, energy, personal charm, and an extraordinary talent. We who were privileged to know him and to work with him will miss his exuberance, vitality, and wisdom. On behalf of the National Association for the Advancement of Colored People, I extend to his family and to the National Urban League our sincere sympathy in this period of bereavement."

All-White Private Academies

The Executive Director urged the Commissioner of the Internal Revenue Service to investigate the tax-exemption of seventeen newly-established all-white private academies in eight Southern states. The commissioner replied to the Executive Director's letter under date of March 4 and stated, "according to our records, five of the seventeen schools that you listed have been recognized by the Service as tax-exempt." They are: Rocky Mount Academy, Rocky Mount, N.C., Jan. 8, 1969; Bowman Academy, Bowman, S.C., Sept. 27, 1966; Cleveland Day School, Cleveland, Tenn., April 14, 1964; Chichahominy Academy, Charles City, Va., August 2, 1967 and York Academy, Mattaponi, Va., Feb. 7, 1964. The Commissioner further stated:

> You may assure your local chapters and their members that specific complaints concerning private tax-exempt schools that practice racial discrimination will be given serious consideration by the service. We will undertake to withdraw recognition of tax exempt status where we find that a school is not in good faith pursuing a non-discriminatory admissions policy.

Food Stamps and Lunch Programs

The Executive Director made two public service tape recording announcements for the U.S. Department of Agriculture to promote its Food Stamp and National School program.

Roy Wilkins, Executive Director
March 1971

Report of the Executive Director for the Board Meeting of the First Quarter 1973

Speaking Engagements

On January 7, the Executive Director attended [a] meeting of the Special Contributions Fund Trustees, and later that evening attended the Association's Fellowship Dinner in New York City; on January 8, attended annual meeting of the Association, and the Board of Directors meeting in New York City; attended staff meeting on January 10; testified at hearing of the Senate Committee on Labor and Public Welfare against [the] President's nomination of Peter J. Brennan as Secretary of Labor in Washington, D.C., on January 18; was honorary pallbearer at funeral services for Elmer Carter on January 19 in New York City; attended memorial services for President Lyndon Baines Johnson at City Hall in New York City on January 24; and on January 25, attended funeral service for President Johnson in Washington, D.C.; on January 29, attended annual meeting and annual dinner of the Leadership Conference on Civil Rights.

On February 1, the Executive Director was interviewed via telephone conference call by Carl Rydingsword, Nora Harris, and Nate Jackson in connection with [a] book they are writing; on February 2, was interviewed by poetess Nikki Giovanni and author Ida Lewis of *Encore* Magazine in New York City; on February 5, attended meeting of "The Wednesday Group" (Republican congressmen) with Clarence Mitchell and Nathaniel Jones in Washington, D.C.; on February 6, was interviewed by Nick Kotz of the *Washington Post* in New York City; on February 7, met with Chief Gasha Buthelizi, Chairman of the Executive Council, Zulu Homeland, South Africa, in New York City; and was interviewed that same day by Vernon Jarrett for the *Chicago Tribune*; on February 9, testified in behalf of Judge Otto Kerner at his trial in Chicago, Ill.; on February 13, chaired the Interracial Colloquy which met in New York City; on February 14, lectured at Columbia University Law Forum in New York City; and on February 19, lectured at the Jewish Community Center Forum in Cincinnati, Ohio; on February 26, spoke at Rededication of the Willkie Memorial Building in New York City; and was interviewed by Godfrey Hodgson of the *Washington Post* in New York City on February 27.

On March 1, the Executive Director and Jack Greenberg taped interview with Summer Glimcher of Mass Communications, Inc. in New York City; lectured at Vanderbilt University in Nashville, Tenn., March 2 and 3; met with Atlanta Branch President, Legal Redress Chairman, and Southeast Regional Director, Chairman and Vice Chairman of the Board on March 6; spoke at dinner meeting of the EDGES Group, Inc. in New York City, on March 7; on March 12, spoke at luncheon sponsored by the President of International Telephone and Telegraph in New York City; and later that afternoon, met with a delegation (fourteen) from Northern Ireland, at the request of Dr. Richard Brown (of Bluefield, W.Va.) in New York City; on March 13, attended Executive Committee meeting of Leadership Conference on Civil Rights in New York City; and was photographed with Cleveland Mallory, of U.S.S. Kitty Hawk fame; on March 15, was guest on KMOX Radio's "At Your Service" program from St. Louis, Mo., via telephone; and lectured at Eckerd College Free Institution's Forum on March 19 and 20 in St. Petersburg, Fla.

N.A.A.C.P. Urges Senate to Reject Nomination of Peter Brennan for Secretary of Labor

The Executive Director called upon the Senate Committee on Labor and Public Welfare to reject the nomination of Peter J. Brennan, former president of the New York Building and Construction Trades Council and sponsor of the so-called New York Plan, as Secretary of Labor. The Executive Director said, "The record speaks for itself in New York where Mr. Brennan has been the chief spokesman for the A.F.L.–C.I.O. construction unions. Again and again Federal and state courts have found local affiliates of the Building and Construction Trades Council, headed by Mr. Brennan, to be guilty of, as one Federal Judge said, 'a broad and pervasive pattern of racial discrimination.'"

Death of Lyndon Johnson

The Executive Director released the following statement on former President Lyndon Baines Johnson who died on January 22.

The passing of Lyndon Baines Johnson marks the end of an era during which unprecedented progress was made towards elimination of racial bias, providing for the basic needs of the nation's poor, and lifting the horizons of disadvantaged groups within the American society. Many persons and various social forces contributed to that era of change, but foremost of all was President Johnson. It was his dedication, his uncompromising commitment, and his skillful leadership which wrought a revolution of national conscience in regard to race and poverty.

His Voting Rights Act of 1965 restored the ballot to millions of black Americans. His Civil Rights Act of 1964 abolished racial discrimination in public accommodations and tackled the complex bias in employment. His 1968 Fair Housing Act affirmed freedom of residence to Negro citizens.

A man of southern origin, he broke with the traditions of his region and boldly espoused the Great Society in which each person would be valued on his individual merit. Never before in the history of the United States of America had this great goal of human equality been championed from the White House.

Death of Elmer A. Carter

A wire was sent to the family of Elmer A. Carter: "The National Association for the Advancement of Colored People extends our profound sympathy in the death of your father Elmer A. Carter. He was a distinguished public servant whose career spanned some four decades in the field of human rights. A former commissioner and subsequently Chairman of the State Commission Against Discrimination and as Special Assistant to the Governor for Intergroup Relations, he spearheaded programs which helped to eliminate many barriers designed to deny members of minority groups their full citizenship right. His death is an immeasurable loss not only to his family but to the hosts of those who admired and respected him and benefited from his dedicated service."

The Executive Director served as honorary pallbearer, January 18, at Mr. Carter's funeral.

Atlanta, Ga., School Desegregation Case

The Executive Director gave the following statement on Feb. 26 concerning the school desegregation settlement reached in Atlanta.

The settlement announced last week, whereby some of the Negro plaintiffs and their lawyers in the Atlanta, Ga., school suit have agreed to accept what will be, soon, one-half of the administrative positions in the school system and to forego the mass transportation of pupils is a purely local decision. The constitutionality of the plan is yet to be approved by the court.

The Atlanta agreement must not be mistaken for a national N.A.A.C.P. position on school desegregation and it does not represent any change in the N.A.A.C.P. basic commitment to quality integrated education to be achieved by whatever means are required, including transportation of children for the purpose.

The Chairman of the Board and the Executive Director sent a telegram to Lonnie King, Atlanta Branch President, in which they repudiated the agreement and in which they directed the officers and Executive Committee of the Atlanta Branch to reverse its approval of the plan submitted to the court. The Atlanta Branch not only failed to do this, but reaffirmed its support of the compromise settlement. The Executive Director had no other choice but to suspend the officers and executive committee members for their action, which threatens irreparable harm to the Association, pending a full hearing.

Roy Wilkins, Executive Director
First Quarter 1973

Speeches, Essays, and Articles, 1955–1976

Editor's Note

Roy Wilkins received the following letter from a person who had followed his writings in the many publications he wrote for during his long career. Mrs. Roy Wilkins thought that this letter captured the substance of her husband as a human being and as a leader of civil rights for all Americans. In fact she used the letter as a preface to a collection of her husband's speeches, essays, and articles that she herself published.

August 14, 1967
Roy Wilkins
L.A. Times
Los Angeles, Cal.

Dear Mr. Wilkins:

I feel, that as one of your reader audience, you should know how much you inspire me. You maintain a universal tone in the human dilemma of wanting to love and to be loved, to feel worthwhile, to believe that others feel that we are worthwhile. The Negroes' dilemma is a silhouette of every man's fear of neglect, deprivation, and isolation. In view of the uprising in some of the big cities, it is more important that we keep our cool and plough ahead with our aspirations for mankind.

I know that what I am saying must be terribly moralizing. But I am simply trying to say that you invite love in this world of distrust.

Please think of me as an ardent supporter.
Sincerely yours.

Roy Wilkins used every available opportunity to publicize the achievements of the NAACP. This point is evidenced in the speeches, essays, and articles that follow. They bear consistent themes, including (1) the dangers of separatism as a solution, (2) the dangers of white resistance to the civil rights laws, (3) the need for optimism and involvement, and (4) why white people should be in the civil rights movement.

The War against the United States

One year after the *Brown* decision, the U.S. Supreme Court handed down its decree reaffirming the constitutional principle that racially segregated schools are unconstitutional, and it turned over to the lower federal courts the responsibility of seeing that local school boards moved with "all deliberate speed" to abide by the ruling. The reaction to this decree varied across the nation. School districts in Mississippi declared that they would defy the Supreme Court. Other school districts—in Poteau, Oklahoma; Fayette County, Kentucky, and Oak Ridge, Tennessee—desegregated without friction. In the following article, published in the *Crisis* in December 1955, Roy Wilkins discusses the aftermath of the Supreme Court's 1955 decree.

On May 31, 1955, the United States Supreme Court handed down its decree in the school segregation cases, reaffirming the constitutional principle in its 1954 opinion that racially segregated schools were unconstitutional, and turning over to the lower Federal Courts the task of seeing to it that local school boards made plans and took action with all deliberate speed to abide by the ruling.

The reactions to this decree among our good white people ranged from one extreme to the other. The Richmond, Va., *News Leader* published an angry editorial, "Now It's the South's Turn," on June 1. In effect it called rebellion (although by what it termed legal means), for resistance for fifty years, if necessary, and concluded that in the minds of many Southerners "as soon as possible" meant never at all.

Joining the *News Leader* in language not nearly so finely turned was that eminent journal of the State of Mississippi, the Jackson *Daily News*, which declared in plain street corner phrases that it intended to defy the Supreme Court.

At the other end of the scale was the attorney general of Oklahoma who advised his state that Oklahoma statutes requiring segregation of the races in the public schools were now invalid and that compliance with the Court's decree was in order. Since May 31 approximately 100 communities in Oklahoma, including all major cities, have desegregated their school systems.

There has been no friction. No vigilante groups have been organized to protect this and preserve that. The two races are not looking at each other with suspicion and fear. What our white friends are fond of calling "peaceful relations between the races" have not been upset. Apparently no one is worried to death about his bloodstream. Oklahoma just decided to remain a part of the United States of America and to let God and good sense help it in solving a problem in the American way.

The contrast between Mississippi on the one hand, and Oklahoma on the other, is important because it points up what is actually under way in a number of states in the South today. The unpleasant but plainly discernible fact is that war has been declared and is being fought against the United States of America. It is a war against the right of petition, against legal redress of grievances, against the exercise of the franchise, and against equality under the law.

The immediate and highly visible target of this warfare is the Negro, but the real target is the United States, its Declaration of Independence, its philosophy, and its Constitution, all based upon equality of citizenship. The dissenters will have none of this equality if it is to be brought, as the Supreme Court opinion brings it, to actual practice in everyday life.

As long as equality remained in the archives of the nation, in the speeches in Congress, or in Fourth of July orations, it was acceptable. But the transfer, after so many years of hypocrisy, to the nation's public school classrooms was much too much. For one thing—and an extremely practical thing at that—what would happen to the whole intricate, comfortable and profitable structure of white supremacy if the children and youth should learn, side by side, that group superiority and inferiority based upon color is myth?

A small segment of this predicament is found in the remark of a registrar of voters in Mississippi who protested a new law requiring written examinations for voters. Said he: "When you have written blanks in the files, with maybe a white man's back to back with a Negro's and the Negro has answered the questions correctly and you have disqualified him, how do you explain it? There are some things you don't want known."

So, some of our white people have gone to war against their country. They don't mind the government making statements, but they draw the line at opinions and decrees. In this war other states may choose debate, but Mississippi chooses murder. It was to be expected that Mississippi, with its record of more lynchings than any other state, would be the worst performer. But not even those who knew Mississippi well expected that the hysteria would extend to the killing of a fourteen-year-old boy.

A jury of their neighbors has acquitted the two men accused of the murder, so Emmett Till must technically be listed as having come to his death at the hands of persons unknown. But while his killers were only one or two or three persons out of the whole population of Mississippi, the entire state must take the blame for this death. For the people of Mississippi had created, or had sat by and acquiesced in the creating of an atmosphere of physical violence directed at Negroes.

From no less a forum than the floor of the Mississippi state legislature in September, 1954, came the call to organize councils of white citizens to preserve segregated schools, to keep Negroes from voting in elections, and to act against those whites who seemed to be sympathetic in any way with the aims and aspirations of the colored citizens.

To only a pious and scrupulously correct declaration that the councils did not favor violence were coupled inflammatory calls to "all white people to unite" and instructions on economic pressures to be used to beat the Negroes down. The highest state officials issued their statements. The editors wrote their editorials, often dragging them over from the regular page to page one to secure attention. A United States Senator made a speech defying the Supreme Court and calling for war on the N.A.A.C.P. A circuit judge wrote a book called *Black Monday* and demanded the impeachment of the Supreme Court.

A gubernatorial primary election campaign turned into an anti-Negro circus, with all five candidates trying to outdo each other in inflammatory denunciation of the Negro and his cause. Much of this language, duly reported in the daily press, is sub-gutter, even for politics.

The White Citizens' Councils grew in Mississippi to a claimed membership of 50,000—at a minimum of $5.00 per member. They pursued their "non-violent" methods on Negroes, declaring that any one of them who sought his civil rights would find it impossible to get a job, get credit, maintain a business, or have a home.

In this atmosphere the Rev. G. W. Lee was shot to death in his car in Belzoni, Miss., on May 7. He was the first of his race to register to vote in his county and he had refused, under pressure, to remove his name from the list.

In this atmosphere Lamar Smith was shot to death in broad daylight on the courthouse lawn in Brookhaven, Miss., August 13. He was active in getting Negroes to register and vote. Brookhaven is the home of the judge who wrote *Black Monday* and who would impeach the Supreme Court.

In this atmosphere Emmett Louis Till was murdered in or about the town of Money, Miss., August 28. For the essence of the Mississippi atmosphere is that it is all right to mistreat Negroes, young or old—even to kill them—in order to maintain white supremacy. No one was arrested in the Lee murder; no indictment could be secured in the Smith murder and the accused men in the Till murder were freed after an hour's deliberation.

Some Mississippians deplored the Till murder, but few, if any, have deplored, disavowed, or denounced the reign of terror that made it possible.

In this cold, calculated, officially endorsed campaign Negroes have been the immediate victims, but the real target is the United States. Mississippi is saying "to hell with the Constitution" and it is saying it in the crudest and bloodiest way of any state.

Some other states are saying the same thing without (as yet) bloodshed. The Old Dominion, she of the proud tradition and the aristocratic manner, is pronouncing in rounded phrases what Mississippi says in whoops and hollers.

Virginia has its thirty-day contracts for teachers, a suave but cowardly maneuver, unworthy of a great state or a just and secure people, akin, in effect, to the threat of the night rider. Here we have an attorney general who slanders a whole people as being immoral, diseased, and criminal. Here we have a pillar of journalism, crying in careful but meaningful sentences that the region will never accede to a ruling of the nation's highest court. Here we have the Defenders of State Sovereignty and Individual Liberties knocking down once more that battered old straw man, intermarriage.

In North Carolina there is also defiance, but generally speaking, of the less blatant, less sure nature. One gets the impression that thoughtful North Carolinians would like to find an honorable way out of the ranks of rebellion. In the climate of opinion that has been created by the political hierarchy many Tar Heel residents are reluctant to say they would like to try desegregation, but they aren't by any means sure they want to participate in open defiance of the United States.

Like so many southern states, North Carolina was sure "her" Negroes did not want desegregation. Her officials said only a few members of the N.A.A.C.P. wanted it. But, like all the rest, North Carolina found that more Negroes than she suspected detested segregation and wanted to get rid of it.

It cannot be repeated too many times that Negroes do not tell southern white people what they think about segregation and civil rights. Even the Uncle Toms do not tell whites the truth. Negroes tell whites only what is necessary to keep the peace and get along in the little worlds that we both inhabit.

Well, having discovered that we did not want segregation, some white people organized to make us take it.

Down in Orangeburg, S.C., a state senator made a speech saying white people should talk to the Negroes "in our employ" and show them the value of segregation and the evil of the N.A.A.C.P

And they have been doing just that, from the East Coast to East Texas. Many people who have signed petitions to their school boards have been fired from their jobs. Others have been evicted from their rental homes. The Citizens' Council in Yazoo City, Miss., bought a full-page advertisement in the local daily to publish in big black type the names and addresses of all signers of the petition. All the employed ones were fired in twenty-four hours. One plumber was pulled off a job, refused supplies for further work by a supply house, and had to leave for Michigan.

One grocery store owner got his last delivery from a wholesale house on August 26, the day after the advertisement appeared. On September 18 his shelves held a few crackers, three cans of milk, and some dried up celery. He is out of business and gone to Chicago.

In Ft. Smith, Ark., the president of our N.A.A.C.P. branch returned from the Atlantic City convention to find that his job in a local glass works had been shifted from one at $3.02 an hour to a night shift at $1.82 an hour—and that job was subject to some kind of arbitration hearing. He was told by his foreman that he spent too much time doing N.A.A.C.P. work.

The economic boycott in any case is a dangerous, two-edged sword. When used to force citizens to renounce their rights it is a reprehensible practice. The N.A.A.C.P. does not sponsor boycotts. But in a sense this is a life and death struggle. In such a struggle the word gets around as to who is knifing whom, and with what. In such a struggle innocent bystanders in faraway New York, Ohio, Michigan, and California can get hurt. We don't want any economic squeeze business. An American should not have to choose between his civil rights and his livelihood. That is slavery. We were finished with that ninety-two years ago, and rather than return to it in any form, our people will defend themselves and their rights as free men with every available weapon within decency and the law.

For we are law-abiding citizens. In all this struggle we have voiced hatred for no man. This is our government, our America. We have no other land. We have sweated for it. We have died for it. While suffering its deepest humiliations, we have clung fast to it and defended it from detractors, those without and within.

We are determined that, having helped make it a good land for others, it shall also be a good land, a fair land, a just land for us.

But if the First Amendment to the Constitution is now flouted in flagrant fashion as to the right petition, the Fifteenth Amendment which protects discrimination as to race or color has been disregarded in some states for so long a time that any attempt at enforcement is viewed in some quarters as un-American and subversive!

The circle created by the abrogation of the guarantees of the Fifteenth Amendment is a vicious one. The Negro citizens suffer indignities because they cannot vote, and they cannot vote because of the terror of the indignities. It should be noted that naked intimidation merely buttresses the trickery contrived in studied and open fashion to prevent their entrance to the polling booths. Under the pretense of setting up qualifications for voters, several southern states have devised legislation to bar Negroes from the polls. No one denies this; indeed, it is a subject for unashamed public gloating.

Under this system of denial of the franchise, democratic government in the affected states has been destroyed. In most places the governors, state legislators, town councils and local officials are under no obligation to respond to the wishes or needs of large sections of their populations. Moreover the representatives and senators sent to Washington not only ignore their Negro constituents, but consider it their duty to block any and all legislative or executive efforts on the Federal level to make constitutional government a reality in their bailiwicks.

The defenders of this network of nullification, the perpetrators of this war on America, have declared (when they have bothered to explain at all) that they act as they do to "preserve Anglo-Saxon civilization." The very essence of Anglo-Saxon civilization, of course, is the protection of the precious rights and liberties of the individuals and groups, and from government itself. Nothing could destroy Anglo-Saxon civilization more quickly than the abrogation of the guarantees in our Constitution. We Negroes fight to preserve and enjoy these guarantees not only for ourselves, but for all Americans. We are unwilling to abandon our white fellow citizens to the tyranny that would ensue, even if we were not a factor, if the pattern of abrogation herein outlined should become permanent.

We will win because we are in a time of history when the clock cannot be turned back to the nineteenth century. A slogan is also a truism. Time marches on! The Supreme Court opinion was in great part a recognition of this fact. As we see it, far more was involved than the sitting of a court "different" from that of 1896. Far more, too, than is contained in the easy characterization of the opinion as "political." The dynamism of the American system was at stake. Its ability to change and grow was on trial. On a great moral and political question it had to decide between, roughly, 1880 and 1954.

I repeat that the Negro is the acid test of the American democratic system. It may be, God forbid, that after 179 years we are to discover that the Declaration of Independence will not work as to "all men." Our Western World may founder on the problems of the color lines. It does not have to be so. We can work at it, looking squarely at the realities of the world of 1955 and beyond, the kind of world not envisaged when the Emancipation Proclamation was signed in 1863. Each of us in his own sphere, using his personal skills and good sense, calling upon his moral conviction, or calling, if you will, upon his own self-interest, is obligated to declare himself and to enlist in the crusade.

For the peril to every American embodied in the deliberate defiance of the Constitution is obvious. Under our government there is and must be room for disagreement and debate and there is and must be procedure for orderly and lawful change. There is, however, no room for defiance and rebellion. That way lies disintegration and anarchy.

I cannot put it better than has the distinguished novelist Nobel Prize winner, and native Mississippian, William Faulkner, who, in commenting on the brutal murder of the fourteen-year-old Negro boy on August 28, said:

> Perhaps we will find out now whether we are to survive or not. Perhaps the purpose of this sorry and tragic error committed in my native Mississippi by two white adults on an afflicted Negro child is to prove to us whether or not we deserve to survive.

Integration Crisis in the South

In 1957 when nine black youth attempted to integrate Central High School in Little Rock, Arkansas, at issue was the constitutional power of a state versus the power of the federal government, and equally paramount was the physical safety of the schoolchildren who were involved in this atmosphere of violence. The constitutional authority was resolved when President Dwight Eisenhower ordered federal troops to Little Rock on September 24, 1957, to enforce the 1955 Supreme Court decree desegregating schools "with all deliberate speed." In the face of Eisenhower's actions, the question remained: Why was there still open hostility and violence by so many whites regarding the High Court's order? In the following address to the NAACP Fourteenth Annual State Convention, Roy Wilkins talks about the status of the civil rights movement after Little Rock. This address was given on October 11, 1957.

I am pleased to be able to counsel once again with the delegates to the North Carolina state convention assembled here under President Kelly Alexander and your other fine officers for your fourteenth annual meeting. Much has happened since I spoke to you two years ago at a statewide rally in Raleigh, and although North Carolina has had a period of soul-searching which is not yet ended, the state is struggling toward the right decision.

Its legislature refused to join other states in passing bills which would have restricted the freedom of its citizens to function in the N.A.A.C.P., or the freedom of our organized body to assemble, speak freely, and petition for redress of grievance. In turning its back upon this type of repression, North Carolina has done no special favor to the N.A.A.C.P.; it has, instead, favored itself and the nation by upholding the precious liberties of the individual which are the very foundation stone of America itself, and of the Western World.

Some of the state's newspapers have given leadership to those who want to think on the issue. On June 1, 1955, the *Charlotte News* editorial, "End of an Era," declared: "Racial barriers which have existed for generations must be dissolved. A massive change . . . is about to take place."

Three North Carolina cities have ventured to put their little toes into the waters of public school desegregation and have not yet been drowned, nor even poisoned. We believe they have acted with courage to make a beginning, and that is good. I hope we will be forgiven for offering the wholly natural and expected advice given to all would be swimmers: "Come on in, the water's fine!" Or, you might say, having made a start, they should not be satisfied with a little Methodist water, but should try the Baptist way.

We do not underestimate the difficulties involved in making a great change in a pattern of living, nor do we brush aside lightly the adjustments each person must make. But we would hope that, in North Carolina and in other southern states, millions of white people genuinely desire to attain fairness for their fellow-men and peace for themselves. The inflammatory pronouncements and degrading performances of a noisy minority only serve to highlight the existence of the substantial majority which abhors violence and would seek a just solution to a complex problem.

The events of the past month have added enormously to the expected complications, and needlessly so. Our nation is today faced with the gravest constitutional crisis in our time. Many factors—tradition, law, psychology, politics, and economics—went into the making of the tragedy at Little Rock, but the catalytic agent that set off the explosion was the action of the governor of the state. No one can tell the end result of this tragic situation. Its repercussions are already being felt, not only throughout the South and the entire nation, but also throughout the world.

While the Little Rock affair must bear the blame for the immediate crisis, it must not be forgotten that those organized elements which have preached defiance of the courts, while piously disclaiming violence, have created the climate in which mobs have felt free to act. Self-styled respectable citizens banded together for a campaign of resistance to the decision of the nation's highest court, have given the green light to gangsters.

The manicured hands of the solid citizens did not throw a stone or swing a fist. Their voices did not jeer at six-year-old children in Nashville and their well-bred mouths did not spit upon a girl here in Charlotte. But their exhortations inspired less-restrained members of the communities to overt action. They cannot purge themselves by pointing the finger at another sinner, Orval Faubus.

While all Americans join President Eisenhower in his sadness at the use of troops anywhere, as between troops to obstruct the orders of our court and troops to uphold those orders, there can be but one choice. The President has earned not only the thanks of Negro citizens—hounded by actual mobs and harassed on all sides by the mob spirit—but the thanks as well of millions who saw the fate of the American dream trembling in the balance.

Those politicians who now scream at Federal troops in Little Rock were as silent as a tomb when Arkansas National Guardsmen carrying guns turned back school girls carrying books.

In a larger sense, the Little Rock tragedy opposes a serious political problem which may well re-shape political alignments throughout the country. Clearly the supporters of Governor Faubus are political orphans with no established home in which to seek refuge. Certainly neither party can support the Governor's use of troops to defy a Federal court order. Neither the Republicans nor the Democrats will go before the American people on such a platform. No, the major political parties can only face the people on a platform calling for the observance of law and order and respect for constituted authority.

There is no place for the supporters of Governor Faubus's segregation stand in a national political party because there is no future for a party whose principal plank is the advocacy of racial bigotry. Their only future would seem to lie in the organization of a provincial political clique dedicated to the maintenance of an obsolescent way of life. And no matter what they name it, or who sponsors it, or how its objectives are described, it will still be a party of racial bigotry, as reprehensible as anything sponsored by the late Adolf Hitler. Enlightened southerners recognize the futility of joining any such desperate cabal.

As for the Negro voter, I cannot predict the impact Little Rock will have upon his decisions in 1956 and 1960. He has seen all the pictures from Little Rock. He knows the political affiliations for the leading actors in the drama. He knows who sent what troops to do what. He has noted who supports whom. He knows his own local and state situation. When he enters the polling place it is certain that he will weigh all these factors and a variety of others which affect his daily life.

Even beyond the constitutional crisis, our country faces what might be called a survival crisis. The Soviet satellite that has been traveling around the world this past week is not so much in itself. The United States can and will launch a satellite. The British could launch one. Our uneasiness stems from the fact that we did not believe the Russians had the know-how and the capacity to launch a satellite at this time.

Our country will surely correct its error and revise its calculations. It is unthinkable that we should be at the mercy of the Soviet Union or of any other country. But in re-orienting ourselves, we will need to mobilize all the resources and skills available in our population.

For example, we cannot afford second-class education for any American child, or second-class citizenship for any American adult.

As we face a ruthless and skillful adversary bent upon destroying our way of life, we must educate, train and utilize every ounce of manpower and every brain and skill we possess. It is axiomatic that the segregated school system does not provide that equality of opportunity demanded by our Constitution, or, now, urgently required by national security.

One lone Negro scientist worked on the first atom bomb, but he was educated in Illinois and graduated from the University of Chicago. Hundreds like him should have been graduated from the educational systems of the South to serve their country. Instead, they were condemned to school without adequate mathematics courses, without physics, and chemistry laboratories, and even without proper facilities for useful vocational training.

The separate-but-equal theory has been proved through sixty years of trial to have been merely separate. Those who seek to perpetuate it at all costs are not only trampling upon decency and fairness and the mandates of the American tradition; they are trifling with the security of our country.

It is later, far later, than we think. We can no longer afford the luxury of debating whether nine or ninety, or ninety-nine thousand non-white American children shall have access to the best education alongside white American children. Less than the mutual respect and dedication and unity which such education will provide, and less than the maximum employment of our manpower potential may spell disaster.

In this connection, the mobs which disrupt communities discourage the investment of capital and the location of industry in the affected areas. Thus, they not only retard the development of the areas concerned, but tend to dislocate the program of production dispersal which is a part of security planning. The United States is upon shaky ground, indeed, if it must depend upon workers who take a few days off now and then to chase Negro school children, or to snatch at random a Negro man and mutilate him.

In the end, of course, the real crisis facing us is a moral one. Political and economic expediency are important factors, but they fade before the meeting of man with himself, in his heart and in his conscience. No decision which is not rooted in the hearts of men will have a useful permanence, and this is not to decry the function and persuasiveness of laws and court opinions on our temporal behavior, any more than it is to decry the function and persuasiveness of the tenets of the Bible on our spiritual behavior.

Both whites and Negroes know in their hearts that the system that has been in vogue is morally wrong. As they talk with each other and make the moves dictated by emerging events, they both know the truth.

They know it as they make and hear the baseless charge of communism hurled at every dissenter from the philosophy and practices of the dead and enervating past. The absurdity of this accusation is revealed in the ever-widening circle of those accused. The N.A.A.C.P., the National Council of Churches, Catholic bishops, daily newspapers and magazines, student associations, radio and television networks, organized labor, the United States Supreme Court and the President of the United States! The ridiculous theory is that anyone who opposes segregation is a Communist.

The white people know it as they busy themselves with devices to smash the N.A.A.C.P. and thus deprive Negro citizens of their law-abiding spokesman and defender. A recent national survey by the magazine, *Catholic Digest*, printed in its August issue, found that ninety-four per cent of northern Negroes and ninety-three per cent of southern Negroes support the views of the N.A.A.C.P.

It is pertinent to recall here that in 1955 when the Governor of Mississippi called ninety hand-picked Mississippi Negro leaders to his office and asked them to endorse a voluntary segregated plan, only one supported the Governor. The famed Montgomery, Ala., protest against bus segregation was a wholly indigenous action by local Montgomery Negro citizens, not inspired or led by the N.A.A.C.P.

Thus it would appear that the state legislation aimed at suppressing the N.A.A.C.P. will not kill the determination of Negro citizens to enjoy their constitutional rights. Nor will it kill the N.A.A.C.P., whose members intend that it shall stay alive and press its reasonable and wholly American program along all fronts. These laws deprive citizens of freedom of speech and assembly, and of freedom to pool their knowledge and resources to seek redress of grievances in the courts and in the arena of public opinion.

No more un-American or unconstitutional measures could be imagined, and, until they are stricken down, they are certain to plague white Americans who seek to exercise their freedoms.

Certain white people know this great moral truth even as they incite to violence by means of transparent warnings against violence. In fact, the invocation of violence represents the final dawning of truth. Physical excesses confess the bankruptcy of the host of sham "arguments" and the inevitability of the moral law.

On the upholding of law—spiritual and temporal—the forces for decency and justice can unite. The overwhelming majority of good white citizens of the South has been appalled and shamed by the ugly excesses of the past weeks. Only the mobsters and some weak uneasy politicians have been brazen, one ignorantly and unashamedly so, and the other behind a mask of face-saving phrases.

As Judge Lee Ward of the Twelfth Chancery District of Arkansas writes in his letter to Look magazine: "It is all right to disagree . . . But it is not all right—under our system of government—for us to decide that we will ignore or violate the law as it has been interpreted by the Supreme Court. We do not have any such right . . . There is a vast difference between disagreement and defiance."

Most white southerners do not relish the role of law defiers and would like to work out a plan of compliance, even as did the people of Louisville, as did the people of numerous Texas cities and towns, and as did the people of Little Rock— for it must not be forgotten that Little Rock white citizens devised their own plan. Federal Judge Ronald Davies did not "bring a plan down from North Dakota and cram it down Little Rock's throat" as has been falsely charged.

In the working out of any plan, approached in good faith, southern white people will have the active and understanding cooperation of Negro citizens, as long as the principle of desegregation is the core of the plan.

Immediately after the decision of May 17, 1954, Dr. Channing H. Tobias, National Board Chairman of the N.A.A.C.P., issued a statement to an Atlanta conference of the N.A.A.C.P. held May 22 in which he said:

It is important that calm reasonableness prevail, that the difficulties of adjustment be realized, and that, without any sacrifice of basic principles, the spirit of give and take characterize the discussion.

This is the spirit of the N.A.A.C.P. and Negro citizens today. Three and one-half years after the decision we are still willing to meet and discuss with "calm reasonableness" any good-faith plan of desegregation.

We hate no man and have never used hatred as a weapon. We want only our rights as American citizens and the equal opportunity for our children that America promises to all its children.

Our people in the South have given a magnificent demonstration of their courage and restraint in the teeth of slander, threats, economic reprisals, and mob violence.

Our children, through their courage and dignified behavior before howling mobs, have made us proud and have challenged us not to fail them as they seek their own destiny in the world of 1977 and beyond.

I am confident that the N.A.A.C.P. organization in North Carolina, one of the best in the land, will not fail these children. Despite the present emotional outburst, I remain confident that Americans, black and white, North and South, will not fail them, for they are the very stuff of which America is made.

To suggest that the present difficulties cannot be resolved is to deny the genius of Americans who have built a mighty nation from peoples of many cultures, using the amalgam of individual liberty and equality of opportunity.

To suggest a hopeless impasse is to deny the verities of our religious teaching and to renounce our partnership with God in the task of bringing His kingdom into the hearts of men here on earth.

The devotion and wisdom of the patriots, and the prayers of the righteous and the just will surely avert any such catastrophe.

The Film Industry and the Negro

Since the early 1940s, the NAACP has taken issue over the fact that blacks were not being portrayed in motion pictures in the manner in which they occupy positions in life. In the following address under the auspices of the Association of Motion Picture Producers Roy Wilkins outlines the NAACP's policy on black actors in film roles. This speech was given on October 25, 1957.

I am grateful for the opportunity to discuss with you face to face, at long last, a matter about which there has been a great deal of misunderstanding. After much telephoning and writing back and forth, beginning, I believe, last March or April, you have been gracious enough to arrange this luncheon meeting.

While there has been much talk of an N.A.A.C.P. policy on employment of Negro actors in film roles, and on the type of material involving Negroes and the so-called race question which has found its way into motion pictures, the truth of the matter is that there has never been a clear policy issued by the N.A.A.C.P.

The late Wendell Willkie of Twentieth Century Fox and the late Walter White of the N.A.A.C.P. held several conferences in 1942 with executives of the film industry. Mr. Willkie was concerned with the pictures of America being received by nations around the globe and the effect such impressions were having on our war effort. Mr. White was concerned with this, but also with the damage to the morale of Negro citizens in the war against Hitlerism.

While no written policy came out of these discussions, the clear intent of the talks was indicated by a paragraph in a letter written by Mr. Darryl Zanuck under date July 21, 1942, to other film executives. I should like to quote just that paragraph:

> It seemed to me that Walter White's statement of the problem was simple and direct. What he is actually asking for is that Negroes be used in motion pictures in the same manner in which they occupy positions in life; some are heroic; some are not; some are serious minded; others are comedians; some are industrious; some are lazy; some hold highly responsible positions; some of course are in mental occupations. In other words, they are just like all other human beings. There is no objection to using a Negro occasionally for comedy, but he would like to have them used as often as possible in the more heroic roles—in the position which they occupy in real life, as normal and integral parts of the American and world scenes. All this should be done, of course, without any direct or indirect suggestions of propaganda.

This seems clear, but in some way misunderstanding developed on a fantastic scale. Some figures in the industry apparently used the N.A.A.C.P. discussions as an excuse for restricting employment of Negro actors. Negro film actors thereupon concluded that the N.A.A.C.P., through the suggestions of Mr. White, was keeping them from employment. Some of the allegations which attained wide currency were:

1. The N.A.A.C.P. censors scripts and even in some cases designates the Negro actors who should or should not be employed. This is sheer nonsense. We have not the time, money, staff, or inclination to act as a censor. We believe in freedom of expression for ourselves and for others. Occasionally the N.A.A.C.P. is asked for an opinion on an idea, or a treatment, or, on very rare occasions, on a completed script. We have no list of "dos and don'ts." Therefore, the executives, on any level, or any other persons connected with film production, either for theaters or for television, who say, "We can't do so and so because we would get into trouble with the N.A.A.C.P. code" are merely using us as an excuse and are costing Negro actors jobs.

2. The N.A.A.C.P. has a one-for-one policy, that is, if a Negro actor is cast as a servant, there must be elsewhere in the cast a Negro actor cast in a non-servant role. This is ridiculous and untrue. We have never stated any such position, either verbally or in writing. Just recently we learned that a young Negro actress had been chosen for a maid's role in a television series, but when her picture reached the McCann Erickson advertising agency in New York, she was turned down with the statement that if hired "the N.A.A.C.P. would demand another Negro in the cast on a higher level." We are investigating

this report with McCann-Erickson in order to nail the falsehood once and for all, but in the meantime the N.A.A.C.P. has been used again as an excuse to deny Negro actors jobs.

3. The N.A.A.C.P. will not approve of Negroes as comics, maids, menials, etc. This is not true and nothing can be found in the 1942 discussions to support it. The N.A.A.C.P. does oppose (a) limiting Negro actors to such roles and thus limiting the depiction of Negroes in American life, and (b) stereotyped characteristics such as eye-rolling, shuffling, grinning, and obsequiousness—the kind of thing that perpetuates the image of the Negro as a buffoon whose claims to equality need not be taken seriously.

So that there will be no misunderstanding, please let me recapitulate and emphasize:

1. The N.A.A.C.P. does not now and never has assumed the role of censor.
2. The N.A.A.C.P. does not now and never has had a "one-for-one" policy.
3. The N.A.A.C.P. does not now disapprove and never has disapproved servant and comic roles as such; it has opposed and does oppose exclusive or preponderant casting of Negro actors in such roles, since such casting misrepresents the role of Negro citizens in American life.

I should like to elaborate a bit on the latter point. There have been many changes in the status of Negroes since 1942. The Armed Services, formerly restricted and rigidly segregated, are now desegregated. Negroes now serve in all branches and grades up to and including a general in the Air Force.

Since 1942 we have seen the enactment of fair employment practice laws by states and cities—more than a dozen states and some forty cities. This means that Negroes now occupy better-paying jobs in a wider variety of categories, including white collar and technical.

The organized labor movement has opened up membership and promotions to Negroes under many contracts with management, resulting in an expansion in the number of Negro skilled artisans. There has been too, a growth in the number of Negroes in professional and technical employment. We have more engineers, chemists, laboratory technicians than ever before. Our great industrial concerns now recruit engineering and chemistry graduates from Negro colleges as they have done for years from "white" colleges. It is now commonplace, therefore, to find Negroes as stenographers, bookkeepers, retail clerks, bus drivers, nurses, crane operators, etc.

Since 1942, public school desegregation has progressed under Supreme Court decisions. Since 1950, Negro students have entered and been graduated from state universities in all but five southern states. On the elementary and high school levels, desegregation has been practically completed in the District of Columbia,

West Virginia, and Missouri; it is well along in Maryland, Delaware, Kentucky, and in West and South Texas; small beginnings have been made in North Carolina, Tennessee, and Arkansas.

Moreover, since 1942, there has been a steady migration of Negroes from the South to northern and western states. As a result their political strength has increased, with the further result that their employment in civil service jobs has increased, and their number in elective and appointive political posts has grown.

For examples, in civil service, many state, county and city departments and bureaus have Negro white collar workers in considerable numbers. There have been Negro policemen and detectives for years and years, but now it is not a rarity to be halted by a Negro motorcycle or traffic officer, to have Negroes as dispatchers at headquarters, or to have Negro police academies. The Commissioner of Public Safety for Illinois, in charge of all highway police, is a Negro.

There are Negro firemen and, of course, a vast number of other municipal and state servants. Take a look sometimes at the Los Angeles City Hall or Hall of Justice. Drop into the Municipal Building in New York City, or the State Motor Vehicle Bureau office there, or into the municipal office in Chicago, Cleveland, Detroit, Pittsburgh, Philadelphia, Cincinnati, St. Louis, and Kansas City. For instance, the chief purchaser of drugs for the City of New York is a Negro, and, until he was recently promoted, the Commissioner of Water Supply, Gas, and Electricity for the City of New York was a Negro engineer who was graduated from the University of Montana nearly forty years ago!

There are three Negroes in Congress, many state legislators and city councilmen, judges, members of school boards, and staff members in city and state law departments. A Negro is Borough President of Manhattan in New York City; until recently, one was Vice Mayor of Cincinnati, and one is an elected member of the board of education in Atlanta, Georgia.

Yet with all this, we find that the films seldom picture Negroes as a part of an American crowd scene, either on the streets in normal course of business, or in sports crowds, or at political rallies.

So, it is unrealistic for the movies and TV not to keep pace with the Negro's own progress. It is not fair to the race or to Negro actors.

Besides, I suggest strongly that the industry has a duty to become more accurate. In 1942 we were in a shooting war. In 1957 we are in a Cold War. We have had Little Rock and Sputnik. Each has damaged the prestige of our country. With Little Rock we were forced into hasty and emergency measures to counteract the damage done. Our Ambassador to Britain was rushed into a defensive speech before a distinguished British gathering in London. One of our delegates to the United Nations, Mr. George Meany, president of the AFL–CIO, was delegated to make a speech on Little Rock and the American race situation before the United Nations. The Voice of America frantically tried to explain Little Rock to the world.

But the film industry can do this every day. Television can do this every day. If the films had been doing the job that they know how to do so well, the picture of the Negro in American life would have been before the world and Little Rock would have been seen in perspective. There would have been no need for the unseemly (and hence suspect) scrambling to try to make clear the nation's position. Yes, the proper portrayal of the Negro American is a patriotic duty which the film industry ought to perform.

I cannot close without mentioning that there have been changes in the Negro himself. He is more alert, more aware of himself and of the place of his nation in the world. He knows what the great conflict between democracy and dictatorship is all about. He knows that our democratic ideals are at stake and that he is a part of the test. He has traveled and his young men have fought all over the globe. He has the movies, radio, television, newspapers, and magazines, and he evaluates the information he thus receives.

He has seen India and Indonesia attain independence. This year he saw Ghana, an independent African nation, come into being. He knows that in a year or two Nigeria will be independent. With all this happening about him, it seems foolish to him that the American film industry should be so far behind the times in depicting him as a citizen of the world's greatest showcase nation of democracy. Mind you, he does not want and does not expect exaggeration or "overplaying"; he just wants an honest, balanced picture of himself in these times of decision. World War II gave him a sense of importance and the Cold War has emphasized it.

There will continue to be scrutiny and criticism by the N.A.A.C.P. of the products of the film industry touching this area. The old stereotypes, for example, must give way to new portrayals. The N.A.A.C.P. will continue to fulfill its role of trying to represent the best interest of the race as a whole. It will not seek to dictate to the industry, but will attempt to see that sixteen million Americans, struggling to attain their rightful place in the life of the nation and the world, are not handicapped by misrepresentation in a medium which speaks powerfully to people everywhere.

Your presence here today indicates your interest in exploring how the task can be accomplished. I think I can assure you that in that exploration you will have the full cooperation of Negro actors, agencies, and organizations, as well as the gratitude of the rank and file of Negro Americans themselves.

Address Given at the National Negro Publishers' Association

Roy Wilkins believed that no one person could adequately represent black America as its leader. He further contended that the goal for full equality was a complex and multifaceted struggle that required many group leaders with specialized skills. In this address to the National Negro Publishers' Association Wilkins speaks about "leadership." He argues that no so-called "race leader" in the traditional sense can be expected to have the wisdom and skill to speak and act on behalf of all black Americans. He contends, however, that there are numerous convergent areas that should bring black leaders together. This speech was given on May 18, 1958.

I appreciated the invitation to participate in this conference of leaders, but after reading the first two articles in a series on Negro leadership published by the New York *Amsterdam News* which were devoted exclusively to me, I have a feeling that I do not belong here. According to that newspaper's criteria, anyone who associates with white people or who fails to visit regularly the taverns in Harlem is definitely not a leader. Since I have associated with white people all my life, and since I do not drink, either in taverns or outside them, I would seem to be disqualified from participating here as a full-fledged "leader." Perhaps, however, you will indulge me as just a plain citizen who has worked in the civil rights field for many years.

In passing, a word might be said on the ever popular topic of leadership. Twenty years ago in a speech in Detroit, Mich., the late James Weldon Johnson stated what was then apparent to all knowledgeable persons, namely, that Negro Americans had progressed to a point where no one leader could be said to "speak for the race." The days of Frederick Douglass and Booker T. Washington are over, not because they lacked qualities of leadership, but because times have changed.

Today no one man can speak for all Americans. The President is our national leader and on all matters vital to the nation's welfare the majority of the nation follows him. But even he has his troubles, as is shown by the Pentagon reorganization fight, the foreign aid program, reciprocal trade, and the farm policies, to say nothing of public power and many other issues. Americans are led by group leaders who speak for special interests or who are experts in certain lines.

Similarly, Negro Americans are divided into many groups. Many of these are skilled and successful in their special fields. No so-called "race leader" in the traditional sense, can be expected to possess the wisdom and the skill to speak and act for all segments of Negro life. But all of us can come together to consider the one common thread that runs through all phases of our section of the American population: our status as citizens. We can assess the enjoyment, or lack thereof, of our citizenship of civil rights. As a representative of the organization that has specialized in this field for forty-eight years, I am happy to contribute what I can to this conference, reviewing a situation which is not unknown to every person here, and offering suggestions which, I suspect (since very little is new in human relations), have occurred to many of you.

Civil rights is the central issue because until Negro Americans enjoy them in full, no effort in any separate or specialized field will be free to attain full success.

The long campaign for unrestricted employment opportunities which, since 1941, has proceeded under the banner of fair employment practices, is a good example of this inter-relationship. Our merchants, professional men, churches, insurance companies, publications, banks, real estate dealers, and independent contractors, large and small, are all dependent upon increased opportunity in employment for Negro workers. Yet the FEPC idea, one of the main sections of the civil rights program, has received spotty and indifferent support from many of those individuals and groups whose welfare depends upon the increased earning power of workers. An increase of $5.00 a week for 200,000 workers means an increase of fifty million dollars a year in payrolls for them. The upgrading on merit into new skilled categories of 10,000 Negro workers at an average, say, of fifty cents an hour means $5,000 an hour into their pay envelopes, some of which will be fed into the Negro business and professional community.

Therefore, any state or national campaign for the FEPC idea should receive the whole-hearted backing of the Negro community. The candidates for public office, regardless of party, should be queried on this question. Both parties have good and bad records on employment opportunities. The Republicans under Governor Dewey of New York passed the first state FEPC law in the nation, but the Republicans in Illinois and Ohio have continued to defeat a similar law there. The Democrats, while passing more state FEPC laws than the Republicans, fiddled around with President Truman's Committee and did nothing to improve the situation in areas of Federal employment. The Republicans came in with the war cry that the Democrats had merely talked about civil rights and done nothing; but the present President's Committee on Government Contracts has an outstanding record of achievement, despite a few small successes here and there.

Some of the big unions have an excellent record of continued activity in this area, with regular departments and staff to work on the problem in their spheres. In addition, these unions have given skilled and immensely important support to the general civil rights program. Neither they nor I contend that the difficulties have been licked and that discrimination has been wiped out, but it is certainly true that they have done more than, say, the National Association of Manufacturers or the Chambers of Commerce.

The right to vote is still being denied or abridged in many areas and this civil right should claim the attention of all thoughtful citizens. The hallmark of a democratic society is that the people are free to choose their government. Negro citizens are not free to do this in many parts of the South. They are either threatened or tricked out of their right to the ballot. There is no need, in this kind of audience, to review in detail the methods by which they are restricted. These form an old story.

The salient fact is that this denial has perpetuated a political system in the South which not only denies both white and Negro citizens there a full voice in government, but which, through the Southern representatives in Washington, acts to block and curtail the civil rights of citizens who live outside the South. These representatives accomplish their work through their own votes, but more importantly, through their influence on their Northern and Western colleagues.

A case in point is the Jenner–Butler Bill, now out of the Senate Judiciary committee, which would restrict the powers of the United States Supreme Court. One of the provisions of this bill would prohibit the Supreme Court from reviewing the regulations of the various states as to admission to the bar.

It is plain to all who can read, and who know the times in which we live, that if this bill should pass, any white or Negro lawyer who argued a segregation case in certain states would be subject to disbarment and loss of his license to practice law. Virginia has passed such a law which has been challenged by the N.A.A.C.P. in the Federal court and thrown out. But Tennessee has such a law. Other Southern states such as Georgia, Alabama, South Carolina, Arkansas, Mississippi, and Texas have indicated they may interpret their present barratry statutes to mean that racial segregation law suits will endanger the lawyers involved.

In committee this bill was supported by four Southern Senators headed by Senator James O. Eastland of Mississippi. By themselves they did not have enough votes to get it reported out. But, galloping to their aid were five Republican Senators: Jenner of Indiana, Butler of Maryland, Dirksen of Illinois, Hruska of Nebraska, and Watkins of Utah.

The Republican in this conference, and especially the newspaper publishers who lean toward the Republicans, should inquire of the party about this collaboration with the enemies of Negro civil rights. What is Senator Dirksen doing supporting this bill? Is he not in line for Senate leadership of his party? Does he represent the official party stand on this issue?

This bill will hog-tie the Negro citizens in their fight for their rights. They will be left to the mercy of Southern state courts, with no appeal to the United States Supreme Court. Already they are blocked on the home front from securing any redress at the ballot box. Now, this bill would block them from securing relief through the courts. Is that what the Republican party thinks is proper and fair for Negro citizens?

This action on the Washington front interlocks with the action of certain Southern state legislatures back home in the wide campaign to turn back the clock on Negro civil rights. Many new and special laws have been enacted to cripple or drive out of business the N.A.A.C.P. I am happy to state that despite these attacks, the N.A.A.C.P. is still in business in all the Southern states except Alabama. The Alabama injunction barring us from operating there was secured without notification or a hearing of any kind, and in addition, we were fined $100,000 for failing to submit the names and addresses of our members in that state. The case is now before the U.S. Supreme Court and a decision is expected soon.

However, these attacks and their threats of reprisals against members of the N.A.A.C.P. have made our people jittery and have caused some drop in the membership in some of the states. So far, the Northern and Western states have done very well, indeed, in increasing their support, but they cannot be expected to make up completely for the Southern losses.

In the face of these attacks the N.A.A.C.P. has pressed its program and will continue to do so. The Negro parents in the South who want their schools desegregated can consult with their school boards. If they get no satisfaction they can sue in the courts. If they request help from the N.A.A.C.P. we will assist them in every way possible.

The publishers of our weekly newspaper have given this program their full support both in their news and editorial columns, as they have to civil rights generally, and with their continuing help the steady campaign of desegregation will register new gains.

We have also embarked upon a voter-registration campaign in the Southern states and this, too, has been given support by the weekly press. The effort is on the block and precinct level and the groundwork is being laid in careful educational work with the people themselves. The vote is the key. When we attain it and use it effectively in the North as well as in the South, we shall go far down the highway to full citizenship.

The whole struggle for full citizenship status, needless to say, now revolves around desegregation in the public schools and in all the public phases of American life. Regardless of the progress made in other fields (and steady progress is being made) we will be judged by the desegregation question. We are on the threshold of a new era. Some parts of the old, die-hard South are resisting with every weapon within reach. Some of their antics are funny and some are tragic. In Alabama, two leading contenders for the governorship are riding the race issue, but hard. One says he put the N.A.A.C.P. out of business in Alabama and if elected will banish it from the entire South. The other says he will throw FBI agents in jail.

While these are amusing, other actions, notably bombings and violence, are not amusing. The recent bombing of a Negro school and a Jewish center in Florida indicated a South-wide interstate conspiracy to incite violence. This is no guess of mine, but a finding of *Southern* white officials on the scene. They have set up machinery to run down the bombings, with a number of states cooperating. This is commendable and we wish it success. But the question arises, if Southern white officials recognize this as an interstate conspiracy, why does the Federal Department of Justice stand aloof in Washington? Have we come to the place where Southern state officials are more interested in halting interstate violence than Federal officials who are supposed to be concerned with interstate matters?

God knows it would be fine if Southern white people and Southern Negroes would get together in honor and good faith to solve their problems honestly, with fairness for all. The Federal Government ought to step in only when the states deprive citizens of their rights. But until that fair day dawns, the Federal agencies have a duty to protect the rights of United States citizens wherever they may live.

President Eisenhower did act last September by sending troops into Little Rock. He had no other course. A Federal court order had been defied by the state government which called out its troops to bar little children from school. If troops had not been called, the authority of the Federal Government would have been nullified and the law of the land and the courts which are charged with its enforcement would have gone down the drain. In its stead, we would have had anarchy. The President deserves credit for this action at Little Rock. He laid to rest the doctrine of interposition and we have heard no more about that.

But in this desegregation crisis the Federal Government can do more than send troops after the mobs take over. It can take preventive, educational action to hold up the hands of the good citizens in the South who want to find a way toward compliance with the law. There are hundreds of thousands, perhaps millions of these. They have been intimidated by the organized minority of their own people. They dare not speak; they hardly dare to think.

When the foreign aid program was in danger the White House called a huge conference in Washington. Regional conferences have been held. The public has been educated on the necessity of foreign aid. Why not a conference on school desegregation? Why not a pooling of knowledge and skills on this important domestic question? Let's prevent another Little Rock, not with troops, but with truth, and law and order.

Let our nation get on with desegregation not by hamstringing the N.A.A.C.P. and other groups who are working for civil rights, or by shutting up individuals who fight for the cause, but by acting to secure for all our citizens those rights to which they are entitled, and by aiding those who want to obey the courts.

A great spokesman for civil rights is now under indictment on the allegation that there was a difference of $3,700 in the amount he said his income was and the amount the government says it was. The tax involved is $1,600.

It does not matter whether we like Adam Powell personally or approve of all his actions and speeches. Regardless of this, many Negro Americans (and white ones as well) are asking themselves whether Adam is being singled out because he does not bite his tongue on civil rights for his people. He is a fighter, sometimes right and sometimes not diplomatic, but always a fighter. Fighters are what we need and fighters are what the other side does not want us to have. All eyes will be on the government as it proceeds on the Powell case.

Obviously the whole range of civil rights could not be covered in this brief talk, but an effort has been made to show some of the relationships between the Negro citizen and the governmental forces which affect his status. There is a great task ahead of all of us, a task far more complex than many seem to realize. The opposition is desperate, as evidenced by the bombings. It is organized and well-financed. Some of our allies outside the south have grown timid. They don't mind sparring, but they dislike the slugging.

After all, the people who want freedom must take the lead in fighting for it. We must be smarter than ever before. We must cooperate as never before. No matter what our special interests may be, we must rally to the great battle, we must clean up and educate and organize our own people, not because they must be perfect in order to be accorded their rights, but because they cannot be first class citizens in truth until they appreciate the responsibilities of the station.

We stand to win because it is unthinkable in this day and age, and in this, the world's greatest democracy, that a program of degradation on the basis of race can become the badge of either America or Western democracy.

Mr. Wilkins Replies

At the end of an hour-long documentary report on the school desegregation issue in Atlanta, aired on February 1, 1959, Chet Huntley, television commentator of the National Broadcasting Company, came to the shocking conclusion that "there would be more chance of desegregating schools if there were less reliance on the courts and on the federal power." In terms of this issue, that "the NAACP may have outlived itself," and "militant Negro leadership must be abandoned." In the following televised address of February 8, 1959, Roy Wilkins replies to Chet Huntley.

Mr. Huntley, I think first of all, Mr. Waring's reference to the National Association for the Advancement of Colored People and its alleged subversion is probably best answered by J. Edgar Hoover, who is acknowledged to be the authority on communism. In his book, *Masters of Deceit*, there is a chapter on "Communism and Minorities," where, on pages 246 and 247, Mr. Hoover details how the N.A.A.C.P. is not communist, how it has fought communism, and sets forth the record.

The rest of what Mr. Waring has said, of course, is familiar and will be answered in due course.

But in suggesting that the N.A.A.C.P. remove itself from the desegregation campaign, Mr. Huntley brands it as an "extremist" organization.

On May 22, 1954, five days after the historic Court ruling, Dr. Channing H. Tobias, chairman of our national Board of Directors sent a policy statement to a meeting of our leaders in Atlanta. This "extremist" message reads as follows:

> It is important that calm reasonableness prevail, that the difficulties of adjustment be realized, and that without any sacrifice of basic principles, the spirit of give and take characterize the discussions. Let it not be said of us that we took advantage of a sweeping victory to drive hard bargains, or to impose unnecessary hardships upon those responsible for the working out of the details of adjustment.

Accordingly, our very first act was to advise our people to present peaceful petitions to their school boards asking them to devise plans to comply with the Supreme Court ruling. The result was widespread publication in local newspapers of the names and addresses of the petition signers. Two hundred of these names appeared in Mr. Waring's newspaper with addresses. In consequence, individual petitioners lost their jobs, were denied credit, had their mortgage foreclosed, and were in some cases driven out.

The "loud" noise of desegregation, to use Mr. Huntley's phrase, does not come from Negro leaders, or Negro citizens. It comes from southern state legislatures, from southern governors, from some national politicians, from many state and local politicians, from certain daily papers, and from the dynamiters. The "loud" noises Mr. Huntley hears are those of the rending of the Constitution and the tumbling down of the temple of individual rights, America's most sacred shrine.

Negro Americans did not rise up in rebellion in 1896 when the Supreme Court established the separate but equal doctrine in the Louisiana case of *Plessy* vs. *Ferguson*; yet that decision was an interpretation of the constitutionality of a state railroad segregation law, just as the 1954 decision was an interpretation of state school segregation laws. But Negro citizens lived with the 1896 setback, and with the humiliation and handicaps which Jim Crow status imposed upon them. "Separate but equal" became immediately separate but unequal (as Mr. Waring has admitted when he says if we integrated, the standards of the white schools would fall. They would fall because the white schools have been placed so far out in front of those for Negroes) and this spread from railroad trains to every walk life.

The N.A.A.C.P., founded fifty years ago this week, first appeared in the United States Supreme Court in 1915 on a voting registration case, but it was not until

1944, nearly thirty years and many law suits later, that it finally broke through a major legal barrier to the franchise. Now, the franchise battle is not yet won, as Alabama events have demonstrated, but this long struggle illustrates the belief of the N.A.A.C.P. in orderly legal procedure.

Our Association, then, and the Negro, believe in the law, in the Constitution, in the courts of the nation. If that be extremism, then we are extremists. To equate this firm and reasonable adherence to law with the doctrine of defiance which has sprung up since 1954 is to mangle Americanism beyond recognition.

But what of Mr. Huntley's basic contention that if the N.A.A.C.P., the courts and federal power were withdrawn from the arena there would be more chance for desegregating schools, or his assertion that other elements are anxious "to do the decent thing" but "will not come forward while extreme passions are in control."

All the history of race relations in the South refutes this thesis. Never in its history has the South as a region, without outside pressure, taken a step to grant the Negro his citizenship rights. Paternalistic good feeling has existed; individual toleration on a purely personal basis has been in effect. But citizenship rights on an equal basis, no.

A great many southerners want nothing more than that the Negro's destiny shall be left to their decision. This is their historic position. This is their cry today in the school desegregation issue. Nothing in the history of the past five years suggests even faintly that if the N.A.A.C.P. were to bow out, school desegregation would have a better chance of success. No so-called moderate group has ever intimated it would get on with desegregation if the N.A.A.C.P. were not in the picture. There is nothing to prevent these groups, if they exist, from acting at this very moment, if they so desire, for there are hundreds of school districts where no law suits have been filed and hundreds of towns where there is no N.A.A.C.P. unit.

But Mr. Huntley's moderates will not do this, not because they are fearful of the N.A.A.C.P., but because they are fearful of the extremists among their own people, those who counsel defiance and preach hatred, and encourage violence. If this element is to be left in undisputed dominance, it will not atrophy, as Mr. Huntley hopefully imagines. It will flourish, and genuine moderates will find that they have been undercut and abandoned, their future efforts rendered futile.

One such moderate, Albert Barnett of Decatur, Georgia, wrote in *The Christian Century*, May 30, 1956: "As a southerner, I am thankful for the N.A.A.C.P. The N.A.A.C.P. seeks the implementation of rights guaranteed in the Constitution by strictly legal processes. . . . In no case has 'privilege' surrendered of its own accord. Nor will it. If to go slow is to relax pressure through the courts and public opinion, no social change will be effected."

Yes, the diehards want to remove the N.A.A.C.P. from the picture, not to speed desegregation, but to halt it completely.

Mr. Huntley suggests that another Negro leadership might find a better reception than the Association. Where is such a leadership? A 1957 survey by *Catholic Digest* magazine found ninety-three per cent of American Negro citizens in agreement with the N.A.A.C.P. We have no doubt as to whether we are backed or not, or whether there is a split. And the best testimony is that southerners have not found any considerable segment of the Negro population on which they can fasten and claim that it disagrees with this position. The Rev. Dr. Martin Luther King of Montgomery, Alabama, the National Urban League, the Negro church and the Negro press have been pilloried, persecuted, and rejected because they have stood firmly with us.

Now, Mr. Huntley flatly declares that never in history has society been changed by law. Does anyone seriously maintain that the Magna Carta did not change society, or, say, that the Code of Hammurabi had no effect on mankind? It cannot be denied that even the 1896 decision profoundly affected society in America.

Mr. Huntley argues that the product of dependence upon the courts is closed schools, tension and violence. The N.A.A.C.P. is uncompromisingly opposed to closing any schools. We regard this as disastrous in the face of the Soviet challenge. But this has been a condition which white citizens have imposed upon themselves. We did not thrust it upon them, nor upon their bewildered young people. No colored man sits in any southern state legislature. No vote of ours decreed the closing of schools.

If it is contended that Negro Americans should renounce their constitutional rights, and the redress of their grievances in the courts, we believe this is more than anyone has a right to ask of a people. It amounts to a request that we and our children sit by the side of the road while others zoom past us into the space age.

We cannot do it, and we shall not do it. We would have no right to be Americans, or to enjoy the respect of our fellows, or to receive the love and honor of our children if we voluntarily accepted a lesser status.

As for violence, we have been the victims, not the perpetrators. We reject violence and place our faith in order and law. And tensions are a part of great social change. They have been throughout history, and they will be in the future. All good citizens hope for decreased tension on this issue.

But in the words of Charles L. Black, a Texan on the Yale Law School faculty: "No social evil of this hugeness and long-rootedness can be plucked out without pain." Every thoughtful American with a spark of fair play in his veins (and this includes thousands of white people in the Deep South) wants this issue settled in justice under law. Any other method would betray not merely Negro citizens, but the moral giant that is America, our country, man's best hope for a free life in this mid-century's fresh threats of dark dictatorship.

At Youth for Integrated Schools

More than 15,000 college students participated in the Second Youth March for Integrated Schools in Washington, D.C., on April 18, 1959. The march was led by Roy Wilkins, A. Philip Randolph, Martin Luther King, Jr., Daisy Bates, Jackie Robinson, Harry Belafonte, and others. Its purposes were to dramatize the dissatisfaction of America's black youth with the slow pace of school integration and to show their support for the Supreme Court's May 17, 1954 ruling on school desegregation. Roy Wilkins was very interested in the youth of America in general and African-American youth in particular. In the following address he praises the youth for demonstrating their feelings and taking action on the issue of desegregation in public schools.

It is most fitting and proper that the youth of this nation should make their feelings known in plain fashion on the issue of desegregation in the public schools.

Education has always been a matter of deep concern to young people and their parents and in the age in which the uses of machines have climbed to a new high level, when electronics, engineering, chemistry, and the atom have sent our world forward at unprecedented speed, education is more necessary than ever.

Literally, one must be trained in order to live. The day is long past when what you don't know won't hurt you. Ignorance and lack of skill not only will hurt, but may well destroy.

But the world's mechanical and scientific progress has made more necessary than ever before an adequate education in human relations. The whole world is instantly aware of the revolt in far-off Tibet, where once news from that country might have taken weeks to reach Washington. The Prime Minister of Great Britain can be in Moscow on Sunday and in Washington or Ottawa on Tuesday. An African leader is jailed in Nyasaland and a Japanese Prince is married in Tokyo. The stories are in our newspapers and the pictures on our television screens within hours, often minutes. The story of the Montgomery bus protest is on the front pages of papers in Stockholm, Rome, and New Delhi as soon as it is printed in Chicago.

In this kind of a world, it is silly to talk about segregating people because of their color, because they wear robes or veils, because they speak French or because they are Swahili, Buddhists or Moslems, or Presbyterians, or because their spiritual leaders are called ministers or priests or rabbis.

Yet, here in the greatest country in the world, in the country which has grown great in the minds and hearts of mankind everywhere because it has been built on the guarantee of equality and individual liberty, we are engaged in degrading debate on whether American children, regardless of race, shall be educated together in our public schools.

Our highest court has held that they shall be so educated in accordance with the equal protection clause of the Fourteenth Amendment to our Constitution. It has said plainly that racial segregation in public schools is unconstitutional and denies to Negro children equality of opportunity in education.

But instead of complying with the Court's opinion and taking advantage of the leeway it had allowed local communities in planning to make beginnings in good faith, several of the states and many localities have refused to obey the ruling. They are defying the Court and tearing up the Constitution.

This resistance is the plan of adults, not of young people. Many of the leaders of the resistance have lived their lives, or are so far along that they cannot, or will not, change. Their world is behind them. They don't understand India any more than Kipling did. They don't know—and don't care—about the difference between Viet Nam and Ghana, or between Ecuador and Ethiopia. What is Kenya and where is Leopoldville?

What kinds of people live in these places? What are their colors, their religions, their eating habits? Our segregationists cry, who cares—what do they have to do with the United States?

So, living in their world of yesterday, they fight the uprooting of segregation and inequality which they nurtured in the land of the free. Yesterday it did not matter much to the rest of the world what the Governor of Arkansas did to nine Negro children, or to nine thousand. Today it matters a great deal. When Alabama sentenced a Negro man to death for the robbery of $1.95 the mail flooded into United States embassies in every part of the world and mounted to such a volume as to cause the Secretary of State to communicate formally and officially with the Governor of Alabama. The Jimmie Wilson case damaged the image of America in the eyes of the world—and the image of America in these delicate and dangerous days must be the concern of every citizen.

It is *your* concern because this is the world in which you will have to grow up and serve. This is the world in which you will choose a career, marry, rear children, govern and be governed. It is a world in which education will be a tool without which men cannot live and function or know happiness, satisfaction, and peace.

For education will give us the knowledge of each other, the mutual respect and dedication to the ideal of liberty and equality which will keep us all free. It has been the fashion to talk in terms of the damage which segregation has done to Negro children, and to forget the corrosive injury it has done to white youngsters. No more revealing or tragic story has come out of the desegregation campaign than that from the small town of Clay, Ky., where a white girl of fourteen declared: "I'd rather grow up to be an idiot than to go to a school with a nigger in it." The segregated system made this girl a useless citizen for the world of 1970 by the time she had barely reached her teens.

That is why it is not merely silly to talk about maintaining segregation in public education; it is well-nigh suicidal. It could lose us the struggle for the hearts of men, be it cold or hot.

So you are here to say by your presence and in your resolutions that you want integrated schools for all American children. You have every right to say this to your government and to all among the citizenry who will listen. No one has a better right, for in so speaking, you are demanding only that the high pronouncements and glorious traditions of this beloved bastion of freedom be vindicated, and that we be about the business of building the kind of world in which your generation can preserve freedom.

Finally, in this time of world-wide tension, youth, together with their allies, reaffirm their determined opposition to totalitarianism, wherever it occurs, in whatever form. Our unceasing struggle for equality in America demands our dedication to the achievement and maintenance of democracy in all parts of the world. The cause of democracy must triumph, for there can be no civil rights except within the framework of a democracy society.

We wish to express appreciation to the Attorney General's Office for the role it has played in advancing the cause of civil rights, but urge it to do more.

Let us not be dismayed by the long, hard struggle ahead, for we will win if we fight and faint not.

Freedom, Franchise, and Segregation

The NAACP and The Cooper Union for the Advancement of Science and Art in New York City have a very special relationship that extends to the founding of the Association in 1909. The founders often met at Cooper Union to bring forth plans for the development of the NAACP. In the centennial year of Cooper Union, Roy Wilkins underscores the unswerving and unyielding forward push of the Association and its accomplishments since its founding. In his optimistic fashion he expresses his belief that success is inevitable. This address, given in 1959, was broadcast on Station WNYC in New York City.

It is a privilege to have a small part in the celebration of the centennial year of The Cooper Union for the Advancement of Science and Art and to speak here in this famous Forum where so many issues of importance to our nation and to the world have had an airing.

In many a year since the founding of our country it must have seemed to anxious students that freedom of speech and freedom of assembly were about to be curtailed, if not abolished. The tensions that develop with wars, the fervors distilled in political and economic conflict, and the emotions stirred by debate over human rights, here and abroad, have threatened these and other precious freedoms from time to time. The Bill of Rights has escaped, often by the skin of its teeth. The courts which dared to interpret it and other clauses in our Constitution have had to meet and defeat challenges of greater or lesser intensity.

Through it all, America has lived and grown, meeting and overcoming crisis after crisis. I suggest that her survival and the preservation of her credo of individual liberty and of government by consent of the governed have been due in substantial measure to the fealty accorded these ideals by Cooper Union and similar institutions throughout our land.

I have a peculiar interest in this place, this celebration, and this topic. It was just fifty and one-half years ago that here in this Great Hall was held a mass meeting which helped to bring forth the National Association for the Advancement of Colored People.

On the night of May 31, 1909, Judge Wendell Phillips Stafford of the Supreme Court of the District of Columbia presided at a mass meeting here at which John E. Millholland was one of the speakers. The meeting was part of a two-day conference described by the *New York Times* as one "to consider the uplifting of the Negro. . . ."

A commentary on those times and a small indication of the distance we have come on this question may be found in the heading which *The Times* of June 1, 1909, placed over its account: "WHITES AND BLACK CONFER AS EQUALS." In the story of the Cooper Union meeting, *The Times* said:

> Cooper Union was three-quarters filled with men and women of both races. Negro men and white women sat side by side. On the platform were leaders of the movement, both black and white.

The conference committed itself to "union of the races in the public schools as against segregation of the Negroes as is now the case in the South," thus disposing of the popular 1956 argument in the Deep South that the N.A.A.C.P. thought up public school desegregation day before yesterday. Resolutions adopted at the final session have a familiar ring today: demanding the enforcement of the Fourteenth Amendment, demanding equal education opportunities, and demanding the right to register and vote under the Fifteenth Amendment. Lynching was scathingly denounced.

The conferees were called radicals and Booker T. Washington, Seth Low, Andrew Carnegie, and other conservatives would have none of it. When the gavel fell upon the last speech the continuation committee named by Chairman Charles Edward Russell began the formal organization of the National Association for the Advancement of Colored People. Russell was to be a member of its board until his death and Dr. W. E. B. Du Bois was to be its editor and spokesman and board member for twenty-five years, until his resignation in 1934.

Thus, the Cooper Union centennial has a special significance for the N.A.A.C.P. In the light of the stormy desegregation debates of the past ten years, and especially those of the six years since the Supreme Court's ruling on racially segregated public schools, the scheduling of this discussion tonight by this speaker is clue enough to the continuing independence and vigor of a hale centenarian. May Cooper Union live and continue to mold sinewy thought throughout its second hundred years and more.

The freedom bestowed upon the Negro as a result of the Civil War proved soon to be an April Fool's day wallet with string attached. It was there in plain sight; it was in the speeches and in the Congressional debates and Constitutional Amendments; but when one sought to pick it up, to hold it and use it, the substance was not there.

It is a temptation to assert that the overall objective of the South after Appomattox appeared to be to keep the Negro in the same personal, economic, and citizenship status he had occupied during slavery. Much of ante-bellum history as well as post-bellum activity—even to the present day—suggests the validity of this thesis, although, of course, the region was not (and is not) unanimous in support of such a goal. A fair analysis compels the recognition of many factors which shaped policy, but the control and exploitation of the Negro population was a ready and powerful weapon in evolving a new role for the defeated region. Its almost universal and enthusiastic employment has given color to the theory of some researchers that such activity in itself was the end objective.

The reaction of the Confederate States to the benevolent policy applied by the Federal Government as hostilities ended was denial of Negro suffrage and enactment of the Black Codes which baldly continued slavery with the exception that bodies were not bought and sold. The codes provided, among other things, that

> Persons of color might not carry arms unless licensed to do so; they might not testify in court except in cases involving their own race; they must make annual contracts for their labor, and if they ran away from their "masters" they must forfeit a year's wages; they must be apprenticed, if minors, to some white person, who might discipline them by means of such corporal punishment as a father might inflict upon a child; they might, if convicted of vagrancy, be assessed heavy fines, which, if unpaid, could be collected by selling the services of the vagrant for a period long enough to satisfy the claim. Former owners were given first option on these services.

Then Congress moved in with military government and the South responded with the terror and bloodshed of the Ku Klux Klan. The view has been cultivated assiduously that this Reconstruction period was a "tragic era" in which illiterate and unscrupulous Negroes were forced into public office and that these along with scalawags and Yankee carpetbaggers fostered an intolerable era of corruption and incompetence upon competent and upright Southerners. The period (or the professional Southern interpretation of it) is cited as "proof" of the necessity for barring the Negro from voting or holding public office.

Of course, as we look about us in government today the plaint of the orthodox Southerner about the Negro and Reconstruction assumes its proper proportion as the incantation of a religious cult, with tough subservient to fervor. The infinitesimal bonuses voted to themselves by some black-and-tan legislatures were as nothing compared to the percentages now extracted daily by resourceful political operators in and out of the South. Texas sought recently to extradite a former state official from South America in connection with a huge insurance deal. Georgia has had her trouble with the operation of her ports. A year or two ago the state treasurer of Illinois was convicted in a theft of nearly two million dollars. A Surrogate in wealthy and aristocratic Westchester County, N.Y., has pleaded guilty in a $718,000 land deal. The Borough President of Manhattan, New York City, the lone Negro in this series, is under indictment for conspiracy in connection with his alleged acceptance of $5,500 worth of repairs upon his apartment.

Obviously the "tragedy" in the Reconstruction period was not in the alleged irregularities, but in the color and regional background of those who benefited.

The Hayes-Tilden compromise accomplished the withdrawal of Federal troops and made automatic the departure of the carpetbaggers. The North was weary of the struggle and anxious to reap the rewards of a boom time. It turned its back and the conservative Southerners busied themselves with the building of a political structure that would serve their needs. They came up eventually with a system of restrictive franchise laws that guaranteed the dominance of the white majority politically and that made widespread racial segregation convenient, comfortable, and profitable.

The headlines in the newspapers of only five days ago, telling of the Eisenhower administration's new proposal for protecting the right of Negro citizens to vote, testify to the enduring nature of the disfranchisement structure fashioned by white Southerners seventy-five years ago. Poll taxes, grandfather clauses, literacy tests, property tests, criminal disqualifications, lengthened residence requirements, intimidation and violence, staggered registration periods, and restriction of the Democratic primary to white persons were instituted and, while some have been successfully challenged, others persist until today.

The six-year-old N.A.A.C.P. participated in 1915 through an *amicus* brief in a Supreme Court action which resulted in outlawing the grandfather clauses which had been adopted by a number of states. These clauses provided in general that all persons whose grandfathers were eligible to vote prior to the Civil War were now eligible to vote, thus effectively excluding all descendants of slaves.

Eight years later in 1923 the N.A.A.C.P. assisted a Texas Negro dentist in the first of three challenges of the constitutionality of the White Democratic Primary. Three cases were carried to the U.S. Supreme Court before the device was banned in 1944.

Only five Southern states still retain the poll tax as a prerequisite to voting— Virginia, Alabama, Arkansas, Texas, and Mississippi, but other devices are effective in barring Negro citizens from the ballot box. The Civil Rights Commission last year found a registrar who had given a literacy test and had reported in writing that a Negro applicant had made a mistake in "spilling." The word and the unique spelling were used twice in the report.

Registration books are moved to the homes of registrars. Offices are opened parts of days. Often only one applicant at a time is admitted to the registry room. Applicants frequently wait five and six hours to take their turns. One state requires the recording of age in years, months, and days. Miscounting by one day disqualifies a would-be registrant. In some states systems are changed frequently and fresh re-registration required. Too many localities countenance intimidation, threats of economic reprisal and of bodily harm.

It is no wonder, then, that on a South-wide basis, only twenty-five percent of the Negro citizens of voting age is registered, whereas sixty percent of such white citizens is registered. There are wide variations between states and still wider variations between counties within states. Texas has the greatest number of non-whites registered, 226,495, but Florida has the greatest percentage of its Negro eligibles registered, 39.5.

Mississippi, the bottom state, has only 3.89 percent of its eligible Negro citizens registered. This state has fourteen counties with a total Negro population of 109,000 in which not a single Negro was registered to vote in 1955. One of these counties is Tallahatchie where the fourteen-year-old Negro Emmett Till was murdered in 1955 by two white men who were subsequently acquitted in court. The jury panel contained no Negroes since only voters are eligible for jury service.

Another Mississippi county without a single Negro registrant is Pearl River, where in April of last year a Negro truck driver, Mack Charles Parker, was taken from the jail at Poplarville and lynched. A grand jury there refused even to read a report on the lynching prepared by the FBI. This report is said to contain the names of the men who helped to kill Parker and throw his body into the river, as well as the name of the man who made the jail keys available to the mob.

No clearer examples of the advantages to the ruling white clique of racial disfranchisement on the local level can be found than the Till killing and the Parker lynching, but the ramifications extend beyond county lines and help to erect protective ramparts for segregation far from the Pearl and Tallahatchie rivers. Indeed, this local system has formed the base of a blackjack operation upon the rest of the country designed to forestall any interference with what is solemnly proclaimed to be the Southern way of life.

Through the disfranchisement of citizens of both races (the deprived whites being soothed by the knowledge that the Negroes are on the bottom), Congressmen and Senators are elected and re-elected from the one-party South until their seniority gives them a disproportionately powerful influence on the nation's legislative business.

When the Democratic party is in control of the Congress they become chairmen of most of the committees, as they are in this session. Not content with protecting their own brand of apartheid back home, they have not hesitated to demand the extension of their racial philosophy and practices to the rest of the nation.

Senator James O. Eastland of Mississippi is a case in point. His seniority has brought him to the chairmanship of the powerful Senate Judiciary Committee. In this capacity he reviews all nominations for the Federal bench and for United States attorneys, questioning nominees as to their views on racial segregation. Civil rights bills have been bottled up in his committee and on one occasion Chairman Eastland boasted to his constituents in Mississippi of his carrying of one such bill around in his pocket so the committee could not act upon it.

A look at the total vote for Senator Eastland in his last election and the vote for a Senator from a state with a population comparable to Mississippi's suggests forcefully that the racially disfranchisement system is much more than a matter between the Eastlands and the Negroes.

The 1950 population of Connecticut was just 7,000 more than two million and the population of Mississippi was but 171,000 more, yet the total vote for Senator in Connecticut in 1956 was 1,090,289, whereas the total vote for Senator in Mississippi in 1954 was 105,526—just a fraction under one-tenth of the Connecticut vote. In the 1958 election the figures are even more arresting: the total Connecticut vote for Senator was 965,463 and that in Mississippi was 61,039—just about one-sixteenth of the Connecticut vote.

In the House the story is the same. The Thirtieth California District (San Diego) polled 202,931 votes in 1958 from its population of 426,00, but the Fourth Mississippi District, also with 426,000 population, polled only 8,665 votes.

The tail is wagging the dog. The Southern states are pulling the wool over the eyes of the rest of the country as they did from the earliest days of the Republic

when they insisted—for purposes of representation—that slaves be counted as three-fifths of a person. Today the Southerners want the disfranchised Negro citizens counted to enable a disproportionate number of Dixie representatives to come to Washington to browbeat the rest of the nation and to use the machinery and privileges of government to spread their arrogant racist theories.

This system deprives the citizens of Connecticut and other free election commonwealths of the influence in the nation's government to which they are entitled. If the South remains stubborn on Negro disfranchisement, the disadvantaged Northern states ought to insist on a cut in the Congressional representation from the offending states. This step would decrease the Dixie House members by twenty to twenty-five percent and clothe them, so to speak, in the proper size britches.

In the North the Negro citizen has become a significant political factor in large urban centers and his vote, on occasion, has had a bearing on the outcome of gubernatorial contests as well as on the results in the Presidential electoral college. In close elections, and with certain racial issues at stake, Negro voters can become the balance of power.

In general, the Negro tends to vote according to his interests as a citizen and only secondarily (barring a hot racial issue) as a Negro. Negro citizens are interested in national defense, foreign affairs, taxes, health and welfare, cost of living, education and jobs and wages, as are other Americans. They are also interested in civil rights, in attacking prejudice and bigotry in American life.

Negro voters were largely Democratic under Presidents Roosevelt and Truman, but there was a move back to the Republicans on the Presidential level in 1956. Whereas Mr. Eisenhower had received but twenty-one per cent of the Negro vote in 1952, he received thirty-eight percent of it in 1956. Characteristically, the Republicans did not regard these statistics as presenting an opportunity but asserted querulously that Negro citizens "did not seem to appreciate all that the Administration had done for them since 1952." Party leaders forgot that since 1932 the Democrats had been building great strength among Negroes in state and local machines and that this is not weaned away quickly nor with old Republican cliches.

On the racial issue, the Republicans seem to lack the ability to improve, to change pace, to deal with fresh developments, to concede, to advance a seed of crop with an eye to the later harvest. Whatever else they may be, the Northern Democrats are seldom inept in this area. If they had picked up seventeen points in 1956, they would have worked at picking up seventeen more by 1960. Not so the sulky Republicans. At this very moment their leader in the House, Rep. Charles A. Halleck of Indiana, is blocking a civil rights bill by officially frowning upon the signing by Republican members of a petition to get the bill discharged from the Rules Committee where it is buried.

With an obtuseness that could stem only from the McKinley era, Mr. Halleck blandly explains that he and his fellow Republicans believe in the committee system and cannot support unorthodox methods of bringing up legislation! The plain meaning is that the Republicans do not want to unbottle civil rights legislation. It is on this kind of performance that the Republicans expect Negro voters to rush to the GOP banner next November, but I suggest that this maneuver is as reprehensible as the smothering tactic of Democratic Senator Eastland. No one can predict now or later exactly what the Negro voter will do on election day, but as of today he does not like much of what he sees in the behavior of either party.

Segregation is bound up with politics and never more so than during the period since World War II, particularly since the Supreme Court public school ruling of May 17, 1954.

The great stride forward against racial segregation was the integration of the armed services. This began on a small scale without a formal policy during World War II, but it progressed officially from the day in July, 1948, when President Truman signed the Executive Order on the non-discriminatory use of manpower in the armed services.

In the past twenty years Supreme Court decisions have outlawed segregation in tax-supported colleges and universities and in public elementary and secondary schools, in public recreation and in interstate travel. Within the past two weeks a Federal court has ruled that Negro passengers may not be segregated in the airport dining room in Atlanta, Ga.

Discrimination in employment has been banned by law in a growing number of states and municipalities and discrimination in public and private housing is also forbidden under state laws that differ in content and scope, but seek the same goal.

It was the public school decision of 1954, however, that brought the segregation issue into fresh focus and precipitated the great human rights debate of this century.

Six years after the Supreme Court ruled racially segregated public school systems to be violative of the equal protection clause of the Fourteenth Amendment, only four Deep South states have retained completely segregated educational systems. These are South Carolina, Alabama, Georgia, and Mississippi. Louisiana has Negro students in its colleges and state university, but in no other public school.

This enumeration sounds as though spectacular progress has been made, since originally there were seventeen states and the District of Columbia with separate schools. While there has been substantial desegregation in the border states of Maryland, West Virginia, Kentucky, Missouri, Kansas, and Oklahoma, and in the District of Columbia—complete desegregation in some of these—only token action has occurred in others. The partially desegregated states may be ranked about as follows in terms of the number of Negro children involved: Texas, Delaware, Virginia, Tennessee, Arkansas, North Carolina, and Florida. This record disposes of the contention that the N.A.A.C.P. and the Negro citizens are moving too fast. It also suggests that, contrary to the optimism in some quarters, much work remains to be done.

Everyone knows of the dramatic episodes in the Little Rock story. It is clear now that Little Rock was chosen by the die-hard segregationists to test two theories: (a) that school segregation could be maintained by interposing the power of the state—through state armed forces, if necessary—between its citizens and a Federal procedure; and (b) that public schools could be closed and private ones opened and operated effectively for white students only.

Despite denials in Georgia and in Arkansas by Governor Orval E. Faubus, it is reasonable to conclude that the 1957 visit of the then Governor Marvin Griffin to Governor Faubus just prior to the drastic actions of the latter in the Central High School case did influence Faubus to carry on an "ultimate resistance" experiment in behalf of the Deep South states. It was reported at the time that Roy E. Harris, long a power in the Talmadge forces in Georgia and an extreme segregationist, was the chief salesman in Little Rock of the resistance idea. If so, there is a kind of irony in the recently disclosed letter to Harris by the Georgia State Superintendent of Schools to the effect that closing of the Georgia public schools to avoid some integration would be disastrous.

Whether Georgia sold the idea to the previously neutral and comparatively mild Faubus, or whether the Arkansas Governor suddenly turned from a tabby into a tiger on his own, the tests failed. The Federal Government, with an order of its courts being flouted by state militia, could do nothing less than move in its troops to back up its courts—especially with the whole world watching. The nine Negro children attended Central High School and, despite annoying difficulties suffered by them, the point was made that Federal court orders in such cases had to be obeyed. In the second test the parents and business community became so alarmed over the harm being done by the closed high schools and the improvised lily-white private schools that a series of moves was initiated which resulted in the re-opening of the schools on an integrated basis.

In Virginia, the parents and businessmen and enlightened citizenry finally rejected a "massive resistance" policy which involved closed schools with the result that six Virginia communities now have desegregated public schools. These have ten times as many Negro students involved as are included in the extremely token desegregation of the neighboring "liberal" state of North Carolina. Since the North Carolina total is disgracefully small, Virginia's number is not large, but the two states illustrate how the application of pupil placement laws function to slow desegregation to a crawl.

Even so, the existence and functioning of these laws declare to the nation that the segregationists have retreated from the "never, never" line. Georgia is now in the throes of a debate and an "agonizing reappraisal" of its declared policy to close schools and cut off state funds whenever a court order requires the admission of Negro students. The Atlanta school board is under such a court order and the state legislature is being asked to modify the state law so as to permit Atlanta to obey the order.

As in Little Rock and in Virginia, a movement has developed among responsible white citizens in Georgia to "Save Our Schools." The oratory of the state legislatures and the whooping and hollering when these emotion-laden laws were passed have been replaced by sober reflection upon the crippling effect of closed schools on Georgia's youth of both races. The Southern politicians have become the prisoners of their own racial spellbinding and have been made deaf by their own rebel yells.

The Southern people, white and Negro, are, as usual, the victims of a racial policy that refuses to recognize the history of the last ninety years. The difference today is that the hardship attendant upon the maintenance of segregation is plainly to be seen and felt by Southern white people. Heretofore, segregation was something created for and endured by the Negro population. Its imposition and operation brought no discomfort to whites and certainly no deprivation. But these schemes imposed by politicians to defy the U.S. Supreme Court by closing down the public schools for white children alter the time-honored formula. The 1960 white parents and businessmen have taken a look at it and found it not good.

In fact, it is the change in the times that has caught the professional segregationists upon the hip and that will defeat their effort to cling to the nineteenth century. The South is changing rapidly from a region with a predominantly rural economy to one of diversified, high-mechanized agriculture, industry, and finance. Giant government installations, wangled for the region by segregationist politicians, dot the South.

However, the technicians, supervisory and administrative personnel for these and for the hundreds of private plants that have been built in the South want no part of re-fighting the Civil War as a condition of employment in 1960. If there is to be turmoil over public schools, if action upon every public and business question is to be influenced by ante-bellum attitudes and practices on race, then they will choose to work elsewhere in the nation. They don't want their children and their wives in such an atmosphere.

Of course, changes on the race question in America outside the South, plus the profound changes in the world, doom the South's plan to adhere to an 1870 philosophy. With Negroes in the African Congo voting and about to become independent of Belgium, how much longer can Negroes in Mississippi be denied the ballot in the world's greatest democracy?

The black and brown people of Africa and Asia, winning their freedom from great colonial powers, refute the die-hards of our Deep South who revere the dead doctrine of Kipling.

Indeed, the American Negroes within their state borders refute them, for since 1954, no significant segment of the Negro population of any Southern state has been found to support the continuance of segregation. Instead, Negro citizens and their children have given heroic notice of their determination to secure all their rights as citizens and to do away with the humiliations and inequalities in the segregationist system. They have withstood economic reprisals, shootings, bombings and killings. The Montgomery bus protests dramatized this determination as did the behavior of Negro students who dared to attend schools under the personal abuse of adults and of white fellow students.

Segregation as a philosophy is dead. In practice it is alive, but it is being eliminated at a faster pace than many persons realize.

The pace will be speeded by the functioning of the underlying and basic American ideal of fair play, by active support for constitutional guarantees and for law and order, and by increased adherence to the Judeo-Christian ethic. The great religious faiths have played an influential part in the segregation debate thus far on the side of the right and the just. The tone they have set is reflected in the modification of community attitudes in many affected areas.

Complete change will not take place overnight, but it requires no crystal ball to assert with assurance that the segregated life as we have known it in America is on its way out, and, as social movements go, swiftly. The N.A.A.C.P. is proud of its fifty-year role in stimulating the change.

It has been and is now not merely a contest in which Negro Americans would emerge as the sole beneficiaries. It is a struggle which America must win, which white citizens must help to win because it is a struggle for the individual freedoms precious to all men everywhere. Abridgment or denial of the freedoms of Negro citizens constitutes a threat to the freedoms of white Americans.

The best hope of mankind to achieve liberty and human dignity is our own America, founded upon the immortal proposition that

> all men are created equal, that they are endowed by their Creator with certain unalienable Rights, that among these are Life, Liberty, and the pursuit of Happiness. That to secure these rights, Governments are instituted among Men, deriving their just powers from the consent of the governed.

Testimony to the continued dedication of our nation to these ideals was given by our outrage at the beating down of the Hungarian freedom fighters and by our quick aid to them. It would appear that we can react no less positively to the pleas of the freedom fighters within our own borders.

The Meaning of the Sit-ins

On February 1, 1960, in Greensboro, North Carolina, four African-American students at North Carolina A&T State College took a bold step by staging sit-ins. The sit-in action spread to other colleges: Michigan State University, University of Washington, Howard University, and others. A majority of the protests were organized and led by NAACP youth members. Most of those arrested were defended by attorneys provided by local NAACP branches. In addition, branches, NAACP officers, and members provided an appreciable portion of bail monies. In the following address, Roy Wilkins speaks before the City Club Forum of Cleveland about the meaning and results of sit-ins on April 16, 1960.

Since February 1, 1960, the so-called race problem has taken a fresh and dramatic turn. Beginning on that date in Greensboro, N.C., a wave of sit-ins by Negro college students at lunch counters of variety stores has swept across the South, from Florida to West Texas.

Back in the early 1940s, Howard University students, members of the college chapter of the National Association for the Advancement of Colored People, initiated sit-in demonstrations designed to break the color bar at lunch counters in

Negro areas in Washington, D.C. The present generation of youth renewed the demonstrations, also under N.A.A.C.P. auspices, in Wichita, Kansas, and Oklahoma City, Oklahoma, in the summer of 1958.

As the result of these well-organized and peaceful demonstrations by orderly young Negroes, colored citizens may now be served at nearly 100 lunch counters which previously barred them in Oklahoma City and other urban centers in the state. Similar success crowned the efforts for the young people in Wichita when a state-wide drugstore chain abolished the color bar at its lunch counters.

For some undetermined reason, the 1958 successes in Oklahoma and Kansas caused no immediate visible ripple in North Carolina or Tennessee. In February, 1958, the movement was revived by Negro and white students at Washington University in St. Louis. A year later it burst out spontaneously in city after city. It has made men and women of the Negro youths overnight. It has electrified the Negro adult community with the exception of the usual Uncle Toms and Nervous Nellies. It has baffled law enforcement officers. It has stirred white college students from coast to coast as they have not been stirred on any issue since Pearl Harbor. It has upset the managements of the chains of variety stores (although they won't admit it publicly) and it has set the politicians, in this election year, to calculating anew.

What is the importance of the lunch counter campaign of hundreds of Negro college students? Obviously, this effort is not a student prank. Obviously, too, it had only relative concern with freedom to sit down into a public business establishment and eat a hamburger or a slice of pie and drink a cup of coffee.

The message of this movement is plain and short: Negro youth is finished with racial segregation, not only as a philosophy, but as a practice. The overwhelming response of Negro adults to the bold venture of their children signals that they, too, whatever the myth to the contrary, are finished with segregation.

Among the first to sit down in North Carolina was a veteran who had served in the United States Air Force. He said he served cheerfully in the unsegregated air arm of his country's defense force. He trained, studied, ate and played with white boys in uniform. His unit was in the Far East where the United States was trying to demonstrate the advantage of democracy in the face of the growing strength of Chinese communism.

When this young man came to his native North Carolina to begin belated study to be a doctor, the old pattern of segregation by skin color seemed silly and cruel. It just did not make sense. The Supreme Court had spoken. The government had a national policy. The Air Force had a policy. The United States was preaching democracy to Indonesia and to Vietnam. Yet in North Carolina, U.S.A., he could not sit down in a Woolworth store and eat a sandwich.

So he and his friends sat on the stools waiting for service and by this simple act forced a nation to take a new look at the old race problem. For suddenly it was not Greensboro alone, but Durham and Raleigh and Chapel Hill and Tallahassee and Chattanooga and Nashville and Norfolk and Richmond and Atlanta and Orangeburg and Memphis and East Texas and San Antonio.

The South brought the sit-downs upon itself. The process began decades and decades ago, nurtured in the time of slavery which seems, in retrospect, to have done more harm to the minds and hearts of the free southern white men and their descendants than it did to the slaves and their descendants. In modern times it is propped up by the South's refusal to abandon the *Dred Scott* decision of 1857. That decision held that since Scott was a slave he was not a citizen and thus was not protected by the Constitution. "A black man," it said in effect, "has no rights which a white man is bound to respect."

The Dred Scott ruling was reversed by the Emancipation Proclamation, by the Civil War, and by the Amendments for the Constitution, but for the South, on the Negro question, there was no Civil War verdict and there were no Amendments to the Constitution. Aided by a monumental indifference on the part of the North and frequently by open collusion, the South, in effect, maintained the Dred Scott opinion, practically intact, until the outbreak of World War II.

The Dred Scott concept was maintained by means of intimidation, terror, and mob violence (short-memoried citizens tend to forget that as late as 1935 twenty-five persons were lynched, twelve of them in July, August, and September—an average of one every seven and a half days).

It was sustained, also, by widespread disfranchisement of Negro citizens and by the consequent perpetuation in office of those who kept the system in force. It was sustained through restrictive legislation enacted by the southern state legislatures and by the ruthless application of economic and cultural force wielded by those whom the system benefited.

In his classic dissent to the "separate-but-equal" ruling of the United States Supreme Court in 1896 in *Plessy* vs. *Ferguson*, Mr. Justice Harlan wrote these prophetic words:

> If laws of like character (that is, segregation laws) should be enacted in the several states of the union, the effect would be in the highest degree mischievous. Slavery as an institution tolerated by law would, it is true, have disappeared from our country, but there would remain a power in the states, by sinister legislation, to interfere with the full enjoyment of the blessings of freedom; to regulate civil rights common to all citizens upon the basis of race; and to place in a condition of legal inferiority a large body of American citizens. . . .

There did, indeed, "remain a power in the states . . . to interfere with the full enjoyment of the blessings of freedom" and the southern states have exercised that power to the *nth* degree.

They have restricted the employment opportunities of Negroes and have enforced, as long as possible, and wherever possible. a racial differential in wages.

They subscribed to the ghetto idea, finding it useful not only in maintaining status, but in facilitating control of a population segment.

They instituted and wove into a smothering pattern a thousand different personal humiliations, both public and private, based upon color. Through legal and extra-legal machinery, through unchallenged political power, and through economic sanctions, a code of demeaning conduct was enforced which cast down children before they could dream, and eroded manhood after it came of age.

As best they evaded the Fifteenth Amendment and at worst they contemptuously ignored it: Negro citizens were denied the right to register and vote. The persistence in this tactic is there for all to see.

Given the green light by the *Plessy* decision in 1896, Southerners happily set up the segregated Negro public school which neither they nor the indifferent North ever pretended was equal to the public schools for white children.

The shocking statistics of this inequality over the decades cannot, of course, tell us how many hundreds of thousands of Negro youngsters from, say, 1900 through 1959 have been cheated and crippled as men and as citizens by being deprived, wholesale, of the same education offered their white fellows.

How many in this country were surprised to learn that in much of the South Negroes are barred from public libraries, zoos, and art galleries? But they are.

With due allowance for many unknown factors, was the deprived number 100,000 a year? 2000,000? Does our Negro population today lack the greater stability, the steadier guiding force and the higher achievement factors which would have been added to it by the presence of five million better educated ones?

The sixty-year record notwithstanding, the Deep South resisted and has continued to resist compliance with the 1954 Supreme Court ruling outlawing segregated public education as violative of the equal protection clause of the Fourteenth Amendment because it was not legally ratified; even if it exists, it does not apply to public schools; even if it exists, the Supreme Court had no right to rule upon the question as such ruling would be "legislation"; and even if the Amendment exists and the Supreme Court has ruled, no compliance is possible because desegregated schools will lead to intermarriage and *intermarriage* is unthinkable.

The South, however, has not been the only performer on this human rights stage. The North has helped to drive home to Negro college youth that one must act, rather than wait, if one would attain and enjoy the dignity and rights which belong to American citizens and to humans beings. If the South has been contemptuous and ruthless, the North has been timid and hypocritical, a seeker of racial-quiet-at-any price.

Except for a few zealous crusading lovers of freedom for all men and a few unashamed descendants of the abolitionists, the North has cautioned the Negro to be calm and to go slow. It has grasped every opportunity, no matter how slender, to "see the point of view" of the South.

It has swallowed whole the elaborate fabrication, delineated and redelineated to this day, of the "Tragic Era" of Reconstruction. This oft-told tale, repeated in speech, song, story, films, scholars' tomes, and political tirades, furnished the pretext for (a) the exclusion of the Negro from politics and (b) the reiterated demand upon the North to keep "hands off" the race question henceforth since the North was held to be responsible for the South's period of torment.

And the North, by and large, has kept its hands off and has allowed the South to do with the Negro pretty much as it pleased. There is no need to recount here the record of shadow-boxing over anti-lynching and civil rights bills in the Congress, with Northerners frequently (with notable exceptions) in coalition with the South.

Since the public school decision in 1954, the North has eagerly absorbed the massive propaganda material of the hard-core southern states, of the admittedly extremist elements in Dixie.

It was a northern national magazine that in 1956 carried to its millions of readers Mississippi Novelist William Faulkner's cry to the N.A.A.C.P. and to the North to "Go Slow" on school desegregation. Northern editors, speakers, college professors, ministers, conferees, and truck drivers appropriated Faulkner's wail and made it their own.

In April of 1960, a national newspaper, surveying what it called the "ordeal" of the South (not the ordeal of the Negro), served up not only the old plaint that the issue is being "rammed down the South's throat" and being pressed "too fast," but another popular refrain: the North, on race discrimination, is as guilty as the South. It aired the hyperbole that the Negro is as bad off in the North as he is in the South and that the South loves him, while the North wants none of him.

Well, how fast is desegregation proceeding? The Southern School Reporting Service in Nashville, Tenn., which has been at work as a fact-recording agency on this problem since 1954, released figures in April, 1960, revealing that in the six years since the Supreme Court decision, six per cent of the Negro school children in the southern and border states have been admitted to desegregated classes.

Ninety-four per cent have not been affected. Slightly more than 2,500,000 Negro children out of just 3,000,000 in affected areas are still in Jim Crow school systems six years after the Supreme Court said such schools should be abolished.

The blinding speed of one per cent a year is what the South is screaming about—and what the North has accepted as "going too fast." And judging by the leather-lunged opposition to a civil rights bill by Southerners and by raucous vows of never to comply with the school ruling, no one is ramming anything larger than a cough drop down the throat of the South.

Of course, this assertion that the Negro is no better off in the North than he is in the South is always a lie, sometimes plausible, sometimes crude. If a Negro can stay in ninety per cent of the hotels in Ohio, but in not a single hotel in Alabama, does that make Ohio "as bad as" Alabama?

There is not a single Negro white collar worker in a city hall or state house in the entire South. Compare that to the Negro white collar worker in the state house in Columbus, Ohio, or in Lansing, Mich., or Harrisburg, Pa., or Albany, N.Y., or Sacramento, Calif.

In the school year 1956–57, Oregon spent $356 per pupil in attendance in her unsegregated schools, but in the school year 1956–57, Mississippi spent $107 per pupil in attendance in her segregated Negro schools. This fact, according to the propaganda, makes the Negro child in Oregon "no better off" than the Negro child in Mississippi. Ohio last year spent $330 per pupil in its mixed schools, while South Carolina spent less than half as much on its Negro pupils. Yet the North is listening in dewy-eyed sympathy to the dixie fairy tale that "the North shouldn't point the finger at us because it is as bad as we are."

The Negro students have been impelled to their action program in lunch counters because they are no longer able to stomach this humbuggery from the non-southern states. They know all about the old days in the South; they know what their mothers and fathers had to accept, and what their grandfathers and grandmothers endured.

They know about going to the back door, using the freight elevator, riding in the rear of the bus, living on dirt streets, forgetting about election day, being thankful for food and shelter on a farm—and no cash. They know about the insults, the beatings, the whippings, the killings. They went into Woolworth's and bought a lipstick or a tablet or costume jewelry, but when they wanted to buy a hamburger, that was "social."

They did not see how the North could agree with all this and they looked vainly for some understanding and moral support. But the North has been "busy" and ever so wary of becoming involved in a sticky business like a racial dispute involving, of all things, justice.

So the Negro students sat down, asking only simple justice. From the northern white people who are so much more free than the southern white people, the Negro students have received mixed messages. The northern white students have rallied with funds and vocal moral support. They have manned protest picket lines. Even in the South, white students have joined in the demonstrations and some have suffered arrest and abuse in consequence.

Some northern adults, including, I am ashamed to say, some Negroes who have the appearance of adults, have brushed off the whole thing with either indifference or condemnation. They do not know how late it is in the day nor how gray their acquiescence to injustice has made their little world.

The ponderous process of the law and the dexterous deception of politics also helped propel the Negro students on the lunch counter protest. All during the sit-ins the Congress was debating a civil rights bill aimed, it was said, at protecting the right of the Negro to vote in the South.

From day to day and week to week there were cloakroom huddles over parliamentary maneuvers. What rule would permit what? How could this clause be best challenged? What was the word from the Senate leadership? Can six words be slipped into Title VI and thus nullify the whole title? Shall this be done on Thursday, or held over until next Tuesday? What does the White House say? Will the Attorney General accept this change? How about the Laushe amendment? Registrars or referees?

The bill that finally emerged from the House and Senate is nothing about which to loose hosannas to the skies; it is a severely trimmed version of the Administration civil rights proposals which, when advanced in 1959, were termed "moderate" by no less an authority on moderation than President Eisenhower.

It is probable that under this bill it will not be easier for a Negro in certain areas of the South to register and vote. It may be no more difficult, but it is not likely to be easier. There seems to be only one tiny gain and that is that this bill empowers the Federal Government itself to enroll Negro citizens under certain conditions.

Certainly either political party is welcome to claim whatever credit it can for this bill. There is precious little credit to be shared. The Democrats did their dirty work and the Republicans did theirs. In fact, at times one did not know whether

Senator Dirksen, the Republican Minority Leader, was pushing the Administration bill or tearing it to pieces.

The Majority Leader, Senator Lyndon B. Johnson, keeps saying the legislation is a "good bill." He and Senator Dirksen and President Eisenhower were described as "happy" over the final bill. It is not recorded, however, that any of these three ever suffered discrimination at the polling place so that their joy over the bill is not to be confused with the feelings of Negro citizens on the subject.

In any case, the civil rights minuet under the Capitol dome did not stir the pulse of the Negro students. It had no freedom beat. And they are deaf to any note except the freedom note. It does not have to be a ringing declaration. It can be a soft logical remark like that of Governor LeRoy Collins of Florida who said if a store served Negroes at one counter it ought to serve them at its food counter. A little thing, but so right, so wrapped up in the essence of human dignity.

These Negro young people are right. The need of the times is for decency and dignity among men. We Americans are properly revolted over the slaughter of men, women, and children with automatic weapons by the police in the Union of South Africa. The world is outraged over the use of armored cars and tanks against unarmed men and women, the invasion of homes and merciless lashing with whips, the mass arrests, the herding, imprisonment and banishment. Civilized men everywhere condemn this senseless and corrupting cruelty.

It has to be cause for shame, then, that within our own United States, the Mississippi House on April 12 passed a resolution commending the government of South African for its "firm segregation policies."

The commendation includes, it is fair to conclude, the shooting down of civilians who demonstrated their objection to the degradation embodied in racial segregation. It must include, also, the whipping of men and women from their homes in order to force them to work.

Against this animalism the Negro college students sit undaunted in protest. Who can say them nay? Is the distance so great between the contempt of lunch counter exclusion and the crack of a bull whip or the death rattle of a Sten gun?

Nor is Johannesburg, South Africa, so far in spirit and practice from Birmingham, Alabama. A stark and frightening report from the Alabama city in the *New York Times* for April 12 pictures there "the emotional dynamite of racism."

In a way, the Negro college students are seeking to save what has been so precious about our America and what bids fair to be lost; our love of individual liberty and our readiness to fight for it in the face of the grossest manifestations of tyranny, in the teeth of massive state power.

This is the *real* United States underneath the mask which cowardly, cruel, crafty, and greedy men have sought to hold in place. As these young Negro students recover their freedom, they will be recovering America's, also, and redeeming its promise of life, liberty, and the pursuit of happiness for all under government by consent of the governed.

We owe them and their white student cooperators a debt for rearming our spirits and renewing our strength as a nation at a time when we and free men everywhere sorely need this clear insight and this fresh courage, so quietly and so humbly offered.

It is no extravagance to venture that they, in a sense, constitute another beacon in an Old North Church, another hoofbeat under a Paul Revere.

Medgar W. Evers: In Memoriam

The following are remarks by Roy Wilkins at the funeral of Medgar W. Evers on June 15, 1963, in Jackson, Mississippi. Evers, NAACP field secretary for Mississippi, died after being shot down from ambush in front of his home in Jackson on June 12.

There have been martyrs throughout history, in every land and people, in many high causes. We are here today in tribute to a martyr in the crusade for human liberty, a man struck down in mean and cowardly fashion by a bullet in the back.

The N.A.A.C.P. has had its share of sufferers: John R. Shillady, one of the earliest N.A.A.C.P. executive secretaries who was badly beaten by a mob in Austin, Tex., in 1919; Elbert Williams, secretary of the Brownsville, Tenn., N.A.A.C.P. who was lynched in 1940; Rev. George W. Lee, officer of the Belzoni, Miss., N.A.A.C.P., who registered to vote and was assassinated in 1955; Harry T. Moore, N.A.A.C.P state secretary for Florida and his wife, both murdered in their beds in Mims, Fla., by a bomb on Christmas night, 1951.

Now in 1963, Medgar W. Evers, N.A.A.C.P. state secretary for Mississippi, was shot June 12, 1963.

We tend to forget pioneer fighters. We say, unfeelingly and thoughtlessly, "No one really acted before now." "These marches were the first." "This death shot in the dark was the first." The truth is that through all the years before our time men have fought for freedom. Now it is our turn, not to re-write the record, but to add to it, not to preach that there never was a Columbus because there is now a Gordon Cooper.

The lurking assassin at midnight June 11–12 pulled the trigger, but in all wars the men who do the shooting are trained and indoctrinated and keyed to action.

The southern political system put him behind that rifle: the lily-white southern governments, local and state; the Senators, governors, state legislators, mayors, judges, sheriffs, chiefs of police, commissioners, etc. Not content with mere disfranchisement, the officeholders have used unbridled political power to fabricate a maze of laws-cushioned and economic practices which has imprisoned the Negro.

When at times it appeared that the rest of the nation might penetrate the Kingdom of Color, there were those ready always to beat back the adherents of decency and justice. Speaking of the public school decision of 1954 of the United States Supreme Court, Senator James O. Eastland told a 1955 Sentorobia, Miss., audience, "You are obligated to disobey such a court."

In faraway Washington, the southern system has its outposts in the Congress of the United States and by their deals and maneuvers they helped put the man behind the deadly rifle on Guynes Street this week. The killer must have felt that he had, if not an immunity, then certainly a protection for whatever he chose to do, no matter how dastardly.

Today as Americans and their President try to recover from their horror and to devise ways to correct the evils now so naked in our national life, these men in Congress, abetted by the timorous, the technical and selfishly ambitious are raising the familiar—and by now sickening—chorus of negations. With surgery required, they talk of ointments and pills. With speed the essence, they cite their rituals of procedure. Man may die and children may be stunted, but the seniority system and the filibuster rule must remain inviolate.

There appears to be a very real question as to whether the white man, so long an exemplar of bold and venturesome ingenuity in many fields is not committing spiritual suicide here in the land he fashioned as the home of free men. "All men" he said in his Declaration of Independence. But today he is shocked at the eruptions on every hand against his amendment of the "all men" doctrine.

In their moment of truth our opponents are striving frantically to drive away the reality of their decline. In something of the manner of the Maginot Line their defenses have been breached or by-passed. A southern state hires a retired professor to write a book setting forth the inferiority of the Negro race—twenty years after a Negro mathematician had helped in the calculations for the first atomic bomb! The opposition has been reduced to clubs, guns, hoses, dogs, garbage trucks, and hog wire compounds.

Obviously, the opposition is nearing bankruptcy. Fresh material is in short supply and strategy is stale and ineffective. Obviously, nothing can stop the drive for freedom. It will not cease here or elsewhere. After a hundred years of waiting and suffering, we are determined, in Baldwin's language, not upon a bigger cage, but upon no cage at all.

Medgar Evers was the symbol of our victory and of their defeat. Contrary to the view of a Jackson city official, Medgar was more than just an opponent. In life he was a constant threat to the system, particularly in his great voter registration work. In the manner of his death, he was the victor over it.

The bullet that tore away his life four days ago tore away at the system and helped to signal its end.

They can fiddle and they can throw a few more victims to the lions of repression and persecution, but Rome is burning and a new day is just over yonder.

At his arrest with me two weeks ago today, Medgar found that the man in the fingerprint room was from his hometown, Decatur, Miss. There they were, the one hometown boy carrying out the routine of the old order, unaware, perhaps, that the other, calm and smiling, was the herald of that future day when no man, white or black, even in Mississippi, will be fingerprinted and photographed under a felony charge merely for seeking his manhood rights as an American citizen.

We in the N.A.A.C.P. loved him for himself, for his sincerity and integrity. We mourn him, but we are not cast down. For a little while he loaned us and his people the great strength of his body and the elixir of his spirit. We are grateful for this blessing. For him we shall all try harder to hold our nation to the concept of "all men." If he could live in Mississippi and not hate, so shall we, though we will ever stoutly contend for the kind of life his children and all others must enjoy in this rich land.

Many years ago an N.A.A.C.P. executive secretary, James Weldon Johnson, wrote the words to the anthem, "Lift Ev'ry Voice and Sing."

These words belong here today to this heroic fallen N.A.A.C.P. officer who believed in his people and fought each waking hour for the realization of their destiny; who believed in his country and in its high principle of individual freedom and human dignity.

Stony the road, we trod,
Bitter the chast'ning rod,
Felt in the days when hope unborn had died;
Yet with a steady beat,
Have not our weary feet
Come to the place for which our fathers sighed?
We have come over a way that with tears has been watered,
We have come, treading our path through the blood of the slaughtered.
Out from the gloomy past,
Till now we stand at last
Where the white gleam of our bright star is cast.

Lift ev'ry voice and sing
Till earth and heaven ring,
Ring with the harmonies of Liberty;
Let our rejoicing rise
High as the listening skies,
Let it resound loud as the rolling sea.
Sing a song full of the faith that the dark [past] has taught us,
Sing a song full of the hope that the present has brought us,
Facing the rising sun of our new day begun,
Let us march on till victory is won.

We Want Freedom Now!

In this keynote address to the Fifty-fourth NAACP Convention, Roy Wilkins told the audience, "There will be a march on Washington as a living petition for the redress of old grievances, a march of decency and dignity." Secretary Wilkins's declaration was ratified by the convention, and a resolution was passed committing the NAACP to "cooperate, support, and participate in a March on Washington or other mass demonstrations which may be jointly sponsored, planned, and executed by those organizations and individuals similarly commited to enactment." The following is Wilkins's speech at the 1963 March on Washington for Jobs and Freedom.

I want to thank all of you for coming here today because you saved me from being a liar. I told them you would be here. They didn't believe me because you always make up your mind at the last minute, and you had me scared. But isn't it a great day. I want some of you to help me win a bet. I want everybody out here in the open to keep quiet and I want to hear a yell and a thunder from all those people out there under the trees. Let's hear you. There is one of them in the tree! I just want to let you know, those of you who are sitting down front here, that there are a whole lot of people out there under the trees.

My friends; we are here today because we want the Congress of the United States to hear us in person say what many of us have been telling our public officials back home and, that is, WE WANT FREEDOM NOW! We came here to petition our lawmakers to be as brave as our sit-ins and our marchers, to be as daring as James Meredith, to be as unafraid as the nine children of Little Rock, and to be as forthright as the Governor of North Carolina, and to be as dedicated as the Archbishop of St. Louis. We came to speak to our Congress, to those men and women who speak here for us in that marble forum over yonder on the Hill. They know from their vantage point here of the greatness of this whole nation, of its reservoirs of strength and of the sicknesses which threaten always to sap the strength and to erode in one or another selfish and stealthy and specious fashion the precious liberty of the individual which is the hallmark of our country among the nations of the earth.

We have come asking the enactment of legislation that will affirm the rights of life, liberty, and the pursuit of happiness and that will place the resources and the honor of the government of all the people behind the pledge of equality in the Declaration of Independence. We want employment and with it we want the pride and responsibility and self-respect that goes with equal access to jobs— therefore, we want an FEPC bill as a part of the legislative package.

Now for nine years our parents and their children have been met with either a flat refusal or a token action in school desegregation. Every added year of such treatment is a leg iron upon our men and women of [1980]. The civil rights bill now under consideration in the Congress must give new powers to the Justice Department to enable it to speed the end of Jim Crow schools, South and North. We are sick of those jokes about public accommodations. We think, for example, that if Mrs. Murphy, rugged individualist as she must be, has taken her chances with the public thus far, she can get along without solicitous protection of the august Senate of the United States. It is true, of course, that Mrs. Murphy might get a Negro traveler here and there in her boarding house, or in her tourist home, but then we must remember this, she might get a white procurer, or a white embezzler too. So Congress must require non-discriminatory accommodations.

Now, my friends, all over this land and especially in parts of the Deep South, we are beaten and kicked and maltreated and shot and killed by local and state law enforcement officers. It is simply incomprehensible to us here today and to millions of others far from this spot that the U.S. Government which can regulate the contents of a pill apparently is powerless to prevent the physical abuse of citizens within its own borders. The Attorney General must be empowered to act on his own initiative in the denial of any civil rights, not just one or two, but any civil rights in order to wipe out this shameful situation.

Now the President's proposal represents so moderate an approach that if it is weakened or eliminated the remainder will be little more than sugar water. Indeed, as it stands today, the package needs strengthening and the President should join us in fighting to be sure that we get something more than pap.

And finally, we hear talk of protocol and procedures and rules, including the Senate filibuster rule. Well, we have a thought on that. We declare that rules are made to enable the Congress to legislate and not keep it from legislating and we are tired of hearing rules cited as a reason why they can't act. Now we expect the passage of an effective civil rights bill. We commend those Republicans in both Houses who are working for it. We salute those Democrats in both Houses who are working for it. In fact, we even salute those from the South who want to vote for it but don't dare do so and we say to those people, just give us a little time and one of these days we will emancipate you! It will get to the place where they can come to a civil rights rally too. If those who support the bill will fight for it as hard and as skillfully as the southern opposition fights against it, victory will be ours.

Just by your presence here today we have spoken loudly and eloquently to our legislature. When we return home, keep up the speaking by letters and telegrams and telephoning and, wherever possible, by personal visit. Remember that this has been a long fight. We were reminded of it by the news of the death yesterday in Africa of W. E. B. Du Bois. Now, regardless of the fact that in his later years Dr. Du Bois chose another path, it is incontrovertible that at the dawn of the 20th century his was the voice that was calling for you to gather here today in this cause. If you want to read something that applies to 1963 go back and get a volume of the *Souls of Black Folk* by Du Bois, published in 1903.

Well, my friends, you got religion here today. Don't backslide tomorrow. Remember Luke's account of the warning that was given to us all: "No man," he wrote, "having put his hand to the plow and looking back is fit for the Kingdom of God."

Thank you.

At American Association of Advertising Agencies

This speech was made in the aftermath of the March on Washington, the Kennedy and Evers assassinations, and the bombing of four little children in Birmingham, Alabama. Job opportunities were opening, but, these available jobs were in automation. Job that had been long held by the unskilled poor were being eliminated with no hope or plans for replacement. In this speech Roy Wilkins explains the need for black people to put into action the concept, "Don't Buy Where You Can't Work." This speech was given on November 18, 1963.

It is no mere coincidence that the Negro protest movement attains its greatest thrust in a period of rising expectations on one hand and of shattering despair on the other. Within the Negro community two divergent economic trends are clearly discernible—one hopeful, the other despairing. Each contributes to the discontent and ferment among the nearly 20,000,000 Negroes comprising the country's largest racial minority.

For the trained and talented Negro new opportunities in an expanding range of occupations are opening up at a faster rate than ever before. Meanwhile, automation is threatening the unskilled and semi-skilled Negro with economic extinction. There are entrenched barriers to his free entry into the artisan class. Training and opportunity are denied him. He faces the grim prospect of permanent unemployment. The unemployment rate among Negroes is already more than twice that among white workers and may well soar higher.

The Negro revolt in the United States is not, as some seem to believe, of 1963 vintage. Historically, the Negro has always been in revolt against inferior status imposed upon him. The genesis of the Negro revolt is deeply rooted in American history. During the three and a half centuries of his residence here he has expressed this discontent in many ways, including armed insurrection against and flight from slavery; non-violent agitation, law suits, political action, economic pressures and demonstrations. For more than a half century now, the organized resistance to the status quo has largely been directed by and channeled through the National Association for the Advancement of Colored People.

Why then did this revolt come to a climactic head in 1963 and not, say, in 1959 or 1940, or in some other earlier year? The discontent and the essential ingredients of the present ferment have long been with us. Why was it possible to bring nearly a quarter of a million persons to Washington on August 28 for a massive demonstration, an achievement which would have been impossible ten years ago, or, perhaps, even last year?

There have been many factors contributing to this upsurge of militancy, especially since the United States Supreme Court's historic anti-segregation ruling of May 17, 1954. There has been disillusionment over the slow pace of school desegregation. There has been mounting anger stemming from the brutally repressive measures used by the police against civil rights demonstrations. There has been fury because of the unpunished assassination of Medgar W. Evers in Jackson, Miss., and the bomb murders last September 15 of four Negro children in Birmingham. There has been increasing distress because of the failure of the Federal Government to act effectively to protect basic human rights. And there has been hope for an early end to a century of denial of equal rights, suppression of traditional American liberties, and negation of the country's basic democratic tenets.

Significantly, the August 28 demonstration was known as the "March on Washington for Jobs and Freedom." What the Negro demands today is equality in job opportunity and in the exercise of citizenship rights. These goals, he fully realizes, are unattainable within the framework of segregation. Segregation was instituted to keep the Negro in his place, that is, to preserve the patterns of slave regime. It was not devised to keep the races apart, especially in the South where the two races had been in intimate contact for more than 250 years. As long as segregation remains a fact of American life, the Negro will be deprived of his full citizenship rights of his opportunities for job equality.

The divergent economic trends within the Negro Community bring this issue into sharp focus. It is true, more Negroes are holding better jobs in industry and government than ever before. Between 1955 and 1961, the percentage of Negro families with annual incomes above $5,000 doubled, jumping from 14.2 to 28.4. In the $10,000 and above bracket the increase was five-fold, from .6 to 5.6 pecent. But when it is realized that 17.1 per cent of white families are in the $10,000 and above bracket, it becomes apparent that Negroes have not advanced in proportion to their numbers and their readiness. Obviously, there is a burgeoning Negro middle class composed of people of good training and substantial and steady income comprising an expanding market for quality goods.

Nevertheless, the average college-trained Negro encounters far more difficulty in obtaining employment and advancement than his white counterpart. There are jobs for which he is qualified which remain closed to him solely because of his race. The fact that some Negroes—admittedly more than ever before—are moving into new jobs with greater responsibilities and higher pay accentuates the frustrations of the many to whom the door of opportunity is still closed.

During and immediately following World War II the gap between the median incomes of white and Negro families was somewhat narrowed. Alarmingly, since 1952, that trend has been reversed. The median income for Negro families, which in 1952 was 56.8 percent of that of white families, had dropped to 53.4 by 1961. The indications are that this downward trend continues—spreading despair, swelling the relief rolls and piling up human wreckage.

One of the problems confronting the Negro community is the excessive dropout rate among young colored people. A Bureau of Labor Statistics study affords a revealing answer as to why so many Negro boys and girls fail to complete high school. According to this study, the median income for a family headed by a Negro high school graduate was less than that of a white family whose head had completed only the eighth grade. The incentive for further schooling, particularly for those with no hope of going on to college, is too often lacking. They see too little to gain.

At the very time new opportunities are opening up for some of the better trained young Negroes, jobs long held by the undertrained masses are being steadily eliminated with little or no hope of restoration. These trends have led to increasing economic and cultural stratification within the Negro community. But what is apparent to all is the star fact that the freedom of the successful Negro is as much circumscribed as that of his less advantaged brother. Neither enjoys the freedom of the most ordinary white person. Neither is welcome at the Dinkler-Tutwiler Hotel in Birmingham. Prevailing color proscription ignores the class structure within the Negro community.

Racial discrimination is an inescapable burden for every known Negro in the country. He knows that at any moment he may encounter the racial slur or rebuff. He knows that, no matter how eminent his position or how fat his bankroll, he is, in the eyes of his white fellow citizens, a man apart. He realizes that in the land of his nativity he is regarded as a stranger, subject always to a group evaluation and never wholly accepted on the basis of individual merit.

The Negro protest movement has involved not only the limited and dispossessed, but also the economically secure and the talented. These latter were in Washington by the thousands, not in pursuit of jobs for themselves, but in demand for freedom and equality for everyone. They realized that without these, they themselves would never be free, never really secure. They recognized that, as long as the color bar remains, their fate is inextricably linked with that of the jobless auto worker in Detroit, the unlettered field hand in Mississippi, the rejected applicant for apprenticeship training in New York City, the displaced mechanic in Chicago.

Jobs and Freedom, yes. But also the white man's image of the Negro. The denial of jobs and freedom stems largely from the distorted image the white majority has of the Negro. How persistent and pervasive this stereotype of the Negro as not only a different, but also a lesser, creature is revealed by the Louis Harris poll published in the October 21 issue of *Newsweek*. According to this poll, the majority of white Americans believes that Negroes are a happy-go-lucky people with little ambition, and that they are careless about their persons, their morals and their homes. Half of the white people believe Negroes have less native intelligence than white persons.

This stereotype is daily re-inforced by all the media of mass communications— the press, radio, television, and films. The N.A.A.C.P. has long been engaged in efforts to eradicate this image which has consistently been invoked to deny Negroes jobs, decent housing, access to public accommodations, justice in the courts, and, in the South, the right to vote. Some gains have been made, but the stereotype persists.

What the Negro asks of the communications industry and particularly of you gentlemen in the advertising field is not special treatment nor a crusade for civil rights—that's our job and we will carry it on. What we in the Negro protest movement ask is realistic treatment of the Negro in the roles he actually plays in American life today. Only recently, and still too rarely, has the viewer of television commercials had any reason to believe that the United States is populated by any persons other than White Anglo-Saxon Protestants.

Negroes in the United States represent a huge consumer market. Some estimate it as high as $20 billion annually. They buy refrigerators, washing machines, automobiles, clothing, food, detergents, and deodorants. They consume drinks— soft, hard and in-between. They smoke pipes, cigars, and cigarettes, at the same risk of lung cancer as white people. Yet to look at television commercials and read advertisements in the daily press and the mass circulation magazines, one would never realize this. Only when one turns to *Ebony* Magazine or to the Negro newspapers is one made aware of the existence of Negro consumers.

The time has come for a change. Your clients sell their products to Negroes and they want more purchasers. There is every reason why they should let this fact be known through the advertisements, not only in the Negro media, but also in their television commercials and in the press of general circulation. In doing so they will not only present a true picture of the Negro, projecting a new, realistic image, and help product sales; they will also provide new employment opportunities for Negro models and discharge an act of justice.

Increasingly, Negro consumers are concerned about jobs and image. They like to spend their money where Negroes can get employment and with businesses which do not distort the Negro image either by ignoring the existence of Negroes or by utilizing unacceptable portrayals. Increasingly, they are making their desires known, preferably in conferences and negotiations, that is why I am here today; but if need be, on the picket line, where I may be tomorrow. The pursuit of new job opportunities extends also into the offices of advertising agencies.

Selective buying and picketing for jobs are not new. They date back at least to the late 1920s when a militant Negro newspaper *The Chicago Whip* launched its "Don't Buy Where You Can't Work" campaign against stores in the city's Black Belt. These demonstrations were given constitutional sanction by a United States Supreme Court decision handed down in 1938.

"Race discrimination by an employer," the decision declared, "may reasonably be deemed more unfair and less excusable than discrimination against workers on the ground of union affiliation."

The movement originated in Chicago, spread to Cleveland, Detroit, New York City, Washington, and other cities across the land. In recent years, there's hardly a major city that has escaped selective buying campaigns, in the South as well as in the North and West. They have proved productive when well organized and consistently maintained as, notably, in Philadelphia, Pa.; Columbus, Ohio; Oklahoma City; Camden, N.J; Durham, N.C.; Savannah, Ga.; and Charleston, S.C., to name a few places. Unless new employment opportunities are speedily opened up, there certainly will be more such campaigns on the local level and, possibly, nationally against certain chain stores and products, the manufacturers of which continue discriminatory employment practices.

The N.A.A.C.P. and other civil rights organizations are prepared to mobilize the Negro's considerable purchasing power in the fight for jobs and freedom. What is more important, the Negro public in 1963 is more responsive than ever to the call to exert economic pressure in pursuit of legitimate goals and aspirations. They are equally responsive to those products and companies which indicate in their advertisements and policies their desire to cultivate the Negro market.

The N.A.A.C.P. does not set racial quotas, nor does it advocate the lowering of reasonable standards. Such steps may prove self-defeating. On the other hand, it rejects tokenism in employment as in other areas. To employ a Negro as a show-piece is no answer to today's needs. Moreover, no one is deceived by such a maneuver. The answer is a thoroughly non-discriminatory policy in employment and promotions based on individual merit. Competent Negro personnel is available, even though in some instances difficult to reach.

A measureable increase in job opportunities for Negroes redounds to the benefit of the total economy. It does not mean fewer jobs for white persons. On the contrary, it means more jobs for the whole community. Negroes do not enjoy a reputation as hoarders of money. They spend perhaps a larger share of their income than do similarly situated white persons. New millions of dollars in circulation would create more jobs for all. Employable Negroes could come off the relief rolls thus reducing the tax burden and releasing more money for circulation.

But these new job opportunities will not be made available on a significant scale unless the Negro mobilizes his full economic and political strength and unless the old stereotype of the Negro, as a shiftless, irresponsible person is demolished. We will undertake the job of mobilizing that strength and we call upon you for assistance in getting rid of that false image by projecting through the media the diverse roles Negroes play in American life today. Not all doctors and lawyers and business men, to be sure. But also, not all menials and clowns and criminals.

At Conflict '66—Virginia Polytechnic Institute

Race and color have permeated American history since its beginning. No state, however, has the right to abridge the constitutional rights of any individual. Indeed, it is the responsibility of the state to protect an individual's constitutional rights. In the aftermath of the Supreme Court's ruling in the *Brown* decision, many southern states attempted to and in some cases did obstruct the High Court's ruling to desegregate public education. In the following speech, Roy Wilkins explains why the states' rights doctrine on the constitutional rights of African Americans has outlived its time.

I offer first my thanks for the opportunity given me by your kind invitation to participate in Conflict '66. And then I extend my congratulations to the student body of Virginia Polytechnic Institute for its decision to explore an issue which has been a factor, open or concealed, in every move of our country since the first white men landed at Jamestown in 1607 and the first black men arrived there twelve years later.

A debate of a kind has been in progress from that time to this very day over the abilities of black people. In the beginning, of course, the sentiment was almost unanimous that they were inherently inferior; indeed, they were thought to be just a cut above animals. Today that opinion exists as a belief, not as an intellectual exercise—in South Africa, officially, and in certain backwaters of the United States.

A distinguished Virginian, Thomas Jefferson, wrote in 1809 what is almost the theme of my remarks:

My doubts [as to the inherent abilities of Negroes] were the result of personal observation in the limited sphere of my own state, where the opportunities for the development of their genius were not favorable, and those of exercising it still less so. . . . But whatever be their degree of talent, it is a measure of their rights.

The present civil rights struggle is essentially an effort by the American Negro minority, handicapped above other minorities by skin color and a slave background, to find "favorable opportunities," in Jefferson's words, for the "development" and "exercise" of "their genius."

Four days ago the United States Supreme Court ruled that the United States could invoke an 1870 law and prosecute those who conspire to deny a Negro and his fellow campaigners their right to physical safety, including their lives, and not leave such matters exclusively to the state courts. The decision grew out of a ruling by a lower Federal court that the United States could not act against all the accused men in the 1964 murders of three civil rights workers in Philadelphia, Miss., but only against the accused law officers.

As this hairsplitting of the sixties suggests, the struggle has been a long one, running throughout the history of this country, before and after it became an independent nation. It is altogether likely, with blackouts on certain subjects being what they are, that the continuing thread of the racial issue through our political, economic and social history should have escaped not only Virginia students, but those in New England as well.

We built the economy of the entire South first on black slave labor and then on black plantation sharecroppers and tenants. Our jobs were divided into racial categories; our wage scales were racial.

But the states' rights doctrine on the Negro had outlived its time. Despite all the elaborate restrictions and the still more elaborate propaganda, enough Negroes had forged ahead to make the system look ridiculous as well as cruelly unfair. Two World Wars had come along. Increasing numbers of Negroes had become politically active—and influential—in states outside the South.

The Supreme Court was chipping away at the separate-but-equal doctrine of constitutionality, finally to renounce it in the *Brown* case. Great Britain abandoned its empire role and African colonies became free nations.

Resistance to the *Brown* decision and to the trend toward change sparked the direct action protest demonstrations over the nation. Virginia was so determined upon a policy of "massive resistance" to school desegregation that in 1956 it enacted what became known as an anti-N.A.A.C.P. package of laws. One of these sought to punish not only an organization that offered legal aid to those seeking desegregation, but the person seeking such aid!

The Civil Rights Act of 1964 followed the highly emotional year of 1963, the centennial of the Emancipation Proclamation and the date of the assassination of the beloved John F. Kennedy. In 1963, also, the fiction that "only a few agitators" want civil rights was laid to rest by the 200,000 people from all corners of the nation who marched in Washington on August 28 to petition Congress by their presence to enact the civil rights bill proposed by President Kennedy and urged by President Johnson.

The 1964 statute is the most comprehensive civil rights law ever enacted. Its ten titles covered all matters except housing. The voting title was deemed inadequate for the problems presented by the "hard core" counties and the Voting Rights Act of 1965, proposed by President Johnson, came into being.

While these two Acts have won pleasantly surprising support in the South, even if on a token basis, the usual dissents are heard, the usual evasions and delays are uncovered and the usual wails arise about invading the province of the states.

The resisters to school desegregation have not been deterred. Compliance with Title Six of the Civil Rights Act which requires desegregation as a condition to the allocation of Federal funds to a school district is spotty. Some districts are complying in good faith; others are complying on paper only and others are proceeding in their segregated ways without Federal funds.

In the realm of discrimination in employment the rugged individuals and the states' righters are protesting and digging in their heels, but are inclined toward compliance, even if slowly. The overall picture is not encouraging because the Negro who was displaced from the farms is not being taken into Southern industry, but it is not as bleak as it once was. The new industrial South cannot reap full benefits from its new economy if it keeps its Negro consumer market on domestic servant wage levels.

Loud protests went up from politicians and voting machinery officials against the Voting Rights Act and its provision for sending Federal registrars in counties where the regular registration machinery had failed conspicuously to enroll Negro applicants.

But politicians are believers in adjustment. When the increased Negro registration became a fact of political life, Alabama, for example, erased the slogan, "For White Supremacy" from the state's Democratic party ballots. There are still threats in some localities. There is still murder as an attempted deterrent, as we had in the ghastly Vernon Dahmer fire bombing in Hattiesburg, Mississippi, in January—only because Dahmer had announced that he would receive poll tax receipts.

But the climate is steadily better. The poll tax is gone with the Supreme Court ruling in the Virginia case. Negroes are filing as candidates and most hitherto loud voices on race and politics are now muted.

As we look back and contemplate the deadening racial poison that ran virulently for decades in our land, as we count the stunted, the maimed, and the dead in the racial conflict and as we attempt to estimate what might have been, it seems inescapable to this reviewer that while the states' rights doctrine may have been good for an uneasy few, it was poison for the Negro and a moral and physical shackle upon our nation.

Every student of public affairs can take heart from the emergence of a new white South. This South is unsure about procedures and about the speed of change, but it is sure that it is not going to repeat the follies of the past.

Every student is apprehensive over the stubbornness of Northern urban complexes over their failure to meet challenges in locked-in slums, in *de facto* school segregation, in police-minority relations, in training and opportunity for minority youth. The deprivation has been generations-deep and the correction will take extra time, extra skill, [and] extra money.

Regardless of the loud noises from the extremists, the great body of Negroes knows that it has a responsibility in these changing times. They know, however, that they cannot be expected to make bricks without straw. They must have help—

extraordinary help and understanding. Their upward climb against the literally heartbreaking odds of the past 100 years of states' rightsism is indication enough that they will come through if the openings and the training are available.

And what of states' rights? Of course the states have certain rights. They also have responsibilities. But these rights and these responsibilities are encompassed within the framework of the Constitution of the United States of America. No state has the right to abridge the constitutional rights of any citizen or group of citizens upon the basis of race or color. The rights that inhere in statehood are rights which must be extended equally to all citizens of the respective states. And it is the responsibility of the states to see that these individual rights are safeguarded.

With the new legislation already enacted, together with that proposed on protection for those seeking their constitutional rights, we have useful tools for making progress.

Let a Watts not dismay us, but spur us to accelerated action. With respect to slavery, but with words that fit our times, Jefferson wrote in 1797:

The day which begins our combustion must be near at hand; and only a single spark is wanting to make that day tomorrow . . . every day's delay lessens the time we may take for emancipation.

We—the Negro citizen and our country—seek justice. The Negro has been thwarted by obstacles of size, intensity, and duration he had no right to expect in this land, founded on individual liberty. In the eloquent words of our President, a man from Texas, in his speech at Howard University last June:

. . . American justice is a very special thing. . . . We have pursued it faithfully to the edge of our imperfections. And we have failed to find it for the American Negro. . . . It is the glorious opportunity of this generation to end the one huge wrong of the American Nation and, in so doing, to find America for ourselves. . . .

At White House Conference
"To Fulfill These Rights"

When Lyndon B. Johnson succeeded John F. Kennedy as president in 1963, Roy Wilkins found Johnson much more aggressive on civil rights than Kennedy had been. Yet even after Johnson signed the 1964 Civil Rights Bill into law, Wilkins knew there was still much to be done. At the time of this White House conference, the *Brown* decision was twelve years old. The expectations in the black community had been high after *Brown*, and now blacks were growing impatient with the roadblocks to civil rights that some states had put into place. Since 1619 the plight of African Americans had been a matter for the states and private institutions. The issue of race relations lacked the country-wide recognition of what should have been a national concern. In the following speech, Wilkins discusses President Johnson's White House Conference "to fulfill these rights."

This conference, which we are concluding tonight, is properly but an expansion of the revolution of rising expectations which has been in being among Negro citizens and their allies since the date of the Second Emancipation, May 17, 1954.

On that date, the legal blessing which had been bestowed for fifty-eight years upon the doctrine of separate-but-equal constitutional citizenship was withdrawn in the historic *Brown* decision of the U.S. Supreme Court.

These past two days have brought the first-in-history White House Conference "To Fulfill These Rights." There have been White House Conferences on health, children, foreign policy, education, and other issues vital to our national welfare. Now, for the first time, the issue which has plagued both the national policy and the American conscience from Jamestown in 1619 to Watts in 1965, has moved to the center of the national stage.

Through most of our history it has been a matter for the states and for private organizations. We have cried out our anguish, voiced our protests and worked feverishly in patchwork efforts within the States, but we lacked the national recognition of, and attention to, what we know to be a national concern.

The handicap of the state perspective has been underscored no more effectively than by the correspondence in 1809 of Thomas Jefferson. He wrote to a friend:

My doubts (as to the inherent abilities of Negroes) were the result of personal observation in the limited sphere of my own state, where the opportunities for the development of their genius were not favorable and those of exercising it still less so . . . but whatever be their degree of talent, it is no measure of their rights.

The present civil rights struggle is essentially an effort by the Negro American minority, handicapped above other minorities by skin color and a slave background, to find, in Jefferson's words "favorable opportunities" for the "development" and "exercise" of "their genius."

Our conference today, called with uncommon courage by our President, has substituted for Jefferson's personal observation a White Paper of formidable facts, of fearless analysis and arraignment and of bold chartings of action reaching to the heart of the democratic ideal.

Since a survey of the vast variety of disabilities stemming from racial exploitation would require a month-long conference and several volumes of reports and recommendations, four critical areas of living and citizenship were selected. No mere history of hardship, this, but a frank 1966 look at the present and into the future.

Our economic security and welfare: ". . . no more ugly and urgent crisis facing this Nation today than the economic insecurity of Negro Americans . . . employment and income problems are complex, long-standing and rooted deeply. . . . Negro unemployment is of disaster proportions . . . creative and large scale action must be taken to achieve full and fair employment for the Negro working-age population."

On education: "American schools today are failing to fulfill" their purpose of preparing children "to be independent persons in an open society. . . . It is incontestable that we have different qualities of education and therefore widely varying levels of opportunity through schooling for the Negro child and the white child . . . more than ninety percent (of school children) is educated in racially segregated schools . . . (which) provide inferior education through their failure to prepare their pupils for life in our pluralistic society, and ever-shrinking world . . . defacto segregation continues as the prevailing pattern in the North and West, and, if anything, has become more, rather than less rigid."

On housing: "The consequence of the slums and the ghettos and the barriers to freedom of choice in housing loom large. The dimensions of this program (of massive building and rehabilitation programs) are staggering but they are no larger than America's space ventures. . . ."

On administration of justice three categories were set forth embracing protection of Negroes and civil rights workers in connection with the exercise of their rights: equal justice in the operation of the machinery of the law—juries, courts, court officials and law enforcement agents and police minority group community relations.

The material in the Council report, including the recommendations for action, has received critical scrutiny and has benefited from broadening and strengthening corrections and amendments including home rule for D.C. by the conferees in the twelve committees. Each of these urgent suggestions, born of intimate experience on local and state levels, has become a part of the record and will be submitted as a part of the report to the President, as will the specific resolutions adopted in the committees this afternoon.

The urgent, recurring stated duty upon every conferee is to multiply his experience here in the communication he will effect among his fellow citizens back home. He must carry the message, the call to community action on the local level, the stirring of interrelated and purposeful state and regional action and the wide use of the newly-acquired tools and channels provided by Federal policy and legislation.

The new four-part civil rights bill of 1966, now at or near the committee hearing stage in both the House and the Senate, offers a chance for immediate action this summer, not next winter, on aspects of three topics of this Conference.

A section of the bill, H.R. 14765, broadens the authority of the Attorney General to initiate school desegregation actions without waiting for the filing of complaints by parents.

Another section would close some of the loopholes in the jury selection process in both state and Federal courts which now permit racial discrimination—or exclusion—in that process.

A third selection is in line with our Conference's recommendation on the administration of justice in providing for the handling in Federal courts of the assailants of the civil rights workers and their friends who seek the free exercise of constitutional rights.

Finally, the new legislation would ban discrimination in the sale or rental of housing, a prime target of the participation in this Conference.

Each Congressman and Senator should be impressed, in this election year, with the need for enactment of this legislation. After every gigantic and seemingly impersonal gathering such as this, people tend to ask "what can one person do?"

Each section of the Council report, the White Paper of this Conference, contains specific enumeration of what can be done. But here, in this pending legislation, now before the Congress, is a task that can be undertaken in the next twenty-four hours.

In fact, urgency is the key word not only with respect to this Conference, but with respect to the whole deadly infection of racism in our national life.

In either intellectually patronizing or in stridently sneering tones it has been held in some quarters that conferences such as this are but "talk." The answer is that in an honest and accurate sense, they are talk. But so, too, was the Sermon on the Mount. So was Patrick Henry's deathless oration in the Virginia Assembly. So were the Lincoln–Douglas debates.

What were the lamentations of the ancient Hebrews but talk to revive their people and to restore their relationship to God and to hope? What, indeed, were the spirituals of the slaves of our own South but talk set to the chants for a new day of freedom and dignity?

There is room always for dissent on emphasis and tactics, but none on goals. The destiny of twenty millions of Americans and of the nation to whose welfare that destiny is bound, cannot be left solely to the flippant doctrinaire conformists who brook no dissent and who, lately, have begun to classify believers by the color of their skins.

In this long climb, Negroes have had white allies since the first white Southerner violated the law by teaching slaves to read and write. The devils have been overbalanced, by far, by the quiet unafraid friends—the students of recent years who went into the Southern hinterlands and the dedicated men and women of all three great religious faiths who have brought a new fervor and a fresh courage to the whole freedom movement. We need them and they need us.

Students and observers have recognized that the bravery and resourcefulness and everlasting energy of the Negro American have marked the climb of all our people, white and black, to an awareness of the enormous task before our country.

As the President remarked in an aside last night, the Negro has ploughed a steady furrow. There has been this unremitting drive ahead by the black millions who, when darkness was all around and hope but a distant glimmer in the pervasive night, fought their way upward.

The mood today is not one of despair, but one of escalating expectation. The need is for urgency, for our nation's neglect of the past is about to rendezvous with a worldwide technological expansion. The repercussions are felt from Biloxi to Bombay to Nairobi to London to Washington.

Urgency is the word. After the Watts riot last August, the McCone report declared: ". . . our Commission has made many costly and extreme recommendations." But in addition, it called for a "revolutionary attitude" toward the problems of the city.

Revolutionary attitude means a discarding of the past routines, a welcome to daring, to innovation, to unorthodoxy. It means a looking forward, not looking back.

Undergirding all, it means a commitment to more than structure and method and even precise objectives. It means a commitment to a morality broader and higher than that concerned with self and group.

We must truly see others as ourselves and all as our nation—our common and glorious heritage built upon man and his freedom. For that is what our country is about. If at times some of us become irritable or uneasy over the expectations of our largest minority population, let them read again the eloquent and perceptive words from the President's Howard University speech. He said:

> The Negro, like these others (the white minorities) will have to rely mostly on his own efforts. But he just cannot do it alone. For they did not have the heritage of centuries to overcome. They did not have a cultural tradition which had been twisted and battered by endless years of hatred and hopelessness. Nor were they excluded because of race and/or color—a feeling whose dark intensity is matched by no other prejudice in our society.

And the President concluded as we here tonight might well conclude: For what is justice?

> It is to fulfill the fair expectations of man. American justice is a very special thing. . . . We have pursued it faithfully to the edge of our expectations. And we have failed to find it for the American Negro.
>
> It is the glorious opportunity of this generation to end the one huge wrong of the American Nation, and, in so doing, to find America for ourselves . . . a home for freedom.

Sail Our N.A.A.C.P. Ship "Steady as She Goes"

Roy Wilkins declared in 1965 that a new generation had appeared on the civil rights scene whom he considered limited on their history and long on petulance. They accused the NAACP of being out of touch with the civil rights movement. These young activists hurled names at Roy Wilkins such as "Uncle Tom," and "so-called Negro leader." In the face of this dissension within the civil rights movement, Wilkins remained steadfast in his fundamental objective for the Association—that no group would sway the NAACP from its course toward the full participation of black Americans in all phases of American life. He viewed this division as a "warring generational gap." In the following address, given on July 5, 1966, he tells the NAACP Fifty-seventh Annual Convention that there are serious divisions in the civil rights movement, and he adds: "If there is a lesson in this [division], it is that youth, energy, and passion are not enough to keep the civil rights movement on course. Age, wisdom, and experience are as vital."

In transition period of the civil rights movement, 1966 is developing into a critical year. The Fifty-seventh Annual Convention of our N.A.A.C.P. is thus a gathering of more than ordinary significance.

All about us are alarms and confusions as well as great and challenging developments. Differences of opinion are sharper. For the first time since several organizations began to function where only two had functioned before, there emerges what seems to be a difference in goals.

Heretofore there were some differences in methods and in emphases, but none in ultimate goals. The end was always to be inclusion of the Negro American, without racial discrimination, as a full-fledged equal in all phases of American citizenship. The targets were whatever barriers, crude or subtle, which blocked the attainment of that goal.

There has now emerged, first, a strident and threatening challenge to a strategy widely employed by civil rights groups, namely, nonviolence. One organization, which has been meeting in Baltimore, has passed a resolution declaring for defense of themselves by Negro citizens if they are attacked.

This position is not new as far as the N.A.A.C.P. is concerned. Historically our Association has defended in court those persons who have defended themselves and their homes with firearms. Extradition cases are not as frequent or as fashionable as they once were, but in past years we have fought the extradition of men who had used firearms to defend themselves when attacked.

We freed seventy-nine Arkansas sharecroppers in a four-year court battle beginning in 1919. They had returned gunfire directed at a meeting they were holding in a church.

We employed the late Clarence Darrow in 1926 to defend a man and his family when a member of a mob that threatened his newly-purchased Detroit home was shot and killed. The N.A.A.C.P. has subscribed to nonviolence as a humane as well as a practical necessity in the realities of the American scene, but we have never required this as a deep personal commitment of our members. We never signed a pact either on paper or in our hearts to turn the other cheek forever and ever when we were assaulted.

But neither have we couched a policy of manly resistance in such a way that our members and supporters felt compelled to maintain themselves in an armed state, ready to retaliate instantly and in kind whenever attacked. We venture the observation that such a publicized posture could serve to stir counter-planning, counter-action, and possible conflict. If carried out literally as instant retaliation, in cases adjudged by aggrieved persons to have been grossly unjust, this policy could produce—in extreme situations—lynchings, or, in better-sounding phraseology, private, vigilante vengeance.

Moreover, in attempting to substitute for derelict law enforcement machinery, the policy entails the risk of a broader, more indiscriminate crackdown by law officers under the ready-made excuse of restoring law and order.

It seems reasonable to assume that proclaimed protective violence is as likely to encourage counter-violence as it is to discourage violent persecution.

But the more serious division in the civil rights movement is the one passed by a word formulation that implies clearly a difference in goals.

No matter how endlessly they try to explain it, the term "black power" means anti-white power. In a racially pluralistic society, the concept, the formation and the exercise of an ethnically-tagged power, means opposition to other ethnic powers, just as the term, "white supremacy" means subjection of all non-white people. In the black–white relationship, it has to mean that every other ethnic power is the rival and the antagonist of "black power." It has to mean "going-it-alone." It has to mean separatism.

Now separatism, whether on the rarefied debate level of "black power" or on the wishful level of a secessionist Freedom City in Watts, offers a disadvantaged minority little except the chance to shrivel and die.

The only possible dividend of "black power" is embodied in its offer to millions of frustrated and deprived and persecuted black people of a solace, tremendous psychological life, quite apart from its political and economic implications.

Ideologically it dictates "up with black and down with white." In precisely the same fashion that South Africa reverses that slogan.

It is a reverse Mississippi, a reverse Hitler, a reverse Ku Klux Klan.

If these were evil in our judgment, what virtue can be claimed for black over white? If, as some proponents claim, this concept instills pride of race, cannot this pride be taught without preaching hatred or supremacy based upon race?

Though it be clarified and clarified again, "black power" in the quick, uncritical and highly emotional adoption it has received from some segments of a beleaguered people can mean in the end only black death. Even if, through some miracle, it should be enthroned briefly in an isolated area, the human spirit, which knows no color or geography or time, would die a little, leaving for wiser and stronger and more compassionate men the painful beating back to the upward trail.

We of the N.A.A.C.P. will have none of this. We have fought it too long. It is the ranging of race against race on the irrelevant basis of skin color. It is the father of hatred and the mother of violence.

It is the wicked fanaticism which has swelled our tears, broken our bodies, squeezed our hearts and taken the blood of our black and white loved ones. It shall not now poison our forward march.

We seek, therefore, as we have sought these many years, the inclusion of Negro Americans in the nation's life, not their exclusion. This is our land, as much as it is any American's—every square foot of every city and town and village. The task of winning our share is not the easy one of disengagement and flight, but the hard one of work, of short as well as long jumps, of disappointments and of sweet successes.

In our Fight for Freedom we choose:

1. The power and the majesty of ballot, the participation of free men in their government, both as voters and as honorable and competent elected and appointed public servants. Year in and year out, the N.A.A.C.P. voter registration work has proceeded. No one except the Federal Government has registered more Negro voters in Mississippi than the N.A.A.C.P. In six weeks last summer more than twenty thousand new names were added by our workers alone, with additional thousands during an intensive renewal last winter. That work is continuing under the leadership of our Mississippi state president, Dr. Henry Aaron, and of our state director, Charles Evers. Later this month a summer task force will be at work in Louisiana. Already our South Carolina N.A.A.C.P. is busy on registration, as is our Alabama organization.

We are aware that a Louisiana young man, born along the Mississippi border, has been named and confirmed as one of the seven governors for the Federal Reserve Bank. We know that his extraordinary ability finally tipped the scales, but we know also, that, without ballot power, he would not even have been on the scales ready to be tipped.

2. We choose employment for our people—jobs not hidden by racial labels or euphemisms, not limited by racial restrictions in access and promotion, whether by employers or organized labor. We commend a growing number of corporations for expanding their employment of Negro applications in technical and professional posts, but we insist that only the surface has been scratched.

We commend the "Good guys" among the trade unions for the improvement in opportunities and advancement for the Negro worker, but we condemn the policies of some unions which have either barred or heavily handicapped the Negro worker. Negro employment is in a crisis stage. The rate of unemployment ranges from twice that of whites to four and five times the white rate in some areas. The answer to the complaint of employers that workers are not trained is to institute in-plant training, just as they have in other shortages. The apprentice training stranglehold must be broken, the racially separate seniority lines, the still-persisting segregated local and the remaining crude segregation in plant facilities must be abolished. The demonstrations before the U.S. Steel Corporation offices and plants under the cooperative leadership of Dr. John Nixon, our Alabama president, and Henry Smith, our Pennsylvania president, had wide and beneficial impact.

The Negro migrant worker, the forgotten man in the employment picture, must have attention.

In the Watts district of Los Angeles last year the unemployment rate was more than thirty per cent, a rate higher than that during the great, nationwide Depression of the 1930s. The Negro teenage rate is nearly twenty-five per cent as against thirteen per cent for white teenagers.

Negro employment is a disaster area demanding the strict enforcement of Title VII of the 1964 Civil Rights Act. The N.A.A.C.P. has filed more than one thousand complaints with the Equal Employment Opportunity Commission and will file more until the law accomplishes what it was enacted to do. As evidence of his continuing concern, Congressman Augustus Hawkins of Los Angeles succeeded in having his bill relating to Federal employment passed by the House as an amendment to Title VII of the 1964 Civil Rights Act.

3. We choose to combat the color line in housing. In one breath our opinion-makers decry the existence of the poverty and filth and crime and degradation of the slums, but in the next decry low-cost housing and fair-housing laws. Here in California the hysteria over whether Negro Americans should live in gullies or be pushed into the sea reached the Proposition 14 stage which the state's highest court has declared unconstitutional. But who cares about the Constitution when a Negro might be enabled to move into the neighborhood? One could think black Americans were men from Mars. Instead, we have been here, side by side with the white folks (some of whom just got here), for 345 years.

They tell us to work hard and save our money, to go to school and prepare ourselves, to be "responsible," to rear and educate our children in a wholesome and directed family atmosphere, to achieve, to "get up in the world."

After we do all this, they look us in the eyes and bar us from renting or buying a home that matches our achievements and one in keeping with our aspirations for further advancement.

Some public officials, including mayors of cities and many candidates for election to public office, are not above public double talk and private single talk on this issue. Any candidate who orates about basic Americanism or "the American way," but who hems and haws over fair housing legislation is no friend of the Negro citizen.

The Administration's civil rights bill of 1966 with its vital section barring discrimination in the rental or sale of housing must be enacted with the amendment, already inserted by the committee, providing for administrative redress as well as court action.

Your congressmen and senators are at home until July 11 celebrating Independence Day—Freedom Day for the United States. See them or have your branch officers back home see them in person. Urge them to rub some freedom off on twenty million loyal Americans by voting for a strong civil rights bill. Of course the section on punishing in the Federal courts those who attack civil rights workers must pass. And we must have indemnification for victims.

4. Most of all, we choose to secure unsegregated, high quality public education for ourselves and our children. A new report, made public only last week, is a jolt for anyone who thought the 1954 Supreme Court decision or subsequent legislation solved the problem.

The report says officially and professionally what we have contended all along: that predominantly Negro schools are inferior to those attended largely by whites. Also that the achievement gap widens between the first grade and the twelfth. In other words, the longer our children attend racially segregated schools, the farther they fall behind white children.

And, lest the non-Southerners feel smug, the report found that segregation for both whites and Negroes is more complete in the South, but "is extensive in other regions where the Negro population is concentrated: the urban North, Midwest, and West."

The Federal Government, whose Office of Education has made some strong statements, must follow up with a strong enforcement of Title VI of the 1964 law. The empty promises of school officials and the defiance of the whole State of Alabama must not be accepted meekly by Federal officials. The furor over the guidelines issued by HEW is another version of the Dixie bluff on race which has worked so well for so many decades. The guidelines are mild. They are legal and not illegal, as Governor Wallace proclaimed to his state's educators. They ask the Southerners to do what is for them: obey the school desegregation law. On this point the Federal Government must not yield. The Attorney General and the Department of Justice must back up resolutely the legality of Federal action. There can be no temporizing.

Outside the South the call is for unrelenting activity to wipe out de facto school segregation. Boston, Massachusetts, has proved to be the Mississippi of the North. In fact, in fairness to Mississippi and in consideration of the starting points and traditions of the two places, Boston is below Mississippi on this issue. The details, the traps, the methods, and the progress will be covered in workshop discussions, but here it must be said that before we can get jobs to earn increased income to buy and rent better homes, before we can contribute to the enrichment of our nation, we must have free access to quality education.

The man who shoots and burns, and drowns us is surely our enemy, but so is he who cripples our children for life with inferior public education.

5. We also choose to wrestle with the complex problems of urban life, all of which include an attitude toward and a treatment of millions of Negro citizens. The solution of urban problems will become the solution of living into the last third of our century since more than seventy per cent of Americans now live in urban communities.

Last summer you had an upheaval that shook the world. To many of us who looked from afar, it appeared to be a wild, senseless rampage of hate and destruction. But that was far from the whole truth.

There was powder in Watts, piled up and packed down through the years: wide-scale unemployment, both adult and teenage, slum housing, crowded schools, non-existent health facilities, inadequate transportation and—the Parker police attitude. Everyone was suspect and everyone was subject to harassment in one form or another. The community smoldered under the peculiar brand that police place upon a whole section with their constant sirens, their contemptuous searches, their rough talk, their ready guns, and their general "God Almightiness."

The lesson they and city officials have learned from last year is to seek not correction and improvement, but still more repression. Mayor Yorty and whoever writes his scripts testified in Sacramento in support of a so-called riot-control bill.

The only thing one has to remember about this bill is that it would allow a policeman to judge whether an utterance of an act is an incitement to riot! On his own judgment he could arrest or club or otherwise deter—or shoot—a person whom he (not the law or the courts) deemed to be an inciter of riot. Down the drain goes freedom of speech and down, too, possibly, goes a life.

The McCone Report on the 1965 riot called for "costly and extreme" remedies for Watts, undertaken with a "revolutionary attitude." The answer of the City of

Los Angeles was to vote down a hospital bond issue. The answer of Mayor Yorty and of his man, Chief Parker, is a trampling-tough riot-control bill which, if enacted, would loose the police, almost without restraint, upon a populace sick to death—literally—of race control. To blot out any remaining fitful light, one of the gubernatorial candidates, full of disavowals, is the darling of those ultraconservatives who believe in iron control of what they call "violence in the streets"— their code name for Negroes.

If this is the best that a great city can bring to a hard urban problem, one largely of its own making, then God pity both the whites and the Negroes!

We have no panacea for all these problems. We do not proclaim that what we declare here this week is going to change the course of the whole civil rights movement. We do not know all the answers to the George Wallace problem in Alabama, the James Eastland problem in Mississippi, or the Boston, Massachusetts, school committee and its Louise Day Hicks problem.

We certainly don't know the answers to foreign policy and to tax and interest rate puzzlers.

But in this unsettled time when shifts are the order of the day and when change is in the air, we can sail our N.A.A.C.P. ship "steady as she goes," with more drive to the turbines, more skill at the wheel, but no fancy capers for the sake of capers.

We can follow down into each community the really advanced blueprint of the White House Conference "To Fulfill These Rights," which covered four principal areas: economic security and welfare, education, housing, and the administration of justice.

We can expand and point up the community services of our N.A.A.C.P. branches, each of which is, in reality, a citizenship clinic. Just as medical clinics need specialists to cure physical ills, so our branch clinics should recruit volunteer specialists to diagnose and minister to social ills.

We must involve people in the communities in the solution of our problem— not limiting ourselves to our church or lodge or club group.

We must keep the pressure on our local and state education systems through the employment of every legitimate technique: protests, surveys, discussions, demonstrations, picketing, and negotiation. Nothing should be overlooked in fighting for better education. Be persistent and ornery, this will be good for the lethargic educational establishment and will aid the whole cause of public education.

Our branches are at work in their territories. In Baltimore, the N.A.A.C.P. won a case against the police commissioner which the Fourth Circuit Court of Appeals declared revealed the most flagrant police practices ever to come before the court. The Blair County, Pennsylvania, N.A.A.C.P. is busy rooting out the remaining discrimination in public accommodations in Clearfield, Pennsylvania.

The Wilmington, Ohio, N.A.A.C.P. has a program for tutoring adults and dropouts and has recruited college professors and students and textbooks to make the project effective. The Bay City, Michigan, N.A.A.C.P. also has a tutorial program under way as well as continuous work on industrial employment practices and housing. The Stillwater, Oklahoma, N.A.A.C.P. is active on a child care center project and on high school desegregation.

And the Montgomery County, West Virginia, N.A.A.C.P. bless her heart, is 112 per cent above last year in membership and 500 per cent above last year in funds raised.

Thirty-one branches found time and funds to be present at the Meredith march rally in Jackson, Mississippi, even though the Association, at the last minute, was insulted by the barring of Charles Evers as an N.A.A.C.P. spokesman.

This is only part of the chronicle of "steady as she goes," in a world where the Mayor of Los Angeles is yelling "riot control," where Rhodesia says "never!" to black representation while in America SNCC raises the chant of black power, where the Federal Government at long last is committed, but both the far right and the far left offer vocal and vicious objection, someone has to drive the long haul toward the group goal of Negro Americans and the larger ideal of our young nation.

Our objective is basically as it was laid down in 1909 by the interracial founders of our N.A.A.C.P. Back there Oswald Garrison Villard expressed the strong feeling that the first N.A.A.C.P. conference "will utter no uncertain sound on any point affecting the vital subject. No part of it is too delicate for plain speech. The republican experiment is at stake, every tolerated wrong to the Negro reacting with double force upon white citizens guilty of faithlessness to their brothers."

As it was then, so it is today. The republican experiment is at stake in 1966. More than that, the dream of a brotherhood in equality and justice is imperiled.

Our fraternity tonight, as it was then, is the fraternity of man, not the white, or brown, or yellow, or black man, but man.

Voluntary Segregation—A Disaster

In the following article, written in March 1969, Roy Wilkins argues against the theory that "a little voluntary racial segregation might not be a disaster." He proclaims that racial separation is the principal tool for white supremacy.

San Bernardino, Calif.—In California one gets the impression from spokesmen and apologists for militant elements that a little voluntary racial segregation might not be a disaster.

The so-called settlement of the four and one-half months of strife at San Francisco State College is spurring discussion. It leaves the students with less than they sought and much less public support than they had in the beginning.

Once the door to the policy of official, imposed racial separation is opened, the darkness begins to descend. Particularly is this true in nations where the non-whites are a small numerical minority and a still more vulnerable economic and political minority. Also, where the whites have control of the government machinery and can enact legislation and execute policies that can rivet tactical inferiority upon a whole people.

The United States is just emerging from many generations in which inferiority was imposed upon Negro citizens. Those black youngsters who today are seeking absolute blackness in all things don't know, of their own experience, what racial segregation can do to a people. They think they know. They read an account of the workings of segregation in this or that instance. Their eyes flash and their fists clench, but they are still reacting to but one tiny facet of enveloping apartheid.

If Negro young people are truly students of their race's present position, and not merely hell-raising opportunists riding the currently popular bandwagon, they will take a look at the proposed constitution for Rhodesia. This is a clear example of what those in control of government can do to enforce inequality. Rhodesia has racial segregation in capital letters.

In fact, racial separation is the basic requirement for control. The Rhodesian constitution is designed to insure that there will "never" be black rule in the nation. The prime tool is separate lists of voters. The black list (no pun intended) can elect only sixteen out of sixty-six members of parliament, the other fifty would be elected by non-blacks. The difficulties of blacks in urging or opposing government policies are crystal clear. They can throw rocks, but they cannot control government.

Racial segregation, preached and urged by a youthful minority of Negro Americans, can be the means of plunging their race back behind the barbed wire of restriction, inferiority, persecution and death to both the spirit and the body. The black youth of today owe it to themselves to study the appalling effects of segregation. When one asks for a little bit of it in order to go off in a corner and counsel together, one asks for the whole bit.

There are individuals (millions of them) and organized forces in the nation itching to respond to the disruptive clamor of Negroes themselves for separation. One day it will be separate, all-black studies centers. The next it will be not only a quota system on jobs, but one on the types of jobs in separate black buildings under black bosses. Then it will be separate (and inferior) schools and residential areas (like South Africa) and the completely separated elective offices so that the impact of a black bloc within a predominantly white party will be nil. Not humanity against evil. Just white against black.

There are many flaws in the present system. They cry for overturning. But the surest way to postpone their downfall is to split into skin-color camps, into enclaves motivated by national and religious myths and hatreds.

If Negro youth will think beyond their understandable frustration and their impatience with their elders, they will surely realize that they cannot commit suicide by opening Pandora's box of racial separatism.

Toward a Single Society

The President's Kerner Commission Report stated in its introduction that "our nation is moving toward two societies, one black, one white—separate and unequal." In the aftermath of the *Brown* decision and, the Civil Rights Acts of 1957, 1964, and 1965, the nation was shocked at the killing of six college students at Jackson State College and Kent State University, by highway patrolmen and national guardsmen. As Roy Wilkins states in the following speech, "The siren song of separation has been sung again and again in Negro Americans. Each time separatism has been rejected." In this speech to the NAACP Sixty-first Convention on June 30, 1970, he tells the audience that America cannot continue to pursue its present course of division.

Few Americans were not shocked at the killing this spring of six students—two at Jackson State College in Mississippi and four at Kent State University in Ohio, by state highway patrolmen and National Guardsmen. Despite the difference in geography, the basic reaction of the two state governments was the same. In Mississippi, there was an unashamed attempt at a cover-up, while in Ohio the state officials toned down their public statements but maintained their law and order stance.

On sober reflection, after the sorrow over the taking of young life, these two tragedies must be viewed as incidents supporting the warning in the report of the President's National Commission on Civil Disorders, known popularly as the Kerner Commission. Said the report's introduction:

"Our nation is moving toward two societies, *one black and one white—separate and unequal.*

"This deepening division is not inevitable. The movement apart can be reversed." The report said our course must be changed. "To pursue our present course," it said, "will involve the continuing polarization of the American community and ultimately the destruction of basic democratic values.

"The alternative is not blind repression or capitulation to lawlessness. It is the realization of common opportunities for all within a single society."

As it has been since its founding, the National Association for the Advancement of Colored People is dedicated to achieving "the realization of common opportunities for all within a single society." So that in this day of double talk and obscurantism in a highly-charged emotional atmosphere generated by viciously executed murders of Negro young people, such as those at Jackson State, we make it clear that our stand is for integration and against black separatism.

To paraphrase a famous line, "We intend to fight it out on this line if it takes all summer and, indeed, if it takes forty more summers." And we intend to keep at it in spite of frontal attacks upon us by the haters, in spite of trickery from the left and misrepresentation from the right, and in spite of sabotage and betrayals from within the ranks of black people themselves.

Even if we were not committed to our anti-polarization work, even if we did not believe steadfastly in making real, for black as well as white Americans, the great dream of equal opportunity of our young nation, tactically, for a numerical minority of about one-tenth, and an economic, political and social minority of far less strength, integration is the only way to go. The word "integration" is not used here to mean assimilation. No one is advocating loss of identity, loss of color distinction, the burying of a culture and a complete merging into the general population. The anti-integrationists have sought to give that impression of the integrationist position. We seek no elusive "melting pot." Instead we use the dictionary definition of integration: "The making up of a whole by adding together or combining the separate parts or elements."

We seek to become a part of the whole, an equal part of the whole, to be on the inside with other Americans, rather than on the outside looking in. We want to make our country whole, to give it its missing tenth, to fill the ugly gap in the teeth, to enable it to throw away the crutches and hobbling gait of the color line and to replace the stuttered apology with strong straight talk.

We believe in all God's children and that means that today, as in the beginning, the N.A.A.C.P. does not discriminate against people because they are white. A fighter for freedom is a fighter for freedom. That is the way black people want to be judged and that is the way we should judge white people—by what they are, not by how they look.

Despite the clamor of a minority of our minority, despite the penetration of its medicine men into key spots, the overwhelming majority of Negro Americans, ranging from ninety-five per cent on down to seventy-eight per cent, chooses integration. More than half of those "under thirty" are included and in some part of the country the "under thirty" percentage runs above seventy per cent. Every opinion poll has shown this trend.

The siren song of separatism has been sung again and again in Negro Americans. Each time separatism has been rejected. Someone broached the subject as early as 1714, ninety-five years after 1619. It was given a great push by the American Colonization Society and for fifty years from 1816, the Society spent $2,500,000 and managed to coax only 12,000 freedmen to Africa. This was an average of 240 a year and half of these had to go because they were freed on condition that they go. Thus only 120 a year went voluntarily. Hardly a gold rush crowd.

Then Marcus Garvey and his "Back to Africa" movement appeared in the 1920s. Garvey had his native intelligence and his uniforms, plumes, gold braid, and medals going for him, as well as the titles he bestowed, but he also had a reverse racism. Everything black was good and everything white was evil. He got together a goodly following, but again Negro Americans rejected a return to Africa.

The Communists tried again in the 1930s with their "self-determination for the black belt," but when the party line changed in far-off Moscow, the few Negro Americans who had been attracted to the black separatist line were dumped down the drain and told to forget separatism, forget Jim Crow and fight Mother Russia's enemies.

So the present-day agitation for separatism may be in new bottles, but it is old wine. And the new packaging will not save it from the rejection accorded the other old wine. For Negro Americans are more sophisticated than they once were. They have always known that racial segregation was a device by which their daily goings and comings and their very horizons could be controlled. We resent so much the personal mistreatment and humiliation in racial segregation that we tend to forget that it is a system of control that means degradation and death to the race. Today Negro citizens know that the subtle forms of control must be resisted and routed just as were the elder, cruder forms—lynching, the White Primary, the Negro job and pay scale, and the shanty school.

Today, too, they know that no matter who advocates it, or in what honeyed and beguiling terms it is couched, the deadly poison is there. It does not matter whether it comes out of a white mouth, as with the 1930 communists, or of a black mouth, as in the case of Garvey, whether it is pushed with government funds, as with the American Colonization Society, or whether it is yelled in cadence by the young black separatists of 1970, it is the tranquilizer that precedes the suicide of a people.

The young black separatists, including a small percentage of black students, are giving aid and comfort to the enemy by calling for separation. Negroes are dismayed and whites cannot believe their good fortune. Just when white Americans thought they must at last give in and open the doors to opportunity and equality wider and wider, a small school of vociferous young Negroes, including, of all people, some Negro college students, are chanting, "We want to be alone." In many places they have rudely rejected all contact with whites and declare they want to build a black society all to themselves. They talk a complete apartheid except on one point: they want white money. They preach black manhood established with white financing. The news for them is that manhood purchased on that basis is worthless in the marketplace of self-respect in which every man, white, black, yellow or brown, must face himself before his secret mirror.

The black militants, who number among them the smaller total of black separatists, have done their race a service by attacking college admissions policies and demanding increased Negro enrollment. They have urged, either politely or impolitely but justly, an increase in black faculty members and the setting up of black studies departments. They are to be cheered for this advocacy, for no one can deny that the image (and progress) of Negro Americans has been damaged seriously by the blotting out of their contributions to America and to the world in the textbooks and study courses in our schools and colleges.

However, their insistence on a full black studies department in universities of varied sizes, excellence, and accessibility all across the nation has raised questions. A recent estimate by a black professor, friend, and beneficiary of the black studies departments, was that eighty-five percent of them were ineffective exercises rather than solid contributions to the knowledge of black people and their history. They are bound to be skimpy and incomplete because it requires a large appropriation to staff a department with competent faculty, to set up an adequate library and all the other services that go with a full department.

Another error is the insistence upon black professors and only black students in the courses. Many black studies departments are merely devices set up by the universities to enable blacks to talk to blacks. The same holds true for so-called black student centers. These provide rooms for black student bull sessions. Here they can talk to themselves, indulging in language and mannerisms inexplicable as an activity with national characteristics and value, however clear they may be as jargon of a group—a kind of tribe.

One of the chief values of black studies is lost if whites are not registered in the courses. One of the racial stumbling blocks in America has been the abysmal ignorance of whites on the Negro side of the race question. Now that students have managed to milk our black studies departments, they immediately kick over the bucket by demanding the exclusion of white students. It is one with the insistence that only blacks know enough to teach blacks about blacks. This is silly. Some whites come on, Man, and some blacks throw threes. Black dormitories and black student residences deserve the same comment as black students centers. They delight Governor John Bell Williams of Mississippi and Governor-elect George C. Wallace in Alabama and do little if anything to prepare the Negro student to take his place in the world.

The youngsters have performed a necessary and valuable task, however, in the stimulus to racial pride. They have helped the Negro American to be proud of himself, his race and the accomplishments of the race. Our people have been working at it for years, chalking up a few converts each year. But in four short years, the black militants have made race pride a household word. More importantly, they have woven it into the backbone, used it to lift the head and the chin, lighted a fire in the eye and made it to calm the nerves and spur the spirit. If pride can be kept from becoming arrogance, we will leap forward as never before.

The present mood of many of our young people is rooted, understandably, in the slow progress of the goals of complete freedom. They are discouraged, as we all are, by the setbacks. We are bracing ourselves this week in fearful anticipation of a setback. Some weeks ago, the Nixon Administration astonished all civil rights activists by announcing that it might grant income tax exemption to those who gave money to set up the private segregated schools for white children in the South. But between that indication of dismaying White House support for sabotage of the 1954 Supreme Court decision and of the 1964 Civil Rights Act, the President, apparently, had second thoughts. I do not know what those thoughts are (who can know the Nixon mind?), but I hope that they do not herald one of those acts which have so "fed up" black young people that they turn inward for what seems for a moment to be relief, but which is truly ingrown debilitation and death.

Their elders know these setbacks. They know too well the heartaches and disappointments. Their fathers had these before their sons and daughters came along. It was not comfortable and pretty. On the contrary, it was like a disease. Sometimes it killed, but more often it crippled and hobbled and held back forward motion.

But the elders did not run away and hide. They did not drag themselves into the black corner and cut off other men, whether they were friend or foe, or half-friend. They did not retreat and turn away from the harsh competition of life— much of it with the cards stacked against them. They looked the Grandfather Clause and the White Primary in the eye and licked both of them. They are getting the vote and it has brought the race 1,200 elected black officeholders. Only three of the southern states still have lily white legislatures. The latest mayor is Kenneth Gibson of Newark, N.J., who takes office tomorrow, July 1, And we must not forget Mayor Howard Lee, elected in Chapel Hill, N.C., by white and black votes.

The elders fought lynching down to the bricks, reversing the national public opinion in thirty years. It fought its way through the administration of justice and is still fighting for law and order and justice, frequently against the forces of law and order.

The segregated school was outlawed and the diehards are being pursued. The older Negroes battled employers, unions, and public opinion. Gates were opened, others were cracked and still others are yielding, but only inch by inch. The FEP idea, which was only a gleam in A. Philip Randolph's eye in 1939, is full blown today and is embodied in Title VII of the 1964 Civil Rights Act, as well as in the laws of scores of states and cities.

Housing and urban development has become a department of government because Negro Americans, among others, never ceased fighting segregation. It is foisted upon them, but they have never let up in their protests. The N.A.A.C.P. won its first Supreme Court case against segregated housing in 1917. The N.A.A.C.P. housing department led off on what some said was the impossible dream of seeking a change in the sacred land-use practices of suburbs so that low-income housing might be built. Today HUD is behind the idea, and the Supreme Court will hear a case on the issue.

The list is long—travel, recreation, public places, churches, service clubs, Greek letter societies, hospitals, health program—all these were on the continuing agenda of the "over thirty" Negro Americans. They did not run from light, hard, bare-knuckled fighting for their rights and the rights of their children. They did not withdraw into a comfortable familiar segregation. They knew that only in open competition is true worth discovered and skin color eventually put in its proper place.

These people understand the anger and frustration of Negro youth. Anyone who saw the bullet holes in all five floors of the women's dormitory at Jackson State College can understand and share the anger of Negro youth. The building was literally sprayed with bullets. Remember this was a women's dormitory and so far no one has claimed that the girl students were firing on the state highway patrolmen from the windows of their dormitory. No, the conclusion is fairly drawn and seems inescapable that the Mississippi highway patrol came to the Jackson State campus determined to kill black students. They were out for blood, not for keeping the peace. Yes, yes—and no one is pooh-poohing the righteous anger of students.

But Negro citizens are not about to permit anyone, repeat, anyone, to put Negro Americans back behind the eight ball of racial segregation. In South Africa and in Rhodesia, racial segregation or apartheid is the national policy. It is the law to keep black Africans, in the words of the Kerner Commission, "separate and unequal." By law black Africans may hold only certain kinds of jobs and may live in only certain areas. They must carry passes to be shown to anyone who makes an inquiry. Their children may attend only certain schools and they may vote only if certain conditions are met. In South Africa they may not elect any of their own to the general assembly. In Rhodesia they may elect only sixteen out of sixty-six in Parliament, so that they will never have any influence in government. The laws permit their arrest, detention, and imprisonment without any specification of the charges against them.

This is what segregation means to them.

In 1831, an anti-colonization convention of free Negroes in New York declared, "We do not believe that things will always continue the same. This is our home and this is our country. Here we were born and here we will die." Their people were to go through the valley of the shadow of death, through a bloody Civil War, through Reconstruction and the revival of the Ku Klux Klan, through the Hayes–Tilden betrayal, the separate-but-equal hocus-pocus, the dark decades of the early twentieth century, the indifference and hostility of the U.S. Supreme Court, the unbelievable racial segregation in the nation's capital under President Woodrow Wilson and all the other marks of segregation.

The only redeeming feature was that, contrary to South Africa, it was possible here to organize and protest and try for change. In this age the N.A.A.C.P. was born in 1909. That has been what has been happening. The goal has been achieved only in part; there is still much to be done. The murders at Jackson State and the bare-faced defense for the killings by state officials are evidence of the size of the task ahead.

The Kerner Commission report declared that: "This . . . will require a commitment to national action—compassionate, massive and sustained, backed by the resources of the most powerful and the richest nation on this earth. From every American it will require new attitudes, new understanding and, above all new will."

In the Negro community this new will should be expressed by a close working relationship between those elders who have carried on a magnificent battle against great odds and those young militants who can bring to the fray so much talent and energy and innovative efforts and skill and unselfishness and fearless negotiation plus increasing political know-how, so that progress toward true integration under their leadership will be speeded.

Everything that old folks have done has not been perfectly suited to the needs of the struggle. There have been the inevitable mistakes, but the course has been charted and the contest for life, liberty, and the pursuit of happiness has been pressed. The old soldiers need now to welcome the new, young soldiers and to cease the mean and meaningless sneering. The young people, who have so much to give, should also cease the eternal talk about a generation gap and about nothing having been done until they came along. We can win if these forces will join in mutual self-respect and mutual marching forward.

Such a combination can help to save the nation, save the white people from themselves and save democratic participation in government. "To pursue our present course will involve the continuing polarization of the American community," the commission report said, "and ultimately the destruction of basic democratic values."

A racial minority cannot live except in a democracy. In saving it, we save ourselves.

Ego and Race

Roy Wilkins noted that some black parents were against integration because they believed it meant "begging" to be with whites. He further contended that many of these parents believed that race pride could be taught only in segregated educational settings. He explains in the following article, written in June 1971, why the slow pace of integration is better than seeking quality education in a separate system.

In the whole black-and-white field, a more emotional topic than that of racial integration in the public schools will be hard to find unless it is racial integration in housing.

The idea of Negro and white children going to school together somehow seems to rouse both black and white parents to peaks of feeling. Whites, of course, want a good and exclusively white thing to continue.

They don't fancy black children, whom they have heard come from strange and even terrible backgrounds, sharing the classrooms, toilet facilities, and cafeterias with white children. These latter, if white adult tales are to be believed, come from 100 percent high-class homes, morally and physically.

Some black parents, on the other hand, see moves toward integration as "begging" to associate with whites. They want none of it. They talk endlessly about pride of race as though this can be developed only in an all-black school. They say they want quality education for their children, not integration. This view conveniently overlooks the fact that all-black schools, with but few exceptions, have turned out to be something very much less than quality education.

Both the white and black parents stand solidly on the adult concepts of race. Neither is very much concerned with the welfare and education of the child. It is not the egos and politics and social strategies of adults that should be determining factors, but the education of black and white children. Federal Judge Damon Keith, in his 1970 ruling in a Pontiac, Mich., case that has just been upheld by the Sixth Circuit Court of Appeals, put it this way:

> The harm to another generation of black children while awaiting implementation of long-range plans to integrate simply cannot be tolerated, and no degree of expense is unbearable when placed alongside the unbearable situation which exists for those black children.

Much of the accusation that the Nixon Administration is anti-Negro stems from its confused statements and counterstatements on public school integration. One day the President opposes the business of pupils. The next week his "strict constructionist" Chief Justice of the Supreme Court hands down a unanimous 8–0 opinion upholding busing.

The President says he will enforce the law, but he does not propose to cut off federal funds to obdurate school districts although such cut-offs are provisions in the law. To please Northern whites who have many all-black neighborhoods and schools (the devil take the Negroes) he re-emphasizes his personal opposition to busing, even though the Supreme Court has ruled otherwise.

The President and some of his advisers no doubt have listened to some black parents (and some of black haranguers) who say they will accept all-black schools because such schools will mean more black teachers and principals and more emphasis on Negro history. Negroes in this category are properly disgusted with the seventeen-year creeping pace of school desegregation ordered in 1954.

Whatever good might come from such a course, the fatal flaw is in the source of the school funds. Salaries for teachers and other personnel, upkeep of plans, purchase of textbooks and supplies, selection of sites and land purchase funds plus other costs, ad infinitum, all come from a public that in most cases is overwhelming white, through school boards with similar racial membership.

Black Americans have ended the dual school system on the clearly demonstrable ground that it was racially unequal. Better by far to organize and fight—even at an unsatisfactorily slow pace—for quality education within an integrated system than to repeat the heartbreaking and futile task of battling for quality education in a separate system.

Ralph J. Bunche

Ralph Johnson Bunche (1904–1971), born in Detroit, became one of the most successful men of his time. In 1948 he led the peace-seeking Palestine Commission that brought temporary peace to the Arab–Israeli conflict in 1949. As a result of his efforts in the Middle East, he was awarded the Nobel Prize for Peace in 1950. In the following article, Roy Wilkins pays tribute to Ralph Bunche after his death on December 9, 1971.

Ralph J. Bunche was truly concerned with mankind, no matter what its location on the earth, its nationality or color. He did not forget his domestic racial difficulties or his unhappy experiences with them (how could he?), but he sensed early and knew later that war and hunger and hatred were the enemies of man. His life was devoted to efforts to bring about peace.

It is possible that his encounters with prejudice against his race—the refusal, for example, of the honor society at Jefferson High School in Los Angeles to elect to membership the Ralph J. Bunche who was class valedictorian—gave him that extra quality of understanding and compassion in his later dealings between nations on the world stage.

It may now be said publicly what his intimate friends already knew; never in his soaring career was Ralph Bunche apart from or indifferent to the treatment visited upon his people in his native land. He conceived it to be a matter of honor not to allow his title or his activities in the United Nations to intrude in any official way into the internal affairs of a member nation.

However, in scores of permitted ways he found channels that allowed him to condemn the philosophy and the practices that demeaned and denied his race. When the West Side Tennis Club in Forest Hills, New York City, apologized for barring Dr. Bunche and his son from membership, Dr. Bunche refused the tendered membership. He felt it skirted broad racial policy and was offered only because of his position.

Before 1945, when the United Nations was formed in San Francisco, he went on a picket line of the National Association for the Advancement of Colored People in Washington in 1937. He won the Nobel Prize in 1950 for his successful Arab–Israeli mediation.

Among his flood of medals and honorary degrees from universities all over the world is the N.A.A.C.P.'s Spingarn Medal, presented to Dr. Bunche in 1949. The citation describes Dr. Bunche as "brilliant scholar, faithful international servant and successful practitioner of man's noblest profession," the quest for peace.

We Americans do not mourn this man, except in that tiny part of our nature which reflects that we shall be deprived, on occasion, of the richness of his wisdom, the variety of his wit and his down-to-earth comments on everything from international affairs to the scores and standings of athletic teams.

Rather, we are proud. He was of us, but he was, in every sense, of the world. His practiced skills, his wondrous talents, his dedications and his hatred of the waste of war—whether between nations or races—were at the disposal of those who sought peace. Of all the capable men produced by Negro America, he was the only one to have achieved success in the general field of international diplomacy in endeavors not strictly in behalf of his race.

Of many men it has been said, and justly, that their lives were inspirations for others. Of Ralph Bunche this, too, may be said. Perhaps in the tensions of our times it is more true today that what his life stood for deserves the emulation of young and old, but of the young, particularly. He knew Africa, for example, and the manifold problems of dependent territories, not from picture books, but from living there with the people. This is a priceless heritage.

For his family, too, we know that this pride is inextricably mixed with the sadness of this parting. But the sadness will fade. The heritage of a man of peace will endure and shine into the darkness of this world. Our thanks to you, Ralph Johnson Bunche.

Adam Clayton Powell, Jr.

Adam Clayton Powell, Jr., was born in 1908 in New Haven, Connecticut, and raised in New York City. In 1931 he succeeded his father as senior pastor of Abyssinian Baptist Church in Harlem. In 1944 he was elected to Congress as a representative from Harlem. Powell became chairman of the powerful House Committee on Labor, a post that afforded him the chance to exercise

more power than any previous black congressman. In the following article,
Roy Wilkins pays tribute Powell, who died on April 4, 1972.

The Negro American who caused white Americans more worry than any other
single black individual is dead. Adam Clayton Powell, Jr., former U.S. Congressman
from Harlem, died peacefully in a Miami, Fla., hospital April 4, 1972.

Adam was a perfect example of a man who made the system work for his
people. He thoroughly enjoyed all his endeavors as he worked to benefit his constituents, whom he believed to be not just those in his Harlem district, but all the
disadvantaged in the nation. How he prodded the system, lashing with a brash,
disrespectful vocabulary at first one, whom he in his scornful estimation classed
as an enemy, then, without warning, at another.

It is the fashion among "black" historians and commentators to believe that
the civil rights struggle began in the 1960s with the marches and jailings. Nothing,
of course, could be farther from the truth. These events were but a new phase of
an old struggle to which many unsung black and white heroes and heroines had
contributed. In 1945, Powell's book, *Marching Blacks*, was published and he, too,
saw the emergence of a "new" Negro. The marches 15 years later were not new
under the sun because Adam Powell in his Harlem had preached and practiced
them in a dark time.

Let no one assert that Adam was so busy with his fancy plans that he ignored
the plight of his people. In his Abyssinian Baptist Church, during the years of the
Great Depression, he had a staff of more than twenty persons operating a grocery
store, a day nursery for working mothers and many other services for his congregation. He got jobs on 125th Street by demands, marches, and selective buying
campaigns.

But his great service to his district and to Americans generally was rendered
after his election to Congress. His talents and his ability to cut through the booby
traps of legislation to find the harm directed at the poor and black populations
confirmed him as a maverick. It was his continued re-election that finally brought
him the chairmanship of the powerful House Committee on Education and Labor.
As long as seniority was the game, Harlem voters gave him the seniority that
some Southerners had used for years to become the heads of Congressional committees.

Adam Powell showed how the system could work if one worked at it. He had
a brilliant career as a committee chairman and helped speed the enactment of
social legislation, including Title 7 of the Civil Rights Act of 1964.

He ran afoul of the moral astigmatism that abounds in America. People who
benefited from practices which were not 100 per cent kosher ganged up on Adam
for what they considered his unorthodox behavior. Most Negro Americans are
firmly convinced that the punishment meted out Adam was "by the book" primarily because he was black, because he thumbed his nose at his accusers and
because he was unafraid.

He was controversial, even among his own people. But he was also colorful
and acted his part on the world stage with a style (whether one agreed with him

or not) that evoked reluctant admiration. So, he went off on racial and personal tangents? What matter, even if his barbs made one wince?

He showed to a superb degree how the American electoral and legislative processes can be made to work for an abused citizenry. For this alone, disregarding his flamboyance and his puckish sallies, white America, plagued on the race problem with a horde of raucous imitators who lack his skills, should say a prayer for Adam Clayton Powell.

In Back of the Busing Issue

Roy Wilkins proclaimed that the busing issue was never the real issue. The real issue, he argued, was desegregated quality education. In the following article, written in August 1972, he discusses what he believes to be the real issues behind the highly charged question of busing.

Not much more can be said on the highly emotional topic of busing children to school for the purpose of aiding the desegregation of the public school system.

Except that busing is not the real question, but only the excuse behind which forces, for a variety of reasons, move against the real issue: Desegregated quality education. This, said the Supreme Court in 1954, belongs to every child, irrespective of race, color, or place of residence.

In this election year, many politicians in Washington are busy passing legislation to curb busing. They are getting their votes on record against busing so that the folks back home will vote for them next November.

Others in Washington have spent the past eighteen years seeking to turn back to the untroubled (for whites) old days. A Senator from Mississippi spoke at Senatobia, Miss., in 1955, saying, in effect: "You are obligated to disregard the Supreme Court."

Today, Rep. William Colmer of Mississippi, chairman of the Rules Committee, has scheduled an anti-busing bill for a vote August 17. Even if Rep. Colmer, 82, subscribes to the racial theories of fifty years ago, that was thirty-two years after he was born. The Congress is following this leadership today.

Not only is the Congress following it, but President Nixon (who is also campaigning for re-election, but on what has been described as a high level), is a disciple of anti-busing. The Supreme court ruled unanimously, 8–0, in a 1971 case that busing was a tool that should be used. Mr. Nixon was unimpressed.

The language of the bills all forbid the courts, regardless of the evidence, to order the busing of children to correct the inequities revealed. This would seem to make Congress supreme instead of one of the three branches of government. Whatever may be the inequalities, no busing may be ordered.

Negro parents, and, indeed, the broad generality of black Americans, are increasingly bitter at this racial by-passing. They had a hard struggle to pull themselves up from an average fourth grade education. Now, just as they are getting more youngsters finishing elementary and high schools and more are going to college, the white folks, led by the President, are getting all high and mighty about busing. Of course, no one is fooling anyone. Every black person knows it is not busing, but education, just as the houses were not sold or the apartments not rented or the jobs not filled when blacks showed up.

The short, ugly version is that black children must subsidize the comfort of white parents and children. So that later in life these whites can discuss how the black population needs "more training." Or how black workers can't be promoted because they lack the required education, how black families must be barred from decent housing because they are "below standard."

It fits into the pattern of 1896, the separate-but-equal constitutionality that was always separate but never equal. It has not worked in seventy years for white Americans. It has not worked for black Americans, either, except that they developed stronger bodies because they had steeper hills to climb and longer roads to travel.

The often-tried forcing of black children to stay back-through moratoriums— a few more years (and decades and generations) hasn't worked any better. Nothing but the actual practice of equality will bring racial peace. Either we make the "all men" doctrine work, including all minorities, or we go down the drain.

A black citizen mused, "Busing to support segregation was O.K., but busing supporting desegregation is sinful! Man, man. . . ."

A. Philip Randolph

A. Philip Randolph (1889–1979) was born in Crescent City, Florida. In 1925 Randolph organized the Brotherhood of Sleeping Car Porters (BSCP), and ten years later he negotiated a collective bargaining agreement with the Pullman Palace Car Company. As an official of the AFL-CIO, Randolph joined other prominent civil rights leaders in organizing the 1963 march on Washington. In the following article Roy Wilkins pays tribute to Randolph for conceiving the idea of the march on Washington. This article was written in August 1972.

The ninth anniversary of the famous March on Washington by the civil rights organizations and their followers is August 28. It seems only yesterday that 220,000 white and black people—an estimated 40,000 white—presented their petition and their personal presence to their government, at its seat, in behalf of civil rights for all Americans.

August 28 offers also an opportunity to pay a tribute to the father of the March on Washington idea, A. Philip Randolph, who is several years past his 80th birthday. Randolph attained nationwide notice for his work in the 1920s with the organizing period of the Brotherhood of Sleeping Car Porters. Few people know of those hard days, for the trains are gone.

Today is not the time to review the battle of Randolph's incipient union of poor and powerless Pullman porters with the rich and arrogant Pullman company. That is a story of steadfast integrity which might well inspire every black young person who seeks black heroes. One does not have to go to far-off Africa for black kings and fearless warrior tribes. One can find the greatness, the sacrifice, the suffering and the inspiration right here in America.

After the union was a growing concern of proud men, Randolph pursued his dream of an outpouring in Washington in support of jobs and the whole range of civil rights. He drove FDR up a tree in 1941 with the March on Washington idea of jobs for minorities just as Great Britain was calling for more production of war goods and black workers were being refused factory jobs.

President Roosevelt signed Executive Order 8802 and the concept of fair employment practice was born. It went from the toothless, wartime FEP to where it is today, solidly rooted in our economic and political thinking, regardless of breaches in the practice.

Randolph waited impatiently for the right climate of opinion for his march. He got it in the summer of 1963 after the assassination of Medgar Evers, the Birmingham battle between "Bull" Connor, and the civil rights forces of Rev. Martin Luther King. A week after the Evers killing, President John F. Kennedy went on nationwide television announcing that an omnibus civil rights bill was being sent to Congress.

The time was ripe. July 2, 1963, saw the organizing meeting in New York City. The next eight weeks were crammed with activity under the tireless direction of Bayard Rustin, assistant to Randolph.

Except for the many behind-the-scenes crises, the story of August 28 is a public record. Martin Luther King, assigned the clean-up spot, went on to deliver his now world-famous speech, "I Have a Dream."

Perhaps because of this, the practice has grown among writers on King, to call the August 28, 1963, gathering "his" march. It has been so stated in newspaper and magazine articles, on television and on radio. Nothing could be farther from the truth. Nothing could be more unfair to A. Philip Randolph.

Martin Luther King, Jr. with his matchless oratory, his mellifluous cadences, and his great charisma, was the star above the star-studded cast of civil rights speakers. But the man who dreamed the dream that brought 220,000 American to Washington in behalf of the black and all minorities, should have the acclaim that is rightly his. Dr. King, who was assassinated in 1968, would be the first to hail Randolph on his anniversary.

Today, the ideals of America are endangered and again the question is, "What shall be the United States' stand on opportunity and equality for blacks and other non-whites?" This time it is school busing that masks the denial of equal education.

August 28 is a sobering date in our national history.

Mayor Tom Bradley of Los Angeles

Tom Bradley (1912–1998) was born in Culvert, Texas, and moved to Los Angeles in 1919. In 1940 he joined the Los Angeles police department, where he remained for twenty-two years and rose to the rank of lieutenant—the highest ranking position ever held by an African American. In 1973 he became the first black mayor of Los Angeles. In the following article, Roy Wilkins hails Tom Bradley on his mayoral victory.

The white voters of Los Angeles, the nation's third largest city, have combined with the black voters and the Mexican-American ones to elect Tom Bradley as the city's first black mayor.

In doing this voters piled up a margin of 97,000 votes for the former Texas sharecropper, police lieutenant and city councilman over the total of Mayor Sam Yorty, who has occupied the office for twelve years.

Bradley's performance was strictly in the tradition of every candidate of an American minority. Since the black population of Los Angeles amounts to about eighteen per cent, the first task was to win support from among eighty-two per cent non-black voters. Bradley did this, enlisting almost fifty per cent of the white voters and about fifty-one per cent of the Mexican-Americans.

The Task Ahead

Roy Wilkins believed that many of the youth who took part in the civil rights movement in the 1960s and 1970s were deficient in their history and motivated strongly by impatience and anger. In the following address to the NAACP Sixty-fourth Annual Convention on July 3, 1973, he discusses some of the historical highlights of African Americans in this nation, the progress made by the race, the obstacles to full equality, and the tasks that remain ahead.

Any history of Negro Americans in this country since 1619, even if casually worded, must record their persistent efforts to be included as a part of the nation, equal with other parts. Not to separate themselves from other Americans, but to be included among them. Not to set up a land of their own, but to win and hold a portion of this land, in the same manner that others have won a foothold, running the same risks—but no greater—as others have run.

The first item, naturally, was freedom from slavery. At first the idea was of a return to the African scene that had been a homeland for most of them. Later it became a desire to make a home in this new land. Our forefathers wanted to share in this land, to share in this brave and newly declared government that Thomas Jefferson was later to immortalize in the Declaration of Independence.

So they had to get rid of the repeated lie that they were "happy" as slaves. They did this in a thousand ways, by appealing to individual avarice or compassion, by singing and praying in a tongue which had double meaning for them and for white listeners.

Or by "misunderstanding" the meaning of orders, by defiance up to the limit, by cunning and by the deadly (and outwardly futile) actual revolutions. The lie that they were happy has persisted until today, assisted by too many accommodating blacks, but the small band of leaders, in the pews as well as the pulpit, in the schools and kitchens, destroyed the myth by their very existence.

Throughout this struggle, right down to this very minute, it has been the ideas that we have had to combat. The physical tortures of the body were bad enough, that is, the whippings, beatings, brandings, and killings. The tortures came with a slave regime: rape of slave women, the separation of families, and the destruction of the idea of marriage between slaves. All these sufferings of the body were subordinate to the concept—the idea—of human beings as chattel property. The idea that slavery was right and proper—and demonstrably profitable—hurt worse than physical torture.

Thomas Jefferson set forth in writing, in the Declaration of Independence in the last third of the eighteenth century, the idea of individual freedom and its protection by a government. He wrote:

We hold these truths to be self-evident, that all men are created equal and are endowed by their Creator with certain unalienable rights—that among these are Life, Liberty and the Pursuit of Happiness. Governments are created among men, deriving their just powers from the consent of the governed.

This was what the leading dissenters on human slavery had been waiting for. They, white and black alike, set about bringing black slaves under the formulated ideas of the new government. I am not sure that the N.A.A.C.P. idea did not start at least when Jefferson wrote down the creed that was to be the backbone of the new government.

They had 5,000 black soldiers fighting in George Washington's army. They had the frank debates on slavery at the Constitutional Convention of 1787 as set forth by W. E. B. Du Bois in the first volume of the Harvard Classics, published in 1895. They had black sailors with Perry's fleet in 1812. They had the insurrections of Denmark Vesey and other daring slaves. They had the famous Manifesto of Daniel Walker in 1829, the infamous *Dred Scott* decision in 1857, and the continuing oratory and pamphleteering of the Abolitionists up to and through the war.

Some results of the counter-idea war were spectacular. A nation only eighty-five years old risked its existence and waged a bloody civil war over a moral idea—the abolition of human slavery.

It did not matter that economics was forging to the front and that, in this sense, a nation could not exist half slave and half free. It did not matter that service in the Army was unpopular, that there were draft riots and other violent objections—what did we have in the Vietnam War? It did not matter whether

Abraham Lincoln said he would hit slavery hard, or whether, as President, he said he would keep slavery if he could save the Union. The point is that as a result of the war, four million black slaves were freed and could embark thereafter in the perilous pursuit of happiness as free men.

Thus, despite the roadblock idea of their status in a slave regime that lasted 250 years, the freed descendants were on their way to winning equality here in America, the only home most of them had ever known. The overwhelming majority spurned the offer of the American Colonization Society to return to Africa.

They had their ups and downs after the war. There were peaks of achievement, such as the election of U.S. Senators, Representatives and members of state legislatures and other state officeholders. For me the greatest thrill, more significant than the election of Senator Blanche K. Bruce of Mississippi, was the fact that some 500 schools were owned by the former slaves and that against the government's appropriation of $3,500,000 in a seven-year period to the Freedmen's Bureau the ex-slaves themselves contributed $500,000.

There were, also, the bitter disappointments: the Hayes-Tilden Compromise, which withdrew Federal troops from the South and told that region, in effect, that it would be free to treat the ex-slaves as it saw fit; the nullification of the civil rights laws; the rise in the terror and killing by the Ku Klux Klan; and finally the constitutional legalization of racial discrimination under the 8–1 decision of the United States Supreme Court in *Plessy* vs. *Ferguson* in 1896.

The last was the most crippling blow of all. It was to enthrone the iniquitous and wholly untrue doctrine of "separate but equal." This doctrine was to last through fifty-eight years until Thurgood Marshall and his band of lawyers upset it through a unanimous ruling of the U.S. Supreme Court, May 17, 1954, in *Brown* vs. *Board of Education* of Topeka, Kansas. It put a stranglehold on relations between the races, affecting red, yellow, and brown, as well as black. With only a breather here and there, it was a veritable apartheid in America.

There was nothing for Negro Americans to do except to begin at the bottom, setting out again to establish the equality they had wanted back in 1619. The separate-but-equal myth spread from a Louisiana railroad train to public schools, to employment, to housing, to voting, to interstate, restaurants, hotels.

Then to taxicabs, parks, playgrounds, municipal auditoriums, swimming pools, and beaches. And to separate drinking fountains, toilets and separate tax windows. It was "understood" that in stores whites would be waited on before Negroes and that the latter would not be able to try on articles of clothing, contenting themselves with a verbal guess on size.

American whites settled into their routine of the deprivation of blacks. Each year the customs grew more entrenched and rigid. Millions of white youngsters in their separate schools studied nothing about blacks, since their textbooks contained no information whatsoever. The blacks were locked out of education and remained ignorant, by and large, were frozen out of jobs and thus had little money. They were barred from the ballot box and thus had no political influence.

But the impoverished blacks took their cue from Mr. Justice Harlan's lone dissent in *Plessy* vs. *Ferguson*. He wrote:

If laws of like character should be enacted by the several states of the Union, the effect would be in the highest degree mischievous. Slavery, as an institution tolerated by law, would, it is true, have disappeared from our country; but there would remain a power in the states, by sinister legislation, to interfere with the full employment of the blessings of freedom, to regulate civil rights, common to all citizens, upon the basis of race, and to place in a condition of legal inferiority a large body of American citizens. . . .

Elsewhere he wrote the famous and most quoted passage:

The white race deems itself to be the dominant race in this country, and so it is . . . but in the view of the Constitution, in the eye of the law, there is in this country no superior, dominant ruling class of citizens. There is no caste here. Our Constitution is color-blind. In respect to civil rights all citizens are equal before the law.

With this theory of the U.S. Constitution as their blueprint, Negro Americans began again the long, painful, and heartbreaking struggle for equality against the greatest odds ever. When the definitive history is written, this fifty-eight year period undoubtedly will show the greatest sacrifices, the greatest unity, the most dogged determination in the face of implacable opposition from political, economic and social (in the broad sense) fountainheads. Blacks had literally to pick themselves up off the floor and inch upward by their own bootstraps.

We can charge that they were not relevant, that they made mistakes, that they lacked self-respect, that they grinned like Aunt Jemima and shuffled like Stepin Fetchit. But they made it. They brought the race issue out of the political corridors and put it smack in the middle of committee discussions and floor debate. They had sense enough to hop by the thousands into the new industrial unions of the 1930s and thus pushed wider the doors of the old-line unions with their vise-like hold on jobs. They pounded at every crack they made in public education. They fashioned a moral issue out of their general treatment on all fronts and made America choose between a conscience and no conscience.

They are still at it, slugging away like Hammering Hank Armstrong. An increasing number of black youngsters who knew not Joseph have turned their jeers to cheers and have thrown their fresh young strength and their wide-ranging knowledge into the fray.

For today the phase of this age-old contest is one, not merely for survival, but for life itself. I know that there is talk about black people over the world, of their looking to Negro Americans for inspiration, strength, and knowledge. But no people ever helped another when it failed in its quest for equality in its own house. How can a race, some members of which have not won respect and equal treatment in their own country, aid other peoples? One cannot offer repeatedly for one's shortcomings the old excuse of a white majority's dislike of blacks, its sweeping or strategic policies of racial discrimination.

No matter what the obstacles are, physical or psychological, no matter how long it requires, no race can have it put in a permanent record that it folded under pressure and persecution, that it quit the fight for equality because it did not relish the rules. We need to observe the rules. If that is the way it is, then we should study how to make the rules work for us. The time will come when we will feed on the meat of power, a time when we are ready, not unready and prepared only to tear up the pea patch.

And in these 1970s the old enemies are their ideas to hamper and to halt forward progress.

From Stanford, one of our great universities, Dr. William Shockley has spouted the poison of his pet idea—the genetic inferiority of blacks. He received invaluable assistance from a learned and scholarly journal at Harvard University, probably in the interest of truth or science or some other objective, deemed not to be worthy in some thinking by someone. Anyway, Dr. Shockley maintains that Negroes are inherently and innately inferior to whites and that no matter what legislation is enacted, what opinions courts may have and what administrative policies are pursued, black American are just plain unable to cope—from their mothers' womb.

The great danger here is that this theory, instead of being examined exhaustively to discover its worth, if any, will find its way into educational policy. Who can doubt, after the revelations of these weeks, that bright young men in Washington (or in your local and state school systems) are busy planning new laws and policies based upon the Shockley theory? As eagerly as thousands of teachers and principals seized upon the idea that black children were uneducable, who can say that they would not embrace Shockley, unproven as the man may be?

Who can assert, with certainty, that Federal appropriations to the states for education, that local and state school budgets and that elaborate administrative maneuvering are not influenced by notions out of Stanford, served up by Harvard? Who knows what scholars are working upon "reports" or "research" (financed by grants) that sooner or later will be woven into policy on the education of Negroes?

Or take another theory developed in detail by Dr. Christopher Jencks at Harvard University. Dr. Jencks maintains that education, little or much, does not affect the getting and holding of a job—any job. In other words—and this could be an oversimplification—the type of job secured does not depend on one's amount of schooling.

The adoption of this thesis would dump all black protests on educational inequality into the ash can. It would stop the education of blacks promptly. It would play havoc with the system which whites have built so painstakingly to frustrate other whites and particularly to block blacks. What becomes of the tests which all candidates for a job or for a classification are supposed to take? What about the Air Force Qualification Test (AFQT), used by all the Armed Services to determine which recruits shall be restricted to certain careers in the service?

Black sailors in the Navy, black soldiers in the Army and black airmen in the Air Force all brand the AFQT as the chief devil in racial discrimination in the Armed Service. In Germany a black NCO complained bitterly to an N.A.A.C.P. investigating team that this test had been given him on enlistment "when I had a substandard education compared to white boys. Now the slot has got me and no matter how hard I study, I can't catch up or otherwise improve myself." Black sailors on the aircraft carrier *Kitty Hawk* made the same complaint to their N.A.A.C.P attorneys.

The Jencks theory, like that of Dr. Shockley, may creep or be deliberately thrust into education policy and practice on the education of blacks. Disaster would follow. A street sweeper would not know what to do in the age of space.

To an extent, these obstructive ideas, which pose very real threats to the progress of the black minority to equality under the Constitution, are aided unconsciously by the actions of certain minorities (and I emphasize minorities) within the black minority. These barrier ideas are buttressed in the popular and uncritical mind by crime actually committed by, or attributed to, Negroes. It is impossible to state with any degree of accuracy just how solid a feeling has been built up against black employment, black housing and black education by real or alleged black crime.

Crime statistics are of little help. By the time principal categories are broken down, by the time the arrests are separated from the convictions and by the time the prejudice of arresting officers and of various law enforcement officials all are taken into account. Negro crime takes its proper place, away from the inflammatory accounts and the news flashes on radio and television.

But, in the meantime the harm has been done to the aspirations of millions of law-abiding Negroes. The FBI once reported mere arrests as though they were convictions. Our departed and dearly beloved friend and co-worker. William R. Ming, once told me his law firm appeared in behalf of eleven persons and finally released eight of them as innocent! The media duly recorded eleven arrests and this was what remained in the minds of the fearful and unthinking white housewives.

Recently a whole neighborhood in New York City, Canarsie by name, barred thirty black children living in a public housing project from a Canarsie school. White parents physically kept the little black pupils on board a bus and stood guard to see that they did not enter the school. A strike was called. The Board of Education was picketed. New policy was made, based upon the color of the children and the public housing project from which they came.

I do not have to tell this audience that a segment of the Forest Hills community in New York City kept yelling until it forced a revision in a housing project originally planned for low-income families. The contention was that low-income families would be largely black and that blacks were "crime-oriented." They made no bones about black crime being kept out of the neighborhood. In the school case crime was only implied. In Forest Hills it was mentioned, loud and clear and often profanely.

It is difficult to estimate the tens of thousands of upright black families, having no connection with crimes, which have been barred from decent housing by actual physical threats, by hostile neighbors, by circumventing the fair housing laws or by realtors in combination with banks and mortgage lenders.

The executive branch of the present Administration in Washington has not helped black families in this predicament. The President himself has added to the public's fancies and fears on black crime. A rallying cry of the Nixon Administration has been for "law and order," by which it meant "law and order for Negro criminals." Last October 28, just before the election, President Nixon said in a radio speech:

> Most Americans are united in demanding respect for the law. . . . We will not be satisfied until all our city streets are safe . . . that is my philosophy in appointing judges to the bench, from the Supreme Court on down. They must by qualified jurists, but they must be jurists who recognize that the first civil rights of all Americans is the right to be free from domestic violence.

Let no one say that he did not use the code words which mean Negro crime or that the threat to law enforcement was lost on millions of white listeners.

We shall not comment on the irony of a "law and order" Administration punishing penny ante Negro crime while plotting in the highest echelons of government the theft of the liberties and freedom of a whole people. Not that Negro crime, in instances, is not heinous and horrible. Not that murder is pretty, whether the accused be black or white. But nothing can match the oily preachments on law of one whose dark code is a belief that the end justifies the means.

In heartening contrast, Mrs. Mattie Cook, administrative director of Malcolm-King College in Harlem, takes her students the hard, long, slow way around. She and her students do not take the easy path of planning and executing breaking and entering, forging cablegrams and staging reprisals against those who do not agree with them.

"It is evident," says Mrs. Cook, "that the better jobs are not open unless you have credentials, academic degrees. Society demands it and if that's what it takes to move up. . . ."

Mrs. Cook and the 750 students at Malcolm-King College, about ninety per cent black and nearly all the rest Puerto Rican, are planning and working only for equal opportunity for their race in America.

If they had been thinking of separation and of starting anew in another land, they would not be at college in Harlem in 1973. They would not be responding to society's demand for credentials. They would not be seeking, earnestly and industriously, to "move up."

Everyone within the sound of my voice knows how much we have given. Yesterday and last night in moving speeches we counted some of the freedom's martyrs in this ever-present crusade for mankind.

Each one of us here can add his bit from his own life. But we're here this week to mark another anniversary in the old struggle. We have an investment in America, an investment in blood and tears, in lives dead and revered, and in lives which are triumphant over insults and barriers and persecution.

We aren't going anywhere. We are staying right here. This is our land. For good or bad, it owns us. And we own it! We have bought it and our futures here with sacrifice and heroism, with humility and love. It belongs to us and we shall never give up our claim and run away.

We are proud of our race, of our color, of our history as Americans. We are so proud of it that we demand that it be accepted on an equality with every other minority or majority in this nation. We want to stand on an equal footing with our fellow Americans and help make our country what it was supposed to be.

"Our Constitution is color-blind," wrote Mr. Justice Harlan, a lone voice in 1896.

Today, that voice and that tough ideal has become—because of you and those from every race like you—the sound and fervor of a multitude.

Your victory is certain if you finish the task you have so magnificently advanced.

"Come over into Macedonia and Help Us!"

The NAACP and the church have been partners since the association's inception. The NAACP's church program was established to involve religious groups in the civil rights movement. The church wing of the Association worked with religious groups to register voters, recruit members, support organized marches, provide meeting places, and raise funds. In the following address to the Ninety-third Annual Session of the National Baptist Convention, Roy Wilkins describes some of the pressing challenges before the NAACP and the Association's need for continued church support. This speech was given on September 7, 1973.

I am here at this convention of churchmen in signal of this body, a body well acquainted with struggle and strain and with the healing effect of the spirit and of the faith, for aid at this juncture. My cry is the well-known one of the Bible: "Come over into Macedonia and help us!"

We have been partners—the church and the National Association for the Advancement of Colored People—for the six-and-a-half decades of our life as an organization. Together we have seen the marching ahead, the stalemates, the marking time, the joyous times when the Lord was compassionate and the people were prayerful and righteous. We have muddled together through periods of dark despair, but never gave up, never abandoned the faith that one day it would be all right.

The church took us under its wing. It nurtured us, gave us, in our local units, the service and guidance of its ministers of all denominations and faiths. When the inns of our nation turned their flinty faces against us and we had no place to meet, it was the church which threw open its doors and ministered to our needs, both spiritual and physical.

More than 1,000 Baptist churches are Life Members of the N.A.A.C.P., fully paid up in the $500 membership. The leader, Dr. J. H. Jackson, president of the National Baptist Convention, is a fully-paid Life Member, as are many individual ministers, church members, as well as clubs that have a church connection. We have a partnership not made with hands, but with the instant and mutual recognition of the rights of men, whatever their color or station in life. Thousands of church members of the N.A.A.C.P., who have joined on the minimum membership basis, testify to this partnership.

The story never changes. Man's need never changes. In this hurly-burly world, so prone to brush aside man's rights here on earth and his salvation in the time to come, the church and the N.A.A.C.P. have a mission.

We ask help in winning, for those who care, access to employment, to jobs. Recent figures from the 1970 Census show the median family income of Negro Americans to be $6,854, but the median family income of whites to be $11,549. These figures tell the whole story. The gap, overall, is growing not narrower, but wider.

We ask help in equalizing opportunity for access to the best education. Without the preparation inherent in good schooling, we can't get very far in housing, employment, and political affairs. All are interlocking. A very present danger is the mobilizing of the idea that black children are genetically inferior and will never be able to equal whites. In the prestigious universities in this country and in England and in forbidding tomes in scholarly journals and on the printing presses, this poisonous and wholly untrue thesis is being readied for use in more popular journals, in boards of education and in legislation.

We need decent housing for black Americans, unrestricted as to location. The same 1970 Census revealed that thirteen times as many whites moved to the suburbs as did blacks. Of course, there were obstacles, deliberately laid, to hog-tie the blacks into the rotting inner cities.

We need help to fight crime amongst us, to take positive, not punitive measures to keep our youth out of crime. Every statistic shows that Negro Americans suffer more at the hands of criminals than any other segment. We will be helping ourselves, as well as society generally, if we not only condemn crime, but turn our faces against it and actively work to cut crime to the minimum.

We need help in turning around our youth. Not in slowing them down, but in returning them to the goals which are good for any people, white, brown, red, Oriental, or black. No one seems to know what has got into the youth of every race on the face of the earth. They should be impatient with things as they are. They should expand to new ground, new discoveries and new methods. This is the way it should be from generation to generation. But this coldness, this hardness, this snap-judgment, purely on the basis of age, this lack of toleration for dissent! And the maimings and killings because they cannot do as they wish—this is frightening. We need help with our young people, among all majorities and minorities. In addition to those on the right track (and there are many) there are others who must be got off the suicidal "Kick" of these times. They can destroy the image that has been built so painstakingly over the past thirty-five decades. Just as you are beginning to head the race in the right direction, some of them, in just a few minutes, dash all your hopes to the ground and you have to start all over again. Yes, we need help—every organization of any people needs help with its youth.

We need help in voter registration and in marshaling the full power of our electorate, not only to elect qualified black men to office, but to elevate good government for the whole community. We should double the present 2,600 black elected officials.

We need help in building black economic power, not as a threat, but as legitimate expression of our desire to make a contribution for the economic community.

To do this we need members and money. If we have the members, the money will follow. Therefore our appeal is for more individual members. At the end of 1973, we should have between 425,000 and 450,000 enrolled.

But this number should be at the very least a million. Will you help? The Life Members at $500 should be continued and we must have more of them. They are thrice welcome. But we need thousands of $4.00 and $5.00 members. Go back to your home cities and towns and begin soliciting minimum memberships in the N.A.A.C.P. Ministers can spread the word on memberships in their congregations. The totals by December 31, 1971, can be cause for pride.

Some ask why we need members in mounting numbers. One answer is that we in the N.A.A.C.P. want to continue this as an organization where people make things happen.

Right now there is an amendment sponsored by Congressman Charles Diggs of Michigan to have the United States increase its aid to the famine region of Africa. It will help. It will show concern for humanity if only twenty people urged their Senators to vote for the amendment to a foreign aid bill. But how much more effective if 20,000 urged such a course? We need members in order to win battles for freedom. In this sophisticated time, when smiles are used to cover up evil, when a sinister or selfish thing is buried in the fine print, we need members to get the job done properly.

And now, let me turn from a brief comment on the N.A.A.C.P. program and our continuing needs for the future, to a pervasive question for the American people. Any organization which concerns itself with rights of minorities, and which tries to shape its program to get its government to guarantee those rights, has to have a deep interest in this question.

Any church body that is properly concerned with morality and which gives support to a lay organization whose active program is so oriented, must give attention to the question posed.

If there is one passage of the Scriptures that sheds a light and a comfort on the American people in this time of stress it is in the verses to be found in the fourth chapter of the second epistle of Paul to the church of Corinth. You will remember that Paul encouraged them against troubles. "Blessed be God," he wrote, "who comforted us in all our tribulation, that we may be able to comfort them which are in any trouble. . . ."

We Americans are in trouble, bad trouble. We are sick and uneasy as a nation. But Paul has reassured us as he did the Corinthians, with these rallying words, beginning at the eighth verse:

8. We are troubled on every side, yet not distressed, we are perplexed but not in despair;

9. Persecuted, but not forsaken; cast down, but not destroyed . . .

13. We have the same spirit of faith, according as it is written . . .
18. While we look not at the things which are seen, but at the things which are not seen: for the things which are seen are temporal; but the things which are not seen are eternal.

Perplexed, but not in despair, cast down, but, thank the Lord, not destroyed.

How did these clouds come upon our horizon? How did we come, as a people, to the brink of the destruction of our inner selves? How did our faith make us cling to "the things which are not seen" so that we were "troubled on every side, yet not distressed"?

Perhaps we were plunged into our predicament by our simple and naive trust. As Paul says in his second verse: "not walking in craftiness, nor handling the word of God deceitfully. . . ." We trusted. We believed. It did not occur to us until long afterward, until we heard the men we had trusted declare out of their own mouths a cynical belief in other gods.

A god of expediency and ruthless and unfeeling power. No compassion. No love of humanity. A game with pawns and kings and queens. And at the apex, at the very peak, the quintessence of raw power, the planned distillation of ever tightening control.

Paul writes of "not walking in craftiness." Little did he know of the American troubles of the 1970s! Little did he know of men struggling toward freedom who barely escaped being changed into robots. Craftiness, indeed! Deception with an open face. Lies. Partial truths. Pretense. And strong arm-men, able and willing to demolish any obstacle to their ambition and to their thirst for power.

It was a simple operation whose thoroughness and completeness depended upon the child-like beliefs of some of us, the unquestioning temperament of some of us and the greed for power and profit of the rest of us. Control was to be through men and placed in every strategic place of influence.

And these were to report to a control center whose word would be absolute, because its control would be absolute. All dissenters from the New Order would be pictured as traitors, no matter how high their station. Rivals would be pinioned by untruths in falsified letters and other communications. If necessary, a smooth and thoroughly plausible chain of events would be manufactured out of the whole cloths.

All would be made to move and function by a mountain of gold, conveyed hither and yon by special couriers whose loyalty was insured and whose curiosity was silenced by their handsome stake in the proceedings.

Beside these monumental moves, having no less a grand design than the serfdom of a whole people, the craftiness of which Paul speaks is petty, indeed. For the uncritical, it was presented as a contest between two men and their followers. We were told that no one knew of this vast plot to take over the liberties of a people. One after another, from the highest to the next highest to the middle and to all the rest, each has denied that he directed or ordered or discussed this wholesale theft of manhood. These denials have ignored a coordinated plan whose very existence points to much more than a Topsy-like growth.

Moses, preaching and scolding the children of Israel, says at one point (Deuteronomy 32: 18,28) "There are . . . children who have no faith. For they are a nation void of counsel, neither is there any understanding in them."

Some among us did not lose our faith. That is a great song for this convention. "We've Come This Far by Faith." And so true.

We have looked hard at the things which are not seen. These are eternal. Not here today and gone tomorrow. Eternal. Not smothered with soft lies, angry lies, smooth lies. Eternal.

This is why we are perplexed, but not in despair. Because we know the truth underneath the things that are seen. Eternal. This is why we discovered the truth and separated it from the falsehoods that were betraying our country.

We are cast down; it is true, but not destroyed. We were stopped at the abyss. We were stopped and our loved ones and all those on the other side were saved by the things that are eternal, like truth and honor and integrity.

Why do we in the National Baptist Convention invoke a moral stand in this time of peril to our country? Because we are among those who are keepers of the faith. "We having the same spirit of faith as it is written," said Paul to Corinth. Down through the centuries, we have inherited that "same spirit or faith." We are its trustees throughout our lifetime. Whenever it is challenged, whenever a brazen scheme of so monstrous a proportion as to boldly plot to take over the destiny of a people, we of the Baptist persuasion and all like-minded members of every faith must not keep silent. We must cry out. We must call, "Watchman, what of the night?"

Paul, the good apostle of all of us, had a few words in his letter to the small church at Ephesus. I commend them to you now, not only in the present crisis, but in the unending struggle between good and evil in whatever place on the earth it may be, between people of the same race and those of different races.

In the eleventh and twelfth verses of the sixth chapter he wrote these enduring words of battle:

Put on the whole armour of God that ye may be able to stand against the wiles of the devil.

For we wrestle not against flesh and blood, but against principalities, against powers, against the rulers of the darkness of this world, against spiritual wickedness in high places

These words bear repeating. You are called to your covenant against evil, against the rulers of the darkness of this world, against spiritual wickedness in high places. You are called to aid man's continuing quest for freedom and peace, for equality of opportunity for all the races of mankind.

Here in this place, and when you return to your homes and wherever you may be next year or in the years to come, the call rings out: "Come over into Macedonia and help us!"

No more ennobling task faces men of good will today. Indeed, the stars in that figurative crown will glow with your deeds to those now in darkness who seek the light. The song says, "We've Come This Far by Faith." We could add only two words to encompass completely our appeal tonight: "and deed."

Black Power or Black Pride

Roy Wilkins was unyielding in his belief that the move toward full integration was the only way to a united America. He frequently challenged the so-called separatists and militants about their beliefs that a system that was centuries old could be eradicated overnight. In the following article, written in March 1974, he offers a definition of black power.

There is considerable indication, cropping up here and there, that some aspects of the black power hysteria that spread into all race relations when it was first voiced in 1966 are on the way out. In fact, among more advanced thinkers these aspects are dead.

Negro political leaders in New York City, fresh from their soul-searching in the hectic and discouraging experience of the nomination and appointment of a black deputy mayor, were among those who redefined "black power." Its real meaning is far from the sloganeering of marches, demonstrations, and confrontations. It is fully as far from the chip-on-the-shoulder bragging of some of its less thoughtful early proponents.

Percy E. Sutton, borough president of Manhattan, the highest elective office held by a black man in New York City, quotes the late Malcolm X as saying wisely, "Power is best used quietly, without attracting attention."

It was the exercise of this quiet power on one occasion that had a police lieutenant shaking his head in disbelief.

There had been an automobile accident in Harlem and a crowd had gathered. Malcolm X had been called and he conferred with the police. Soon, either by signal or by swift word of mouth, the crowd melted away. The police lieutenant said that it was not good for one man to have such control over a crowd.

Percy Sutton echoed Malcolm X when he said, "There are a lot of ways that black power is going to be exercised and you're not going to know a thing about it."

Extremist movements, say black leaders, are dead. Followers of the separatists and ultra-militarists, always a tiny minority, have almost vanished. No one in his right mind expects radical changes over the weekend.

If the black community really wants to exercise this quiet power, it must first of all get black voters registered. There are about one million Negroes in and around New York City, but some estimates say they have fewer citizens registered than are registered in Mississippi. Black people in New York have never had the kind of machine politics based upon the number of registered black voters that Chicago, for example, has had.

The late Congressman William L. Dawson, of Chicago's first district, once advised a conference of black intellectuals to solve race problems at the ballot box. Years ago, black Chicagoans were an important part of the Republican "Big Bill" Thompson machine, just as they are today a part of the Democratic Daley machine.

It was the late Charles Wright who declared then from the witness chair, "I am the third ward," in response to a question during a federal investigation. No black man has ever had such power in New York City.

The other important need in New York is money in larger denominations than hundred dollar bills. The relative poverty of the black community must be overcome. It takes a million dollars to just "sit in the game" of running for mayor, for example. Other candidates have personal fortunes or can call on inherited or business wealth. The situation is different for a black candidate.

Out of this New York experience has come one more reassurance that the raucous phase of black power is on the wane. This is a plus for every community that has a black population. Black power may continue to show itself in all its original glory, with its pitiful empty boasts, but it is dying.

In its place is proper pride in blackness, determination to qualify for public service to all citizens and an exercise of power for the good of minorities and for the benefit of the majority as well.

How Old the Civil Rights Movement

When Roy Wilkins wrote the following article in 1975, the NAACP was in its sixty-sixth year. But for many young black activists, the civil rights movement began when three college students sat down at a lunch counter in Greensboro, North Carolina, on February 1, 1960. In this essay he emphasizes the Association's many years of work in the civil rights movement and acknowledges that the seventeenth-century slave revolts started the civil rights movement.

It is good to know that someone recognizes that something was afoot on the civil rights front before 1960. If one reads about civil rights these days, one would get the clear message that before February 1, 1960, when four Negro young men sat down in a restaurant in Greensboro, N.C., nothing had happened. They say it all started there. The daily press, radio, and television have fed the idea.

Elias M. Schwarzbart, who was one of the host of attorneys who worked on the case, had a newspaper piece called, "The Scottsboro Case, A Lightning Flash," recalling for readers of this generation the excitement of 1931–44.

But even Mr. Schwarzbart says the case "signaled the reawakening of the civil rights movement after the long sleep since Reconstruction—a movement that was to break into full flame in the . . . 1960's and culminate in the historic Civil Rights Act of 1964 and the Voting Rights Act of 1965. We have come a long, long way. . . ."

There it is, the admission that there was something stirring in the civil rights movement at least thirty years before 1960, despite skipping over the years 1863–1931 with the author's "long sleep since Reconstruction." The period included the KKK upsurge, Roman Holiday lynchings, the Black Codes, disfranchisement, peonage, legal approval in *Plessy* vs. *Ferguson* of dual racial constitutionality. The race was barely staying alive with no time to organize demonstrations.

But after forty-four years no one seeks to take "credit" for the mixed "victory" in the case. The Scottsboro affair was a milestone in establishing the Negro as a human being entitled to all the rights and privileges of a citizen. The most telling ruling that came out of it was Judge James Horton's setting aside of the conviction on the ground that it was contrary to credible evidence. This was a body blow at the system of jurisprudence as it affected Negroes accused of crime.

It became apparent that, in spite of Judge Horton's ruling, the Scottsboro defendants would not be free as long as they were defended by the International Labor Defense, the legal arm of the American Communist Party.

So the N.A.A.C.P. joined with the American Civil Liberties Union, the International Labor Defense, the League for Industrial Democracy, the Church League for Industrial Democracy, the Methodist Federation for Social Service, the Brotherhood of Sleeping Car Porters, and the National Urban League (as a sponsoring organization) to form the Scottsboro Defense Committee. Samuel Liebowitz, famous criminal lawyer, volunteered to defend the men without fee. Liebowitz was given his transportation to Alabama and the insufficient sum of $3,000 for expenses.

In the 1934 printed report of the N.A.A.C.P., it is stated that the total "so far expended by the association is $11,854.70." This was in the same year that the total income of the N.A.A.C.P., exclusive of special funds, was $44,176.91.

The point is that the N.A.A.C.P., now entering its sixty-sixth year, never wavered from its determination to win discrimination-free citizenship for all minorities. It weathered the Scottsboro case with its vitriolic misrepresentation. It was at work on torture-confession cases, the second and third of the four Texas primary cases, school segregation cases, etc.

Slave revolts started the civil rights struggle in the seventeenth century. This is an acknowledgment that the pre-1960 years were not a desert of inactivity.

Black Mayors

In 1976 when Roy Wilkins wrote this article, Maynard Jackson was mayor of Atlanta, Georgia, and Richard Hatcher was mayor of Gary, Indiana. At the time, both mayors were accused of allowing race to divide their respective cities. In the following article, Wilkins discusses what he believes to be some of the reasons behind the racial dissension in cities headed by black mayors.

It was not to be expected that all the cities which elected black mayors would be, in a few years, miraculously recovered from their serious problems, although many people felt that the black mayors were to do this. They would be backed by either the black minority or the fifty per cent and more majority.

Well, it hasn't worked out that way. The new black mayors, as with new white mayors, used up a year getting acquainted with the cities and who really runs them. They found that they had been elected by cities more bankrupt than usual. They found the tax base shriveling. They found that the Negroes who had been complaining (and rightly so) made up a fat percentage of the low or nonpaying tax groups. At the same time, these black citizens needed expensive municipal services, like hospitals, clinics, police and fire protection, water, light, and sewage services, schools and many others.

The new black mayors were not responsible for these and other problems connected with the general economy any more than the average white was responsible for 350 years of deprivation. The former President didn't help matters much by returning to the states more than 30 billion dollars in revenue-sharing funds. This, in effect, gave the money to factions in the states that regarded black mayors with skepticism.

Mayor Maynard Jackson of Atlanta, Ga. and Mayor Richard Hatcher of Gary, Ind. have been the subject of long articles in recent weeks. The one on Atlanta is speculative, at the end of the first year of a four-year term and the one on Gary is a pre-election piece.

It is difficult to believe that Maynard Jackson, with his background and his intelligence, would deliberately seek to block the Atlanta white community and to push blacks to the fore. Mayor Jackson is not consciously the head of a racist regime.

It may be that some members of his official family or its periphery are fanning the racial fires. It may even be that Mayor Jackson has made remarks that may seem to be heavily laced with race. If so, these are no more serious than the efforts of all politicians seeking support from a part of the population. It is not wise, but it is no sin.

It would be extremely foolish for Maynard Jackson or anyone else to head a racially divided city. It would be disastrous for there to be a rift between blacks who have political but little economic leadership and whites who rely on their economic strength but lack political dominance. If such a rift is developing it should be nipped in the bud. Atlanta's progress depends upon a biracial approach.

In Gary, one of the first cities to elect a black mayor, Richard Hatcher has made a good record against great odds. Of course, he has his powerful enemies; one cannot hold public office and not have enemies.

However, both men are accused of allowing race to divide their cities. In Gary and Atlanta, the word "racist" is being bandied about far too much by whites and blacks alike. Most of what happens to each race is political, not racial. Negroes have been kept off the political gravy train for so long that they are exuberant at even temporary relief, and whites just hate to be where they cannot call the political shots.

More wisdom in dealing with all segments of the population is indicated in each city. For decades blacks cried this to whites. Now the roles are reversed. They should get together, for the time grows shorter for the cities.

Integration the Only Way

When Roy Wilkins wrote this article in 1975, he believed that many African Americans had wandered off the path of integration in search of a quick panacea. In this essay he counters the "go-it-alone" theory.

Nearly every day some evidence appears that more and more black Americans who have wandered off the path of creeping progress in search of a more speedy resolution of the race's destiny are returning to the fold. They have found out their men, no matter how dedicated, need help and cooperation.

The "go it alone" theory has been tried and it won't work, at least for now. At one time it was thought the magic of black alone would be sufficient. Black was added to every enterprise and although some blacks, here and there, made some extra money by taking advantage of a fad, and although some egos were twisted unrecognizably, it was found, after a brief time, that in few instances was the race advanced.

Truth to tell, integration is the only philosophy that goes anywhere under the present circumstances where there is a minority of ten to ninety. Until black people build up their retail field, reduce their number of household domestics, improve their land-holding class (farmers and non-farmers) find a way to employment in all brackets, fight their way to good solid education and are housed freely in all kinds of neighborhoods, they might as well forget going it by themselves.

Blackness is not enough. It helps by instilling knowledge and pride, but it falls short. When it gets down to the money-on-the-table stage and to the subsequent operating phases, there are few who will come up with the cash and have the discipline enough to operate a business and see that costs are met.

Years ago the Woodlawn organization in Chicago, cheek by jowl with the University of Chicago, was trying to build a neighborhood. Under their leader, the late Saul Alinsky, they raised the cry of community cooperation when hostility against newcomers, mostly blacks, from the South was the normal reaction.

Now the Woodlawn Organization has eschewed protest and demonstrations. Gang wars and fires of unknown origin have all but disappeared. New Housing and the rehabilitation of old housing is going forward. The neighborhood has lost some of its rundown look. One apartment house (like many an urban university) is attracting a good mix of black and white families, mainly from the university. Another apartment house is receiving money from Washington to aid with its financial problems. The Woodlawn people themselves are rehabilitating 100 buildings that are structurally sound. In addition they run a profitable theater and supermarket.

But the Woodlawn Organization has taken another step and that is to declare boldly that it is part of the establishment. Leon D. Finney, 37, a good dresser and the valuable president of the organization, talked freely of the shift. He counters the view that Woodlawn will never attract middle class families because people remember that it was a ghetto. President Finney says:

> A lot of our black friends have been critical, but now we know that there is no way Woodlawn is going to make it as an all-black community. . . . We not only want residents here, but also white business. Woodlawn cannot develop by black money alone; black capital must participate with white capital. . . . But being establishment means that we are a responsible organization that doesn't go off half-cocked as we did sometimes in the past. We don't loosely or cavalierly use our authority.

Woodlawn is not out of the woods, but it is on its way. It just might be the races that stay in the inner cities, rather than those who ran away to the suburbs, may find the answers to Americans living together.

Intelligence Tests

In the following article, written in May 1975, Roy Wilkins discusses the harm done to black children by so-called intelligence tests. These imperfect conclusions by scholars, he writes, allow politicians and society at large to perpetuate myths and lies about a race and ultimately act on their negative views.

Among the crosses a black child has to bear are tests of various kinds, particularly so-called intelligence tests.

These prove little, if anything, about intelligence, but the harm to a race can be measured in the use which the political system makes of them. And scholars, too, permit their imperfect conclusions to be cited by politicians and schools of thought to support some restrictive measure against a whole race.

Dr. Robert L. Williams, a black psychologist on the faculty of Washington University in St. Louis, is pictured in a feature article as conducting a lone campaign against the use of tests to set limits on minorities. Dr. Williams would be the first to acknowledge that the black community, far from just becoming aware of these tests, has been inveighing against them certainly since before World War II.

Dr. Williams had the experience common to thousands of black kids of passing an intelligence test, but by a margin insufficient in his counselor's mind. His mark was an eighty-two and the counselor "advised me not to go to college, but to take up a trade because I was good with my hands." He ignored the advice and went on to college.

Lest he feel that geography was a factor, Dr. Williams would be surprised to hear that counselors in Boston, Mass., high schools told Negro students they should study how "to cook and clean and sew."

Negro advisers were telling black students a few years ago that there were no black chemists and counseled against such college careers.

Julius Hobson upset the track system used then by the District of Columbia schools by winning a lawsuit in a federal court. The court held that the tracks to which black students were assigned on the basis of race were "inaccurate and misleading scores."

A classic case is *Griggs* vs. *Duke Power Company* in which the company was forbidden in 1971 by the U.S. Supreme Court to use tests "not job-related." The promotion involved coal handlers who wished to move up on the scale. In some other tests black men have been queried about Beethoven, Mozart, and Shakespeare.

Some idea of the test of black resolution on the various examinations is to be found in the 250 million tests administered annually. In addition to having to decide what tests to ignore, black families are up against constant harassment that may affect a whole life. Dr. Williams believes that a high proportion of blacks are hindered early in life after scoring low on intelligence tests. Despite this, he does not wish to be rid of all tests, "only those that discriminate against any culture."

The universal complaint is that tests reflect "middle class" culture. Dr. T. Anne Cleary, a psychologist in New York, says she shares many of the concerns of Dr. Williams. But she adds the tests will indicate "how well a student will do in a middle-class educational environment of the future." If black students hope to make a success in a middle-class environment, her statement means that they ought to be tested on middle-class values.

The lifetime effect of substandard education and tests is told with poignancy by a black soldier: "I got a substandard education compared to the white NCO's my age. No matter how hard I study, I can't advance now. On a promotional exam . . . I have to be damn near perfect. That is what is killing us."

Black History Missing

In the following article, Roy Wilkins responds to a study by the *Journal of American History* that it may be too late to include black history into textbooks of American schools. He writes here that the distortions, untruths, and myths that have hurt a race for more than 200 years only serve to perpetuate further racial strife. The article was written in August 1975.

Just when black Americans are struggling to put black history into the textbooks of the nation comes news that the contest may be too late. History, says a study which will appear in the September issue of the *Journal of American History*, may be on the way out as it was studied years ago.

It is not that black people contend that every single item must be included in the history texts. This is not, in their minds, a question of including everything "black" in black history. Negroes will want some things that seem superfluous to whites. It can be assumed without doubt that black people, whose history has been "blacked out" for more than 200 years, would seek to get everything in. This may be meritorious—in the strict sense of history—or not, but weighs little beside the hurt of a race neglected for so many generations.

One of the untruths that black people have had to suffer because they could find no word in history to back up their position is that they were "happy" in slavery and "contented" in their lot.

The truth is that they were not happy and that the numerous slave revolts pictured their discontent. Even many spirituals, while seeming to concentrate on heaven, were songs of revolution. There is not a word in histories used by high school and college students about these revolts, or the suicides of those who chose death to slavery, or those who took over ships from their captors and sailed to the West Indies.

Word has filtered out about Benjamin Banneker, the clockmaker and architect who helped the French city planner who laid out Washington, D.C. While every school child knows about Crispus Attucks, one of those killed on Boston Common, who knows that 5,000 black soldiers were in George Washington's army? Who knows about Peter Salem at the battle of Bunker Hill? When the fighting was over, who knows that McCoy, a black man, invented the oil cup on stationary engines and a variation used on trains?

These are just a few out of many nominees that Negroes would like to see included in histories. It would bolster the pride of a race and it would help the white people of the nation. Whatever helps racial peace is good for the United States. How much better it would be if today we did not have hostility in Boston but had an appreciation (not necessarily love) generated by year after year of history book accounts of blacks for the past 200 years.

A small white segment of the Boston population believes in a black and white country. That is the way it used to be. Today it is a lost cause, but it illustrates graphically what black history, taken in by generations of school children, could do to save racial peace in, say, the unlikely place of South Boston.

Now history is giving way to current events taken out of their historical perspective. Decent laws mandating consumer education have led districts in Illinois to substitute courses in economics and career education for history. In Alabama, "students have no time to study the past." In the east, "history is in an especially weak position" as far as teacher qualification is concerned.

There is a school of thinking among blacks which holds that every time the blacks are about to begin to catch up, whites change the rules. Maybe they don't really want racial progress. Maybe they want the Boston strife. Maybe our 200 years have been for nothing except building skyscrapers. Somehow this columnist does not believe this is true.

Paul Robeson

Paul Bustill Robeson (1898–1976), actor, singer, and activist, was born in Princeton, New Jersey. Robeson appeared in Eugene O'Neill's *The Emperor Jones* in 1925. That same year he gave his first concert of Negro spirituals. He performed in such plays as *All God's Chillun Got Wings, Porgy and Bess, Showboat, Othello,* and *The Hairy Ape.* After World War II he campaigned vigorously for the rights of African Americans. His activism attracted the attention of anti-Communists and he was denied a passport; his passport was not reissued until 1958. In the following article, Roy Wilkins pays tribute to the late Paul Robeson.

The name "great" had been misapplied to many men, white and non-white, but there is one among the citizens of this country who eminently deserved the title "great"—Paul Robeson.

Robeson was a man ahead of his time. He believed passionately in his people and, therefore, in the cause of humanity. The son of a slave who became a minister, there was no need to tell him of the exploitation of those who worked with their hands. He did not care that he could not speak their language. He knew poignantly what they suffered. He sang to them of the glory of victory over big and little wrongs. His rendition of a Negro spiritual, the battle song of slavery, needed no translation.

At Rutgers, Robeson attended on scholarship, which should have been a tip-off on his scholastic ability. Before he had finished his four years he won All-America honors in football two years in a row, 1917 and 1918. Walter Camp, who chose him for All-American, called him "the greatest defensive end that ever trod the gridiron." He was not only a great athlete, but he won a Phi Beta Kappa Key.

It was not until he had been graduated from Columbia Law School that his career on the stage began. Sometimes in London and sometimes in New York, he played roles in "The Emperor Jones," "Porgy," "Showboat," and "Othello." The latter was on Broadway longer than any other Shakespearean play. In between he gave concerts. A new fledgling concert bureau in Kansas City came under his largesse ($250 off the guaranteed sum). Anything to spread black culture and manhood was his lifelong doctrine.

Robeson found a life that he was to do his best to change. When he found what the Soviet Union, as he saw and interpreted it, was doing for the poor, he did not see why he, personally, should be restrained by a Senate from lending his encouragement. He tangled with Senator Joe McCarthy and had his passport lifted for eight years. Robeson's friends and associates need only reflect that any Negro who protested the treatment of the black citizens was called a communist or worse.

Paul Robeson was a great civil rights expatriate in the sense that he was impatient with conditions facing the blacks in this country from a comfortable existence in Europe. Negroes wanted instant manhood with all its rights and privileges, with individual and small group adjustments to be ironed out later. But freedom first! Of course, the white majority was unwilling to give (in the final analysis, they had at that time most of the police, the army and the navy). That created a stalemate.

Some expatriates were fond of loosing criticism (between ships as it were), telling the home civil rights leaders what was wrong in the view of Paris or London or Bonn cliques. Robeson was not as bad as all this. He kept referring to this country as his and in one magnificent passage told a Senate committee: "Because my father was a slave and my people died to build this country and I am going to stay right here and have a part of it, much like you."

Any man has the right to range himself on the side which seems to get to the goal in good shape. Robeson proudly and consistently paid the price for his beliefs. That is why we salute him. That is why he was great.

Harassment of Dr. King

After Martin Luther King, Jr., was assassinated on April 4, 1968, information released from FBI files revealed the animus toward King that was held by many FBI officials. In the following article, written in January 1977, Roy Wilkins discusses the harassment of Dr. King during his lifetime by the FBI.

Little by little the story of the assassination of Dr. Martin Luther King, Jr. is emerging, and in a matter of months the world may possibly know the truth.

Those who know something of the hatred of some officials of the F.B.I. for the dead man may put two and two together and guess the answer to the puzzle. Why was James Earl Ray, the confessed killer, able to get out of Memphis to Canada and England with no money and no ability to get about in foreign lands? Who were the men, if any, behind him? What was the real basis of his quarrel with his attorneys?

Of course the fresh inquiries into the assassination of President John Fitzgerald Kennedy are helping along the Martin Luther King matter. JFK was shot in Dallas, Texas, November 22, 1963, and only about fifteen per cent of the American people believe the official version of his killing contained in the Warren Report.

The rest of the population, if it has any opinion at all, leans toward a conspiracy and especially toward a conspiracy connected in some way to Cuba. The American people, it has been demonstrated again and again, are suckers for communism.

In fact, the late director of the F.B.I. was not above trotting the Communists out every so often to frighten the people and the Congress. As for the race question, every Negro knows that he has only to speak up for his people to be accused of being a Communist.

Last week Attorney General Edward H. Levi announced that J. Stanley Pottinger and Richard L. Thornburgh, top level assistant attorneys general, would examine the King file and report to him. Mr. Levi was quoted as saying "this is not in itself a reopening of the matter." Mr. Levi was said to be convinced that the King case had been thoroughly investigated.

What led to the new examination was the harassment of Dr. King and a letter, unrevealed by the F.B.I. until recently, that Dr. King had been egged on to possible suicide by the F.B.I. The letter said, "There is only one thing left for you to do. You know what that is. You are done. There is but one way out for you."

Dr. King is said to have interpreted this as an attempt to drive him to suicide. Previous harassment is said to have included an attempt to interfere with his being awarded an honorary degree by a college. It even extended to efforts to have the award of the Nobel Peace Prize in 1964 to Dr. King in some manner reversed.

One setback for the anti-King forces in the F.B.I. was their failure to cast cold water on his "I Have a dream" speech to the 220,000 people at the March on Washington August 28, 1963.

The way in which a government agency was used to harass a citizen going about his business of civil rights is something the Ford Administration ought to examine. James B. Adams, a top official of the Federal Bureau of Investigation, told the Senate Select Committee on Intelligence headed by Senator Frank Church, that there was "no statutory basis or justification" for the F.B.I. letter to Dr. King. In other words it was illegal.

Dr. King, it is just being found out, endured this illegality, but no other citizen will have to endure such vindictive, cruel, and embarrassing treatment if the Ford Administration, after an official record, is sufficiently clear and emphatic in condemning such actions—as clear and emphatic as the instructions to the C.I.A. on plotting assassinations.

Appendix A

The National Association for the
Advancement of Colored People (NAACP)

A Chronology
(January 1909-July 1977)

1909   In January, several people meet in William English Walling's apartment to discuss the idea of creating a national biracial organization to help right social injustices. They are Dr. Henry Moskowitz, a socialist and social worker among New York immigrants; Miss Mary White Ovington, a social worker and descendant of abolitionists; and Walling, a wealthy Southerner, a socialist, and a writer whose article in the Springfield, Illinois, periodical, *The Independent*, on the 1908 riots arouses widespread sympathy over the treatment of African-Americans; Charles Edward Russell, a close friend of Walling's, and Oswald Garrison Villard, publisher of the liberal *New York Evening Post*. It is agreed that a public campaign should open on Lincoln's birthday to obtain the support of a much larger group of citizens. This initial group is made biracial by the inclusion of Bishop Alexander Walters of the African Methodist Episcopal Zion Church and the Rev. William Henry Brooks, minister of St. Mark's Methodist Episcopal Church of New York. Augmenting this group are such other black leaders as W. E. B. Du Bois, Ida Wells Barnett, W. L. Bulkley, the Rev. Francis J. Grimke, and Mary Church Terrell, all of whom sign the Lincoln Day Call. In a letter of encouragement to the conferees, William Lloyd Garrison, Jr., son of the Boston abolitionist, expresses the hope "that the conference will utter no uncertain sound on any point affecting the vital subject."

On February 12, over the signature of sixty persons, the Lincoln Day Call is issued calling for a meeting on the concept of creating an organization that will be an aggressive watchdog for African-American liberties. This date marks the founding of the National Association for the Advancement of Colored People.

Based on the "NAACP Highlight" (a pamphlet), 1980.

On May 31 and June 1, the National Negro Conference is held in the Charity Organization Hall in New York City. The theme is based on efforts to refute pre-Civil War beliefs that African Americans are physically and mentally inferior. A Committee of Forty on Permanent Organization is chosen to prepare for the incorporation of a National Committee for the Advancement of African-Americans.

Notable among the participants in this conference is Dr. W. E. B. Du Bois, a signer of the Lincoln Day Call, who had organized the Niagara Movement in 1905 in an attempt to stem the curtailment of political and civil rights of blacks.

1910   On May 12 the Second Annual Conference of the National Negro Committee is held in the Charity Organization Hall in New York. The theme is "Disfranchisement." An executive committee selects the following as officers: William English Walling, chairman; John Millholland, founder of the Constitution League; Oswald Garrison Villard, treasurer; and Frances Blascoer, the "incumbent Secretary." On May 25 the executive committee meets to develop a permanent structure. The title "director of publicity and research" is agreed on, and the functions of this office are made distinct from others such as "secretary" or "chairman" of the executive committee. The first issue of the *Crisis* is published in November.

At a meeting on Oswald Garrison Villard's program [the Call] on November 29, it is decided that the NAACP should be incorporated. J. E. Spingarn, chairman of the Department of Comparative Literature at Columbia University, is elected to the executive committee.

The Committee on Permanent Organization suggests to the annual conference the name National Association for the Advancement of Colored People and the name is accepted.

1911   A New York NAACP branch is organized in January, with J. E. Spingarn as chairman. His brother, Arthur B. Spingarn, a distinguished attorney, becomes a member of the New York branch vigilance committee, which seeks to publicize and prosecute cases of injustice against blacks in the Metropolitan area. In July the NAACP officially challenges Booker T. Washington's philosophy on the international scene by sending four delegates to the First Universal Races Congress in London, a conference aimed at developing closer understanding and cooperation between the races. Du Bois is one of the NAACP delegates; representatives of Booker T. Washington also attend.

The NAACP is incorporated on June 20. The by-laws provide for a board of directors of thirty members, which is to supplant the executive committee.

The second annual conference is held in Boston at the Park Street Church on March 30–31.

1912   On January 4 the executive committee meets and presents a slate of thirty board members for nomination. Oswald Garrison Villard is elected chairman of the board. The Association now has 329 members.

The *Crisis* circulation reaches 16,000 and is circulated in every state except South Dakota.

Three branches of the Association are in existence: New York, Chicago, and Boston. Du Bois's book, *History of the Negro Race*, is published by Henry Holt and Company. The third annual conference is held in Chicago.

1913   In May, Oswald Garrison Villard presents to President Wilson a plan for a National Race Commission, whose members will be appointed by the President. Their duty will be to conduct "a non-partisan, scientific study of the status of the African Americans in the life of the nation, with particular reference to their economic situation."

At the annual conference in Philadelphia in April, J. E. Spingarn institutes the Spingarn Medal, a gold medal which will be awarded annually to an African American of "highest achievement" for the preceding year or years.

1914   In January, Oswald Garrison Villard retires as chairman of the board and is elected chairman of the finance committee. The NAACP has twenty-four branches and 3,000 members.

Joel E. Spingarn is elected chairman of the board.

The NAACP protests the drawing of the color line in the American Bar Association and wins the admission of blacks to the woman's suffrage parade in Washington.

The Sixth Annual NAACP Conference is held in the Lyric Theater in Baltimore.

Oswald Garrison Villard intervenes with the judge advocate general of the Army and eventually wins freedom for a black soldier, Private Anderson of Honolulu, who had been sentenced by a court martial to five years in prison for burglary.

The NAACP hires two newsmen as lobbyists for each branch of Congress to report on the introduction of hostile bills.

1915   On February 15 "The Birth of a Nation," probably the most controversial and racially biased film in the history of the motion picture industry, is released. Even before its release, a vigorous campaign was launched in California to halt its production, since it was based upon Thomas Dixon's notorious anti-black novel, *The Clansman*. The novel and the film glorify the Ku Klux Klan and vilify the role of African Americans in the Reconstruction period after the Civil War.

Professor Ernest E. Just of Howard University Medical School is awarded the first Spingarn Medal for "distinguished research in physiology and biology."

Booker T. Washington dies on November 14, ending an era in the civil rights movement.

1916   At the January 10 board meeting, Mary White Ovington becomes acting secretary, replacing Miss Nerney. Roy Nash is appointed secretary in February.

Following the death of Washington in 1915, W. E. B. Du Bois proposed that the regular annual meeting be postponed because a memorial meeting for the Tuskegee leader was scheduled to be held on that day. At his suggestion, a meeting of reconciliation, known as the Amenia Conference, is held instead this year. This meeting, which is attended by the heads of all large black organizations, is held at "Troutbeck," the estate of J. E. Spingarn in Amenia, New York.

James Weldon Johnson is appointed field secretary in November.

In an attempt to raise funds to end the widespread brutality against blacks, an anti-lynching committee is formed. The five-member committee determines that the NAACP should (1) gather and compile facts on lynching, (2) investigate such cases, and (3) organize southern businesses and political leaders who are willing to speak out against the crime. A fund-raising drive is launched, and more than $10,000 is collected. The development of the public's awareness of lynching as a national problem is regarded as the year's most important achievement.

1917   J. E. Spingarn leads the NAACP fight to have the War Department provide a training camp to train black officers. In April the NAACP is notified that this facility will open on June 17 at Des Moines, Iowa.

Roy Nash resigns as secretary in May.

On July 2 the East St. Louis, Illinois, riots break out. As a result of the widespread brutality against black residents, the NAACP sends Martha Gruening and Du Bois to investigate. The Association also raises special funds to finance the legal defense and provide assistance for African Americans left destitute.

On Saturday, July 28, the NAACP leads a "Silent Protest Parade" to the sound of only muffled drums down New York City's Fifth Avenue to protest the mass murders, discrimination, and segregation in East St. Louis and other parts of the nation.

On December 10, 1910, Baltimore had become the first of a number of cities to enact ordinances that segregated blacks into residential districts. Several state courts, including the Maryland Supreme Court, threw out these ordinances on the grounds that they were unconstitutional. Other state courts, however, upheld them. On November 15 of this year, in *Buchanan* vs. *Warley*, an NAACP case originating in Kentucky, the U.S. Supreme Court rules unequivocally that these ordinances are "in direct violation" of the Fourteenth Amendment. This is often referred to as the Louisville case.

1918   John R. Shillady is appointed secretary in January, and Walter White is selected assistant secretary.

Because of long-standing NAACP pressure, President Wilson finally makes a public statement on July 26 against lynching. The association distributes 50,000 copies of the message.

Following the summary execution of thirteen members of the Twenty-fourth Infantry who had been accused of participating in the Houston riot, sixteen more are condemned to die. Consequently, the NAACP collects 12,000 signatures on a petition which is presented to President Wilson on February 19. On September 3 the president commutes ten of the death sentences and affirms six.

On December 1 Du Bois leaves for France on a threefold mission: (1) to serve as representative of the NAACP and the *Crisis* to the Peace Conference following the end of the World War, (2) to collect material for an NAACP history of the African Americans in the war, and (3) to summon a Pan-African Congress as a representative of the NAACP.

1919   At the annual meeting in January, Mary White Ovington is elected chairman of the board. Arthur B. Spingarn is elected a vice-president.

The Pink Franklin case finally ends in January, nearly nine years after the NAACP started the fight to free the farmhand who had killed a white law officer who broke into his cabin at 3:00 A.M. to arrest him for breaking his contract. South Carolina Governor Richard I. Manning paroles Franklin for good behavior. This is the first legal redress case undertaken by the Association.

Du Bois's trip to the Peace Conference in France lasts until early spring. The three-day Pan-African Congress is held February 19–21. It adopts a resolution stating that it is the right of the people of African descent to have a voice in their own government and that whenever there is an abuse of this right, it is the duty of the League of Nations to publicize these conditions. These resolutions are presented to the Peace Conference.

The anti-lynching fight is stepped up. In April the Association publishes its *Thirty Years of Lynching in the United States*, which covers the years 1889 to 1918. A "call" for an anti-lynching conference is sent out, bearing about 120 signatures. The conference is held the first week of May at Carnegie Hall.

This year marks the development of a new militancy among blacks. Tired of being easy targets for lynching and mass murders, they begin to strengthen their defense against the opposition.

Because of this new fighting spirit which is displayed in several cities, beginning with Longview, Texas, and because of the NAACP investigations and campaigns, efforts are begun to curtail the Association's work. The first move is made by the Texas attorney general, who subpoenas the Austin NAACP branch president to turn over all of the association's records to the court. Such a move threatens the existence of all thirty-one NAACP branches in Texas, so the national office steps in to protect its operation. To lead the fight against the subpoena, NAACP Secretary John Shillady travels to Austin. But he is beaten unconscious by a group of men one morning on the courthouse steps as he leaves the attorney general's office, where he himself is questioned in a "court inquiry." County Judge Dave J. Pickle is a leader of the mob against Shillady.

A national commemoration of the tercentenary of the landing of the slaves at Jamestown, scheduled for August, is canceled because Du Bois is unable to devote sufficient time to planning, as a result of the Peace Conference.

1920   Following the United States takeover of Haitian finances in 1915 and the occupation of that Caribbean nation the following year by the U.S. Armed Forces, the NAACP begins receiving reports of widespread atrocities there. In Du Bois's words, the NAACP becomes concerned because Haiti is "a continuing symbol of black revolt against slavery and oppression, and has a capacity for self-rule."

The board sends James Weldon Johnson to investigate the actions of the U.S. Armed Forces. He spends six months on the island country, and his findings are published in *The Nation*, The *Crisis*, *The Christian Herald*, and other magazines. The Ku Klux Klan is strengthened under the leadership of Imperial Wizard William Joseph Simmons with headquarters in Atlanta. Through its publication, *The Searchlight*, the Klan announces that the NAACP is its archenemy.

The NAACP eleventh annual conference is held in Atlanta, the hotbed of the Klan, from May 30 to June 2.

Secretary John Shillady's recovery is slow from the beating in Austin. In August he resigns as secretary.

Upon congress's adoption of the Nineteenth Amendment, granting the vote to women, the NAACP launches an expanded voter education campaign to bring people into the political process. The NAACP dramatizes black people's political impotence in its pamphlet, "Disfranchisement of Colored Americans in the Election of 1920."

Led by James Weldon Johnson and Walter White, NAACP representatives testify in Washington before the House Committee on the Census on the vicious tactics that southern states use to bar blacks from the ballot boxes. They ask that Congress investigate the 1920 elections in those states. Where it is determined that the vote is being denied black people, the NAACP demands that no representative from those areas be seated in the House.

1921   Newly appointed NAACP Secretary James Weldon Johnson visits President-elect Warren G. Harding at his home in Marion, Ohio, and outlines the concerns and problems of his people. He informs Mr. Harding that black people are interested primarily in the enactment of measures to relieve the oppressive conditions under which they live. Subsequently, the NAACP secretary arranges a meeting between the president and a group of black southerners. Johnson meets once more with the president. He presses for action on lynching, disfranchisement, peonage, and the end of American atrocities in Haiti. Johnson also calls for the abolition of segregation in federal agencies and offices.

As a measure of the NAACP's unrelenting fight against lynching, 45,000 pieces of literature are sent out by the national office on lynching in this year.

W. E. B. Du Bois and Walter White are among the thirty-five U.S. delegates who attend the Second Pan-African Congress in Europe.

The NAACP presents a petition signed by 50,000 persons to President Harding requesting the pardon of soldiers from the Twenty-fourth Infantry who had been imprisoned at Fort Leavenworth on charges arising from a riot in Houston in 1917.

1922   During the previous year, on April 11 Congressman L. C. Dyer of St. Louis reintroduced his anti-lynching bill at the opening of the Sixty-seventh Congress. On January 26 the House passes this bill by a vote of 230 to 119. The following day, the bill is sent to the Senate Judiciary Committee. The NAACP is the lonely force pushing for the passage of anti-lynching legislation and is to be credited for bringing the issue to the fore of the nation's consciousness during thirteen years of unrelenting work. The NAACP's greatest single stroke this year in this fight is the placing of full and half-page advertisements entitled, "The Shame of America," in nine major dailies and two weeklies across the nation to present the facts of this crime to the world. On June 30 the Judiciary Committee reports the bill to the Senate floor, where it dies in November because of a filibuster by Southern Democrats. The NAACP, however, wins four ancillary but decisive victories as a result of this fight. In Delaware, New Jersey, Michigan, and Wisconsin, congressmen who had voted against the Dyer bill are defeated at the polls as a result of their votes in Washington.

The fight against peonage reaches a significant stage after the NAACP assumes the defense of twelve Arkansas farmers near Elaine who had been sentenced to death for rioting in 1919. The case of six of the men is scheduled to be argued before the U.S. Supreme Court the third week of January this year. The NAACP had twice won reversals of death sentences for the other six in the Arkansas Supreme Court. After the second reversal, the NAACP wins a change of venue to Lee County.

1923   The NAACP wins a significant victory in its fight for due process when the Supreme Court reverses a lower court order dismissing a petition for a writ of habeas corpus in the Arkansas riot case. NAACP lawyer Moorfield Storey argues the case of the six men before the

Supreme Court on January 9. On February 19 the Supreme Court hands down its decision in the case, *Frank Moore et al.*, reversing the convictions. The majority opinion is delivered by Justice Oliver Wendell Holmes. By this decision, the Supreme Court also reverses itself on the principle that federal courts have no right to interfere in certain cases even though it is shown that the trial was dominated by a mob atmosphere.

In September 558 delegates attending the Fourteenth NAACP Annual Conference in Kansas City, Missouri, journey to Leavenworth federal prison in Kansas to visit fifty-four members of the Twenty-fourth Infantry who had been convicted for rioting in Houston in 1917. James Weldon Johnson leads the delegates. November 11 is designated "Houston Martyrs' Day." Thirteen members of the Twenty-fourth Infantry had been summarily hanged in 1917 and another six at a subsequent date.

1924   On February 7 President Calvin Coolidge receives at the White House a delegation of fourteen African Americans headed by James Weldon Johnson. The delegation presents the president with a petition of 125,000 signatures requesting the release of the Twenty-fourth Infantry soldiers from the Leavenworth prison. As a result of this long campaign which began in 1917, the sentences of the men remaining in prison are reduced. Twenty of these men are released during the year; all the other sentences are reduced. Thus the NAACP wins reductions for a total of fifty-five soldiers.

The Court of Appeals rules on June 2 in *Corrigan et al.* vs. *Buckley*, better known as the Curtis case, that residential covenants are not unconstitutional. Immediately the national office joins the D.C. office in appealing the case to the Supreme Court.

1925   The system permitting only whites to vote in the Texas Democratic primaries is challenged by Dr. L. A. Nixon, a prominent black physician living in El Paso, after he is barred from voting. The El Paso branch of the NAACP files suit against local election officials. The case is dismissed. Hence the National Office of the NAACP is asked to enter.

The NAACP leads successful fights against anti-intermarriage bills in Ohio, Michigan, and Iowa.

Thirteen more members of the Twenty-fourth Infantry are released. Three of these soldiers had been sentenced to die and the others were facing life imprisonment. Twenty-two soldiers now remain in prison.

On September 9 one member of a mob attacking the Detroit home of Dr. Ossian Sweet is killed. Dr. Sweet and his family had just moved into the newly bought home in a white neighborhood. Sweet, his wife, two brothers, and seven other persons are arrested and jailed on charges of murder in the first degree. Celebrated attorney Clarence Darrow is retained by the NAACP to take charge of the defense. The first trial ends on November 27 with a deadlocked jury.

1926   The outstanding legal victory of the year is the acquittal of Henry Sweet (brother of Dr. Ossian Sweet) by a Detroit jury. Because of its importance, the national office of the NAACP and the Detroit branch assume full responsibility of the case. Assisting Clarence Darrow are Arthur Garfield Hays of New York, and Detroit attorneys Walter Nelson, Julian Perry, Cecil O. Rowlette, and Charles Mahoney.

Congressman L. C. Dyer had introduced a new anti-lynching bill in the House in December of the previous year, and this was followed by the introduction of another in the Senate by William B. McKinley. On February 16 James Weldon Johnson testifies on the McKinley bill before the subcommittee of the Senate Judiciary Committee and submits facts on lynching.

NAACP Assistant Secretary Walter White delivers a most telling blow against the crime of lynching by conducting a bold investigation on October 8 into the lynching of the Lowman family. White had obtained a detailed story of the lynchings, including sworn affidavits, in Aiken, S.C., in regard to the murder of three persons—Bertha, Demon, and Clarence Lowman—and obtained the names of persons, including law enforcement officers, who had been members of the mob or assisted it. White sends these names to South Carolina Governor Thomas McLeod and turns over details of the mob action to the *New York World*. The newspaper consequently sends its correspondent, Oliver H. P. Garrett, to Aiken. His stories not only arouse the South Carolina press but also win the support of the nation's editors, who join the demand for a federal anti-lynching law.

1927   On March 7 the U.S. Supreme Court in a unanimous decision rules that the Texas white primary, in *Nixon* vs. *Herndon*, is unconstitutional.

In July a Michigan judge dismisses all remaining cases in the Sweets' trial.

The board of directors establishes the $500 Life Membership Program to provide another source of funds for the Association.

1928   Although the courts had earlier ruled that black people could not be barred from voting in Texas Democratic primaries because of their color, the party devised alternate means to continue their illegal actions in Texas and other states. Political committees and party members are now personally preventing qualified black Democrats from voting.

Four cases in which the association participate this year challenge the constitutionality of enabling acts in Virginia (*West* vs. *Biley*), Texas (*Nixon* vs. *Condon*), Florida (*H. O. Goode* vs. *Thomas Johnson et al.*), and Arkansas (*Robinson, et al.* vs. *Holfman et al.*).

1929   Now twenty years in existence, the NAACP demonstrates the wisdom and prescience of its founders and the need for its continuing existence. When it was founded, many people thought the race relations problems could be solved by concentrating on the economic question alone. But now, after it has confronted racism on a determined and organized basis for twenty years, there is the realization that a broad attack upon all phases of the problem is required. Emphasis is shifted away from racial brutalities as lynchings have declined. The NAACP resources are now being concentrated on gaining free access to the ballot, eliminating residential segregation, and ending employment discrimination.

Attorney Louis Marshall, who worked with Moorfield Storey to win the five great victories for the NAACP in the U.S. Supreme Court and who had participated in a number of other significant cases, dies in September in Zurich, Switzerland. Replacing Marshall on the NAACP board is New York Lieutenant Governor Herbert H. Lehman. Harvard Law School Professor Felix Frankfurter joins the National Legal Committee.

Moorfield Storey, national president, dies at his home in Lincoln, Massachusetts, on October 23.

1930   The political strength of the Association is dramatically displayed when Walter White engineers the strategy and leads the successful fight against the nomination of Judge John J. Parker of North Carolina to the U.S. Supreme Court. The series of fast-moving events last just five weeks from the time the NAACP launches an inquiry into the record of President Hoover's nominee. But the consequences are of such great importance that the fight is nothing less than one of the most bitter in the nation's political history. The NAACP's opposition to Judge Parker had been sparked by a speech he made ten years before in which he approved an amendment to his state's constitution that provided for a poll tax and literacy tests for voters. This clause, like the other two aspects of Judge Parker's proposals, violates basic equal rights of black Americans. The NAACP urges President Hoover to withdraw the nomination, citing a precedent that was set on February 8, 1912, when President Taft withdrew the nomination of Judge Hook after the NAACP protested. In the face of President Hoover's adamant support of his man, the NAACP launches a national campaign. As a result, the Senate rejects his confirmation on May 7 by a vote of 41 to 39.

At its December meeting the board of directors elects J. E. Spingarn to succeed Moorfield Storey as president. Spingarn had served as chairman of the board from 1914 to 1919 and as treasurer from 1919 to this time.

On December 17 James Weldon Johnson resigns as secretary.

1931   On March 30 nine black youth are returned to the Scottsboro courthouse in Alabama to be charged with raping two white girls. The
"Scottsboro" case arose on March 25 when the youths, aged fourteen
to twenty, were removed from a freight train at Pain Rock, Alabama,
after a fight with a group of white boys who were also traveling on
the train in search of work. Eight of the youths are tried and sentenced to death in April. For the fourteen-year-old, the state asks for
life imprisonment. The boys are at first represented by the NAACP,
but because of conflicts with the Communists, who are operating
through the International Labor Defense, NAACP lawyers Clarence
Darrow and Arthur Garfield Hays of New York withdraw from the
case. The I.L.D. is now solely responsible for the defense.

Walter White, who had been acting secretary since 1929 when
James Weldon Johnson took a leave of absence, is named secretary.
Roy Wilkins, former managing editor of the *Kansas City Call*, joins
the staff as assistant secretary.

1932   The NAACP vigorously protests to President Hoover the inhuman
conditions under which blacks are working on the Mississippi Flood
Control Project. Hoover responds to the Association's repeated complaints by appointing a commission to investigate the charges. New
York Senator Robert F. Wagner also promises to introduce in the
Senate a resolution demanding an investigation of conditions on the
project as a result of the NAACP's charges.

The NAACP also joins the National Bar Association in protesting
the refusal of the Hoover Dam contractors to hire black workers. In
July the NAACP board of directors authorizes a contribution of
$1,000 to the Legal Defense Fund for use in the defense of the Scotts-
boro boys. The cases are argued before the Supreme Court on October 10 and November 7. A decision is handed down reversing the
death sentences. The court grants a new trial.

The Texas white primary case is concluded when the Supreme
Court in a 5–4 decision declares the party's actions unconstitutional.
This decision thus makes it impossible for state party committees to
bar black voters from the primaries. Nevertheless, a third Texas white
primary develops when the election judges refuse to allow Dr. L. A.
Nixon of El Paso to vote in the general election.

1933   At the height of the Great Depression, Franklin D. Roosevelt begins
his first term as president. His revolutionary programs for social and
economic development hold an initial promise for the betterment of
black as well as white Americans. Walter White reaches the president
through the First Lady. He bombards Mrs. Roosevelt with letters and
telegrams, using the powerful issue of lynching.

NAACP Assistant Secretary Roy Wilkins and George S. Schuyler,
a writer, are sent to investigate inhumane working conditions for
blacks on the Mississippi Flood Control Project. They spend three

weeks in the state disguised as laborers. As a result of their efforts, the secretary of war announces that unskilled workers will have their pay raised and hours shortened.

The NAACP continues contributing funds to the I.L.D. for the defense in the Scottsboro case.

On August 7 an accord is signed between the United States and Haiti providing for the withdrawal of American troops by October 1, 1934, and for modification of U.S. control of Haitian finances. The NAACP had been fighting the battle for Haitian sovereignty since 1920.

A second Amenia Conference is held on the Troutbeck estate of J. E. Spingarn in Amenia, New York, August 18–21. The conference is called to consider the role of blacks in a changing America and the world. The conference concludes that a union of white and black workers is needed in the labor movement to direct economic and political life. The conference condemns the traditional labor movement in America as ineffective.

1934 On February 19 and 20 hearings are held on the newly introduced Costigan–Wagner Anti-Lynching Bill. The Senate Judiciary Committee reports out the bill, but it is not called up on the floor because of lack of support. Among the supporters of the bill are the Young Women's Christian Association and the Women's International League for Peace and Freedom. The bill's defeat arouses even more sympathy for its passage. Consequently, by year's end, organizations representing more than 42 million persons are openly committed to its passage and plan to support it the following January when it is scheduled to be reintroduced in Congress. Other organizations that are committed to fighting for the bill include the American Federation of Labor, the Episcopal Church, and several southern groups.

With the effects of the Great Depression now being felt in every corner of society, the NAACP finds itself increasingly involved in fighting to end employment discrimination.

The Association continues its militant opposition to the numerous codes of fair competition created under the National Industrial Recovery Act, which blatantly discriminates against black people. The NAACP's position is that the NRA is condemning African Americans to industrial slavery. Most of the NAACP's effort to end these injustices is waged through the Joint Committee on National Recovery, which is composed of twenty-two national, racial, and interracial organizations. The chairman is Dr. George E. Haynes of the Federal Council of Churches.

In March the NAACP fights the closed-shop provisions of the Wagner Labor Disputes Act, which is aimed at providing bargaining machinery. The NAACP knows that thousands of black workers are being shut out from membership in AFL unions and also excluded from jobs by the closed-shop provisions.

The NAACP continues protesting discrimination on the Boulder Dam construction site near Las Vegas. It furthermore reports to President Roosevelt similar employment discrimination on the Tennessee Valley Authority construction project.

On June 26 Dr. Du Bois tenders his resignation as editor of the *Crisis* because he strongly differs with the board of directors on many issues, but particularly over what stance the association should take on segregation. The resignation follows an extended discussion on the issue by the board and among branch leaders across the country. On July 9 the board accepts the resignation "with the deepest regret."

Roy Wilkins is elected acting editor of the *Crisis*. He also continues his duties as assistant secretary.

The NAACP hails the withdrawal of the last contingent of U.S. troops from Haiti in August.

1935   Dr. Louis Tompkins Wright is elected chairman of the board.

The NAACP receives a grant to establish a legal department. Charles Hamilton Houston is named special counsel.

Youth councils develop rapidly throughout the country.

The Joint Committee on National Recovery forces the Maid-Well Garment Company of Forest Park, Arkansas, out of business because, despite fifteen months of protests, it continues to pay only fifty cents of the specified code wages to black employees. The company is deprived of its permit to operate and closes its doors rather than pay $5,000 in back wages to black workers.

The Association accelerates its fight to end racial discrimination on federal construction and relief projects. NAACP Vice President James Weldon Johnson, now a Fisk University professor, is offered a high post with the National WPA in October, but the offer is suddenly withdrawn, and no satisfactory explanation is ever given by the Roosevelt administration.

The Association on March 1 launches a nationwide drive to enlist public support for passage of the Costigan-Wagner Anti-Lynching Bill, but after protracted and bitter debates, on May 1 the bill is killed for this session by a Senate filibuster. Most striking is the fact that the Commission on Interracial Cooperation of Atlanta gives its last-minute endorsement to the measure. The support from all areas, particularly the South, is greater than ever. The sharpest increases in lynchings and mob violence against blacks within a decade take place this year.

The NAACP's legal staff, under the direction of attorney Charles H. Houston, wins its first major victory when the Baltimore City Court orders the University of Maryland Law School to admit Donald

Murray if he qualifies. The university appeals the case in November and loses. Murray's lawyers are Houston and Thurgood Marshall of Baltimore.

In June, at the Twenty-sixth Annual Conference in St. Louis, the board of directors adopts a broadened and more intensive program encompassing a universal concern for economic, legal, and educational problems. A new legal offensive arises from this approach, which is directed against the fundamental basis of racial discrimination in education. In a sense, this marks a turning point in strategy—from a chiefly defensive stance against the onslaught of racism to an aggressive offensive upon segregation and other forms of discrimination.

On July 19 the American Civil Liberties Union, the International Labor Defense, the League for Industrial Democracy, and the NAACP form the Scottsboro Defense Committee and provide funds for an attorney. The Methodist Federation for Social Service later joins, and the National Urban League becomes a sponsoring organization. The Reverend Allan Knight Chalmers agrees to be chairman of the committee. In late December the American Scottsboro Committee disbands to permit the newly formed committee to take over.

Field Secretary William Pickens is appointed director of branches in September.

On December 13 the NAACP warns the League of Nations about the dangers of the proposed Franco–British Peace Agreement, which is supposed to settle the Italo–Ethiopian War by giving half of the African nation to Italy.

1936   Senator Frederick Van Nuys of Indiana, at the opening of the Seventy-fourth Congress, introduces a resolution calling for an investigation of the fourteen lynchings since the Costigan-Wagner Bill was killed on May 1 of the previous year by a filibuster. However, Congress adjourns before any action is taken on the resolution.

The Association wages a sustained fight against educational barriers. In a case similar to Murray's, the NAACP seeks the court's assistance to have the University of Missouri Law School admit Lloyd L. Gaines, age 23. But the judge rules that the state has a right to separate black from white students in schools.

The NAACP opens an attack on unequal salary scales for black teachers in Maryland. Assistant Special Counsel Thurgood Marshall appears before the state board of education to argue the case.

The Scottsboro Defense Committee now includes the Church League for Industrial Democracy and the Brotherhood of Sleeping Car Porters. A request for a change of venue from Decatur, Alabama, is denied. At the conclusion of his fourth trial, Haywood Patterson is found guilty and sentenced to seventy-five years in prison.

On September 12 William English Walling, a founder of the NAACP, dies.

1937   Roy Wilkins is named editor of the *Crisis* in January.

A major victory is won when the House approves the Gavagan Anti-Lynching Bill by a vote of 277–119 on April 15. Opponents in the Senate succeed in blocking any decisive action on the measure by waging a filibuster. The NAACP continues its fight to open up state universities to black students by challenging the University of Tennessee's policy of providing professional training for whites but denying it to blacks. In response to an NAACP suit against the university, the legislature subsequently passes a bill that provides scholarships for black students attending universities outside Tennessee.

In another case, NAACP Counsel Houston leads the court battle to have the University of Missouri admit Lloyd Gaines to its law school. However, the State Supreme Court upholds a lower court decision that dismisses Gaines's petition. The NAACP then moves to take the case to the U.S. Supreme Court.

E. Frederick Morrow is appointed coordinator of branches.

William H. Hastie is elected to the national board of directors.

1938   Despite another effort to gain the enactment of an anti-lynching bill, Senate opponents once more defeat the measure on the floor by a filibuster. Hope is sustained, however, by the support of the two warring labor federations, the Congress of Industrial Organizations and the American Federation of Labor. Mrs. Franklin D. Roosevelt also expresses her support for such a bill at the November 22 Southern Conference on Human Welfare meeting in Birmingham.

The Association continues its fight to end segregation at the Tennessee Valley Authority. Charles H. Houston and Thurgood Marshall conduct a third NAACP investigation of working conditions there and submit a report to a joint committee of Congress that had been appointed to study repeated complaints of racial discrimination.

The last two Houston martyrs are freed from the Leavenworth Federal Penitentiary on April 19, after twenty-one years of imprisonment.

James Weldon Johnson dies in an automobile accident in Wiscassett, Maine, on June 26.

Donald Murray graduates from the University of Maryland Law School.

The U.S. Supreme Court rules on December 12 that the University of Missouri Law School cannot exclude a student (Lloyd Gaines) because of his color. It also rules that states must provide equal educational facilities for black students and that the provision of scholarships outside a state does not constitute equality.

1939   The most concerted drive ever is made to gain enactment of an anti-lynching law. Despite the continued backing of groups like the CIO and the AFL, however, Congress adjourns without acting on a measure.

The Missouri legislature appropriates $200,000 to provide graduate study for black students at Lincoln University. The NAACP opposes the establishment of such a school, because it believes that such a school would be inadequate.

Marian Anderson is barred by the Daughters of the American Revolution from giving a concert at Constitution Hall in Washington. With the help of Harold Ickes, secretary of the interior, the NAACP arranges to have her appear at the Lincoln Memorial on Easter Sunday. More than 75,000 people attend the open-air concert, which is broadcast nationally on the radio.

After being appointed to the U.S. Supreme Court, Justice Felix Frankfurter resigns from the national board of directors.

The NAACP Legal Defense and Educational Fund, Inc. is formed on October 11. Its incorporators are Dr. William Allan Nielson, president of Smith College, Arthur B. Spingarn, federal judge William H. Hastie, New York Governor Herbert H., Lehman, Mary White Ovington, municipal judge Charles E. Toney, and New York City tax commissioner Hubert T. Delany.

J. E. Spingarn, president of the NAACP, dies. His brother Arthur replaces him as president.

1940   The NAACP finds it necessary to step up its efforts to end discrimination in the Armed Services and win justice for black servicemen. Walter White, along with A. Philip Randolph, president of the Brotherhood of Sleeping Car Porters, and T. Arnold Hill, an executive officer with the National Youth Administration, lead a series of nationwide demonstrations to publicize their opposition to segregation in the military. In response to such protests, the Roosevelt administration promotes Col. Benjamin O. Davis, Sr., of the 369th New York Infantry to brigadier general, the first such office ever held by a black man in the Army. William H. Hastie is named a civilian aide to the secretary of war. Another black man, Major Campbell C. Johnson, is named administrative assistant to the Selective Service director.

On September 9 the board of directors passes a resolution offering the NAACP's legal services to any American who finds it difficult to enlist in the Army or Navy because of race or color.

The NAACP writes seventy-five senators urging them to amend the Selective Service Act before its passage to provide for the drafting of blacks into the Army and Navy without consideration of race. Later in the year the Association urges its branches to seek the appointment of blacks to local draft boards. Consequently, a greater number of African Americans are appointed to draft boards than during World War I.

Some encouragement is gained when the CIO union the United

Electrical, Radio and Machine Workers of America declares at its convention that it will work to end racial discrimination. But the AFL, under its president, William Green, does not take any such positive action.

The Gavagan-Fish Anti-Lynching Bill passes the House by a vote of 252–131 but is killed in the Senate by a filibuster.

When the first defense contract is awarded in mid-July, the NAACP immediately urges black workers to apply for jobs in plants and offers its assistance to persons who are barred from employment because of their race. Walter White presents a clear picture of the problems black workers face in the defense industry in the December 11 issue of the *Saturday Evening Post*.

Thurgood Marshall is appointed special counsel when Charles Hamilton Houston returns to private practice.

1941   On June 18 Walter White and A. Philip Randolph meet at the White House with President Roosevelt, Secretary of War Henry L. Stimson, Secretary of the Navy Frank Knox, and other officials to discuss the impending march on Washington as a protest against employment discrimination. Finally, to avoid the march, the president on June 25 issues Executive Order No. 8802, which sets up the Committee on Fair Employment Practices and bans discrimination in industries that receive government contracts.

The NAACP continues its fight against segregation in graduate schools and against the discriminatory practice, prevalent in the South, of paying black teachers considerably less than their white counterparts. Nevertheless, progress is slow. In Missouri, the State Supreme Court upholds a lower court decision of the previous year against Lucile Bluford, who had been barred from registering in the state university's graduate school of journalism. The court refuses to issue an order to have the university register her and dismisses her suit. The NAACP consequently files a new suit in federal court to have her admitted. Other institutions that the NAACP is actively battling include the universities of Tennessee and Kentucky.

On December 7 the Japanese attack the U.S. naval base at Pearl Harbor, Hawaii, precipitating U.S. entry into World War II.

1942   The NAACP opposes the creation of a Jim Crow blood bank by the American Red Cross and fights the creation of segregated service clubs by the Red Cross.

The NAACP protests the many forms of discrimination in the war industries. In February it demands that the AFL permit thirty black workers who had been restricted to jobs as painter's helpers to sign up for better-paying jobs. Nineteen of them are skilled boilermakers.

A notable NAACP success on the East Coast is the establishment of the Committee on Discrimination in Employment of the State of New York War Council.

The NAACP repeats to Chief of Staff General George C. Marshall its proposal that the Army establish a volunteer division that is free of segregation and discrimination. Other protests against segregation are continued.

The NAACP Washington Bureau is established in June. As a result of NAACP demands, Dorie Miller, a black mess attendant, is commended by the secretary of the navy for his bravery during the attacks on Pearl Harbor.

The Navy modifies its practice of restricting black enlisted men to the mess halls, but the NAACP continues to protest the new policy as being racially restrictive, since they are still generally barred from serving on ships as sailors, gunners, and technicians.

The NAACP continues to fight against voter discrimination in three areas: white primaries, poll tax, and general registration barriers. The Association seeks passage of the Geyer Anti–Poll Tax Bill, which passed the House but is defeated by a filibuster in the Senate.

In another Texas case, *Smith* vs. *Allright*, the NAACP loses a bid to have the Fifth Circuit Court of Appeals reverse a lower court which had refused to grant an order permitting blacks to vote in Democratic primaries.

1943   Job opportunities and racial discrimination in the Armed Services are the principal concerns this year. The NAACP repeats its demands several times that the War Department establish a mixed voluntary unit. Other actions include protesting the exclusion of blacks from the Army and Navy specialized programs that are being offered in colleges and defending several soldiers who had been convicted on various charges.

The *Smith* vs. *Allright* case reaches the Supreme Court.

The NAACP files several informal complaints with the Interstate Commerce Commission on the refusal of railroads to serve black passengers in dining cars. The Association begins preliminary steps to challenge interstate commerce segregation in the courts.

Cases challenging dual pay scales are now pending in twelve southern states.

NAACP branches in Detroit and Harlem, N.Y., work to quell violent riots that erupted. In Detroit, Walter White and Thurgood Marshall work with local NAACP officials to protect the rights of black residents. Walter White and Roy Wilkins help New York Mayor LaGuardia to end the disturbance. Riots also break out in Beaumont, Texas; Mobile, Alabama; Los Angeles, and Philadelphia.

1944   Walter White spends three months touring the European and Mediterranean theaters to observe the U.S. war machine in operation. Upon his return, he submits to the War Department a fourteen-point memorandum in which he makes recommendations for improving opportunities for black soldiers. Two of his recommendations are that the services create nonsegregated bomber crews and a special court-martial review board.

On April 3 the U.S. Supreme Court rules in *Smith* vs. *Allright* that the right to vote is protected by the Constitution. Consequently, black citizens are now able to vote in Texas, where the case originated because they had been barred from participating in Democratic primaries. Nevertheless, the South Carolina legislature continues its attempts to disfranchise black residents by abolishing its laws on primaries and thus providing election officials with unlimited discretion as to who should vote. But in Alabama, Georgia, Florida, and Mississippi, blacks are still openly and officially barred from voting in Democratic primaries.

The Washington Bureau vigorously protests discrimination by the Federal Housing Administration by submitting to President Roosevelt a comprehensive statement on the agency's racial policies and actions.

W. E. B. Du Bois returns to the staff in September as director of special research after an absence of ten years, during which time he taught at Atlanta University.

1945   Walter White's book, *A Rising Wind*, which is based on visits to Armed Service bases in Europe, the Mediterranean, and the Pacific, is published.

Continuing its attack on discrimination against black soldiers, the NAACP demands that the Veterans Administration end hospital segregation and other forms of racial bias. The Association fights to free fifty seamen who had been convicted of mutiny at Port Chicago, California. The Association is responsible for reversing the convictions of fifty-two soldiers who had also been convicted of mutiny in Hawaii, where they are stationed.

1946   The U.S. Supreme Court hands the Association an important legal victory when it rules in *Morgan* vs. *Virginia* that a state law requiring separation of the races on motor carriers cannot apply to interstate passengers. The bus companies then circumvent this ruling by creating their own regulations.

The NAACP launches a new attack on segregation in universities, in the cases of *Sweatt* vs. *University of Texas; Sipuel* vs. *University of Oklahoma; Hatfield* vs. *Louisiana State University*, and *Johnson* vs. *Louisiana State University*. In the case of *Mendez* vs. *Westminister School District*, in which the NAACP participates, a federal court declares for the first time that segregation is a denial of the equal protection clause of the Constitution.

The NAACP negotiates pardons for eleven of twenty-six servicemen by petitioning the secretary of war for clemency in their behalf, and it gains a review of their cout-martial convictions.

The NAACP makes some progress in its fight against discrimination in the Veterans Administration. These positive steps include the hiring of a black assistant to the administrator, the certification of a veteran for educational benefits to attend Harvard University, and the admitting of black patients by eleven of the twenty-two veterans' hospitals that had previously refused to do so.

Clarence Mitchell is appointed national labor secretary and assigned to the Washington Bureau.

Walter White leads a delegation from the National Emergency Committee against Violence to the White House for an audience with President Truman.

1947   W. E. B. Du Bois organizes the preparation of a 155-page petition, "An Appeal to the World," which documents the history of racism in America. This petition is presented to the United Nations. The issues in the petition are raised before the world body following a debate on the treatment of blacks and minorities in South Africa, Southwest Africa, Palestine, and Asia. The NAACP petition is debated for two days at a meeting in Geneva by the Drafting Committee of the United Nations Human Rights Commission.

The NAACP Church Department is established on March 1 to coordinate its civil rights activities with similar work by religious institutions.

A very significant development in the nation is the shift in the federal government's attitude toward segregation and discrimination, a result of President Harry S. Truman's address to the NAACP's Thirty-eighth Annual Conference in Washington, D.C., in June. The president declares:

We can no longer afford the luxury of a leisurely attack upon prejudice and discrimination. There is much that state and local governments can do in providing positive safeguards for civil rights. But we cannot, any longer, await the growth of a will to action in the slowest state or the most backward community. Our national government must show the way.

The president appoints three bodies to further clarify the government's policies on race: the Commission on Higher Education, the Civil Rights Committee, and the Advisory Commission on Military Training. The Civil Rights Committee is particularly significant to the NAACP, since it is the direct result of a meeting between Mr. Truman and civil rights groups, of which the NAACP is the leader.

The U.S. Supreme Court had established nine years earlier, in *Lloyd Gaines* vs. *the University of Missouri*, the right of black students to equal public educational facilities. Nevertheless, graduate schools around the nation are still barring blacks. The NAACP therefore begins to create a legal strategy to tear down the entire structure of segregation in all levels of education.

Because of its persistent attacks on restrictive housing covenants, the NAACP wins the support of several other ethnic groups and starts to move to take its case to the U.S. Supreme Court. A national conference of lawyers and sociologists sponsored by the NAACP Legal Department meets in New York on September 6. Four cases are subsequently prepared for the High Court. These are *Hurd* vs. *Hodge* and *Urciolo* vs. *Hodge*, which are handled by private lawyers, and *Shelley* vs. *Kramer* and *McGhee* vs. *Sipes* are handled by the NAACP lawyers.

1948   Twenty-two national black organizations respond to an NAACP call and meet in New York to formulate a "Declaration of Negro Voters," a guide on candidates for the November elections. This guide demonstrates that black voters are not wedded to a single party or special candidate. Consequently, President Truman is reelected with the help of three key states—Ohio, California, and Illinois—with a sizable margin of black votes.

The United Nations General Assembly approves for submission to member-nations the Declaration of Human Rights and a Genocide Convention. Walter White also works to have the American delegation support a United Nations trusteeship for Somaliland, a former Italian colony in Africa

The NAACP further positions itself for an all-out attack on school segregation when the board of directors approves a legal strategy for the Association to file only cases that challenge the constitutionality of racial separation. The professional and graduate school cases had all been tried on this issue; therefore, various precedents had been established. Attention is therefore turned to extending these principles to elementary and secondary schools.

The NAACP wins fights for equalization of teachers' salaries in several cases.

The NAACP succeeds in having President Truman issue Executive Order No. 9980, prohibiting racial discrimination in the federal service. Although the practice does not end, by the end of the year at least eighteen agencies establish procedures for handling complaints.

On July 26 President Truman issues Executive Order No. 9981, which establishes the Committee on Equality of Treatment and Opportunity in the Armed Forces. This order does not meet the NAACP's demand for an end to racial segregation in the military, but it is viewed as a step in that direction.

W. E. B. Du Bois leaves the NAACP for a second time. Sparking this second departure is the refusal of the board of directors to renew his contract because he supports certain ideologies that are inconsistent with the program of the Association.

1949   The NAACP files suits in federal courts attacking public school segregation in Lumberton, North Carolina, and Irwin County, Georgia.

A petition against segregation is also filed with the school board in Clarendon County, South Carolina.

On February 1 the NAACP submits a 21-page memorandum to President Truman in which it charges that the Federal Housing Administration is supporting and perpetuating residential segregation. As a result of such pressures, the U.S. solicitor general announces on December 2 that the federal government will end policies that directly contribute to the creation of racial ghettos.

President Truman issues an executive order ending segregation in the Armed Service.

The Joint Committee on Civil Rights is organized by the NAACP on February 5, for the purpose of coordinating twenty-two organizations seeking enactment of civil rights legislation. The Joint Committee gives priority to the enactment of a Fair Employment Practices Law by the federal government. The committee also supports efforts to enact bills against lynching, poll tax, and Jim Crow travel.

President Truman establishes a Federal Fair Employment Board, which immediately responds to some of the issues the NAACP has raised.

On April 8 an NAACP conference on colonialism is held in New York. Nineteen organizations attend and adopt a statement prepared by Dr. Rayford Logan, a consultant to the Association. One purpose of this conference is to support the establishment of an international trusteeship for Southwest Africa and the former Italian colony of Somaliland. It also calls for the independence of Indonesia.

Walter White submits his resignation as executive secretary, effective June 1, because of ill health. The national board of directors rejects it, however, and instead gives him a year's leave-of-absence beginnning June 1. Roy Wilkins is named acting secretary.

The NAACP wins its twenty-fifth victory before the Supreme Court on July 22, when the murder conviction of Austin Watts is reversed. The Court states that the Marion County, Indiana, police denied Mr. Watts due process in preparing his case.

NAACP founder Oswald Garrison Villard, author of the NAACP's "Call" in 1909, dies on October 2.

The Civil Rights Committeee meets in New York on October 15 to announce its objectives of calling "upon the American people to join in a crusade to remove the stigma of discrimination and segregation from our national life." Other groups, including the CIO, are also invited to lobby for these civil rights goals.The goals of the Emergency Civil Rights Committee are announced to the branches by Roy Wilkins, who is a key strategist. Following the October 15 meeting by the planning committee, a conference is held on November 10 with twenty-two national, church, labor, civic, and trade organizations to map plans for developing widespread support for their civil rights program.

The NAACP urges the repeal of the Taft–Hartley Act, because it believes that its union shop requirement is a bar to the employment of black workers in the construction industry.

1950   More than 4,000 delegates representing 100 organizations that comprise the National Emergency Civil Rights Mobilization meet in Washington January 15–17 to demonstrate for civil rights laws. The mobilization is authorized by a resolution that was adopted at the Association's annual convention in 1949 in Los Angeles. Roy Wilkins, who is the general chairman of the demonstration, leads a delegation that meets with President Truman at the White House to ask the president for his active support in securing passage of the FEPC bill that is being considered in the Senate. Mr. Truman assures the delegation that he will support the civil rights program.

The U.S. Supreme Court takes decisive steps toward ending the "separate but equal" doctrine that was established in 1896. In one case, the Court rules that the University of Texas could not bar Herman Marion Sweatt from its law school because of his race. It further rules that the separate law school that the state had established to accommodate Sweatt is not and cannot be equal to that at the University of Texas. In another case, the High Court rules that the University of Oklahoma cannot segregate G. W. McLaurin within its graduate school once he is admitted. In a third case, brought by Elmer Henderson against the Southern Railway Company, the Supreme Court declares that segregation of dining car facilities is unconstituional. The Sweatt and McLaurin cases are NAACP actions, while the Association supported the Henderson action by filing a brief.

Clarence Mitchell is appointed director of the Washington Bureau on August 1.

Former NAACP Special Counsel Charles Hamilton Houston dies on April 3 in Washington, D.C.

1951   Encouraged by the U.S. Supreme Court decisions invalidating segregation in state-supported professional and graduate schools, the NAACP launches a well-planned "Equality Under Law" campaign to overturn racial separation at its roots—in elementary and secondary schools. The drive is launched with the filing of lawsuits against school districts in Atlanta and in Wilmington, Delaware.

Special Counsel Thurgood Marshall responds to complaints from black G.I.s by personally investigating the conditions of segregated units in Korea. He confers with soldiers and top-level Army personnel in Japan and Korea, including General of the Army Douglas MacArthur. Marshall uncovers a shocking pattern of racial discrimination.

1952   A NAACP delegation, consisting of Arthur B. Spingarn, president; Channing H. Tobias, assistant treasurer; Theodore Spaulding, board member; and Walter White, executive secretary, meet with President-elect Dwight D. Eisenhower. The president-elect gives the delegation assurance that he will use his executive powers to eliminate racism in federal establishments.

Dr. Louis T. Wright, chairman of the NAACP board of directors, dies on October 8.

The five precedent-shattering school desegregation cases reach the Supreme Court and are argued on December 9–11. The cases now involve Clarendon County, South Carolina; Topeka, Kansas; Prince Edward County, Virginia; Wilmington, Delaware; and Washington, D.C.

1953   Financially pressed by the heavy load of legal cases and other aspects of the civil rights battle, Dr. Channing Tobias, newly elected chairman of the NAACP board of directors, launches the Fight for Freedom Fund Campaign at the annual convention in St. Louis. The slogan is "Free by '63," and the goal is to eliminate all state-imposed racial discrimination and segregation by the time of the Centennial of Lincoln's Emancipation Proclamation. The convention unanimously adopts a resolution to raise $1 million annually.

Membership continues to climb for the fourth consecutive year, reflecting the increased activity of the NAACP and high expectations throughout black communities.

1954   On May 17 the Supreme Court hands down its decision overturning the "separate but equal" doctrine of the land. This historic victory for the NAACP marks the dramatic opening of a new, intensified front in the battle for equality. Six days later the NAACP issues its "Atlanta Declaration," offering to negotiate so that segregated schools will be eradicated in a spirit of "calm reasonableness."

In response to this Supreme Court decision the White Citizens Councils is formed. These councils are established first in Mississippi, then in other states, with the aim of maintaining the separate school system and continuing the restriction on civil rights for blacks.

Economic reprisals are invoked in several communities in Mississippi, South Carolina, and Alabama against the signers of desegregation petitions. To counter this pressure, the NAACP induces churches, as well as fraternal, civic, and labor organizations to make deposits in the Tri-State Bank of Memphis, a black-owned bank, to enable it to expand its loans to persons in need.

1955   Walter White dies of a heart attack on March 21 at his home in New York City.

In April, Roy Wilkins is named secretary by the board of directors.

On May 31, the U.S. Supreme Court hands down its ruling outlining the procedures to be followed in implementing its May 17, 1954 decision. The May 31 order states that "all provisions of Federal, state, or local law requiring or permitting" segregation in public

education "must yield to" the principle that had been announced in the 1954 decision.

The NAACP continues to grow despite an unprecedented level of attacks from die-hard segregationists. For the first time since 1947, membership passes 300,000 to a record high of 309,000. These members are drawn from every region, including the South, where affiliation with the NAACP often means physical harm and even death. On November 25 the Interstate Commerce Commission bans segregation in interstate travel, including railways, bus stations, and airports. This action is taken in response to a petition from the NAACP that had been filed in December 1953. The carriers are given until January 10, 1956, to cease all such segregation. The Montgomery, Alabama, bus boycott is launched. Actively involved are local NAACP branch officials. Dr. Martin Luther King, Jr., leads this year-long boycott.

1956   Despite several attempts to outlaw the NAACP throughout the South, the civil rights organization presses forward with its programs. The first attempt to outlaw the Association comes in late March when the Louisiana attorney general dusts off a 1924 anti-Ku Klux Klan law requiring the filing of membership lists by organizations and attempts to use it against the NAACP. The Louisiana branches refuse to file their lists, so the following month the state obtains an injunction barring the NAACP from operating in Louisiana. Similar injunctions are obtained in Georgia and Virginia.

The desegregation of the Montgomery bus system is finally achieved by an NAACP suit decided by the U.S. Supreme Court. The Court rules that segregation in intrastate travel is unconstitutional.

Roy Wilkins's effort to bring various civil rights and labor organizations under one umbrella comes together in early March when fifty national organizations cooperate to bring 2,000 delegates from thirty-eight states to Washington to attend a three-day National Delegate Assembly for Civil Rights.

1957   Foremost among the year's achievement is enactment of the Civil Rights Act of 1957, the first civil rights legislation Congress has passed since the Reconstruction era. Aided by local and state units, Roy Wilkins and Clarence Mitchell are credited for their tireless efforts to secure passage of this legislation. Also supporting the measure are organized labor, minority group organizations, civic and fraternal organizations, and U.S. representatives and senators themselves. The act provides for expanded registration and voting in the South.

A federal court order to desegregate Little Rock, Arkansas, schools sparks widespread violence as the first nine black students attempt to enter Central High School. President Eisenhower federalizes the Arkansas National Guard and orders 1,000 members of the 101st

Airborne Division into Little Rock to restore and maintain order. Courageously directing the desegregation strategy that eventually leads to victory over arch-segregationist Governor Orval Faubus are local NAACP leaders Mr. and Mrs. L. C. Bates.

1958   This year is probably the most significant for the NAACP since the historic 1954 Supreme Court desegregation decision. The Supreme Court, in *Cooper* vs. *Aaron*, states in even stronger language than in 1954 that state-imposed segregation, which had been the issue in the Little Rock school case, violates the Constitution. The decision is timely, since other southern states such as Virginia are laying out plans for massive resistance to the High Court's edict.

The Supreme Court reverses a $100,000 contempt fine that Alabama had levied against the NAACP for refusing to turn over its membership lists to the state. The decision is a triumph in that it removes a major threat to the existence of the Association. Such legal and extralegal roadblocks include punitive legislation, state court orders, and administrative regulations.

Efforts to bar the NAACP from providing blacks with legal aid becomes an issue. The state of Virginia leads the way by accusing the NAACP of unlawful solicitation of clients and passes statutes that attempt to subject the association to heavy fines and threaten its attorneys with disbarment. But a U.S. District Court rules in *NAACP* vs. *Patty* that these laws are unconstitutional. The state of Virginia appeals the decision to the U.S. Supreme Court.

The Oklahoma City Youth Council launches the forerunner of the sit-in demonstrations. A similar sit-in is conducted by the Wichita, Kansas, Youth Council.

The NAACP ends an eight-month boycott of Budweiser beer following agreement by the national and local Teamsters Union officials to eliminate alleged job discrimination in the industry.

Roy Wilkins, A. Philip Randolph, Lester Granger, and Martin Luther King, Jr., meet with President Eisenhower and conclude that the president lacks an understanding of the race problem.

1959   The NAACP celebrates its Golden Anniversary. The year opens with the launching of a full-scale assault upon what is thought to be the remnants of discrimination in organized labor and closes with an intensified campaign to increase the number of black registered voters in the South by more than a million.

Roy Wilkins rejects Chet Huntley's remarks on national television. Huntley had earlier stated that "there would be more chance for the desegregation of schools if there were less reliance on the courts and federal power. The NAACP may have outlived itself."

More than 15,000 college students and youth participate in the Second March for Integrated Schools in Washington, D.C. This march is led by Roy Wilkins and other civil rights leaders.

1960   The NAACP proudly salutes the involvement of its youth in the sit-in demonstrations that start on February 1 in Greensboro, North Carolina, in an effort to desegregate lunch counters.

Dr. Robert C. Weaver is elected chairman of the national board of directors. Subsequently, he resigns to become administrator of the Federal Housing and Home Finance Agency, the highest position ever held by a black man in the federal government.

1961   The NAACP Youth Division shifts its emphasis from sit-in demonstrations to demands for jobs and the upgrading of black workers. This tactical change yields immediate and tangible benefits in Durham, North Carolina; Dallas, Texas; Jacksonville, Florida; Columbia, South Carolina; Oklahoma City, Oklahoma; Kansas City, Missouri; and other cities. More than 700 NAACP youths are arrested in these demonstrations.

Bishop Stephen Gill Spottswood is elected chairman of the board of directors on April 1.

As chairman of the Leadership Conference on Civil Rights, Roy Wilkins along with Conference Secretary Arnold Aronson on August 29 present to President John F. Kennedy a comprehensive sixty-page memorandum, "Federally Supported Discrimination," which documents federally supported racial discrimination. Wilkins and Aronson call on President Kennedy to "promulgate a general Federal Civil Rights Code governing the operation of the whole Executive branch of government." The memorandum further urges the president to "direct all departments and agencies of the federal government to assure nondiscrimination" in all its activities, programs, institutions, and services.

1962   As a result of a lawsuit by the NAACP Legal Defense Fund, James H. Meredith is admitted to the University of Mississippi on September 30, as the first known black student at the university. U.S. marshals and troops are required to help him enroll and protect him from harm. Students and townsfolk stage riots to prevent the enrollment of Meredith.

1963   The Centennial of the Emancipation Proclamation is a year of hope and excitement for the civil rights movement. There is an increase in membership, which reaches a new high of 534,741. General income exceeds one million dollars.

NAACP Mississippi Field Secretary Medgar Wiley Evers is assassinated on June 12.

In Washington, the NAACP Bureau leads the fight for a comprehensive civil rights bill in Congress. President Kennedy introduces a bill on June 19. Roy Wilkins appears twice before the House Judiciary Committee to testify on the need for the bill.

Around the nation, the NAACP wages direct-action campaigns to desegregate public facilities and other areas of American life. The

Oklahoma City NAACP Youth Council is successful in its five-year campaign to desegregate public facilities.

W. E. B. Du Bois dies in self-imposed exile in Accra, Ghana, on August 27.

The NAACP is a cornerstone among the organizations participating in the August 28 "Jobs and Freedom" March on Washington. In preparation for the massive demonstration, the NAACP mobilizes its financial and human resources for what is to become the nation's greatest mass demonstration for civil rights.

President John F. Kennedy is assassinated on November 22 in Dallas.

1964   On June 1, after four appeals to the U.S. Supreme Court, the NAACP ends efforts by southern states to cripple it by winning a unanimous decision that upset an injunction banning it from operating in Alabama. The Association had been barred from that state for eight years. This time the High Court rules that the NAACP has a right to register in the state as a foreign corporation. On October 29 the NAACP again files registration papers in Alabama and resumes operation.

The most outstanding gains are legislative, in contrast to earlier years, when achievements were predominantly judicial or executive. The 1964 Civil Rights Act, enacted with the full support of the NAACP and signed by President Lyndon B. Johnson on July 2, is the most sweeping in the nation's history.

Other measures for which the NAACP works are the passage of the Twenty-fourth Amendment to the Constitution, which bars the poll tax as a requirement for voting in federal elections, and the passage of the Economic Opportunity Act, both of which are signed on August 24.

Moving to shift the civil rights struggle from the streets, Roy Wilkins announces that the NAACP intends to step up its drive to register black voters. This campaign, with the help of several other organizations, registers a record total of 6 million black voters in time for the presidential election.

1965   The NAACP plays a pivotal role in the passage of another major civil rights law, the Voting Rights Act. President Johnson signs the Act on August 6. The Southern Christian Leadership Conference sponsors the Selma demonstrations to dramatize the denial of the vote to blacks.

1966   The NAACP Voter Education Project accomplishes marked successes in registering more black voters in the South. With the assistance of sixteen federal examiners, the Association helps 27,589 voters to register in thirty-five Mississippi counties during the first five months of the year. An overall total of 163,000 are registered by the federal examiners themselves and other civil rights groups.

Robert C. Weaver, former NAACP board chairman, becomes the first member of his race to hold Cabinet rank when President Johnson appoints him secretary of the Department of Housing and Urban Development.

Arthur B. Spingarn, NAACP president since 1940, retires and Kivie Kaplan is elected to succeed him.

1967   On July 29 President Johnson names Roy Wilkins to the eleven-member National Advisory Commission on Civil Disorders to investigate the causes and consequences of the urban riots and to recommend remedial action.

On August 30 the Senate confirms Thurgood Marshall as associate justice of the Supreme Court, the first of his race to be named to the High Court.

1968   The National Advisory Commission on Civil Disorders, of which Roy Wilkins is a member, releases its report on March 1, affirming that white racism is the root cause of the nation's racial tensions and conflicts.

Roy Wilkins is designated chairman of the U.S. Delegation to the International Conference on Human Rights, which meets in Tehran, Iran, under the auspices of the United Nations. As leader of the delegation, Wilkins presents the American position on human rights to the convention.

Dr. Martin Luther King, Jr., is assassinated in Memphis, on April 4.

The passage of another major civil rights law, the Fair Housing Act, is achieved largely through the adroit efforts of NAACP Washington Bureau director Clarence Mitchell. The act ends a long, arduous struggle by civil rights forces to remove some of the most obvious practices of housing discrimination.

1969   The civil rights momentum, which had slackened, picks up as the Nixon administration reveals its policies for the nation. Among the NAACP's most notable achievement this year is defeating President Nixon's nominee to the U.S. Supreme Court, Clement F. Haynsworth.

Julius Williams, a World War II veteran, is appointed NAACP Director of Armed Services and Veterans Affairs. His job is to lead the attack against racism in the military.

1970   Barely two months after the Senate rejected Haynsworth, by a vote of 55 to 45, because of his racist record, President Nixon nominates another anti-black judge, G. Harrold Carswell, to the Supreme Court. The NAACP vigorously launches another attack to bar Carswell's confirmation. In April the Senate rejects the nominee 51 to 45.

In the field of housing, the creation of the National Housing Development Corporation is approved. This nonprofit affiliate is to assist local NAACP units to sponsor moderate and low-income housing. The Glen Cove, New York NAACP branch distinguishes itself by becoming one of the first units to benefit from the program.

In the area of military justice, NAACP General Counsel Nathaniel R. Jones and Armed Services and Veterans Affairs Director Julius Williams visit the U.S. Air Force base at Goose Bay, Nova Scotia, to investigate complaints of racism. Their investigation results in the dropping of unfounded charges against a group of black servicemen and the transfer of the commanding officer. At the end of the year, Mr. Jones, Mr. Williams, and Legal Department attorney Melvin Bolden start preparations for similar investigations on U.S. bases in West Germany.

The first NAACP day care center is opened by the Jamaica, New York NAACP Branch.

1971   In Mississippi, the NAACP makes national headlines when it assists striking black as well as white pulpwood workers. The NAACP Southern Labor Office organizes picket lines and provides technical assistance in the workers' struggle for higher wages. An NAACP contribution of more than $5,000 in strike benefits aids the workers in winning a fair settlement.

The NAACP publishes its comprehensive military justice report, "The Search for Military Justice," which is based on investigations in West Germany by an NAACP team headed by general counsel Nathaniel Jones. The report sparks several legal and administrative reforms by the Department of Defense.

Arthur B. Spingarn, NAACP president since 1940, dies on December 1.

Ralph J. Bunche of United Nations fame and a member of the NAACP board dies on December 9.

1972   The Washington Bureau again plays a crucial legislative role in the passage of the Equal Employment Opportunity Act of 1972.

The first NAACP prison branch is chartered at Lewisburg Federal Penitentiary in Pennsylvania on July 6.

1973   As a result of a long-standing NAACP suit, a federal court orders the U.S. Steel Corporation and the United Steelworkers of America at Fairfield, Alabama, to eliminate discriminatory seniority lines of promotion and to replace them with a new plant-wide seniority structure. The order requires a systemic promotion of black workers and imposes goals and timetables for hiring blacks in hitherto all-white job classifications. Black workers receive over $200,000 in compensation and other forms of relief for the many years of discrimination they endured.

1974   Boston, like Little Rock, Arkansas, in 1967 commands the full resources of the NAACP in the fall, when public schools in the largely black areas of Roxbury and Mattapan and the mostly white South Boston and Hyde Park start the first phase of Judge W. Arthur Garrity's integration order. White opponents launch boycotts of some schools and demonstrate against the cross-district integration plan. Roy Wilkins and other NAACP officials lead the Association's fight to ensure that the plan will not be scuttled or weakened. They assist in getting protection from city, state, and federal officials to protect the children. On December 1 Judge Garrity issues his final ruling on the case. His guidelines are the carbon copy of the NAACP's recommendations.

On December 1 Stephen Gill Spottswood dies at his home in Washington, D.C.

1975　　Margaret Bush Wilson is elected chairman of the board of directors.

Fifty thousand people demonstrate in Boston on May 17 to commemorate the historic *Brown* decision.

On August 6 President Gerald Ford signs H.R. 6210, amending and extending certain provisions of the 1965 Voting Rights Act, culminating a two-year effort by the NAACP Washington Bureau and cooperating organizations.

Kivie Kaplan, president of the Association, dies on May 5.

1976　　On November 29 Clarence Norris, the last of the "Scottsboro boys," returns to Montgomery, Alabama, to receive his pardon for a rape conviction from the Alabama Pardons and Parole Board. Until this time, he had been a fugitive and a parole violator. The legal matters are handled by NAACP lawyer James Myerson.

William H. Hastie, the first black federal judge in the United States, dies.

1977　　The NAACP charges that the nation's school boards are failing to uphold educational standards in public schools. The Association releases a comprehensive report to assist local units in developing programs to bring about quality education in their communities.

The NAACP extends its full support to U.N. Ambassador Andrew Young, who is being criticized for his comments on racism and minority white rule in South Africa.

Roy Wilkins, after forty-six years of service with the NAACP, bids the Association an emotional farewell at the Sixty-eighth Annual Convention.

Appendix B

"The Call":
A Lincoln Emancipation Conference

To Discuss Means for Securing Political and
Civil Equality for the Negro

The celebration of the centennial of the birth of Abraham Lincoln widespread and grateful as it may be, will fail to justify itself if it takes no note and makes no recognition of the colored men and women to whom the great emancipator labored to assure freedom. Besides a day of rejoicing, Lincoln's birthday in 1909 should be one of taking stock of the nation's progress since 1865. How far has it lived up to the obligations imposed upon it by the Emancipation Proclamation? How far has it gone in assuring to each and every citizen, irrespective of color, the equality of opportunity and equality before the law, which underlie our American institutions and are guaranteed by the Constitution?

If Mr. Lincoln could revisit this country he would be disheartened by the nation's failure in this respect. He would learn that on January 1st, 1909, Georgia had rounded out a new oligarchy by disfranchising the negro after the manner of all the other Southern states. He would learn that the Supreme Court of the United States, designed to be a bulwark of American liberties, had failed to meet several opportunities to pass squarely upon this disfranchisement of millions by laws avowedly discriminatory and openly enforced in such manner that white men may vote and black men be without a vote in their government; he would discover, there, that taxation without representation is the lot of millions of wealth-producing American citizens, in whose hands rests the economic progress and welfare of an entire section of the country. He would learn that the Supreme Court, according to the official statement of one of its own judges in the Berea College case, has laid down the principle that if an individual State chooses it may "make it a crime for white and colored persons to frequent the same market place at the same time, or appear in an assemblage of citizens convened to consider questions of a public or political nature in which all citizens, without regard to race, are equally interested." In many States Lincoln would find justice enforced, if at all, by judges elected by one element in a community to pass upon the liberties and lives of another. He would see the black men and women, for whose freedom a hundred thousand soldiers gave their lives, set apart in trains, in which they pay first-class fares for third-class service, in railway stations and in places of entertainment, while State after State declines to do its elementary duty in preparing the negro through education for the best exercise of citizenship.

Added to this, the spread of lawless attacks upon the negro, North, South and West—even in the Springfield made famous by Lincoln—often accompanied by revolting brutalities, sparing neither sex, nor age nor youth, could not but shock the author of the sentiment that "government of the people, by the people, for the people shall not perish from the earth."

Silence under these conditions means tacit approval. The indifference of the North is already responsible for more than one assault upon democracy, and every such attack reacts as unfavorably upon whites as upon blacks. Discrimination once permitted cannot be bridled; recent history in the South shows that in forging chains for the negroes, the white voters are forging chains for themselves. "A house divided against itself cannot stand"; this government cannot exist half slave and half free any better to-day than it could in 1861. Hence we call upon all the believers in democracy to join in a national conference for the discussion of present evils, the voicing of protests, and the renewal of the struggle for civil and political liberty.

Miss Jane Addams, Chicago
Ray Stannard Baker, New York
Mrs. Ida Wells-Barnett, Chicago
Mrs. Harriet Stanton Blatch, New York
Mr. Samuel Bowles, (*Springfield Republican*)
Prof. W. L. Bulkley, New York
Miss Kate Claghorn, New York
E. H. Clement, Boston
Prof. John Dewey, New York
Miss Mary E. Dreier, Brooklyn
Prof. W. E. B. Du Bois, Atlanta
Dr. John L. Elliott, New York
Mr. William Lloyd Garrison, Boston
Rev. Francis J. Grimke, Washington, D.C.
Prof. Thomas C. Hall, New York
Rabbi Emil G. Hirsch, Chicago
Rev. John Haynes Holmes, New York
Hamilton Holt, New York
William Dean Howells, New York

Rev. Jenkin Lloyd Jones, Chicago
Mrs. Florence Kelley, New York
Rev. Walter Laidlaw, New York
Rev. Frederick Lynch, New York
Miss Helen Marot, New York
Miss Mary E. McDowell, Chicago
Prof. J. G. Merrill, Connecticut
Mr. John E. Milholland, New York
Dr. Henry Moskowitz, New York
Miss Leonora O'Reilly, New York
Miss Mary W. Ovington, New York
Rev. Charles II. Parkhurst, New York
Rev. John P. Peters, New York
J. G. Phelps-Stokes, New York
Louis F. Post, Chicago
Dr. Jane Robbins, New York
Charles Edward Russell, New York
William M. Salter, Chicago
Joseph Smith, Boston
Mrs. Anna Garlin Spencer, New York
Judge Wendell S. Stafford, Washington, D.C.

Lincoln Steffens, Boston
Miss Helen Stokes, New York
Mrs. Mary Church Terrell,
    Washington, D.C.
Prof. W. I. Thomas, Chicago
President Charles F. Thwing,
    Western Reserve University
Oswald Garrison Villard, New York
Mrs. Henry Villard, New York
Miss Lillian D. Wald, New York
Dr. J. Milton Waldron, Washington,
    D.C.
William English Walling, New York
Bishop Alexander Walters, New
    York

Dr. William H. Ward, New York
Mrs. Rodman Wharton,
    Philadelphia
Miss Susan P. Wharton,
    Philadelphia
Horace White, New York
Mayor Brand Whitlock, Toledo
Rabbi Stephen S. Wise, New
    York
President Mary E. Wooley, Mt.
    Holyoke College
Rev. M. St. Croix Wright, New
    York
Prof. Charles Zueblin, Boston

Appendix C

The Committee of Forty

National Negro Committee, 1909

William English Walling, Chairman, New York
Rev. William Henry Brooks, New York
Prof. John Dewey, New York
Paul Kennaday, New York
Jacob W. Mack, New York
Mrs. Mary Maclean, New York
Dr. Henry Moskowitz, New York
John E. Milholland, New York
Miss Leonora O'Reilly, New York
Charles Edward Russell, New York
Prof. Edwin R. A. Seligman, New York
Oswald Garrison Villard, New York
Miss Lillian D. Wald, New York
Bishop Alexander Walters, New York
Rabbi Stephen S. Wise, New York
Miss Mary White Ovington, Brooklyn, New York
Dr. Owen M. Walle, Brooklyn, New York
Rev. John Haynes Holmes, Yonkers, New York
Prof. W. L. Bulkley, Ridgefield Park, New Jersey
Miss Maria Baldwin, Boston, Massachusetts
Archibald H. Grimke, Boston, Massachusetts

Although provision was made for forty members, only thirty-eight names appear on this list. An additional name, the Reverend Joseph Silverman, New York, is included in Minutes, National Negro Committee, March, 1909, but is not included in *Proceedings of the National Negro Conference 1909: New York May 31 and June 1*, p. 225.

Albert E. Pillsbury, Boston, Massachusetts
Moorfield Storey, Boston, Massachusetts
Pres. Charles F. Thwing, Cleveland, Ohio
Pres. W. S. Scarborough, Wilberforce, Ohio
Miss Jane Addams, Chicago, Illinois
Mrs. Ida Wells-Barnett, Chicago, Illinois
Dr. C. E. Bentley, Chicago, Illinois
Mrs. Celia Parker Woolley, Chicago, Illinois
Dr. William Sinclair, Philadelphia, Pennyslvania
Miss Susan Wharton, Philadelphia
R. R. Wright, Jr., Philadelphia, Pennsylvania
L. M. Hershaw, Washington, D.C.
Judge Wendell P. Stafford, Washington, D.C.
Mrs. Mary Church Terrell, Washington, D.C.
Rev. J. Milton Waldron, Washington, D.C.
Prof. W. E. B. Du Bois, Atlanta, Georgia
Leslie Pinckney Hill, Manassas, Virginia

Appendix D

Resolutions

Adopted by the National Negro Committee
June 1, 1909

We denounce the ever-growing oppression of our 10,000,000 colored fellow citizens as the greatest menace that threatens the country. Often plundered of their just share of the public funds, robbed of nearly all part in the government, segregated by common carriers, some murdered with impunity, and all treated with open contempt by officials, they are held in some States in practical slavery to the white community. The systematic persecution of law-abiding citizens and their disfranchisement on account of their race alone is a crime that will ultimately drag down to an infamous end any nation that allows it to be practised, and it bears most heavily on those poor white farmers and laborers whose economic position is most similar to that of the persecuted race.

The nearest hope lies in the immediate and patiently continued enlightenment of the people who have been inveigled into a campaign of oppression. The spoils of persecution should not go to enrich any class or classes of the population. Indeed persecution of organized workers, peonage, enslavement of prisoners, and even disfranchisement already threaten large bodies of whites in many Southern States.

We agree fully with the prevailing opinion that the transformation of the unskilled colored laborers in industry and agriculture into skilled workers is of vital importance to that race and to the nation, but we demand for the Negroes, as for all others, a free and complete education, whether by city, state, or nation, a grammar school and industrial training for all, and technical, professional, and academic education for the most gifted.

The Resolutions are reported in this form in *Proceedings of the National Negro Conference 1909: New York May 31 and June 1*, pp. 222–25.

But the public schools assigned to the Negro of whatever kind or grade will never receive a fair and equal treatment until he is given equal treatment in the Legislature and before the law. Nor will the practically educated Negro, no matter how valuable to the community he may prove, be given a fair return for his labor or encouraged to put forth his best efforts or given the chance to develop that efficiency that comes only outside the school until he is respected in his legal rights as a man and a citizen.

We regard with grave concern the attempt manifest South and North to deny to black men the right to work and to enforce this demand by violence and bloodshed. Such a question is too fundamental and clear even to be submitted to arbitration. The late strike in Georgia is not simply a demand that Negroes be displaced, but that proven and efficient men be made to surrender their long followed means of livelihood to white competitors.

As first and immediate steps toward remedying these national wrongs, so full of peril for the whites as well as the blacks of all sections, we demand of Congress and the Executive:

(1) That the Constitution be strictly enforced and the civil rights guaranteed under the Fourteenth Amendment be secured impartially to all.

(2) That there be equal educational opportunities for all and in all the States, and that public school expenditure be the same for the Negro and white child.

(3) That in accordance with the Fifteenth Amendment the right of the Negro to the ballot on the same terms as other citizens be recognized in every part of the country.

The committee on permanent organization in its report proposed a resolution providing for "the incorporation of a national committee to be known as a Committee for the Advancement of the Negro Race, to aid their progress and make their citizenship a reality, with all the rights and privileges pertaining thereto." It presented also a resolution calling for a committee of forty charged with the organization of a national committee with power to call the convention in 1910.

We deplore any recognition of, or concession to, prejudice or color by the federal government in any officer or branch thereof, as well as the presidential declaration on the appointment of colored men to office in the South, contradicting as it does the President's just and admirable utterance against the proposed disfranchisement of the colored voters of Maryland.

Appendix E

NAACP Officers, Executive
Committee, and General Committee
December, 1910

NATIONAL PRESIDENT
Moorfield Storey

CHAIRMAN OF THE EXECUTIVE COMMITTEE
William English Walling

TREASURER
John E. Milholland

DISBURSING TREASURER
Oswald Garrison Villard

DIRECTOR OF PUBLICITY AND RESEARCH
Dr. W. E. B. Du Bois

EXECUTIVE SECRETARY
Miss Frances Blascoer

EXECUTIVE COMMITTEE

Miss Gertrude Barnum
Rev. W. H. Brooks
Mr. Paul Kennaday
Mrs. F. R. Keyser
Mrs. M. D. Maclean
Rev. A. Clayton Powell
Mr. Charles Edward Russell
Rev. Joseph Silverman
Rev. John Haynes Holmes
Miss M. W. Ovington
Dr. O. M. Waller

Mr. W. L. Bulkley
Mr. Albert E. Pillsbury
Miss Jane Addams
Mrs. Ida B. Wells-Barnett
Dr. C. E. Bentley
Mrs. Celia Parker Woolley
Dr. N. F. Mossell
Dr. William A. Sinclair
Mrs. Mary Church Terrell
Rev. J. Milton Waldron

From *Crisis*, I (November, 1910).

GENERAL COMMITTEE

Prof. John Dewey
Miss Maud R. Ingersoll
Mr. Jacob W. Mack
Rev. Horace G. Miller
Mrs. Max Morgenthau
Mr. James F. Morton, Jr.
Dr. Henry Moskowitz
Miss Leonora O'Reilly
Mr. Jacob H. Schiff
Prof. E. R. A. Seligman
Mrs. Anna Garlin Spencer
Mrs. Henry Villard
Miss Lillian D. Wald
Bishop Alexander Walters
Dr. Stephen S. Wise
Rev. James E. Haynes
Miss M. R. Lyons
Mrs. M. H. Talbert
Hon. Thomas M. Osborne
Mr. George W. Crawford
Miss Maria Baldwin
Mr. Francis J. Garrison
Mr. Archibald H. Grimke

Mrs. Florence Kelley
Dr. Charles Lenz
Mr. William Monroe Trotter
Dr. Horace Bumstead
Miss Elizabeth C. Carter
President Charles F. Thwing
Mr. Charles W. Chesnutt
President H. C. King
President W. S. Scarborough
Miss Sophonisba Breckinridge
Mr. Clarence Darrow
Miss Susan Wharton
Mr. R. R. Wright, Jr.
Mr. W. Justin Carter
Rev. Harvey Johnson
Hon. William S. Bennet
Mr. L. M. Hershaw
Prof. Kelly Miller
Prof. L. B. Moore
Justice W. P. Stafford
President John Hope
Mr. Leslie P. Hill

Notes

Introduction

1. James Weldon Johnson, "The Militant N.A.A.C.P.," 1929.
2. See the NAACP board minutes, June 1914.
3. August Meier and Elliott Rudwick, "The Rise of the Black Secretariat in the NAACP, 1909–1935," *The Crisis* (February 1977): 65.

Part I

1. Eugene Levy, *James Weldon Johnson: Black Leader, Black Voice* (Chicago: University of Chicago Press, 1973), p. 186.
2. See NAACP board minutes, June 1914.
3. Levy, *James Weldon Johnson*, p. 186.
4. Tony Martin, *Race First: The Ideological and Organizational Strategies of Marcus Garvey and the Universal Improvement Association* (Dover, Mass.: The Majority Press, 1976), p. 13.
5. Ibid.
6. Stephen Fox, *The Guardian of Boston: William Monroe Trotter* (New York: Atheneum, 1971), p. 140.
7. Ibid.
8. Ibid, p 143.
9. August Meier and Elliott Rudwick, "The Rise of the Black Secretariat in the NAACP, 1909–1935," p. 65.
10. Ibid.
11. Ibid.
12. E. E. Schattschneider, *The Semisovereign People: A Realist's View of Democracy in America* (Hinsdale, Ill.: Dryden Press, 1975), p. 45.
13. Warren Bennis and Burt Nanus, *Leaders: Strategies for Taking Charge* (New York: HarperBusiness, 1997), p. 46.
14. James Weldon Johnson, *Along This Way* (New York: Viking Press, 1933), p. 373.

Part II

   1. Roy Wilkins, *Standing Fast* (New York: Viking Press, 1982), p. 219.
   2. Walter White, *A Man Called White* (New York: Viking Press, 1948), p. 12.
   3. Genna Rae McNeil, *Groundwork: Charles Hamilton Houston and the Struggle for Civil Rights* (Philadelphia: University of Pennsylvania Press, 1983), p. 138.
   4. Ibid.

Part III

   1. Roy Wilkins, *Standing Fast*, p. 320.
   2. Ibid, p. 317.
   3. Ibid, pp. 214–15.
   4. See preface to *Talking It Over with Roy Wilkins*, ed. by Aminda Wilkins (Norwalk, Conn.: M & B Publishing, 1977)

Bibliography

Printed Materials

Anderson, Jervis. *A. Philip Randolph*. New York: Harcourt Brace Jovanovich, 1972.

Aptheker, Herbert, ed. *The Correspondence of W. E. B. Du Bois*, Vol. I. Amherst: University of Massachusetts, 1973.

———. ed. *A Documentary History of the Negro People in the United States, 1910–1932*. Secaucus, N.J.: The Citadel Press, 1977.

New York: HarperBusiness, 1997.

Bell, Derrick A. *Race, Racism, and American Law*. Boston: Little, Brown & Co., 1973.

Bennis, Warren, and Burt Nanus. *Leaders: Strategies for Taking Charge*. New York: HarperBusiness, 1997.

Branch, Taylor. *Parting the Waters: America in the King Years, 1954–1963*. New York: Simon and Schuster, 1988.

Carmichael, Stokely, and Charles V. Hamilton. *Black Power: The Politics of Liberation in America*. New York: Random House, 1967.

Carter. Dan T. *Scottsboro: A Tragedy of the American South*. New York: Oxford University Press, 1969.

Cruse, Harold. *Crisis of the Negro Intellectual*. New York: William Morrow, 1967.

———. *Plural but Equal*. New York: William Morrow, 1987.

Du Bois, W. E. B. *Autobiography of W. E. B. Du Bois*. New York: International Publishers, 1968.

Foner, Philip S., ed. *W. E. B. Du Bois Speaks: Speeches and Addresses, 1890–1919*. New York: Pathfinder Press, 1970.

Fox, Stephen. *The Guardian of Boston*. New York: Atheneum, 1971.

Franklin John Hope. *From Slavery to Freedom*. New York: Alfred A. Knopf, 1967.

——— and August Meier. *Black Leaders of the Twentieth Century*. Urbana, Ill.: University of Illinois Press, 1982.

Garrow, David J. *Bearing the Cross: Martin Luther King, Jr. and the Southern Christian Leadership Conference*. New York: William Morrow, 1986.

Greenberg, Jack. *Crusaders in the Courts*. New York: Basic Books, 1994.

Harlan, Louis. *Booker T. Washington: The Wizard of Tuskegee*. New York: Oxford University Press, 1983.

Higginbotham, A. Leon, Jr. *In the Matter of Color, Race and the American Legal Process: The Colonial Period.* New York: Oxford University Press, 1978.

———. *Shades of Freedon: Racial Politics and Presumptions of the American Legal Process.* New York: Oxford University Press, 1996.

Huggins, Nathan Irvin. *Harlem Renaissance.* New York: Oxford University Press, 1971.

Johnson, James Weldon. *Along This Way: The Autobiography of James Weldon Johnson.* New York: The Viking Press, 1933.

———. *Black Manhattan.* New York: Alfred A. Knopf, 1930.

———, ed. *The Book of American Negro Poetry.* New York: Harcourt Brace, 1922.

———. *Negro Americans, What Now?* New York: The Viking Press, 1934.

——— and J. Rosamond Johnson, eds. *The Books of American Negro Spirituals.* New York: Da Capo Press, 1983.

Kellogg, Charles Flint. *NAACP: A History of the National Association for the Advancement of Colored People, Volume I: 1909–1920.* Baltimore: Johns Hopkins Press, 1967.

Kluger, Richard. *Simple Justice. The History of Brown v. Board of Education.* New York: Vintage, 1977.

Levy, Eugene. *James Weldon Johnson: Black Leader Black Voice.* Chicago: University of Chicago Press, 1973.

Lewis, David Levering. *W. E. B. Du Bois: A Biography of a Race.* New York: Henry Holt Co., 1994.

Logan, Rayford. *What the Negro Wants.* Chapel Hill: University of North Carolina Press, 1944.

——— and Michael Winston, eds. *Dictionary of American Negro Biography.* New York: W. W. Norton & Co., 1982.

McNeil, Genna Rae. *Groundwork: Charles Houston and the Struggle for Civil Rights.* Philadelphia: University of Pennsylvania Press, 1983.

Martin, Tony. *Race First: The Ideological and Organizational Struggles of Marcus Garvey and the Universal Negro Improvement Association.* Dover, Mass.: The Majority Press, 1976.

Meier, August, and Elliot Rudwick. *Along the Color Line.* Urbana: University of Illinois Press, 1976.

Myrdal, Gunner. *An American Dilemma.* New York: Harper and Row, 1944.

National Association for the Advancement of Colored People. Annual Reports, 1911–1969.

———. *The Crisis.* 1920–1977.

———. Minutes of the Board of Directors, 1909–1977.

———. *Highlights,* 1982.

O'Reilly, Kenneth. *Racial Matters: The FBI Secret File on Black America, 1960–1972.* New York: The Free Press, 1989.

Ovington, Mary White. *The Walls Came Tumbling Down.* New York: Harcourt, Brace, and World, 1947.

Ross, Barbara Joyce. *J. E. Spingarn and the Rise of the NAACP, 1911–1939.* New York: Atheneum, 1972.

Saint James, Warren D. *NAACP Triumphs of a Pressure Group, 1909–1980.* Smithtown, N.Y.: Exposition Press, 1980.

Schattschneider, E. E. *The Semisovereign People: A Realist's View of Democracy in America.* Hinsdale, Ill.: The Dryden Press, 1975.

Tushnet, Mark V. *The NAACP's Legal Strategy against Segregated Education, 1925–1950.* Chapel Hill: University of North Carolina Press, 1987.

Van Deusen, Martin. *J. E. Spingarn.* New York: Twayne Publishers, 1971

Watson, Denton. *Lion in the Lobby: Clarence Mitchell, Jr.'s Struggle for the Passage of Civil Rights Laws*. New York: William Morrow, 1990.

White, Walter. *How Far the Promised Land*. New York: The Viking Press, 1955.

————. *A Man Called White: The Autobiography of Walter White*. New York: The Viking Press, 1949.

Wilkins, Aminda, ed. *Talking It Over with Roy Wilkins*. Norwalk, Conn.: M & B Publishing, 1977.

Wilkins, Roy. *Standing Fast: The Autobiography of Roy Wilkins*. New York: The Viking Press, 1982.

———— and Ramsey Clark. *Search and Destroy: A Report by the Commission of Inquiry into the Black Panthers and the Police*. New York: Metropolitan Applied Research Center, 1973.

Wilson, Sondra Kathryn, ed. *The Selected Writings of James Weldon Johnson*, Vols. I and II. New York: Oxford University Press, 1995.

Zangrando, Robert L. *The NAACP Crusade Against Lynching, 1909–1950*. Philadelphia: Temple University Press, 1980.

Manuscripts

The James Weldon Johnson Papers, The James Weldon Johnson Memorial Collection of Negro Arts and Letters, Beinecke Library, Yale University, New Haven, Conn. (hereafter: JWJMC)

The Walter White Papers, JWJMC.

The Roy Wilkins Papers, The Library of Congress, Washington, D.C.

The N.A.A.C.P. Papers, The Library of Congress, Washington, D.C.

The N.A.A.C.P. Papers (microfilm), Schomburg Center for Research in Black Culture, The New York Public Library

Personal Files

Edward B. Muse, New York City

O. Jewel Sims Okala, New York City

Mildred Bond Roxborough, New York City

Jane White Viazzi, New York City

Sondra Kathryn Wilson, New York City

Index

513